CRIMINOLOGY REVIEW YEARBOOK

Volume 2

CRIMINOLOGY REVIEW YEARBOOK

Associate Editors

Volume 2

CRIMINOLOGY REVIEW YEARBOOK

Edited by
Egon Bittner
and
Sheldon L. Messinger

SAGE PUBLICATIONS   Beverly Hills   London

For information address:

SAGE Publications, Inc.
275 South Beverly Drive
Beverly Hills, California 90212

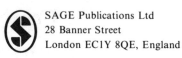

SAGE Publications Ltd
28 Banner Street
London EC1Y 8QE, England

Printed in the United States of America

International Standard Book Number 0-8039-1309-5

International Standard Serial Number 0163-9056

FIRST PRINTING

CONTENTS

INTRODUCTION

EGON BITTNER

SHELDON L. MESSINGER

Like the first, this second volume of the CRIMINOLOGY REVIEW YEARBOOK is intended to assist students of crime and crime control stay abreast of their burgeoning field by presenting especially prepared essays and recently published work on these subjects. Both students interested in crime and crime control, and associated phenomena, as subjects in their own right, and that increasing band of scholars concerned with these matters because they facilitate study of other topics of theoretical importance, such as learning processes, will find materials worthy of contemplation in the following pages.

Preparing the second volume served to confirm some impressions gaining in preparing the first. Much is published on crime and crime control that is barely if at all worth reading; and again as much, perhaps, that is of interest mainly to criminal justice technicians. Further, there is considerable redundancy in the more generally readable published materials, both books and journal articles often covering the same areas in similar ways. Even so, there are more publications of wide criminological interest in any given year or two than can possibly be discussed, much less reprinted, in a single, usable volume. Also, the range of perspectives brought to bear, theories proposed and partially tested, and issues raised and analyzed is dizzyingly diverse.

The successive volumes of the YEARBOOK are one response to this frustrating situation.[1] They represent the results of the efforts of the editors and their associates (1) to sort through a substantial part of the mass of yearly publications to find those most worth reading because they communicate trenchant ideas about crime and crime control phenomena old and new and (2) to commission essays that bring together for analysis and comment materials on particular aspects of these phenomena. Any given volume might be regarded as a platform, so to speak, for discussion and debate amidst a rather large and churning sea of ideas. Even the series as a whole, however, will doubtless provide little more than a series of platforms with large spaces between them, spaces through which significant materials which should have been reprinted, and issues and perspectives which should have been developed at length, will unfortunately fall from view. It would be easy to become depressed about this, and the only antidote we know is to worry less about what cannot be accomplished with the resources at hand.

So, we are necessarily committed to selectivity in the topics covered and the materials reprinted. The absence of anyone's favorite topic or recently published piece may be a sign of oversight; but it is equally likely to be the result of the need, if one would avoid a potpourri, to make discriminations that are not intended to imply a judgment about relative importance. Thus, among the matters not treated sufficiently if at all in this volume or the last, on which some worthy recent publications exist, are surely race, crime and crime control; women offenders and prisoners; biosocial approaches to deviance and crime; the import of victim surveys and self-report studies for the interpretation of official crime rates; the move toward increased "determinacy" in sentencing; the sources and implications of increased rates of imprisonment during the 1970s; and the fate of the "new" criminology. Essays and materials on these important topics will likely be included in future volumes of the YEARBOOK—though we make no promises: The possibilities are too many.

Roughly following the practice initiated for the first volume, three essays were commissioned for this one to deal, respectively, with perspectives on crime within a scholarly discipline whose practitioners have recently shown renewed interest in the subject; with the character and implications of knowledge about a problem of long-standing concern to students of crime and crime control; and with thinking about a complex congery of forms of crime and associated control efforts that are increasingly the subjects of scholarly inquiries and practical debates. John Monahan and Stephanie Splane prepared the first, providing an overview of salient contemporary psychological perspectives on crimes. John Conrad undertook to summarize and evaluate work on criminal violence for the second. For the third, Jack Katz essayed his view of the nature of the recent movement, perhaps already peaked, to indict and prosecute white-collar criminals. These essays, plus current work that illustrates and amplifies their themes and arguments, make up Parts I, II, and III of this YEARBOOK.

Parts IV and V consist of outstanding recent work on the ecology of crime and on crime victims. The first is a subject that has never fully lost fashion in criminology. Recently there has been a resurgence of good work that may fairly be described as "ecological" and which, in our judgment, deserves the wider audience that reprinting may help to engender. Study of crime victims, on the other hand, is relatively recent as a concerted effort; resultant work seems ready for wide consideration and criticism.

We have also added a new section to this volume, Part VI, entitled "Continuities and Controversies." As explained more fully in the introduction to that section, in future years we hope to publish brief original contributions under this rubric that expand on or take issue with matters raised in earlier volumes. The final section of this volume, as the last, consists of an essay especially prepared by Joseph G. Weis and James G. Henney to serve as a source of recent statistical data on crime and crime control, emphasizing those aspects of these phenomena treated in this volume.

We are jointly responsible for final decisions about topics, essays, and reprinted work. In reaching these decisions, we were ably assisted by the associate editors and by the essayists; we are grateful to them for this assistance. To the essayist, additionally, our thanks for their thoughtful, prompt written contributions to the volume. We also want to thank Pattricia Lawson for tireless, accurate, and cheerful secretarial assistance. Finally, our thanks to the many authors and publishers who permitted reprinting of the articles and book chapters included in this volume.

NOTE

1. Another response is the newly initiated series edited by Norval Morris and Michael Tonry, entitled CRIME AND JUSTICE: AN ANNUAL REVIEW OF RESEARCH. (Volume 1 has recently been published—University of Chicago Press, 1979.) We highly recommend the series as another antidote to frustration with the plenty and fragmentation of the criminological enterprise. Every volume will contain about eight especially prepared papers, each designed to survey and integrate knowledge on some criminological subject.

Other responses include SNI (Selective Notification of Information) published by the National Criminal Justice Reference Service (Box 6000, Rockville, MD 20850), which abstracts current literature on a variety of criminological topics; "selected bibliographies" published by the National Institute of Law Enforcement and Criminal Justice (for example, Carolyn Johnson and Marjorie Kravitz, OVERCROWDING IN CORRECTIONS INSTITUTIONS, February 1978; and J.T. Skip Duncan, Robert N. Brenner, and Marjorie Kravitz, POLICE STRESS, June 1979); and lists of sources published by the National Institute of Law Enforcement and Criminal Justice, such as Susan S. LaPerla, David M. Horton, and Marjorie Kravitz, CRIMINAL JUSTICE PERIODICALS, February 1979.

Ironically, it has become nearly impossible to read through the available abstracts and annotated bibliographies or even, at times, to keep track of the latter, much less read them. The *selected* bibliography of CRIMINAL JUSTICE PERIODICALS suggests the size of the problem: it lists 113 periodicals devoted to criminal justice.

Part I:

PSYCHOLOGICAL APPROACHES IN CRIMINOLOGY

Turf claims in criminology by psychologists and sociologists are familiar. Sociologists make assumptions about individuals but, according to psychologists, fail to examine them sufficiently; moreover, sociologists are not sufficiently sensitive to individual differences. Psychologists assume that social forces are at work but, from the standpoint of many sociologists, fail to examine *them* with due care or to give them enough weight. One useful if indirect form of turf claim comes when psychologists and sociologists undertake to criticize the work purported to support the assumptions of the "other" grouping. Criticism of studies ostensibly showing the importance of family backgrounds or the results of "personality tests" in a differentiating criminal from noncriminal provide familiar examples. Equally familiar are demonstrations that sociological theories of criminal behavior fail in the end to account for the behavior of most persons confronting similar situations.

In their essay prepared for this volume, John Monahan and Stephanie Splane review some of these claims and counterclaims. We concur with their conclusion that, in the end, any theory purporting to offer a comprehensive account of criminality will necessarily include psychological and sociological (and indeed other) elements. One could take the view, however—and this may be their view, too—that accounting for criminality in a comprehensive way has its problems, and need not be the effective aim of many, if any, criminologists, whatever their disciplinary persuasions. "Criminality," of course, is probably not sufficiently specific to be of much use as a dependent variable, the single term covering a vast variety of behaviors. Further, attempting a "comprehensive" explanation is only one possible tack; one might instead seek to account for some aspects of criminality, or, perhaps, some aspect of some particular form of criminality. Finally, though much more could be said, eschewing any hope or even care for a comprehensive explanation, one might seek to press the explanatory powers of chosen variables to the limit in the interest of clarifying and systematizing the relations among *them*.

Seen in this light, both Durkheim's and Sutherland's antipsychological penchants, noted by Monahan and Splane, were understandable and even useful. Both used psychological formulations of the causes of crime as foils to facilitate clarification of distinctively social independent and dependent variables and the relations among them. Whether Durkheim and Sutherland would have agreed that explaining criminality, or even any given form of criminality, in its phenomenal fullness could not be accomplished given their interests and tactics is arguable, but this may be less important than what they achieved. The same should be said, we think, for those "tireless warriors" from the psychological camp, for example, Freud. Learning what a discipline can contribute to the explanation of a phenomenon, including how it can aid in analyzing the latter, *and* learning how study of a phenomenon can help the discipline articulate and systematize its theoretical framework strike us as achievements of high value.

Monahan and Splane provide a number of examples. Focusing on deviant and criminal behavior may assist learning theorists in isolating special conditions or processes of effective, and ineffective, learning. Some favorite studies, of course, may lead psychologists to decide that cetain phenomena call for a different framework for effective analysis; even this helps to specify the limits of a psychological perspective—and, thus, its distinctive relevances. Though one can predict with confidence that such studies will not stop, data to date suggest that explaining criminality via mental illness mainly muddies an already difficult distinction. The fascinating findings on the increased frequency of violent behavior among former mental patients in recent years, on the other hand, suggest a phenomenon that should be explored from a sociological and economic perspective, as Monahan and Splane suggest. Changes in the composition of mental hospital populations point to changing decision patterns and conditions in the broader apparatus of social control. Continuing work aimed at differentiating criminals and noncriminals in terms of their psychological characteristics, if it withstands the almost certain attacks to come, suggests further distinctively psychological studies to be done—and intervening variables that sociologists may want to take into account.

We have included seven recent contributions by psychologists, selected in consultation with Monahan and Splane, that exemplify and amplify the work they discuss. The lengthy treatise by David P. Farrington analyzes experimental studies of deviance, with particular reference to dishonesty. Very much in the "generalist" tradition identified by Monahan and Splane, Farrington is incidentally concerned with criminal behavior per se as part of larger classes of conduct ("deviance," "dishonesty") that are more amenable to conceptualization within a psychological framework and to experimental manipulation. His review of the threats to the validity of experimental studies of deviance and criminality, as well as special limitations and values of such studies, should be particularly instructive for the majority of criminologists whom, we believe, do not use experimental methods.

The pieces by Sarnoff Mednick, by Minoru Masuda and his associates, and by John S. Carroll all illustrate various approaches to criminality via learning theory. Joan McCord's further follow-up of subjects of the Cambridge-Somerville study speaks to a traditional concern of learning theorists—whether child-rearing practices affect learning.[1]

Mednick offers a formulation emphasizing the physiological underpinnings of learning and the results of "empirical tests . . . that could have disconfirmed this hypothesis," but did not. He describes the "Mauritius Project," now in progress, which will permit further articulation and tests of the theory. Cautious in his statements and claims, Mednick leaves a large role for "social forces" in his formulation but, both typically and understandably, does little to explore their character or import. Notwithstanding the explicit inclusion of such social factors, Mednick's work raises strong objections from other social scientists, including many psychologists. It deserves, and likely will receive, careful scrutiny, keeping one aspect of the traditional antagonism in criminology alive.

Masuda et al. furnish data to support the "stress" theory discussed at some length by Monahan and Splane. As Masuda et al. note, such theorizing is in its early stages; this is reflected in the article. How to evaluate the stress induced by various events is not entirely clear, nor is it clear why—or, better, how—such stress leads to crime or the conditions under which this is the case. John S. Carroll, responding to the models of choice used by economists and sociologists studying deterrence, brings to bear a model, at once simpler and more articulated, drawn from work by experimental learning psychologists. His conclusions (though threatened, we think, by their possible lack of external validity) suggest that incentives may play a greater role than penalties in deterring criminal behavior for most persons; further, so far as penalties are taken into account, it seems from his work that severity rather than certainty is the more important. Caroll's work links with that of Philip J. Cook printed elsewhere in this volume (Part VI). Both emphasize how potential criminals respond to opportunities; Carroll, characteristically, emphasizes differential responses and the need for choice models allowing for them.

Joan McCord provides convincing evidence that family atmosphere during childhood affects subsequent behavior. More specifically, she attempts to show that differences in child-raising—indexed by mother's affectionate conduct, parental supervision and expectations, and parental conflict—predict later differences in criminal behavior—as indexed by recorded convictions. Predictions markedly improved on chance. The study does little to explain *how* child-raising works to affect later behavior, but does go some considerable distance toward confirming the relevance of further study of this question. Some earlier studies, which she summarizes, had questioned its relevance in light of ambiguous and even negative findings.[2]

Two further contributions complete this section. Often choosing the individual as the locus of causal forces, it is understandable that psychologists are committed to documenting individual differences.[3] Jack D. Edinger presents data to show that a prisoner typology—developed by E. I. Megargee and generated by responses to the Minnesota Multiphasic Personality Inventory—is valid and generalizable to other prisoner populations. Edinger asserts that the typology has significant implications for both the treatment and management of prisoners.

The final article, a report by a task force of the American Psychological Association, deals with the ethical problems posed for psychologists in the criminal justice system and with one problem posed for the system by the presence of psychologists in it. The discussion and recommendations should be of wide interest because, as the report makes clear, the questions of loyalty and competence raised for psychologists and the problem of predicting criminal behavior are matters that confront in some measure all students of crime and criminal justice. We particularly want to call to attention the discussion of the need "to differentiate obligations owed to organizational as opposed to individual clients." An "employee's ethic," as contrasted with one for "sole proprietors," would help us all in this age of burgeoning bureaucracy.

The essay by Monahan and Splane, as well as most of the readings in this section, focus on the psychological sources of criminal conduct. (See also the papers by Leonard Berkowitz and Hans Tock in Part III.) As Monahan and Splane note, psychologists are also deeply involved in studies of the criminal justice system and in studies of treatment modalities. The first volume of the *Yearbook* contains several articles displaying these involvements that continue to merit examination: see there the article by Joan McCord, already mentioned, and those by Robert M. Garber and Christina Maslach, by Stephen Pfohl, and by Robert R. Ross and H. Bryan McKay. In a future *Yearbook,* we hope to commission essays that will critically analyze psychologists' work on these two topics.

NOTES

1. Volume 1 of the *Yearbook* contains an earlier follow-up by McCord demonstrating some negative side effects of the "treatment" given Cambridge-Somerville experimental subjects.

2. Belief in the consequences of family atmosphere for character formation and later conduct is a firm part of common sense—and many social science theories. Understanding the bases and evidence for this belief is at least as important as understanding the support for deterrence theory or the rehabilitative ideal. Indeed, it is more important since a great deal more than crime is at issue. Perhaps a national commission could examine the evidence.

3. Such differences provide the variations that individually focused theories require for explanatory purposes.

PSYCHOLOGICAL APPROACHES TO
CRIMINAL BEHAVIOR

JOHN MONAHAN and STEPHANIE SPLANE

According to common wisdom, scientific study of criminal behavior was born in economics, had its infancy in biology and psychology, is currently experiencing its adolescence in sociology, and will shortly go home again to mature in the discipline of its birth. From Beccaria and Lombroso, through Freud and Wolfgang, and back to Ehrlich is the accepted sequence of exemplars. While depicting criminology as such a succession of paradigms has occasional merit as a gross index of academic interest, "the older paradigms, are, it turns out, simply quite healthy academic disciplines that have turned their attention elsewhere" (Hirschi and Rudisill, 1976: 15).

In this chapter we made the case for psychology as an intellectual approach with something to contribute to the study of criminal behavior. Psychologists, it is true, are not as often studying crime as they once were; they surely are outnumbered at present by those from the sociological tradition. Still, something of a renaissance of interest in the topic of crime is developing in psychology (Toch, 1979; Sales, 1977; Tapp, 1976; Tapp and Levine, 1977; Lipsitt and Sales, 1979; Sarbin, 1979; Monahan, 1976, in press; Farrington et al., 1979; Konecni and Ebbesen, in press). No doubt the relative largess of research funding on crime has helped whet the appetite of many in the psychological community.

We do not intend, however, to serve notice to criminologists that "the psychologists are coming!" We do intend to argue that psychology as a generic mode of intellectual analysis has never left criminology and, in fact, forms the core of almost all contemporary theories of criminal behavior. It simply happens that the psychology in question has often been formulated by those formally outside the discipline. Making or failing to make this point, we shall then specify the attributes that characterize criminological research when it is performed by professional psychologists and, finally, selectively review several of the salient themes pursured by contemporary psychologists of crime.

To expedite our agenda, we shall restrict the scope of inquiry to the *etiology and description of criminal behavior* and omit consideration of both the criminal justice system as a means for controlling crime and psychology as a tool for reforming those who engage in it. Extensive treatments of both topics from a psychological point of view are available elsewhere (American Psychological Association, 1978; Sechrest et al., 1979). Likewise, and due only to our relative expertise, we shall neglect approaches that are sometimes called "psychological" but which we believe are better characterized as "biological," such as the psychobiology of aggression or the genetic transmission of antisocial propensities.

One preemptory disclaimer is made. Some of what follows may appear to be a revisionist history of criminology in the service of psychology and at the expense of sociology. No such imperialism is intended. There can be no question that sociology has been "the major parent discipline of criminology for perhaps fifty years" (Hirschi and Rudisill, 1976: 15) and remains so today. Yet this professional primacy, we believe, is "because of accidents of national academic history, and not on logical grounds" (Inkeles, 1963: 318). The allocation of the field of criminology to the more general area of sociology has been as much a matter of professional turf-taking as it has been a rational division of intellectual labor. The tone of much of the writing in the area, at least until recently, has reflected this professional antagonism. "The discussion of delinquency in recent sociological theory," Bordua noted, "seems to be distinguished more by a desire to avoid 'psychologizing' than by a desire to understand delinquency" (1962: 249). If a boy is humiliated by his teacher, that is "social class" and admissible in criminological theory. But if he is humiliated by his father, that is child psychology and inadmissible (Bordua, 1962; Empey, 1978). What Kornhauser stated about one leading criminologist is true of others, "In the long battle between sociology and psychology for dominance in explanations of delinquency, Sutherland was a tireless warrier" (1978: 189). Now that both sociology and psychology are entrenched academic disciplines, dissipating energy in such conflicts seems wasteful. The taboo against the incorporation of psychological constructs in sociological theory "may have been necessary to an infant science, as protective barriers are to an immature national economy; it may later become just as obsolete and dysfunctional" (Catton, 1966). We detract nothing from the sociological pioneers of modern criminology in pointing out that some of what they did is more properly construed as psychology.

We believe that not only may psychology have something to contribute to understanding crime but also the process of studying crime may contribute to the development of general psychological theories of human behavior and of broadly applicable psychological research methods. Psychological theory and method have always been shaped by the problems to which they have been applied. The study of abilities and intelligence once led to the development of influential theories of individual differences and sophisticated psychometric techniques. More recently, the application of psychology to the problems of the physical and social environment is spawning new and generalizable insights into the ecological context of all human behavior and is refining field methodology for the discipline as a whole. A serious attempt to understand crime from a psychological perspective could illuminate numerous questions of general relevance to psychology, including: (1) the relationship between self-reported and actual behavior; (2) the effects of institutional processing ("labeling") upon psychologial development; (3) the role of risk-benefit cognitive processes in decision making; (4) the existence of individual differences in affective learning ability; and (5) maturational influences on aggression and conformity. In studying crime, psychologists are undoubtedly shaped by the traditions and biases they bring to the problem. But the study of crime, like the study of other problems in the past, can enlarge those traditions and reduce those biases so that the field itself may undergo useful transformation.

PSYCHOLOGY IN CRIMINOLOGICAL THEORY

Psychological theories of criminal behavior must be distinguished from theories put forth by persons who identify with the discipline of psychology

To appreciate the role of a psychological perspective on criminal behavior, one must see psychology as something other than what people called psychologists do. Failure to do this will result in a severe underestimation of the contribution of psychology to the field of criminology. Psychologists may have been less than stellar in rising to the challenges of criminological analysis. Psychology, on the other hand, is part of the essential foundation of almost all modern criminological thought.

Alex Inkeles, a sociologist, addressed this issue in the more general context of "social" psychology:

> It would not be at all difficult to assemble a set of fity or one hundred recent articles in social psychology, half chosen from the psychological and half from the sociological journals, which would be so much alike that no one judging without knowledge of source or author could with any precision discriminate those written by professional sociologists from those written by psychologists. Several considerations follow from this simple fact. Clearly the two disciplines cannot be defined in terms of what psychologists and sociologists respectively "do," since they often do the same thing. Recourse to the different history and development of the disciplines, while of intrinsic interest, must be treated as irrelevant to the appropriate formulation of their present nature [1963: 318].

In criminology, the point that formal disciplinary affiliations do not strictly dictate an approach to a problem is made most clearly when sociologists perform what is by any account psychological analysis (e.g., Hirschi and Hindelang's, 1977, study of IQ and delinquency; the numerous sociologists in Toch's, 1979, edited volume, *The Psychology of Crime and Criminal Justice*); when psychologists engage in explicitly sociological research (e.g., the numerous psychologists in Simon's, 1977, edited volume, *Advances in Law and Sociology*); and when psychologists and sociologists collaborate on joint projects without either group assuming a supporting role (e.g., Gottfredson et al.'s, 1978, work on parole decision making).

Theories of criminal behavior are psychological to the extent that they use the individual as a unit of analysis

If psychology is not what psychologists do, then what is it? There is no shortage of definitions, "the study of the mind" being the most frequent. In the context of the study of crime, Cohen notes that theories "that seek answers in differences among persons, in the situations they face, and in the interactions between them we may call *psychological*" (1966: 45). Nettler (1978), another sociologist, refers to psychological approaches to criminal behavior as those that take the individual as a unit of analysis. To the extent that a theory of criminal behavior finds it necessary or even useful to make references to an individual's expectations, motivations, learning, or other inferred states or processes that occur within the skin of the individual human being, according to Nettler, the theory would be a psychological one (see Carroll, 1978, in press). A theory may, to be sure, operate on both the sociological and the psychological levels simultaneously (i.e., "social psychology"). This would be the case when system variables (e.g., social class, subculture) are held to have an influence upon individual ones (e.g., self-concept, aspirations). Virtually all existing theories of crime, it will shortly be argued, are sociological in the sense that they are interested in system-level factors that affect crime, and psychological in the sense that they find it impossible to make the link between social variables and crime without first articulating the effect of those social variables on individual offenders. As Cohen has put it:

> Sociologists—or people who are asking sociological questions, whatever they call themselves—are no less interested in motivation than are psychologists, but they are interested in it from a special point of view: how the culture and the organization of the social system help to determine the ingredients and the processes of motivation, and the distribution of different kinds of motivation within and between social systems [1966: 65].

Virtually all existing theories of criminal behavior are, in part, psychological theories

Nettler has noted, regarding criminal behavior, that "sociological explanations that omit reference to individuals do not always satisfy" (1978: 164). Indeed, if the intellectual history of criminology is a guide, such theories virtually never satisfy. The principal reason for the felt necessity of criminological theorists to turn—however reluctantly and surreptitiously—to psychological variables lies in *the obstinate refusal of individual differences in criminal behavior to yield to sociological explanation.*

Enrico Ferri long ago spoke to this issue. Regarding "poverty" as a sociological explanation for crime, he wrote:

> If you regard the general condition of misery as the sole source of criminality then you cannot get around the difficulty that of the one thousand individuals living in

misery from the day of their birth to that of their death, only one hundred or two hundred become criminals. . . . If poverty were the sole determining cause, one thousand out of one thousand poor ought to become criminals. If only two hundred become criminals, while one hundred commit suicide, one hundred end as maniacs, the other six hundred remain honest in their social condition, then poverty alone is not sufficient to explain criminality [1906: 60].

Ferri's defense of psychological analysis might be termed the *individual difference* argument. Inkeles's complementary position might be called the *intervening variable* argument:

> Specification of the *consequences* of different institutional arrangements, that is, of the structural aspects of a social system, often depends on correct estimation of the given arrangements' meaning for, or effect on, the human personality. Since all institutional arrangements are ultimately mediated through individual human action, the consequence of *any* institutional arrangement will, at least, *in part*, depend upon its effects on the human personality. To estimate the influence of one aspect of social structure on another one must, therefore, consider the role of the personality system as the main intervening variable [1963: 320; italics in original].

The proper role of psychological explanation in sociological theory is, of course, one of those "great debates" in social science that is never so much resolved as it is tucked away in footnotes. Durkheim is generally held to be the champion of the antipsychologists: "the determining cause of a social fact should be sought among social facts preceding it and not among the states of the individual consciousness" (1951. 110). Homans holds down the other end of the continuum. He referred to himself as "the ultimate psychological reductionist" (1958: 279). Homans believed "that the chief intellectual task of sociologists at the moment is to show how individual human choices can produce and maintain social organizations. When this task is well done, the arbitrary line we draw between the psychological and the social will disappear" (1974: 13). Sociologists, Homans believed, suffer from a "trained incapacity to recognize the role played by psychological propositions in social theory" (1966: 543).

We kick this horse only to remind the reader that it is just sleeping and not dead. One need not swallow Homans whole and conclude that all sociologists are really practicing psychology without a licence in order to appreciate the role the psychology plays in *some* social theory. Knowledge of the social structure can be improved if bodies of psychological findings are used not for ad hoc explanations to fill in gaps when sociology fails, "but as a base upon which new principles of social structure and structural change are built" (Emerson, 1969).

So important and yet easily fobbed off or forgotten is the observation that modern criminological theories have their foundation in psychological reasoning that a brief review of them is justified. General familiarity with each theory will be assumed. We shall arrive at the conclusion of the sociologist Donald Black that existing theories of crime explain data "with the principles that motivate an individual to violate the law."

For example, one theory explains this motivation with deprivation, such as poverty or a lack of opportunity (e.g., Cloward & Ohlin, 1960); another with marginality, such as lack of family or friends (e.g., Hirschi, 1969); another with participation in a subculture (e.g., Miller, 1958); and still another with the consequences of labeling a deviant as such (e.g., Lemert, 1967). Whatever the details may be, each explains illegal behavior with the motivation of the individual [1976: 9].

Social Disorganization Theories

Shaw and McKay's (1931) theory of criminal behavior, emphasizing economic status, residential mobility, and cultural heterogeneity, is often taken as an exemplar of "pure" sociological analysis. It is true that in this theory "the psychological consequences of the environment for personality development remain unexplored, unsystematized, and indeed only vaguely sensed" (Inkeles, 1963: 341). Yet Shaw himself found it necessary to supplement the sociological aspects of his theory with a case study, *The Jack-Roller: A Delinquent Boy's Own Story*. His justification for so doing is explicitly psychological.

> The case-study approach to delinquency is of primary importance as a device for ascertaining the personal attitudes, feelings and interests of the child; in other words, it shows how he conceives his role in relation to other persons and the interpretations which he makes of the situation in which he lives . . . the child reveals his feelings of inferiority and superiority, his fears and worries, his ideals and philosophy of life, his antagonisms and mental conflicts, his prejudices and rationalizations [1930: 3; see also Toch, 1979].

Opportunity or Strain Theory

The psychological nature of Cohen's (1955) exceedingly influential version of strain theory is revealed most starkly in Kornhauser's (1978: 151) excellent summary. Cohen stated:

> Delinquency, especially in its subcultural form, has the strategic function for working-class youth of serving as a mechanism of defense against the anxiety provoked by violating moral values and flouting achievement values that they have, after all, internalized. The threat that would be posed by conscious awareness of guilt at wrongdoing or same at failure to gain respectable status is met by repressing conventional norms. Repressed but not extinguished, these norms when violated give rise to a pervasive anxiety that is met by the mechanism of reaction formation, a defense in which the ego wards off recognition of repressed impulses by overreacting in a direction opposite to the wishes secretly harbored. By his exaggerated repudiation of middle class norms, the delinquent youth persuades himself that he really hates what he unconsciously desires [1955: 133].

Likewise, Cloward and Ohlin's (1960) version of opportunity theory is replete with references to "internalizations," "aspirations," and "anticipations" that plainly characterize the individual deviant or would-be deviant, rather than the social system in which he or she functions.

Differential Association Theory

Sutherland and Cressey's position that a person commits a crime "because of an excess of definitions favorable to violation of law over definitions unfavorable to violation of law" (1970: 75) is psychological on its face. It posits a differing balance "within each actor among *the definitions* he or she has learned to associate with categories of conduct defined by law as legal or criminal. These 'definitions' are attitudes. They are evaluations. As such, they are presumed to be motivating. The central idea of the differential-interactional explanations: that *cognition causes conduct"* (Nettler, 1978: 264). Sutherland and Cressey's (1970) emphasis upon "drives," "motives," and "learning" is sufficient to make the point that the individual has a central explanatory role in their perspective. The fact that Burgess and Akers (1966) could so easily translate the "sociological" theory of differential association into straightforward psychological learning theory reinforces this interpretation.

Labeling Theory

At first blush, labeling theory (e.g., Lemert, 1951) is not only without a psychological component it is also rabidly antipsychological. According to Nettler, labeling theory "denies . . . the casual importance and explanatory value of personality variables. In fact, labeling theorists regard as futile the search for personality differences that might distinguish categories of more or less criminal persons" (1978: 301).

Henshel and Silverman (1975), on the other hand, find the psychological assumptions of labeling theory "obvious." It is, for them, largely a theory based on psychological perceptions. "Even though the word itself rarely appears in discussions, the notion of perception is ubiquitous in the labeling framework. In fact, . . . it plays a dual role, appearing first in the initial application of the label and then again in subsequent change of self-image" (i.e., secondary deviance; 1975: 346).

Schur (1975), one of the leading proponents of the labeling perspective, notes the seeming inconsistency between interpretation such as that of Nettler and those of Hershel and Silverman. "Paradoxically," he states, labeling theory "seems to emphasize the individual deviator (at least his personal and social characteristics) less than did previous approaches and at the same time to focus on him more intensively, seeking the meaning of his behavior to him and the nature of his self-concept as shaped by societal reactions" (1975: 440). Schur goes on to note, however, "the labeling school's social-psychological focus" which "incorporates from symbolic interactionism a view of the actor as significantly shaping his own projects and lines of action" (1975: 446).

Control Theory

Control theory—the theory that takes crime for granted and asks why some people do *not* commit it—is the most explicitly psychological of modern approaches in criminology. According to Hirschi's version of control theory, delinquent acts result "when an individual's bond to society is weak or broken" (1969:16). The elements of this "bond" are the individual's *attachment* to others, *commitment* to conventional behavior, *involvement* in conventional activities, and *belief* in the validity of social rules. The individual here is clearly the principal unit of analysis. Hirschi refers to attachment as "the sociological counterpart of the super ego or conscience" and commitment as "the counterpart of the ego or common sense" (1969: 20). William James is cited in support of the concept of involvement and Jean Piaget, to explain the nature of belief. It is unclear why Hirschi would choose to depict these concepts as "sociological" in any sense—other than the disciplinary one that he himself happens to be a sociologist—since each of his variables has its effect upon the minds and emotions of individual human beings.

Black's "Behavior of Law"

Of the recent "sociological" attempts to understand criminal behavior, only the positivistic theory of Donald Black (1976) is without a psychological foundation. Black specifies a series of propositions about variations in law across differing social conditions (e.g., "Law varies directly with rank," 1976: 13) and explicitly eschews, as a matter of principle, "explaining" the propositions themselves in terms of psychological constructs (see also Black, 1979; Gottfredson and Hindelang, 1979). Black stated:

> Theory of this kind predicts and explains social life without regard to the individual as such. . . . It neither assumes nor implies that he is, for instance, rational, goal directed, pleasure-seeking, or pain-avoiding. It has no concept of human nature. It has nothing to say about the responsibility of an individual for his own conduct or about its causes. Theory of this kind, then, has nothing to do with the psychology of law (compare, e.g., Schwartz, 1954). It is not at odds with psychological assumptions or theories, however, but is simply a different kind of explanation, a different way to predict the facts [1976: 7].

It is important not to overstate the psychological nature of criminological theory. While sociologists have found it necessary to invoke psychological constructs to explain crime, their *emphasis* have clearly been on the system-level determinants of the internal states and processes they describe. The puzzles that sociological criminologists have tried to solve have by and large been social puzzles, despite the fact that it took some individual pieces to complete the picture. Likewise, psychological criminologists uniformly employ sociological constructs such as "social class" or the "community" in their accounts of crime, but then focus largely on how the individual offender experiences and reacts to these social forces. While sociologists and psychologists of crime each find it necessary to rely upon the work of the other in generating their own explanations of crime, the direction of their intellectual interests corresponds to their larger commitment to the study of social or individual processes.

CRIMINOLOGICAL RESEARCH
PERFORMED BY PSYCHOLOGISTS

Kluckhohn and Murray once stated that every man is "like *all* other men, like *some* other men, and like *no* other men" (1949: 35). Carlson (1971) used this tripartite distinction to categorize psychological research strategies in the field of personality description, and her account provides a useful framework for viewing what is distinctive about various types of psychological research on criminal behavior.

> The psychologist working from this perspective seeks universals, the discovery of general laws of human nature. The emphasis is upon psychological processes; persons are essentially "carriers" of the variables under investigation. Research methods reflected the basic assumptions of this approach: persons are interchangeable; random assignment to treatment conditions is employed to insure control of idiosyncratic qualities which are "noise" in the generalist's inquiry [Carlson, 1971: 208].

The generalist approach to psychological research on criminal behavior is best exemplified in social learning theory (see below). Criminal behavior is seen as a function of the same processes, e.g., reinforcement and modeling, that account for the learning of other more prosocial behaviors. Reinforce someone—anyone—with enough status and prestige for stealing hubcaps and he or she will become a hubcap thief.

When applied to the study of crime, the generalist approach has several ramifications for the kinds of research psychologists do. The belief that the processes involved in learning to do anything else results in the "criminal" aspect of criminal behavior being de-emphasized and the "behavior" aspect increasing in salience. Since the *processes* of learning and cognition as independent variables are most important, the *outcome* of criminal behavior as a dependent variable assumes a secondary position. This allows the psychologist of the generalist persuasion to study what might be called "mock criminality." The psychologist assumes "crime" to be a broad concept, with a largely common-sense quality, for which many indices short of conviction or even arrest will suffice. Since official records are often unreliable and, in any event, are unlikely to be easily affected by brief manipulations, the generalist psychologist uses "laboratory analogies" of what he or she ultimately wishes to address. Thus, psychological studies on television and "violent crime" may use as their dependent measure whether a child hits an inflatable rubber Bo-Bo doll after having watched fighting on television. Crime here is viewed as a subset of a larger psychological construct, that of "aggression." Likewise, psychological research on "theft" is often studied by analyzing how many people return a letter containing money that they "find" in the street. Theft here is also a subset of a larger psychological construct, that of "dishonesty" (cf. Farrington, 1979).

The major implication of the generalist strategy for the psychologist studying crime, however, is the one mentioned by Carlson: reliance upon the true experiment as the analytical method of choice. She found that 75% of the research published in the field of personality description employed experimental (as distinguished from correlational) methods. Psychological research on crime appears to be similarly weighted in favor of the generalist's penchant for randomization (see Farrington et al., 1979).

> This tradition studies psychological processes and their organization in different *kinds* of subjects; its aim is that of identifying group differences that make a difference. Such inquiry establishes typologies, charts the influence of moderator variables, and, substituting measurement for manipulation, tends to employ correlational methods (broadly conceived, in all their contemporary variations) [Carlson, 1971: 208].

The "differential" approach in psychological research applied to crime is best exemplified in the work of Eysenck and Megargee (see below). In the former case, the goal of the research is to isolate those personality characteristics that distinguish offenders from nonoffenders; in the latter, to divide offenders into groups based on their personality types.

It is interesting to note that psychologists of the "differential" sort who study crime do so in very different ways than psychologists of the "generalist" sort. Since they are interested as much in *kinds of people* as in *kinds of processes*, they pay more attention to case-finding considerations. If one assumes, as does the generalist, that psychological processes operate substantially the same in all people, then the choice of research subjects becomes largely a matter of convenience, and college sophomores will do as good as any. But if one believes, as does the differential psychologist, that entirely different processes may operate in one kind of person compared to another kind, one chooses research subjects with care. Thus psychologists of crime from the differential orientation tend to use convicted and imprisoned persons, or at the very least those who admit to having committed a crime, as subjects in their largely nonexperimental research.

> The clinical tradition, in its concern for mapping the intricate organization of psychological processes within the unique individual is the prototype; however, the individual approach includes less comprehensive kinds of inquiry. . . . While the potency of the case method in the development of personality study should be so obvious as to require no special emphasis, the particular quality of the contempor- ary (American) *zeitgeist* imposes a special problem: the "clinical" tradition has come to connote a "helping" orientation totally extraneous to the method itself [Carlson, 1971: 208].

Psychologists of the clinical sort who study crime, as Carlson pointed out, generally do so with therapeutic intent. Attempts to understand individual offenders are made not to gain insight into how they came to crime (etiology), or how they currently function as criminals (description), but to serve as an aid in selecting the best available technique of returning them to the ranks of nonoffenders. As Carlson also pointed out, there is no *necessary* connection between case ("n = 1") research and rehabilitative treatment. Yet descriptive psychological case studies of individual offenders not performed in the context of treatment are rare (see, however, Berkowitz, 1978). Such recent studies as are available (e.g., Yokelson and Samenow, 1976) tend to be so ideological as to lack scholarly credibility.

EMERGING PATTERNS OF PSYCHOLOGICAL RESEARCH

We wish now to highlight several topics or problem areas on which the efforts of psychological criminologists have converged in the later half of the 1970s and which will in all likelihood be influential well into the decade that is beginning. As mentioned, we shall concentrate on the etiology and description of criminal behavior, rather than on psychological treatment or the psychology of criminal justice decision makers. The topics that will be considered are (1) psychological *theories* of criminal behavior; (2) the relationship between crime and psychological *disorder*; and (3) psychological *characteristics* of criminal offenders. As will be noted, most psychological research has focused on *violent* crime. To the extent psychologists have considered nonviolent forms of crime, it has often been as examples of "dishonesty," such as classroom cheating. There are very few accounts of the psychology of white-collar crime (but see Monahan et al., 1979; Monahan and Novaco, 1979).

Psychological Theories of Criminal Behavior

Social learning theory. Far and away the most influential modern psychological theory addressing the performance of criminal behavior is social learning theory. It has most frequently been applied to the topic of "aggression," which is viewed as broader than, but inclusive of, violent crime.

Bandura (1979) has recently summarized the massive body of psychological research on aggression. His analysis is presented in Figure 1. The *origins* of aggression, Bandura believes, are to be found in (1) *observational learning*, i.e., in modeling the aggression of others; (2) in reinforced performance, i.e., in *direct experience* in aggression that is rewarded; and (3) in *structural factors* of the organism, such as physical strength and hormonal level. Bandura distinguishes these three factors that account for how aggressive behavior is learned in the first place from factors that activate it in given situations. These *instigators* of already-learned aggression include four forms of modeling influences: watching others aggress may (1) *disinhibit* the fear or guilt one would feel in engaging in the behavior oneself; (2) teach one that acting aggressively often produces *rewards*; (3) generate *emotional arousal* in the observer, which in turn can influence the level of his or her own aggression: and (4) enhance the *salience* of aggressive stimuli (e.g., guns) for the individual observing the aggression.

The most common instigators of aggression are aversive or unpleasant events. These are held to influence aggression in four ways. People are more likely to engage in aggression when they have (1) been physically assaulted, (2) been verbally threatened or insulted, (3) had their reinforcements for performing some activity reduced, or (4) been frustrated in seeking a goal they desire.

SOCIAL LEARNING ANALYSIS OF BEHAVIOR

ORIGINS OF AGGRESSION	INSTIGATORS OF AGGRESSION	REGULATORS OF AGGRESSION

Observational learning
Reinforced performance
Structural determinants
	Modeling influences
	  disinhibitory
	  facilitative
	  arousing
	  stimulus enhancing
	Aversive treatment
	  physical assaults
	  verbal threats and insults
	  adverse reductions in reinforcement
	  thwarting
	Incentive inducements
	Instructional control
	Bizarre symbolic control
		External reinforcement
		  tangible rewards
		  social and status rewards
		  expressions of injury
		  alleviations of aversive treatment
		Punishment
		  inhibitory
		  informative
		Vicarious reinforcement
		  observed reward
		  observed punishment
		Self-reinforcement
		  self-reward
		  self-punishment
		  neutralization of self-punishment
		    moral justification
		    palliative comparison
		    euphemistic labeling
		    displacement of responsibility
		    diffusion of responsibility
		    dehumanization of victims
		    attribution of blame to victims
		    misrepresentation of consequences

Figure 1: Schematic outline of the origins, instigators, and regulators of aggressive behavior in social learning theory. From Bandura (1979).

Bandura also posits three other instigators to the performance of aggression. Incentive inducements to aggression are what the individual expects to obtain by means of the aggressive encounter, such as money or prestige. Instructional instigators of aggression are forms of "following orders" such as occurs in the military. Delusional beliefs such as divine mandates can also instigate aggressive acts.

Finally, Bandura's (1979) social learning account of aggression considers the factors that *regulate* or maintain aggression once it has been initiated. External reinforcements not only can account for the origins and instigation of aggression but also can account for its maintenance as well. These external reinforcements can be in the form of (1) tangible rewards such as money; (2) social rewards, such as approval; and (3) expressions of injury on the part of the victim (which can regulate aggression either by inhibiting it, if the aggressor has any empathy for the victim, or by augmenting it, as when people take pleasure in the misfortune of those they hate). Aggression is also influenced by whether the aggression is successful in the alleviation of aversive treatment that the aggressor had been receiving at the hands of the person who is now the victim. If the only way for children to keep their parents from ignoring them is to be aggressive, for example, aggression is likely to be maintained.

Aggression can be regulated through the threat of punishment, and punishment can serve an informative role as well in giving notice as to behaviors that are socially undesirable. Both the rewards and punishments that regulate aggression may be experienced vicariously, by observing others, in addition to experiencing them oneself.

Bandura (1979) holds that a wide variety of mechanisms regulating aggression are self-generated. People adopt certain cognitive standards for rewarding and for punishing themselves regarding aggression. Aggression, for example, may reinforce one's sense of pride or physical prowess or it may evoke feelings of self-reproach and anger. People are also adept at techniques for disengaging these internal standards and controls. They may (1) use moral justifications for aggression, such as occurred with the Spanish Inquisition; (2) compare their own aggressive acts with the even more aggressive acts of others so as to appear relatively benign; (3) label their behavior in nonaggressive terms, as when scatter bombs become "antipersonnel devices"; (4) displace responsibility for the aggression of others; (5) diffuse respnsibility among as many people as possible; (6) view victims as less than human and, therefore, unworthy of concern; (7) perceive victims as responsible for their own demise; and (8) misrepresent to the point of denial that they are being aggressive at all.

Bandura's (1979) social learning account of aggression is an obviously complex and comprehensive one, to which a brief summary cannot do justice. While it is not a theory of "crime" per se, it would seem to have great relevance both to those theories of crime and delinquency that hold that people "learn" to commit crime and to those theories that posit that people are "naturally" criminal and must learn to inhibit or control their criminal tendencies.

One might observe a certain "laundry-list" quality to many of the factors given as influencing the occurrence of aggression. This is due to the so-called pragmatic orientation of behavioral psychology compared to the more theoretical orientation of sociological criminology. Thus, while a sociological theory of crime will generally attempt to tie all its postulates fairly directly to a few central constructs (e.g., "disorganization," "strain," "bond"), social learning theory incorporates any factor believed to relate to the learning or performance of the behavior in question, without regard to the theoretical connections among the various factors. "Bizarre symbolic control," for example, in Bandura's (1979) account of aggression, is related to "verbal threats and insults" only in the functional sense that both are believed to instigate aggression. Their relationship is not of the same order as the relationship between "attachment" and "involvement" in Hirschi's (1969) sociological theory. Behavioral psychologists appear to be more concerned with the usefulness of their theories in preventing or treating crime, while sociologists have placed a higher value on conceptual elegance.

Eysenck's extraversion-neuroticism-psychoticism theory. A second psychological theory relating to criminal behavior is that of Hans Eysenck, the British psychologist and major nemesis of psychoanalysis. While Eysenck's theory of crime appears more popular in England than in the United States and has nowhere near as many adherents as social learning theory, it is one of the few psychological theories explicitly formulated to account for criminal behavior.

Eysenck (1977) has developed and tested a theory of personality and crime based upon the positions that persons occupy on three major personality dimensions: extraversion (E), neuroticism (N), and psychoticism (P). A high E score indicates sociability, impulsivity, aggressiveness, and a craving for activity and excitement. A high N scorer tends to be moody, anxious, sensitive, and rigid. A high P scorer is characterized by being solitary, lacking in empathy, sensation seeking, and aggressive toward others.

Eysenck's basic thesis is that persons occupying different positions on these dimensions will respond differently to the same learning experiences. Extraverts and high N scorers are postulated to be the least responsive to social training, particularly training that relies upon the emotion of "fear." Eysenck has posited a physiological basis for extraversion and neuroticism, but has not yet done so for psychoticism. Extraverts are held to have a lower level of cortical arousal than introverts and, therefore, to learn less rapidly and less strongly than introverts. People high on neuroticism are believed to have an excessively labile autonomic nervous system and to react with extreme fear to painful stimuli, which in turn inhibits efficient learning. With regard to criminal behavior, the following hypotheses emerge from Eysenck's theory: (1) the neurotic extravert (high E, high N) will have the highest level of offending; (2) the stable introvert (low E, low N) will have the lowest level of offending; (3) neurotic introverts (low E, high N) and stable extraverts (high E, Low N) will exhibit intermediate levels of offending. Thus, offending is predicted to be directly proportional to scores on E, N, and P.

juveniles were found to have a nonpsychotic mental disorder. "Personality disorders" were reported for 21.0% of the adults and 25.2% of the juveniles. Monahan et al. (in press) found that police officers estimate that 30% of the persons they arrest are at least "somewhat" mentally ill, but only 12% are either "moderately" or "severely" mentally ill. Roth and Ervin concluded that "psychiatric morbidity in criminal populations is probably somewhere between 15 and 20 percent" (1971: 429). Finally, Koenigsberg et al. (1977) studied 255 males known to the juvenile courts 25 years previously. Of these adjudicated delinquents, 6% had later contact with both the criminal justice and mental health systems, 6% with the mental health system only, and 28% with the criminal justice system only. Thus, 12% of the delinquent sample acquired a history of treated psychological disorder within 25 years.

Considering that the President's Commission on Mental Health recently concluded that "as many as 25 percent of the population are estimated to suffer . . . emotional disorders at any time" (1978: 8) and given that the social class from which "street" offenders are drawn are disproportionately represented in that figure, the findings of Bolton (1976), Monahan et al. (in press), and Roth and Ervin (1971) do not indicate an increased rate of mental illness among jail inmates.

The most comprehensive study of rates of psychiatric disorder among offender populations has been performed by Guze (1976, Martin et al., 1978). Guze's review of the literature is representative of the conclusions of others (e.g., Brodsky, 1973):

> Overall, the other studies may be summarized as follows. Psychosis, schizoprenia, primary affective disorders, and the various neurotic disorders are seen in only a minority of identified criminals. There is no complete agreement as to whether any of these conditions is more common among criminals than the general population, but it is clear that these disorders carry only a *slightly* increased risk of criminality if any at all [Guze, 1976: 35: italics in original].

Guze's own study of 223 male and 66 female felons in Missouri arrived at the following findings:

> Sociopathy, alcoholism, and drug dependence are the psychiatric disorders characteristically associated with serious crime. Schizophrenia, primary affective disorders, anxiety neurosis, obsessional neurosis, phobic neurosis, and brain syndromes are not. Sexual deviations, defined as illegal *per se*, are not, in the absence of accompanying sociopathy, alcoholism, and drug dependence, associated with other serious crime.

Diamond, commenting on Guze's earlier work, notes that sociopathy, alcoholism, and drug dependence "are precisely those psychiatric states which are less easily definable and less generally agreed to be illnesses at all" (1974: 448). Indeed, Guze defined "sociopathy" for the purposes of his research as follows:

> This diagnosis was made if at least two of the following five manifestations were present in addition to a history of police trouble (other than traffic offenses): a

history of excessive fighting . . . school delinquency . . . a poor job record . . . (and) a
period of wanderlust or being a runaway. . . . For women, a history of prostitution
could be substituted for one of the five manifestations [1976: 35].

If all prostitutes who have ever been truant in school or all unemployed males
with a period of "wanderlust" in their history are counted as "sociopaths," it is
not difficult to understand why 78% of all male and 65% of all female felons were
so diagnosed.

With the exception of a higher prevalence of the "disorders" of alcoholism and
drug dependence, therefore, prisoners do not appear to have higher rates of
diagnosable mental illness than their class-matched peers in the open community.

Violent behavior among ex-mental patients. An interesting pattern exists in
the data on violent crime rates of former mental patients. Almost without
exception, studies performed in the 1950s and earlier found that released patients
had a *lower* rate of arrest for violent behavior than the general population
(Ashley, 1922; Pollock, 1938; Cohen, 1955; Brill and Malzberg, 1954), while
studies performed in the 1960s and 1970s have consistently found a *higher* rate of
violent behavior among former patients than among the nonpatient population
(Rappaport and Lassen, 1965; Giovanni and Gurel, 1967; Zitrin et al., 1976;
Durban et al., 1977; Sosowsky, 1978). What accounts for this wholesale shift in
the research findings?

According to Cocozza et al. (1978; see also Steadman et al., 1978), the
apparently increased crime rate among former patients reflects "the changing
clientele of state hospitals." They examined the arrest records of almost 4,000
patients released from New York State mental hospitals in 1968 and 1975 using a
19-month follow-up period. Particular attention was paid to whether or not the
ex-patient had ever been arrested *prior* to being sent to the hospital. Since their
findings for both years were similar, only the 1975 data are presented in Table 1.

A striking pattern of results emerges. While it is true that former patients, as a
group, do have a substantially higher arrest record for all types of crime than
does the general population, patients without an arrest record *prior* to going to
the hospital have a *lower* arrest rate than the general population. Patients with
one arrest prior to going to the hospital have a slightly higher than average arrest
rate for violent crime once they get out of the hospital (except for sex criminals
whose rates are substantially higher). Patients with *two or more* prior arrests
have a drastically higher violent crime rate than the general population. *Thus,
compared with the general population, the higher rate of violent crime
committed by released mental patients can be accounted for entirely by those
patients with a record, particularly an extensive record, of criminal activity that
predated their hospitalization.* This is consistent with the literature on violent
crime among criminal populations: A record of past violence is the best predictor
of future violence.

But why the *increase* in violent crime rates among released patients in recent
years? Steadman et al. (1978) compared their findings with those reported by

TABLE 1
Annual Arrest Rates per 1,000 for Felonies—1975 Sample*

	General Population	Total Patient Sample	Patients with no prior arrest	Patients with one prior arrest	Patients with two or more prior arrests
	(N=12,320,540)	(N=1938)	(N=1428)	(N=187)	(N=323)
Total Arrests	32.51	98.50	22.06	138.00	413.50
Arrests for Violent Crimes	3.62	12.03	2.21	3.37	60.46
Arrests for Potentially Violent Crimes	2.83	6.18	0.88	3.37	31.21
Arrests for Sex Crimes	0.45	2.60	0.44	6.74	9.75

*From Cocozza et al., 1978.

Brill and Malzberg (1954) on a comparable population of New York patients released in 1947. The results of the two studies are almost identical except that *only 15% of the 1947 patients had a prior arrest record, while 40% of the 1975 subjects did.* As Brill and Malzberg noted 25 years ago:

> Arrests in the ex-mental hospital patients were largely concentrated in a relatively small, rather well-demarcated group of persons with a previous criminal record, and their anti-social behavior was clearly correlated with well-known factors which operate in the general population and was not correlated with the factors of mental illness except in a negative way. . . . An attack of mental illness with hospitalization does not tend to leave an inclination toward criminal activity greater than that which existed prior to the illness and . . . does not produce such a tendency if it did not previously exist [1954: 12].

Rabkin came to a similar conclusion in her exhaustive review of every study published on the topic:

> At the present time there is no evidence that released patients' mental status as such raises their arrest risk; rather, antisocial behavior and mentally ill behavior apparently coexist, particularly among young, unmarried, unskilled poor males, especially those belonging to ethnic minorities [1979: 25].

The real issue, therefore, is not what psychological factors account for the increased crime rate among released mental patients, but rather what socio-logical and economic factors underlie the administrative and political decision to send more criminals to mental hospitals in the first place. As chronic-geriatric patients—who have a very low crime rate—are being deinstitutionalized from mental hospitals into nursing homes, the proportion of beds that are being filled by younger and more violent persons—who in the past might have been sent to jail or prison (Stone, 1975)—is rising. As Steadman et al. have noted, "If one were to gather a group of men of whom 40 percent had previously been arrested, from the general population, it is quite likely that the arrest rates found among the 1975 former patient group would be duplicated or exceeded" (1978: 820).

In terms of specific psychiatric diagnoses, the New York study found a significant association between patients diagnosed as drug or alcohol abusers of "Personality Disorders" and future criminal behavior. While no more than 8% of any other diagnostic category was subsequently arrested, 18% of patients with alcohol- or other drug-related diagnoses were arrested as were 28% of those diagnosed as "personality disorder" (Steadman et al., 1978). With the substitu-tion of "sociopathy" for "personality disorder," these are the same three factors identified in Guze's (1976) study of mental illness in a prison population. As was the case with sociopathy, it is unclear what personality disorder means in this context and how independent it is from a history of past criminal behavior.

Is there, then, a relationship between crime and psychological disorder? Judging from the research that exists, the answer would appear to be a fairly definitive no. Prisoners do not seem to have higher rates of psychological disorder than their age-, sex-, and class-matched contemporaries in the community, and people who are released from mental hospitals seem to be no more likely to commit crimes than others with equivalent criminal records who have never been in mental hospitals.

The last word on this topic, however, may yet to be uttered. Institutional status—being or having been a prisoner or a mental patient—is only the grossest and most extreme index of whether one has committed a crime or experienced a psychological disorder. Surely the majority of people who at one time in their lives commit criminal or disordered acts manage successfully to avoid state institutionalization, whether due to lack of detection and apprehension or to the vagaries of criminal justice and mental health system processing. Future research in this area might profitably be directed toward methods of case-finding less crude than residence in an institution and might ask questions less global than "does crime relate to psychological disorder?" Which forms of psychological disorder (if any) are associated with which forms of criminal behavior under what circumstances may be a more fruitful overarching question than has been articulated in the research to date.

Psychological Characteristics of Criminal Offenders

The study of the personality characteristics of criminal offenders, particularly as compared with nonoffenders, has a long but not illustrious history. Schuessler and Cressey, in a widely quoted review of over 100 psychometric investigations, concluded that "not a single trait was shown in these series of studies to be more characteristic of delinquents than nondelinquents" (1974: 1962). Waldo and Dinitz (1967), however, found the 81% of the Minnesota Multiphasic Personality Inventory (MMPI) studies, and 75% of the non-MMPI studies published in the subsequent 15 years were able to distinguish criminal and noncriminal groups at statistically significant levels.

The MMPI has been the instrument most frequently chosen in recent years to describe the personality of criminal offenders. Rader (1977), for example, compared the MMPI profiles of rapists, exhibitionists, and assaultive persons and concluded that the rapists differed from the other two groups on a variety of scales, but that assaultive persons and exhibitionists did not differ from each other in their personality patterns. Adams (1976) found several scales that could distinguish between incarcerated multiple and first-time offenders. Other investigations have used the MMPI successfully to distinguish assaultive from nonassaultive inmates (McCreary, 1976; Holland and Holt, 1975; Suther et al., 1978).

By far the most comprehensive program of research using the MMPI to distinguish *among* offender groups is that of Megargee (1977; Mergargee and Bohn, 1979). In a series of studies, Megargee and his colleagues have shown that the MMPI profiles of young male prisoners can be reliably placed into 1 of 10 categories that differ from one another in many respects (Meyer and Megargee, 1977; Megargee and Dorhout, 1977; Megargee and Bohn, 1977). Edinger (1979) attempted to validate Megargee's system with a sample of over 3,000 state and federal prisoners. Over 85% of the prisoners could be classified by a computer into 1 of the 10 types. Significant differences in age, sex, commitment offense, and prison rule infractions were found among the groups. The principle use of the MMPI research to date has been to assist in prisoner classification as an aid to prison management. Bohn (1978), for example, reported a 46% reduction in prison assaults when the Megargee system was used to assist in prison dormitory assignments.

Megargee (1966, 1970) has postulated that there are two distinct personality types related to antisocial behavior: the undercontrolled and the overcontrolled aggressive. The Overcontrolled Hostility Scale (Megargee et al., 1967) was developed to distinguish the two types. The first type scores low on this scale and simply lacks the ability to control aggressive impulses. the highly overcontrolled group, on the other hand, appear to have aggressive impulses which are pent up over time due to strong inhibitions against their expression, making this group prone to sudden, violent outbursts. Thus, overcontrolled persons would be expected to be overrepresented in groups of persons who have committed very violent acts such as murder, rape, or aggravated assault. Several studies have supported the hypothesis that high schores on the Overcontrolled Hostility Scale relate to episodic acts of violence (Megargee, 1966; Wheeler, 1971). Other studies, however, have failed to find this relationship (Hoppe and Singer, 1977; McGurk and McGurk, 1979).

One non-MMPI characteristic of offenders that has received attention is that of temporal orientation. Morris and Zingle (1977) administered the Wallace Temporal Perspective Technique and the Life Orientation Test to a group of male prison inmates and a sample of noncriminals and found that the inmates tended to be less future-oriented than noncriminals. Landau (1975) investigated the assumption that both delinquency and institutionalization independently have a limiting effect on future time perspective (FTP). The results confirmed the hypotheses: Institutionalized delinquents had the shortest FTP, while noninstitutionalized nondelinquents had the longest. Institutionalized nondelinquents and noninstitutionalized delinquents fell in the middle range. In a second study, Landau (1976) investigated the temporal orientation of delinquents and nondelinquents while controlling for institutionalization. The data indicated that delinquents tended to perceive the past as more negative and the future as more positive than did nondelinquents.

In addition, Andrew and Bentley (1976) conducted an investigation which confirmed prior findings that time seems to pass slowly for delinquents as compared to the perceptions of normal samples. Davids and Falkof (1975) did a comparative study of institutionalized delinquents in 1959 and 1974 on measures of time orientation and delay of gratification. They concluded that the 1974 delinquents were more impulsive, present-oriented, and in need of immediate gratification than the 1959 delinquents.

Farley (1973) and Farley and Farley (1972) have characterized adolescent delinquents as having an exaggerated need for stimulation. Farley and Sewell

(1976) found that delinquents were in fact significantly higher than nondelinquents in stimulation-seeking as measured by the Sensation Seeking Scale. Farley et al. (1979) investigated delinquent behaviors among institutionalized male drug addicts. The dependent measure was type of discharge: delinquent (result of rule infractions) or normal (upon successful completion of the program). Two independent measures were employed: physiological arousal and sensation-seeking motive as measured by the Sensation Seeking Scale. A significantly greater frequency of delinquent discharges were found among low arousal/high sensation-seeking persons relative to high arousal/low sensation-seeking persons. Significantly more normal discharges were found in the latter group.

Finally, it is worth noting that psychological studies of IQ as a characteristic distinguishing offenders from nonoffenders—so long dismissed in criminological theory—have achieved a new-found respectability due to Hirschi and Hindelang's (1977) comprehensive review and reinterpretation of IQ as a mediating variable in determining school performance.

CONCLUSIONS

Psychological research on how one learns to commit crime or to refrain from committing it, on the relationship between crime and mental disorder, and on the traits and processes that characterize people who commit crime would seem clearly relevant to current theory in crime and delinquency, particularly since that theory is so psychologically oriented in the first place.

Why, then, has there been such little rapprochement between criminologists of the sociological and the psychological traditions, and why has *explicitly* psychological research—that is, research directed to understanding the individual—had so little influence on contemporary criminological thought? We have already alluded to disciplinary squabbles as historical factors accounting for the development of criminology within sociology. Yet the reluctance of sociological criminologists to admit to reliance upon the individual as a unit of analysis appears to be maintained by more than disciplinary rivalry. We believe that it has to do with the *erroneous belief that the level of causal analysis determines the level of preventive and rehabilitative intervention.* It is as though directing attention at the personality characteristics associated with people who commit crime necessarily means that one favors psychotherapy as the treatment of choice for criminal offenders or parent education programs as the preferred prevention strategy. But such need not be the case. If social conditions influence the development of certain patterns of psychological functioning, then research on those patterns can assist in designing changes in the social conditions as well as in the psychological functioning itself. In any etiological model of crime that implicates *both* system-level and individual-level factors—as virtually all current models do—the choice of interventions for prevention and rehabilitation becomes more a political than a scientific matter. It is true that psychologists may have a trained incapacity to see the social forest for the individual trees. As Judge

David Bazelon (1973) said to a group of psychological criminologists, "I think you would do well to consider how much less expensive it is to hire a thousand psychologists than to make even a miniscule change in the social and economic structure." What the field of criminology needs, it appears to us, are sociologists who use psychological intervening variables without embarrassment and psychologists who are aware of the social roots of the individual processes they study.

We anticipate that the future will see psychological research on criminal behavior develop in the direction of *comprehensive empirically based theories* to rival in breadth the sociologically oriented theories currently in existence. As psychologists gain more proficiency in criminological research and become more comfortable with criminological concepts, the tendency toward single variable, nonprogrammatic investigations will decrease. Such theories will no doubt at first rely heavily upon psychological metaphors drawn from other domains. In time, however, psychological explanations indigenous to criminal behavior will appear.

Sociologists have had the field of criminology largely to themselves for the past half-century. Economists in the decade just ending have thrown down a conceptual gauntlet that has precipitated some of the most lively paradigm clashes in the history of criminological theory. Psychologists, in the decade to come, may provide a similarly invigorating challenge. Indeed, on the topic of crime, "the debate between sociologists and economists has now become a forum" (Carroll, 1978: 1520).

NOTE

1. As Inkeles points out, even Durkheim "finally found it necessary to refer to human psychology" (1963: 323) in order to explain suicide. Where society was not integrated, Durkheim stated the individual, having "too keen a feeling for himself and his own value . . . wishes to be his own only goal, and as such an objective cannot satisfy him, drags out languidly and indifferently an existence which henceforth seems meaningless to him" (1951: 356).

REFERENCES

Adams, T.C. Some MMPI differences between first and multiple admissions with a state prison population. *Journal of Clinical Psychology*, 1976, 32(3), 555-558.

Allsopp, J.F. and Feldman, M.P. Extraversion, neuroticism and psychoticism and anti-social behavior in school girls. *Social Behavior and Personality*, 1975, 2, 184.

Allsopp, J.F. and Feldman, M.P. Item analyses of questionnaire measures of personality and anti-social behavior in school. *British Journal of Criminology*, 1976.

American Psychological Association. Report of the Task Force on the Role of Psychology in the Criminal Justice System. *American Psychologists*, 1978, 33, 1099-1113.

Andrew, J.M. and Bentley, M.R. The quick minute: delinquents, drugs and time. *Criminal Justice and Behavior*, 1976, 3(2), 179-186.

Ashley, M. Outcome of 1,000 cases paroled from the Middletown State Homeopathic Hospital. *State Hospital Quarterly*, 1922, 8, 64-70.

Bandura, A. The social learning perspective: mechanisms of aggression. In H. Toch (Ed), *The Psychology of Crime and Criminal Justice.* New York: Holt, Rinehart & Winston, 1979, pp. 198-236.

Bazelon, D. Psychologists in corrections—Are they doing good for the offender or well for themselves? In S. Brodsky, *Psychologists in the Criminal Justice System.* Urbana: University of Illinois Press, 1973.

Berkowitz, L. Is criminal violence normative behavior? *Journal of Research in Crime and Delinquency,* 1978, *15,* 148-161.

Black, D. *Behavior of Law.* New York: Academic Press, 1976.

Black, D. Common sense in the sociology of law. *American Sociological Review,* 1979, *44,* 18-27.

Bohn, M. Classification of offenders in an institution for young adults. Paper presented at the Nineteenth International Congress of Applied Psychology. Munich, 1978.

Bolton, A. A study of the need for and availability of mental health services for mentally disordered jail inmates and juveniles in detention facilities. Unpublished report, Arthur Bolton Associates, Boston, Mass., 1976.

Bordua, David J. Some comments in theories of group delinquency. *Sociological Inquiry,* Spring, 1962, *33,* 245-460.

Brill, H. and Malzberg, B. Statistical report on the arrest record of male ex-patients, age 16 and over, released from New York State mental hospitals during the period 1946-48. Unpublished manuscript, New York State Department of Mental Hygiene, 1954.

Brodsky, S. *Psychologists in the Criminal Justice System.* Urbana: University of Illinois Press, 1973.

Burgess, R. and Akers, R. Differential association—reinforcement theory of criminal behavior. *Social Problems,* 1966 *14,* 128-147.

Carlson, R. Where is the person in personality research? *Psychological Bulletin,* 1971, *75,* 203-219.

Carroll, J. A psychological approach to deterrence: the evaluation of crime opportunities. *Journal of Personality and Social Psychology,* 1978, *36,* 1512-1520.

Carroll, J. Committing a crime: the offender's decision. In V. Konecni and E. Ebbesen (Eds), *Social Psychological Analysis of Legal Processes.* San Francisco: W.H. Freeman, in press

Catton, W. *From Animistic to Naturalistic Sociology.* New York: McGraw-Hill, 1966.

Cloward, R.A. and Ohlin, L.E. *Delinquency and Opportunity.* New York: Macmillan, 1960.

Cocozza, J., Melick, M. and Steadman, H. Trends in violent crime among ex-mental patients. *Criminology,* 1978, *16,* 317-334.

Cohen, A.K. *Delinquent Boys: The Culture of the Gang.* New York: Macmillan, 1955.

Cohen, D. *Deviance and Control.* Englewood Cliffs, N.J.: Prentice-Hall, 1966.

Davids, A. and Falkof, B.B. Juvenile delinquents then and now: comparison of findings from 1959 and 1974. *Journal of Abnormal Psychology,* 1975, 84(2), 161-164.

Dershowitz, A. The origins of preventing confinement in Anglo-American law. Part I: the English experience. *University of Cincinnati Law Review,* 1974, *43,* 1-60.

Diamond, B. The psychiatric prediction of dangerousness. *University of Pennsylvania Law Review,* 1974, *123,* 439-452.

Dinitz, S. Chronically antisocial offenders. In J. Conrad and S. Dinitz *In Fear of Each Other: Studies of Dangerousness in America.* Lexington, Mass., Lexington Books, 1978.

Durban, J., Pasewark, R., Albers, D. Criminality and mental illness: a study of arrest rates in a rural state. *American Journal of Psychiatry,* 1977, *134,* 80-83.

Durkhiem, E. *Suicide.* New York: Macmillan, 1951.

Edinger, J.D. Cross-validation of the Megargee MMPI typology for prisoners. *Journal of Consulting and Clinical Psychology,* 1979, *47*(2), 234-242.

Emerson, R. Operant psychology and exchange theory. In R. Burgess and D. Peushell (Eds), *Experimental Analysis and Social Process: Implications for a Behavioral Sociology.* New York: Columbia University Press, 1969.

Empey, L. *American Delinquency: Its Meaning and Construction.* Homewood, Ill.: Dorsey Press, 1978.

Eysenck, H.J. *Crime and Personality.* London: Routledge & Kegan Paul, 1977.

Farley, F.H. A theory of delinquency. Paper presented at the American Psychological Association annual meeting, Montreal, August 1973.

Farley, F.H. and Farley, S.V. Stimulus-seeking motivation and delinquent behavior among institutionalized delinquent girls. *Journal of Consulting and Clinical Psychology*, 1972, *39*, 94-97.

Farley, F.H. and Sewell, T. Test of an arousal theory of delinquency: stimulation-seeking in delinquent and nondelinquent black adolescents. *Criminal Justice and Behavior*, 1976, *3*, 315-320.

Farley, F.H., Steinberger, H., Cohen, A., and Barr, H.L. Test of a theory of delinquency: "delinquent" behaviors among institutionalized drug addicts as a function of arousal and the sensation-seeking motive. *Criminal Justice and Behavior*, 1979, *6*(1), 41-48.

Farrington, D. Experiments on deviance with special reference to dishonesty. *Advances in Experimental Psychology*, 1979, *12*, 207-252.

Farrington, D., Hawkins, K., and Lloyd-Bastock, S. (Eds) Psychology, Law and Legal Processes. New York: Macmillan, 1979.

Feldman, M.P. *Criminal Behavior: A Psychological Analysis*. New York: John Wiley, 1977.

Ferri, E. *The Positive School of Criminology*. Chicago: Kerr, 1906.

Giovanni, J. and Gurel, L. Socially disruptive behavior of ex-mental patients. *Archives of General Psychiatry*, 1967, *17*, 146-153.

Gottfredson, M.R. and Hindelang, M.V. Response: theory and research in the sociology of law. *American Sociological Review*, 1979, *44*, 27-37.

Gottfredson, D., Wilkins, L., and Hoffman, P. *Guidelines for Parole and Sentencing*. Lexington, Mass.: Lexington Books, 1978.

Greenland, C. The prediction and management of dangerous behavior. Social Policy Issues, Law and Psychiatry Symposium, Clarke University, 1978.

Guze, S. *Criminality and Psychiatric Disorders*. New York: Oxford University Press, 1976.

Henshel, R.L. and Silverman, R.A. (Eds) *Perception in Criminology*. New York: Columbia University Press, 1975.

Hirschi, T. *Causes of Delinquency*. Berkeley: University of California Press, 1969.

Hirschi, T. and Hindelang, M. Intelligence and delinquency: a revisionist review. *American Sociological Review*, 1977, *42*, 571-587.

Hirschi, T. and Rudisill, D. The great American search: causes of crime 1876-1976. *Annals of the American Academy of Political and Social Science*, 1976, *423*, 14-22.

Holland, T.R. and Holt, N. Prisoner intellectual and personality correlates of offense severity and recidivism probability. *Journal of Clinical Psychology*, 1975, *31*(4), 667-672.

Homans, G. Reply to Razak. *American Sociological Review*, 1966, *31*, 543-544.

Homans, G. Social behavior as exchange. *American Journal of Sociology*, 1958, *63*, 597-606.

Homans, G. *Social Behavior: Its Elementary Forms*. New York: Harcourt Brace Jovanovich, 1974.

Hoppe, C.M. and Singer, R.D. Interpersonal violence and its relationship to some personality measures. *Aggressive Behavior*, 1977, *3*(3), 261-270.

Inkeles, A. Sociology and psychology. In S. Koch (Eds), *Psychology: A Study of a Science* (Vol. 6). New York: McGraw-Hill, 1963, pp. 317-385.

Kluckhohn, C. and Murray, H. *Personality in Nature, Society and Culture*. New York: Knopf, 1949.

Koenisberg, D., Balla, D.A., and Lewis, D.O. Juvenile delinquency, adult criminality, and adult psychiatric treatment: an epidemological study. *Child Psychiatry and Human Development*, 1977, *7*(3), 141-146.

Konecni, V. and Ebbesen, E. (Eds) *Social Psychological Analysis of Legal Processes*. San Francisco: W.H. Freeman, in press.

Kornhauser, R. *Social Sources of Delinquency*. Chicago: University of Chicago Press, 1978.

Landau, S.F. Delinquency, institutionalization, and time orientation. Journal of Consulting and Clinical Psychology, 1976, *44*(5), 745-759.

Landau, S.F. Future time perspective of delinquents and nondelinquents: the effect of institutionalization. *Criminal Justice and Behavior*, 1975, *2*(1), 22-36.

Lazarus, R., and Launier, R. Stress-related transactions between persons and environment. In L. Pervin and M. Lewis (Eds), *Internal and External Determinants of Behavior*. New York: Plenum, in press.

Lemert, E. The concept of secondary deviation. *In Human Deviance, Social Problems and Social Control.* Englewood Cliffs, N.J.: Prentice-Hall, 1967.

Lemert, E.M. *Social Pathology.* New York: McGraw-Hill, 1951.

Lipsitt, P. and Sales, B. (Eds) *New Directions in Psycholegal Research.* New York: Van Nostrand Reinhold, 1979.

Martin, R.L., Cloninger, C.R., and Guze, S.B. Female criminality and the prediction of recidivism. a prospective six-year follow-up. *Archives of General Psychiatry,* 1978, *35*(2), 207-214.

Masuda, M., Cutler, D.L., Hein, L., and Holmes, T.H. Life events and prisoners. *Archives of General Psychiatry,* 1978, *35*(2), 197-203.

McCreary, C.P. Trait and type differences among male and female assaultive and non-assaultive offenders. *Journal of Personality Assessment,* 1976, *40*(6), 617-621.

McGrath, J. *Social and Psychological Factors in Stress.* New York: Holt, Rinehart & Winston, 1970.

McGurk, B. and McGurk, R. Personality types among prisoners and prison officers. *British Journal of Criminology,* 1979, *19*, 31-49.

Mechanic, D. *Medical Sociology: A Selective Review.* New York: Macmillan, 1968.

Megargee, E.I. The need for a new classification system. *Criminal Justice and Behavior,* 1977, *4*(2), 107-114.

Megargee, E.I. The role of inhibition in the assessment and understanding of violence. In E. Singer (Ed), *The Control of Aggression and Violence: Cognitive and Physiological Factors.* New York: Academic Press, 1970, 125-147.

Megargee, E.I. Undercontrolled and overcontrolled personality types in extreme antisocial aggression. *Psychological Monographs,* 1966, *80*(3), 611.

Megargee, E.I. and Bohn, M.J., Jr. *Classifying Criminal Offenders.* Beverly Hills, Calif.: Sage Publications, 1979.

Megargee, E.I., Cook, P.E., and Mendelsohn, G.A. Development and evaluation of an MMPI score of assaultiveness in overcontrolled individuals. *Journal of Abnormal Psychology,* 1967, *73*, 519-528.

Megargee, E.I. and Dorhout, B. Revision and refinement of the classificatory rules. *Criminal Justice and Behavior,* 1977, *4*(2), 125-148.

Meyer, J. and Megargee, E.I. Initial development of the system. *Criminal Justice and Behavior,* 1977, *4*(2), 115-124.

Miller, W. Lower class culture as a generating milieu of gang delinquency. *Journal of Social Issues,* 1958, *15*, 5-19.

Monahan, J. (Ed) *Community Mental Health and the Criminal Justice System.* Elmsford, N.Y.: Pergamon Press, 1976.

Monahan, J. *The Clinical Prediction of Violent Behavior.* Washington, D.C.: Government Printing Office, in press.

Monahan, J., Caldiera, C., and Friedlander, H. The police and the mentally ill: a comparison of arrested and committed persons. *International Journal of Law & Psychiatry,* in press.

Monahan, J. and Geis, G. Controlling "dangerous" people. *Annals of the American Academy of Political Science,* 1976, *423*, 142-151.

Monahan, J.T., Novaco, R.W., and Geis, G. Corporate violence: research strategies for community psychology. In T. Sarbin (Ed), *Community Psychology and Criminal Justice.* New York: Human Sciences Press, 1979.

Monahan, J.T. and Novaco, R.W. Corporate violence: a psychological analysis. In P. Lipsett and B. Sales (Eds), *New Directions in Psycholegal Research.* New York: Van Nostrand Reinhold, 1979.

Morris, G.B. and Zingle, H. Irrational beliefs, life orientation and temporal perspective of prison inmates. *Canadian Counsellor,* 1977, *11*(2), 76-82.

Nettler, G. *Explaining Crime.* New York: McGraw-Hill, 1978.

Novaco, R.W. Anger and coping with stress. In J. Foreyt and D. Rathjen (Eds), *Cognitive Behavior Therapy: Theory, Research and Practice.* New York: Plenum, 1978.

Novaco, R.W. The cognitive regulation of anger and stress. In P. Kendal and S. Hollon (Eds), *Cognitive-Behavioral Interventions: Theory, Research and Procedures.* New York: Academic Press, 1979, pp. 241-285.

Novaco, R.W. The function and regulation of the arousal of anger. *American Journal of Psychiatry,* 1976,*133,* 1124-1128.

Passman, R.H. and Mulhern, R.K. Maternal punitiveness as affected by situational stress: an experimental analogue of child abuse. *Journal of Abnormal Behavior,* 1977, *86*(5), 565-569.

Pollock, H. Is the paroled client a menace to the community? *Psychiatric Quarterly,* 1938, *12,* 236-244.

President's Commission on Mental Health, *Report to the President.* Washington, D.C.: Government Printing Office, 1978.

Rabkin, J.G. Criminal behavior of discharged mental patients: a critical appraisal of the research. Psychological Bulletin, 1979, *86*(1), 1.

Rader, C.M. MMPI Profile types of exposers, rapists, and assaulters in a court services population. *Journal of Consulting and Clinical Psychology,* 1977, *45*(1), 61-69.

Rappaport, J. and Lassen, G. Dangerous-arrest rate comparisons of discharged patients and the general population. *American Journal of Psychiatry,* 1965, *121,* 776-783.

Roth, L. and Ervin, F. Psychiatric care of federal prisoners. *American Journal of Psychiatry,* 1971, *128,* 424-430.

Rule, B. and Nesdale, A. Emotional arousal and aggressive behavior. *Psychological Bulletin,* 1976, *83,* 851-863.

Sales, B.D. *Psychology in the Legal Process.* New York: Spectrum Publications, 1977.

Sarbin, T. (Ed.) *Challenges to the Criminal Justice System.* New York: Human Sciences Press, 1979.

Schuessler, K. and Cressey, D. Personality characteristics of criminals. *American Journal of Sociology,* 1950, *55,* 476-484.

Schur, E. A critical assessment of labeling. In R. Henshel and R. Silverman (Eds), *Perception in Criminology.* New York: Columbia University Press, 1975, 437-454.

Schwartz, R. Social factors in the development of legal control: a case study of two Israeli settlements. *Yale Law Journal,* 1954, *63,* 479-491.

Sechrest, L., White, S., and Brown, B. (Eds) *The Rehabilitation of Criminal Offenders: Problems and Prospects.* Washington, D.C.: National Academy of Sciences, in press.

Shaw, C. *The Jack-Roller: A Delinquent Boy's Own Story.* Chicago: University of Chicago Press, 1930 (reprinted 1966).

Shaw, C. and McKay, H. *Social Factors in Delinquency.* Washington, D.C.: Government Printing Office, 1931.

Simon, R. (Ed) *Research in Law and Sociology.* Greenwich, Conn.: JAI Press, 1977.

Sosowsky, L. Crime and violence among mental patients reconsidered in view of the new legal relationship between the state and the mentally ill. *American Journal of Psychiatry,* 1978, *135*(1), 33-42.

Steadman, H. and Cocozza, J. Selective reporting and the public misconceptions of the criminally insane. *Public Opinion Quarterly,* 1978, *4,* 523-533.

Steadman, H.J., Cocozza, J.J., and Melick, M.E. Explaining the increased arrest role among mental patients: the changing clientele of state hospitals. *American Journal of Psychiatry,* 1978, *135*(7), 816-820.

Stone, A. *Mental Health and the Law: A System in Transition.* Washington, D.C.: Government Printing Office, 1975.

Suther, P.B., Allain, A.N., and Geyer, S. Female criminal violence and differential MMPI characteristics. *Journal of Consulting and Clinical Psychology,* 1978, *46*(5), 1141-1143.

Sutherland, E.H. and Cressey, D.R. *Criminology,* 8th edition. Philadelphia: Lippincott, 1970.

Sutherland, E. and Cressey, D. *Criminology,* 9th edition. Philadelphia: Lippincott, 1974.

Tapp, J.L. Psychology and the law: an overture. In M.R. Rosenzweig and L.W. Porter (Eds), *Annual Review of Psychology* (Vol. 27). Palo Alto, Calif.: Annual Reviews, 1976.

Tapp, J.L. and Levine, F.J. (Eds) *Law, Justice, and the Individual in Society: Psychological and Legal Issues.* New York: Holt, Rinehart & Winston, 1977.

Toch, H. *Psychology of Crime and Criminal Justice.* New York: Holt, Rinehart & Winston, 1979.

Toch, H. *Violent Men.* Skokie, Ill.: AVC, 1969.

Waldo, G. and Dinitz, S. Personality attributes of the criminal: an analysis of research studies, 1950-1965. *Journal of Research in Crime and Delinquency*, 1967, *4*, 185-201.

Wheeler, C.A. Overcontrolled hostility and the perception of violence. *FCI Research Report*, 1971, *3*, 1-19.

Yochelson, S. and Samenow, S. *The Criminal Personality, Volume I: A Profile for Change.* New York: Jason Aronson, 1976.

Zitrin, A., Hardesty, A., Burdock, E., and Drossman, A. Crime and violence among mental patients. *American Journal of Psychiatry*, 1976, *133*, 142-149.

1

EXPERIMENTS ON DEVIANCE WITH SPECIAL REFERENCE TO DISHONESTY

DAVID P. FARRINGTON

With comparatively few exceptions (e.g., Steffensmeier & Terry, 1975), the field of deviance is dominated by nonexperimental research. Most of this is by sociologists and can be described as hypothesis generating rather than hypothesis testing. The common methodologies used are participant observation, cross-sectional surveys, and case histories. Hypothesis-generating research is necessary for the advancement of knowledge, but it needs to be followed by hypothesis testing. These methodologies are unsuitable for testing hypotheses because of their low internal validity or the low extent to which they can demonstrate unambiguously that changes in one factor have produced changes in another (Campbell & Stanley, 1966). They can establish correlations between

From David P. Farrington, "Experiments on Deviance with Special Reference to Dishonesty," pp. 207-252 in Leonard Berkowitz (ed.), *Advances in Experimental Social Psychology* (Vol. 12). Copyright 1979 by Academic Press. Reprinted by permission.

deviance and other factors, but they cannot establish causal relationships and they cannot decide between alternative explanations of observed findings.

The most conclusive methodology for testing hypotheses is experimentation, which distinctly characterizes research by psychologists. However, with comparatively few exceptions (e.g., Bickman & Henchy, 1972), psychological experiments have been carried out in rather artificial laboratory settings with undergraduate psychology students as subjects. This means that their external validity, and especially the extent to which their findings can be generalized to real life, is likely to be low. Gradually, however, naturalistic experiments are becoming more common, and psychological journals are becoming more concerned with external validity (e.g., Wyer, Dion, & Ellsworth, 1978).

The argument in this essay is that, by using the experimental method, psychologists can make a great contribution to our understanding of deviance. The major barriers which need to be overcome are the ethical and practical difficulties of devising operational definitions and methods of measuring deviance which enable experiments with high internal and external validity to be carried out. The first aim of this contribution is to review operational definitions of deviance which have been used so far in experiments, and to indicate which are the most satisfactory and where improvements may be made. The second aim is to review the advances in our knowledge about one specific kind of deviance—dishonesty—which have been achieved by experimental psychological research.

I.   Deviance and Experimentation

A.   DEFINITION OF "DEVIANCE"

Deviance may be defined as behavior which violates a norm or breaks a rule, but this is a rather unsatisfactory definition for research purposes. This is because different groups of people have different norms, and consequently the same act may be deviant by the standards of one group but not by the standards of another. Furthermore, an individual may simultaneously be a member of several different groups with different behavioral norms, and it may be difficult to discover the norms of any particular group. In order to study deviance, it is desirable to devise an unambiguous method of classifying any given act as deviant or not, assuming that deviant behavior is a category rather than a continuum.

This article concentrates on deviant behavior which is prohibited by the criminal law or which violates other widely recognized moral norms of Western society at the present time. This definition acknowledges that laws and norms vary with time and place. It is somewhat arbitrary and ambiguous, but it will serve as a guiding rule. In practice, the major focus of interest here is on various kinds of dishonesty (stealing, lying, and cheating) and on other illegal acts. It is hardly necessary to point out the practical importance for our society of understanding these kinds of deviant behavior and the social benefits which would follow from a decrease in their frequency. In order to reduce this contribution to a manageable length, no attempt is made to review experiments on aggression here.

Simmons and Chambers (1965) asked a quota sample of the United States population to list acts or types of persons which they regarded as deviant. While 252 different things were mentioned by the 180 subjects, the most frequent responses were homosexuals, drug addicts, alcoholics, prostitutes, murderers, criminals, lesbians, juvenile delinquents, beatniks, mentally ill people, and perverts. In all cases, the acts which characterize these types of persons would come within my definition of deviance. There is a difference, of course, between deviant acts and deviant persons. Hood and Sparks (1970, p. 129) have pointed out that calling someone a murderer because he has committed one murder is rather like calling someone a golfer because he has played one round of golf. Perhaps someone should not be called a deviant person unless he commits deviant acts with a certain degree of regularity. The emphasis here is on deviant acts, but some experiments studying deviant persons (e.g., drunks: Piliavin, Rodin, & Piliavin, 1969) are mentioned.

One important issue is the extent to which any empirical variable is a valid measure of the theoretical construct of deviance. This falls within the topic of external validity. What is needed is correlational research to investigate the strength of the relationship between the measure used in the experiment and some external criterion of the theoretical construct. Social psychologists have been much less concerned with this aspect of external validity than have users of psychological tests (e.g., Cronbach, 1970). It is particularly important to establish the relationship between verbal measures—for example, predicted behavior in hypothetical situations—and actual behavior. The reliability of verbal reports of mental processes is doubtful (e.g., Nisbett & Wilson, 1977), and there is a great deal of inconsistency between verbal reports and behavior (e.g., Deutscher, 1973). Even more inconsistency might be expected with deviance than with other topics, since frank admissions of deviant acts or tendencies are likely to attract social disapproval. In the interests of drawing general conclusions about deviance in real life, this article concentrates on experiments using behavioral measures.

So far, deviance has been discussed as if it were a single category or dimension. This seems unlikely, in view of the apparent heterogeneity of prohibited acts such as stealing, assault, vandalism, rape, and possessing drugs. However, the extent to which it is possible to generalize from one kind of deviance to another, and the extent to which all kinds of deviance obey the same causal laws, are empirical questions. One theoretical implication of generalization might be that each person can be placed at some point on a single dimension reflecting a tendency to commit deviant acts of all kinds.

In agreement with this, there is little evidence of specialization in the crimes committed by convicted delinquents. West and Farrington (1973, 1977) showed that most juveniles and young adults convicted of aggressive, damaging, and drug offences in England had other convictions for crimes of dishonesty. In the United States Wolfgang, Figlio, and Sellin (1972) found that the probability of committing any type of crime did not depend on the type of crime committed on the last occasion. Other indications of the versatility of delinquent behavior are obtained in research with self-reported delinquency questionnaires. Farrington (1973), in England, found that those who admitted theft and burglary also tended to admit aggressive and damaging offences and even minor deviant acts, such as playing truant from school and drinking under age. Similar results were obtained by Hindelang (1971) in the United States. There is some evidence that older and more experienced offenders do tend to specialize, for example, in violent as opposed to property crimes (Buikhuisen & Jongman, 1970; Peterson, Pittman, & O'Neal, 1962), but even here there is conflicting evidence that the majority of older offenders convicted for a violent crime also have convictions for property crimes (McClintock, 1963; Walker, Hammond, & Steer, 1967).

These questions about the generality or specificity of deviant behavior are very important in developing theories of deviance, but they are not discussed further in this contribution. The major theoretical concern (in Section III) is with dishonesty.

B. DEFINITION OF "EXPERIMENT"

An experiment, of course, is a study of the effect of changes in one or more independent variables on one or more dependent variables, its defining feature being the control of independent variables by the experimenter. There should also be some attempt to control extraneous variables that may influence the dependent variables, and the most satisfactory way of doing this is to randomly allocate subjects to different conditions of the independent variable. Another method is to give all the treatments to each subject in a random order, but this is beset with the problems of the effects of prior treatments and the interaction of treatments. Another possibility is to individually match the subjects in each condition in advance, but it is impossible to match for every factor which may affect the dependent variable. One of the least satisfactory experimental methods, because of the lack of control, is to give different treatments to different naturally occurring groups of subjects (e.g., classes in a school) and then to check subsequently to see if any of the preexisting differences between the groups reached statistical significance. Experiments using all these methods are included in this review but the selection bias is in favor of experiments which appear to have high internal validity, in randomly allocating subjects to conditions, and also high external validity, in being carried out in realistic field settings with members of the general public as subjects, rather than in the artificial conditions of the psychological laboratory with introductory psychology students as subjects.

From the point of view of internal and external validity, nonreactive field experiments using unobtrusive measures (cf. Webb, Campbell, Schwartz, & Sechrest, 1966) are especially desirable. If a subject does not know that he is serving in a psychological experiment, he is likely to behave typically rather than be affected by such reactive factors as experimenter expectancy and demand characteristics (e.g., Miller, 1972). These kinds of experiments raise ethical problems (see Section II,E). They also create methodological questions, particularly in regard to manipulation checks. It is very difficult to carry out a manipulation check during a nonreactive experiment without its becoming reactive. If the check is carried out after the experiment has been completed, the subject's response in the check might be influenced by the way he has just responded in the experiment (see also Kidd, 1976). The deviance literature indicates that persons who have committed deviant acts will seek to justify or defend them or to minimize their own responsibility (e.g., Sykes & Matza, 1957), in order to avoid disapproval or sanctions from other people. It would be possible to carry out a separate study to do a manipulation check, but, as mentioned above, there is no guarantee that subjects would be able or willing to make verbal statements in the check reflecting either their mental processes or their likely behavior in the experiment.

A manipulation check is just one kind of validity check. It is desirable to check that the independent variable in an experiment is a measure of the specified theoretical construct by correlating it with some other measure of the same theoretical construct, preferably obtained externally to the experiment. This is essentially what is done in a manipulation check, but demonstrating one significant correlation is not enough. The independent variable may actually be measuring some construct other than the intended one, a construct which is correlated with the intended one for some reason. It would be better to investigate the correlations between the independent variable and a variety of measures of different theoretical constructs, to demonstrate that the highest correlation is with the measure of the intended construct. It is also desirable to check that the dependent variable in an experiment is a measure of a specified theoretical construct, in the same way. However, both of these checks become less important as the independent and dependent measures become more similar to the theoretical constructs, which is usually true in naturalistic research. The desirability of manipulation checks should only be considered as part of the wider question of internal and external validity.

C. AN ALTERNATIVE METHODOLOGY

There are many hypotheses about deviant behavior which, for ethical and practical reasons, are difficult or impossible to test experimentally in Western society at the present time. The main argument in this paper is that, whenever possible, experiments should be carried out. However, when experiments are not possible the next best methodology, in terms of internal and external validity, is probably the quasiexperiment (Campbell & Stanley, 1966). This has been almost completely ignored by psychologists and sociologists alike, despite some interesting published demonstrations of its value (e.g., Campbell & Ross, 1968; Ross, Campbell, & Glass, 1970; Schnelle & Lee, 1974).

As an example of the use of the quasiexperimental methodology, Farrington (1977) tested a hypothesis derived from labeling theory (e.g., Becker, 1963; Lemert, 1972), namely that persons who are publicly labeled as deviants will become more deviant as a result. Public labeling was operationally defined and measured by convictions in court for criminal offenses, and deviant behavior was operationally defined and measured by self-reports of the commission of certain delinquent and socially disapproved acts. It would be difficult to test this hypothesis experimentally using these operational definitions, because it would be difficult to persuade the police and the courts to randomly allocate people either to a group who were to be found guilty in court or to a group who were not to be officially processed or labeled in any way. The hypothesis could be tested experimentally using other operational definitions of public labeling, but it might then be difficult to generalize the results to the real-life situation with which the labeling theorists were concerned.

The research described by Farrington (1977) was part of a longitudinal survey called the Cambridge Study in Delinquent Development (West & Farrington, 1973, 1977). Nearly 400 working-class London youths were given self-reported delinquency questionnaires (Farrington, 1973) successively at ages 14, 16, and 18 approximately, and their scores on these questionnaires were used as measures of their deviant behavior. Each youth was given a percentile rank score at each age, and it was found that the scores of the 53 youths who were first convicted between ages 14 and 18 had significantly increased by the later age, in agreement with the hypothesis.

This was a satisfactory outcome, but it was then necessary to systematically investigate a number of alternative explanations of the results, or threats to the internal validity of the quasiexperiment (Campbell & Stanley, 1966). First of all, the results could not have been caused by maturation (processes within the subjects operating as a function of the passage of time), history (events occurring between the first and second test), testing (the effects of taking one test on the scores in a second) or instrumentation (changes in the measuring instruments or scoring methods). Each of these factors would be expected to affect the whole sample equally, but the scoring method (percentile rank scores at each age) meant that the scores of the convicted youths increased relative to the scores of the whole sample. Second, the results could not have been caused by mortality (differential loss of subjects from the comparison groups), because the analysis was based on only the 383 youths who were interviewed at all three ages (over 93% of the original sample of 411 at age 8 years). Third, statistical regression to the mean could not explain the results, because the scores of the convicted youths became even more extreme at age 18 than they had been at age 14.

This left only two of Campbell and Stanley's factors, namely selection effects and the interaction between selection and other factors, especially maturation and history. It is plausible to suggest that the convicted youths differed from the remainder even before they were convicted, and that one of these preexisting differences rather than the conviction caused their relative increase in deviant behavior. In an attempt to counteract selection factors, the 53 convicted youths were individually matched at age 14 with 53 other youths not found guilty up to age 18, not only on their self-reported delinquency scores but also on an index of deviant behavior derived from teacher and peer ratings and on a combination of five nonbehavioral factors which were known to predict delinquency (parental criminality, low family income, large family size, low IQ, and a global index of poor parental behavior: see West & Farrington, 1973). It was hoped that this matching technique would produce two groups which were comparable in every factor except for the occurrence of a conviction. In the event, the scores of the convicted youths still increased significantly relative to the scores of the matched unconvicted youths, so the conclusion about the effect of convictions was unchanged.

There is another threat to internal validity which was not listed by Campbell and Stanley but which was tested in this research, namely the question of causal order. It is possible that the increased deviant behavior of the convicted youths caused rather than was caused by their convictions. This was investigated using the self-reported delinquency scores at age 16, and the fact that 26 of the 53 convicted youths were not found guilty until after they had been interviewed at 16. These youths had significantly higher scores at 18 than their matched unconvicted youths. If the increase in deviant behavior preceded the conviction, it might be expected that the convicted youths would already have had higher scores at age 16 than their matched unconvicted youths. If the conviction preceded the increase in deviant behavior, however, the two groups should have had similar scores at age 16, and this was in fact what was found. This result is in agreement with the hypothesis that the conviction caused the increase in the deviant behavior, rather than the reverse. Attempts were also made to elucidate intervening variables in the causal chain (see Farrington, 1977).

Since this work was done, a further analysis using self-reported delinquency scores at age 21 has been completed (Farrington, Osborn, & West, 1978). In agreement with the labeling prediction and with the earlier results, youths first convicted between ages 18 and 21 significantly increased their self-reported delinquency between these ages, in comparison with other youths. However, these demonstrations that being found guilty in court tends to increase deviance are by no means as conclusive as field experiments would have been. Where they are ethically and practically feasible, field experiments on deviance should be carried out, but the quasi-experimental methodology should be considered in other instances. It may be better to sacrifice some internal validity and carry out a quasiexperiment than to sacrifice some external validity and carry out a laboratory experiment.

II. Operationally Defining and Measuring Deviance in Experiments

A. DISHONESTY AS A DEPENDENT VARIABLE

In order to carry out an experiment with deviance as a dependent variable, it is necessary to give subjects an opportunity to commit deviant acts under controlled conditions. The most influential early research in which this was arranged was concerned with dishonesty. It was undertaken by Hartshorne and May (1928), although they did not carry out experiments. They devised a variety of methods of measuring cheating, lying, and stealing by children aged about 10-14, in school, in athletic contests, and in party games.

Cheating was operationally defined as achieving a falsely good performance on a test by disobeying instructions, reporting scores incorrectly, or making illegitimate use of an answer key. It was either detected directly, for example by comparing a child's test paper before and after he was allowed to score it himself, or indirectly, from improbably good performance. The indirect method was less satisfactory, since there was always some doubt, however small, about whether or not cheating actually had occurred. Two methods of measuring lying were used, one based on admissions or denials of cheating a week or more after the tests were taken, and the other based on improbable answers on a questionnaire (e.g., saying "Yes" to "Do you always do today things that you could put off until tomorrow?"). The disadvantage with the former method is that only the cheaters were exposed to the risk of lying, while the problem with the latter method is that a saint would appear to be a liar. Hartshorne's and May's tests of stealing involved children having opportunities to steal coins which were given to them for use in games or puzzles. Stealing was detected either by noting surreptitiously that a child failed to return a coin which he had been given or by giving the children coins in inconspicuously numbered boxes which were later checked.

The methods used by Hartshorne and May to study cheating have been used in experiments by many subsequent researchers. A favorite method has been to allow subjects to score their own tests after they have been secretly copied or scored by confederates of the researcher (e.g., Heisler, 1974; Keehn, 1956; Schachter, 1971; Stephenson & White, 1970; Tittle & Rowe, 1973). More in-genious methods of recording subjects' original answers have also been devised (e.g., Dienstbier & Munter, 1971; Mills, 1958). Cheating has also been studied by arranging for subjects to obtain a predetermined set of scores in a game and allowing them to score themselves (e.g., Grinder, 1962; Hill & Kochendorfer, 1969; Lepper, 1973). Improbably good reported performance has also been used as an index of cheating in tests (e.g., Stephenson & White, 1968; Vitro & Schoer, 1972) and in guessing games (e.g., Dmitruk, 1971; Kanfer & Duerfeldt, 1968). Disobeying instructions to achieve a good performance has also been studied (e.g., Aronson & Mettee, 1968; O'Leary, 1968). The research by O'Leary is especially interesting, as he is one of the few researchers actually to have observed and recorded cheating as it happened. In his experiment, 6-year-old boys were told to press a telegraph key to obtain a marble, which was exchangeable for a prize, only when a certain stimulus appeared on the screen. The experimenter watched through a one-way mirror to see whether each boy violated the rules and pressed the key when other stimuli were shown. Diener and Wallbom (1976) also used a one-way mirror to observe and record cheating, defined as disobeying instructions in a test by continuing after the time limit.

Lying has not been studied a great deal as a dependent variable in experi-ments, although the dividing line between cheating and lying is sometimes arbi-trary. In some of the researches mentioned above, cheating consisted of telling lies about performance rather than making illegitimate use of an answer key. Two other studies in which subjects were given opportunities to tell lies were carried out by Medinnus (1966) and by Taylor and Lewit (1966). Medinnus presented children with a list of book titles, some of which were fictitious, and asked them to check those which they had read. Taylor and Lewit gave adoles-cents a dynamometer which was programmed to produce the same series of readings for each boy and asked them to report their grip strengths. Bleda, Bleda, Byrne, and White (1976) placed subjects in a situation where each had to tell a lie in order for a confederate to benefit from his or her cheating. In the research of Quigley-Fernandez and Tedeschi (1978), subjects were given the opportunity to tell lies about whether they had previously heard the answers to a test which they had to take.

Stealing has not been investigated under controlled conditions to any great extent, but in recent years a number of field experiments have been carried out. In most of these, subjects were given an opportunity to steal or dishonestly accept money in situations where the owner of the money was either unknown or absent or both. It is doubtful that some of these studies would conform to legal definitions of theft. For example, in England, the Theft Act of 1968 specifies that a person is not committing theft if he appropriates property in the belief that the person to whom the property belongs cannot be discovered by taking reasonable steps.

In a naturalistic study, Feldman (1968) pretended to pick up money in the street and offered it to members of the public, asking if they had dropped it. The subjects therefore had an opportunity to claim the money dishonestly. Feldman also gave cashiers and store clerks too much money when buying items, giving them an opportunity to keep the money dishonestly, and Korte and Kerr (1975) used the same method. Bickman (1971) carried out an experiment in which coins were left in telephone booths and the users of the booths were then asked whether or not they had picked them up. Again, the users had the opportunity to keep the money dishonestly, and Franklin (1973) and Kleinke (1977) used the same method. Lenga and Kleinke (1974) unobtrusively observed customers in a department store taking shopping bags without paying. Diener, Fraser, Beaman, and Kelem (1976), after telling children that they could take one candy from a dish in a house, observed the stealing of extra candies, or of money from an adjacent dish, using a peep hole in curtains. In a campus-bound experiment, Penner, Summers, Brookmire, and Dertke (1976) left unobtrusively coded dollar bills in various locations where students would find them and recorded whether the dollars were returned, ignored, or taken dishonestly. Steinberg, McDonald, and O'Neal (1977) gave female students the opportunity to steal shampoo in dormitory shower rooms.

Stealing has also been involved in experiments intended primarily to investigate helpful behavior. Hornstein, Fisch, and Holmes (1968); Hornstein (1970); and Tucker, Hornstein, Holloway, and Sole (1977) left a wallet containing $2 in cash in an envelope on the street for members of the public to pick up. While returning the envelope constituted helpfulness, keeping it constituted stealing. White (1972), in an experiment intended to investigate the donating of 5ᶜ gift certificates exchangeable at a local store, also observed children stealing these certificates, using a one-way mirror in a mobile laboratory. Mention should also be made of the experiments on stealing carried out by hypnotists. Beigel (1962) gave subjects a posthypnotic suggestion to steal a (marked) $10 bill from a book at the rear of a lecture theatre. Nineteen out of 20 subjects complied, in comparison with only one who thought he might in the waking state, and none out of 20 unhypnotized controls complied. Coe, Kobayashi, and Howard (1972) carried out an experiment in which subjects were given posthypnotic suggestions to steal a copy of a master's degree examination paper from a secretary's office for the graduate student experimenter.

The field experiments on stealing and financial dishonesty seem to me to be the nearest approach yet to the experimental study of delinquent behavior. Systematic observation and recording of delinquent behavior as it happens are rare but they may advance our knowledge of the reality of delinquency more than the official statistics, with all their known biases (e.g., Hood & Sparks, 1970). Furthermore, if it is possible to experimentally manipulate delinquent behavior, this holds out the likelihood of controlling it, at least in principle. McNese, Egli, Marshall, Schnelle, and Risley (1976) and Switzer, Deal, and Bailey (1977) carried out naturalistic experiments designed to reduce stealing. McNees et al. measured shoplifting in a department store by checking 25 key items each day and found a considerable decrease in stealing following the introduction of antishoplifting signs. Switzer et al. placed 10 items in a classroom each day and found that the theft of these items decreased after the children were made aware that the whole group would suffer if stealing occurred.

I have been involved in a number of researches which have investigated stealing or financial dishonesty under controlled conditions (see Farrington & Knight, 1979a). In the first of these, carried out in collaboration with William S. Knapp and Bonnie E. Erickson, 25 youths in Cambridge, England, were invited to participate in a survey about gambling and risk taking and were interviewed in a van parked in the street. During part of this interview, the youths were left alone in the van with a bag of money and were asked to sort the coins as fast as possible into a sorting box. They were given the (incorrect) impression that the interviewer did not know how many coins were in the bag, and had the opportunity to steal some of the coins. The number and value of coins stolen (if any) were ascertained later by the interviewer. This study indicated that stealing was not impulsive, since youths only stole when they knew in advance what was involved in the interview. Another result was that the behavioral measure of stealing was not closely related to verbal measures based on reports of past behavior or assessments of likely behavior in hypothetical situations.

The second study, carried out in collaboration with Robert F. Kidd (Farrington & Kidd, 1977), was based on the method used by Feldman (1968). The experimenter walked past a member of the public in the streets of Cambridge, England, pretended to pick up a coin, and then ran after the subject, offering him the coin and asking whether he had dropped it. The subject had the opportunity to dishonestly accept the coin. One problem in this study was the very marked experimenter effect, because subjects were nearly twice as likely to take the money from the male experimenter as from the female experimenter.

In view of this experimenter effect, the third study used a nonreactive paradigm and was based on the technique of Hornstein et al. (1968). It was carried out in collaboration with Barry J. Knight (see Farrington and Knight, 1979b). One hundred stamped, addressed, apparently lost, unsealed letters, each containing a handwritten note and also (apart from control conditions) a sum of money, were left on the streets of London, England, and were picked up by members of the public. The experimenter, who was blind to the condition of each letter, noted down the personal characteristics and behavior of each subject. Each subject was free to post the letter and money to the intended recipient or to steal the money. The results obtained in this experiment, and in another using the same paradigm, are discussed in Section III, A.

Virtually all the researchers mentioned so far in this section have used behavioral measures of dishonesty. Others have used verbal measures, as for example in the "ethical risk taking" studies of Rettig and his collaborators (e.g., Rettig, 1964, 1966; Rettig & Pasamanick, 1964; Rettig & Rawson, 1963; Rettig & Turoff, 1967) and later Krauss (e.g., Krauss & Blanchard, 1970; Krauss, Coddington, & Smeltzer, 1971; Krauss, Robinson, Janzen, & Cauthen, 1972). In some well-known recent research, West, Gunn, and Chernicky (1975) asked some students whether they would participate in a burglary and other students whether they thought they would agree to participate in a burglary in the hypothetical situation of being asked to do so.

The external validity of verbal statements about dishonesty in relation to real dishonest behavior is not securely established. In studying it, verbal and behavioral measures need to be obtained from the same people. Shotland and Berger (1970) lent pencils to female workers to fill in the Rokeach value scale and found that those who returned the pencils rated the value of honesty more highly than those who kept them dishonestly. In agreement with this result, Henshel (1971) found a negative correlation between the rated value of honesty and cheating on a spelling test, and Lepper (1973) found a negative correlation between cheating and self-perceived honesty. However, Santrock (1975) found little correlation between cheating and verbal measures of honesty (self-ratings and moral judgments) and, as mentioned above, Farrington, Knapp, and Erickson found little correlation between verbal and behavioral measures of stealing.

The final question which can be asked is whether it is reasonable to treat dishonesty as a unidimensional variable, or whether different theories are required for different kinds of dishonesty. Hartshorne and May (1928) found that their measures of cheating were significantly correlated with teachers' ratings of dishonesty in class, while Hill (1934) showed that institutionalized delinquents cheated more than nondelinquents, and Heisler (1974) found that cheating by students was significantly related to their self-reports of law violations. These results indicate that cheating in experiments is related to more serious kinds of dishonesty. They may seem surprising in the light of Hartshorne's and May's famous conclusion, based on the small positive correlations between their different tests, that dishonest behavior is largely determined by situational factors. However, in a reanalysis of their data, Burton (1963) found that most of the low correlations were contributed by tests with very low reliabilities and concluded that, although situational factors were very important, there was an underlying general factor of honesty. Nelsen and his collaborators (Nelson, Grinder, & Biaggio, 1969; Nelsen, Grinder, & Mutterer, 1969) gave six cheating tests to more than 100 children and came to much the same conclusion. Although there are not many studies intercorrelating different behavioral measures of dishonesty, the indications are that it is reasonable to suggest the existence of a single underlying dimension or general factor.

B. OTHER DEPENDENT MEASURES OF DEVIANCE

In experiments on deviant behaviors other than dishonesty, the dependent variable of deviance has usually been measured by self-reports or official records. As mentioned earlier, deviant behavior has rarely been observed directly. This is true with sexual deviance, for example, and the few observational studies (e.g., Humphreys, 1970) have almost all been nonexperimental. There are obvious difficulties in observing sexual deviance under controlled conditions. Most types of it occur primarily in private, and those acts which take place in public tend to be relatively infrequent. Providing the ethical problems could be overcome, it would be possible in principle to study types of sexual deviance which occurred in public places with a reasonably high frequency, such as male homosexuality in certain public toilets.

Almost the only question in the area of sexual deviance which has been studied experimentally is the effect of pornography, but the occurrence of sexually deviant behavior before and after exposure to pornography has been measured by self-reports rather than by observation (e.g., Mann, Sidman, & Starr, 1970). Probably the nearest approach to a behavioral experiment on sexual deviance was carried out by Kline (1958, 1972). In this, a male student was hypnotized to indecently expose himself in what appeared to be a public place, although in fact the area had been sealed off by the police. In an interesting recent experiment using a verbal measure, Mathes and Guest (1976) asked students to say how willing they were to carry a sign saying "masturbation is fun!"

It is surprising that more experiments have not been carried out on deviant behaviors which occur frequently and which do not raise insurmountable ethical difficulties, such as dropping litter and traffic offences. As an example of what might be done, Buikhuisen (1974) studied the effect of a police and newspaper campaign on the incidence of worn tires on cars. Before and after the campaign, his students recorded the incidence of worn tires in two towns in Holland, by checking all cars parked in a representative sample of streets between 1:00 a.m. and 5:30 a.m. Fortunately for the research, few car owners in these towns had garages. The police and newspaper campaign was mounted in one town, and the other was used as a control. Because only one town was compared with one other town, rather than many towns being randomly allocated to the two conditions, this experiment was not high in internal validity. Sigelman and Sigelman (1976) also showed the possibility of experimenting with traffic offenses using observational measures, in investigating right turns by cars against a red light, and Lefkowitz, Blake, and Mouton (1955) observed the behavior of pedestrians in conforming to or violating traffic signals. Mention should also be made of the recent experiments on litter dropping, an illegal behavior (e.g., Baltes & Hayward, 1976; Burgess, Clark, & Hendee, 1971; Finnie, 1973; Kohlenberg & Phillips, 1973; Krauss, Freedman, & Whitcup, 1978).

With other kinds of deviance, there have been isolated examples of behavioral experiments. One of the best known was carried out by Zimbardo (1969), who left a car in the street with its hood open and license plates removed and filmed vandalism directed against it. Unfortunately, because of the inadequate control of independent and extraneous variables, this study would not come within my definition of an experiment. The research of Coe, Kobayashi, and Howard (1973) was more clearly experimental. They studied whether or not students sold heroin off campus to a confederate, in relation to the presence or absence of hypnosis and the presence or absence of a relationship with the experimenter.

Much more common are experiments in which official statistics are used to measure the dependent variable. For example, Törnudd (1968) studied the effect on drunkenness of a reduction in the likelihood of prosecution. The police in three towns in Finland cooperated by halving the proportion of arrested drunks who were prosecuted, and these towns were compared with three control towns in which this proportion did not change. The three experimental towns were chosen at random from the six towns participating, and all six towns were comparable in size. None of the six police forces was supposed to change the likelihood of arresting drunks, and the incidence of arrests for drunkenness was used as the dependent variable. However, it is difficult to be sure that police policies did not change in an experiment of this kind. In any experiment using official statistics, it is hard to disentangle changes in deviant behavior from changes in the behavior of the official agencies. This is less of a problem when the official agencies can be kept blind to the conditions of the experiment and where they play a less active role in the production of the official statistics. For example, Schwartz and Orleans (1967) studied the effect of threats of sanctions and appeals to conscience on income tax fraud. Their dependent variable, based on information supplied by the income tax authorities, was the total paid by randomly chosen groups of taxpayers in 1 year in comparison with the previous year. A relative increase in income tax paid, by experimental groups in comparison with a control group, was taken to indicate a decrease in the incidence of income tax fraud.

The Schwartz and Orleans study can be regarded as an experiment in the prevention of crime. It differs from the experiments by Buikhuisen (1974) and

Törnudd (1968) in that the preventive measures were applied to specific individuals rather than aimed at the community as a whole. This is true of most prevention experiments, but the dependent variable is usually general delinquency obtained from records held by criminal justice agencies, rather than a specific type of crime.

In the classic Cambridge–Somerville experiment, for example (McCord & McCord, 1959), boys were chosen at random to receive either regular friendly attention from specially appointed counselors or the usual resources of the community. The counseling began at age 11 and continued for 5 years, on the average, and the major dependent variable was whether each boy had been convicted by 15 years after the beginning of the project. As is usual in experiments on delinquency prevention and treatment, the experimental and control groups did not differ significantly in their conviction histories, suggesting that the counseling had been ineffectual in preventing delinquency. A further followup 30 years after the end of the treatment showed that, if anything, the treated group was more criminal (McCord, 1978). A more intended result was obtained in the prevention experiment of Bowman (1959), who found that low-achieving children taught in special classes having one sympathetic teacher had fewer recorded offenses during a 2-year period than low-achieving children taught in regular classes. The experiment by Reckless and Dinitz (1972), in which boys thought to be vulnerable to delinquency were randomly allocated to regular or special classes, is especially notable, because the police records of offenses were supplemented by self-reports. However, the experimental and control groups were not significantly different on either measure.

The dependent variable of general delinquency obtained from official records also predominates in experiments on the treatment of delinquency, which are more numerous than prevention experiments. One exception, in concentrating on a specific kind of delinquency, is the experiment of Berg, Hullin, and McGuire (1979). In this, boys brought before the courts for truancy were randomly allocated either to have their case adjourned or to be supervised by social workers, and the subsequent records of truancy for both groups were then investigated. The adjourned group showed less truancy, suggesting that social work supervision was less effective than adjournment in the treatment of truancy. In an experiment on a related, although nondelinquent, kind of deviance, Palmer (1967) showed that boys who were punished by detention for arriving late at school were more likely to repeat this offence than those who were reprimanded.

Most treatment experiments have been intended to investigate the relative efficacy of different methods of treating convicted persons, rather than their absolute efficacy in comparison with no treatment. However, there have been a few experiments which come close to being comparisons between treatment and no treatment. Venezia (1972) randomly allocated juveniles apprehended for crimes either to receive unofficial probation or to be released without further official action. Neither group was taken to court, and the groups were not significantly different in the dependent variable of re-referral to the probation service during a 6-month follow-up period. In a rather similar experiment, Rose and Hamilton (1970) randomly allocated juveniles either to be cautioned and supervised for 6 months or only to be cautioned and again found no difference in subsequent offenses known to the police.

Most treatment experiments compare what are essentially different varieties of the same treatment rather than different treatments, and this may be one reason why null results predominate in the literature. For example, Kassebaum, Ward, and Wilner (1971) randomly allocated offenders sent to a new prison to receive small or large group counseling or no counseling. There was little difference in reconviction rates between the groups, but it could be argued that the differences in treatment between the groups were negligible in comparison to the similarities resulting from the fact that they were all in the same prison. After all, the counseling sessions occupied only 1 or 2 hr/week. In other prison experiments, Berntsen and Christiansen (1965) and Shaw (1974) found that prisoners selected at random for special welfare treatment were less likely to be reconvicted than others, but Fowles (1978) did not find that prison welfare treatment was effective.

Experiments have also been carried out on institutional treatment for juveniles and young adults, and on probation and parole. Jesness (1971) randomly allocated boys entering a juvenile institution either to a small, well staffed living unit or to a larger, poorly staffed one, and found that, at least in the short term, those leaving the smaller unit had lower recidivism rates. Cornish and Clarke (1975) randomly allocated boys entering an approved school either to a unit run as a therapeutic community or to a more traditional unit and found no difference in reconvictions during a 2-year follow-up period. Williams (1975) randomly allocated Borstal boys to three institutions, one with a traditional regime and the other two dominated by casework and group counseling, respectively; he found that the boys in the casework Borstal had significantly lower reconviction rates. Folkard, Smith, and Smith (1976) randomly allocated men on probation either to probation officers with specially reduced caseloads or to regular probation officers and found no effect on reconviction rates. Similarly, Reimer and Warren (1957) randomly allocated parolees to officers with large or small caseloads without finding any effect on subsequent arrest rates, but Adams (1970) found that parolees who were given special intensive counseling were less likely to be returned to custody.

Very few treatment experiments have been carried out in which offenders were randomly allocated to radically different sentences. Empey and Erickson (1972) and Empey and Lubeck (1971) compared recidivist juvenile offenders allocated to regular institutions with those given special treatment in the community emphasizing guided group interaction. There was little difference between the groups in subsequent arrest rates. Palmer (1971) also compared regular institutional treatment with individualized community treatment and found that the juveniles receiving community treatment had lower recidivism rates. However, the dependent measure of recidivism was parole revocation, and Lerman (1975) showed that Palmer's groups did not differ in recorded offending but did differ in their likelihood of parole revocation. Lerman concluded that the community treatment program had changed the discretionary decision-making behavior of the adults but had not changed the delinquent behavior of the juveniles. This highlights once again the problems of using official records as a dependent measure of deviant behavior.

The review of research in this section may give the impression that experiments on delinquency prevention and treatment using random allocation are commonplace, but this is far from true. As in other areas of deviance, the majority of research on prevention and treatment is nonexperimental and hence has low internal validity. This is at least partly because of the difficulty of persuading judges and other people in the criminal justice system to randomly allocate offenders to different treatments. To many of these people, experimentation and justice seem incompatible. As a result, offenders are being allocated to treatments whose effects are essentially unknown. In my opinion, the social benefits consequent upon the advancement of knowledge from treatment experiments are likely to exceed the costs of injustice to the individuals concerned. If the medical profession had been as opposed to experimentation as the legal profession is now, we would know very little about the relative effectiveness of different medical treatments.

In theory, the kinds of experiments reviewed so far in this section should have high internal and external validity. Their internal validity is boosted by the random allocation of subjects to different conditions, which leads to the control of extraneous variables. Their external validity is boosted by the fact that they are concerned with real-life deviant behavior, rather than with the laboratory behavior of introductory psychology students. Furthermore, these kinds of experiments are likely to have important implications for theories of deviant behavior. Theories about the causes of delinquency are likely to lead to predictions about the prevention and treatment of delinquency and, conversely, the results of prevention and treatment experiments can be used in deciding between competing theories. Yet experimental social psychologists have shown little interest in carrying out these kinds of experiments and, partly because of this, the existing experiments are rather inadequate.

One of the major problems of the existing experiments is to specify the independent variable. Most treatments vary along many dimensions and, even if a positive result is obtained, it is difficult to know to which aspect of the treatment it can be attributed. Furthermore, most treatments are not based upon explicitly stated theories about the causes of deviant behavior, and hence the results of the experiments are difficult to use in testing theories. Another problem is that few researchers try to use a double-blind technique in which neither the subjects nor the criminal justice personnel know what is going on, making it impossible to control for the Hawthorne effect, for example. Finally, as mentioned before, the methods of measuring the dependent variable of delinquency leave much to be desired and lead to the kinds of problems highlighted by Lerman (1975).

On the basis of the experimental social psychology literature, it might be expected that prevention and treatment experiments designed and carried out by experimental social psychologists would try to avoid the above problems. This is one of the reasons why I have argued that they could make a great contribution to the field of deviance. However, they would have to face rather unfamiliar practical difficulties, such as the problem of obtaining the cooperation of criminal justice staff who have a well-founded suspicion that the results of the research will indicate that their work is ineffectual (cf. Clarke & Cornish, 1972). They would have to be prepared to carry out research over a much longer time period than the average laboratory experiment and would have to accept the associated threat to their productivity, at least in terms of quantity. They would also have to accept that results which fail to show a significant difference are worth reporting. Such results are conspicuous by their absence in the experimental social psychology literature, presumably because of the policies of journal editors. The selection of significant results for publication ensures that the proportion of spurious results in the literature is considerably greater than the $p = .05$ level.

One kind of deviance which has not been studied experimentally to any great extent is vandalism or property damage. This is puzzling, because it occurs frequently in public and is not such an ethically sensitive subject as sexual deviance, for example. Furthermore, it can usually be measured by unobtrusive, observational methods, and there is often a permanent record which is easier to measure than in the case of, say, shoplifting. Whereas experimenters might not wish to be victims of physical violence, it is more feasible that they should be victims of vandalism. After theft and other forms of dishonesty, this might be the deviant act which is most susceptible to real-life experimentation. It is usually regarded as a more serious crime, and a more serious social problem, than either dropping litter or traffic offenses.

C. DISHONESTY AS AN INDEPENDENT VARIABLE

In most experiments with deviance as an independent variable, the subject is exposed to the deviance of another person (usually a confederate) and is then expected to evaluate or react to this in some way. The other person's deviance is presented in real life, in a film or videotape, or in a written description. In a minority of experiments with deviance as an independent variable, the subject himself is induced to behave deviantly or to feel deviant, and the focus of interest is then on his subsequent behavior.

It has been argued above (Section II,B) that real-life experiments in which the subjects do not realize that they are participating in an experiment are likely to have the greatest internal and external validity. In studying dishonesty as an independent variable, a number of these kinds of experiments have been carried out, often involving staged thefts. Harari and McDavid (1969) had a confederate child steal money in a classroom while the teacher was called out, and then interviewed the children to see if they would report the "thief." Latane and Darley (1970) carried out two experiments to study the reporting of thefts. In the first, students waiting to be interviewed observed another student steal cash, while in the second members of the public in a beer store observed the theft of a case of beer. Gelfand, Hartmann, Walder, and Page (1973); Steffensmeier and Terry (1973); Bickman and Green (1975); Bickman (1976); and Bickman and Rosenbaum (1977) also staged thefts in shops to investigate reporting by members of the public. Moriarty (1975) staged thefts on a beach to investigate bystander intervention, and Harris and Samerotte (1976) staged thefts in restaurants to study the effect of transgression on altruism. Campus-bound experiments on reporting or bystander intervention were carried out by Dertke, Penner, and Ulrich (1974) and Bickman (1975), who staged thefts in university bookstores, and by Shaffer, Rogel, and Hendrick (1975), who staged thefts in a university library.

One of the major methodological problems in this kind of research is to ensure that the subjects observed the theft. It seems that little reliance can be placed on their statements about this in postexperimental interviews. Latane and Darley (1970) reported that observers watching the subjects through one-way mirrors were convinced that many of those who claimed that they had not noticed the theft had in fact done so. Bickman and Green (1975) included as subjects in their analysis people who said that they had not seen the theft, providing that their observers thought that the people had seen it. Many members of the public deliberately turn a blind eye to thefts in shops. Steffensmeier and Terry (1973) found that their shoplifting incident had to be carried out very blatantly and right next to the shoppers before anyone would report. All of the researchers appear to have been successful in avoiding damaging publicity during the course of their experiments. For example, Gelfand *et al.* (1973) staged shoplifting incidents in two drugstores over an 8-month period and gave every subject a printed handout explaining the study, but only one subject said that he suspected that the shoplifting had been staged. Apparently, no subject had learned about the research from a previous subject, and no subject gave the printed handout to his local newspaper.

Staged thefts have also been used in nonexperimental research on eyewitness testimony (e.g., Buckhout, Alper, Chern, Silverberg, & Slomovits,

1974) and in other correlational research. For example, Denner (1968) investigated the reasons given by students for reporting or not reporting a staged theft from a handbag. A staged cheating incident was used in an experiment by Savitsky and Babl (1976). In this, students witnessed a confederate cheating and later had the opportunity to deliver aversive ,oise to him as punishment for mistakes in a learning task. In the research of Heisler (1974), a confederate was apprehended for cheating, and the influence of this event on later cheating by students was studied. It is rare for subjects to be cheated out of money by experimenters, but this happened in the study of Fromkin, Goldstein, and Brock (1977). Members of the public riding in taxis were overcharged by a large or a small amount in an attempt to manipulate high or low frustration. It is less rare for subjects to be deceived by experimenters, of course (e.g., Carlson, 1971), and some researchers have tried to investigate the effects of being deceived on subjects' later behavior (e.g., Silverman, Shulman, & Wiesenthal, 1970).

Subjects have often been shown films or videotapes of dishonest behavior or have listened to dishonesty. Brickman and Bryan (1975, 1976) showed children a film in which a girl stole and then asked them to evaluate her, while people heard a violent theft occurring in the bystander intervention research of Schwartz and Gottlieb (1976). Savitsky, Muskin, Czyzewski, and Eckert (1976) showed incarcerated juvenile offenders a videotape in which a confederate cheated, again requiring evaluative decisions, while Lingle, Brock, and Cialdini (1977) also showed a videotape of cheating in a study of entrapment attempts. Films including thefts have been used in experiments on eye-witness testimony (e.g., Marshall, 1966) and on the perception of people and events (Tickner & Poulton, 1975). In an experiment on the detection of deception, Ekman and Friesen (1974) showed students videotapes of people telling lies or being honest. One problem is that it may not be possible to generalize from results obtained with videotapes of dishonesty to results obtained with real dishonesty, as Bickman (1976) found.

Written descriptions of dishonesty have also been used as independent variables. Mudd (1968) gave these to students in an experiment relating recommended sanction severity to the degree of behavior deviation and the relevance of the norm, while Efran (1974) gave students written descriptions of cheating in a simulated jury experiment. Maier and Lavrakas (1976) gave subjects written descriptions of lies and asked them to rate the lies for reprehensibility. Maier and Thurber (1968) studied the accuracy of detection of deception in relation to whether lies were presented in written descriptions or whether the subjects watched or listened to the deceivers. In real-life experiments on reactions to dishonesty, Buikhuisen and Dijksterhuis (1971) and Boshier and Johnson (1974) sent letters applying for jobs to companies, in some conditions including the information that the applicant had been convicted for theft. The applicant was less likely to be called for an interview in these conditions than when his letter included no mention of the conviction.

The simplest way of arranging experiments in which the subject himself behaves dishonestly is to instruct subjects to be dishonest. For example, Burns and Kintz (1976) instructed students to tell lies to a confederate and found that they gazed longer into the confederate's eyes when lying than when telling the truth. This method is difficult to distinguish from role playing, which has also been used. For example, Maier and Lavrakas (1976) measured the GSRs of subjects instructed to play honest or lying roles, and subjects have pretended to commit thefts in lie detection experiments (e.g., Lykken, 1959). One problem with role playing is that the subjects are aware of at least some of the aims of the experiment and can pretend to behave in a way that they would not actually behave in real life. For example, Shaffer *et al.* (1975) described the library theft to some students as a role-playing exercise. Many more of the role-playing subjects said that they would intervene to prevent the theft than actually did in the experiment (85% as opposed to 40%).

It is more satisfactory to induce the subject to act dishonestly in an experiment whose true purpose he does not know. However, it is difficult to avoid self-selection of subjects and to achieve experimental control over dishonesty, so that all subjects in one condition are dishonest, for example. This can only be achieved when the dishonest behavior is universal. Freedman, Wallington, and Bless (1967) and McMillen (1971) came close to this in experiments in which a confederate, posing as a previous subject, gave the subject information about a test the subject was about to take. When asked by the experimenter if they had heard anything about the test before, all subjects, except one in the Freedman *et al.* experiment, told a lie and denied this. The focus of interest in the two experiments was on compliance after transgressing, but they have important implications for the reliability of verbal measures obtained from subjects (e.g., in postexperimental questionnaires).

D. OTHER INDEPENDENT MEASURES OF DEVIANCE

It is very rare for subjects to be exposed to kinds of deviance other than dishonesty in naturalistic experiments. This is surprising, for it is possible in principle to stage acts of violence or vandalism, for example, in front of subjects. In a campus experiment, Shotland and Straw (1976) staged a fight between two actors in front of introductory psychology students and found that most believed it to be realistic. In contrast, when shown a videotaped fight, nearly half of the students said they did not believe that it was genuine and was really happening.

Most experiments with deviance as an independent variable have involved subjects being presented with written descriptions. This has happened, for example, in the large number of researches in which students have been asked to recommend a sentence for an offender on some interval scale convenient for statistical analysis (e.g., 1–25 years). The student subjects are often referred to as simulated jurors, but a more accurate term would be simulated judges, since with few exceptions (e.g., Sealy, 1975; Valenti & Downing, 1975) they have rarely discussed the case in groups and arrived at a group decision. Descriptions of many kinds of deviance have been used, including rape (e.g., Jones & Aronson, 1973; Scroggs, 1976) and murder (e.g., Hendrick & Shaffer, 1975; McGlynn, Megas, & Benson, 1976; Stephan, 1974). Similar descriptions have been used in experiments on attribution of responsibility (e.g., Hill, 1975) and on legal procedures (e.g., LaTour, Houlden, Walker, & Thibaut, 1976).

Few researchers have presented written descriptions to people who have to make legal decisions in real life, but Shea (1974) and Ebbesen and Konecni (1975) did. The research of Ebbesen and Konecni is especially notable, because they compared decisions made by judges in simulated cases with decisions made by the same judges in real cases. On the basis of a multiple regression analysis, it appeared that real decisions (about bail) depended only on the District Attorney's recommendation, whereas in the simulation experiment two other factors appeared to influence the decision as well. In another realistic study, Schwartz and Skolnick (1962) used the methodology mentioned in Section II,C in making job applications to employers. Some of the applications mentioned that the applicant had been convicted for assault, some that he had been tried for assault and acquitted, and some did not mention any court appearance. As before, the employers did not realize that they were participating in an experiment.

Written descriptions of deviance also have been used extensively in experiments on moral judgment. In a typical experiment, Bandura and McDonald (1963) presented children with pairs of stories, each contrasting a well-intended act resulting in material damage with a maliciously motivated act having only minor consequences. With each pair, the children were asked to say which act was the naughtier and why. Several other researchers have used these kinds of moral dilemmas in experiments (e.g., Birnbaum, 1972; Cowan, Langer, Heavenrich, & Nathanson, 1969; Dorr & Fey, 1974; Le Furgy & Woloshin, 1969; McManis, 1974; Walker & Richards, 1976). The experiment by Prentice (1972) is notable, because he compared moral judgments and delinquent behavior, as measured by official records. His subjects were convicted delinquents, and they were randomly allocated either to a control group or to experimental groups that were exposed to modeling techniques designed to change their moral judgments. Prentice succeeded in changing moral judgments as he intended, but he found no difference between the groups in recorded delinquency during a 9-month follow-up period. Few researchers have compared verbal and behavioral measures as he did, and fewer still have carried out experiments over a comparatively long period to investigate the persistence of experimentally induced changes (cf. Sternlieb & Youniss, 1975). However, both of these are desirable.

In other experiments using written descriptions of deviance, Walker and Argyle (1964), Berkowitz and Walker (1967), and Kaufmann (1970) studied moral evaluations of acts in relation to whether or not they were prohibited by the law. A number of experimenters (e.g., Bord, 1971; Kirk, 1974; Phillips, 1963; Schroder & Ehrlich, 1968) have studied the evaluation of persons displaying mentally abnormal behaviors in relation to the label given to the behavior (e.g., mentally ill, wicked, under stress) and the labeler (e.g., a psychiatrist, the person himself, his family, or sane people). Videotaped interviews have also been used in studying reactions to mentally abnormal behavior (e.g., Caetano, 1974). In the research by Lerner and Agar (1972), students were asked to evaluate drug addicts in relation to the perceived causes of their addiction, while Weissbach and Zagon (1975) studied reactions to homosexuals.

This brings us to the study of deviant persons rather than deviant acts. Field experiments are conspicuous by their absence in the present section, but a number have been carried out to investigate how members of the public react to deviant persons, such as hippies (e.g., Raymond & Unger, 1972) and drunks (e.g., Piliavin *et al.*, 1969). It is significant that the dependent variable in both of these experiments was helpfulness, because this is the one area of social psychology in which large numbers of field experiments have been carried out. As an example of experiments in which subjects were induced to feel deviant, Bramel (1962, 1963) made male subjects feel homosexual by showing them photographs of nude men and giving them false feedback about their GSRs to lead them to believe that they were sexually aroused.

E. SOME ETHICAL ISSUES

Many of the methods of operationally defining and measuring deviance described so far in this contribution may be considered unethical by some psychologists. Some methods may even be considered illegal by some lawyers (e.g., Nash, 1975; Silverman, 1975). Ethical problems arise in naturalistic field experiments, and these are magnified when the topic being studied is deviance. The ethical problems are likely to be greatest when the experimenter deliberately provides opportunities for people to commit deviant acts, rather than tries to influence a naturally occurring deviant behavior, such as shoplifting.

Most official statements about ethics by professional bodies in psychology suggest that the decision about whether or not to carry out an experiment should depend on the relationship between its costs (especially the harm suffered by subjects) and its benefits (especially the advancement of knowledge). Furthermore, it has been argued that ethical decisions should be informed by empirical research about the reactions of potential subjects, such as that carried out by Wilson and Donnerstein (1976). Perhaps rather surprisingly, subjects in experiments on deviance have not complained about their treatment. For example, even after being cheated out of money, no subject in the Fromkin *et al.* (1977) experiment expressed regrets or reservations about participating, and this has been a common finding (e.g., Schwartz & Gottlieb, 1976). As pointed out by West and Gunn (1978), follow-up research on even experiments employing highly stressful and deceptive procedures has uniformly failed to find that the subjects have suffered any long-term consequences. It seems unlikely that existing psychological research has had anything other than a negligible impact on the lives of the subjects. As Sullivan and Deiker (1973) discovered, psychologists are more concerned with ethics than are their subjects, but this is as it should be.

No one should embark lightly on research which may cause harm or stress to the subjects. However, real life is full of stresses, strains, and moral dilemmas for most people, full of opportunities to be deviant and to react to deviance. Anything done by psychologists in experiments on deviance will almost certainly be negligible in comparison with the harm caused by deviants to their victims, and with the harm caused by society to deviants. Being cheated out of a few cents pales into insignificance in comparison with being raped or mugged or in comparison with being incarcerated in degrading conditions for many years. If a psychologist sincerely believes that his experiment will have a negligible impact on the lives of his subjects and will advance our knowledge about deviance, is it not worth taking some small ethical risks in the hope of avoiding large social costs?

III.   Experiments on Dishonesty

A.   FACTORS INFLUENCING DISHONEST BEHAVIOR

In the remainder of this paper I shall discuss theories and experimental results on dishonest behavior, concentrating on experiments using behavioral measures. The focus of interest is on why people commit dishonest acts and on how people react to dishonesty. Numerically, crimes of dishonesty predominate in the official criminal statistics of most countries. This means that conclusions about delinquency in general will be similar to conclusions about dishonesty alone.

Most theories proposed in the area of deviance or delinquency have been intended to apply to deviance or delinquency in general rather than to a specific type of deviant or delinquent behavior. Furthermore, most have been dynamic or process theories, in which present behavior is explained by reference to a sequence of past events, rather than static theories, in which present behavior is explained in relation to the immediate influences of the moment. This is equally true of psychological approaches, such as social-learning theory (Trasler, 1973), and sociological perspectives, such as labeling or social reaction (Taylor, Walton, & Young, 1973). Another feature of the existing theories is that they treat delinquency as a dichotomous variable and try to explain why some people become "delinquents" and others remain "nondelinquents." This kind of approach emphasizes individual consistency over situations. By and large, the nonexperimental, empirical investigations follow the theories in treating delinquency as dichotomous and in studying historical factors. Typically, a group of officially convicted delinquents is compared with an unconvicted group on social background factors, such as broken homes and family size. This approach encounters problems both in the definition of the groups (e.g., the biases in official statistics) and in the measurement of historical factors (e.g., retrospective bias and faulty memory).

The experimental studies of dishonesty have very different theoretical foundations. No doubt because of the very short time scale within which they have been carried out and their static independent variable–dependent variable design, they have been concerned with immediate influences on dishonesty. Furthermore, their emphasis is on individual variability over situations, and hence the importance of situational factors. The situational factors which have been studied most are the costs and benefits of dishonesty, and several experiments have been inspired by the theory that dishonest behavior is largely determined by rational or hedonistic factors.

This theory has much in common with the theory of deterrence, dating back to Jeremy Bentham, which still has a great deal of influence on the sentencing practices of judges. Bentham thought that people acted rationally and hedonistically, weighing the pleasure of crime against the pain of the legal punishment, and that it was necessary to increase the severity of the punishment to tip the scales in favor of law-abiding behavior. However, he also realized that there was an interaction between the certainty and the severity of punishment and concluded that, as a punishment became less certain, it should be more severe to maintain its deterrent effect (Geis, 1955). The most popular method of investigating the theory of deterrence has been to correlate crime rates, usually in different states of the United States, with indices of the severity and certainty of punishment in each state (e.g., Chiricos & Waldo, 1970; Logan, 1972; Tittle, 1969). However, such studies can never be conclusive, partly because of their reliance on official statistics and partly because of the problem of drawing causal inferences in correlational research. In order to make unambiguous causal inferences, experimental research is needed.

If dishonesty depends on rational considerations, it should increase with the rewards which might be gained and with the increasing likelihood of a reward, and should decrease with the punishment which might follow and with the increasing likelihood of punishment. In general, the likelihood of cheating increases with the rewards which are consequential upon it. Mills (1958) found increased cheating with a more valuable prize at stake, Dmitruk (1971) found more cheating with more attractive incentives, and Vitro and Schoer (1972) found more cheating in a test when the results of the test were made more important to the subject. Farrington and Kidd (1977) did not find that financial dishonesty increased with the amount of money which could be gained, but it could be argued that the amounts involved in their research were too small to have a significant effect.

Most of the research studying the negative consequences of dishonesty has varied the likelihood of negative consequences rather than their severity. However, Heisler (1974) varied the severity of the penalty for cheating by students by negatively sanctioning a confederate in front of them and found that cheating decreased as the consequences became more severe. Mills (1958) found that cheating decreased when he increased the likelihood of detection by suggesting to children that their scores would be checked, and similar results were obtained by Burton, Allinsmith, and Maccoby (1966); Hill and Kochendorfer (1969); and Vitro and Schoer (1972). Tittle and Rowe (1973) found that cheating by students decreased when they were made aware of the likelihood of negative consequences, and Kanfer and Duerfeldt (1968) found that merely warning children not to cheat was effective in reducing cheating.

Despite the differing operational definitions of costs and benefits, most of the above experiments indicate that the likelihood of dishonesty varies with the costs and benefits which might follow from it. I shall now attempt to specify this theory more exactly. The theoretical variable of interest is the probability of committing a dishonest act, given an opportunity to do so. The importance of opportunity should not be neglected, despite individual variations in awareness of opportunity. For example, Wilkins (1964) showed that the number of thefts from cars increased over the years in direct proportion to the number of cars registered. It is suggested that this probability is transformed into actuality according to processes which can be regarded as random. In other words, whether or not a person commits a delinquent act in a certain situation, within the constraints of his probability of doing so, depends on a random process. Given the indeterminancy of human behavior, it seems more realistic to build probabilistic processes into the model than deterministic ones.

The most general theory suggests that the probability of committing a dishonest act in any situation depends on a large number of factors, only some of which correspond to costs and benefits. A very simple additive model might be specified as follows:

$$P = a_0 + a_1x_1 + a_2x_2 + a_3x_3 + a_4x_4 + a_5x_5 + \cdots + a_nx_n \qquad (1)$$

In Eq. (1), P is the probability of committing a dishonest act, $x_1, x_2, \ldots, x_n$ are theoretical variables, and $a_0, a_1, a_2, \ldots, a_n$ are coefficients. [In order to ensure that P falls between 0 and 1, it would be better to have $\log (P/1 - P)$ on the left-hand side of this equation, as in a logistic regression. However, I will ignore mathematical complications of this kind, which do not affect the argument.] In

Eq. (1), x_1 might correspond to the costs of the dishonest act and x_2 to its benefits, assuming for simplicity that these can be expressed as unidimensional variables. However, x_3 then might correspond to some individual factor, such as strength of conscience, and x_4 and x_5 might correspond to other situational factors, such as the presence of a dishonest model and characteristics of the victim (again treated as unidimensional variables). It is easy to see how this equation could be extended to allow for theoretical variables which are not unidimensional (e.g., by putting in several x terms for each) or interactions (e.g., by having such terms as $a_5 x_5 x_6$). The problems come in operationally defining the theoretical variables in order to apply the equation to empirical variables.

The most specific theory would suggest that the probability of committing a dishonest act in any situation depended only on the costs and benefits present in that situation, and that all factors influenced this probability only insofar as they could be treated as costs or benefits. An equation is then required which relates the probability of committing a dishonest act to costs and benefits and their associated probabilities. One of the most obvious candidates is based on the subjectively expected utility model which has been so influential in explaining single-stage risky decision making (e.g., Becker & McClintock, 1967; Edwards, 1961; Rapoport & Wallsten, 1972; Slovic, Fischhoff, & Lichtenstein, 1977). The decision to commit a dishonest act is a risky decision, and theories of risky decision making should therefore have some relevance.

The subjectively expected utility (SEU) of an event or outcome is the product of the subjective probability of its occurrence and its utility, or subjective value, attractiveness, benefit, or cost. In a risky decision, each alternative choice has a certain SEU, which is the sum of the SEUs associated with each outcome of the choice. The SEU theory is deterministic and suggests that a person chooses the course of action with the greatest SEU. It is inspired by the fact that, in gambling, a person can maximize his winnings by choosing the bet with the greatest expected value (the product of objective probability and objective value). The SEU theory has been derived and tested in gambling experiments. Because of the maximization involved, it can be argued that the SEU theory prescribes the "rational" course of action. It is not suggested that subjective probabilities and utilities are calculated and combined at the conscious level, but only that people behave as if they are maximizing SEU.

Converting the SEU theory into a probabilistic theory yields the following rather general equation:

$$P = a_0 + a_1 \sum p_1 u_1 + a_2 \sum p_2 a_2 + \cdots + a_n \sum p_n u_n \quad (2)$$

What Eq. (2) indicates is that the probability of committing a dishonest act depends on the SEU of each possible course of action. For example, imagine someone in a shop considering whether or not to steal something, and for simplicity imagine that he has two possible courses of action, stealing and not stealing. The SEU of stealing might be as follows:

$$\text{SEU} = p_{11}u_{11} - p_{12}u_{12} \tag{3}$$

In Eq. (3), u_{11} is the positive utility of the item which is stolen, and this is multiplied by the probability of stealing (p_{11}), which in this course of action is 1; u_{12} is the negative utility (cost) of an uncertain outcome, being caught by the store detective, and p_{12} is the subjective probability of this event. This is again a simplification, since only two possible outcomes have been included in the equation. The SEU of stealing is then compared with the SEU of not stealing, obtained by a similar process of multiplication, and the probability of stealing depends on the relative size of the two SEUs. The probability of stealing increases with the SEU of stealing.

In attempting to test either of the theories outlined here, the general theory and the more specific SEU theory, it would be necessary to simplify them by making restrictive assumptions. It is doubtful that the theories could be tested quantitatively at the present time, given our present ability to quantify human behavior. However, mathematical specification of theories is valuable, if only to force theorists to make all their assumptions explicit.

The SEU theory has been stated here deliberately in an extreme version. It seems implausible to suggest that dishonesty depends only on costs, utilities, and their associated probabilities or, alternatively, that all factors influence dishonesty only insofar as they are costs and utilities. However, it is valuable to begin with a very simple theory and to see which results cannot be included within it. The most useful theory is a simple theory which explains a large number of results. In trying to explain every possible result, it may be necessary to postulate a very complex theory which is less useful, and indeed less testable, than the simple theory. There is always the danger that the number of free parameters in the theory may approach the number of degrees of freedom in the data.

Some experiments on dishonesty have been designed to investigate factors other than costs and utilities, and some researchers have tried to compare cost factors with moral factors. Tittle and Rowe (1973) found that making students aware of the sanctions for cheating was more effective in reducing it than was a moral appeal, emphasizing the immorality of cheating. This result seems to conflict with that of Schwartz and Orleans (1967) showing that income tax fraud decreased more after taxpayers were interviewed and given moral reasons for compliance then after they were reminded of the possible penalties. However, moral factors, such as a sense of guilt or an uneasy conscience, could be regarded as costs which are taken into account in decisions about dishonesty.

Some other experimental results could also be explained from a cost–utility perspective. For example, Diener et al. (1976) found that children were more likely to steal in conditions of anonymity than when their names were known to the potential victim. This result could be explained by suggesting that the important theoretical construct being varied was probability of being caught, which was less in the anonymous condition. A similar explanation could be offered for another result obtained by Diener *et al.*, namely that children were more likely to steal in groups than alone, and for Penner's *et al.* (1976) demonstration that students were more likely to steal money which had no identifiable owner than money with an identifiable owner. Even Bickman's (1971) results, showing that members of the public were more likely to steal from someone in lower class dress than from someone in higher class dress, could be explained by reference to variation in the probability of legal consequences, since rich people are more likely to invoke the support of legal agencies than poor people are. The plausibility of these explanations could be tested in further experiments measuring both the probability of being caught and anonymity (for example), to see whether anonymity had an effect on stealing over and above the effect resulting from variations in the probability of being caught.

Other experimental results are less easy to explain on the extreme SEU theory outlined above. For example, Schachter (1971) found that students cheated more after being given chlorpromazine, which reduces arousal or fear, than after taking a placebo. This is understandable if arousal or fear tends to inhibit cheating. Dienstbier and Munter (1971) and Dienstbier (1972) gave students a placebo, but told them to expect side effects of either a pounding heart or yawning. They found more cheating in the pounding heart condition, and suggested that this was because the students could attribute their arousal to the effects of the drug rather than to the cheating. Just as arousal has been found to be an important factor in aggression (e.g., O'Neal & Kaufman, 1972; Zillman, 1971; Zillman, Katcher & Milavsky, 1972), it seems likely that it should be included in a theory of dishonesty.

Arousal might possibly be involved as an explanatory factor in the social facilitation of dishonesty. For example, Taylor and Lewit (1966) found that delinquent boys were most likely to tell lies in reporting their grip strengths when another boy would be aware of their performance, and several experimenters (e.g., Dmitruk, 1973; Hill & Kochendorfer, 1969; Shelton & Hill, 1969) found that children were more likely to cheat to do well in a test or to win a prize if they believed that their peers had done well.

Other experimental results are harder to explain in relation to either costs and utilities or arousal. Diener and Wallbom (1976) found less cheating when subjects were made aware of what they were doing by performing in front of a mirror, and O'Leary (1968) found that children cheated less when they were required to verbalize the task instructions. Cheating was also more likely among subjects who believed that they had done relatively badly on a test (Millham, 1974), or who believed that their responses were deviant from those of their peers

(Lepper, 1973), or who had lowered self-esteem for another reason (Aronson & Mettee, 1968). Children were also more likely to cheat if they had been justly privileged or unjustly deprived in comparison with their peers (Stephenson & Barker, 1972; Stephenson & White, 1968, 1970). In order to explain all these results, it seems likely that the more general theory is needed. However, it may also be valuable to investigate the range of applicability of the more specific SEU theory.

I have carried out two experiments, in collaboration with Barry J. Knight, inspired by the SEU theory. They were intended to investigate three basic hypotheses, namely that (a) the probability of stealing increases with increasing utility of the theft, (b) the probability of stealing decreases with increasing cost of the theft, and (c) the probability of stealing decreases with increasing probability of apprehension by the police. If these three hypotheses were not verified, the importance of costs, benefits, and probabilities in the explanation of dishonesty would require reconsideration. These hypotheses were investigated in nonreactive field experiments with members of the public unwittingly participating as subjects.

The experiments were based on the lost letter technique. This was originally used by Merritt and Fowler (1948) to study dishonesty. They showed that letters left on the street and containing a lead slug which felt like a 50¢ piece were less likely to be returned unopened than letters merely containing a message. As mentioned earlier, Hornstein *et al.* (1968), Hornstein (1970), and Tucker *et al.* (1977), in studies of helpfulness, also left money in an envelope on the street. In these experiments, failing to return the letter constituted stealing, but this was not true in later research on helping using this technique (e.g., Deaux, 1973; Gross, 1975; Hornstein, Masor, Sole, & Heilman, 1971; Korte & Kerr, 1975; Lowe & Ritchey, 1973; Sole, Marton, & Hornstein, 1975). The lost letter technique has been used primarily to measure political and social attitudes (e.g., Georgoff, Hersker, & Murdick, 1972; Himes & Mason, 1974; Jacoby & Aranoff, 1971; Milgram, Mann, & Harter, 1965; Wicker, 1969; Zelnio & Gagnon, 1977).

In the first experiment, 100 stamped, addressed, apparently lost, unsealed letters, each containing a handwritten note and in most cases also a sum of money, were left on the streets of London, England, and were picked up by members of the public. The experiment employed a 2 × 2 × 2 between-subjects factorial design, with two levels of utility (low or high), two levels of cost (low or high), and two levels of probability of apprehension (low or high). The dependent variable was whether the letter and its contents were returned intact to the intended recipient (Barry J. Knight). Ten letters were dropped in each of the eight main conditions of the experiment, and 10 letters in each of two control (no money) conditions. The experimenter who dropped the letters was blind to the conditions.

An attempt was made to manipulate the utility of stealing by varying the amount of money contained in the letter, either 20p (low utility) or £1.00 (high utility). An attempt was made to manipulate the cost of stealing by varying the content of the note. In the low-cost condition, the intended recipient was the male secretary of a yachting association, and the note indicated that the sender was enclosing money for a yachting magazine. In the high-cost condition, the intended recipient was an old lady, and the note indicated that the sender was refunding money from a Senior Citizen's outing to her. It was thought that stealing in the low-cost condition would be more pleasant, because the victims were less deserving. The probability of apprehension was varied by the form in which the money came, either cash (low probability) or an uncrossed postal order (high probability). It is necessary to forge the signature of the intended recipient of a postal order to obtain the money, and it is possible that someone doing this might be asked for identification evidence and hence detected.

One problem with the operational definition of stealing as failure to return a lost letter containing money is that it is impossible to separate honesty and helpfulness. Those who return the letter are displaying both. The 20 control (no money) letters were intended to investigate helpfulness in the absence of dishonesty. Ten had a very similar note to that used in the low-cost condition, and 10 had a very similar note to that used in the high-cost condition. The 100 letters were made up in a random order, with the restriction that each of the 10 conditions occurred once in each block of 10 letters. A further 20 control letters, two in each condition, were made up and posted by the experimenters during the same period and in the same areas in which letters were dropped. These 20 letters were intended to check the efficiency of the Post Office, and all were delivered safely.

Twenty-three of the 80 letters in the main experiment were not returned. An analysis of variance showed that the main effects of cost and probability were statistically significant and that there was a significant interaction between cost and probability. The results are clear when simple percentages are presented. The nonreturn rates in the low-cost and high-cost control conditions were identical (20%), giving a base rate for unhelpfulness or carelessness in not returning letters. The nonreturn rate in the low cost–low probability condition, at 75%, was significantly greater than the control rate (15 out of 20 in comparison with 4 out of 20; $\chi^2 = 10.03$ with 1 d.f., $p < .002$). However, the nonreturn rates of other conditions were not significantly greater than the control rate. It can be concluded that a low cost and a low probability of apprehension produced a high level of stealing. The fact that the experimental manipulations of cost and probability had clear-cut effects shows that they were very powerful, in view of the many sources of variation which were controlled only by the random allocation.

The utility manipulation did not have a significant effect on stealing (32.5% nonreturn out of 40 in high-utility conditions, as opposed to 25% nonreturn out of

40 in low-utility conditions). This replicates the result of Farrington and Kidd (1977), who found no difference between 10p and 50p in inducing financial dishonesty. However, it could be argued that these utility manipulations were too weak, so that for the majority of subjects the difference between 20p and £1 was not sufficient to have a significant effect on stealing. The second lost letter experiment was carried out to investigate this. It was very similar to the first lost letter experiment, except that only utility was manipulated. Sixty letters were left on the streets of London, England, and picked up by members of the public. The note in each letter indicated that the intended recipient was an old lady, and each letter contained either no money, £1, or £5 (in cash).

The utility manipulation in the second experiment did have a significant effect. The proportion of letters not returned was 5% in the control condition, 25% in the £1 condition, and 45% in the £5 condition ($N = 20$ in all cases: $\chi^2 = 8.69$ with 2 d.f., p < .025). Thus, taken together, the two lost letter experiments are in agreement with the hypotheses, in showing that the probability of stealing increases with increasing utility, with decreasing cost, and with decreasing probability of apprehension. In turn, this leads to increasing confidence in both of the theories outlined above, the general theory and the SEU theory. Given that stealing is influenced by costs, utilities, and probabilities, the next step is to carry out experiments which systematically investigate the importance of other factors, preferably in comparison with the above factors.

B. EVALUATING AND REACTING TO DISHONESTY

The process of reacting to crime by criminal justice agencies usually begins when a crime is officially recorded by the police and hence becomes an entry in the official criminal statistics. Before a crime can be recorded, some person must become aware that a criminal act has been committed and, unless that person is a policeman, he must decide to report it to the police. Most entries in the official statistics are initiated by citizen reports rather than by the police themselves (e.g., Black & Reiss, 1970). Therefore, citizens play an important role in defining and hence creating crime, and the study of factors influencing a person's decision to report a crime has important practical implications. Furthermore, some states of the United States have "Good Samaritan" laws requiring citizens to intervene to prevent crimes. It is clear that crime would be reduced if more citizens were to intervene in this way, and therefore the study of factors influencing citizens' intervention also has practical importance.

There have been a number of nonexperimental studies of crime reporting. Most of these have used the victim survey technique, which involves asking people about crimes which have been committed against them rather than about crimes they have observed. For example, Ennis (1970) reported the result of a victim survey based on a random sample of 10,000 American households, in which people were asked about crimes committed against them in the previous year. As is usual in such surveys, this victim survey revealed twice as much major crime as the official statistics in the Federal Bureau of Investigation *Uniform Crime Reports*. The rates of homicide and car theft in the victim survey were similar to those in the official statistics. In the case of car theft, the high rate of reporting to the police was at least partly caused by the requirements of insurance companies. For other major crimes, the victim survey rates were higher than those in the official statistics. The victim survey revealed four times as much forcible rape, three times as much burglary, twice as much theft over $50, twice as much aggravated assault, and 50% more robbery than the official statistics.

In general, the more serious crimes were more likely to be reported to the police. Whenever anyone was victimized and did not report to the police, he was asked to give the reason. Much the most common reason (55%) was the belief that reporting would be a waste of time, because the police would not want to be bothered or would not catch the offender. A further 9% did not want to take the time or trouble to get involved with the police or were too confused. Of the rest, 34% thought that it was not a police matter or did not want the offender to be harmed, and 2% feared reprisals from the offender's friends or from insurance companies (in cancelling the insurance or increasing its cost).

This nonexperimental research is based on what people say. There has also been some experimental research on the reporting of thefts by observers rather than victims, but I will begin by discussing some experiments on the evaluation of dishonesty. It might be hypothesized that the evaluation of the offence and offender (if known) is a stage which precedes the decision to report. On the basis of research on simulated jurors and moral judgments mentioned in Section II, D, it might be expected that this evaluation would depend, at least, on the intentions and personal characteristics of the offender and on the consequences of the offence. Some of these factors have been studied in experiments. Brickman and Bryan (1975) showed girls a film of a girl stealing 10¢ tokens and found that whether the tokens were stolen to increase or decrease equality had no effect on the evaluation of the thief. Savitsky *et al.* (1976) showed incarcerated juvenile offenders a videotape of someone cheating and found that whether or not the cheating had good consequences (a charity benefitted) did not affect their evaluation of it. However, Savitsky and Babl (1976) found that introductory psychology students delivered more aversive noise in a learning task to someone who had cheated if he had gained by the cheating than if a charity had gained. Maier and Lavrakas (1976) studied evaluations of lying and found that lies with less harmful consequences were rated more acceptable, and that it was considered more reprehensible to lie to a friend than to a stranger. More research on the evaluation of dishonesty is required, preferably using real-life staged thefts, varying such factors as the kinds of offender and victim and the intentions and consequences of the theft.

As mentioned in Section II,C, staged thefts have been used in experiments on crime reporting and bystander intervention in crime. Harari and McDavid (1969) found that schoolchildren who had observed a theft were less likely to name the thief if she was a high-status girl rather than a low-status boy. Steffensmeier and Terry (1973) found that a shoplifter dressed as a hippie was more likely to be reported than one dressed conventionally, but Gelfand *et al.* (1973) found that hippie dress did not affect the reporting of shoplifting. Both Steffensmeier and Terry (1973) and Dertke *et al.* (1974) found that the sex of the thief did not affect reporting, but Steffensmeier and Terry found that subjects were more likely to report shoplifters of the opposite sex. Dertke *et al.* found that black shoplifters were more likely to be reported than whites. Bickman and Green (1975) found an interaction between the cost of the item stolen and the previous contact between the shoplifter and the subject. With a low-cost item, subjects were more likely to report if the shoplifter had previously been rude to them, but with a high-cost item reporting was not related to previous contact.

Shaffer *et al.* (1975) and Moriarty (1975) found that bystanders were more likely to intervene to prevent a theft if they had previously been asked to do so, and Bickman and Rosenbaum (1977) showed how confederates could encourage bystanders to report. However, Bickman (1975) found that a mass media campaign designed to encourage intervention had little effect. Harari and McDavid (1969) discovered that schoolchildren were more likely to name a thief if they were questioned alone rather than in pairs, and Latane and Darley (1970) also found that witnesses to a theft were more likely to report if they were alone rather than with another person. Similarly, Shaffer *et al.* (1975) found that bystanders were more likely to intervene to prevent a theft if they were alone than if they were in the presence of a nonreactive confederate.

As with the commission of dishonest acts, several researchers have proposed a cost–benefit model to explain the reporting of theft. For example, Gelfand *et al.* (1973) pointed out that the rewards of reporting were minimal, since reporters received no money or gratitude and only had the satisfaction of bringing a criminal to justice. These rewards could be contrasted with the potential costs of causing harm to the accused person, being sued by the accused, and the inconvenience of appearing in court. Both of the models outlined in Section III, A could be applied to the reporting of theft. In the general case, it could be suggested that the probability of reporting in any situation depends on a large number of factors, some of which are costs and benefits. In the more specific case, it could be suggested that this probability depends only on the costs and benefits present, and that all factors influence this probability only insofar as they can be treated as costs or benefits.

Up to the present time, no researchers have tried to vary costs and benefits systematically in an experiment and to relate reporting to them. The theory fits in with the nonexperimental results mentioned above. People do seem to be considering costs and benefits when they say that reporting would be a waste of time because the police would not catch the offender, that they do not want to take the time or trouble to get involved with the police, that they do not want the offender to be harmed, or that they fear reprisals from the offender's friends. Furthermore, some of the experimental results could be explained within this theory. It is possible that people are more willing to report low-status thieves, hippies, and blacks because the potential costs are less with these groups, in view of their relative lack of power. Alternatively, it may be that people get more pleasure from reporting these groups than they do from reporting others. Steffensmeier and Terry (1973) found that some of their subjects were enthusiastic about reporting the hippie shoplifter and made statements which reflected their prejudiced feelings toward hippies. People may also get more pleasure from reporting shoplifters who have previously been rude to them than from reporting those who have previously been polite. Within a cost–benefit theory, it is harder to explain the greater reluctance of people to report when in the presence of others than when alone, but in general this theory seems worthy of experimental research designed to investigate it more directly.

IV. Conclusions

Throughout this paper, I have argued that field experimentation with members of the public unwittingly participating as subjects is likely to have the greatest internal and external validity of any research method. Most research on deviance is nonexperimental and hence has low internal validity, while most research by experimental social psychologists has tended to have low external validity, in being far removed from real life. In order to advance our knowledge about deviance, more field experiments with behavioral measures of deviance should be carried out. These need to be backed up by correlational research, to establish the extent to which experimental results can be generalized to real life and to establish which theoretical constructs are being measured. When true experiments involving random allocation cannot be arranged, quasiexperimental analyses should be considered.

One of the major problems in carrying out experiments with deviance as either a dependent or an independent variable or both is to operationalize deviance, and this contribution has reviewed operational definitions used in experiments up to the present time. Of the more serious deviant acts, it seems most possible to study theft and vandalism, and a number of experiments investigating why people steal and why people report or intervene in stealing have been reviewed. Of the less serious acts, further studies of litter dropping and traffic offenses seem feasible and potentially valuable.

Special attention has been given to experiments on dishonesty. These have tended to investigate immediate influences and situational factors, both of which have been neglected in the nonexperimental research. Many of the experiments have been inspired by a cost–benefit theory, in relation to both committing and reporting dishonest acts. This promising theory requires a systematic program of experimental research to investigate the importance of costs and benefits in comparison with other factors and eventually to lead to an explicitly formulated theory with a wide range of applicability. One practical implication which may be drawn from it is that crime prevention efforts which aim to change immediate situational factors may be more successful than the traditional forms of treatment aimed at individuals. It has been argued that experimental social psychologists should undertake practical experiments on the prevention and treatment of deviance.

Real-life experiments on deviance are much harder to arrange than laboratory experiments on less sensitive topics. When it comes to research with ethical difficulties, even on topics perceived to be "relevant," funding agencies are likely to err on the side of caution. Yet our knowledge about the causes, prevention, and treatment of deviance could be advanced greatly by real-life experimentation, and the quality of life of most people would improve if it were possible to reduce deviant behavior prohibited by the criminal law. It is to be hoped that psychologists will have the ingenuity, determination, and social responsibility to meet the challenge of experiments on deviance.

REFERENCES

Adams, S. The PICO project. In N. Johnson, L. Savitz, & M. E. Wolfgang (Eds.), *The sociology of punishment and correction.* New York: Wiley, 1970.

Aronson, E., & Mettee, D. R. Dishonest behavior as a function of differential levels of induced self-esteem. *Journal of Personality and Social Psychology,* 1968, **9**, 121–127.

Baltes, M. M., & Hayward, S. C. Application and evaluation of strategies to reduce pollution: Behavioral control of littering in a football stadium. *Journal of Applied Psychology,* 1976, **61**, 501–506.

Bandura, A., & McDonald, F. J. Influence of social reinforcement and the behavior of models in shaping children's moral judgments. *Journal of Abnormal and Social Psychology,* 1963, **67**, 274–281.

Becker, G. M., & McClintock, C. G. Value: Behavioral decision theory. *Annual Review of Psychology,* 1967, **18**, 239–286.

Becker, H. S. *Outsiders: Studies in the sociology of deviance.* New York: Free Press, 1963.

Beigel, H. G. Experimental production of anti-social acts in hypnosis. *British Journal of Medical Hypnotism,* 1962, **14**, 11–19.

Berg, I., Hullin, R., & McGuire, R. A randomly controlled trial of two court procedures in truancy. In D. P. Farrington, K. Hawkins, & S. Lloyd-Bostock (Eds.), *Psychology, law and legal processes.* London: Macmillan, 1979.

Berkowitz, L., & Walker, N. D. Laws and moral judgments. *Sociometry,* 1967, **30,** 410–422.

Berntsen, K., & Christiansen, K. O. A resocialization experiment with short-term offenders. In K. O. Christiansen (Ed.), *Scandinavian studies in criminology* (Vol 1). London: Tavistock, 1965.

Bickman, L. The effect of social status on the honesty of others. *Journal of Social Psychology,* 1971, **85,** 87–92.

Bickman, L. Bystander intervention in a crime: The effect of a mass-media campaign. *Journal of Applied Social Psychology,* 1975, **5,** 296–302.

Bickman, L. Attitude toward an authority and the reporting of a crime. *Sociometry,* 1976, **39,** 76–82.

Bickman, L., & Green, S. Is revenge sweet? The effect of attitude toward a thief on crime reporting. *Criminal Justice and Behavior,* 1975, **2,** 101–112.

Bickman, L., & Henchy, T. (Eds.), *Beyond the laboratory: Field research in social psychology.* New York: McGraw-Hill, 1972.

Bickman, L., & Rosenbaum, D. P. Crime reporting as a function of bystander encouragement, surveillance and credibility. *Journal of Personality and Social Psychology,* 1977, **35,** 577–586.

Birnbaum, M. P. Anxiety and moral judgment in early adolescence. *Journal of Genetic Psychology,* 1972, **120,** 13–26.

Black, D. J., & Reiss, A. J. Police control of juveniles. *American Sociological Review,* 1970, **35,** 63–77.

Bleda, P. R., Bleda, S. E., Byrne, D., & White, L. A. When a bystander becomes an accomplice: Situational determinants of reactions to dishonesty. *Journal of Experimental Social Psychology,* 1976, **12,** 9–25.

Bord, R. J. Rejection of the mentally ill: Continuities and further developments. *Social Problems,* 1971, **18,** 496–509.

Boshier, R., & Johnson, D. Does conviction affect employment opportunities? *British Journal of Criminology,* 1974, **14,** 264–268.

Bowman, P. H. Effects of a revised school program on potential delinquents. *Annals of the American Academy of Political and Social Sciences,* 1959, **322,** 53–61.

Bramel, D. A dissonance theory approach to defensive projection. *Journal of Abnormal and Social Psychology,* 1962, **64,** 121–129.

Bramel, D. Selection of a target for defensive projection. *Journal of Abnormal and Social Psychology,* 1963, **66,** 318–324.

Brickman, P., & Bryan, J. H. Moral judgment of theft, charity, and third-party transfers that increase or decrease equality. *Journal of Personality and Social Psychology,* 1975, **31,** 156–161.

Brickman, P., & Bryan, J. H. Equity versus equality as factors in children's moral judgments of thefts, charity, and third-party transfers. *Journal of Personality and Social Psychology,* 1976, **34,** 757–761.

Buckhout, R., Alper, A., Chern, S., Silverberg, G., & Slomovits, M. Determinants of eyewitness performance on a lineup. *Bulletin of the Psychonomic Society,* 1974, **4,** 191–192.

Buikhuisen, W. General deterrence: Research and theory. *Abstracts in Criminology and Penology,* 1974, **14,** 285–298.

Buikhuisen, W., & Dijksterhuis, F. P. H. Delinquency and stigmatization. *British Journal of Criminology,* 1971, **11,** 185–187.

Buikhuisen, W., & Jongman, R. W. A legalistic classification of juvenile delinquents. *British Journal of Criminology,* 1970, **10,** 109–123.

Burgess, R. L., Clark, R. N., & Hendee, J. C. An experimental analysis of anti-litter procedures. *Journal of Applied Behavior Analysis,* 1971, **4,** 71–75.

Burns, J. A., & Kintz, B. L. Eye contact while lying during an interview. *Bulletin of the Psychonomic Society,* 1976, **7,** 87–89.

Burton, R. V. Generality of honesty reconsidered. *Psychological Review,* 1963, **70,** 481–499.

Burton, R. V., Allinsmith, W., & Maccoby, E. E. Resistance to temptation in relation to sex of child, sex of experimenter and withdrawal of attention. *Journal of Personality and Social Psychology,* 1966, **3**, 253-258.

Caetano, D. F. Labeling theory and the presumption of mental illness in diagnosis: An experimental design. *Journal of Health and Social Behavior,* 1974, **15**, 253-260.

Campbell, D. T., & Ross, L. The Connecticut crackdown on speeding: Time-series data and quasi-experimental analysis. *Law and Society Review,* 1968, **3**, 33-53.

Campbell, D. T., & Stanley, J. C. *Experimental and quasi-experimental designs for research.* Chicago: Rand-McNally, 1966.

Carlson, R. Where is the person in personality research? *Psychological Bulletin,* 1971, **75**, 203-219.

Chiricos, T. G., & Waldo, G. P. Punishment and crime: An examination of some empirical evidence. *Social Problems,* 1970, **18**, 200-217.

Clarke, R. V. G., & Cornish, D. B. *The controlled trial in institutional research—paradigm or pitfall for penal evaluators?* London: HMSO, 1972.

Coe, W. C., Kobayashi, K., & Howard, M. L. An approach toward isolating factors that influence antisocial conduct in hypnosis. *International Journal of Clinical and Experimental Hypnosis,* 1972, **20**, 118-131.

Coe, W. C., Kobayashi, K., & Howard, M. L. Experimental and ethical problems of evaluating the influence of hypnosis in antisocial conduct. *Journal of Abnormal Psychology,* 1973, **82**, 476-482.

Cornish, D. B., & Clarke, R. V. G. *Residential treatment and its effects on delinquency.* London: HMSO, 1975.

Cowan, P. A., Langer, J., Heavenrich, J., & Nathanson, M. Social learning and Piaget's cognitive theory of moral development. *Journal of Personality and Social Psychology,* 1969, **11**, 261-274.

Cronbach, L. J. *Essentials of psychological testing* (3rd ed.). New York: Harper, 1970.

Deaux, K. Anonymous altruism: Extending the lost letter technique. *Journal of Social Psychology,* 1973, **92**, 61-66.

Denner, B. Did a crime occur? Should I inform anyone? A study of deception. *Journal of Personality,* 1968, **36**, 454-465.

Dertke, M. C., Penner, L. A., & Ulrich, K. Observer's reporting of shoplifting as a function of thief's race and sex. *Journal of Social Psychology,* 1974, **94**, 213-221.

Deutscher, I. *What we say/What we do.* Glenview: Scott Foresman, 1973.

Diener, E., Fraser, S. C., Beaman, A. L., & Kelem, R. T. Effects of deindividuation variables on stealing among Halloween trick-or-treaters. *Journal of Personality and Social Psychology,* 1976, **33**, 178-183.

Diener, E., & Wallbom, M. Effects of self-awareness on antinormative behavior. *Journal of Research in Personality,* 1976, **10**, 107-111.

Dienstbier, R. A. The role of anxiety and arousal attribution in cheating. *Journal of Experimental Social Psychology,* 1972, **8**, 168-179.

Dienstbier, R. A., & Munter, P. O. Cheating as a function of the labeling of natural arousal. *Journal of Personality and Social Psychology,* 1971, **17**, 208-213.

Dmitruk, V. M. Incentive preference and resistance to temptation. *Child Development,* 1971, **42**, 625-628.

Dmitruk, V. M. Intangible motivation and resistance to temptation. *Journal of Genetic Psychology,* 1973, **123**, 47-53.

Dorr, D., & Fey, S. Relative power of symbolic adult and peer models in the modification of children's moral choice behavior. *Journal of Personality and Social Psychology,* 1974, **29**, 335-341.

Ebbesen, E. B., & Konecni, V. J. Decision making and information integration in the courts: The setting of bail. *Journal of Personality and Social Psychology,* 1975, **32**, 805-821.

Edwards, W. Behavioral decision theory. *Annual Review of Psychology,* 1961, **12**, 473-498.

Efran, M. G. The effect of physical appearance on the judgment of guilt, interpersonal attraction, and severity of recommended punishment in a simulated jury task. *Journal of Research in Personality,* 1974, **8**, 45-54.

Ekman, P., & Friesen, W. V. Detecting deception from the body or face. *Journal of Personality and Social Psychology,* 1974, **29**, 288-298.

Empey, L. T., & Erickson, M. L. *The provo experiment: Evaluating community control of delinquency.* Lexington: Heath, 1972.

Empey, L. T., & Lubeck, S. G. *The silverlake experiment: Testing delinquency theory and community intervention.* Chicago: Aldine, 1971.

Ennis, P. H. Crime, victims and the police. In M. Lipsky (Ed.), *Law and order: Police encounters.* Chicago: Aldine, 1970.

Farrington, D. P. Self-reports of deviant behavior: predictive and stable? *Journal of Criminal Law and Criminology,* 1973, **64**, 99-110.

Farrington, D. P. The effects of public labelling. *British Journal of Criminology,* 1977, **17**, 112-125.

Farrington, D. P., & Kidd, R. F. Is financial dishonesty a rational decision? *British Journal of Social and Clinical Psychology,* 1977, **16**, 139-146.

Farrington, D. P., & Knight, B. J. Four studies of stealing as a risky decision. In P. Lipsitt & B. D. Sales (Eds.), *New directions in psycholegal research.* New York: Van Nostrand-Reinhold, 1979, in press. (a)

Farrington, D. P., & Knight, B. J. Two non-reactive field experiments on stealing from a "lost" letter. *British Journal of Social and Clinical Psychology,* 1979, **18**, in press. (b)

Farrington, D. P., Osborn, S. G., & West, D. J. The persistence of labelling effects. *British Journal of Criminology,* 1978, **18**, 277-284.

Feldman, R. E. Response to compatriot and foreigner who seek assistance. *Journal of Personality and Social Psychology,* 1968, **10**, 202-214.

Finnie, W. C. Field experiments in litter control. *Environment and Behavior,* 1973, **5**, 123-144.

Folkard, M. S., Smith, D. E., & Smith, D. D. *Impact. Vol 2: The results of the experiment.* London: HMSO, 1976.

Fowles, A. J. *Prison Welfare.* London: HMSO, 1978.

Franklin, B. J. The effects of status on the honesty and verbal responses of others. *Journal of Social Psychology,* 1973, **91**, 347-348.

Freedman, J. L., Wallington, S. A., & Bless, E. Compliance without pressure: The effect of guilt. *Journal of Personality and Social Psychology,* 1967, **7**, 117-124.

Fromkin, H. L., Goldstein, J. H., & Brock, T. C. The role of "irrelevant" derogation in vicarious aggression catharsis: A field experiment. *Journal of Experimental Social Psychology,* 1977, **13**, 239-252.

Geis, G. Pioneers in criminology: VII. Jeremy Bentham. *Journal of Criminal Law, Criminology and Police Science,* 1955, **46**, 159-171.

Gelfand, D. M., Hartmann, D. P., Walder, P., & Page, P. Who reports shoplifters? A field-experimental study. *Journal of Personality and Social Psychology,* 1973, **25**, 276-285.

Georgoff, D. M., Hersker, B. J., & Murdick, R. G. The lost-letter technique: A scaling experiment. *Public Opinion Quarterly,* 1972, **36**, 114-119.

Grinder, R. E. Parental child-rearing practices, conscience, and resistance to temptation of sixth-grade children. *Child Development,* 1962, **33**, 803-820.

Gross, A. E. Generosity and legitimacy of a model as determinants of helpful behavior. *Representative Research in Social Psychology,* 1975, **6**, 45-50.

Harari, H., & McDavid, J. W. Situational influence on moral justice: A study of 'finking. *Journal of Personality and Social Psychology,* 1969, **11**, 240-244.

Harris, M. B., & Samerotte, G. C. The effects of actual and attempted theft, need, and a previous favor on altruism. *Journal of Social Psychology,* 1976, **99,** 193–202.

Hartshorne, H., & May, M. A. *Studies in deceit.* New York: Macmillan, 1928.

Heisler, G. Ways to deter law violators: Effects of levels of threat and vicarious punishment on cheating. *Journal of Consulting and Clinical Psychology,* 1974, **42,** 577–582.

Hendrick, C., & Shaffer, D. R. Murder: Effects of number of killers and victim mutilation on simulated jurors' judgments. *Bulletin of the Psychonomic Society,* 1975, **6,** 313–316.

Henshel, A-M. The relationship between values and behavior: A developmental hypothesis. *Child Development,* 1971, **42,** 1997–2007.

Hill, F. A. Attribution of responsibility in a campus stabbing incident. *Social Behavior and Personality,* 1975, **3,** 127–131.

Hill, G. E. Cheating among delinquent boys. *Journal of Juvenile Research,* 1934, **18,** 169–174.

Hill, J. P., & Kochendorfer, R. A. Knowledge of peer success and risk of detection as determinants of cheating. *Developmental Psychology,* 1969, **1,** 231–238.

Himes, S. H., & Mason, J. B. A note on unobtrusive attitude measurement: The lost letter technique. *Journal of the Market Research Society,* 1974, **16,** 42–46.

Hindelang, M. J. Age, sex, and the versatility of delinquent involvements. *Social Problems,* 1971, **18,** 522–535.

Hood, R., & Sparks, R. *Key issues in criminology.* London: Weidenfeld and Nicolson, 1970.

Hornstein, H. A. The influence of social models on helping. In J. Macauley and L. Berkowitz (Eds.), *Altruism and helping behavior.* New York: Academic Press, 1970.

Hornstein, H. A., Fisch, E., & Holmes, M. Influence of a model's feeling about his behavior and his relevance as a comparison other on observer's helping behavior. *Journal of Personality and Social Psychology,* 1968, **10,** 222–226.

Hornstein, H. A., Masor, H. N., Sole, K., & Heilman, M. Effects of sentiment and completion of a helping act on observer helping: A case for socially mediated Zeigarnik effects. *Journal of Personality and Social Psychology,* 1971, **17,** 107–112.

Humphreys, L. *Tearoom trade: A study of homosexual encounters in public places.* London: Duckworth, 1970.

Jacoby, J., & Aranoff, D. Political polling and the lost-letter technique. *Journal of Social Psychology,* 1971, **83,** 209–212.

Jesness, C. F. Comparative effectiveness of two institutional treatment programs for delinquents. *Child Care Quarterly,* 1971, **1,** 119–130.

Jones, C., & Aronson, E. Attribution of fault to a rape victim as a function of respectability of the victim. *Journal of Personality and Social Psychology,* 1973, **26,** 415–419.

Kanfer, F. H., & Duerfeldt, P. H. Age, class standing, and commitment as determinants of cheating in children. *Child Development,* 1968, **39,** 545–557.

Kassebaum, G., Ward, D., & Wilner, D. *Prison treatment and parole survival.* New York: Wiley, 1971.

Kaufmann, H. Legality and harmfulness of a bystander's failure to intervene as determinants of moral judgment. In J. Macauley & L. Berkowitz (Eds.), *Altruism and helping behavior.* New York: Academic Press, 1970.

Keehn, J. D. Unrealistic reporting as a function of extraverted neurosis. *Journal of Clinical Psychology,* 1956, **12,** 61–63.

Kidd, R. F. Manipulation checks: Advantage or disadvantage? *Representative Research in Social Psychology,* 1976, **7,** 160–165.

Kirk, S. A. The impact of labeling on rejection of the mentally ill: An experimental study. *Journal of Health and Social Behavior,* 1974, **15,** 108–117.

Kleinke, C. L. Compliance to requests made by gazing and touching experimenters in field settings. *Journal of Experimental Social Psychology,* 1977, **13,** 218–223.

Kline, M. V. The dynamics of hypnotically induced antisocial behavior. *Journal of Psychology,* 1958, **45**, 239-245.

Kline, M. V. The production of antisocial behavior through hypnosis: New clinical data. *International Journal of Clinical and Experimental Hypnosis,* 1972, **20**, 80-94.

Kohlenberg, R., & Phillips, T. Reinforcement and rate of litter depositing. *Journal of Applied Behavior Analysis,* 1973, **6**, 391-396.

Korte, C., & Kerr, N. Response to altruistic opportunities in urban and nonurban settings. *Journal of Social Psychology,* 1975, **95**, 183-184.

Krauss, H. H., & Blanchard, E. B. Locus of control in ethical risk taking. *Psychological Reports,* 1970, **27**, 142.

Krauss, H. H., Coddington, R. D., & Smeltzer, D. J. Ethical risk sensitivity of adolescents in legal difficulty: First contact and repeat contact groups. *Journal of Social Psychology,* 1971, **83**, 213-217.

Krauss, H. H., Robinson, I., Janzen, W., & Cauthen, N. Predictions of ethical risk taking by psychopathic and non-psychopathic criminals. *Psychological Reports,* 1972, **30**, 83-88.

Krauss, R. M., Freedman, J. L., & Whitcup, M. Field and laboratory studies of littering. *Journal of Experimental Social Psychology,* 1978, **14**, 109-122.

Latane, B., & Darley, J. M. *The unresponsive bystander: Why doesn't he help?* New York: Appleton, 1970.

LaTour, S., Houlden, P., Walker, L., & Thibaut, J. Procedure: Transnational perspectives and preferences. *Yale Law Journal,* 1976, **86**, 258-290.

Lefkowitz, M., Blake, R. R., & Mouton, J. S. Status factors in pedestrian violation of traffic signals. *Journal of Abnormal and Social Psychology,* 1955, **51**, 704-706.

Le Furgy, W. G., & Woloshin, G. W. Immediate and long-term effects of experimentally induced social influence in the modification of adolescents' moral judgments. *Journal of Personality and Social Psychology,* 1969, **12**, 104-110.

Lemert, E. M. *Human deviance, social problems and social control* (2nd ed.). New York: Prentice-Hall, 1972.

Lenga, M. R., & Kleinke, C. L. Modeling, anonymity, and performance of an undesirable act. *Psychological Reports,* 1974, **34**, 501-502.

Lepper, M. R. Dissonance, self-perception, and honesty in children. *Journal of Personality and Social Psychology,* 1973, **25**, 65-74.

Lerman, P. *Community treatment and social control.* Chicago: University of Chicago Press, 1975.

Lerner, M. J., & Agar, E. The consequences of perceived similarity: Attraction and rejection, approach and avoidance. *Journal of Experimental Research in Personality,* 1972, **6**, 69-75.

Lingle, J. H., Brock, T. C., & Cialdini, R. B. Surveillance instigates entrapment when violations are observed, when personal involvement is high, and when sanctions are severe. *Journal of Personality and Social Psychology,* 1977, **35**, 419-429.

Logan, C. H. General deterrent effects of punishment. *Social Forces,* 1972, **51**, 64-73.

Lowe, R., & Ritchey, G. Relation of altruism to age, social class, and ethnic identity. *Psychological Reports,* 1973, **33**, 567-572.

Lykken, D. T. The GSR in the detection of guilt. *Journal of Applied Psychology,* 1959, **43**, 385-388.

Maier, N. R. F., & Thurber, J. A. Accuracy of judgments of deception when an interview is watched, heard and read. *Personnel Psychology,* 1968, **21**, 23-30.

Maier, R. A., & Lavrakas, P. J. Lying behavior and evaluation of lies. *Perceptual and Motor Skills,* 1976, **42**, 575-581.

Mann, J., Sidman, J., & Starr, S. Effects of erotic films on sexual behavior of married couples. In *U.S. President's commission on obscenity and pornography.* Technical Report 8. Washington, D.C.: Government Printing Office, 1970.

Marshall, J. *Law and psychology in conflict.* Indianapolis: Bobbs-Merrill, 1966.

Mathes, E. W., & Guest, T. A. Anonymity and group antisocial behavior. *Journal of Social Psychology,* 1976, **100,** 257–262.

McClintock, F. H. *Crimes of violence.* London: Macmillan, 1963.

McCord, J. A thirty-year follow-up of treatment effects. *American Psychologist,* 1978, **33,** 284–289.

McCord, J., & McCord, W. A follow-up report on the Cambridge-Somerville Youth Study. *Annals of the American Academy of Political and Social Sciences,* 1959, **322,** 89–96.

McGlynn, R. P., Megas, J. C., & Benson, D. H. Sex and race as factors affecting the attribution of insanity in a murder trial. *Journal of Psychology,* 1976, **93,** 93–99.

McManis, D. L. Effects of peer-models vs. adult-models and social reinforcement on intentionality of children's moral judgments. *Journal of Psychology,* 1974, **87,** 159–170.

McMillen, D. L. Transgression, self-image, and compliant behavior. *Journal of Personality and Social Psychology,* 1971, **20,** 176–179.

McNees, M. P., Egli, D. S., Marshall, R. S., Schnelle, J. F., & Risley, T. R. Shoplifting prevention: Providing information through signs. *Journal of Applied Behavior Analysis,* 1976, **9,** 399–405.

Medinnus, G. R. Age and sex differences in conscience development. *Journal of Genetic Psychology,* 1966, **109,** 117–118.

Merritt, C. B., & Fowler, R. G. The pecuniary honesty of the public at large. *Journal of Abnormal and Social Psychology,* 1948, **43,** 90–93.

Milgram, S., Mann, L., & Harter, S. The lost-letter technique: A tool of social research. *Public Opinion Quarterly,* 1965, **29,** 437–438.

Miller, A. G. *The social psychology of psychological research.* New York: Free Press, 1972.

Millham, J. Two components of need for approval score and their relationship to cheating following success and failure. *Journal of Research in Personality,* 1974, **8,** 378–392.

Mills, J. Changes in moral attitudes following temptation. *Journal of Personality,* 1958, **26,** 517–531.

Moriarty, T. Crime, commitment, and the responsive bystander: Two field experiments. *Journal of Personality and Social Psychology,* 1975, **31,** 370–376.

Mudd, S. A. Group sanction severity as a function of degree of behavior deviation and relevance of norm. *Journal of Personality and Social Psychology,* 1968, **8,** 258–260.

Nash, M. M. "Nonreactive methods and the law." Additional comments on legal liability in behavior research. *American Psychologist,* 1975, **30,** 777–780.

Nelson, E. A., Grinder, R. E., & Biaggio, A. M. B. Relationships among behavioral, cognitive-developmental, and self report measures of morality and personality. *Multivariate Behavioral Research,* 1969, **4,** 483–500.

Nelsen, E. A., Grinder, R. E., & Mutterer, M. L. Sources of variance in behavioral measures of honesty in temptation situations: Methodological analyses. *Developmental Psychology,* 1969, **1,** 265–279.

Nisbett, R. E., & Wilson, T. D. Telling more than we can know: Verbal reports on mental processes. *Psychological Review,* 1977, **84,** 231–259.

O'Leary, K. D. The effects of self-instruction on immoral behavior. *Journal of Experimental Child Psychology,* 1968, **6,** 297–301.

O'Neal, E., & Kaufman, L. The influence of attack, arousal and information about one's arousal upon interpersonal aggression. *Psychonomic Science,* 1972, **26,** 211–214.

Palmer, J. W. Punishment—A field for experiment. *British Journal of Criminology,* 1967, **7,** 434–441.

Palmer, T. B. California's Community Treatment Program for delinquent adolescents. *Journal of Research in Crime and Delinquency,* 1971, **8,** 74–92.

Penner, L. A., Summers, L. S., Brookmire, D. A., & Dertke, M. C. The lost dollar: Situational and personality determinants of a pro- and anti-social behavior. *Journal of Personality*, 1976, **44**, 274-293.

Peterson, R. A., Pittman, D. J., & O'Neal, P. Stabilities of deviance: A study of assaultive and non-assaultive offenders. *Journal of Criminal Law, Criminology and Police Science*, 1962, **53**, 44-48.

Phillips, D. L. Rejection: A possible consequence of seeking help for mental disorders. *American Sociological Review*, 1963, **28**, 963-972.

Piliavin, I. M., Rodin, J., & Piliavin, J. A. Good samaritanism: An underground phenomenon? *Journal of Personality and Social Psychology*, 1969, **13**, 289-299.

Prentice, N. M. The influence of live and symbolic modeling on promoting moral judgment of adolescent delinquents. *Journal of Abnormal Psychology*, 1972, **80**, 157-161.

Quigley-Fernandez, B., & Tedeschi, J. T. The bogus pipeline as lie detector: Two validity studies. *Journal of Personality and Social Psychology*, 1978, **36**, 247-256.

Rapoport, A., & Wallsten, T. S. Individual decision behavior. *Annual Review of Psychology*, 1972, **23**, 131-176.

Raymond, B. J., & Unger, R. K. 'The apparel oft proclaims the man': Cooperation with deviant and conventional youths. *Journal of Social Psychology*, 1972, **87**, 75-82.

Reckless, W. C., & Dinitz, S. *The prevention of juvenile delinquency: An experiment*. Columbus: Ohio State University Press, 1972.

Reimer, E., & Warren, M. Special Intensive Parole Unit. *NPPA Journal*, 1957, **3**, 222-229.

Rettig, S. Ethical risk sensitivity in male prisoners. *British Journal of Criminology*, 1964, **4**, 582-590.

Rettig, S. Group discussion and predicted ethical risk-taking. *Journal of Personality and Social Psychology*, 1966, **3**, 629-633.

Rettig, S., & Pasamanick, B. Differential judgment of ethical risk by cheaters and noncheaters. *Journal of Abnormal and Social Psychology*, 1964, **69**, 109-113.

Rettig, S., & Rawson, H. E. The risk hypothesis in predictive judgments of unethical behavior. *Journal of Abnormal and Social Psychology*, 1963, **66**, 243-248.

Rettig, S., & Turoff, S. J. Exposure to group discussion and predicted ethical risk taking. *Journal of Personality and Social Psychology*, 1967, **7**, 177-180.

Rose, G., & Hamilton, R. A. Effects of a juvenile liaison scheme. *British Journal of Criminology*, 1970, **10**, 2-20.

Ross, H. L., Campbell, D. T., & Glass, G. V. Determining the social effects of a legal reform: The British 'Breathalyser' crackdown of 1967. *American Behavioral Scientist*, 1970, **13**, 493-509.

Santrock, J. W. Moral structure: The interrelations of moral behavior, moral judgment and moral affect. *Journal of Genetic Psychology*, 1975, **127**, 201-213.

Savitsky, J. C., & Babl, J. Cheating, intention, and punishment from an equity theory perspective. *Journal of Research in Personality*, 1976, **10**, 128-136.

Savitsky, J. C., Muskin, R., Czyzewski, D., & Eckert, J. The cheating and intention of a partner as determinants of evaluative decisions among juvenile offenders. *Journal of Abnormal Child Psychology*, 1976, **4**, 235-241.

Schachter, S. *Emotion, obesity and crime*. New York: Academic Press, 1971.

Schnelle, J. F., & Lee, J. F. A quasi-experimental retrospective evaluation of a prison policy change. *Journal of Applied Behavior Analysis*, 1974, **7**, 483-496.

Schroder, D., & Ehrlich, D. Rejection by mental health professionals: A possible consequence of not seeking appropriate help for emotional disorders. *Journal of Health and Social Behavior*, 1968, **9**, 222-232.

Schwartz, R. D., & Orleans, S. On legal sanctions. *University of Chicago Law Review*, 1967, **34**, 274-300.

Schwartz, R. D., & Skolnick, J. H. Two studies of legal stigma. *Social Problems,* 1962, **10,** 133-142.

Schwartz, S. H., & Gottlieb, A. Bystander reactions to a violent theft: Crime in Jerusalem. *Journal of Personality and Social Psychology,* 1976, **34,** 1188-1199.

Scroggs, J. R. Penalties for rape as a function of victim provocativeness, damage, and resistance. *Journal of Applied Social Psychology,* 1976, **6,** 360-368.

Sealy, A. P. What can be learned from the analysis of simulated juries? In N. Walker & A. Pearson (Eds.), *The British jury system.* Cambridge: Institute of Criminology, 1975.

Shaffer, D. R., Rogel, M., & Hendrick, C. Intervention in the library: The effect of increased responsibility on bystanders' willingness to prevent a theft. *Journal of Applied Social Psychology,* 1975, **5,** 303-319.

Shaw, M. *Social work in prison.* London: HMSO, 1974.

Shea, M. A. A study of the effect of the prosecutor's choice of charge on magistrates' sentencing behaviour. *British Journal of Criminology,* 1974, **14,** 269-272.

Shelton, J., & Hill, J. P. Effects on cheating of achievement anxiety and knowledge of peer performance. *Developmental Psychology,* 1969, **1,** 449-455.

Shotland, R. L., & Berger, W. G. Behavioral validation of several values from the Rokeach value scale as an index of honesty. *Journal of Applied Psychology,* 1970, **54,** 433-435.

Shotland, R. L., & Straw, M. K. Bystander response to an assault: When a man attacks a woman. *Journal of Personality and Social Psychology,* 1976, **34,** 990-999.

Sigelman, C. K., & Sigelman, L. Authority and conformity: Violation of a traffic regulation. *Journal of Social Psychology,* 1976, **100,** 35-43.

Silverman, I. Nonreactive methods and the law. *American Psychologist,* 1975, **30,** 764-769.

Silverman, I., Shulman, A. D., & Wiesenthal, D. L. Effects of deceiving and debriefing psychological subjects on performance in later experiments. *Journal of Personality and Social Psychology,* 1970, **14,** 203-212.

Simmons, J. L., & Chambers, H. Public stereotypes of deviants. *Social Problems,* 1965, **13,** 223-232.

Slovic, P., Fischhoff, B., & Lichtenstein, S. Behavioral decision theory. *Annual Review of Psychology,* 1977, **28,** 1-39.

Sole, K., Marton, J., & Hornstein, H. A. Opinion similarity and helping: Three field experiments investigating the bases of promotive tension. *Journal of Experimental Social Psychology,* 1975, **11,** 1-13.

Steffensmeier, D. J., & Terry, R. M. Deviance and respectability: an observational study of reactions to shoplifting. *Social Forces,* 1973, **51,** 417-426.

Steffensmeier, D. J., & Terry, R. M. (Eds.). *Examining deviance experimentally.* Chicago: Alfred, 1975.

Steinberg, J., McDonald, P., & O'Neal, E. Petty theft in a naturalistic setting: The effects of bystander presence. *Journal of Social Psychology,* 1977, **101,** 219-221.

Stephan, C. Sex prejudice in jury simulation. *Journal of Psychology,* 1974, **88,** 305-312.

Stephenson, G. M., & Barker, J. Personality and the pursuit of distributive justice: An experimental study of children's moral behaviour. *British Journal of Social and Clinical Psychology,* 1972, **11,** 207-219.

Stephenson, G. M., & White, J. H. An experimental study of some effects of injustice on children's moral behavior. *Journal of Experimental Social Psychology,* 1968, **4,** 460-469.

Stephenson, G. M., & White, J. H. Privilege, deprivation, and children's moral behavior: An experimental clarification of the role of investments. *Journal of Experimental Social Psychology,* 1970, **6,** 167-176.

Sternlieb, J. L., & Youniss, J. Moral judgments one year after intentional or consequence modeling. *Journal of Personality and Social Psychology,* 1975, **31,** 895-897.

Sullivan, D. S., & Deiker, T. E. Subject-experimenter perceptions of ethical issues in human research. *American Psychologist*, 1973, **28**, 587-591.

Switzer, E. B., Deal, T. E., & Bailey, J. S. The reduction of stealing in second graders using a group contingency. *Journal of Applied Behavior Analysis*, 1977, **10**, 267-272.

Sykes, G. M., & Matza, D. Techniques of neutralization: A theory of delinquency. *American Sociological Review*, 1957, **22**, 664-670.

Taylor, I., Walton, P., & Young, J. *The new criminology: For a social theory of deviance*. London: Routledge and Kegan Paul, 1973.

Taylor, S. P., & Lewit, D. W. Social comparison and deception regarding ability. *Journal of Personality*, 1966, **34**, 94-104.

Tickner, A. H., & Poulton, E. C. Watching for people and actions. *Ergonomics*, 1975, **18**, 35-51.

Tittle, C. R. Crime rates and legal sanctions. *Social Problems*, 1969, **16**, 409-423.

Tittle, C. R., & Rowe, A. R. Moral appeal, sanction threat, and deviance: An experimental test. *Social Problems*, 1973, **20**, 488-498.

Törnudd, P. The preventive effects of fines for drunkenness. In N. Christie (Ed.), *Scandinavian studies in criminology* (Vol 2). London: Tavistock, 1968.

Trasler, G. B. Criminal behaviour. In H. J. Eysenck (Ed.), *Handbook of abnormal psychology* (2nd ed.). London: Pitman, 1973.

Tucker, L., Hornstein, H. A., Holloway, S., & Sole, K. The effects of temptation and information about a stranger on helping. *Personality and Social Psychology Bulletin*, 1977, **3**, 416-420.

Valenti, A. C., & Downing, L. L. Differential effects of jury size on verdicts following deliberation as a function of the apparent guilt of a defendant. *Journal of Personality and Social Psychology*, 1975, **32**, 655-663.

Venezia, P. S. Unofficial probation: An evaluation of its effectiveness. *Journal of Research in Crime and Delinquency*, 1972, **9**, 149-170.

Vitro, F. T., & Schoer, L. A. The effects of probability of test success, test importance and risk of detection on the incidence of cheating. *Journal of School Psychology*, 1972, **10**, 86-93.

Walker, L. J., & Richards, B. S. The effects of a narrative model on children's moral judgments. *Canadian Journal of Behavioral Science*, 1976, **8**, 169-177.

Walker, N., & Argyle, M. Does the law affect moral judgments? *British Journal of Criminology*, 1964, **4**, 570-581.

Walker, N., Hammond, W., & Steer, D. Repeated violence. *Criminal Law Review*, 1967, 465-472.

Webb, E. J., Campbell, D. T., Schwartz, R. D., & Sechrest, L. *Unobtrusive measures: Nonreactive research in the social sciences*. Chicago: Rand-McNally, 1966.

Weissbach, T. A., & Zagon, G. The effect of deviant group membership upon impressions of personality. *Journal of Social Psychology*, 1975, **95**, 263-266.

West, D. J., & Farrington, D. P. *Who becomes delinquent?* London: Heinemann, 1973.

West, D. J., & Farrington, D. P. *The delinquent way of life*. London: Heinemann, 1977.

West, S. G., & Gunn, S. P. Some issues of ethics and social psychology. *American Psychologist*, 1978, **33**, 30-38.

West, S. G., Gunn, S. P., & Chernicky, P. Ubiquitous Watergate: An attributional analysis. *Journal of Personality and Social Psychology*, 1975, **32**, 55-65.

White, G. M. Immediate and deferred effects of model observation and guided and unguided rehearsal on donating and stealing. *Journal of Personality and Social Psychology*, 1972, **21**, 139-148.

Wicker, A. W. A failure to validate the lost-letter technique. *Public Opinion Quarterly*, 1969, **33**, 260-262.

Wilkins, L. *Social deviance*. London: Tavistock, 1964.

Williams, M. Aspects of the psychology of imprisonment. In S. McConville (Ed.), *The use of imprisonment*. London: Routledge and Kegan Paul, 1975.

Wilson, D. W., & Donnerstein, E. Legal and ethical aspects of nonreactive social psychological research. *American Psychologist*, 1976, **31**, 765-773.

Wolfgang, M. E., Figlio, R. M., & Selling, T. *Delinquency in a birth cohort*. Chicago: University of Chicago Press, 1972.

Wyer, R. S., Dion, K. L., & Ellsworth, P. C. An editorial. *Journal of Experimental Social Psychology*, 1978, **14**, 141-147.

Zelnio, R. N., & Gagnon, J. P. The viability of the lost letter technique. *Journal of Psychology*, 1977, **95**, 51-53.

Zillman, D. Excitation transfer in communication-mediated aggressive behavior. *Journal of Experimental Social Psychology*, 1971, **7**, 419-434.

Zillman, D., Katcher, A. H., & Milavsky, B. Excitation transfer from physical exercise to subsequent aggressive behavior. *Journal of Experimental Social Psychology*, 1972, **8**, 247-259.

Zimbardo, P. G. The human choice: Individuation, reason, and order versus deindividuation, impulse, and chaos. In W. J. Arnold, & D. Levine (Eds.), *Nebraska symposium on motivation, 1969*. Lincoln, Nebraska: University of Nebraska Press, 1970.

2

A BIOSOCIAL THEORY OF THE LEARNING OF LAW-ABIDING BEHAVIOR

SARNOFF A. MEDNICK

Students of civilization have attempted to understand the origins of antisocial behavior by study of those who defy or ignore society's sanctions. This chapter takes a slightly different tack; it attempts to examine the bases of obedience to society's sanctions. It assumes that law-abiding behavior must be learned and that this learning requires certain environmental conditions and individual abilities. Lack of any of these conditions or abilities would hinder socialization learning and might, conceivably, be partly responsible for some forms of antisocial activities.

How do people learn to be law-abiding? This chapter describes socialization learning in terms of the interaction of early family training and individual physiological characteristics. If there are lacks in either of these spheres the learning of law-abidance will be incomplete, retarded and/or unsuccessful.

Most offenders are convicted of having perpetrated only one, two or three relatively minor offenses. These offenders are doubtless instigated by socio-economic and situational forces. There is, however, a small group of offenders (perhaps only 1% of the male population) which may be characterized as extremely recidivistic. In a Copenhagen birth cohort of over 30,000 men described in Chapter 10 we found that this minute fraction of the male population accounts for *more than half of the offenses*

From S. A. Mednick, "A Biosocial Theory of the Learning of Law-Abiding Behavior," pp. 1-8 in S. A. Mednick and K. O. Christiansen (eds.), *Biosocial Bases of Criminal Behavior*. New York: Gardner Press, 1977. Reprinted with permission.

committed by the entire cohort. Similar results have been reported for the city of Philadelphia by Wolfgang, Figlio, and Sellin (1972). It is especially this small active group of recidivists that are hypothesized to have had their socialization learning influenced by deviant physiological characteristics. In emphasizing biosocial interactions the approach also seeks to help in the explanation of those cases of antisocial behavior which seem to have no apparent social cause as well as those cases in which an individual seems extraordinarily resistant or invulnerable to powerful criminogenic social forces (criminal family, extreme poverty, broken home background, etc. . . . See Chapter 2 for an example of this method of study).

Hidden crime.

Before going further with this exposition, perhaps I should make clear that I define a criminal as an individual who is registered as having been convicted of a violation of the penal code. In no case will this mean that our studies have utilized a prison population. All the individuals studied were functioning in society. We are concerned about the possibility that hidden crime may be governed by a different set of laws of nature from registered crime. We are, however, encouraged to continue working with registered crime by relatively strong evidence that the hidden criminal is the less serious, less recidivistic criminal (Christie, Andenaes and Skerbaekk, 1965).

LAW-ABIDANCE LEARNING IN CHILDREN

Children almost certainly do not come into the world with a set of inborn behaviors which unfold into civilized behavior. An objective consideration might in fact suggest that the behavior of young children is dominated by rather uncivilized immediate needs and passions. Becoming civilized consists in part of learning to inhibit or rechannel some of these passions.

Hare (1970b), Trasler (1972), and others have discussed the possibility that the psychopath and criminal have some defect in avoidance learning that interferes with their ability to learn to inhibit asocial responses. Much of this has been inspired by the 1957 study by Lykken indicating the difficulties psychopaths have in learning to avoid an electric shock. These results have found some empirical support. Hare has suggested that the empirically observed and reobserved autonomic hyporeactivity of the psychopath and criminal may be, partially, the basis of this poor avoidance learning. To better understand this, let us consider the avoidance learning situation. In particular, let us follow Trasler (1972), and consider how the law-abiding citizen might learn his admirable self-control. When one considers the modern urban center in terms of the temptations and, in fact, incitements it offers to a variety of forms of asocial behavior, one is impressed with the restraint and forebearance of the 80–90% of the population, who apparently manage to avoid committing repetitive or heinous crimes. Reading of books such as *The Lord of the Flies* and observation of intersibling familial warfare suggests that there actually *are* some strong instincts and passions that society must channel and inhibit to maintain even the poor semblance of civilization we see around us. The type of learning involved in this civilizing process has been termed passive avoidance; the individual avoids punishment or fear by *not* doing something for which he has been punished before.

Let us consider the way children learn to inhibit aggressive impulses. Frequently, when child A is aggressive to child B, child A is punished by his mother. After a sufficient quantity or quality of punishment, just the thought of the aggression should be enough to produce a bit of anticipatory fear in child A. If this fear response is large enough, the raised arm will drop, and the aggressive response will be successfully inhibited.

What happens in this child after he has successfully inhibited such an asocial response is critical for his learning of civilized behavior. Let us consider the situation again in detail.

1. Child A contemplates aggressive action.
2. Because of previous punishment he suffers fear.
3. He inhibits the aggressive response.
What happens to his fear?
4. It will begin to dissipate, to be reduced.

We know that fear reduction is the most powerful, naturally occurring reinforcement psychologists have discovered. Thus the reduction of fear (which immediately follows the inhibition of the aggression) can act as a reinforcement for this *inhibition* and will result in the learning of the inhibition of aggression. The fear-reduction-reinforcement pattern increases the probability that the inhibition of the aggression will occur in the future. After many such experiences, the normal child will learn to inhibit aggressive impulses. Each time such an impulse arises and is inhibited, the inhibition will be strengthened by reinforcement. What does a child need in order to learn effectively to be civilized (in the context of this approach)?

1. A censuring agent (typically the family) *AND*
2. An adequate fear response *AND*
3. The ability to learn the fear response in anticipation of an asocial act *AND*
4. Fast dissipation of fear to quickly reinforce the inhibitory response.

Now I wish to concentrate on point 4. The speed and size of reinforcement determines its effectiveness. An effective reinforcement is one that is delivered *immediately* after the relevant response. In terms of this discussion, the faster the reduction of fear, the faster the delivery of the reinforcement. The fear response is, to a large extent, controlled by the autonomic nervous system (ANS). We can estimate the activity of the ANS by means of peripheral indicants such as heart rate, blood pressure, and skin conductance. The measure of most relevance will peripherally reflect the rate or speed at which the ANS recovers from periods of imbalance.

If child *A* has an ANS that characteristically recovers very quickly from fear, then he will receive a quick and large reinforcement and learn inhibition quickly. If he has an ANS that recovers very slowly, he will receive a slow, small reinforcement and learn to inhibit the aggression very slowly, if at all. This orientation would predict that (holding constant critical extraindividual variables such as social status, crime training, and poverty level) those who commit asocial acts would be characterized by slow autonomic recovery. The slower the recovery, the more serious and repetitive the asocial behavior predicted. Note that although we have concentrated on electrodermal recovery (EDRec), the theory also requires another ANS characteristic, hyporeactiveness, as a predisposition for delinquency. The combination of hyporesponsiveness and slow EDRec should give the maximum ANS predisposition to delinquency.

TESTS OF THE THEORY

To test this notion we first turned to a longitudinal study of some 13 years duration (Mednick and Schulsinger, 1968). We have been following 311 individuals whom we intensively examined in 1962. This examination included psychophysiology. Since 1962, 36 have had serious disagreements with the law (convictions for violation of the penal code). We checked and noted that, indeed, their EDRec was considerably slower than that of controls. Those nine who have been clinically diagnosed psychopathic have even slower recovery.

Siddle et al. (1973) examined the electrodermal responsiveness of 67 inmates of an English borstal. On the basis of 10 criteria, these inmates were divided into high, medium, and low asociality. Venables suggested to Siddle et al. that they also measure EDRec in their sample. Speed and rate of EDRec varied inversely as a function of asociality. EDRec on a single trial was surprisingly effective in differentiating the three groups. (See Chapter 13.)

Bader-Bartfai and Schalling (1974) reanalysed skin conductance data from a previous investigation of criminals, finding that criminals who tended to be more "delinquent" on a personality measure tended to have slower EDRec.

In view of the relationships that have been reported between psychophysiological variables and asocial behavior, and in view of our interest in better understanding the apparent genetic predisposition to asocial behavior, we next turned to a study of the heritability of psychophysiological behavior. We (Bell, Mednick, Gottesman, and Sergeant) invited pairs of male 12-year-old twins into our laboratory. Interestingly enough, EDRec to orienting stimuli proved to have significant heritability (consistently higher for left hand than for right; see Chapter 14). This finding would suggest that part of the heritability of asocial behavior might be attributed to the heritability of EDRec. Thus a slow EDRec might be a characteristic a criminal father could pass to a biological son, which (given the proper environmental circumstances) could increase the probability of the child failing to learn adequately to inhibit asocial responses. Thus we would predict that criminal fathers would have children with slow EDRec. In Table 1 we present data on the electrodermal behavior of children with criminal and noncriminal fathers. As can be seen, the prediction regarding EDRec is not disconfirmed. It is interesting that the pattern of responsiveness of these children closely resembles that which we might anticipate seeing in their criminal fathers (Hare, 1970b). Results of other studies in our laboratory have replicated these findings.

Hare (1975b) has recently tested this ANS-recovery theory on a sample of maximum-security prisoners. More-psychopathic prisoners show significantly slower EDRec than serious, but less psychopathic, maximum-security prisoners. In one figure Hare plots the EDRec of the prisoners along with that of male college students. The prisoner and student curves are worlds apart! Hinton (personal communication, 1975) also finds the EDRec of more asocial prisoners (in an English maximum-security prison) to be slower. In an ongoing study we are finding that criminals reared in a noncriminal milieu have slow EDRec. Children reared in a criminogenic milieu who resist criminality evidence fast EDRec (see Chapter 2).

Table 1

Skin Conductance Behavior During Orienting Response Testing in Children with Criminal and Noncriminal Fathers

Skin Conductance Function (Right hand)	MEAN SCORE		F	df	p
	Noncriminal Father	Criminal Father			
Basal level skin conductance	2.51	2.33	.09	1,193	n.s.
Amplitude (in micromhos)	.031	.016	.03	1,193	n.s.
Number of responses	2.79	1.55	8.51	1,187	.01
Response onset latency (in seconds)	2.11	2.18	.07	1,97	n.s.
Latency to response peak (in seconds)	2.05	2.38	5.32	1,95	.05
Average half recovery time (in seconds)	3.75	5.43	4.26	1,90	.05
Minimum half recovery time	2.26	4.33	8.80	1,90	.01

Note: During Orienting Response testing, the child was presented 14 times with a tone of 1000 cps.

In a rather compelling study, Wadsworth (1976) traced all the males registered for delinquency from a sample of the 13,687 births which occurred in England, Wales and Scotland between March 3 and 9 in 1946 (Douglas et al., 1958). They had had their pulse taken in 1957 just before a school medical examination (deemed to be a mildly threatening event). This pre-examination pulse rate predicted whether or not a boy would achieve a record of serious delinquency by the age of 21 years. These results must be given special consideration in view of the representativeness of the population.

Here is what we have said so far:

1. There is a theory of social learning of law-abiding behavior that has as a unique and key element, the specification of specific autonomic nervous system factors as useful aptitudes for effectively learning to inhibit asocial behavior.

2. Some empirical tests were described that could have disconfirmed this hypothesis. No grounds were found for rejection of the hypothesis in experiments conducted in Denmark, Sweden, England and Canada under a rather large variety of situational conditions and criterion group definitions.

Please note that my emphasis of these physiological factors in this chapter should only be understood as an attempt to call attention to this type of approach. The percent of text devoted to the physiological variables does not relate to their perceived importance in the total field of criminology.

MAURITIUS PROJECT

To obtain a meaningful answer to the question of the relevance of these ANS variables for the etiology of asocial behavior, one useful research design would involve testing 100% of a reasonably large population of children, following them, and determining the relative probability of antisocial behavior among those who are physiologically predisposed. In terms of our theoretical orientation, such predisposed children would be those who are among the slowest in autonomic recovery and the weakest in autonomic response. In Mauritius, a group of investigators (Schulsinger, Mednick, Venables, Raman, Sutton-Smith, and Bell, 1975) have tested the entire population of 3 year olds in two well-defined areas (Vacoas and Quatre Bornes). From smallpox vaccination records, all the 1800 three year olds in the two areas were located and invited in for testing. The tests included:

1. Psychophysiology (heart rate, bilateral skin conductance, and skin potential).
2. EEG—(not the entire population).
3. Birth data (not the entire population).
4. Cognitive development.
5. Medical examination.
6. Laboratory observation ratings.

These children are now in school, and we are developing a system for the collection of behavior ratings. This work is being organized by Cyril Dalais. At this point we know that the children with slow EDRec are those who did not cry in the laboratory, were less concerned and frightened about the testing, and were less anxious.

With respect to the understanding of the etiology of antisocial behavior, the critical question is whether (as in the 1976 Wadsworth study) the autonomic variables will predict which of the 1800 children in this cohort will evidence serious antisocial behavior. We are planning to follow these children to attempt to answer this question. The answer will have some importance in planning of prevention of delinquency (see Mednick and Lanoil, 1977). Also of importance to such attempts at prevention is the determination of what other outcomes are observed from the children with autonomic deviance. Perhaps weakness in learning socially conforming modes of living is accompanied by some increase in potential for creativity or originality. We must ascertain all possible outcomes before we take any action in this sensitive area. Clearly it is a desirable goal to reduce the frequency of delinquency. Before doing this, however, we must be clear, via longitudinal study, about any additional unwanted effects intervention may have. (See Chapter 3 for further discussion of problems in primary prevention of delinquency.)

Sarnoff A. Mednick is Professor of Psychology and Research Associate in the Social Science Research Institute of the University of Southern California. He is the coeditor of An Empirical Basis for Primary Prevention: Prospective Longitudinal Research in Europe *and also of* Longitudinal Research: Methods and Uses *(both in press from Oxford University Press).*

3

LIFE EVENTS AND PRISONERS

MINORU MASUDA
DAVID L. CUTLER
LEE HEIN
THOMAS H. HOLMES

● This study explores retrospectively the relationship of the accumulation of life events as it relates to prison incarceration and extends further the concept that coping with increasing environmental changes results in a variety of overt behaviors. The prison sample comprised 176 male inmates of a federal prison (McNeil Island, Washington) and a state penitentiary (Walla Walla, Washington). Life change scores were derived from the Schedule of Recent Experience (SRE). There was an escalation of annual life change scores of prisoners, indicating the mounting frequency of occurrence of life events prior to incarceration. The SRE may have value in the prediction of socially deviant behavior as with health changes. Variables seen as influencing life change scores were race, age, and education.

Analyses of life event frequencies as compared to a normative group indicated that prisoners have evolved a coping life-style that reflects antisocial and criminal behavior.

(Arch Gen Psychiatry 35:197-203, 1978)

O ver the past several years an increasing amount of information has been generated that indicates that the accumulation of life events is associated with the onset of illness.[1] The data indicate that the magnitude of accumulated life change is significantly related to the time of disease onset. In addition, when illness is experienced, the greater the magnitude of life change present at time of onset, the more serious is the chronic illness experienced.[2] The illness experience covered a wide spectrum of disease states.[1]

The ability to make a magnitude estimation of psychosocial readjustments to various life events led to the development of the Social Readjustment Rating Scale (SRRS).[3] The incorporation of the SRRS items into the Schedule of Recent Experience (SRE) allowed for the periodic quantification of accumulated life changes as they might relate to illnesses.[4,5]

The concept of the psychosocial readjustment required in the responses to life events has expanded into that area of conventional illness onset into other behavioral areas, including the academic performance of both teacher[6] and

student,[7] and job performance.[8] In addition, studies have shown a positive relationship between the magnitude of life change and injuries in collegiate football players[9] and traffic accidents.[10] Recent studies have also shown that suicide attempters accumulate significantly greater numbers of life events in the year prior to the attempt than do controls.[11,12]

To our knowledge, there are no published reports of the relationship of life events and onset of incarceration in prison. The maladaptive responses to environmental challenges that lead to greater disease risks may also manifest themselves in those susceptible to deviant social behavior. This study explores retrospectively the relationship of the accumulation of life events as it relates to prison incarceration and extends further the concept that coping with increasing environmental change results in a variety of overt behaviors. The evolving behavior, whether illness, incarceration in prison, job performance, etc, appears to be an epiphenomenon of the individual's psychobiological adaptive or coping style.

SUBJECTS AND METHODS
Sample Populations

McNeil Island Inmates.—McNeil Island is a federal penitentiary located in the southern portion of Puget Sound in the state of Washington. At the time of the study (summer 1971), the prison population was 1,027, all men. The volunteer subjects were randomly selected from inmates who had been in prison five years or less. Of a group of 120, the responses of 98 subjects were satisfactory. The men were informed of the voluntary nature of the exercise and filled out the forms in groups of one to ten. One of the investigators was present at all times to read the directions and answer questions.

Walla Walla Inmates.—Walla Walla prison is a state corrections institution in the southeastern rural part of the state. It is the oldest of the state institutions and receives the most serious offenders. At the time of this study (summer 1973) there were 1,300 inmates, all men. The sample was selected from inmate volunteers with initial solicitation from organizations such as black, Indian, lifer, and white inmate clubs. This produced insufficient numbers and, with prison approval, eight inmate volunteers canvassed the entire population one evening. Two hundred names were selected from a total of 350 volunteers. Of these, 121 men filled out questionnaires of which 78 were usable.

Significant numbers of questionnaires were discarded, in spite of the fact that experimenters were present to administer the questionnaires to small groups of up to 20 in order to explain and answer questions. Many forms were incomplete and many contained gross responses that indicated confusion as to directions or to event chronology, as well as possibly deliberate distortions.

Accepted for publication June 20, 1977.

From the Department of Psychiatry and Behavioral Sciences, University of Washington, Seattle. Dr Cutler is now with the Southern Arizona Mental Health Center, Tucson. Dr Hein is currently in private practice in Highland, Calif.

Reprint requests to Department of Psychiatry and Behavioral Sciences RP-10, University of Washington, Seattle, WA 98195 (Dr Masuda).

Schedule of Recent Experience

This is a self-reporting questionnaire[3] that asks subjects to indicate the yearly occurrence and frequency of 40 life events over a period of ten years. This yielded life change data for five years (−1 to −5) prior to imprisonment and up to five years after imprisonment (+1 to +5). Each life event has a numerical score, derived from the SRRS. For example, marriage has a score of 50, while death of a spouse is 100; divorce, 73; business readjustment, 39; change in living conditions, 25; vacation, 13, etc. The number of yearly occurrences of an item is multiplied by its score, and the sum of products of all items yields the annual Life Change Units (LCU).

RESULTS
Comparison of Groups

McNeil Island Total Population vs Study Sample.—A comparison of the total population of the McNeil Island prisoners and the study sample of 98 showed that the two groups were similar except that the study sample had a greater representation of ages 21 to 30 than the prison population (45% vs 34%) and a lesser representation of those over 31 years of age. Data for a similar comparison of the Walla Walla inmates with the study sample were not available.

Characteristics of McNeil Island and Walla Walla Samples.—A comparison of the demographic characteristics of McNeil Island and Walla Walla samples indicated relative homogeneity in the two study populations. The only significant differences in distribution between the two samples were the following:

1. Race. There were more blacks at McNeil Island (26% vs 11%).

2. Occupation. At McNeil Island there were more people in skilled, clerical, and managerial positions, while at Walla Walla there were more students and salespeople.

3. Criminal offenses. In the McNeil Island sample, there were no murders and more armed robbery, grand larceny, forgery, and drug violations; in the Walla Walla sample, there were murders, more burglaries, assaults, and sexual offenses.

4. Number of siblings. The McNeil Island sample had a larger percentage of prisoners with three or more brothers.

Since 18 of 22 demographic variables investigated showed no significant differences in distribution, the data of the two prison surveys were combined. This homogeneous population (Table 1) exhibited the following characteristics: 73% were white and 19% were black; 90% between the ages of 21 and 45. Only 25% were married, the rest were divorced, separated, widowed, or never married. Fifteen percent had only an elementary school education, 50% had attended high school, and 23% had a college education. More than half had been born and spent most of their lives in larger cities. About 97% were at least second-generation Americans. Although many of the prisoners' parents were still living (78% of the mothers and 56% of the fathers), the data indicate that during the formative years (age 0 to 20) 11% of the mothers and 20% of the fathers had died. Of the crimes, 70% were against property and 17% were against persons.

Black and White Prisoners.—The racial distribution according to age, educational levels, and criminal offense is

Table 1.—Characteristics of Combined Sample	
	% of Prisoners (N = 176)
Race	
White	73
Black	19
American Indian	3
Other	5
Age, yr	
< 21	1
21-30	43
31-45	47
46-65	9
Religion	
Protestant	40
Catholic	18
Jewish	3
Other	12
None	27
Marital status	
Married	25
Divorced	33
Separated	12
Widowed	2
Never married	28
No. of marriages	
None	29
1	40
2	17
3	10
4	4
No. of divorces	
None	49
1	34
2	11
3	5
4	2
No. of spouses who died	
None	95
1	4
≥ 4	1
Education	
Elementary	15
High school	50
Technical	12
College	22
Graduate	1
Time at present residence, yr	
1	34
2	41
5	15
10	2
> 10	8
No. of moves in last 5 yr	
1	18
2	25
3	22
4	9
5	8
6	3
7	1
9	15
Place of birth	
Canada	2
Central America	1
Don't know	1
United States	97
Europe	1
Where most of life spent	
Pacific Coast	50
Other	4
East	9
South	8
Southwest	9
Midwest	12
Rocky Mountains	6
Alaska	2
Population of birthplace	
Rural	20
< 5,000	8
5,000-50,000	17
50,000-500,000	22
> 500,000	32

Table 1.—Characteristics of Combined Sample—
continued

	% of Prisoners (N = 176)
Population where spent most of life	
Rural	18
< 5,000	5
5,000-50,000	15
50,000-500,000	24
> 500,000	38
Place of father's birth	
Canada	2
South America	1
Central America	1
Don't know	3
United States	86
Western Europe	4
Eastern Europe	2
Place of mother's birth	
Canada	5
South America	1
Central America	2
Don't know	3
United States	84
Western Europe	3
Eastern Europe	1
No. of brothers	
None	28
1	26
2	22
3	12
≥4	13
No. of sisters	
None	27
1	33
2	17
3	12
≥4	12
Birth order	
Only	12
Oldest	33
Youngest	26
Middle	30
Age at mother's death, yr	
Mother alive	78
0-5	6
6-10	3
10-15	1
15-20	1
> 20	10
Age at father's death, yr	
Father alive	56
0-5	6
6-10	4
10-15	3
15-20	7
> 20	25
Occupation	
Service	2.9
Skilled	42.1
Student	4.7
Unskilled	8.8
Armed Forces	2.9
Clerical	4.1
Managerial	5.3
None	10.5
Professional	6.4
Sales	6.4
Other	5.8
Crime	
Murder (first degree)	2.4
Murder (second degree)	1.8
Armed robbery	28.7
Grand larceny	13.4
Robbery	16.5
Assault	6.1
Fraud	0.6
Forgery	10.4
Escape	0.6
Sexual	6.7
Drugs	12.2
Probation violation	0.6

not significantly different although there was a trend ($P < .10$) for blacks to be involved in more armed robberies and drug offenses.

Significant differences were seen in marital status. A greater percentage of blacks than whites were married and separated from their wives, but fewer were divorced or never married. More blacks had spent most of their lives on the Pacific Coast, the East Coast, in the Rocky Mountains, and in Alaska. The most striking difference was that 70% of the blacks came from cities of greater than 500,000 as compared to 30% of the whites.

The blacks had higher percentages of students and unskilled workers while the whites had higher percentages of all the other categories, except in the skilled category where percentages were similar.

Life Change Magnitude

The mean annual life change scores for the combined prison samples for years prior to and years after imprisonment are shown in Fig 1. The life change magnitude escalates from a mean of 170 (year -5 and year -4) to a peak at year -1 of 361 LCU and then decreases in prison to 156 LCU in years $+4$ and $+5$. The life change score for year -1, the year prior to incarceration, is significantly higher ($P < .0005$) than the scores of the other years. In addition, the scores for years -4 and -5 were significantly lower than years -3, -2, -1, $+1$, and $+2$. No significant differences were seen in the annual life change scores while in prison. The McNeil Island and Walla Walla samples showed similar annual life change patterns.

Analysis of the pattern of mean annual life change scores is not significantly influenced by religion, marital status, where most of life was spent, birth order, occupation, or type of offense. However, race, age, and level of education are associated with different life change profiles (Fig 2).

Black prisoners (N = 33) experienced lower LCUs in all years compared to white prisoners (N = 126), and a muted peak is seen in the pattern. The life change scores of the blacks are significantly ($P < .002$) lower than those of the white prisoners for the year prior to incarceration (-1) and the first year of incarceration ($+1$) (Fig 2, top).

In the years prior to incarceration, the younger prisoners accumulate the most LCUs, then the middle-aged, and finally the older age group (Fig 2, center). The mean scores of the young group are significantly higher than those of the other two age groups in years -4, -3, and -2. They are also higher than those of the middle age group in years $+1$, $+2$, and $+3$. There were no differences in any of the annual life change scores between the 31- to 45-year group and the 46- to 65-year group. While the LCUs of the first two age groups decrease with incarceration time, the LCUs of the older age group peak at years $+1$ and $+2$ and remain high.

The life change scores of the grade school group are significantly different from those of the other educational groups (Fig 2, bottom). These scores are significantly lower than those of the high school group in years -5, -4, and -1, and lower than those of the college group in years -4, -3, -2. There was no statistical difference between the other two educational groups. Neither was there any

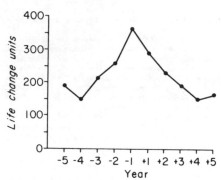

Fig 1.—Annual life change units before and during imprisonment for combined sample.

Fig 2.—Annual life change units according race (top), age (center), and education (bottom) for combined sample.

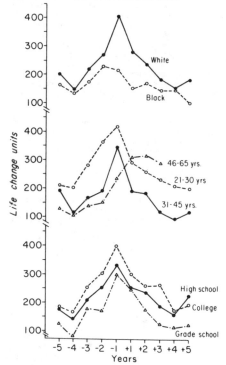

Table 2.—Annual Frequency of Occurrence* of Life Events

Life Event	White Middle-Class Group (N = 969)		Prisoners (N = 176)	
	Frequency	Rank†	Frequency	Rank†
Vacation	1.06	1	.35	5.5
Mortgage or loan less than $10,000	.53	2	.34	7
Change in health of family member	.51	3	.15	18.5
Change in work hours or conditions	.40	4	.37	4
Change in financial state	.36	5	.21	11
Outstanding personal achievement	.35	6	.25	10
Personal injury or illness	.34	8	.15	18.5
Death of spouse	.34	8	.01	40
Change in living conditions	.34	8	.27	9
Sex difficulties	.32	10	.13	24.5
Change in sleeping habits	.30	11	.13	24.5
Change in social activities	.29	12.5	.18	13
Change in responsibilities at work	.29	12.5	.30	8
Change in recreation	.28	14.5	.16	15.5
Change in number of arguments with spouse	.28	14.5	.12	27.5
Change in eating habits	.27	16.5	.13	24.5
Death of close family member	.27	16.5	.10	32
Change in number of family get-togethers	.26	18.5	.14	21.5
Son or daughter leaving home	.26	18.5	.02	39
Change in church activities	.23	21	.09	34
Death of close friend	.23	21	.14	21.5
Gain of new family member	.23	21	.18	13
Revision of personal habits	.22	23	.18	13
Change in residence	.21	24	.79	1
Wife beginning or stopping work	.18	25	.15	18.5
Trouble with in-laws	.15	26.5	.11	29.5
Minor violations of the law	.15	26.5	.57	3
Change to different line of work	.14	28	.35	5.5
Trouble with boss	.13	29	.11	29.5
Business readjustment	.11	30.5	.13	24.5
Mortgage over $10,000	.11	30.5	.05	36.5
Beginning or ending school	.10	32	.10	32
Marital separation	.06	33.5	.16	15.5
Change in schools	.06	33.5	.12	27.5
Marriage	.05	35.5	.10	32
Retirement	.05	35.5	.03	38
Foreclosure of mortgage or loan	.04	37	.05	36.5
Divorce	.02	38.5	.06	35
Fired at work	.02	38.5	.15	18.5
Jail term	.01	40	.62	2
Total	9.55		7.75	

*Frequency of occurrence is item incidence/individual/year.
†Frequency rank order correlation; $r_s = .336$ $(P < .02)$.

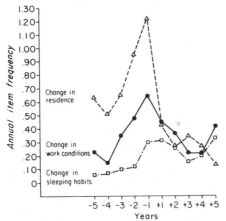

Fig 3.—Selected Schedule of Recent Experience item frequencies for combined sample.

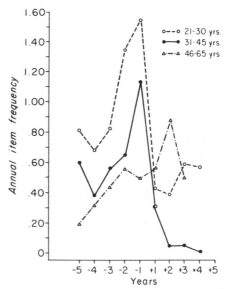

Fig 4.—Item frequency (change in residence) for age groups of combined sample.

significant difference between pairs of groups in any of the years while in prison. However, there was an interesting trend. In all years there is a gradation of LCUs–the college-educated with the highest scores; the high school-educated, the middle; and the elementary school-educated, the lowest scores.

Frequency of Occurrence of Life Events

The frequency of occurrence of the life change events in prisoners provides a qualitative and quantitative description of the life-style of the prisoners. Table 2 compares the annual frequency of occurrence of life event items in the five preprison years as recorded by prisoners with the occurrence of life events in a white, middle-class group. This is unpublished data from a combined group of television program responders (N = 364) and health cooperative members (N = 605). The frequency of events is not similar in these socially disparate groups, and the rank order correlation coefficient (r_s) of the item frequencies is a relatively low 0.336 ($P < .02$). In addition, the total annual frequency is lower for the prisoners. However, the frequencies of jail term and minor violations of the law are 0.63 and 0.57, respectively, ranking second and third. For the normative group the frequencies are .01 and .15, respectively, ranking 40 and 26.5. Change in residence ranks first in the prisoners, but is 21 for the normatives; the prisoners move about four times more frequently. In work-related items, prisoners change more often to a different line of work and have a much greater propensity for being fired at work. In spouse-related categories, the prisoners experience more marriages, divorces, and marital separations.

The frequency of occurrence of individual life events in general parallels the magnitude of total life change and peaks in the year prior to imprisonment. The data on white and black prisoners also show the same phenomena, as did the data separated according to levels of education.

In Fig 3, examples of life events of graded frequency magnitude are compared. The clear separation of item occurrences prior to imprisonment disappears in prison, as prison life forces a stabilization. However, life in prison does not always mean stabilization for all. Figure 4 illustrates the influence of age on a single item, frequency of change in residence. Preincarceration, the young moved most often, then the middle-aged, and the elderly moved the least. But in prison, the elderly prisoner reported more moves in the first two years of prison than did the other two age groups. Even in prison, residence changes for the young and the older are considerable.

COMMENT

The following profile of persons incarcerated in the state and federal prisons under study can be deduced from the data. The prisoner is a white, Protestant man between the ages of 21 and 45, who has been incarcerated for a crime involving property or money. He is the eldest or only son of native-born American parents and had as equal a probability of being born in a rural area as in a city. His early life was seriously disrupted by the death of a parent. After achieving a high school education, he spent most of his life in an urban area occupied as a skilled worker. He has had at least three residential moves and frequent job changes in the last five years. He is currently unmarried. He has had a recent previous prison record and at least one citation for a minor violation of the law.

More life events have been experienced by the young than the old prisoners: they are more mobile, have more problems at work, and more financial difficulties. This finding is similar to that of Holmes,[1] who used the SRE to construct a ten-year profile of events for general hospital patients.

The life-style of prisoners with a college education is characterized by the occurrence of more life events than that of prisoners with other educational experience. Half of the items occur more frequently in those subjects with a college education, while only two occur less frequently. The increase occurs in (1) social items, such as change in recreation and residence; (2) occupation and finance, such as change in working conditions and responsibilities, financial state, and securing loans of less than $10,000; (3) family relationships, such as separation or change in health of family member; (4) personal items, such as sex difficulties, personal injury, or illness; and (5) education, such as change in schools and beginning or ending school. These data suggest the drive to attend college also impels these people to seek new experiences and a wider horizon. College graduates who are criminals are at a greater risk for larger amounts of life change.

The life change magnitude for the elderly incarcerated while in prison is significantly higher than for the young. This is despite the fact that 32 of the 40 items occur equally or less frequently in the old than in the young age groups. Among the items that occur more frequently for the old are death of a close family member, death of a close friend, change in health of a family member, mortgage or loan less than $10,000, and foreclosure of a mortgage or loan. These events are of higher magnitudes, clearly occur outside the prison, and are congruent with the age of the subjects. Although the fact of incarceration may have, in part, evoked these events, these are not occurrences associated with the life style in prison.

The older prisoners moved more often within the prison confines. Movement within prison indicates placements into greater or lesser security, usually dictated by prisoner behavior and status, subject to prison authorities. Inasmuch as the great majority of within-prison life events occurred less frequently in prison amongst the elderly, it would lead to the speculation that their behavior was more stable and exemplary. This might lead to changes in prison residence toward lesser security and greater trust.

Both black and white prisoners showed a rising accumulation of life change units prior to incarceration in prison, but with the blacks showing lower magnitudes. This was a reflection of the fact that blacks had experienced consistently lower numbers of life events. There may be two alternative explanations for this. One might be a speculated difference in "psychological threshold" between blacks and whites that triggers behavior leading to imprisonment. The second alternative is that the low LCUs of the blacks are an artifact deriving from the use of SRRS scores obtained from a sample of white, middle-class subjects that was assumed to reflect the American average. However, the study by Komaroff and colleagues[1] on black ghetto residents showed that for them, life events required significantly greater psychosocial readjustments, ie, their SRRS scores were decidedly higher. These higher scores encompassed the range of life events related to work, finances, housing, and life-style. If the black SRRS

scores obtained by Komaroff et al had been used, the LCUs for blacks would have been similar to those for white prisoners. The SRRS scores obtained from many different subcultural and cross-cultural studies[1] show significant differences from the original SRRS. This places a caveat on using inappropriate life event magnitude estimations to estimate life change scores.

Although there are many similarities between the prisoners and the normative group, there are distinct qualitative and quantitative differences in life event occurrences. Prisoners are less stable, more mobile, and at times even transient. They have greater frequencies of change in residence, change to a different line of work, being fired, and more financial problems. Instability is also indicated by more divorces and separations, more marriages, and more trouble with in-laws. Prior jail terms and minor violations of the law are clearly the province of the prisoner's life style. The prisoners experienced one of these two events at least once every two years.

The life history of convicted felons reveals that social and economic forces have played an important part in influencing their careers.[1] There is a common history of severely disordered family and social backgrounds—there is poverty, broken homes, and there may be parental criminality and alcoholism. Poor social and familial backgrounds leading to restricted opportunities and unhappy internal adjustments provide fertile ground for criminal activities.

But it is also clear that social, economic, and racial forces are not the only answer, for only a small fraction of those so exposed become criminals, and there are criminals who have not known poverty, racism, and social limitations. Other factors must enter into the equation and, of these, a salient factor must be the individual—his development and personal characteristics.

The criminal and his peers live in an American subculture with value orientations at variance with the majority society. Peer group values, loyalty demands, codes of conduct, and denials of society's values are a differentiating part of the criminal subculture. Thus, the criminal's life-style reflects antisocial behavior (as society perceives it) that is a part of his subcultural norm.

This life-style is reflected in the quantitative differences in life event frequencies, displaying a profile of life events that is almost identical to problem areas in the life histories of convicted felons as delineated by Guze.[1] This is further indication of cultural transmission of values from earlier into adult years.

The criminal's world and the life-style he embraces are represented by the total of his life event behaviors of which criminal activity is but one and inseparable part. The same values and orientations by which the criminal lives are reflected in the total spectrum of living activities whether relating to marital, work, financial, or living concerns. Separation into criminal behavior and other behaviors, as to primary causation, is seen as inappropriate in viewing the escalation of life events associated with prison incarceration.

This study has shown a mounting accumulation of life change events and an increase in life change magnitude that achieves crisis proportions in the year prior to incarceration in prison. This pattern of life change frequency and magnitude is similar to that observed at the time of onset of a wide variety of health changes.[1,17] It has been suggested elsewhere[18] that these events, by evoking maladaptive behavior, increase susceptibility to biological and psychological disease. These life change data suggest that the commission of, apprehension, and incarceration for crime parallel the signs and symptoms of an illness. Marital problems or being fired from work may well trigger or accompany a series of events that could lead to illness and hospitalization or to criminal activity and imprisonment.

The data cannot address the issue of criminal behavior that goes unchecked. It addresses itself only to unsuccessful criminal behavior that leads to incarceration. It may be that escalating life changes lead to a "malfunctioning" of previously successful criminal activities such as to bring about apprehension and imprisonment.

A time gap may occur between the time of the criminal act and apprehension and between apprehension and incarceration in prison. If such time gaps of at least a year do occur in sufficient numbers of cases, then year −2 should also show some elevation of life change. There is such a tendency as exemplified for black and younger prisoners in Fig 2, top and center, for change in residence and change in work conditions items in Fig 3, and for change in residence item in Fig 4.

Prison life obviously changes the lives of prisoners; this is reflected in the gradual reduction of life changes experienced. This reduction to preprison levels, however, is not abrupt, indicating that prison imposes a set of new living conditions to which adjustment must be made. Stabilization occurs with time as adaptation follows the restrained and regimented life that is led within prison walls, away from spouse, family, work, etc.

In all retrospective studies there is the issue of accuracy in the recall of life events. Studies[19,20] have shown that there is a decrement in the reporting of life events, ie, events of lesser saliency tend to be lost to recollection with time. But Casey et al[19] have shown that there is a significant correlation between events remembered one year later (0.74), three years later (0.67), and six years later (0.67). Therefore, there is a considerable degree of reliability in recalling of life events.

In the case of this study's prisoner sample, 100% were in the second year of prison and 52% were in the third year, tapering off to 28%, 19%, and 14% in their fourth, fifth, and sixth years, respectively. All subjects gave SRE responses to years −5 through year +1, but there were reduced numbers of responses in years +2 through +5. Thus, the most immediate years of recollection (and ostensibly the most accurate) varied from years +1 to year +5. This spread would tend to negate the possibility that the most recent year of recollection was an important factor in the shape of the escalating curve of life events prior to imprisonment. The possibility that the year of incarceration was the most vividly remembered is also negated by the above consideration and the fact that the average prisoner experiences 0.62 jail terms a year. It seems unlikely, in view of this history, that imprisonment is that vivid a psychological landmark of reference.

A recent study by Guze[16] of male felons in Missouri correction centers indicated that 78% were classified as antisocial personalities, with added percentages due to alcoholism, drug dependence, and frank psychotic illnesses. Guze's demographic data are congruent with the felons' data in this study. This suggests that a similar distribution of disorders also prevails in the prisoners in the present report.

Dudley et al[21] used the SRE to study populations of alcoholics and heroin addicts. Alcoholism and addiction were common in the felons studied by Guze; recent jail term was also a common life event in the two groups of addicts. It appears that crime and alcohol and heroin addiction commonly coexist in the same populations and have similar natural histories.

This research was supported in part by Psychiatry Basic Residency grant 5-TO1-MHO5557-20 and Undergraduate Training in Human Behavior grant 5-TO2-MHO7871-10 from the Public Health Service; Undergraduate Training in Psychiatry grant 5-TO2-MHO5939-22 from the Institute of Mental Health; the O'Donnell Psychiatric Research Fund; and the Stuht Psychiatric Research Fund.

References

1. Holmes TH, Masuda M: Life change and illness susceptibility, in Scott JP, Senay EC (eds): *Separation and Depression: Clinical and Research Aspects*, publication 94. Washington, DC, American Association for Advancement of Science, 1973, pp 161-186.
2. Wyler AR, Masuda M, Holmes TH: Magnitude of life events and seriousness of illness. *Psychosom Med* 33:115-122, 1971.
3. Holmes TH, Rahe RH: The Social Readjustment Rating Scale. *J Psychosom Res* 11:213-218, 1967.
4. Rahe RH, Meyer M, Smith M, et al: Social stress and illness onset. *J Psychosom Res* 8:35-44, 1964.
5. Holmes TH, Rahe RH: *Booklet for Schedule of Recent Experience (SRE)*. Seattle, University of Washington, 1967.
6. Carranza E: *A Study of the Impact of Life Changes on High-School Teacher Performance in the Lansing School District as Measured by the Holmes and Rahe Schedule of Recent Experience*, thesis. Michigan State University, College of Education, East Lansing, 1972.
7. Harris PW: *The Relationship of Life Change to Academic Performance Among Selected College Freshmen at Varying Levels of College Readiness*, thesis. East Texas State University, Commerce, 1972.
8. Clinard JW: Life change events as related to self-reported academic and job performance. *Psychol Rep* 33:391-394, 1973.
9. Bramwell ST, Masuda M, Wagner ND, et al: Psychosocial factors in athletic injuries: Development and application of the Social and Athletic Readjustment Rating Scale (SARRS). *J Human Stress* 1(2):6-20, 1975.
10. Selzer ML, Vinokur A: Life events, subjective stress, and traffic accidents. *Am J Psychiatry* 131:903-906, 1974.
11. Paykel ES, Prusoff BA, Myers JK: Suicide attempts and recent life events: A controlled comparison. *Arch Gen Psychiatry* 32:327-333, 1975.
12. Cochrane R, Robertson A: Stress in the lives of parasuicides. *Soc Psychiatry* 10:161-171, 1975.
13. Holmes TS: *Adaptive Behavior and Health Change*, thesis. University of Washington, Seattle, 1970.
14. Komaroff AL, Masuda M, Holmes TH: The Social Readjustment Rating Scale: A comparative study of Negro, Mexican and white Americans. *J Psychosom Res* 12:121-128, 1968.
15. Masuda M, Holmes TH: Life events, life event perceptions, and life style, abstracted. *Psychosom Med* 38:66, 1976.
16. Guze SB: *Criminality and Psychiatric Disorders*. New York, Oxford University Press Inc, 1976.
17. Rahe RH: Life crisis and health change, in May PRA, Whittenborn R (eds): *Psychotropic Drug Response: Advances in Prediction*. Springfield, Ill, Charles C Thomas Publisher, 1969, pp 92-125.
18. Wolff HG: Life stress and bodily disease—a formulation. *Res Pub Assoc Res Nerv Ment Dis* 29:1059-1094, 1950.
19. Casey RL, Masuda M, Holmes TH: Quantitative study of recall of life events. *J Psychosom Res* 11:239-247, 1967.
20. Rahe RH: The pathway between subjects' recent life changes and their near-future illness reports: Representative results and methodological issues, in Dohrenwend BS, Dohrenwend BP (eds): *Stressful Life Events: Their Nature and Effects*. New York, John Wiley & Sons Inc, 1974, pp 73-86.
21. Dudley DL, Roszell DK, Mules JE, et al: Heroin vs alcohol addiction—quantifiable psychosocial similarities and differences. *J Psychosom Res* 18:327-335, 1976.

4

A PSYCHOLOGICAL APPROACH TO DETERRENCE
The Evaluation of Crime Opportunities

JOHN S. CARROLL

The present analysis of deterrence views potential criminals as making a few simple comparisons and partial examinations of crime opportunities. It is argued that the relevant data for studying responses to crime opportunities are individual judgments rather than aggregate statistics. Adult and juvenile male subjects, offenders and nonoffenders, evaluated three-outcome gambles consisting of four dimensions: (a) the probability of a successful crime, (b) the money obtained if successful, (c) the probability of capture, and (d) the penalty if caught. Subjects based their judgments primarily on a single dimension, although dimensional preferences varied greatly across subjects. Only minor differences existed among the types of subjects. Money was the most important dimension, followed by penalty, probability of success, and probability of capture. These findings support the proposed approach and suggest that making crime less profitable in comparison to noncrime opportunities may have stronger effects on crime rates than increasing the likelihood and severity of punishment.

The deterrence hypothesis is one of the oldest and most controversial issues in crime control. Simply stated, it proposes that an increase in the certainty or the severity of punishment for crime reduces the incidence of crime. In the last 10 years there has been a large number of empirical investigations of the deterrence hypothesis, with conflicting results (e.g., summary by Blumstein, Cohen, & Nagin, 1978). In part, the existing conflict is between disciplines with differing approaches and ideologies. As stated by Palmer (1977),

Although there is a danger of oversimplification, it is probably safe to say that many economists have concluded that an increase in the expected punishment does reduce crime, while many sociologists have concluded such an increase does not deter crime or has too small an effect to be considered a useful instrument of social policy. Therefore, to some extent the debate about the deterrence hypothesis is a debate between disciplines. (p. 9)

Deterrence as Viewed by Economists, Sociologists, and Psychologists

The economists' approach is in agreement with the classical school of criminology, which proposes that crime is a rational choice aimed at receiving maximum pleasure for minimum pain. Economists assume that people evaluate the expected utility (EU) of alternatives and select the alternative with highest utility (Becker, 1968). Expected utility is defined as expected gains less expected losses. These expectations come about by multiplicatively combining outcome values with their associated probabilities. In highly simplified form, the expected utility of a particular crime opportunity might be considered as

$$EU = p(S) \times G - p(F) \times L, \quad (1)$$

where $p(S)$ is the probability of success, G is the gain (perhaps an amount of money), $p(F)$ is the probability of failure, and L is the loss (perhaps a given prison sentence).

I wish to express my gratitude to the staff and participating subjects at the State Correctional Institution and the Shuman Juvenile Detention Center, Pittsburgh. John W. Payne made many helpful comments.

Requests for reprints should be sent to John S. Carroll, Department of Psychology, Loyola University, 6525 N. Sheridan Road, Chicago, Illinois 60626.

Sociologists are frequently more committed to rehabilitation ideals and the orientation of the positive school of criminology, focusing on the etiology of crime in prior environmental circumstances (e.g., Cloward & Ohlin, 1960; Reckless, 1961). Psychologists who have been involved in criminology have tended to view crime as a product of mental illness, of biology or early childhood experiences. For example, psychoanalytically oriented writers make statements such as "When a person commits a crime, he does not think of the consequences. The offender commits a crime because criminality is his particular outlet, just as the seriously mentally ill person's outlet is a psychosis" (Abrahamsen, 1960, p. 274).

A New Approach to Deterrence

The purpose of this article is to introduce a different approach, arising from experimental psychology. This approach views the person as a thoughtful decision maker who chooses among alternative courses of action, both criminal and noncriminal. Although similar to the economists' position in focusing upon mental evaluations of situations, the process by which these alternatives are evaluated is quite different. Drawing upon the idea of *limited rationality* (Simon, 1957) and information-processing approaches in behavioral decision theory (Slovic, Fischhoff, & Lichtenstein, 1977), it is proposed that people use a variety of strategies in which simple comparisons and partial examinations of alternatives are made. Support for this idea has been found in studies of preferences for simple monetary gambles composed of four dimensions: (a) probability of winning, (b) amount of money to be won, (c) probability of losing, and (d) amount of money to be lost. Payne (1973) provides a review of several such studies.

A second important characteristic of this approach is the unit of observation. Economists and sociologists studying deterrence have generally used statistics that aggregate across large numbers of offenders (crime rates, arrest rates, average prison terms) to focus on jurisdictional differences in crime rates and criminal justice activities. This approach contains serious flaws (Manski, 1978). In contrast, the psychological approach focuses explicitly on the individual person's judgments about his or her options.

The proposed approach thus offers a new model of how the person decides about crime opportunities. He or she is not viewed as the "economic person," making exhaustive and complex calculations leading to an optimal choice. Rather, it is the "psychological person," who makes a few simple and concrete examinations of his or her opportunities and makes guesses that can be far short of optimal. The appropriate way to discover how these decisions are made is to examine the judgments of individual persons on tasks designed to provide evidence about underlying decision processes. This method offers distinct advantages over the use of aggregate statistics and over the use of clinical interview reports.

Overview of the Study

The present study serves to illustrate this approach, requiring subjects to evaluate a series of crime opportunities consisting of four dimensions: (a) the probability of a successful crime, (b) the amount of money to be obtained if successful, (c) the probability of capture, and (d) the penalty if caught. The study addresses the question of how people combine this information into a judgment of the desirability of the crime opportunity.

There are several conflicting predictions about behavior on this task that can be drawn from work in economics, sociology, and psychology. Proponents of expected-utility theory might predict that these four dimensions would combine as in Equation 1: Expected gain is a multiplicative product of probability of success and money, expected loss is a multiplicative product of probability of capture and penalty, and expected gain and loss combine additively. Sociologists might predict that we would find little deterrent effect of probability of capture, and even less of penalty (e.g., Zimring & Hawkins, 1973). The work of Tittle and Rowe (1974) suggests that probability of capture may only be effective above a "critical level for a tipping effect," which they found to be $p = .3$. Decision-making research in psychology suggests yet a third possibility. In evaluations of gambles, Slovic and Lichtenstein (1968) found that subjects tended to combine dimensions additively rather than multiplicatively. Individual subjects used some dimensions much more than others, and different subjects had very different dimensional preferences. Overall, probability of winning and amount of money to be won were more important than probability of losing and amount of money to be lost.

Generalizing From the Study to Crimes

The present study should not be considered a model of criminal behavior. We have not assessed whether criminals or noncriminals code situations into these, and only these, dimensions. Even if this task were more than a suggestive metaphor, we would have to know how criminals and noncriminals translate situations into probability judgments and expectations of reward and punishment. For example, Claster (1967) found that delinquents were more likely than nondelinquents to believe that they could evade arrest if they committed a hypothetical crime.

Instead, the present study is an attempt to demonstrate that given a *simplification* of the complex situation of a crime opportunity, evaluations of the simplified stimuli will be even further simplified. We expect that people will adopt simple, additive, perhaps unidimensional strategies. If so, this would imply that "real-world" situations are also highly simplified and that the expected-utility viewpoint is unlikely to be valid. Ebbesen, Parker, & Konečni (1977) found, in a study of drivers choosing whether to make a left turn before or after an oncoming car has passed, that field observation of drivers revealed even simpler decision strategies than those exhibited in laboratory simulations. They suggest that unidimensional strategies may be quite common in real-world decisions. Insofar as the present study *does* capture some of the elements of real crime opportunities, it may also lead to useful new hypotheses about deterrence.

Method

Subjects

Subjects were 23 adult male offenders from a state prison, 13 adult male nonoffenders from a community college night class, 23 juvenile male offenders from a juvenile detention and diagnostic center, and 20 juvenile male nonoffenders from a high school. These four samples were selected in different ways and are not necessarily representative of their respective groups. Males were used as subjects because the large majority of crime is committed by males and because a sample of female offenders was difficult to obtain.

The median adult offender was 27 years old, with a range from 20 to 50 years. The median educational level was 12th grade, ranging from 8th grade to college graduate. Eighty-three percent of these offenders had a prior record. Thirteen were convicted of armed robbery or robbery, 5 of assaultive crimes including one murder, 3 of theft or burglary, and 1 each of selling marijuana and bribery. Over two thirds of the offenders were black. The median adult nonoffender was 27 years old, with a range from 20 to 30 years. The median educational level was 2 years of college, ranging from 12th grade to 2 years of college. Over 90% of these subjects were white.

The median juvenile offender was 15 years old, with a range from 13 to 18 years. The median educational level was 9th grade, ranging from 7th grade to 12th grade. Over two thirds of these subjects were white. Seven were convicted of auto theft, 6 of assaults including two murders, 4 of burglary or theft, 1 of robbery, 2 of drug possession, 2 of runaway, and 1 of trespassing. Seventy percent had prior records. The median juvenile nonoffender was 17 years old, ranging from 16 to 18 years. He had a 12th grade education, ranging from 11th to 12th grade. Eighty-five percent of this group were white.

Stimuli

The stimuli were 72 three-outcome gambles (Payne, 1975), consisting of three levels of each of four risk dimensions varied orthogonally. An example of one such gamble is presented in Figure 1. Probability of success was .1, .3, or .8; amount of money to be gained if successful was $100, $1000, or $10,000; probability of capture was .05, .15, or .4; and expected penalty if captured was probation, 6 months in prison, or 2 years in prison. The $3 \times 3 \times 3 \times 3$ design was incomplete because probability of success of .8 and probability of capture of .4 could not be present in the same stimulus. Thus the design was considered an $8 \times 3 \times 3$ with planned comparisons used to test other specific effects of interest.

The levels of the risk dimensions were selected to be illustrative of the ranges that might be found in real life. Probability of capture of .4 was chosen to include a value above the "critical level for a tipping effect" of Tittle and Rowe (1974), which

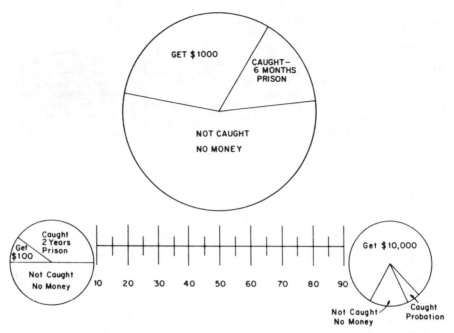

Figure 1. Sample crime opportunity with response scale.

may determine whether probability of capture has an effect.

Procedure

Subjects were run individually by one of 10 interviewers.[1] Subjects were told that they were to evaluate a series of opportunities for committing a crime, represented by a "pie picture." They were shown the example in Figure 1 and each part of the pie was explained. They were told, "There is some chance that your crime will succeed and get you some money . . . there is also some chance that your crime will result in getting caught and receiving a penalty . . . [and] there is some chance that your crime opportunity will be interrupted or disappear so you get no money, but are not caught either." The idea of probabilities was explained through placing a spinner on the pie and demonstrating several times that bigger segments were more likely to occur. The range of possibilities in each dimension was explained and subjects were handed the response scale (see Figure 1), which consisted of a large line marked off from 10 to 90, anchored on the low end by the worst crime opportunity and on the high end by the best crime opportunity in the set. Subjects were told to evaluate each crime opportunity verbally using any

number between 10 and 90, "such as 33, 62, and so forth."

Each subject evaluated all 72 crime opportunities in one fixed random order, followed by 18 crime opportunities randomly chosen from the set of 72 as a measure of within-subjects consistency. Thus, each subject made 90 judgments, generally in 20 to 30 minutes. After these judgments, the interviewer asked a set of background questions.

Results

Analysis of Individual Subjects

Within-subjects error terms were computed using the 18 repeated trials. Averaging these trials as estimates of the respective cells, 8 (probability combinations) × 3 (levels of money to gain) × 3 (levels of penalty) analyses of variance were computed for each subject. Contrasts were computed to examine

---

[1] The interviewers were Jacqueline Barbour, Darlene Baugh, Vanessa Browne, Carolyn Englund, Sue Keller, Gwen Holland, Conchita Harrington, Sharon Sclabassi, Tom Schwartz, and Paula Winner.

Table 1
Relative Importance of Crime Opportunity Dimensions

Dimension	% variance explained		% subjects for whom effect is significant	% subjects classified	
	M within subjects	M between subjects		7 effects	4 dimensions
Probabilities	17.5	8.4	68.3	34.2	
Success[a]	9.7	4.8	60.1		17.7
Capture[b]	4.4	1.8	41.8		7.6
Money	25.6	14.9	83.5	45.6	50.6
Penalty	13.7	7.3	67.1	17.7	24.1
Probabilities × Money	1.0	.6	16.4	1.3	
Success × Money[c]	1.7	.4	27.8		
Probabilities × Penalty	.3	.4	12.6	.0	
Capture × Penalty[d]	.4	.0	11.4		
Money × Penalty	2.1	.3	30.4	1.3	
Probabilities × Money × Penalty	.0	.6	10.1	.0	

Note. An 8 (probabilities) × 3 (money) × 3 (penalty) analysis of variance (ANOVA) was computed for each individual subject. Mean % variance explained across 79 subjects is given in the first column for main effects, interactions, and important planned comparisons. The effect explaining the most variance for each subject classified the subject as to what his judgments were based upon most heavily, either among the seven effects in the ANOVA or among the four dimensions of the stimuli. A similar ANOVA across all subjects also provided % variance explained given in the second column.
[a] Estimated using two orthogonal planned comparisons: (a) low versus medium probability of success and (b) low and medium versus high probability. To be classified as significant, at least one comparison had to be significant in the appropriate direction and neither significant in the inappropriate direction.
[b] Estimated using two planned comparisons similar to probability of success.
[c] Estimated using two orthogonal planned comparisons: (a) low probability of success/low money and medium probability of success/high money versus low probabilty/high money and medium probability/low money and (b) low and medium probability/low money and high probability/high money versus high probability/low money and low and medium probability/high money. Classification procedure was as in superscript a.
[d] Estimated using two planned comparisons similar to Success × Money.

the probabilities of success and capture individually and the interactions of Probability of Success × Money and Probability of Capture × Penalty, which represent the multiplicative terms in the expected-utility model. An estimate of the percentage of variance explained by each effect was computed as in Dwyer (1974).[2]

As presented in Table 1, the first dramatic finding is that nearly all the explainable variance is due to the four main effects of the dimensions. These four effects total over 53% of the variance across subjects, whereas the interactions of Probability of Success × Money and the Probability of Capture × Penalty together total only about 2% of the variance. The amount of money accounts for the most variance (25.6%) and is significant for 83.5% of subjects. This is followed

by the penalty, probability of success, and probability of capture. For 70.9% of the subjects, one dimension explained at least twice as much variance as any other dimension. Thus, most subjects focused principally on one dimension. Classifying subjects by which of the four dimensions accounted for the most variance, 50.6% of subjects focused on the

---

[2] The estimates of variance differ slightly from Dwyer (1974) because of the unusual way the error term was measured. Variance components were treated as though they all came from an analysis with one score for each of 72 cells. The error term from 18 of these cells was calculated separately and was not part of the total sum of squares. This is why estimates of the variance accounted for by a contrast can be larger than the variance accounted for by effects that include the contrast, in the first column of Table 1.

money, 24.1% on penalty, 17.7% on probability of success, and 7.6% on probability of capture. There was at least one subject for each of these dimensions whose evaluations were totally dominåted by that dimension, accounting for over 50% of the variation in ratings.

Differences among the four groups in their use of the four dimensions were detectable although not pronounced. Contingency table analyses of the number of subjects with significant effects in each group found that juveniles used probabilities more than adults, $\chi^2(1) = 8.80$, $p < .005$. They used the probability of success more than adults, $\chi^2(1) = 4.72$, $p < .05$, and they used the probability of capture more than adults, $\chi^2(1) = 4.32$, $p < .05$. Analyses of variance (2×2) computed on the percentage of variance accounted for by each effect also revealed that juveniles made more use of probabilities than did adults, $F(1, 75) = 5.79$, $p < .05$, and marginally more use of the probability of capture, $F(1, 75) = 3.31$, $p < .10$. Adults made marginally more use of the amount of money, $F(1, 75) = 3.90$, $p < .10$. No other differences were found between groups on these four dimensions. Analyses of the numbers of subjects in each group classified as using a dimension showed no significant effects.

Between-Subjects Analysis

Data from all subjects were analyzed together in a 2 (status: offender vs. nonoffender) $\times$ 2 (age: juvenile vs. adult) $\times$ 8 (probabilities) $\times$ 3 (money) $\times$ 3 (penalty) analysis of variance.[3] Although 14 effects were significant by this analysis, only 4 of these accounted for 1% or more of the variance (Dwyer, 1974). As shown in Table 1, these were money (14.9%), probabilities (8.4%), penalty (7.3%), and status (3.7%). Using planned comparisons, as in the within-subjects analysis, probability of success and probability of capture both were substantial effects, accounting for 4.8% and 1.8% of the variance, respectively. The main effect of status was that offenders rated all crime opportunities as more desirable than did nonoffenders.

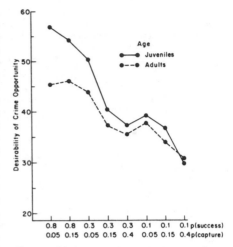

Figure 2. Crime opportunity evaluations as a function of probabilities of success and capture, by subject age group.

Among the significant effects accounting for less than 1% of the variance, juveniles again discriminated more among probabilities than did adults, as shown in Figure 2. Further, juvenile offenders and adult nonoffenders discriminated more among penalties than did the other groups, as shown in Figure 3. It can also be seen in Figure 3 that juvenile offenders rated all crimes particularly high relative to the other groups.

Relative Importance of Dimensions

The relative importance of dimensions, as measured by the effect sizes or numbers of subjects sensitive to each dimension, is heavily dependent upon the range of values included in each dimension. Granting the assumption that the ranges included are somehow representative of real life, we can draw implications about what might be most important in real life. However, establishing what is representative will require further research. Instead, the values in this article

---

[3] Because of the complexity of an unequal-n analysis and limitations built into the analysis programs, scores from random pairs of subjects were averaged to reduce the number of "subjects" to 13 in each group.

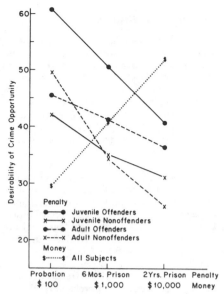

Figure 3. Crime opportunity evaluations as a function of penalty, by status and age, and of money.

constitute a reasonable set from which comparisons can be drawn. For example, the average rating of crime opportunities with $100 to be gained was 29.5, and the average for $1000 inducements was 40.7 (see Figure 3). The average rating for an expected penalty of probation was 49.5; it was 40.2 for a penalty of 6 months in prison and 33.3 for a penalty of 2 years in prison. Thus, other factors held constant, increasing the inducement from $100 to $1000 produced a difference of ratings that could be equivalent to changing the penalty from probation to about 1 year in prison.

The difference between $100 and $1000 is also slightly less than changing the probability of success from .1 to .8 and slightly more than changing the probability of capture from .05 to .4, holding all else constant (see Figure 2). The difference between probabilities of success of .1 and .3 is midway between the difference in probabilities of capture of .05 or .15 and .4; thus, probability of success would seem more important than probability of capture even with equivalent ranges.

The data in Figure 2 can also be used to examine the idea of a "tipping point," interpreted to mean that the probability of capture matters only when it exceeds .3. In contrast to this hypothesis, the difference between .05 and .15 is substantial and nearly as large as the difference between .15 and .4.

Validity of the Task

In response to the question, "Do you think the judgments you made for us are something like the things potential crime-doers think about?" 59% of the subjects agreed. Among the subjects who disagreed, 12 said people do not think (especially about consequences), or they act on impulse, or they do not know what the consequences will be. Seven subjects said people act out of need or desperation, and seven said only the money is considered. The subjects who disagreed were, indeed, more likely to focus on money in their own responses, and less likely to focus upon the probabilities, as judged by their classification into the four dimensions in Table 1, $\chi^2(3) = 8.11$, $p < .05$.

Discussion

Dimensional Preferences

The result that most subjects focus primarily on one dimension and that different subjects focus on different dimensions is strongly supportive of the psychological approach presented and is evidence against the expected-utility approach. The rather weak differences among groups who are so disparate in criminal history, age, and race suggest that this is a widely applicable finding—subjects focus on only a few aspects of a situation and differ substantially in individual preferences. This is a very prevalent finding in decision research (e.g., Ebbesen et al., 1977; Payne, 1975; Slovic & Lichtenstein, 1968).

There are two interrelated interpretations of this result. First, individuals may have previously acquired strong dimensional preferences, which differ across people ("importance beliefs," Slovic & Lichtenstein, 1968). Alternatively, in this abstracted and novel experimental task, subjects may seize upon one feature and spend most of their time examining it. What is salient to a particular subject may be a somewhat accidental aspect of the instructions and the subject's past experience and present attentional state. We would expect some features to be more naturally salient, such as money (cf. Nisbett, Borgida, Crandall, & Reed, 1976). In either case, this general principle implies that persons considering crime opportunities may have different strategies, possibly based on simple comparisons of salient features of the situation: Some are drawn by money, some avoid certain types of risk, and so forth.

The result that offenders and nonoffenders, juveniles and adults, do not appreciably differ should not be taken as evidence that our approach is invalid. Given the translation of crime opportunities into values on the four dimensions, we expected no overall differences. More substantial differences among groups may emerge if we study how a situation is translated into judgments of probability of success, expected payoff, probability of capture, and expected penalty (e.g., Claster, 1967).

Opportunity Cost

The use of a "neutral" alternative in the three-outcome gambles allowed the probabilities of success and capture to be simultaneously manipulated. However, this third alternative may not be truly neutral but may rather represent what economists consider an "opportunity cost" (Palmer, 1977). If this is true, there should be a tendency for evaluations of crimes to be associated with the size of this cost. Examining the eight probabilities in Figure 2, deviations from an additive relationship are apparent in the direction of comparing probabilities and categorizing them into (a) probability of success greater than probability of capture (.8 > .05, .8 > .15, .3 > .05); (b) probabilities roughly equal (.3 ≃ .15, .3 ≃ .4, .1 ≃ .15, .1 ≃ .05); and (c) probability of success less than probability of capture (.1 < .4). Thus, .8/.15 and .3/.05 are evaluated similarly because the ratios of probabilities are alike, even though the probability of an opportunity cost changes from .05 to .65. Thus, subjects seem to be treating the opportunity cost as negligible.

Implications for Deterrence

The psychological approach to judgments about crime opportunities has provided a new kind of information relevant to the deterrence hypothesis. Over the range of monetary incentives and penalties provided in this study, incentives were about twice as powerful as penalties in predicting crime judgments, and probability of success was about twice as powerful as probability of capture. Thus, to the extent we can affect these judgments in potential offenders, we may do better to lower the perceived payoff and chance of success of crime (and raise the incentive for noncrime activities) than to focus upon changes in the penalties and probabilities. However, nearly one third of our subjects could be considered "deterrable" in that their judgments were dominated either by penalty or probability of capture.

The fact that penalties were about three times more effective than probability of capture is at variance with findings from deterrence literature (Zimring & Hawkins, 1973) but agrees with previous research using monetary gambles (Slovic & Lichtenstein, 1968, Table 6). It could be that these penalties are not representative of what offenders think may happen to them if they are caught, which most often would be arrest and release rather than conviction and commitment. Thus, these expected penalties may be far more serious than what offenders typically envision. It could also be that aggregate statistics dealing with differences in penalties over time and place have not been able to detect an actual deterrent effect of penalties.

Conclusions

The results of the present study indicate that the decision to commit a crime is based upon a simple and perhaps unidimensional analysis of crime opportunities. This is in direct contrast to the expected-utility model that describes criminal behavior as the outcome of a complex multiplicative weighing of features. Subjects exhibited strong individual preferences in their reliance on dimensions; these preferences were not strongly related to subject age or criminality. Although it is not clear whether dimensional preferences were characteristic of each subject or created by the task, it seems likely that evaluation of real crime opportunities would also be dominated by simple judgments among a small number of dimensions.

The results provided by this new approach offer suggestive insights into the deterrence issue from a different vantage point. Subjects seemed generally more responsive to changes in the positive payoffs than to changes in the penalties. This suggests that social policies might be directed toward the relative profits of criminal and noncriminal activities as well as toward traditional punitive ends. The addition of new lines of research to an old argument may assist social scientists toward a more definitive statement on this issue. In the meantime, the debate between sociologists and economists has now become a forum.

References

Abrahamsen, D. *The psychology of crime*. New York: Columbia University, 1960.

Becker, G. Crime and punishment: An economic approach. *Journal of Political Economy*, 1968, *76*, 169–217.

Blumstein, A., Cohen, J., & Nagin, D. (Eds.). *Deterrence ·and incapacitation: Estimating the effects of criminal sanctions on crime rates*. Washington, D.C.: National Academy of Sciences, 1978.

Claster, D. Comparison of risk perceptions between delinquents and nondelinquents. *Journal of Criminal Law, Criminology, and Police Science*, 1967, *58*, 80–86.

Cloward, R. A., & Ohlin, L. E. *Delinquency and opportunity: A theory of delinquent gangs*. New York: Free Press, 1960.

Dwyer, J. H. Analysis of variance and the magni-

tude of effects: A general approach. *Psychological Bulletin*, 1974, *8*, 731–737.

Ebbesen, E. B., Parker, S., & Konečni, V. J. Decisions involving risk: Laboratory and field analysis. *Journal of Experimental Psychology: Human Perception and Performance*, 1977, *3*, 576–589.

Manski, C. F. Prospects for inference on deterrence through empirical analysis of individual criminal behavior. In A. Blumstein, J. Cohen, & D. Nagin (Eds.), *Deterrence and incapacitation: Estimating the effects of criminal sanctions on crime rates*. Washington, D.C.: National Academy of Sciences, 1978.

Nisbett, R. E., Borgida, E., Crandall, R., & Reed, H. Popular induction: Information is not necessarily informative. In J. S. Carroll & J. W. Payne (Eds.), *Cognition and social behavior*. Hillsdale, N.J.: Erlbaum, 1976.

Palmer, J. Economic analyses of the deterrent effect of punishment: A review. *Journal of Research in Crime and Delinquency*, 1977, *14*, 4–21.

Payne, J. W. Alternative approaches to decision making under risk: Moments versus risk dimensions. *Psychological Bulletin*, 1973, *80*, 439–453.

Payne, J. W. Relation of perceived risk to preferences among gambles. *Journal of Experimental Psychology: Human Perception and Performance*, 1975, *104*, 86–94.

Reckless, W. C. *The crime problem* (3rd ed.). New York: Appleton-Century-Crofts, 1961.

Simon, H. A. *Models of man*. New York: Wiley, 1957.

Slovic, P., Fischhoff, B., & Lichtenstein, S. Behavioral decision theory. *Annual Review of Psychology*, 1977, *28*, 1–39.

Slovic, P., & Lichtenstein, S. Relative importance of probabilities and payoffs in risk taking. *Journal of Experimental Psychology Monograph*, 1968, *78*(3, Pt. 2).

Tittle, C. R., & Rowe, A. R. Certainty of arrest and crime rates: A further test of the deterrence hypothesis. *Social Forces*, 1974, *52*, 455–462.

Zimring, F., & Hawkins, G. *Deterrence: The legal threat in crime control*. Chicago: University of Chicago, 1973.

Received March 25, 1978 ■

John S. Carroll is Associate Professor in the Psychology Department at Loyola University of Chicago. His research interests center on parole decision making and decisions made by shoplifters. He is a coeditor (with Irene H. Frieze and Daniel Bar-Tal) of New Approaches to Social Problems *(San Francisco: Jossey-Bass, 1979).*

5

SOME CHILD-REARING ANTECEDENTS OF CRIMINAL BEHAVIOR IN ADULT MEN

JOAN McCORD

Records collected during childhood and coded prior to knowledge of adult behavior provided information about the childhood homes of 201 men. Thirty years later, information about criminal behavior was collected from court records. Multiple regression and discriminant function analyses indicate that six variables describing family atmosphere during childhood—mother's self-confidence, father's deviance, parental aggressiveness, maternal affection, parental conflict, and supervision—have an important impact on subsequent behavior.

Despite a massive literature emphasizing the importance of child rearing, conscientious critics (e.g., Clarke & Clarke, 1976; Yarrow, Campbell, & Burton, 1968) have raised legitimate doubts regarding the impact of parental behavior on personality development. Many of the studies that link parental behavior with personality development rely upon a single source of information for both sets of variables; systematic reporting biases could thus cause obtained relationships. Most of the remaining studies have depended upon concurrent measurements, leaving doubt as to the direction of influence between parents' behavior and characteristics of the child. Questions about interpreting the results of both types of studies serve to highlight the importance of longitudinal research.

A few researchers have gathered information through longitudinal studies, using independent sources for measuring child rearing and for measuring personality. Robins (1966) analyzed information from clinic records gathered during childhood and related that information to data gathered when the subjects were adults. Robins pioneered assessment of long-term effects of child rearing, and her study raises doubts about the validity of retrospective reports on family socialization. Nevertheless, since predictor models combined variables describing child rearing with other types of variables (empirically linked with outcome), the research fails to provide convincing evidence that child-rearing differences affected adult behavior.

Block (1971) evaluated character development among subjects in the Berkeley longitudinal studies. Dividing 63 subjects into five types and checking differences in their backgrounds, Block reached the conclusion: "What comes through, for both sexes and without exception in viewing the various types, is an unequivocal relationship between the family atmosphere in which a child grew up and his later character structure" (p. 258). Although Block reports many statistically reliable differences, his analyses do not permit the reader to evaluate the strength of relationships between family atmosphere and character structure.

In 1973-1974, Werner and Smith (1977) retraced 88% of the children born on Kauai Island in 1955. Interviews with the mothers provided evidence about the family environ-

This study was supported by U.S. Public Health Service Research Grant 2 RO1 MH26779, National Institute of Mental Health (Center for Studies of Crime and Delinquency). It was conducted jointly with the Department of Probation of the Commonwealth of Massachusetts. The author wishes to express appreciation to the Division of Criminal Justice Services of the State of New York and to the Maine State Bureau of Identification for supplemental data from criminal records, though they are responsible neither for the statistical analyses nor for the conclusions drawn from this research.

Requests for reprints should be sent to Joan McCord, Department of Psychology and Sociology, Drexel University, Philadelphia, Pennsylvania 19104.

From Joan McCord, "Some Child-Rearing Antecedents of Criminal Behavior in Adult Men," 37(9) *Journal of Personality and Social Psychology* 1477-1486 (September 1979). Copyright 1979 by the American Psychological Association. Reprinted by permission.

ment of subjects when they were newborn infants, age 2, and age 10. Although combined measures tended to account for a relatively high proportion of variance in several problem areas, the authors did not assess specific child-rearing models as predictors of outcome behavior.

Lefkowitz, Eron, Walder, and Huesmann (1977) used a main effects model in stepwise multiple regression for their longitudinal study of aggression. Only two of the six variables that together accounted for about a quarter of the variance in male aggressiveness at age 18 were related to child rearing at age 8. Since the model included both redundant measures of child rearing and heterogeneous variables (e.g., child's preference for girls' games, parents' religiosity, and ethnicity of family), effects of differences in child rearing may have been masked by collinearity (Blalock, 1963; Gordon, 1968; Mosteller & Tukey, 1977).

The paucity of evidence to support a view that child rearing affects personality has led some authors (e.g., Clinard, 1974; Jessor & Jessor, 1977) to the conclusion that home atmosphere during childhood has a negligible effect upon personality development. Such authors present the challenge to which the present research is addressed: if parental behavior has an important impact upon personality development, differences in child rearing ought to contribute to variations in subsequent behavior.

Method

Subjects for this study were selected from a treatment program designed to prevent delinquency. The youths ranged in age, at the time of their introduction to the program, from 5 to 13 ($M = 10.5$, $SD = 1.6$).

Counselors visited 253 boys twice a month, for an average 5-year period between 1939 and 1945. With the exception of one who was a nurse, the counselors had been trained as social workers. After each visit, the counselor recorded observations about the family as well as the child.[1]

Case records from the treatment program described, in detail, whatever activities the counselors had observed on their visits to the homes. The records included reports of conversations with parents, friends, neighbors, and teachers as well as with the boys. Counselor turnover (a potential problem from a treatment perspective) produced a benefit for re-

search: most of the families were visited by more than one counselor.

To justify treatment of family backgrounds as independent units for analyses, only one subject from a family was included. Boys not reared by their natural mothers were also excluded. After eliminating brothers ($n = 21$) and those not reared by their natural mothers ($n = 36$), 201 cases remained for analysis.[2]

In 1957, coders read each case thoroughly in order to form judgments about the home and family interaction. These coders had no access to information about the subjects other than that contained in treatment records. A 10% random sample of the records was read independently by a second coder to yield an estimate of the reliability of the coding.[3] Variables from the coded case records were used in the present study.

The mother's attitude toward her son had been classified as actively affectionate (if there had been considerable interaction, without continual criticism, between mother and child, $n = 95$), passively affectionate (if there had been little interaction between mother and son, though the mother had shown concern for her child's welfare, $n = 51$), ambivalent or passively rejecting (if there had been marked alternations in the mother's attitude toward her son so that she had seemed sometimes to be actively affectionate and sometimes rejecting, or if the mother had seemed unconcerned about the child's welfare, $n = 43$), or actively rejecting (if the mother had appeared to be constantly critical of the boy, $n = 11$). Independent reading of 25 cases resulted in the same ratings for 80%.

Two ratings from the original codes were combined to evaluate effects of supervision. One described whether the child's activities outside of school were governed by an adult. This scale was divided to indicate whether supervision was generally present, occasionally present, or absent. Independent coding yielded identical ratings for 84% of the 25 randomly selected cases The second rating described parental expectations regarding the boys' activities. Coders were instructed to rate expectations as "high" if the

---

[1] The project included a matched control group. Since records on family life, for the control group, were limited to information gathered during the intake interviews supplemented by information from secondary sources, the control group was not used in this study. Originally, 325 boys were included in both the treatment group and the control group. By January 1942, 253 boys remained in each group. (See Powers and Witmer, 1951, for details regarding selection of cases and a description of the treatment program.)

[2] The criteria are not mutually exclusive. Five men were eliminated through both of the selection criteria.

[3] See McCord and McCord (1960) for a complete description of the coding.

child was given responsibility for care of his younger siblings, for preparation of meals, for contributing to the financial support of the family, or for doing "extremely well" in school. Independent ratings yielded agreement for 76% of 25 cases. The scales from the 1957 codes were combined to classify subjects into one of four categories: supervision generally present and high expectations for the child to accept responsibilities ($n = 40$), supervision generally present without evidence that high expectations were placed on the child ($n = 78$), occasional supervision ($n = 60$), and supervision absent ($n = 23$).[4]

A rating of parental conflict was based on counselors' reports of disagreements between the parents. Raters were instructed to look for conflicts about the child and conflicts about values, about money, about alcohol, and about religion. Parental conflict was coded into one of four categories: no indication, apparently none, some, or considerable. For the present research, cases were divided into those whose parents evidenced considerable conflict ($n = 68$) and those coded in alternative categories. Independent readers agreed, for this division, on 80% of the cases checked for reliability.

Three measures from the 1957 codes were combined to identify aggressive parents. Coders classified the aggressiveness of each parent by looking for evidence that the parent "used little restraint" when angry. Case records included reports on parents who threw things (e.g., one father threw a refrigerator down the stairs in the midst of an argument with his wife), hit people, broke windows, and shouted abuses. Independent coders agreed on 84% of the fathers and 92% of the mothers in classifying parents as aggressive. The coders described paternal discipline; the category "consistently punitive" identified fathers who regularly used physical force (e.g., beating a child) or very harsh verbal abuse. Independent coders agreed on 92% of the cases for ratings regarding this classification. If a parent was coded as aggressive or the father was coded as consistently punitive, the child was classified as having an aggressive parent ($n = 75$).[5]

The 1957 codes included a measure of the mother's self-confidence. A rating as self-confident was assigned if that mother showed signs of believing in her own abilities ($n = 55$). Other possibilities for this rating were "no indication of general attitude; evidence that mother saw herself as a victim or pawn in a world about which she could do nothing; and neutral, that is, generally seemed merely to accept things as they came." For this variable, independent raters agreed in classifying 84% of the 25 cases used to estimate reliability.

In 1957, coders rated a father as alcoholic if the case record indicated that he had lost jobs because of repeated drinking, if marital problems were attributed primarily to his excessive drinking, if welfare agencies had repeatedly pointed to the father's drinking as grounds for family problems, or if the father had received treatment specifically for alcoholism. Independent coders agreed for 96% of the ratings on this

variable. In 1948, after termination of the treatment program, criminal records on the family members of subjects were collected; these records were locked in a file separate from the case histories. In 1975, after names had been replaced by numerical identifiers, an assistant unfamiliar with the case records coded these criminal records. For the present study, a father was considered "deviant" if the case record indicated that he was an alcoholic, if the criminal record showed that he had been convicted at least three times for drunkenness, or if his criminal record showed that he had been convicted for a serious crime (i.e., theft, burglary, assault, rape, attempted murder, or murder). These criteria led to identification of 86 fathers as deviant.[6]

Case records included information about family structure. A father was considered "absent" if his residence was not with the subject's mother. Independent coding of 25 cases yielded agreement on 96% regarding whether or not the boy was living with both natural parents.[7] The 71 boys having absent fathers ranged in age, at the time when the loss occurred, from birth to 16 ($M = 7.01$, $SD = 5.03$). The father-absent subjects were subclassified to identify those whose natural fathers had been present during their first 5 years ($n = 48$) and those for whom the absence had occurred prior to the age of 5 ($n = 23$).

These seven variables (mother's affection, supervision, parental conflict, parental aggression, mother's self-confidence, father's deviance, and paternal absence) were used to depict the home atmosphere of subjects during childhood. The first three are regarded as directly related to child rearing. Relationships among these measures are shown in Table 1.

Subjects had been selected from congested urban neighborhoods. Nevertheless, differences in social status could contribute to subsequent differences in behavior. Two measures of social status were available. The case records supplied information about the father's occupation. Coders classified these occupations as white-collar (9.6%), skilled tradesmen (32.8%), or unskilled workers (57.6%). The reliability check yielded agreement on 96% of the ratings. A second measure of social status was provided by a rating of the neighborhoods in which the boys were raised. These ratings had been made, in 1938 and 1939, as part of the selection procedures. The ratings took into account delinquency rates, availability of recreational facilities, and proximity to bars, railroads, and junkyards. These ratings were coded on a 4-point scale from better to worst neighborhoods. The two measures tended to covary, Cramer's $V(6) = .218$, $p = .0044$.

---

[4] Only nine boys exposed to high expectations had not been rated as generally supervised.

[5] Fifty of the subjects were classified as having aggressive parents by the direct description of parental aggression.

[6] Forty-nine had been convicted for serious crimes.

[7] Of the 86 deviant fathers, 40 were also absent fathers.

Table 1

Relationships Among Variables Describing Home Atmosphere (Cramer's V)

	Supervision	Parent conflict	Parent aggression	Mother's self-confidence	Father's deviance	Father's absence
Mother's affection	.241***	.209*	.184*	.199*	.209*	.110
Supervision		.267**	.106	.308***	.230*	.187*
Parent conflict			.188**	.109	.381***	.375***
Parent aggression				.289***	.144*	.024
Mother's self-confidence					.125	.087
Father's deviance						.206*

* $p < .05.$ ** $p < .01.$ *** $p < .001.$

Between 1975 and 1978, the subjects were retraced. Among the 201 men included in the study, 153 (76%) were alive and in Massachusetts at least until the age of 40;[8] 16 (8%) had died prior to their 40th birthdays; 29 (14%) had migrated from Massachusetts; and 3 (1%) remained to be found.

During 1975 and 1976, the names (and pseudonyms) of all the men who had been in the program were checked through court records in Massachusetts.[9] These criminal records were traced and coded by different people from those who coded other records. Coders of the criminal records (and those who traced them) had no access to other information about the subjects. The court records showed the dates of court appearances and the crimes for which the subjects had been convicted. They were coded to show the type of crime and the age of the person when he was convicted. Convictions for serious property crimes (larceny, auto theft, breaking and entering, arson) and serious personal crimes (assault, attempted rape, rape, attempted murder, kidnapping, and murder) were used as dependent measures for this study.

Among the 201 men, 71 had been convicted for at least one serious crime; 53 had been convicted for property crimes and 34 for personal crimes (including 15 convicted for both types). Their ages when first convicted ranged from 8 to 38, with a mean of 18.7 ($SD = 8.7$) and a median of 20. Those convicted prior to their 18th birthdays were classified as juvenile delinquents ($n = 43$); those convicted after reaching the age of 18 were classified as adult criminals ($n = 48$, including 20 who had been juvenile delinquents).

After analyzing the relationship to crime of each of the childhood variables separately, multiple regression analyses (General Linear Model Procedure, Barr, Goodnight, Sall, & Helwig, 1976) were used to ascertain the contribution of child rearing to the variance in number of serious property and personal crimes. To test the degree to which knowledge of home atmosphere could enable accurate prediction of subsequent behavior, the six central variables describing home atmosphere were used in discriminant function analyses to identify criminals.

As a more stringent test of the contribution of home atmosphere to subsequent crime, the discriminant function analyses were also used to predict criminals among the subsample whose criminal records provided the most complete histories of convictions: those men living in Massachusetts at least until the age of 40. If this function identified criminality more accurately for the total group than for those living in Massachusetts, there would be grounds for suspecting an interaction effect between home background and unmeasured variables. If this function identified criminality at least as accurately for those alive in Massachusetts at the age of 40, there would be additional support for a conclusion that home atmosphere during childhood contributes to criminality.

Results

As a first step toward learning whether parental behavior contributes to subsequent differences in criminality, the seven scales describing home atmosphere and the two scales describing social status were individually analyzed for their contributions to the variance in number of serious crimes against property and persons. (See Table 2.)

With the exception of father's absence, each of the scales describing home atmosphere accounted for a statistically significant ($p < .05$) proportion of the variance in number of crimes against property, persons, or both.[10]

---

[8] Among them, 147 were in Massachusetts through their 45th birthdays.

[9] These records were supplemented by court records from the states of New York, Maine, Michigan, Nebraska, and Florida, where some of the men had resided.

[10] The Duncan multiple range test, modified for unequal groups (Kramer, 1956), indicated that boys without supervision, reliably ($p < .05$) more than boys in the other three categories, were convicted

Table 2
Relationships Between Variables Describing Home Background and Crimes

		Property crimes			Personal crimes		
	DF	R^2	F	PR > F	R^2	F	PR > F
Mother's affection	3, 196	.092	6.60	.0003	.029	1.92	.1261
Supervision	3, 197	.152	11.77	.0001	.071	5.04	.0023
Parent conflict	1, 199	.008	1.76	.1866	.035	7.14	.0081
Parent aggression	1, 199	.012	2.38	.1242	.036	7.36	.0073
Mother's self-confidence	1, 199	.022	4.50	.0350	.024	4.98	.0268
Father's deviance	1, 199	.024	4.81	.0295	.000	0.00	.9569
Father's absence	2, 198	.005	0.47	.6286	.026	2.67	.0715
Neighborhood	3, 197	.028	1.87	.1335	.016	1.10	.3513
Father's occupation	2, 195	.008	0.74	.4798	.012	1.15	.3181

Neither of the measures of social status was significantly related to these types of crimes.

Supervision and mother's self-confidence were related to both crimes against property and crimes against persons; mother's affection and father's deviance were related to property crimes (though not to personal crimes); conflict and parental aggression were related to personal crimes (though not to property crimes). The boys who lacked maternal affection, who lacked supervision, whose mothers lacked self-confidence, and whose fathers were deviant were more often subsequently convicted for property crimes. The boys who lacked supervision, whose mothers lacked self-confidence, and who had been exposed to parental conflict and to aggression were subsequently more often convicted for personal crimes.

The relationships to criminality of individual variables describing home atmosphere, though statistically significant, each accounted for a relatively small proportion of the variance. More important, since "criminogenic" conditions tended to be related to one another, these relationships could not be taken as evidence that the differences in home background that they represented resulted in differences in subsequent behavior.

To evaluate the contribution of parental behavior to subsequent behavior, the six central variables describing home atmosphere were divided into two sets. The first set included those variables that described characteristics of the parents, characteristics that might be viewed as antecedent to child-rearing practices: parental aggressiveness, paternal deviance, and mother's self-confidence. The second set included the three variables that described interpersonal behavior: parental conflict, supervision, and mother's affection; these were considered to be direct measures of child rearing. The effect of this division was to classify families in two ways. The first classification took account of relationships among the variables describing the parents; the second took account of relationships among the variables describing child rearing.

Sequential multiple regression models were used. They introduced the measure of social status (the interaction of father's occupation and neighborhood) as the first variable. The regression procedure next evaluated the sequential contribution to explained variance of parental characteristics (the interaction of paternal deviance, maternal self-confidence, and parental aggression). After controlling effects of both social status and parental characteristics, the procedure evaluated effects of child rearing (i.e., the interaction of supervision, parental conflict, and the mother's affection).

Child rearing, as measured in this longitudinal study, clearly accounts for a signif-

---

for both property and personal crimes. This a posteriori test showed that boys rejected by their mothers were most likely to be convicted for property crimes, and boys who had affectionate mothers were least likely.

Table 3
Home Environment and Subsequent Criminality

Sequential contribution	DF	R^2	F	$PR > F$
Predicting property crimes[a]				
Social status	11	.0688	1.55	.1185
Parental characteristics	7	.0610	2.16	.0404
Child rearing	27	.2612	2.40	.0005
Predicting personal crimes[b]				
Social status	11	.0541	1.16	.3222
Parental characteristics	7	.0588	1.97	.0616
Child rearing	27	.2444	2.13	.0023
Predicting total crimes[c]				
Social status	11	.0620	1.40	.0620
Parental characteristics	7	.0691	2.45	.0209
Child rearing	27	.2601	2.39	.0005

[a] Model: $R^2 = .391$, $F(45, 151) = 2.15$, $p = .0003$. [b] Model: $R^2 = .3573$, $F(45, 151) = 1.87$, $p = .0028$. [c] Model: $R^2 = .3912$, $F(45, 151) = 2.16$, $p = .0003$.

icant proportion of the variance in subsequent criminality. Table 3 describes the decomposition of the regression models.

As predictors of property crimes, the model accounts for 39.1% of the variance, $F(45, 151) = 2.15$, $p = .0003$. Parental aggression, paternal deviance, and maternal self-confidence account for 6.1% of the variance after controlling social status, $F(7, 151) = 2.16$, $p = .0404$. Parental conflict, supervision, and maternal affection contribute significantly to the variance after effects of social status and parental characteristics have been controlled, $R^2 = .261$, $F(27, 151) = 2.40$, $p = .0003$.

As predictors of personal crimes, the model accounts for 35.7% of the variance, $F(45, 151) = 1.87$, $p = .0028$. The three more direct measures of child rearing contribute significantly to the variance after effects of social status and parental characteristics have been removed, $R^2 = .244$, $F(27, 151) = 2.13$, $p = .0023$.

As predictors of the total number of serious crimes for which the men had been convicted, the model accounts for 39.1% of the variance, $F(45, 151) = 2.16$, $p = .0003$. Parental characteristics account for 5.9% of the variance after effects of social status have been controlled, $F(7, 151) = 2.45$, $p = .0209$. The child-rearing variables account for 26.0% of

the variance, $F(27, 151) = 2.39$, $p = .0005$, after removing effects of both social status and parent characteristics.

Adding information about whether or not a man had been reared in a home marked by paternal absence did not reliably increase the accuracy of any of the predictions.[11]

Within the (relatively restricted) range of social class represented in the study, the contribution of social status to the variance in crimes was not statistically reliable. On the other hand, both parental characteristics and child-rearing practices were reliably related to the number of crimes for which the subjects had been convicted.[12]

Approximately a third of the 200 men coded on all six variables describing home atmosphere had been convicted for at least one serious crime. A discriminant function based on the variables describing home atmosphere for these 200 men correctly identified 147

---

[11] R^2 was increased by .002 for property crimes, .007 for personal crimes, and .001 for total crimes.

[12] Without controlling for social status, parental characteristics and child-rearing variables accounted for 36.7% of the variance in property crimes, $F(34, 162) = 2.76$, $p \leq .0001$, 30.8% of the variance in personal crimes, $F(34, 162) = 2.12$, $p = .0010$, and 36.3% of the variance in total number of serious crimes, $F(34, 162) = 2.71$, $p \leq .0001$.

Table 4
Results of Discriminant Function Analyses

Dependent and independent variables	Correct as criminals		Correct as noncriminals		Overall accuracy		% improvement over chance	z > p
	n	%	n	%	n	%		
All subjects								
Ever criminal								
Home atmosphere	71	67.6	129	76.7	200	73.5	19.3	.0001
Adult criminal								
Home atmosphere	48	56.3	152	87.5	200	80.0	16.5	.0001
Men living in Massachusetts through the age of 40								
Ever criminal								
Home atmosphere	60	81.7	92	70.7	152	75.0	22.8	.0001
Adult criminal								
Home atmosphere	42	71.4	110	84.6	152	80.9	20.9	.0001
Juvenile delinquency record	42	45.2	110	83.6	152	73.0	13.0	.0011

(73.5%) as criminals or noncriminals; random predictions based on prior probabilities would be expected to identify only 54.2% correctly,[13] $z = 5.48$, $p < .0001$. The function based on parental aggression, maternal self-confidence, paternal deviance, supervision, maternal affection, and parental conflict correctly identified 76.7% of the noncriminals and 67.6% of the criminals. (See Table 4.)

Forty-eight men had been convicted for serious crimes after their 18th birthdays. The six variables describing home atmosphere provided a discriminant function which correctly identified 27 (56.3%) of the 48 adult criminals and 133 (87.5%) of the 152 men without records for convictions as adults. Predictions based on the descriptions of home atmosphere provided a 16.5% improvement over the 63.5% expected from random predictions based on prior probabilities, $z = 4.85$, $p < .0001$. (See Table 4.)

After discarding men who had died before the age of 40, migrated from Massachusetts, or who had not yet been found, 152 men who were living in Massachusetts at least until the age of 40 and whose case records had been coded for all six variables describing home atmosphere remained for discriminant function analyses. Among these men, the discriminant function correctly identified 75.0%, a slight improvement over the rate of correct identification among the total group of men and a 22.8% improvement over random procedures based on prior probabilities, $z = 5.63$, $p < .0001$. (See Table 4.) This discriminant function correctly identified 81.7% of the 60 criminals and 70.7% of the 92 noncriminals.

A breakdown of the results shows that the discriminant function had correctly classified as criminal 78.1% of those convicted only for property crimes, 78.6% of those convicted only for personal crimes, and 92.9% of those

---

[13] The model used to estimate predictions based on chance assumes that the number of predictions as criminal would be proportional to the actual distribution of criminals among subjects. Alternative models that might be considered range from assuming that each individual is as likely to be convicted as not (which would result in an expectation for correct predictions among half the noncriminals and half the criminals) to assuming that all or no individuals would be convicted. Although a "rational bet" would maximize correct predictions by predicting that all individuals would fall into the larger class, this model is inappropriate when the interest is in correct identification of those in the smaller class. An equiprobability model for the discriminant function analysis based on family atmosphere resulted in correct sorting of 68% of the men (62% of the noncriminals and 79% of the criminals) in terms of whether or not they had been convicted for serious crimes.

convicted for both property and personal crimes.

Among the 60 men convicted for serious crimes and still living in Massachusetts at the age of 40, 18 (30.0%) had been convicted only as juveniles, 23 (38.7%) had first been convicted after the age of 18, and 19 (31.7%) had been convicted both as juvenile and as adults. Were one to predict that only and all juvenile delinquents would be convicted as adults, the prediction would be correct for 73.0%, an improvement over an expectation of 60.0% from random procedures based on prior probabilities, $z = 3.27$, $p = .0011$. This prediction would be correct for 45.2% of the adult criminals and for 83.6% of the men not convicted as adults. Predictions based on juvenile records would, of course, be right for *none* of the men first convicted as adults (54.8% of the adult criminals) and for only 51.4% of the juvenile delinquents.

Among men living in Massachusetts at the age of 40, the discriminant function analysis based on home atmosphere during childhood correctly identified 80.9% as criminal or noncriminal after the age of 18. (See Table 4.) Use of the variables describing home atmosphere during childhood resulted in a 20.9% improvement over chance identification, $z = 5.26$, $p < .0001$, and a 7.9% improvement over predictions based on the subjects' juvenile criminal histories, $z = 2.19$, $p = .0282$. This function correctly identified 71.4% of the adult criminals and 84.6% of the noncriminals. The discriminant function based on home atmosphere correctly identified as criminals 65.2% of the men who had first been convicted as adults. In terms of their subsequent criminal records, this discriminant function correctly sorted 78.4% of the juvenile delinquents and 81.7% of those who had not been juvenile delinquents.[14]

Summary and Discussion

Recent criticism of the assumption that child-rearing practices have an important impact on personality development posed the issue addressed in this research. In order to evaluate the assumption, records describing home atmosphere during childhood, recorded during childhood, were linked with records of subsequent criminality, gathered when the subjects were middle-aged. The two sources of information were independent: data collection had been separated by several decades, the data had been coded by different people, and the coders had no access to information other than that which they were coding. Therefore, measures of home atmosphere were uncontaminated by retrospective biases and measures of subsequent behavior were uncontaminated by knowledge of home background.

Records describing home atmosphere had been written between 1939 and 1945. These records were case reports of counselors' repeated home visits to the 201 boys included in this study. The case records were coded, in 1957, to provide descriptions of home atmosphere.

Information about criminal behavior was gathered from court records, 30 years after termination of the program from which descriptions of home atmosphere had been collected. Subjects were considered criminals if they had been convicted for serious crimes (those indexed by the Federal Bureau of Investigation).

In preliminary analyses, six of seven variables describing home atmosphere were reliably related to criminal behavior. Only father's absence failed to distinguish criminals from noncriminals. Considering the emphasis given to broken homes as a source of subsequent criminality (e.g., Bacon, Child, & Barry, 1963; Glueck & Glueck, 1951; Wadsworth, 1979; Willie, 1967), this finding is worthy of note.

Multiple regression analyses indicated that six variables describing home atmosphere in childhood account for a significant proportion of the variance in number of convictions for serious crimes. After controlling effects of differences in social status, parental characteristics and child-rearing variables ac-

---

[14] The "rational bet" that men not convicted as juveniles would not be convicted as adults would be correct for 80% of the men not convicted as juveniles. Since this bet would be correct only for the noncriminals, the prediction would fail to identify correctly any of the critical group: men first convicted as adults.

counted for 32.2% of the variance in number of convictions for property crimes and 30.3% of the variance in number of convictions for personal crimes. The three most direct measures of child rearing (supervision, mother's affection, and parental conflict) accounted for approximately a quarter of the variance in number of convictions for serious crimes—after effects of both social status and parental characteristics had been removed.

Discriminant function analyses based on the six variables describing home atmosphere correctly identified 73.5% of the men as either subsequently criminal or noncriminal; further, these six variables provided a function that for 80% of the men correctly discriminated between those convicted and those not convicted for serious crimes as adults.

As compared with analyses for the total sample, the discriminant function analyses were (slightly) more accurate when used to predict behavior among the men whose criminal records provided the most complete histories of convictions. Among men living in Massachusetts at least to the age of 40, these functions correctly identified 75% as ever criminal or as noncriminal and 80.9% as criminal or noncriminal after the age of 18. Limiting analyses to men living in Massachusetts controlled any differences contributing to migration or early death; therefore, the accuracy of discriminant functions among this subsample is interpreted as supporting the view that home atmosphere during childhood contributes to criminality.

When used to identify men convicted as adults, the discriminant function identified as criminals almost two-thirds of the men first convicted after the age of 18. This function also correctly sorted more than three-quarters of the juvenile delinquents, distinguishing between those who were and those who were not adult criminals.

Although the discriminant functions based on home atmosphere were surprisingly successful in identifying men who were to become criminals, it would be a mistake to conclude that the longitudinal design of this research has led to recognition of the causes of crime. This research is limited not only by its subjects (all of whom were reared in congested urban areas during the thirties and early forties) but also by the hypotheses considered. In this research, parental aggression, paternal deviance, maternal self-confidence, supervision, mother's affection, and parental conflict indexed home atmosphere; unconsidered variables might better describe the features in the child's home that affect his behavior. In this research, the possibly confounding variable of social status was considered; other conditions might account for the apparent link between home atmosphere and crime. Nevertheless, the evidence from this study suggests that parental behavior does have an important impact on subsequent behavior: predictions of adult criminality based on knowledge of home atmosphere were not only markedly more accurate than chance—they were also more accurate than predictions based on the individuals' juvenile criminal records.

References

Bacon, M. K., Child, I. L., & Barry, H. A Cross-cultural study of correlates of crime. *Journal of Abnormal and Social Psychology,* 1963, *66,* 291–300.

Barr, A. J., Goodnight, J. H., Sall, J. P., & Helwig, J. T. *A user's guide to SAS 76.* Raleigh, N.C.: SAS Institute, 1976.

Blalock, H. M. Correlated independent variables: The problem of multicollinearity. *Social Forces,* 1963, *42,* 233–237.

Block, J. *Lives through time.* Berkeley, Calif.: Bancroft Books, 1971.

Clarke, A. M., & Clarke, A. D. B. *Early experience: Myth and evidence.* New York: Free Press, 1976.

Clinard, M. B. *Sociology of deviant behavior.* (4th ed.) New York: Holt, Rinehart & Winston, 1974.

Glueck, S., & Glueck, E. *Unraveling juvenile delinquency.* Cambridge, Mass.: Harvard University Press, 1951.

Gordon, R. A. Issues in multiple regression. *American Journal of Sociology,* 1968, *73,* 592–616.

Jessor, R., & Jessor, S. L. *Problem behavior and psychosocial development.* New York: Academic Press, 1977.

Kramer, C. Y. Extension of multiple range tests to group means with unequal numbers of replication. *Biometrics,* 1956, *12,* 307–310.

Lefkowitz, M. M., Eron, L. D., Walder, L. O., & Huesmann, L. R. *Growing up to be violent: A longitudinal study of aggression.* New York: Pergamon Press, 1977.

McCord, W., & McCord, J. *Origins of alcoholism.* Stanford, Calif.: Stanford University Press, 1960.

Mosteller, F., & Tukey, J. W. *Data analysis and regression.* Reading, Mass.: Addison-Wesley, 1977.

Powers, E., & Witmer, H. *An experiment in the prevention of delinquency: The Cambridge-Somerville youth study.* New York: Columbia University Press, 1951.

Robins, L. N. *Deviant children grown up.* Baltimore, Md.: Williams & Wilkins, 1966.

Wadsworth, M. E. J. *Roots of delinquency.* New York: Barnes & Noble, 1979.

Werner, E. E., & Smith, R. S. *Kauai's children come of age.* Honolulu: University Press of Hawaii, 1977.

Willie, C. V. The relative contribution of family status and economic status to juvenile delinquency. *Social Problems,* 1967, *14,* 326–335.

Yarrow, M. R., Campbell, J. D., & Burton, R. V. *Child Rearing.* San Francisco: Jossey-Bass, 1968.

Received August 7, 1978 ∎

6

CROSS-VALIDATION OF THE
MEGARGEE MMPI TYPOLOGY FOR PRISONERS

JACK D. EDINGER

To cross-validate the Megargee Minnesota Multiphasic Personality Inventory (MMPI) typology for prisoners, one sample consisting of 2,063 male federal offenders and one sample consisting of 1,455 (164 females, 1291 males) state offenders were obtained. By use of a computer typing program, over 85% of these subjects were classified, and all of Megargee's 10 profile types were identified within each sample. Additional data collection and subsequent analyses revealed (a) significant ($p < .01$) age differences among the male state MMPI types; (b) significant ($p < .01$) differences in regard to the proportion of each type found within the male and female state offender samples; (c) significant ($p < .001$) differences among the federal MMPI types in terms of their current offenses; and (d) significant differences among the federal types in terms of the total number as well as the number of verbally aggressive and group-defiant rule infractions committed while incarcerated. It is concluded that the Megargee typology is a valid and generalizable system. Further, implications of the study's findings are discussed, and suggestions for future research are provided.

Although various typologies (Gibbons & Garrity, 1962; Glueck & Glueck, 1956; Hewitt & Jenkins, 1947; Quay & Parsons, 1970; Roebuck, 1967; Warren & Palmer, 1965) have been developed for prisoner classification, none has been employed widely in correctional treatment/management decision making. Perhaps the major reason for their limited use is that these typologies are generally cumbersome to use. In fact, the majority of the available typologies rely on case history and/or interview data that can only be obtained through time-consuming interviews or patience-trying file searching.

The views expressed in this article are exclusively those of Jack D. Edinger and do not necessarily reflect the views of the U.S. Bureau of Prisons.

The author is indebted to R. Fowler and S. Brodsky for making available data from the Alabama state prisoner classification project.

Requests for reprints should be sent to Jack D. Edinger, Bureau of Prisons, Federal Correctional Institution, P.O. Box 1000, Butner, North Carolina 27509.

Thus, these typologies have generally been considered impractical for use in the classification of large offender populations.

To overcome this difficulty Megargee and Dorhout (1977) and Meyer and Megargee (1977) devised a typology that relies solely on Minnesota Multiphasic Personality Inventory (MMPI) data and consists of 10 profile types. In developing this system Megargee and his colleagues used an hierarchical profile analysis and empirically identified 10 MMPI profile types occurring naturally within a prisoner population. Subsequent to labeling these types with nondescriptive names (i.e., Able, Baker, Charlie, Delta, Easy, Foxtrot, George, How, Item, and Jupiter), Megargee and Dorhout (1977) demonstrated that these types are reliable groups that may be both clinically and computer identified in randomly selected prisoner samples.

As suggested in a recent publication (Megargee & Dorhout, 1977), the advantages of this classification system are numerous. Since this typology relies solely on

From Jack D. Edinger, "Cross-Validation of the Megargee MMPI Typology of Prisoners," 47(2) *Journal of Clinical and Consulting Psychology* 234-242 (April 1979). Copyright 1979 by the American Psychological Association. Reprinted by permission.

MMPI results, classification data collection may be accomplished through the administration of a single test. Further, classification data for several prisoners may be collected simultaneously via group testing procedures. Finally, since the Megargee rules can be computerized (Megargee & Dorhout, 1977), the classification of large offender populations may be quickly accomplished when computer access is available.

In addition to supporting this system's reliability and practicality, research has attested to its validity as well. Through numerous demographic and psychometric comparisons, Megargee and Bohn (1977) have documented significant differences among the 10 types and have subsequently developed distinctive descriptions of them. Based on their research, Megargee and Bohn (1977) describe Type *Able* as a forceful, self-confident, and manipulative individual who experiences little guilt for antisocial acts. Type *Baker* individuals seem depressed, withdrawn, and likely to experience difficulty in relating to peers and authorities. Among the more aggressive are Type *Charlie* individuals who seem bitter, hostile, and ready to strike out at others. Somewhat less aggressive are Type *Delta* inmates, who are described as amoral and impulsive individuals who have a notable interpersonal charm that they use to manipulate others. Type *Easy* seems to be a well-adjusted, intelligent, albeit underachieving group, whereas Type *Foxtrot* seems to consist of obnoxious, "streetwise," abrasive individuals who engender much interpersonal conflict. Type *George* in contrast to Type Foxtrot seems to be a submissive, highly adaptable person who experiences fewer interpersonal conflicts. Perhaps the most disturbed are Type *How* individuals, who seem extremely agitated and unstable and whose crimes seem to be only one component of a broad pattern of ineffective functioning. Contrary to Group How, Type *Item* seems to be the most normal and well-adjusted individual whose offenses seem unrelated to interpersonal and intrapsychic problems. Finally, Group *Jupiter* inmates are described as impulsive individuals who make a better than expected adjustment within the correctional environment.

Although research concerning these various types has been compelling, this research has been limited to that performed by Megargee and his colleagues with the young adult male prisoner population incarcerated at the Tallahassee Federal Correctional Institution (FCI). Consequently, questions remaining unanswered are (a) Is this typology applicable to inmate populations other than the Tallahassee sample studied by Megargee and his colleagues? (b) Is this typology applicable to female offenders? (c) If Megargee's 10 types can be identified in other prisoner populations, will they differ on demographic measures? and (d) Does this typology have predictive validity for behaviors occurring within the prison setting? The purpose of the current investigation was to address these questions.

Method

Subjects

Two large samples of prisoners were used for this study. One sample consisted of 2,063 inmates who had been incarcerated at the Petersburg (FCI) prior to June 30, 1976. All of these subjects were young adult males ranging in age from 17 to 29 years (M age = 22.17 years). The second sample consisted of 1,455 inmates drawn randomly from the population of prisoners who participated in the recent Alabama state prisoner reclassification project. One hundred sixty-four of these inmates were females, and the remaining 1,291 were males. The female inmates ranged in age from 16 to 66 years (M age = 28.96 years); the males' ages ranged from 15 to 83 years (M age = 27.30 years).

Procedure

To obtain a sample from the Petersburg FCI, the institution's active and inactive psychology files were reviewed and all inmates who were incarcerated at the FCI prior to June 30, 1976, and who were administered an MMPI on their intake were selected. Of the plethora of inmates reviewed, 2,063 met the selection criteria and, hence, were chosen for use in this study.

To obtain a sample of state prisoners, a request was made to the research directors of the Alabama state prisoner reclassification project. In response to this request, the age, sex, and MMPI validity and clinical scale T scores of a group of 1,455 randomly selected, anonymous Alabama state prisoners were made available.

Once both samples were acquired, the MMPI validity and clinical scale T scores of all subjects were transferred to computer cards, and the Megargee and Dorhout (1977) revised typing rules were translated into computer language. After an initial investigation (Edinger & Auerbach, 1978) with this program, it was revised several times until it identified all 10 types within the current Petersburg sample. Subsequently, the program was used with each sample separately, and the proportions of each of the Megargee 10 types within the FCI, the Alabama State male, and the Alabama state female samples were determined. These proportions, in turn, were statistically compared via chi-square analyses with those proportions reported by Megargee and Dorhout (1977). Additionally, a Type × Sex chi-square analysis was performed on the state sample to determine if the proportions of the 10 types differed across the sexes.

Following these analyses, further data collection was effected with the FCI sample. As a first step, four readily accessible demographic variables were identified and obtained (if available) for each FCI subject from the institution's central card index located in the FCI's record office. The specific demographic data collected were age, current offense, religion, and race of each FCI subject. Having collected these data, I compared the 10 profile types on the variable of age using an analysis of variance procedure. A similar comparison was performed on the state samples, since ages were available for these subjects. Chi-square comparisons were also performed to compare the FCI profile types in terms of the remaining three demographic variables.

To investigate the predictive validity of Megargee's typology, institutional rule infraction data for the FCI sample were utilized. At the time of this study, rule infraction data were available for the period January 1, 1973, through June 30, 1976. Hence, to investigate the infraction patterns of the various types, it was necessary to select only those FCI inmates who (a) were classified as one of Megargee's 10 types and (b) were both committed to and released from the FCI during this 42-month period. Of the 2,063 FCI subjects, 873 met these selection criteria and were used to compare the Megargee types in terms of their infraction patterns.

In collecting infraction data five misconduct measures were determined for each subject. The first four of these measures were (a) the number of verbally aggressive (i.e., threatening, refusing to obey an order, exhibiting insolent behavior, using abusive language, engaging in disruptive conduct) infractions committed; (b) the number group defiant (i.e., rioting, encouraging others to riot, assisting in rule infractions, group demonstrating, destroying property) infractions committed; (c) the number of evasive (i.e. lying, being in an unauthorized area) infractions committed; and (d) the number of pilfering (i.e. stealing, possessing contraband) infractions committed. These specific infraction measures were used, since previous research

(Edinger & Auerbach, 1978) had shown verbal aggression, group defiance, pilfering, and evasion to be the four principal infraction factors occurring at the FCI. In addition to these measures, the total number of infractions of any kind committed by each subject was determined.

Prior to analyzing these misconduct measures, several data transformations were performed. First, each of the subject's five misconduct measures were divided by the number of days that the subject was incarcerated. This procedure, performed for all subjects, was used to control for the varying sentence lengths among the subjects. The scores resulting from this transformation were then multiplied by the constant 30.5 (i.e., the number of days in an average month). The products of this multiplication were then multiplied by 100 to produce derived scores of a more workable magnitude.

To compare the Megargee types, these five transformed misconduct measures were analyzed in separate one-way analyses of variance. Subsequently, Duncan multiple-range tests were used to determine specific differences among the groups on these measures.

Results

Identification of Types

In using the computer typing procedure, 1,763 (85.5%) of the FCI sample, 1,112 (86.1%) of the state male sample, and 143 (87.2%) of the state female sample were classified. Further, all of 10 of Megargee's profile types were identified within each of these samples. Mean T scores of the types found within these samples are presented in Table 1 along with the mean T scores reported by Megargee and Dorhout (1977).

As may be noted, the profile patterns and T-score magnitudes of the two current male samples closely resembled those reported by Megargee and Dorhout (1977). In fact, in comparing corresponding MMPI scales within each type, it was discovered that 77.7% (101/130) of the FCI versus Megargee and Dorhout comparisons and 70.8% (92/130) of the state male versus Megargee and Dorhout comparisons revealed differences of 3 or fewer T-score points. Additionally, no tendency for either male sample to overestimate or underestimate the Megargee and Dorhout T scores was noted.

Greater differences, however, were noted between the current female and the Megargee and Dorhout (1977) samples. Of the

Table 1

Mean T *Scores for the Petersburg Federal Correction Institution, Alabama State, Male and Female, and the Megargee and Dorhout (1977) Samples*

Type	Sample	L	F	K	1	2	3	4	5	6	7	8	9	10
													MMPI scale	
Able	FCI	51	61	52	53	51	54	72	59	57	54	58	79	46
	STM	50	59	52	51	52	54	74	57	57	55	57	77	46
	STF	49	61	50	51	48	55	74	57	60	55	61	76	48
	MEG	52	56	56	50	51	55	70	55	53	53	56	72	44
Baker	FCI	53	57	54	50	60	54	70	62	59	52	55	64	49
	STM	52	55	50	50	58	51	69	59	56	49	52	65	50
	STF	50	43	44	50	53	47	62	61	47	45	40	68	52
	MEG	54	58	51	49	65	54	71	52	57	55	55	61	57
Charlie	FCI	51	77	48	60	65	59	77	61	79	73	90	75	56
	STM	50	76	44	60	65	58	75	61	78	75	89	74	60
	STF	48	76	49	57	61	52	74	51	80	74	88	68	62
	MEG	50	80	46	60	65	59	77	61	81	72	84	75	57
Delta	FCI	51	63	55	53	62	58	88	56	55	56	59	69	48
	STM	51	59	56	53	58	56	86	51	53	56	56	66	48
	STF	47	48	59	48	47	49	74	51	41	50	47	58	53
	MEG	51	61	57	57	65	59	85	58	59	62	63	62	52
Easy	FCI	55	56	58	56	64	61	70	57	56	56	57	59	51
	STM	55	55	56	56	63	60	71	54	54	55	56	58	51
	STF	54	54	54	60	61	65	71	49	59	56	55	55	55
	MEG	57	54	62	59	60	64	68	54	55	58	59	60	49
Foxtrot	FCI	52	68	54	55	57	56	78	56	59	60	74	81	50
	STM	51	67	52	56	57	55	79	56	62	62	75	81	50
	STF	50	73	45	59	60	61	79	51	71	63	77	80	56
	MEG	50	70	51	53	57	55	77	55	60	60	73	81	51
George	FCI	56	59	58	62	68	63	79	58	58	62	62	61	52
	STM	54	58	57	62	66	63	80	56	60	60	60	59	52
	STF	55	56	54	56	71	66	81	41	57	57	56	62	49
	MEG	58	56	59	59	70	61	72	56	53	59	57	56	52
How	FCI	54	72	54	72	82	70	83	64	72	77	84	65	60
	STM	53	70	51	76	85	69	86	67	79	86	91	72	63
	STF	54	69	52	70	79	73	84	48	77	76	80	63	69
	MEG	57	76	54	80	84	76	81	62	71	81	89	65	61
Item	FCI	55	55	55	52	57	55	63	59	55	55	55	62	49
	STM	53	55	53	51	56	54	65	56	55	54	54	62	51
	STF	55	56	51	49	52	51	62	51	57	51	54	58	55
	MEG	54	57	54	54	59	56	61	59	57	57	56	60	52
Jupiter	FCI	50	69	48	53	58	54	61	56	64	70	75	78	51
	STM	47	66	47	54	54	52	61	58	61	72	79	78	53
	STF	50	58	48	37	55	49	60	43	59	79	74	68	62
	MEG	52	65	50	52	58	51	63	56	59	72	79	79	54

Note. FCI = Petersburg Federal Correctional Institution sample; STM = State of Alabama male sample; STF = State of Alabama female sample; MEG = Megargee and Dorhout (1977) sample; MMPI = Minnesota Personality Inventory. *T* scores have been rounded to the nearest whole number.

Table 2
*Percentage of Each of the 10 Profile Types Within the Three
Current and Megargee and Dorhout (1977) Samples*

Population	Type									
	A	B	C	D	E	F	G	H	I	J
Petersburg FCI	6	3	6	1	15	8	7	17	37	1
Alabama state										
Males	8	3	6	2	16	8	8	13	35	2
Females	10	1	4	1	17	4	3	8	51	1
Megargee and Dorhout	17	4	9	10	7	8	7	13	19	3

Note. FCI = Federal Correctional Institution. A = Able; B = Baker; C = Charlie; D = Delta; E = Easy; F = Foxtrot; G = George; H = How; I = Item; J = Jupiter. Numbers reported in the table are rounded to the nearest whole number.

130 corresponding scale comparisons, only 54 (41.5%) revealed differences of 3 or fewer T-score points. In 79 (60.8%) of the 130 comparisons, the female prisoners' mean T scores were lower than those reported for the Megargee and Dorhout (1977) sample. Thus, although Megargee's 10 types were identified within the current female sample, they differed from the Megargee and Dorhout (1977) male types, particularly in regard to scale elevation.

Proportional Distribution of Types

Table 2 displays the percentage of each of the 10 types found within the current and Megargee and Dorhout (1977) samples. Chi-square comparisons revealed significant ($p < .05$) differences between the proportional distribution of the types reported by

Megargee and Dorhout (1977) and those found for each of the three current samples. Further, the proportions of the 10 profile types differed significantly, $\chi^2(9) = 24.06$, $p < .01$, across the sexes in the state sample. The greatest difference between the male and female state prisoners was in regard to the proportion of Types Foxtrot, George, How, and Item found within each sample. A greater proportion of Foxtrots, Georges, and Hows were found within the male sample, whereas a greater proportion of Items were found in the female sample.

Age Comparisons

Table 3 displays the mean ages of each profile type within each sample. Also found in Table 3 are the F values for the comparison of the profile types in terms of age. Of

Table 3
Mean Ages of the Profile Types

Sample	Type										
	A	B	C	D	E	F	G	H	I	J	F value
Petersburg FCI	21.8	22.2	21.7	22.6	22.4	21.6	22.2	22.2	22.3	21.8	1.45
Alabama state											
Males	26.5	29.2	25.4	28.3	29.7	26.1	28.9	25.7	27.2	21.8	4.08*
Females	26.8	27.0	23.5	29.0	32.2	22.0	29.0	31.0	29.1	28.0	1.12

Note. FCI = Federal Correctional Institution. A = Able; B = Baker; C = Charlie; D = Delta; E = Easy; F = Foxtrot; G = George; H = How; I = Item; J = Jupiter.
* $p < .001$.

Table 4
Demographic Characteristics of the Petersburg Federal Correctional Institution

Variable	Type										Overall
	A	B	C	D	E	F	G	H	I	J	
Race[a] (%)											
White	37.1	38.2	34.3	66.7	46.1	35.8	44.7	37.8	43.4	16.7	41.4
Black	62.9	58.8	61.4	33.3	50.6	61.0	54.1	61.3	54.4	83.3	56.7
Other	.0	3.0	4.3	.0	3.3	3.2	1.2	.9	1.7	.0	1.9
n	70	34	70	15	178	95	85	222	472	18	1,259
Religion[b]											
Protestant	60.6	46.9	61.9	53.8	55.5	42.9	66.7	55.0	52.5	50.0	54.5
Catholic	19.7	40.6	28.6	30.8	23.9	29.9	12.8	27.5	26.9	18.0	25.8
Other	6.1	3.1	.0	.0	3.9	5.2	6.4	3.0	7.0	.0	5.0
None	13.6	9.4	9.5	15.4	16.7	22.0	14.1	14.5	13.6	31.2	14.7
n	66	32	63	13	155	77	78	200	427	16	1,127
Offense[c] (%)											
Robbery	26.7	28.6	27.6	20.0	25.8	30.3	27.2	25.8	24.4	42.1	26.1
Violent crimes	6.7	2.9	17.1	6.7	3.8	7.1	3.3	7.4	5.2	15.8	6.3
Property crimes	18.7	37.1	14.5	53.3	25.8	23.2	26.1	27.5	21.9	15.8	23.9
Narcotics violations	13.3	5.7	15.8	.0	21.4	9.1	15.2	11.4	26.3	10.5	18.4
Other	34.7	25.7	25.0	20.0	23.1	30.3	28.3	28.0	22.1	15.8	25.2
n	75	35	76	15	182	99	92	229	479	19	1,301

Note. A = Able; B = Baker; C = Charlie; D = Delta; E = Easy; F = Foxtrot; G = George; H = How; I = Item; J = Jupiter.
[a] $\chi^2(18) = 25.33$, $p > .05$.
[b] $\chi^2(27) = 35.70$, $p > .05$.
[c] $\chi^2(36) = 84.02$, $p < .001$.

the three F values reported, only that for the state male sample was significant. A posteriori comparisons showed that for this sample type, Jupiter subjects were significantly ($p < .05$) younger than the remaining nine types. Also, Type Baker subjects were found to be significantly older than Type Charlie subjects. Aside from these results no significant age differences were observed.

Demographic Variables

Table 4 presents the racial compositions, religious preferences, and current offenses of the FCI types. In regard to race, 41.4% of the total FCI sample were white, 56.7% were black, and 1.9% were of some other race. These figures contrast markedly with the Megargee and Dorhout (1977) population, which was 64.7% white, 34.4% black, and .9% of some other race. A chi-square comparison revealed a significant, $\chi^2(9) = 10.97$, $p < .01$, difference between the current FCI sample and that used by Megargee and Dorhout (1977). Further, although Megargee and Dorhout (1977) reported significant differences among the types in terms of racial composition, no such results were found for the current FCI sample.

Of the 1,127 FCI subjects for whom religious preference data were available, 54.5% were Protestant, 25.8% were Catholic, 5% were of some other religious preference, and 14.7% reported they had no religious preference. In comparing the types within this sample, no significant differences were found in regard to religious preference.

In contrast, the 10 types did differ significantly in terms of their current offenses. Greater proportions of Types Charlie and Jupiter inmates had committed violent crimes against persons (i.e., rape, murder, assault, kidnapping) than had the remaining eight groups. Also, the proportion of Type Jupiter inmates who had committed robbery was greater than the proportions found among the other types in regard to this offense.

Table 5
*Analysis of Variance and Duncan Multiple-Range Test Results
for the Institutional Rule Infraction Data*

Incident type	F value	p <	Ranges*
Verbal aggression	2.75	.005	C A G F H J D I E B
Group defiance	4.78	.001	D G C F H E A I B J
Evasion	1.75	.08	J H G F E C A I D B
Pilfering	1.45	.20	H F B C I G D E A J
Total	2.77	.005	D F C G H A J B E I

* Profile types joined by a common underlining do not differ significantly at the .05 level. Range data are organized with the left side representing the highest mean and the right side the lowest mean. C = Charlie; A = Able; G = George; F = Foxtrot; H = How; J = Jupiter; D = Delta; I = Item; E = Easy; B = Baker.

Types Delta and Baker seemed the most prone of all the groups to commit property crimes (i.e., theft, larceny, burglary, interstate transportation of a stolen motor vehicle), whereas Types Item and Easy were the most prone of the groups to be incarcerated for narcotic violations.

Rule Infraction Data

The analyses of variance and the Duncan multiple-range tests for the rule infraction data are present in Table 5. Significant differences were found among the profile types in terms of verbal aggression, group defiance, and total number of infractions committed. Type Charlie, which displayed the most verbal aggression of all groups, committed significantly more verbally aggressive infractions than did Groups Delta, Item, Easy, and Jupiter. Type Able, which committed significantly more verbally aggressive infractions than did Types Easy and Baker, displayed the second most verbal aggression among the 10 groups.

In contrast, Type Delta committed significantly more group defiant infractions than did the remaining groups. Further, Type Delta also committed a greater number of infractions of all kinds than did the remaining groups. In fact, as revealed by a posteriori comparisons, Type Delta committed significantly more infractions in general than did Types Jupiter, Baker, Easy, and Item. A posteriori comparisons also showed that Type Foxtrot committed significantly more infractions in general than did Group Item. Aside from these findings, no significant differences were found among the types in terms of the institutional misconduct data.

Discussion

The current investigation was effected in an attempt to cross-validate the Megargee typology for prisoners. Specifically, this study was designed to identify Megargee profile types within male and female prisoner samples as well as to explore demographic and behavioral differences among these types. Generally, this study was successful in demonstrating the existence of and differences among Megargee's types in prisoner populations other than those previously used by Megargee and his colleagues.

In reviewing the current results, it appears that this MMPI typology is applicable to both male and female prisoners. In fact, over 85% of each of the current samples were classified by use of this typology. However,

MMPI *T*-score comparisons revealed considerable differences between the female types and Megargee's original types. In regard to these comparisons, the current female types tended to have lower *T* scores than did the Megargee and Dorhout (1977) males. These differences suggest that although the Megargee typology may be useful for female offenders, female types may display somewhat different behavioral tendencies than corresponding male types.

In comparing the proportions of the 10 types found in the current samples with those reported by Megargee and Dorhout (1977), significant differences were noted. These differences, however, are not disturbing when considering the current samples' characteristics vis-à-vis the Megargee and Dorhout (1977) sample. As reported herein, a significant difference existed between the current FCI and the Megargee and Dorhout samples in terms of racial composition. This difference, of course, could account for the proportional differences of the various types found in these two samples. Further, since Megargee and Bohn (1977) suggested that state offender samples might have different frequencies of the 10 types than do federal samples, the noted frequency differences between the current state and Megargee and Dorhout (1977) federal samples might have been expected. Because such proportional differences exist across offender populations, it is necessary to be aware of these differences as they suggest differing treatment/ management needs of these populations.

A closely related implication was suggested by the proportional differences found among the current male and female state samples. These differences, as well as the above mentioned *T*-score differences, suggest that female offender types may present unique behavioral characteristics requiring unique treatment/management approaches. This suggestion, however, is only speculative as research in support of it is yet to be performed.

In addition to these findings, the noted differences among the 10 types in terms of age, current offense, and institution misconduct serve to support the conceptual and empirical integrity of Megargee's system. In regard to the first of these variables, Megargee (1977) hypothesized that age differences among the types should be apparent. Supporting this assumption is his speculation that his typology is dynamic; that is to say, an offender's type may change with maturity. Hence, different proportions of the various types should be present within various age groups. Although longitudinal research is required to document this supposition, the age differences noted among the state, male offender types supports Megargee's assumption. Conservative interpretation of these results, however, is suggested, since age differences among the types were found in only one of the three samples studied.

In regard to the current offense and misconduct data, this study's findings suggest that Megargee's typology successfully discriminates groups of offenders with discrete antisocial behavior patterns. Type Charlie offenders, for instance, seem to possess an extreme amount of interpersonal hostility that they display through violent crimes in the community and through verbal aggression while incarcerated. Deltas seems comparatively less violent than Type Charlies but present a management problem, since they commit the most infractions while incarcerated. In contrast, Types Baker, Easy, and Item seem to commit fewer violent crimes and fewer rule infractions than the other seven types. These findings provide further empirical support for Megargee's (1977) suggestion that the problems presented by the various types differ and require differing treatment/management approaches.

In summary, the current cross-validation effort was successful in demonstrating the applicability of the Megargee typology to both federal and state offenders. Further, this study served to further document the demographic differences among FCI types as well as to suggest the typology's predictive validity. Although the current study failed to explore demographic and behavioral characteristics of state prisoner types, hopefully, the positive findings reported here will encourage such research. Also it is hoped that the demographic and behavioral characteristics of federal and state female types will be investigated in future research. In view of this typology's practicality and empirical documentation, such studies, indeed, seem warranted.

References

Edinger, J. D., & Auerbach, S. M. Development and validation of a multidimensional multivariate model for accounting for infractionary behavior in a correctional setting. *Journal of Personality and Social Psychology*, 1978, *36*, 1472–1489.

Gibbons, D. C., & Garrity, D. L. Definition and analyses of certain criminal types. *Journal of Criminal Law, Criminology, and Police Science*, 1962, *53*, 27–35.

Glueck, S., & Glueck, E. *Physique and delinquency.* New York: Harper, 1956.

Hewitt, L. E., & Jenkins, R. L. *Fundamental patterns of maladjustment: The dynamics of their origin.* Springfield: Illinois State Printer, 1947.

Megargee, E. I. Direction for future research. *Criminal Justice and Behavior*, 1977, *4*, 211–216.

Megargee, E. I., & Bohn, M. J. Empirically determined characteristics of the ten types. *Criminal Justice and Behavior*, 1977, *4*, 149–210.

Megargee, E. I., & Dorhout, B. A new classification system for criminal offenders: Revision and refinement of the classification rules. *Criminal Justice and Behavior*, 1977, *4*, 125–148.

Meyer, J., Jr., & Megargee, E. I. A new classification system for criminal offenders: Initial development of the system. *Criminal Justice and Behavior*, 1977, *4*, 115–124.

Quay, H. C., & Parsons, L. B. *The differential behavior classification of the juvenile offender* (Tech. Rep.). Morgantown, W.Va.: Robert F. Kennedy Youth Center, 1970.

Roebuck, J. B. *Criminal typology.* Springfield, Ill.: Charles C Thomas, 1967.

Warren, M. Q., & Palmer, T. B. *Community treatment project: An evaluation of community treatment for delinquents* (Fourth Progress Rep.). Sacramento: State of California Department of Youth Authority, 1965.

Received April 18, 1978 ■

Jack Donald Edinger is Staff Psychologist in the Mental Health Division of the Federal Correctional Institution in Butner, North Carolina. His research interests are in clinical assessment, correctional programs, and treatment. He is the author of numerous articles on prisonization.

7

REPORT OF THE TASK FORCE ON THE ROLE OF PSYCHOLOGY IN THE CRIMINAL JUSTICE SYSTEM

APA TASK FORCE

ABSTRACT: *APA's Board of Social and Ethical Responsibility for Psychology (BSERP) commissioned a Task Force on the Role of Psychology in the Criminal Justice System to examine the ethical dilemmas faced by psychologists working with police, court, correctional, and juvenile justice agencies. In this final report, the task force makes 10 recommendations regarding the ethical practice of psychology in these areas. Both ethical issues that the criminal justice system creates for psychologists and those that psychologists create for the criminal justice system are addressed. Under the former rubric, questions of the psychologist's loyalty (e.g., confidentiality) and questions of the psychologist's competence (e.g., the effectiveness of services) are the most salient. The most controversial issue faced by the criminal justice system is the use of psychologists as decision makers in the confinement and release of individual offenders (e.g., indeterminate sentences).*

Psychologists are involved in virtually every facet of the criminal justice system. When a person is arrested, it may well be by a police officer who was screened by a psychologist before being hired and trained by other psychologists in ways of handling such potentially hazardous situations as an arrest. Should the police officer use undue force or poor judgment in effecting the arrest, the officer may be sent to the department's psychologist for treatment.

The defendant may then be evaluated by a psychologist to determine whether he or she is competent to stand trial before a jury that other psychologists are in the process of selecting. If competent, the defendant may be examined by a psychologist to determine whether he or she was insane at the time of the offense and so should be sent to a mental hospital for psychological treatment. At the trial, eyewitnesses to the crime may have their perceptions and memories challenged by a psychological expert. The fate of the convicted offender may rest in part on what a psychologist recommends to the judge in a presentence evaluation.

Should the offender be sent to prison, he or she may be classified by one psychologist for the purpose of being treated by another, and the treatment may not end until a third psychologist predicts that the offender can be released into society without risk of recidivism. Remaining free on parole may be contingent upon attendance at outpatient psychotherapy.

Encouraged by Presidential Commissions and supported by federal and foundation funds, a substantial increase in the involvement of psychologists in criminal justice work has occurred in the past decade along with an equally substantial increase in criminal justice and law as topics of in-

Members of the task force were John Monahan (Chair), Seymour Feshbach, William Holder, Ruth Arlene Howe, Nicholas Kittrie, Jane Loevinger, Leah McDonough, Sheldon Messinger, N. Dickon Reppucci, Kenneth Schoen, June Louin Tapp, and Richard Wasserstrom. Staff support was provided by Alan Gross of APA and Rachelle Hollander of the National Science Foundation (NSF).

This report was prepared with the support of National Science Foundation Grant Number OSS76-15832. However, any opinions, findings, conclusions or recommendations expressed herein are those of the authors and do not necessarily reflect views of the Foundation.

Although this report was approved by APA's Board of Social and Ethical Responsibility for Psychology in March 1978, it does not represent the official policy of the American Psychological Association. The entire report, including the commissioned background papers, will be published shortly in book form.

The task force wishes to acknowledge the many people who have assisted us during the two years of our deliberations. Richard Boone was instrumental as a member of BSERP in forming the task force. During its initial phase, Frank Ochberg served as a member of the group, and Fred Strassburger and Serena Stier provided APA staff assistance. The authors of the commissioned background papers (see Reference Notes 1–5) provided an excellent framing of the issues in their various areas. These papers were skillfully critiqued by the participants at our national workshops: Morton Bard, Terry Eisenberg, Patrick Murphy, Martin Reiser, Jerome Skolnick, Paul Lipsitt, Elizabeth Loftus, Richard Millstein, Paul Nejelski, Bruce Sales, Saleem Shah, Carolyn Suber, John Boone, Robert Levinson, and Jane Knitzer.

Requests for reprints should be sent to John Monahan, Program in Social Ecology, University of California, Irvine, California 92717.

terest for psychological research. Numerous recent works have chronicled and conceptualized the burgeoning interactions between the two areas (Brodsky, 1973; Konečni & Ebbesen, in press; Lipsitt & Sales, in press; Meehl, 1970; Monahan, 1976; Sales, 1977a, 1977b; Sarbin, in press; Tapp, 1976; Tapp & Levine, 1977; Toch, in press).

The Task Force

In late 1975, the Board of Social and Ethical Responsibility for Psychology was confronted with requests that it recommend official positions for the American Psychological Association on matters of criminal justice policy involving psychology. Rather than attempting to evaluate each proposal on an ad hoc basis, the Board commissioned a Task Force on the Role of Psychology in the Criminal Justice System to investigate comprehensively the complex ways in which psychologists are involved in the criminal justice system and the ethical issues raised by this involvement.

The task force was composed of 12 members representing psychology and other disciplines having varying perspectives on the criminal justice system and the roles of psychologists in it—law, criminology, social work, corrections, and philosophy—as well as a prisoner union representative.[1] The National Science Foundation's Ethics and Values in Science and Technology Program provided support for four meetings between February 1977 and January 1978 at which the task force members plus invited groups of psychologists and others working in police, court, correctional, and juvenile justice agencies considered prepared background papers (Mann, Note 1; Fersch, Note 2; Brodsky, Note 3; Rappaport, Lamiell, & Seidman, Note 4). In order to guide the selection of topics for debate and to present case material, a survey had been conducted of the 349 psychologists who responded on the 1975 APA Manpower Survey that the criminal justice system was their primary employment setting (Clingempeel, Mulvey, & Reppucci, Note 5).

What follows is our attempt to isolate the key ethical issues for psychologists in criminal justice work and to present recommendations on the ethical course that psychology, as a profession, should set in this area. A detailed summary of the roles occupied by psychologists in the various agencies of the criminal justice system and the myriad ethical quandaries encountered in performing them is beyond the scope of this report. The reader is urged to consult the comprehensive background reports commissioned by the task force.

A Preliminary Consideration

Before addressing ethical issues related to the role of the psychologist in the criminal justice system, we would like to stress a conclusion that became evident early in our deliberations: Many of the ethical issues facing psychologists in the criminal justice system are shared with psychologists working in any other organizational setting.

A principal role conflict and ethical dilemma of psychologists in criminal justice—to help the client, to further the "system," or to serve what they perceive to be the interests of society—is also a principal conflict of psychologists in educational, health, industrial, and governmental settings. The confidentiality of psychologists' records in prisons is no more, and no less, an ethical concern than the confidentiality of psychologists' records in schools, mental health agencies, insurance companies, and the military. The ethical questions of professional competence that arise when psychologists offer their services to screen police candidates are the same as those occasioned by the screening of applicants for the airlines or the Peace Corps.

However, there is a special urgency to address ethical problems in dealing with the criminal justice system, since that system has such a profound impact on the fundamental liberties of the people within its grasp. While other institutions, such as mental hospitals, also restrict individual freedom, the criminal justice system is the principal locus of legitimate force in American society. The consequences of its misapplication may be severe and irreversible. An additional reason for placing a high priority on ethical concerns in criminal justice is that the people processed by that system are likely to be poor or minorities and thus to have little access to conventional means for redressing their grievances.

What psychology appears to lack at the present time is an effective way to differentiate obligations owed to organizational as opposed to individual clients, of which dilemmas in criminal justice work

---

[1] While the large majority of the task force members had experience in working with the criminal justice system, most were primarily employed in academic settings. In retrospect, we would recommend that APA boards strive to achieve a greater balance between "academics" and "practitioners" in the appointment of future panels.

are only one example. Most of the ethical norms of the profession derive from situations in which an individual client freely contracts for services with a psychologist in private practice or voluntarily enters an experimenter–subject relationship. While such arrangements do indeed engender ethical difficulties, principally regarding the best interests of the client versus the broader social good, they fail to reflect the complexities that arise when an organizational third party makes competing claims on the psychologist's loyalty.

Consider the simple example of the psychologist in private practice whose client, in the course of therapy, reveals racist attitudes or behavior. The psychologist, depending upon his or her ethical convictions concerning the relevance of such attitudes or behavior to the appropriateness of continuing therapy with the client, may choose to ignore such attitudes or behavior as irrelevant to therapy, may attempt to alter them, or may, if he or she feels strongly enough, choose to terminate treatment or refer the client elsewhere. But under no conceivable circumstances would it be considered appropriate professional ethics if the psychologist—in furtherance of his or her view of the interests of society—informed the client's employer or wrote an exposé on the client's racism for the local newspaper.

Consider an alternate example. A psychologist working as a consultant to a law enforcement or educational organization discovers, in the course of his or her work, racist organizational policies—perhaps a pattern of discriminatory hiring or a biased application of sanctions. As in the previous example, the psychologist, depending upon his or her ethical convictions, may choose to ignore such behavior as irrelevant to the consultation, may attempt to alter it, or may, if he or she feels strongly enough, choose to terminate the consultation or refer the organization elsewhere. But would it *always* be inappropriate professional ethics for the psychologist to inform the organization's employer (e.g., the city council) or to write an exposé on the organization's racism for the local paper, as it would in the case of the individual client? Might there not be some limited number of severe cases where, all else failing, a "whistle-blowing" breach of confidentiality is the *only* appropriate ethical response, even though a "clear and imminent danger" of physical violence is not present?

We are not suggesting that psychologists should avoid serving in imperfect organizations, only that the perennial debate concerning whether it is better to work from the inside to achieve gradual change or to leave the organization and apply pressure from the outside for reform (Levinson, Note 6) is common to all organizational structures, not just justice system ones, and that such debates are not always enlightened by recourse to analogies based on the ethics of clinical practice. What is right for the psychologist's work with an individual may be wrong for the psychologist's work with an organization—any organization—and vice versa. The question in dealing with organizations is not, on reflection, so much "*Who* is the client?" but rather "*What* is a client?"—What ethical obligations are owed to an organizational, as opposed to an individual, purchaser of psychological services? It is a reflection on ethical issues such as these—how to differentiate the kinds of obligations owed to organizational and to individual clients and how to relate these obligations to the broader concern for human welfare—that the field of psychology currently lacks. Since it is our strong belief that psychologists in criminal justice settings are, as a whole, no less "ethical" than psychologists in other organizational settings (such as universities), we have no desire to single out criminal justice psychologists as scapegoats for the profession's ethical quandaries in dealing with organizations.

The Ethics of Psychology or the Ethics of Criminal Justice?

The charge of the task force was to consider the ethical issues that arise when psychologists work in the criminal justice system. It quickly became evident in our discussions that two related but clearly separable questions were being asked: What are the ethical issues confronting psychologists who work in criminal justice settings, and what are the ethical issues created for the criminal justice system by the presence of psychologists and the ideology that fosters their participation? Despite repeated attempts to remain focused on the former question, the task force found it impossible to consider the ethical dilemmas of the psychologist without repeated reference to the ethical dilemmas of the system in which they work. While recognizing that to address only the larger ethical questions of criminal justice would be insufficient at best and likely ill-advised, since psychologists have no special claim to be the arbiter of ethical issues in criminal justice, the task force concluded that to fail to address at least some of the broader social and ethical issues raised by the presence of psychologists in the criminal justice system would be an even worse failing. It would be to accept blindly the criminal justice system as it is presented to us—to accept without question the goals and nature of that system and their implications for the roles psychologists might be provided. We have chosen, therefore, not to accept such a "take it or leave it" dilemma in regard to the system. The fact that the roles currently open to psychologists in criminal justice are sanctioned by society and therefore "legal" is of only mild consolation, since it is obvious that what is legal can be immoral (e.g., human slavery was at one time legal in the United States) and what is illegal can be moral (e.g., helping persons who were slaves escape to freedom was at one time illegal in the United States) (Wasserstrom, 1963). Bittner (1970) has put it well in the context of the police:

The formulation of criteria for judging any kind of institutional practice, including the police, rather obviously calls for the solution of a logically prior problem. Clearly it is necessary that it be known *what* needs to be done before anyone can venture to say *how* it is to be done well. In the case of the police, this sets up the requirement of specifying the police role in society. (p. 2)

For psychologists to fail to consider the social context that frames their perceived ethical alternatives, we believe, unnecessarily limits the scope of ethical discourse and restricts the range of ethical response. To accept the criminal and juvenile justice systems on their own terms may be to settle for "first order," or cosmetic, change rather than "second order," or more fundamental, improvement in how we conceptualize the roles and ethics of psychologists (Watzlawick, Weakland & Fisch, 1974; Rappaport et al., Note 4).

We have, therefore, attempted to consider both the ethical issues that the criminal justice system creates for those psychologists who work in it as well as the ethical issues created for the criminal justice system by the assumptions that lead it to hire psychologists and employ them in certain roles. We intend our ethical recommendations to be interpreted not as immutable commandments but rather as guides to action and stimuli to provoke self-searching. Circumstances may arise that would justify exceptions from the general principles we offer. While none of us, for example, believes it ethically justifiable to kill political leaders with whom we disagree, just because we disagree with them, if we were colonels in the German Army in 1944, we hope we would have had the courage and the moral judgment to join in the plot to put an end to Hitler. Hard cases do not

make good law. In criminal justice, as elsewhere, an entire constellation of relevant factors must be taken into account before implementing a generally sound ethical principle in any given situation. We recognize that many dilemmas faced by psychologists in the criminal justice system involve clashes of values for which no completely satisfactory solution is possible. In such situations, people of equal integrity and commitment to moral values may arrive at conflicting courses of action. While wishing to promote intensive dialogue and debate on ethical issues, we urge that the self-righteous condemnation that sometimes passes for moral reasoning in this area be avoided.

Ethical Issues the Criminal Justice System Creates for Psychologists

QUESTIONS OF LOYALTY

RECOMMENDATION 1: *Psychologists in criminal justice settings, as elsewhere, should inform all parties to a given service of the level of confidentiality that applies and should specify any circumstances that would constitute an exception to confidentiality. This should be done in advance of the service, preferably in writing.*

RECOMMENDATION 2: *The ideal level of confidentiality of therapeutic services in criminal justice settings should be the same as the level of confidentiality that exists in voluntary noninstitutional settings.*

No question arises more frequently in discussions of the ethics of psychological intervention in the criminal justice system than "Who is the client?" Often the question is asked rhetorically, for any attempt to answer it is dismissed as a "value preference." Since questioning someone's values is viewed as akin to questioning his or her religion, the discussion often ends there. When psychologists do try seriously to articulate who their client is—where their loyalties are to be given—in criminal justice, they sometimes appear to be under the impression that they are constrained to a multiple-choice answer, with the alternatives being (a) the "system" (or "society") and (b) the offender (or police officer or defendant, as the case may be).

It appears to us that there is no need for psychologists to impale themselves on the horns of this dilemma, since "Who is the client?" is not a multiple-choice question. It requires an essay answer.

To us, *both* the offender (or the police officer, etc.) and the criminal justice system may be the clients of the psychologist working in the criminal justice system, but *in different roles and with varying priorities.* There are surely situations in which the psychologist cannot serve two masters, but it does not follow that allegiances must be invariant and that one must always have priority over the other.

In the role of a therapist providing treatment for an offender or a police officer who wants to change his or her behavior, the psychologist, we believe, primarily must be the agent of the individual. This would mean that therapy should only be given on a truly voluntary basis and that it should not be used as a means to pursue administrative ends, such as release or promotion decisions. This is a question of priority rather than an absolute prescription, since in a limited number of defined situations, allegiances may be reordered, such as when information is presented in therapy that a life-threatening act is imminent.

There are other roles in which the criminal justice system may be the psychologist's primary client. Psychological assessments performed for the purpose of selecting police officers and prison guards are the clearest examples. The psychologist's primary goal here is not to assure that applicants achieve their greatest life potential, but rather to help the system improve its odds in choosing those candidates with the highest probability of being able to fulfill job demands.

One psychologist, for example, who works with a large metropolitan police department maintains strict confidentiality concerning the content of therapy sessions with police officers when they themselves initiate the request for help. The psychologist, in this situation, takes the individual officer as his primary client. If, however, an officer is referred by the administration of the police department for treatment of a problem interfering with his or her job, and the department inquires about the progress of treatment, the psychologist may reveal information gained in therapy. In these situations, the psychologist takes the agency as his primary client. Further, the psychologist clearly informs the officer when each of these contingencies apply (Reiser, 1972).

Likewise, a recent report commissioned by the Federal Bureau of Prisons' Executive Staff is generally supportive of a high degree of confidentiality in the limited situations in which it is believed appropriate for psychologists to conduct psychotherapy with prison staff members. Yet the report clearly specifies that there is one situation in which the priorities of allegiance can be reversed: "The responsibility [of psychologists] to keep the Warden advised of staff problems which may affect the overall security of the institution must override keeping staff statements confidential" (Federal Bureau of Prisons, Note 7).

As these two examples indicate, the question of where the psychologist's loyalties lie centers most often on concerns for the confidentiality of information obtained by the psychologist. Fully three out of four of the criminal justice psychologists surveyed by the task force reported that one of the major ethical issues they face concerned confidentiality (Clingempeel et al., Note 5).

While confidentiality dilemmas—which we see as only one manifestation of the larger issue of the psychologist's loyalties—are acute in the criminal justice system, they appear to be a growing concern to all psychologists who engage in treatment. In a far-reaching and bitterly contested decision, the California Supreme Court recently ruled that

public policy favoring protection of the confidential character of patient-psychotherapeutic communication must yield in instances in which disclosure is essential to avert danger to others. The protective privilege ends where the public peril begins.[2]

Some psychologists have interpreted this decision as driving a stake into the heart of psychology. Siegel (1977), for example, has argued that there are no circumstances that ethically can justify the breaking of confidentiality:

When we agree to "exceptional circumstances" under which the confidentiality of information about individuals is waived, we not only violate the civil rights of children and adults, but we violate our essential role as psychologists. (p. 2)

Shah (1977), on the other hand, while agreeing with the importance of confidentiality in psychological practice, does not view specific exceptions to it as necessarily lethal to psychology:

Some clinicians are utterly convinced that therapeutic confidentiality must remain an *absolute* and paramount value over all other societal interests. Such ethnocentric zeal seems to demand that the entire society should accept the value and ideologies of psychotherapists. In other words, what is good for psychotherapists is good for society! (p. 2, emphasis in original).

---

[2] Tarasoff v. Regents of the University of California, Sup. 131 Cal. Rptr. 14 (1976).

The view of the task force is closer to that of Shah (1977) than to that of Siegel (1977). We would note that the APA *Ethical Standards of Psychologists* (1963) have always allowed for an exception to confidentiality "when there is clear and imminent danger to an individual or to society" (Principle 6, p. 4). Surely the psychological assessment of candidates for police and prison work would be meaningless without some "feedback" to the potential employer. In the case of psychological treatment undertaken in criminal justice contexts (whether with prisoner or staff), we would take as a goal that the same standards of confidentiality should apply in criminal justice settings as apply in "free-world," privately contracted therapy—no less, but no more. This would mean that information obtained in treatment not be released without client consent (as a privately contracting client can request to have information revealed to an insurance company). It would also mean that the same specific exceptions to confidentiality in "free-world" settings can apply to confidentiality in criminal justice settings, namely, when knowledge of a "clear and imminent danger" (e.g., a prison riot) is volunteered.

One crucial point in addressing confidentiality, as in addressing other dilemmas of the psychologist's loyalty, is that all parties with a claim on the psychologist's loyalty be fully informed in advance of the existence of confidentiality, or lack of it, and of any circumstances that may trigger an exception to the agreed-upon priorities. The individual being evaluated or treated then has the option of deciding what information to reveal and what risks to confidentiality he or she wishes to bear.

We recognize that many psychologists feel strongly that absolute confidentiality is a prerequisite to the provision of ethical and effective psychological treatment, and at the same time that the pressures to violate confidentiality are extreme and constant in many criminal justice settings. Given the intensity of these feelings regarding confidentiality on the part of many psychologists and the strength of the opposing pressures on the part of the criminal justice system, psychologists would do well to make themselves aware of and come to terms with agency policies on confidentiality before accepting employment in a criminal justice setting.

In a basic sense, confidentiality is a right not so much of the psychologist but of the client. As with release of information to third parties, the pressure to violate the client's "right to know" what is being said about him or her is great in the criminal justice system. While the issue of client access to psychological records is a complex one that is raised in many settings, we believe that, as a minimum, there should be a general presumption that formal psychological reports made to criminal justice agencies be available to the individuals who are subjects of the reports.

RECOMMENDATION *3: Other than for legitimate research purposes, psychological assessments of offenders should be performed only when the psychologist has a reasonable expectation that such assessments will serve a useful therapeutic or dispositional function.*

At the risk of appearing naive, the task force believes that there may be situations in criminal justice work in which the above kinds of conflict among priorities of loyalty do not arise. The psychologist sometimes may be able to serve several masters without slighting any. Training police officers in psychological techniques for nonviolent conflict resolution (Bard, 1969; Driscoll, Meyer, & Schanie, 1973; Novaco, 1977) may be one such situation. To the extent that the techniques are effective, all "clients" of the psychologist—the police officers, the police agency, and the larger society—are better off.

Unfortunately, there is another category of situations where conflicts of loyalty do not arise. Here, however, it is not because the psychologist is serving many masters but because he or she is serving none. The survey conducted by the task force revealed a substantial number of psychologists who were dismayed by their assignment to administer endless batteries of tests to prisoners to assess their suitability for treatment programs, when in fact no treatment programs existed or were likely to. As Corsini (1956) has noted,

correctional psychology is in a chronic state of stagnation, well illustrated by excessive over-emphasis on psychological testing—most of which is either not used or misused. The operation of testing becomes an end in itself: numbers go into folders and there are decently interred. (p. 22)

Brodsky (Note 3), 20 years later, similarly has observed,

When they exist for their own sake, such psychological assessment can be ritualistic and pointless. In [prison] reception and diagnostic centers, these assessments have been described as boring, repetitive and frustrating to the staff, an Edsel-like flop for the system and a disservice and waste of resources for all involved. (p. 7)

Such assessment-without-disposition functions,

when not done for legitimate research purposes (see Recommendation 8), constitute an unethical intrusion into the lives of offenders and an unprofessional squandering of limited psychological resources and limited public funds. Perhaps most objectionably, they give the illusion that psychological services are being provided to offenders and thus serve to legitimate aspects of the criminal justice system that are in serious need of reform.

The answer to the question of where the loyalties of the psychologist in the criminal justice system should be placed, therefore, is a complex one. It depends upon the specific role of the psychologist under consideration, and specified situations may arise within each role that can reorder priorities. It is the precise delineation of these roles and situations, and their unambiguous communication in advance to the various "clients" of the psychologist in the criminal justice system, that is the thrust of our ethical recommendations.

QUESTIONS OF COMPETENCE

RECOMMENDATION 4: *Psychologists who work in the criminal justice system, as elsewhere, have an ethical obligation to educate themselves in the concepts and operations of the system in which they work.*

"Psychologists," according to the 1977 APA *Ethical Standards of Psychologists*, "recognize the boundaries of their competence and the limitations of their techniques" (p. 2). This is essentially a consumer-protection principle with which it is difficult to take issue. As with other products, it is in establishing the precise boundaries and limitations of a psychologist's service that disagreements arise.

"Competence" is not so much a characteristic of the psychologist, in the sense of having the appropriate degrees or license, but rather an interaction between the abilities of the psychologist and the demands of a given setting. A psychologist may be competent in one setting and incompetent in others. A prerequisite to the development of competence in any setting is a thorough knowledge of the system in which the psychologist is operating.

Perhaps the criminal justice system more than other organizations presents an initial challenge to the competence of the psychologist who would work in it. That challenge takes the form of knowing what the system is and how it operates. While all psychologists have been in schools and

many have some acquaintance with the mental health system, their prior interaction with criminal justice often does not go beyond receiving a traffic ticket. Legal education generally is not part of the education of a psychologist, and confusion on the part of mental health professionals in court concerning basic concepts of criminal law appears to be common (McGarry et al., 1973). Given that the decisions made in the criminal justice system on the basis of psychological reports and testimony are so often fateful for the individuals involved, ignorance of relevant legal concepts and the organizational context in which they operate is particularly distressing. Shah (1975) has put it forcefully:

[Psychologists and others] who work in forensic or legal settings, or those who choose to function in situations requiring involvement with the legal system, have a clear and definite responsibility to become properly informed about the relevant legal issues, questions, and criteria pertaining to their roles and functions. It is quite presumptuous, to put it mildly, for mental health and medical professionals to render opinions and recommendations on issues of pretrial competency, criminal responsibility, involuntary civil commitment, sexual psychopathy, and the like, when the relevant legal issues and criteria are not properly understood. Acquiring a sound and accurate understanding of the relevant issues must be viewed as a' *professional and ethical requirement.* (p. ix, emphasis in original)

RECOMMENDATION 5: *Since it is not within the professional competence of psychologists to offer conclusions on matters of law, psychologists should resist pressure to offer such conclusions.*

Those who attempt to educate themselves in criminal justice will soon discover, among other things, that a recurrent criticism of psychologists and other mental health professionals in the courtroom is that they render conclusions that are more properly within the province of the judge or the jury. Psychological testimony, the criticism goes, is often an imposition of the psychologist's personal value preferences into moral or policy issues more appropriately left to other decision makers in a democratic society (Morse, 1978).

A psychologist who, for example, offered the opinion that a given person had a certain probability of committing certain criminal acts in a specified time period, would be making a *professional* or *scientific statement* (although it would likely be grossly inaccurate—see below). However, a psychologist who simply offered that an individual was "too dangerous to be released" would be making a legal or social value statement. The psychologist would be imposing his or her values as to the degree of risk society should bear in releasing the individual. Other examples could be found in the areas of the insanity defense and incompetence to stand trial. We would note that often it is not that the psychologist volunteers such conclusive statements, but that the courts, in an attempt to evade their responsibility to deal with difficult issues, pressure psychologists to answer legal questions for them.

RECOMMENDATION 6: *Psychologists should be clear about what they are trying to accomplish in the criminal justice system and the state of the empirical evidence in support of their ability to accomplish it.*

The history of research in psychotherapy has shown that it is fruitless to attempt to assess the global competence or effectiveness of psychologists in treating psychological disorder. The question needs to be much more task-specific: *How* competent are *which* psychologists at treating *which* people for *what* problems? Likewise, one cannot address the issue of the competence of psychologists in the criminal justice system without specifying the range of tasks on which competence is to be measured.

A close reading of recent literature on the effectiveness of psychological services in criminal justice settings reveals that (a) for some tasks the research is moderately encouraging (e.g., some forms of police training, restoration of defendants for competency to stand trial), (b) for other tasks the research is discouraging (e.g., the prediction and treatment of violent criminal behavior—see below), and (c) for the great majority of tasks there are no data at all.

If one accepts this assessment of the state of the art of empirical research on the competence of psychologists in the criminal justice system, one is not led to throw in the professional towel, since practice has preceded progress in virtually all areas of psychology (and medicine as well). But one *is* led to be exceedingly modest in how psychological services are "promoted" in criminal justice. "Caveat emptor" has long ago given way to "truth in advertising" in other areas, and the need for frankness in representing the effectiveness of psychological services in criminal justice appears to be acute.

Note that we are not recommending that "unproven" or novel programs be abandoned. To do so would be to put the criminal justice psychologist in a classic Catch-22 situation: A program

cannot be documented until it is initiated and cannot be initiated until it is documented. We are recommending frankness and an avoidance of "oversell." If a service has not been adequately researched in the past, it should not be represented as "effective." Rather, the psychologist should inform the police chief, judge, warden, or offender to the effect that "Here is what I would like to do and what I hope it would accomplish. There are theoretical reasons why I think it could be effective, but there has been no good research on the topic, so I cannot be sure. Shall we give it a try and evaluate the results?"

RECOMMENDATION 7: *There is an ethical obligation on psychologists who perform services in the criminal justice system, as elsewhere, to encourage and cooperate in the evaluation of those services.*

Frankness about the limitations of knowledge concerning psychological services in the criminal justice system must be augmented by a commitment to develop that knowledge wherever possible. We do not see empirical research in criminal justice as a luxury to be indulged in after the psychologist's "service" activities are completed. Rather, we see the empirical evaluation of psychological services in the criminal justice system as an *ethical necessity* for the profession. We do not underestimate the formidable methodological difficulties and bureaucratic hurdles confronting the would-be evaluator. We also realize that psychologists are most often hired by criminal justice agencies to provide services, not to perform research. Yet it is worth the effort to climb the ladder of methodological sophistication even if one does not reach the top rung. Much can be learned from nonrandomized designs, and there have been some successful efforts at controlled evaluations of psychological services in criminal justice settings (Kassebaum, Ward, & Wilner, 1971; cf. Quay, 1977). Research provides us with the only way of validating the competence of the psychologist in criminal justice through alerting us to those areas in which psychological services are effective. It provides the empirical basis for making informed ethical decisions on the roles psychologists should assume.

RECOMMENDATION 8: *Psychological research in prisons should conform to the ethical standards proposed by the National Commission for the Protection of Human Subjects.*

Psychologists in the criminal justice system may sometimes feel that, regarding research, they are damned if they do and damned if they don't: condemned as "having something to hide" if they fail to pursue vigorously the evaluation of their services and vilified as turning prisoners into "guinea pigs" as soon as they ask people to fill out a form. It is our belief not only that the pursuit of empirical knowledge regarding psychological services in criminal justice is an ethical necessity for the profession of psychology but that it is ethically possible to obtain such knowledge.

The ethics of research in criminal justice settings is an area that has attracted a great deal of scholarly attention (Bloomberg & Wilkins, 1977). Fortunately, we can benefit from the intensive review and recommendations regarding prison research—and it is in prisons that most criminal justice research by psychologists takes place—recently published by the National Commission for the Protection of Human Subjects of Biomedical and Behavioral Research (1977).

The National Commission identified three broad categories of research in prisons. The first category is one in which research is conducted in the hope of improving institutional or program effectiveness. This would include research on psychological treatments that have "the intent or reasonable probability of improving the health or wellbeing of the individual prisoner" (p. 3080). The second category is one in which the research is inherently related to confined persons but does not have the purpose of benefiting the prisoners, such as research on the psychological makeup of prisoners or "studies of the possible causes, effects and processes of incarceration and studies of prisons as institutional structures or of prisoners as incarcerated persons" (p. 3080). The final category consists of research that uses prisoners as subjects because they are available but does not particularly relate to their status as prisoners—for example research that uses prisoners as subjects for psychopharmaceutical testing.

The National Commission recommended that research whose purpose is to benefit prisoners be allowed only if it is

reviewed by at least one human subjects review committee or institutional review board comprised of men and women of diverse racial and cultural backgrounds that includes among its members prisoners or prisoner advocates and such other persons as community representatives, clergy, behavioral scientists and medical personnel not associated with the research or the penal institution. (p. 3081)

The review committee should consider the risks involved in the research, the provision for ob-

taining genuinely informed consent, safeguards for confidentiality, and other concerns. Parole boards should not take into account prisoners' participation in research.

Research in the second category—related to prisoners but nonbeneficial in intent—is to be conducted only if the above review board approves it and, in addition, only if the studies are such that "they present minimal or no risk and no more than mere inconvenience to the subjects" (p. 3080).

Research in the third category—research on prisoners because they are "there"—is to be conducted only if the above review board approves it and if three additional requirements are satisfied: (a) The research must fill an "important social and scientific need," (b) it must "satisfy conditions of equity," and (c) it must be characterized by "a high degree of voluntariness" on the part of the prisoner. The conditions necessary to infer this voluntariness include uncensored communication to persons outside the prison, a grievance committee composed of elected prisoners, and 17 detailed standards of living in prison, including adequate food, recreation, and living space, a prison staff adequate to provide for inmates' safety, work opportunities that pay the same as the research, and "adequate mental health services and professional staff" (p. 3080).

In approving research of this type, the National Commission noted studies such as that of the University of Michigan's Survey Research Center (Tannenbaum & Cooke, 1976), which found that 80% of the prisoner-subjects interviewed expressed strong support for giving prisoners the option to participate in research. As Brodsky (Note 3) notes, "If these same individuals were free research subjects, it is possible that their evaluations would be more negative." Likewise, one can question the sufficiency of the living standards that the National Commission proposed to assure voluntary participation. For example, some of the task force hold that conjugal visits should be considered a minimal standard of prison life.[3]

In general, the task force believes that the recommendations of the National Commission repre-

---

[3] It should be noted that the Proposed Regulations on Research Involving Prisoners, which is the government's response to the National Commission, would prohibit Department of Health, Education and Welfare funding of any research in this third category (*Federal Register,* January 5, 1978, p. 1053).

sent a significant advance in the protection of prisoners and in the conduct of ethical research by psychologists and others in prisons. We urge psychologists to read and conform to these recommendations.

Ethical Issues Psychologists Create for the Criminal Justice System

RECOMMENDATION 9: *Psychologists should be exceedingly cautious in offering predictions of criminal behavior for use in imprisoning or releasing individual offenders. If a psychologist decides that it is appropriate in a given case to provide a prediction of criminal behavior, he or she should clearly specify (a) the acts being predicted, (b) the estimated probability that these acts will occur during a given time period, and (c) the factors on which the predictive judgment is based.*

The task force considered in detail only one general issue created for the criminal justice system by the presence of psychologists and the assumptions that guide their current role assignments. That issue concerns the nature of imprisonment and the judicial procedures for determining its severity. While, ideally, we would like to have dealt in similar detail with other system-level issues related to psychology, such as the function of the police or the role of psychological factors in the determination of guilt, considerations of time and resources precluded our doing so. Our choice was guided by the fact that the majority (70%) of psychologists working in the criminal justice system are working in correctional institutions and that significant developments in how prisons are to be conceptualized are now taking place across the nation.

On the one hand, there are those who believe that the rehabilitation of offenders through psychological and vocational treatment is a principal justification for imprisonment (Clark, 1970). Advocates of this model see psychologists and other mental health professionals as having a significant role in humanizing prisons and moderating excesses of retributive punishment. They also believe that the diagnostic and therapeutic skills of psychologists can serve important utilitarian functions by protecting society from the release of dangerous persons and by helping offenders overcome antisocial propensities. Indeterminate sentences, to be terminated in part on the basis of psychological reports, are a major component of this model.

On the other hand are those who see the presence of psychologists in decision-making roles in prisons as preventing more basic reform. Psychologists in prisons, according to this view, serve the latent function of legitimizing an "offender-blame" (Ryan, 1971) or individual pathology model of crime that diverts attention from social system factors influencing criminal behavior. Also, by virtue of their scientific and objective image, psychologists unwittingly have usurped or have allowed themselves to be co-opted into making social value decisions, such as how "safe" an offender should be before he or she is released, which more properly should be left to the political and judicial processes (see Recommendation 5 above). Judge David Bazelon (1973) expressed this position to a conference of correctional psychologists:

Instead of facing up to the true dimensions of the problem and society's social and economic structure, we prefer to blame the problem on a criminal class—a group of sick persons who must be treated by doctors and cured. Why should we even consider fundamental social changes or massive income redistribution if the entire problem can be solved by having scientists teach the criminal class—like a group of laboratory rats—to march successfully through the maze of our society? In short, before you respond with enthusiasm to our plea for help, you must ask yourselves whether your help is really needed, or whether you are merely engaged as magicians to perform an intriguing side-show so that the spectators will not notice the crisis in the center ring. In considering our motives for offering you a role, I think you would do well to consider how much less expensive it is to hire a thousand psychologists than to make even a miniscule change in the social and economic structure. (p. 152)

The task force believes that either of these two models, if taken to the extreme, is simplistic. A single-minded focus on changing the behavior of individual offenders can indeed blind us to larger ethical questions of social justice. But one need not perfect the world, or even the criminal justice system, to provide services to individual offenders.

The model of imprisonment that the majority of the task force believes is most conducive to the ethical use of psychologists is the "just-deserts" model (Fogel, 1975, Morris, 1974; Twentieth Century Fund, 1976; von Hirsch, 1976; von Hirsch & Hanrahan, in press). In brief, this perspective holds that the amount of punishment given to an offender, usually operationalized by the length of a prison sentence, must be limited to that which the community believes the offender "justly deserves." It should not be extended beyond that limit by utilitarian considerations such as whether or not an offender needs psychological "rehabilitation" or is predicted to be "dangerous." The principle establishing the upper limit for incarceration is thus an explicitly normative and moral judgment of relative harm and culpability for past behavior, rather than an assessment of relative social risk or the potential for changing behavior in the future. As Norval Morris (1974) has succinctly put it, "Power over a criminal's life should not be taken in excess of that which would be taken were his reform not considered as one of our purposes."

Whether due to outcries of prisoners and prisoner advocates (e.g., American Friends Service Committee, 1971; Mitford, 1973) that "rehabilitation" in prisons often resembles an Orwellian nightmare, or to the research on the lack of effectiveness of prison treatment (e.g., Greenberg, 1977; Martinson, 1974) and the lack of validity of predictions of dangerous criminal behavior (Monahan, 1978), there has been a substantial swing from the "rehabilitative ideal" to "just deserts" in the past few years. Many states and the proposed Federal Criminal Code Reform Act of 1979 are adopting versions of determinate sentencing statutes that eliminate or restrict parole boards and the psychological predictions that feed into them and substitute "presumptive" sentences, in which, for example, every second-offense rapist judged to be similarly culpable receives a similar sentence, regardless of his assumed potential for rehabilitation.

While one can question the extent to which the rehabilitative ideal has been seriously implemented (there are currently fewer than 100 psychologists in the entire Federal Bureau of Prisons, with approximately 30,000 inmates) and the widely accepted conclusion that "nothing works" in prison treatment (cf. Halleck & Witte, 1977; Palmer, 1975; Quay, 1977), we believe that it would be unwise for psychologists to oppose the redefinition of their roles implied by the just-deserts model. The just-deserts model is not without its conceptual difficulties (e.g., How does one arrive at a "just" sentences for a given crime?—Cederblom & Blizek, 1977) or its own ethical quandaries, for "as long as a substantial segment of the population is denied adequate opportunities for a livelihood, any scheme for punishing must be morally flawed" (von Hirsch, 1976, p. 149). And it is surely not lacking the potential for demagogic abuse by those who literally wish to "throw away the key" on offenders. Nonetheless, the just-deserts model appears to us to be "less unacceptable than any

other which can be considered at this time" (Wilkins, 1976, p. 178). It is neither antiscientific nor antipsychological. While it will not ameliorate the horrendous human degradation that is part of many prisons—and *nothing* an offender has done could "deserve" the physical and sexual violence rampant in American "correctional" institutions—it has the important virtue of placing an upper limit on the power of the state to expose persons to such conditions. If it does preclude psychologists from participating in some of their traditional roles in prisons (i.e., release decisions), it more than compensates, in our view, by increasing the fairness of the criminal justice system as a whole and by removing many of the stumbling blocks to the ethical provision of truly voluntary psychological services.[4]

We reject the argument that "somebody has to make predictions" in determining sentence length and that these predictions necessarily will be made at an even lower level of validity—or a higher level of bias—if psychologists "abdicate" their roles as predictors of future crime (Rappaport et al., Note 4). While that is a risk with which psychologists should be concerned, it is also possible that nobody will make such predictions or, at the very least, that predictions for the purpose of incarceration will be made on the basis of actuarial variables that are both open to judicial and public review as well as specifically keyed to the offender's criminal history (Gottfredson, Wilkins, & Hoffman, 1978). The criminal justice system, thus deprived of the opportunity to launder difficult ethical and policy questions as matters of scientific acumen, may begin to confront more honestly the value premises on which it goes about imposing prison sentences. As Watzlawick, Weakland, and Fisch (1974) have stated,

Whether the setting is a maximum-security prison or merely Juvenile Hall, the paradox is the same: the degree to which the offender has supposedly been reformed by these institutions is judged on the basis of his saying and doing the right things because he has been reformed, and not because he has merely learned to speak the right language and to go through the right motions. Reform when seen as something different from compliance, inevitably becomes self-reflective—it is then supposed to be both its own cause and its own effect. This game is

---

[4] The just-deserts model has other implications for the practice of psychotherapy in prisons. If, for example, sentences were set before incarceration began and could not be extended by therapeutic considerations, it would be incumbent upon the psychologist to attend more carefully to constructing a time-limited program of treatment.

won by the "good actors": the only losers are those inmates who refuse to be reformed because they are too
honest or angry to play the game; or those who allow it
to be apparent that they are playing the game only because they want to get out, and are therefore not acting
spontaneously. Humaneness thus creates its own hypo-
crisies, which lead to the melancholy conclusion that in
this specific sense it seems preferable to establish a price
to be paid for an offense, i.e., a punishment, but to leave
the offender's mind alone and thereby avoid the troublesome consequences of mind-control paradoxes. (p. 69)

It is important to note that we take this position more for ethical than empirical reasons. It
does appear from reading the research that the
validity of psychological predictions of violent behavior, at least in the sentencing and release situations we are considering, is extremely poor, so
poor that one could oppose their use on the strictly
empirical grounds that psychologists are not professionally competent to make such judgments.
An analogous conclusion was reached by a task
force of the American Psychiatric Association
(1974): "Neither psychiatrists nor anyone else
have reliably demonstrated an ability to predict
future violence or 'dangerousness.' Neither has
any special psychiatric 'expertise' in this area been
established" (p. 20).

Our position goes further. We hold that even
in the unlikely event that substantial improvements in the prediction of criminal behavior were
documented, there would still be reason to question the ethical appropriateness of extending an
offender's confinement beyond the limits of what
he or she morally "deserves" in order to achieve
a utilitarian gain in public safety.

It is clear, however, that there are no facile answers to this most difficult question of public
policy and professional ethics, especially when one
takes into account "justice" to the potential victims of violent crime, who, like their offenders
and unlike the legislators, judges, and psychologists making decisions in the criminal justice system, are often poor and nonwhite (Shah, 1978).
Likewise, the complexity of accomplishing change
in an organization as large and diffuse as the criminal justice system militated against the task force's
taking a more absolute stand on the question of
psychological predictions of criminal behavior. In
those situations where the realistic alternative to
distinguishing among offenders on predictive
grounds is a draconian sentence uniformly given
to all offenders, it is not clear to us that offering
such predictions is, on balance, always ethically
inappropriate. Nor is there agreement on whether
predictive considerations should play a role in

decisions regarding the release of certain classes of
offenders (e.g., offenders with psychological disorders) from prison to community treatment to
serve the length of their sentences.

While there is broad agreement within the task
force, therefore, that psychological predictions
should not be used to extend an offender's confinement beyond the degree "justly deserved,"
there is disagreement as to whether periods of confinement should be liable to reduction on the
basis of a psychologist's assessment. At a minimum, we urge psychologists to exercise extreme
caution in making predictive judgments, particularly given the history of abuse of such judgments
by the criminal justice system in the past, and to
do so only after considering the broad range of
ethical issues alluded to above.

RECOMMENDATION 10: *Psychologists should be
strongly encouraged to offer treatment services to
offenders who request them.*

What, then, is our position on the ethical context in which prison treatment should occur?
Much has already been implied. We clearly see
no incompatibility between abandoning rehabilitation as the *purpose* of imprisonment and maintaining vigorous rehabilitation programs in prison.
In the context of justly punishing people for what
they have done in the past, we would provide them
with ample psychological resources to aid in changing their behavior for the future and for coping
with their present psychological pains.

As Morris and Hawkins (1977) have recently
put it,

The cage is not a sensible place in which to cure the
criminal, even when the medical analogy makes sense,
which it rarely does. But this does *not* mean that such
treatment programs as we now have in prisons should be
abandoned; quite the contrary, they urgently need expansion. No one of any sensitivity can visit any of our
mega-prisons without recognizing that they contain as in
all countries, populations that are disproportionately il-
literate, unemployed, vocationally untrained, undereduc-
cated, psychologically disturbed, and socially isolated. It
is both in the prisoners' and in the community's best interest to help them to remedy these deficiencies. (p. 67)

Various organizational strategies—for example,
contracting with private therapists for prison treatment or having independent lines of authority for
prison psychologists—may facilitate the provision
of services in a manner consonant with our previous recommendations. We note that Principal 6d
of the 1977 *Ethical Standards of Psychologists*
states that "Psychologists willingly contribute a
portion of their services to work for which they

receive little or no financial return" (p. 5). Prisons would appear an ideal place for psychologists to perform their "pro bono" activity.

Implementing Task Force Recommendations

The recommendations of the task force mentioned so far have dealt with substantive issues regarding the role of psychology in the criminal justice system. We conclude by suggesting several concrete steps the APA might take toward implementing the recommendations we have put forward and toward continuing professional debate on the issues we have addressed.

RECOMMENDATION 11: *The American Psychological Association should strongly encourage graduate and continuing education in the applied ethics of psychological intervention and research.*

While there has been a substantial increase in recent years in the literature on the ethical aspects of psychological intervention and research (Bermant, Kelman, & Warwick, in press; Tapp, Kelman, Triandis, Wrightsman, & Coelho, 1974), this writing has yet to become part of the "mainstream" of psychological education and generally is treated as something the practitioner or researcher will "pick up" as he or she encounters ethical dilemmas. Yet moral crises are better prepared for than reacted to. Troublesome moral issues may be commonplace in criminal justice work, but they also are increasingly present in many forms of psychological research involving human subjects, in all of involuntary hospitalization, and in much of voluntary outpatient treatment, especially in dealing with children, violent persons, the poor, or minorities. The initial problem is not so much *how* these ethical issues are ultimately resolved, but rather that psychologists be prepared to reason them through in a careful manner. This means trying to identify the relevant considerations that may be involved, examining with care the empirical and normative arguments that apply to these considerations and their application to particular cases, and then attempting to assess what—all things considered—is the morally right thing to do.

In the wake of the poverty of moral reasoning ability demonstrated by many attorneys in the Watergate scandal, the American Bar Association in 1974 voted to make a course in professional ethics required in every law school. Rather than waiting for a moral Watergate to occur in psychology, we should see that professional education in applied ethics becomes a part of the curriculum in every graduate program. This might go far to sensitize neophyte psychologists to ethical issues generally, and especially to those issues involved in organizational work, and to carry on the debates begun in this task force and in other groups concerned with ethical problems (e.g., the APA Task Force on Behavior Modification).

There are several ways that APA might take the lead in fostering an awareness of ethical issues. In those areas of psychology in which APA "approves" a graduate program, the Association might make such approval contingent upon the offering or requirement of a course in applied psychological ethics. State licensing boards could be encouraged to reflect ethical reasoning in their examinations, and continuing education programs could likewise place an emphasis upon ethical issues. APA could develop model curricula, background materials, and casebooks for various types of courses in applied ethics, all of which could reflect in part the complexities engendered by work in organizational settings such as criminal justice. The involvement of philosophers and others with interests in applied ethics, as well as practitioners and researchers who have confronted the issues firsthand, should be encouraged.

RECOMMENDATION 12: *The American Psychological Association should take steps to increase awareness among psychologists and those with whom they work of mechanisms to investigate and act upon complaints of violations of its Ethical Standards. Formal advisory opinions should continue to be offered to psychologists requesting an interpretation of the Ethical Standards in specific fact situations.*

To carry out the recommendations of this and similar groups, it appears essential for APA to investigate and take action upon (a) complaints of individuals or organizations that psychologists are violating the Ethical Standards, and (b) complaints by psychologists of unethical behavior on the part of their employers. Before the Association can make such investigations and take such action, however, it must be made aware of those cases that raise ethical difficulty. In the years 1975 through 1977, the Committee on Scientific and Professional Ethics and Conduct—the APA group that deals with complaints of unethical behavior filed against psychologists—handled an average of 80 cases per year. Some of these cases were more violations of professional etiquette (e.g., violations of advertising restrictions) than of professional ethics. Only one case referred to the Committee in this entire 3-year period concerned a psychologist working in the criminal justice system. Likewise, the Committee on Academic Freedom and Conditions of Employment—the APA group that deals with complaints of unethical behavior filed by psychologists against their employers—has handled an average of approximately 30 cases per year for the past 3 years. Only seven cases during this period have been filed by a psychologist against a criminal justice agency. This is in spite of the fact that 82% of the psychologists employed by the criminal justice system who were surveyed by the task force reported personally encountering ethical problems in their work (Clingempeel .et al., Note 5). It appears that much more must be done to make psychologists and those they work with aware of the existence of mechanisms to redress ethical grievances.

Perhaps more important than after-the-fact enforcement of sanctions against those who violate the Ethical Standards, the APA should strengthen its proactive capacity to offer advice and consultation to psychologists who are at ethical choice points. The Association already offers advisory opinions on ethical issues when asked to do so, but its ability to respond quickly to a psychologist's request for an interpretation of the Ethical Standards in a specific fact situation is hampered by a lack of staff resources and the absence of networks of expert consultants in specialized areas (e.g., criminal justice, education) who could offer prompt "peer review" of the ethical implications of a proposed course of action.

As a sign of its commitment to its own Ethical Standards and to taking seriously the work of groups such as this Task Force, APA might begin the upgrading of its educational, enforcement, and advisory responsibilities in the area of applied ethics with all deliberate speed.

REFERENCE NOTES

1. Mann, P. *Ethical issues for psychologists in the law enforcement system.* Report to the APA Task Force on Psychology and Criminal Justice, 1978.
2. Fersch, E. *Ethical issues for psychologists in court settings.* Report to the APA Task Force on Psychology and Criminal Justice, 1978.
3. Brodsky, S. *Ethical issues for psychologists in corrections.* Report to the APA Task Force on Psychology and Criminal Justice, 1978.

4. Rappaport, J., Lamiell, J., & Seidman, E. *Ethical issues for psychologists in the juvenile justice system.* Report to the APA Task Force on Psychology and Criminal Justice, 1978.
5. Clingempeel, G., Mulvey, E., & Reppucci, N. *Ethical dilemmas of psychologists in the criminal justice system.* Report to the APA Task Force on Psychology and Criminal Justice, 1978.
6. Levinson, R. *Changing correctional systems: Influencing change from the "inside."* Paper presented at the Alabama Symposium on Justice and the Behavioral Sciences, Center for Correctional Psychology, University of Alabama, 1973.
7. Federal Bureau of Prisons. *Task force and executive staff report on the role of psychologists in federal prisons.* Washington, D.C.: Federal Bureau of Prisons, 1977.

REFERENCES

American Friends Service Committee. *Struggle for justice.* New York: Hill & Wang, 1971.

American Psychiatric Association. *Clinical aspects of the violent individual.* Washington, D.C.: American Psychiatric Association, 1974.

Bard, M. Extending psychology's impact through existing community institutions. *American Psychologist,* 1969, *24,* 610–612.

Bazelon, D. Psychologists in corrections—Are they doing good for the offender or well for themselves? In S. Brodsky, *Psychologists in the criminal justice system.* Urbana, Ill.: University of Illinois Press, 1973.

Bermant, G., Kelman, H., & Warwick, D. (Eds.). *The ethics of social intervention.* Washington, D.C.: Hemisphere Publications, in press.

Bittner, E. *The functions of police in modern society.* Washington, D.C.: U.S. Government Printing Office, 1970.

Bloomberg, S., & Wilkins, L. Ethics of research involving human subjects in criminal justice. *Crime and Delinquency,* October 1977, 435–444.

Brodsky, S. *Psychologists in the criminal justice system.* Urbana, Ill.: University of Illinois Press, 1973.

Cederblom, J., & Blizek, W. (Eds.). *Justice and punishment.* Cambridge, Mass.: Ballinger, 1977.

Clark, R. *Crime in America.* New York: Simon & Schuster, 1970.

Corsini, R. Two therapeutic groups that failed. *The Journal of Correctional Psychology,* 1956, *1,* 16–22.

Driscoll, J., Meyer, R., & Schanie, C. Training police in family crisis intervention. *Journal of Applied Behavioral Science,* 1973, *9,* 62–82.

Ethical standards of psychologists. Washington, D.C.: American Psychological Association, 1963. (Reprinted and edited from the *American Psychologist,* January 1963).

Ethical standards of psychologists. Washington, D.C.: American Psychological Association, 1977. (Reprinted from the *APA Monitor,* March 1977.)

Fogel, D. *We are the living proof: The justice model for corrections.* Cincinnati: W. H. Anderson, 1975.

Gottfredson, D., Wilkins, L., & Hoffman, P. *Guidelines for parole and sentencing.* Lexington, Mass.: Lexington Books, 1978.

Greenberg, D. The correctional effects of corrections: A survey of evaluations. In D. Greenberg (Ed.), *Corrections and punishment.* Beverly Hills, Calif.: Sage, 1977.

Halleck, S., & Witte, A. Is rehabilitation dead? *Crime and Delinquency,* October 1977, 372–380.

Kassebaum, G., Ward, D., & Wilner, D. *Prison treatment and parole survival: An empirical assessment.* New York: Wiley, 1971.

Konečni, V., & Ebbesen, E. (Eds.). *Social psychological analysis of legal processes.* San Francisco: W. H. Freeman, in press.

Lipsitt, P., & Sales, B. (Eds.). *New directions in psychological research.* New York: Van Nostrand Reinhold, in press.

Martinson, R. What works?—Questions and answers about prison reform. *The Public Interest,* 1974, *35,* 22–54.

McGarry, L., et al. *Competency to stand trial and mental illness* (#HSM 73-9105). Washington, D.C.: U.S. Government Printing Office, 1973.

Meehl, P. Psychology and the criminal law. *University of Richmond Law Review,* 1970, *5,* 1–30.

Mitford, J. *Kind and usual punishment: The prison business.* New York: Random House, 1973.

Monahan, J. (Ed.). *Community mental health and the criminal justice system.* New York: Pergamon, 1976.

Monahan, J. The prediction of violent criminal behavior: A methodological critique and prospectus. In A. Blumstein, J. Cohen, and D. Nagin (Eds.), *Deterrence and incapacitation: Estimating the effects of criminal sanctions on crime rates.* Washington, D.C.: National Academy of Sciences, 1978.

Morris, N. *The future of imprisonment.* Chicago: University of Chicago Press, 1974.

Morris, N., & Hawkins, G. *Letter .to the President on crime control.* Chicago: University of Chicago Press, 1977.

Morse, S. Crazy behavior, morals and science: An analysis of mental health law. *Southern California Law Review,* 1978, *51,* 527–654.

National Commission for the Protection of Human Subjects of Biomedical and Behavioral Research. Research involving prisoners—Report and recommendations. *Federal Register,* 1977, *42,* 3075–3091.

Novaco, R. A stress inoculation approach to anger management in the training of law enforcement officers. *American Journal of Community Psychology,* 1977, *5,* 327–346.

Palmer, T. Martinson revisited. *Journal of Research in Crime and Delinquency,* July 1975, 113–152.

Quay, H. The three faces of evaluation: What can be expected to work. *Criminal Justice and Behavior,* 1977, *4,* 341–354.

Reiser, M. *The police department psychologist.* Springfield, Ill.: Charles C Thomas, 1972.

Ryan, W. *Blaming the victim.* New York: Vintage, 1971.

Sales, B. (Ed.). *Perspectives in law and psychology: The criminal justice system.* New York: Plenum, 1977. (a)

Sales, B. (Ed.). *Psychology in the legal process.* New York: Spectrum, 1977. (b)

Sarbin, T. (Ed.). *Challenges to the criminal justice system.* New York: Human Sciences Press, in press.

Shah, S. Foreword. In A. Stone, *Mental health and the law: A system in transition.* Washington, D.C.: U.S. Government Printing Office, 1975.

Shah, S. Editorial. *APA Monitor,* February 1977, p. 2.

Shah, S. Dangerousness: A paradigm for exploring some issues in law and psychology. *American Psychologist,* 1978, *33,* 224–238.

Siegel, M. Editorial. *APA Monitor,* February 1977, p. 5.

Tannenbaum, A., & Cooke, R. Research in prisons: A preliminary report. In National Commission for the Protection of Human Subjects of Biomedical and Behavioral Research, *Research involving prisoners: Appendix to report and recommendations* (Publication OS-76-132). Washington D.C.: U.S. Department of Health, Education and Welfare, 1976.

Tapp, J. Psychology and the law: An overture. *Annual Review of Psychology,* 1976, *27,* 359–404.

Tapp, J., Kelman, H., Triandis, H., Wrightsman, L., & Coelho, G. Continuing concerns in cross-cultural ethics: A report. *International Journal of Psychology,* 1974, *9,* 231–249.

Tapp, J., & Levine, F. (Eds.). *Law, justice, and the individual in society: Psychological and legal issues.* New York: Holt, Rinehart & Winston, 1977.

Toch, H. *The psychology of crime and criminal justice.* New York: Holt, Rinehart & Winston, in press.

Twentieth Century Fund. *Fair and certain punishment.* New York: McGraw-Hill, 1976.

von Hirsch, A. *Doing justice: The choice of punishments.* New York: Hill & Wang, 1976.

von Hirsch, A., & Hanrahan, K. *Abolish parole?* Cambridge, Mass.: Ballinger, in press

Wasserstrom, R. The obligation to obey the law. *UCLA Law Review,* 1963, *10,* 780.

Watzlawick, P., Weakland, J., & Fisch, R. *Change: Principles of problem formation and problem resolution.* New York: Norton, 1974.

Wilkins, L. Comment. In A. von Hirsch, *Doing Justice: The choice of punishments.* New York: Hill & Wang, 1976.

Part II:

WHITE-COLLAR CRIME

Forty years ago, Edwin H. Sutherland forceably argued that criminologists—by focusing on "crime in the lower class, which is composed of persons of low socioeconomic status," and neglecting "crime in the upper class, which is composed of respectable, or at least respected, business and professional men,"—had been led to a "conception and explanations of crime" which are "misleading and incorrect."[1] Ten years later, he published the results of his investigation of the records of law violations of the 70 largest U.S. industrial and commercial corporations. Some 980 "adverse decisions" were found, though Sutherland was convinced that further search would reveal many more. Every corporation had at least 1 adverse decision recorded; the average number was 14. According to Sutherland, 779 decisions involved criminal conduct by the corporate defendants, most of whom were recidivists.[2]

Sutherland's work helped stimulate a small but steady stream of studies concerning criminality in business and commercial life and, to a lesser extent, the professions.[3] His own work focused on offenses such as the restraint of trade, infringement of patents, and unfair labor practices. His immediate successors turned to such crimes as war-time black markets[4] and embezzlement.[5] More recently, the interests of students of white collar crime have shifted to a degree as legislative and regulatory enactments; and energetic litigation on behalf of consumers have highlighted other forms of white collar criminality—thus the rise of current concern with offenses such as consumer fraud, professional malpractice, corruption of office, and criminal disregard of health and safety.

One could say that while earlier findings demonstrate that businesspeople are frequently dishonest, more recent observations show that the dishonesties of businesspeople, professionals, and officials hurt identifiable persons who are generally poor and easily victimized. These observations underline the class character of white collar crime—a point Sutherland emphasized from the start. It is well known, of course, that common crime can be and is committed by middle and upper class people as easily, if not quite as often, as by lower class people. It does not work the other way, however. To commit white collar crime, it is not enought to have *mens rea;* one must have access to opportunities which are class related. To embezzle, one has to be in a position of trust over valuables. To defraud a customer, one has to be a purveyor of goods or services. To accept a bribe, one has to be in office.

The opportunities for white collar crime, as the term has come to be used by and large, appear to be located within occupational activities. Some occupations appear to offer an abundance of such opportunities; others, few if any. The variation notwithstanding, a crucial distinction between common and white collar crimes is this: Although murder, rape, burglary, robbery, and so on are unalloyed misdeeds, the restaurant owner who causes the death of patrons through neglect of fire safety regulations, to choose one example, does so in connection with performing a valued service. The distinction, although important and useful, is not very precise. A used car dealer who, as part of his merchandizing technique, rolls back odometers is a white collar criminal. But what of the person who sets up a used car dealership to defraud the lender who finances the acquisition of the inventory without engaging in any of the activities normally associated with running a used car business? The former might have been regarded as a sharp businessperson prior to the enactment of laws concerning odometers, while the latter all along was merely a swindler. Still, it could not possibly be a matter of no interest that both crimes are made possible by the existence of a trade, an occupation, an economic mechanism of some sort. And, although, businesses may offer the best advantage for white collar criminality, it is clear that professional practices and political offices are not far behind.

That wherever one does whatever one does to gain a livelihood may be a sphere permeated with crime is inevitably connected with the fact that whatever we might be doing within this sphere—directing traffic, making shoes, setting broken bones, cutting hair, settling disputes, or reporting the news—consists wholly or partly of making money when viewed from the perspective of our interest in it. Throughout most of human history this interest was restrained in two ways. First, by the circumstances that living and making a living could not be distinguished morally, one could not easily say, as we manifestly can, that "business is business" to justify an action that might otherwise be found to be a breach of decency. A second restraint was provided by the regulation of the price people were allowed to ask and accept for goods and services. The institution of "self-regulating" markets in the nineteenth century virtually abolished both of these restraints. The reduction of economic relations to merely economic relations had the removal of all humane scruples as a precondition of its functioning. We are now having second thoughts about the economic liberalism of the nineteenth century, and we are in the midst of a methodological attack on the more predatory aspects of otherwise legal activities.

In the essay commissioned for this volume, Jack Katz identifies the constellation of circumstances that contributed to the focusing of crime control attention on white collar crime in recent years. According to his argument, the ascendancy of white collar crime in the hierarchy of prosecutorial interest is an expression of primarily professional career aspirations of young government lawyers. This became possible, if not inevitable, after the near-collapse of the legitimacy of established law enforcement institutions in the mid-1970s. The complex of events centering around Watergate provided the opportunity for mounting a control effort, but it did not create the conditions that became the target of those efforts. Instead, the relaxation of ties of political obligation created the conditions under which energies could be devoted to tasks that, in the past, were more or less deliberately neglected, and those tasks contained possibilities for conspicuous achievement and career advancement.

The recent prominence of white collar crime, and the modernity of some of its present-day forms, should not obscure the fact that crimes connected with business are as old as business itself. Sheldon and Zweibel survey the history of one species—consumer fraud. Though prenineteenth century analogies are at best quite loose, it would seem that recent efforts to curb economic license show that we are no longer moving away from status toward contract, but are veering off in the direction of a social law of a kind thought past, one that involves the regulation of interpersonal relations.[6]

Clinard and Yeager review the current state of corporate criminality, dealing with both ethical and legal transgressions.[7] Their purpose is to achieve an overall sense of the area in order to identify difficulties connected with obtaining information on white collar crime and on the procedures leading to the imposition of effective sanctions.

The following three articles present information about the nature and extent of certain forms of white collar criminality. The pages by Herlihy and Levine are a segment of a larger article containing a comprehensive review of the "overseas payment problem." Though the materials are drawn from the field of international commerce, this should not divert attention from the likelihood that this form of sabotage of market processes can probably be found wherever trade takes place.

In the next article, drawn from his recent book on the subject, Reisman offers a typology of bribery, consisting of three types of bribe-taking of increasing degrees of culpability. What is of decisive significance here is not that certain forms of bribes are relatively innocuous and at times resemble tipping, but that certain instances of routine transactions acquire a privileged status from which minor benefits accrue to the payer that are denied to others. Thus the world of visible charges becomes padded with invisible charges, and thus another part of reality is not quite what it seems to be, pushing those who participate in it further toward cynicism.

The last of this group of three articles, a chapter from Bequai's book on white collar crime, describes the complicated world of crimes in the capital market. Drawing on his experience as a prosecuting attorney, Bequai leads us to see how the sheer complexity of stock trading and the lack of effective control over it make possible depredations on a vast scale.

The article by Smith technically deals with so-called organized crime—the world of the Godfather and of the Mafia. He argues that whatever the accuracy of the more sensational accounts of organized crime, it is more productive to analyze these activities as illegal ways of exploiting business opportunities. In fact, the analytical scheme of typified business activities he proposes involves kinds of market orientations that range continuously from legal to illegal.

The final article, by Brintnall, illustrates and amplifies points made by Katz. Brintnall explains how resources supplied by the federal government have served to release local initiative in the prosecution of crimes that might otherwise have gone unchecked. Katz and Smith make it quite clear that the needed capacities and interests exist to make white collar crime much more difficult to perpetrate, or to perpetuate without punishment, than it now is. But it is far from clear that these capacities and interests are or will be assured of continued freedom of action.

NOTES

1. Edwin H. Sutherland, "White Collar Criminality," 5 *American Sociological Review* 1-12 (1940), reprinted in Gilbert Geis and Robert F. Meier, *White-Collar Crime*. New York: Macmillan, 1977, pp. 38-49. The quotations are from pp. 38 and 39 of the Geis-Meier text.

2. See Edwin H. Sutherland, *White Collar Crime*. New York: Holt, Rinehart & Winston, 1949. Also see Edwin H. Sutherland, "Crime and Corporations," in Albert Cohen, Alfred Lindesmith, and Karl Schuessler, eds., *The Sutherland Papers*. Bloomington: Indiana University Press, 1956, pp. 78-96. This summary piece is republished in Gilbert Geis and Robert F. Meier, *White-Collar Crime*. New York: Macmillan, 1977, pp. 71-84.

3. See the excellent bibliography in Gilbert Geis and Robert F. Meier, *White-Collar Crime*. New York: Macmilan, 1977, pp. 337-345.

4. Marshall B. Clinard, *The Black Market: A Study of White-Collar Crime*. New York: Holt, Rinehart & Winston, 1952.

5. Donald R. Cressey, *Other People's Money: The Social Psychology of Embezzlement*. New York: Macmillan, 1953.

6. See M. Rehbinder, "Status, contract, and the welfare state," 23 *Stanford Law Review* 941-955 (1971).

7. See also Marshall B. Clinard, Peter C. Yeager, Jeanne Brissette, David Petrashek, and Elizabeth Harries, *Illegal Corporate Behavior*. Washington, DC: USDJ/LEAA/NILECJ, 1979. A study of law violations by the 582 largest publicly owned corporations in the United States, this is the first large-scale effort to extend Sutherland's original effort.

THE SOCIAL MOVEMENT AGAINST
WHITE-COLLAR CRIME

JACK KATZ

In an unpredicted movement over the last decade, "white-collar crime" rose to compete with "street crime" in American consciousness of the crime problem. One indicator of the change has been a diminution of efforts to exploit for political benefit failures of enforcement against common crime. In the 1960s, the books of even liberal politicians often focused on street crime and gave scant attention to white-collar crime.[1] Now ex-members of a fallen "law-and-order" administration flood book sellers with fact and fiction on their experiences in white-collar crime. In the 1968 election, the alleged softness on street crime of Attorney General Ramsay Clark became an issue that threatened to override bread-and-butter differences between the candidates. In the 1976 election, the pardon of Richard Nixon, along with the earlier Republican failures to prosecute white-collar crime, played an analogous role. We may now begin to speculate on the effects on the 1980 elections of the Marston "affair"; the prosecution of President Carter's first budget director, Bert Lance, for bank fraud; allegations of a cover-up after Chappaquiddick; and the trial of John Connolly for corruptly receiving payments from dairy interests.

The change in the last 10 years has been striking because the earlier emphasis on street crime was so strong. In the early and mid-1960s, Presidential commissions drew on the academic community to an unprecedented degree to study juvenile delinquency, urban riots, and violence against political leaders. In the late 1960s and early 1970s, grand jury investigations and prosecutions riveted public attention on clashes between police and war protesters, race leaders, and

Author's Note: For guidance on earlier versions I would like to thank Stanton Wheeler, Ken Mann, the Advisory Committee to the Yale Research Program on White-Collar Crime, and editors Messinger and Bittner. Sheila Balkan provided valuable research assistance. This article is an offshoot of a larger study funded by Law Enforcement Assistance Administration Grant 78 NI AX 0017 to Yale University. Points of view or opinions stated are those of the author and do not necessarily represent the official position or policies of the U.S. Department of Justice, of which the Law Enforcement Assistance Administration is a part.

political radicals. In political rhetoric, in front page news, and in academic focus, the criminal was an outsider attacking "the Establishment" from "the streets."

The change has also been striking because there had been relatively little attention to white-collar crime before the 1970s. To be sure, from 1958 to 1968 there were several dramatic instances of triumphant white-collar crime law enforcement. Massive publicity was given to the criminal prosecution of Westinghouse and General Electric executives for a price-fixing conspiracy in the heavy electrical equipment industry. Early in their administration, the Kennedys prosecuted a prominent Presidential appointee, for tax crimes (James Landis) who had been dean of the Harvard Law School and two U.S. Attorneys of the Eastern District of New York (one acting, Elliott Kahaner; the other, Judge Vincent Keogh, was the brother of a powerful Congressman and had been a prosecutor under Franklin Roosevelt) for promoting judicial bribery in a criminal case. Robert Morgenthau, the U.S. Attorney in Manhattan, became the first prosecutor to make the prosecution of white-collar crime a widely recognized hallmark of his tenure. President Johnson initiated "Operation Snowball" in 1964, a nationally coordinated campaign to prosecute the use of corporations for illegal campaign contributions. There were celebrated charges of corruption against close associates of the Presidents (Sherman Adams, Billie Sol Estes, Bobby Baker). Yet these were isolated events. No patterned expansion of general movement in law enforcement sprang from them.

Consider the range of targets in business and political elites against which criminal law enforcement agencies have mobilized moral indignation in the last decade. In the area of political corruption, in addition to the unprecedented cases against federal officials,[2] charges for the criminal use of gubernatorial powers have been brought in Illinois (Kerner), Oklahoma (Hall), Maryland (Agnew, Mandel), and Tennessee (Blanton). In the early 1970s, 79 federal, state, and local officials were indicted in New Jersey.[3] Between 1971 and 1976, the U.S. Attorney in Chicago indicted 256 individuals in 118 political corruption cases.[4] The public image of corruption at the state level in New York reached the point in 1977 that the major Long Island newspaper ran a computation stating that 1 out of every 32 persons in the state legislature since 1973 had been indicted, compared to a ratio of 1 indictment for every 125 New York State residents.[5]

The movement against white-collar crime has not been directed primarily at politicians. Scores of the nation's largest corporations admitted to criminal political contributions in the 1972 campaign; hundreds acknowledged bribes, or "sensitive payments," to foreign officials. Pervasive systems of business bribery —kickback relations between private company suppliers and private purchasing or inspections agents—were proven in the distribution of a series of products from beer to grain. Law enforcement agencies from the FBI to local police departments have been charged with systematic criminal violations of civil rights. A series of government welfare programs have been characterized as riddled with fraud by private business participants: "Medicaid doctors"; nursing home operators drawing federal health funds; mortgage companies administering Federal Housing Administration subsidies to promote inner-city home ownership; sponsors and vendors in summer feeding programs for school-age children; Small Business Administration loan applicants; lessors of facilities for day care; vocational institutes; suppliers of remedial educational materials. Massive corruption was exposed at General Services Administration, the major federal government contracting agency. Stock frauds (Equity Funding, National Student Marketing, Home Stake Oil) and frauds against banks (C. Arnholt Smith) were publicized as crimes with unprecedented dimensions. Computer-assisted thefts of "astonishing" magnitude have become a recurrent news item.[6]

The last decade has been extraordinary not only in the range of perceived white-collar criminals but also in the widespread character of the social movement making the charges. I have been studying the treatment of white-collar and common crimes in the U.S. Attorney's office for the Eastern District of New York (EDNY), a federal prosecution unit covering Brooklyn, Queens, Staten Island, and Nassau and Suffolk Counties (Long Island). The EDNY has not been the site of the nation's most celebrated political corruption, securities fraud, corporate bribery, government program fraud, or police corruption scandals. We therefore can take the exposure of its public to official charges of white-collar crime as a conservative representation of the experience in many other areas of the country.

In the early 1960s, the cases listed as "most significant" in the annual reports to the Attorney General by the EDNY's U.S. Attorney were against organized crime figures (Gallo, Lombardozzi, Persico). The one white-collar crime repeatedly prosecuted, a crime reflecting the real estate boom on Long Island in the 1960s, was fraud by real estate brokers against the Federal Housing Administration.

In the 1970s, the office prosecuted a series of politicians: William Cahn, Nassau County's Republican District Attorney for 12 years (double-billing Law Enforcement Assistance Administration and the county for expenses to National District Attorney and other conferences); Queens Village's colorful Democratic City Councilman, Matty Troy (tax evasion, embezzlement from law clients); Sam Wright, a poverty program leader and City Councilman from Oceanhill-Brownsville (kickback for school district's purchase of educational materials); officials of the Long Island Park Commission (kickbacks for letting towing contracts); Republican Party workers in Nassau County (extorting 1% salary contributions from civil servants in return for promotions); and, for extorting contributions to a political party in return for public works contracts, the leader of the Nassau County Democratic Party in the 1960s, Marvin Cristenfeld, and Republican Congressman Angelo Roncallo of Oyster Bay (acquitted). The following corporations and corporation executives were prosecuted: Barton's Candy, for adulterated food; Air France and other foreign airlines, for fabricating "groups" eligible for low fares; GTE-Sylvania, for bribing transit officials to buy subway bulbs; several executives at technical publications companies and at Grumman aircraft, Long Island's largest employer, for a kickback arrangement; Pan Am, for negligently transporting hazardous cargo; the Security National Bank and its top executives, for corporate political contributions; Dun & Bradstreet, for covering up Federal Housing Administration frauds (acquitted); executives at Avis and at J. C. Penney, for commercial bribery (the Penney investigation killed the nomination of Kenneth Axelson, a top Penney executive, as Deputy Secretary of Treasury in the Carter Administration). Defendants in government program fraud cases included: 40 individuals (and 10 corporations, among them some of Long Island's largest lending institutions), for fraud and official corruption in a Federal Housing Administration program subsidizing inner-city home ownership; nursing home operators for Medicaid fraud; James Elsbery, who had been an aide in the Carter Presidential campaign, for using his company to bill New York City fraudulently for educational services; several rabbis for fraud in a Department of Agriculture school children summer feeding program; David Greenberg, "Batman" in a highly publicized police team, for a Small Business Administration fraud; and a state-wide network of podiatrists who attempted to bribe the New York legislature to continue Medicaid coverage for podiatry. The office convicted a number of police detectives from an elite unit for extorting money and drugs from narcotics dealers, and brought a tax evasion case related to the theft from the police property clerk's office of the heroin recovered in the so-called French Connection case.

In addition to the impression made by this wave of EDNY-U.S. Attorney prosecutions, the public in the district was exposed to white-collar crime prosecutions brought by the federal prosecutor in Manhattan and by several state prosecutors. To mention only the additional public officials indicted: Thomas Mackell, Queens District Attorney; Brooklyn state legislator and Assembly Speaker, Stanley Steingut; Bronx County Democratic leader and state party head Patrick Cunningham; Suffolk County Republican Chairman Edwin Schwenk; Congressmen Brasco and Podell of Brooklyn; and people described in news stories as "close to" Mayor Beame (Irving Goldman); Brooklyn Democratic leader Meade Esposito (Ronald Parr); Queens Democratic leader Donald Manes (Judge Robert Groh); Attorney General Lefkowitz (his first assistant and other lawyers in his office); and Governor Carey (union leaders Anthony Scotto and Joseph Tonelli). Tonelli admitted to stealing over $350,000 from a pension fund, $50,000 of which went to Georgia lawyers friendly with President Carter and Attorney General Bell in an attempt to stop the investigation.[7]

We have in our own experience an indication that the recently heightened official and public awareness of white-collar crime will soon fade to the relative indifference of the 1960s. I refer to the reaction I presume many readers would have to the review presented above. Even though we all lived through these or similar revelations, we still regard them with a sense that "it's unbelievable," worth at least the immediate response of a head shake or a new expression of cynical disgust. Somehow, in the very near aftermath of officially verified accounts of scandals about our elites, we are inclined to presume their legality.

On the other hand, there is a reason to suggest that attention to white-collar crime has been raised permanently to a new plateau. The movement to prosecute white-collar crime has been justified in the name of equal justice. Consider the career of another recent movement toward equal justice, the movement to provide equal civil legal services to the poor.

Jurisprudence has not been able to define with any degree of rigor the meaning for the poor of "equal access" to legal services. Nor has it given substantive meaning to the value of "even-handed" enforcement against white-collar and common crimes. There is a common, central dilemma. Before we allocate public lawyers to work on defining the wrongs of the rich or the rights of the poor, we are unable authoritatively to gauge the magnitude of the white-collar crime problem or to measure the legal needs of the indigent. As soon as they have gone to work at a professional level approximating that available as a matter of right and routine to wealthy individuals and powerful corporate clients, poverty lawyers and white-collar crime prosecutors have expanded civil protections for the poor and criminal prohibitions against the privileged. Commitments to promote equal justice intensify our appreciation of inequalities. This limitation of legal philosophy has been reflected in an obvious historical reality. The advance of American governmental commitments toward equal justice has not flowed steadily from the implications of a generally embraced political ideology but sporadically, out of contexts of societal crisis: in the case of civil legal services for the poor, the civil rights, social welfare, and anti-war protest milieu of the 1960s; in the case of the movement against white-collar crime, the "Watergate" ambience of the 1970s. But the analogy also indicates that the heightened concentration of law enforcement agencies on white-collar crime may be finding ways to persist as the Watergate 1970s fade. The creation of the national Legal Services Corporation in 1974, after the dissolution of the broader movements of the 1960s, symbolized the continuity of the official public commitment to increase civil justice for the poor. American political movements toward equal justice require the push of external crises to start, but they may acquire their own momentum once in progress. I offer here material to fuel such speculation with an analysis of major themes in the social structure of the movement that has recently turned public and official attentions to white-collar crime.[8]

OFFICIAL VERSUS LAY CATALYSTS

In order to locate a domestic social movement that parallels the generalized outcry over the last decade against criminal behavior in the political and business establishments, we would have to go back to the Progressive movement. If we examine the catalysts of the two movements, we discover in the intervening half century a fundamental shift in the agencies that effectively assert the criminal character of America's elites. The Progressive movement had famous leadership in government,[9] but the movement as a whole had a strong "popular" or "lay" character. In addition to the "settlement house" workers, who have been characterized as "spearheads" of the movement,[10] the agents included rural populists,[11] muckraking journalists,[12] and organizations of "civic-minded" businessmen.[13] In the early 1900s, the immorality of the Establishment was depicted in petition drives to recall corrupt mayors. Lay advocates such as Jane Addams used public oration to spirit state legislators to establish enforcement machinery. In the 1970s, the key agents have been Judge Sirica and Senator Ervin, unraveling the Watergate cover-up; federal prosecutors Thomson and Stern, turning up evidence of systematic political corruption in Illinois and New Jersey; Senator Church, publicly airing murder plots and other crimes by the CIA; Securities and Exchange Commission (SEC) enforcement chief Stanley Sporkin, compelling disclosure of illegal domestic political contributions, and international bribery by American corporations.

Instead of the public exhorting the government to exorcise Establishment criminality, the public of the 1970s has experienced a series of shock waves set off by "revelations" emanating from the government. As the decade's scandals broke, the mass news media began to characterize the moral atmosphere as a popular uprising. Jimmy Carter was ushered into the White House with populist rhetoric. But, up to at least 1975, the scandals could not be attributed generally to popular concern. "Watergate" exploded in the wake of Richard Nixon's landslide 1972 Presidential election. Richard Daley won reelection in 1975 to an unprecedented sixth four-year term, despite the conviction by U.S. Attorney James Thompson of several of the Chicago mayor's powerful political allies. Major American corporations like Exxon and Lockheed were officially damned for bribing foreign political leaders despite the much vaunted "conservatism" of the 1970s, symbolized by the rise in "straight" college student aspirations for corporation careers. The recent movement against white-collar crime has not been an outgrowth of a popular uprising against the elite, but a historically unprecedented series of battles on nonpartisan grounds—Senators Ervin and Church acted as Democrats, but U.S. Attorneys were Republican appointees from 1969 to 1977—within elite circles of power.

Seen as a series of attacks against the Establishment that started within government, the movement against white-collar crime suggests an analogy with the antipoverty program of the 1960s. Moynihan has characterized the community action program of the Office of Economic Opportunity as the first historical manifestation of "the professionalization of reform":

> Increasingly efforts to change the American social system for the better arose from initiative undertaken by persons whose profession was to do just that. Whereas previously the role of organized society had been largely private—the machinery would work if someone made it work—now the process began to acquire a self-starting capacity of its own.[14]

Just as the social welfare reform initiatives of the mid- and late 1960s took shape in the late 1950s and early 1960s, before the proliferation of civil rights protests, urban riots, and anti-war demonstrations, so the movement against white-collar crime in the 1970s took off only after the dissolution of the "anti-Establishment" movement of the 1960s. In the 50-odd years since the end of the Progressive era at the start of World War I, segments of American governmental machinery have developed autonomous capacities to pull the widespread public presumption of legality out from beneath public and private centers of domestic power.

CASE VERSUS INSTITUTIONAL OBJECTIVES

One reason that many of the official catalysts of the recent wave of indignation against the Establishment played at most a minor role in stimulating the Progressive movement is that they either did not then exist (such as SEC and Internal Revenue Service), or, in the case of U.S. Attorneys, existed with only a semblance of their current institutional strength.[15] The institutional incapacity of federal prosecutors to play a significant role against white-collar crime was indicated in the graft prosecution of San Francisco's Boss Ruef in 1907. Ruef was convicted by a federal prosecutor, but only after Fremont Older, the crusading editor of the *Bulletin,* first persuaded a millionaire, Rudolph Spreckels, to guarantee the expense of the investigation, and then persuaded President Roosevelt to lend the services of William Burns, the federal government's star detective, and Francis Heney, one of its best-regarded special prosecutors.[16] Corruption prosecutions by local U.S. Attorney's offices which investigate with little or no guidance from Washington and with autonomous internal resources is a recent pattern.

The emergent capacity of prosecution offices to mobilize autonomously against white-collar crime has changed the dominant motif of movements denouncing illegalities by elites. The paradigmatic legal product of the recent surge of righteous attacks on elites has been the criminally prosecuted case. We have been exposed repeatedly to investigative chases in which fish turn one after the other against big fish, building toward a climax in an adjudication of the guilt of the top figure. Once the fate of the "big enchilada" has been decided, the drama subsides. Compare the dramatic pattern in the campaigns for institutional reform that distinguished the Progressive era. A criminal prosecution would be one moment in the history of a more general movement to replace patronage with a civil service system or to adopt a scheme of prohibitory legislation and regulatory commission designed to govern an industry comprehensively.

The "case" motif for the recent expression of outrage against elites is emphasized by the fact that criminal prosecutions have neither emerged from nor lead movements for institutional reform. Despite the range of officially certified criminality by major corporations and by political officials across the country, the scandals of the 1970s have produced virtually no major institutional reforms.

(An exception is the Federal Election Commission, created by the 1974 amendments to the Federal Election Campaign Act of 1971.) Given the range and intensity of the scandals, the 1970s must be considered an especially sterile period in American political ideology. Legislatures have enacted no sweeping programs to prevent fraud and abuse in government welfare programs. Congress has not devised new criminal prohibitions to reconfirm the successful prosecutions of public officials for using their offices to extort political contributions. No new oversight or regulatory agencies has been created to guard against land and stock swindles or to anticipate computer-assisted crimes.[17]

In fact, to the extent that legislation has taken significant steps toward influencing the movement, it has cut primarily the other way. In 1974, Congress reduced by two years the statute of limitations on criminal contributions to federal election campaigns.[18] On the surface, the Tax Reform Act of 1976 was introduced as a barrier against abuses that were revealed by "Watergate": White House attempts to use criminal tax investigations against political enemies. However, the act's restrictions on Internal Revenue Service disclosure of tax return information were written generally and they have severely reduced informational and, more important, investigative resources previously available to white-collar crime prosecutors. (See note 49 for examples of the costs.) At the state level, grand jury reform in New York, spurred by the fall from grace of corruption prosecutor Maurice Nadjari,[19] has given witnesses the right to have an attorney present as they are asked questions. To many the change seemed to remove an absurd procedural harassment. Previously, defense counsel was available for consultation outside the grand jury room and could be visited after the witness had heard but before he had answered each question. But white-collar crime prosecutors believe the legislation will be strategically significant. The argument is that the new procedure enables defense lawyers who have been supplied to all insiders by the major target to police cover-ups. It restrains insiders who might stray from the fold if they could testify without concern that their words would become known through their counsel to their coconspirators in business or politics. When legislation *has* expanded the definition of white-collar crime, it has come in the wake of scandals and prosecutions rather than in a leadership role. An example is the Foreign Corrupt Practices Act of 1978.

As the vehicle for mobilizing moral indignation against the Establishment has changed from the campaign for institutional reform to the criminal case, the roles played by participating organizations outside of law enforcement have changed correspondingly. When legislators have promoted recognition of "the white-collar crime problem," they have acted not so much by offering bills as by spurring investigations in committee hearings or through their own offices. Exposés of Watergate, Koreagate, the CIA assassinations, FBI-COINTELPRO mail openings and break-ins, and the grain scandal are prominent examples of initiatives in which the powers of the legislature to investigate rather than to legislate have fueled the movement. Courts—famous as *the* recalcitrant governmental unit in the Progressive era for knocking down remedial and protective legislation as unconstitutional—have become the central forum for certifying the elite's immorality. In a series of decisions illustrated in the next section, courts have been receptive to expansive interpretations of criminal penalties pressed by the prosecution.

There has been a related change in the way journalists play a scandal-provoking and sustaining role. In the Progressive era, newspapers and news magazine writers produced a free-lance muckraking that portrayed whole institutions—city governments, meat packers, railroads—as fit for public condemnation, without great concern for the making of particular indictments. Upton Sinclair, Frank Norris, and Theodore Dreiser used the novel as a viable alternative to the news article, showing no professional awe of a sanctified line between fact and fiction. Investigative reporters have played powerful roles in the 1970s—Woodward and Bernstein, Watergate; Seymour Hirsch, My Lai; Jack Anderson in Washington; Jack Newfield and Wayne Barrett of the *Village Voice,* in a long series of exposés in the New York City area—but as promoters of particular scandals and specific cases, with a narrowing concern about facts. The Washington *Post's* requirement for two sources before running Watergate revelations seems to reflect a criminal court's "two witness" requirement for proving key elements of a prosecution's case.[20] In historical perspective, investigative reporters, courts, and even legislators have become assisting players in prosecutive dramas against the elite.[21]

The shift in motifs for expressing public indignation from institutional campaign to criminal case has also meant a major alteration in the perspective of the public. As some observed during "Watergate,"[22] the development of a white-collar criminal case shuts out the public from monitoring the mobilization of official attacks against the elite, possibly blocking the potential for mounting campaigns for institutional reform. Once the lawyers and the courts step in, public access to the contingencies and progress of the inquiry is cut off by doctrines of grand jury secrecy and fair trial and by deals for immunity which deter legislative questioning of witnesses and induce government witnesses to keep a distance from reporters.

As the definition of America's crime problem has changed to feature white-collar crime, the process of defining the crime problem has become less democratic in several respects. The public must rely on officials to learn about the magnitude of the problem; victimization surveys and self-report studies, increasingly used to describe the incidence of common crimes, will not work. In any given case, the public cannot grasp the nature of the behavior being prosecuted by reading the legislated basis of the case. The statutory sections used to indict white-collar crimes—mail fraud, conspiracy to defraud the United States, false statements—are distinctively uninformative. As the process of discovering and acting officially against illegalities of the elite has become a legalized process governed by the criminal prosecutor, the public has changed its posture from that of an exhorting catalyst to a passive audience that receives what doctrines of legality and prosecutive tactics allow it to hear.

EXECUTIVE MORAL ENTREPRENEURS

A major indicator of the dominance of law enforcement executives in the recent movement to depict the illegality of business and political elites has been the innovations achieved by prosecutors. While legislators were essentially inactive in their legislative capacity, prosecutors have developed the legislative capacities of their offices, expanding public attention toward white-collar crime by "making law" and bringing "unprecedented" cases. In a number of cases widely reported as "firsts," prosecutors have extended the criminal sanction to new substantive targets. After Pinto cars became notorious for dangerously placed fuel tanks, a state-level prosecutor in Michigan indicted Ford Motor Company for criminal negligence. Turning the wire fraud statute to a novel use, the U.S. Attorney in Manhattan indicted United Brands for bribing a Honduras official (which itself was not then a criminal offense under American law). In 1976, the U.S. Attorney in Virginia tested pollution law by prosecuting executives of Allied Chemical for poisoning the James River. Major accounting firms became subject to criminal charges for condoning misleading annual corporate financial statements.[23] In what the Tax Division's chief characterized as "perhaps the biggest breakthrough we've ever had in the whole area of fraud in the widespread use of offshore tax shelters," the Justice Department (unsuccessfully) prosecuted a San Francisco lawyer.[24] Criminal charges that would have been unimaginable 10 years ago were brought against high-level FBI officials for violating the civil rights of political dissidents.

The enterprising role of prosecutors in expanding the substantive criminal law to reach previously unprosecuted practices of business and political elites has been much more widespread and innovative at the federal level, where prosecutors are appointed, than at the state level, where they are elected.[25] Federal prosecutors have transcended traditionally accepted federalist barriers on their jurisdiction by innovating statutory bases for major political corruption and business bribery cases. Finding that the federal criminal code failed to provide language specifically reaching many forms of corrupt use of office by nonfederal officials, U.S. Attorneys made the Hobbs Act, originally conceived as an anti-labor "racketeering" statute, into a weapon against local and state politicians.[26] Federal criminal law also fails to condemn domestic commercial bribery directly; and when charges for tax crime have been strategically unfeasible, U.S. Attorneys have applied the richly interpretable language of the mail fraud statute (use of the mails in a "scheme to defraud") in novel ways. The formally vacuous "conspiracy to defraud the United States," expanding for over 100 years,[27] has been put to ever newer uses. Prosecutors in the Eastern District of New York used this section to indict podiatrists for attempting to bribe the inclusion of their specialty in the state's Medicaid program, despite the fact that the federal government had made a policy decision in the statute that podiatry was worthy of subsidy if the state opted.[28] "Filing a false statement" with the federal government may or may not any longer require that the deceiver know he is lying to the *federal* government.[29]

DECENTRALIZED IMPETUS

The impetus behind the movement must be characterized as decentralized. The discussion to this point has emphasized the role of federal prosecutors but, across the country over the last decade, law enforcement executives outside of U.S. Attorney's offices have also played enterprising and controversial roles. Stanley Sporkin, appointed as chief of enforcement at the SEC in 1974, quickly emerged as an innovator in applying the SEC's power of negative publicity to corporations accused of international political bribery and to accounting firms accused of winking at evidence of fraud.[30] In a parallel development, the SEC rapidly built up its enforcement capability in Southern California in the 1970s.[31] Gerald Boltz was appointed Western regional SEC administrator in 1972. He immediately announced plans to move regional headquarters to Los Angeles, which had been an embarrassment to the law enforcement community as an area overripe for large-scale fraud prosecutions, and to increase the Los Angeles staff from 25 to 40. Boltz had previously earned enmity in both political parties as the SEC administrator out of Fort Worth, Texas, who developed the Sharpstown bank case, a multifaceted bank fraud-political corruption scandal that reached Governor Preston Smith and other leading Democratic figures in the state legislature and which forced the resignation of Will Wilson, a Deputy Attorney General under John Mitchell in the early Nixon Justice Department.

The movement against white-collar crime was decentralized in that it characterized a number of independent enforcement agencies, and also in the sense that the impetus came substantially at the field level, not as a result of policy shifts made in Washington headquarters. Boltz and Sporkin worked on parallel policy tracks, but within the SEC bureaucracy they collided frequently and famously.[32] Differences in the relationship between white-collar crime prosecutors and local FBI offices indicate the unsystematic, unregulated character of the bureau's initiatives. Under Neil Welch, the Philadelphia FBI office developed a reputation for leading a change in bureau priorities toward white-collar crime and enjoyed public accolades from the local federal prosecutor.[33] At the same time, the New York Bureau "S.A.C.," Wallace LaPrade, was in frequently bitter conflict with the U.S. Attorneys in Manhattan and Brooklyn. The bicentennial, Independence Day issue of the New York *Times* featured a front-page blast by Eastern District U.S. Attorney David Trager charging the bureau with incompetence and unresponsiveness in white-collar crime investigations.

Perhaps the most dramatically expanded force promoting "the white-collar crime problem" has been the U.S. Attorney's office. The change in 10 years has been so extensive that accounts of the work of federal prosecutors based on research conducted in the 1960s are now substantially misleading. The literature describes assistant U.S. Attorneys as at work on cases that were "substantially made" by investigative agencies before entering the prosecutor's office.[34] This analysis is inapplicable to the investigating prosecutors who currently make up from one-third to one-half of the legal staff of numerous U.S. Attorney's offices.

That the movement has been decentralized (or better, uncentralized) is indicated by the role played by nationally organized feeders of cases to U.S. Attorneys. The pattern is that federal prosecutors have led the investigative agencies which have traditionally presented them cases. A reordering of priorities in the FBI began quite late in the decade. Various investigative offices —in the General Services Administration and in the Departments of Housing and Urban Development; Health, Education and Welfare; Agriculture; and Labor— were reorganized after criminal prosecutions emerged from scandals within the agencies' jurisdiction.[35]

The origins of the movement in U.S. Attorney's offices can be traced back before Watergate, to a time when the Department of Justice in Washington ("main Justice") was rarely supportive and at times pointedly hostile to the trend. The then-unprecedented campaign against political corruption by U.S. Attorneys Lacey and Stern in New Jersey was threatened when Stern, Lacey's first assistant and choice as successor, was held in limbo by the White House as an "acting" U.S. Attorney for a year at a time when the office was shifting emphasis from the Democratic city machines to Republican statewide leaders.[36] The investigation of the Baltimore County political machine, run by assistant U.S. Attorneys Barney Skolnick and Tim Baker, led to the Agnew case without encouragement, much less initiative, from the Justice Department.[37]

There were similar if less dramatic signs of decentralized impetus among federal prosecutors in areas of white-collar crime enforcement other than political corruption. In the early 1970s, the first "environmental protection" and "consumer frauds" sections emerged in some of the larger U.S. Attorney's offices. Frauds sections evolved partly from unanticipated demands for personnel to conduct massive prosecutions of abuses in government social welfare programs. In the Eastern District of New York, as in Detroit, Chicago, and other urban centers, scandals over official corruption and fraud by brokers and mortgage companies in Federal Housing Administration ghetto home subsidy programs encouraged the reorganization of the U.S. Attorney's office. In 1973, the Brooklyn office found itself faced with the need to assign three of its assistants to a nine-month trial. That was about one-tenth of the line criminal staff at the time. Internal adjustments to such unanticipated, prolonged shifts of staff resources prepared the office for the formalization of a separate frauds section.

This pattern of a spontaneous outcropping of simultaneous white-collar crime initiatives by federal prosecutors has continued throughout the decade. While agencies that made decisive contributions to the escalation of the movement in its earlier stages have moved to the sidelines, more and more U.S. Attorney's offices have begun to reorganize their priorities in favor of white-collar crime. The Internal Revenue Service initiated major political (Agnew) and police corruption (New York, Chicago) investigations in the early 1970s, but then was cut back in the mid-1970s when Internal Revenue Service Commissioner Donald Alexander moved his investigators more exclusively to a "tax collection" emphasis. All the while the group of U.S. Attorneys' offices, publicly declaring new "white-collar crime" priorities, expanded. The first set of the decade included New Jersey, Maryland, and Chicago. Then Eastern New York, Pittsburgh, and Los Angeles reordered priorities. Most recently Boston, long a classic example of a politically indebted, quiescent office, has joined the trend. The Philadelphia (Congressman Eilberg) and Georgia (Bert Lance)[38] offices have become famous new entrants in the group. The San Francisco U.S. Attorney announced a blanket policy of nonprosecution for most bank robberies to dramatize the reorientation of his office.

The Justice Department has made a series of efforts over the last few years to get ahead of the trend and give centralized direction. In the first half of the decade, the Justice Department was the leading target of sensational white-collar crime accusations: Henry Peterson, then chief of the Criminal Division, for his relationship to the Watergate cover-up; Attorney General John Mitchell for the Watergate and Ellsberg break-ins; the Vesco matter before the SEC, and the ITT-Hartford insurance ("Dita Beard") merger approval decision. Starting with the Ford Administration,[39] the Justice Department has made a series of moves to direct the movement. Attorney General Levi appointed Richard Thornburgh, who had been U.S. Attorney General in Pittsburgh, as Criminal Division chief and named Manhattan federal judge and ex-Southern District of New York Prosecutor Harold Tyler, Jr., to be Deputy Attorney General. Both had been publicly identified with the movement and became powerful spokesmen for it. Recent announcements from the Justice Department about beefing up fraud and public integrity units indicate that it still perceives the need to be seen as leading the trend. But a view of the Justice Department's role in the last decade shows that the movement overall has been erupting on a series of fronts without a central design. The expansion of the "white-collar crime problem" has been a genuine "social movement," the product of initiatives by people in parallel and independent organizational positions who perceive similar opportunities, not a change integrated by administrative leadership from above.

HISTORICAL ACCIDENT, PERSONAL MOBILITY, AND COMMON-SENSE MORALTIY

What of the philosophy of this newly influential set of enforcement officials? Has a common, historically emergent political perspective in federal executive agencies been responsible for the incorporation of white-collar crime in the collective definition of the crime problem? And what of the influence of Watergate? Was that unique and already fading scandal largely responsible? The movement clearly predated Watergate; long-term trends, not just historical accident, seem to be at work. On the other hand, there is strong evidence that Watergate played an extremely important role in accelerating the development. In an attempt to piece together the relationship between personality and situational opportunity into a comprehensive understanding of the process of change over the last 10 years, it is useful to consider an analogy from the decade of the 1960s—Robert Morgenthau's administration of the U.S. Attorney's office for the Southern District of New York.[40]

Morgenthau received great publicity and professional acclaim for his successful prosecutions of Carmine DeSapio of Tammany Hall and a series of large securities fraud cases. Nothing in Morgenthau's background gave a clear indication that he would make white-collar crime a new priority. Nowhere had he spelled out a jurisprudential or political theory calling for the prosecution of political corruption and business crimes.[41] Assistants who were appointed to run white-collar crime sections in the office knew that *they* had spelled out no such philosophy. The change in the office must be understood as the natural development of an aggressively run, self-consciously elite office in a time of new opportunity.

It should be recalled that in the 1950s the Southern District, by reputation the "premier" prosecution office in the country, had devoted its energies to the punishment of political crimes by Leftists. In the Attorney General's Annual Reports for the years 1950 to 1958, Internal Security was the first priority, and the Southern District cases deemed worthy of specific mention were predominantly prosecutions of Smith Act violations, espionage on behalf of the Soviet Union, and contempts of Congress and false statements growing out of investigations of subversives. After reporting several major judicial reversals in the late 1950s of convictions of Leftists (Jencks, Yates), the Attorney General's report for 1960 showed a general de-emphasis on internal security and, in the Southern District, the emergence of securities frauds prosecutions (Francis Peter Crosby; the Rock Salt scandal—*Fortune* and Anthony Pope; Alexander Guterma). With the installation of the Kennedy Administration and the appointment of Morgenthau in 1961, the office's already ebbing Cold War animus was overtaken by the spirit of meritocratic professionalism in search of an appropriate mission.

It was natural[42] that a group of prosecutors who regarded themselves as the best would seek opportunities to dramatize their excellence. White-collar crime cases were likely to be seen as especially difficult in part because they had to be uncovered and "made," in part because they brought an unusual quality of defense counsel to the other side. Political corruption prosecutions would especially dramatize the office's professional integrity and independence from politics. They would quickly distinguish the office's new staff from the prior regime which, however ethically, played a strong political role as an enforcement arm of nationally led anticommunist campaigns.

The case for emphasizing white-collar crime was put as a matter of enforcement philosophy rather than mere self-celebration: Federal prosecutors should reach where state prosecutors jurisdictionally cannot, and the best federal prosecution staff should reach crimes inaccessible to lesser staffs. In a sense, the most serious crimes are those which attempt to make use of politically powerful or economically elite positions to frustrate detection and prosecution; white-collar crimes define the boundaries of the criminal justice system's capacities and the limits of moral integrity in the economy and polity. The normative statement would require further qualification before it could be embraced as a tenet of a proper social philosophy, but no more elaborate ideology was necessary to motivate the office effectively.[43]

Similarly, the movement in the last decade was propelled as a nationally led, right-wing influence in local offices suddenly dissolved with Watergate. Pre-existing trends were allowed free expression. The trends included a general if gentle meritocratic movement; the rapid expansion of social welfare programs in the 1960s without carefully planned controls; pressure from Naderism for action against consumer fraud; and the cycle of the "Go-Go 60s" and the recession of the early 1970s, which threw many businesses into bankruptcy when the crimes of their pasts were suddenly matters of public record. The early 1970s showed signs of these trends in increased white-collar prosecutions, as well as signs of an expected increase in prosecutions of Democrats by new Republican appointees in Democratic strongholds such as Chicago and Newark. "Watergate" marked the end of repression against war and race protestors and destroyed the "street crime" campaign of the Nixon Administration, removing law enforcement concerns that had obfuscated trends toward increased attention on white-collar crime. Federal criminal prosecutions in the Northern District of Illinois, to take the most glaring example, were no longer represented in the public eye by the trial of the Chicago Eight.

At the same time, Watergate provided historically unprecedented opportunities for professional mobility to a national set of aggressive lawyers. The context was more novel than the personalities. Certainly the lawyers in question entered public office without any distinctive ideological cast. By and large, the leaders of the white-collar crime movement in U.S. Attorney's offices and other enforcement agencies had no clear affiliation in their personal backgrounds with a form of political philosophy that dictated a special animus against the white-collar criminal. In fact, many of the U.S. Attorneys and especially influential assistant U.S. Attorneys in the middle and late 1970s had entered the Justice Department during the early 1970s, when the department was unusually repulsive to social critics. It required a historically distinctive suspension of moral judgment about government to become a federal prosecutor at a time when one's school friends might well become defendants in draft resistance or war protest cases.

In a general pattern, the first Nixon-Mitchell appointees to U.S. Attorney positions were party stalwarts and/or middle-aged, prominent partners in large corporate law firms. This was the case in Los Angeles, Chicago, New Jersey, and Brooklyn. Watergate created power vacuums that enabled younger, less politically connected, and much less career-established assistants to direct the office against white-collar crime, either formally as a new U.S. Attorney or informally as a first assistant or chief of a special prosecutions section. In some offices, the first Republican appointee had already received the appointment as a federal judge that he had anticipated with some confidence before he reached the prosecutor's office, based on his prior political ties and professional stature. His replacement did not have the same credits built up and was likely to be more "hungry." In New Jersey, Stern, an ex-Manhattan assistant D.A. and then an assistant U.S. Attorney, succeeded Lacey, a senior partner in a prestigious corporate firm. In Chicago, Thompson, a young Northwestern University law professor, replaced Bauer, who had had a long career at the Du Page County District Attorney's office as a successful Republican electoral candidate.

Elsewhere, new U.S. Attorneys could rely on the context of the Watergate scandal to neutralize the influence of their offices' traditional political constituencies. In Brooklyn, David Trager and Edward Korman—two lawyers in their 30s who had been close friends from appellate clerkship days through their tenures as assistants in the office's Appeals division in the early 1970s—took over when a bizarre series of events (the suicide of the U.S. Attorney, an unsuccessful prosecution of Long Island Republicans that was brought precipitously by an acting U.S. Attorney) created a vacancy and cut off the control of the selection process that the Long Island Republican organization otherwise would have exercised. The Watergate scandal was a shield for the Maryland office as it developed the Agnew case. By the time the Maryland prosecutors were ready to invite the Attorney General into plea bargaining with Agnew, Elliot Richardson had replaced Richard Kleindienst and was mediating the relation between Nixon and Special Prosecutor Archibald Cox. John Mitchell—who early in the Republican administration had forced the resignation of Maryland U.S. Attorney Stephen Sachs by blocking indictments of public officials—was now the target of several criminal investigations.

In Los Angeles, the first Republican U.S. Attorney under Nixon—Robert Meyer, who had been George Murphy's Senate campaign manager—surprised many with an independent stance. Local police and sheriff's officials then tapped White House connections to stop his investigations of police brutality and corruption.[44] Assistant Attorney General Mardian demanded Meyer's resignation for resisting the inclusion of an official secrets-type charge in the indictment of Daniel Ellsberg.[45] Meyer acceded to the pressure from Washington and left. A resulting power vacuum under the next U.S. Attorney was filled by Stephen Wilson, an enterprising assistant who became chief of Special Prosecutions. Wilson had come to Los Angeles from the Justice Department's criminal Tax Division, after examining carefully the comparative opportunities for personal mobility by travelling to the nation's U.S. Attorney offices as part of his itinerant work.[46] An office whose leadership had been battered and finally purged on partisan and ideological grounds could now choose targets like Dr. Louis Cella, Jr.—the single largest contributor to both Democratic and Republican California campaigns in 1974—without fear of reprisal.

Watergate, in its broad sense as the series of allegations tying numerous Washington headquarters into a seamless scandal, provided protection for controversial executive initiatives in a range of federal enforcement and oversight agencies. About a year after Boltz became Western regional SEC administrator, SEC Chairman G. Bradford Cook was tainted by the investigation of Robert Vesco, Maurice Stans, and John Mitchell for influence peddling at the SEC. His resignation symbolized an extraordinary period of vulnerability to charges of improper commission influence on staff investigations. FBI field leader Neil Welch reportedly had run close to bureaucratic suicide by resisting the FBI's COINTELPRO emphasis on Leftist subversives in the 1960s. He received an unexpected measure of freedom for his unconventional emphases on white-collar and organized crime when the responsibility of J. Edgar Hoover and Wallace LaPrade of the New York office for illegal investigative tactics was exposed. The General Accounting Office (GAO), Congress's investigative arm, exploited the Watergate context to institute a significant new measure of autonomy for provoking scandals about government fraud:

> Between 1972 and 1976, the number of GAO reports that were given nationwide, in-depth media coverage grew from 31 to 180, or about one every other day . . . the traditional audits performed by the GAO—financial reviews—became the basis for national media attention, although the GAO had not suddenly changed its modus operandi.[47]

Awakening to its new opportunities, the GAO threw off a traditional congressional constraint. The agency used to "bury" an audit when the Congressman who ordered it did not care to have the findings released. In 1977, Comptroller General Elmer Staats issued regulations providing for the release of all reports, with or without the specific authorization of the requesting member.

CONCLUSION

The way in which Watergate promoted a general movement against white-collar crime calls to mind Edward Shils's analysis of how charisma works as a modern source of societal integration.[48] On a mass level, citizens silently maintain allegiance to a network of institutions through their transcendant respect for perceived center of collective integrity. The Presidency was suddenly stripped of all shreds of compelling aura by the unprecedented exposure symbolized by the tapes. Sources of political and economic power less central to national identity also became suddenly vulnerable to embarrassing inquiries that previously would have been impossibly impolitic. As a practical matter, the White House temporarily lost its considerable ability to protect lesser power centers from moral attack. Accordingly, the movement against white-collar crime should recede as the Presidency is restored to the insulation of presumptive legitimacy.

There are numerous signs that the movement is in marked decline. Shortly after he took office, President Carter found it costly but in the end politically feasible to fire Philadelphia U.S. Attorney David Marston despite Marston's highly publicized allegations that his dismissal had been promoted by a target of his investigation, Representative Joshua Eilberg. Federal prosecutors have joined to petition for legislative relief from the restrictions of the Tax Reform Act of 1976. They say the act has all but stopped the previously rich production of political corruption cases from tax investigations.[49] Securities fraud prosecutions in Los Angeles have returned to a relatively unexceptional state. The new head of the General Services Administration unabashedly opined that the level of corruption in government contracting, which has been alleged in the indictment of over 115 persons or firms, has been overblown.[50] The Department of Justice announced the formation of white-collar prosecution units in 27 offices, but added the pregnant afterthought that "Budget restrictions will probably prohibit hirings to fill slots."[51]

On the other hand, some degree of institutionalization of the increased emphasis on white-collar crime has been achieved. The FBI was freed from J. Edgar Hoover by natural causes and from its historic priorities on violent criminals, political subversives, and quantitative measures of productivity by a continuing series of scandals. It is now regarded as having shifted its emphasis to white-collar crime even by some of its most severe policy critics. Stanley Sporkin is widely regarded as having become politically unassailable in his command of SEC enforcement. (Some fear his personal power over the agency may rival Hoover's.) Virtually all of the white-collar crime prosecutors mentioned in earlier pages have now left law enforcement, but many have used their fame to move to other positions of public power (e.g., Governors Thompson and Thornburgh), where they may be expected to value a continued reputation for sensitivity to white-collar crime. Judicial decisions validating significant, expansive prosecutive applications of statutes against white-collar crime have in some instances become firm precedents. I would add that an examination of the social organization and symbolic thrust of the movement indicates that it is structured to continue, albeit at a level reduced from the intensity of the 1970s.

There is a long-term market in American political culture for the symbolics of white-collar crime law enforcement. The demand supporting the movement to date has been much more than a utilitarian concern for the efficient deterrence of antisocial conduct. There are, after all, remedies other than the criminal penalty for many of the illegalities that have been newly brought within the prosecutor's reach. In order to redress or attempt to deter insider trading, water pollution, domestic commercial bribery, "sensitive" international business payments, illegal campaign contributions, and food contamination, fines can be assessed, boards of directors restructured, licenses revoked, and punitive damages increased. Public subsidy can be given to the enforcement effort without invoking the criminal law, through administrative agency action and through facilitated access to civil courts for private damage suits. In order to understand the expansion of "white-collar crime," we must understand the demand that unjust enrichment and unjustly acquired power be made criminal; not just that it be made unprofitable but that it be defined officially as abominable, that it be treated as qualitatively alien to the basic moral character of society. The way the criminal law has been expanded by the white-collar crime law enforcement movement suggests a drive described by George Fletcher in the context of an examination of the evolution of larceny law:

> The modern vision of the criminal law seems to be that the proper allocation of each item of property enjoys the full concern of the community; the dishonest displacement of wealth from one person to another therefore becomes a public harm. . . . The end in sight is the criminalization of all cases of dishonest self-enrichment.[52]

Public awareness of white-collar crime has been shaped by government officials. The white-collar crime law enforcement movement has been decentralized. Its agents have been enterprising promoters of morality. Their rhetoric of motivation has been an apolitical indignation about covered-up, publicly indefensible bases of political influence and economic privilege. Motive power has been supplied not by institutionalized bureaucratic authority nor by party loyalty, but by a striving for personal, professional mobility which sincerely and shrewdly exploits a common-sense indignation about social injustice. Once the limits of the criminal sanction have been expanded against "white-collar" crime, it should require no special policies to sustain the expansions. As the trend has developed over the last decade, we may expect that, until it is replaced by another nationally led politicization of "street crime" or centralized campaign against political dissidents, the "white-collar crime problem" will not revert to its insignificance of the 1960s. We should continue to see the criminal law used with distinctive dramatic power to express, however unsystematically and superficially, an official, collective condemnation of social injustice.

NOTES

1. Two Democratic Attorneys General form the 1960s wrote widely read books on "the crime problem." Ramsay Clark, *Crime in America,* New York: Simon and Schuster, 1970, made an occasional rhetorical reference to white-collar crime and the problem of unequal justice, but focused on arguing the causation of crime by urban poverty, drugs, and guns and on the overblown

reputation of organized crime, which he characterized as engaged primarily in efficient street and vice crimes (see p. 74). Robert F. Kennedy's *The Enemy Within* was

> an account of dramatic and sordid crime against organized labor's rank and file, and generally the people of the United States, committed by *gangsters* in trade unions and the cowardly or mercenary employers and lawyers who on occasion criminally conspired with them [New York: Harper, 1960: ix; emphasis added].

Kennedy's Organized Crime Section, particularly the so-called get Hoffa squad, is credited by many federal law enforcement insiders as the first example of a white-collar prosecution office: investigating prosecutors working closely with in-house accountants. Many direct lines can be traced from Robert Kennedy's Washington-based campaign against labor racketeers, through its regional arms, the Organized Crime Strike Forces, to U.S. Attorneys' offices that became renowned for generalized white-collar crime emphases. For example, the careers of Herbert Stern and Jonathan Goldstein, successive U.S. Attorneys in New Jersey, linked the 1960s Kennedy Justice Department with the 1970s (Paul Hoffman, *Tiger in the Court,* Chicago: Playboy, 1973, p. 33). But the role to be attributed to RFK's contribution is at most that of a proven model, and not a "first" nor a sustaining empirical cause of the last decade's social movement against white-collar crime.

2. According to "Federal Prosecutions of Corrupt Public Officials, 1970-1977," A Report Compiled by The Public Integrity Section, Criminal Division, U.S. Department of Justice, August 24, 1978, federal prosecutions of federal officials rose from 9 in 1970 to 129 in 1977. Interestingly, there was a jump from 9 to 58 between 1970 and 1971, and a continuation at that level until 1976, when another jump brought the annual number of federal officials indicted to 111. The statistics on federal indictments of state officials show a similarly timed, two-stage jump, although the pattern is less defined. The same pattern is visible, though even more dimly, in the statistics on local officials indicted federally.

3. Paul Hoffman, *Tiger in the Court.* Chicago: Playboy, 1973, p. 3.

4. *U.S. News and World Report,* February 28, 1977, p. 36. The roles in the Cook County Democratic "machine" of many of the indicted officials are described in Joe Matthewson, *Up Against Daley,* La Salle, Illinois: Open Court, 1974.

5. *Newsday,* November 1, 1977, p. 23.

6. An attempt to outline resulting difficulties for law enforcement is August Bequai, *Computer Crime.* Lexington, Massachusetts: Lexington Books, 1978.

7. A comprehensive review of the recent increase in public attention to white-collar crime would take us beyond the boundaries not only of the Eastern District of New York but also beyond prosecuted cases to the less easily documented atmosphere of scandal. The New York *Times* Index to the N.Y. Times began listing articles under a category for "white-collar crime" only in 1975. The "government investigations" category in the Reader's Guide to Periodical Literature contained about 20 items on white-collar crime or related matters, 13 of which were on Adam Clayton Powell, in volume 27, covering March 1967 to February 1968; and about 69 in volume 37 10 years later.

8. Social scientists have lagged far behind the public and behind government officials in turning their attention toward white-collar crime. Faced with a radically altered public definition of their field, perhaps the best tactic for criminologists would be to hold onto received ideas and research styles and wait for social awareness of white-collar crime to fade. This seems to be the strategy taken by James Q. Wilson, who refuses to turn his mind to white-collar crime in *Thinking About Crime.* New York: Basic Books, 1975. Wilson explains:

> this . . . reflects my conviction, which I believe is the conviction of most citizens, that predatory street crime is a far more serious matter than consumer fraud, antitrust violations [xix].

(Wilson fails to mention political corruption and criminal civil rights violations by law enforcement agents. As he was writing shortly after the Watergate revelations, it is questionable whether his convictions were the same as most citizens.)

9. At all levels of government: John Morton Blum, *The Republican Roosevelt.* Cambridge: Harvard University Press, 1977, chapters 5 and 7. David P. Thelen, *Robert M. La Follette and the Insurgent Spirit.* Boston: Little, Brown. 1976. Ray Ginger, *Altgeld's America.* New York: New Viewpoints. 1973. Melvin G. Holli, *Reform in Detroit: Hazen S. Pingree and Urban Politics,* New York: Oxford University. 1969.

10. Allen F. Davis, *Spearheads for Reform: The Social Settlements and the Progressive Movement. 1890-1914.* New York: Oxford University. 1967.

11. Lawrence Goodwyn, *Democratic Promise: The Populist Movement in America.* New York: Oxford University, 1976.

12. See Arthur and Lila Weinberg, eds., *The Muckrakers.* New York: G. P. Putnam's Sons, 1961.

13. Robert H. Wiebe, *Businessmen and Reform.* Chicago: Quadrangle, 1962.

14. Daniel P. Moynihan, *Maximum Feasible Misunderstanding.* New York: Free Press, 1969, pp. 22-23.

15. There is not decent history of the office of U.S. Attorney. For a passing mention of a very few of the many themes that a thorough history would have to develop, see Whitney North Seymour, Jr., *United States Attorney.* New York: Morrow, 1975, pp. 19-41.

16. Walton Bean, *Boss Ruef's San Francisco.* Berkeley: University of California Press, 1952. Federal authority was also significant for its absence from the movement that brought down New York City's boss. The Tweed "Ring" was turned out of power by local popular forces in the general state election of 1871 after a civic reform group, The Committee of Seventy, and the New York *Times* had developed and published detailed evidence of fraud and corruption. Indictments came only after the stunning electoral victory, which led to the appointment of a special investigator at the state level, Henry J. Taintor, who then fed incriminating evidence into criminal prosecutions for years. Alexander B. Callow, *The Tweed Ring.* New York: Oxford University, 1966, pp. 253-279. These examples suggest not just that the autonomous power of federal law enforcement has risen but also that the autonomous power of local newspapers to turn out corrupt municipal systems has fallen dramatically.

17. Cf. the scale and criminal penalties of the Water Pollution Control Act of 1972.

18. P. I. 93-443, Title IV, 410 (a), 88 Stat. 1304. Oct. 15, 1974. 93rd Congress, 2d Session.

19. Nadjari was appointed by Governor Rockefeller in September 1972 to investigate and prosecute corruption in the New York City criminal justice system. He expanded his jurisdiction to reach political figures not formally within the criminal justice system, such as Patrick Cunningham, a Bronx-based, state Democratic leader with influence over the appointment of criminal court judges. Nadjari was dismissed by Governor Carey in 1976, after most of his cases had been thrown out at trial or reversed after conviction on appellate judicial objections to his investigative procedures. See his own tally in *A Public Accounting: September 18, 1972 to February 29, 1976.* Office for the Investigation of the New York City Criminal Justice System. 2 World Trade Center, New York, 1976.

20. The Bernstein-Woodward behind-the-scenes book on their reporting is full of indications of role modeling on the criminal trial:

"I was absolutely convinced in my mind that there was no way that any of this could have happened without Haldeman, [Washington *Post* Executive Editor Ben Bradlee told Woodward and Bernstein]. . . . But . . . I was determined to keep it out of the paper until you could prove it. . . ." Bradlee served as prosecutor, demanding to know exactly what each source had said. . . . "I want to hear exactly what you asked him and what his exact reply was." "What did the FBI guy say?" The reporters gave a brief summary. "No . . . I want to hear exactly what you asked him and what his exact reply was."

This meeting with Deep Throat produced the most serious disagreement between Bernstein and Woodward since they had begun working together. . . . The question was whether a convincing and well-documented account of Mitchell's and Colson's roles could be written. . . . Bernstein reworked the story three times. . . . Each time . . . Woodward said he didn't think it should run until they had better proof. Bernstein argued that the story was legitimate, that the newspaper didn't have to offer definite evidence.

All the Presidents Men. Carl Bernstein and Bob Woodward. New York: Warner, 1974, pp. 203; 273.

21. The investigative reporter's concern for discovering legally provable facts is one of many indicators of a historical shift in journalism from an explicitly normative role to a commitment to "objectivity." See generally, Michael Schudson, *Discovering the News.* New York: Basic Books, 1978.

22. Anthony Lewis, "Great Care is Needed if Prosecution is the Goal," New York *Times,* October 19, 1975, Part 4, p. 1.

23. The 1970s increased the stock of institutional gadflies such as Abraham Briloff, who wrote a series of business magazine articles depicting the near and the fully criminal involvement of "independent" auditors in major investment frauds. See his *More Debits Than Credits: The Burnt Investor's Guide to Financial Statements.* New York: Harper & Row, 1976.

24. "Taxes and Civil Liberties," New York *Times.* February 20, 1977, p. 11.

25. State-level district attorneys have acted against white-collar crime primarily by attacking consumer frauds. See *Fighting the $40 Billion Rip-Off: An Annual Report from the Economic Crime Project.* Washington, D.C.: National District Attorneys Association, 1976. As nonelected state-level special prosecutors, Charles Hynes, appointed by Governor Carey to investigate and prosecute corrupt nursing home operators, and Nadjari are exceptions that prove the rule.

26. Herbert J. Stern, "Prosecutions of Local Political Corruption Under the Hobbs Act," *Seton Hall Law Review* 3 (Fall 1971), pp. 1-17, developed the early justifications for expansion.

27. Abraham Goldstein, "Conspiracy to Defraud the United States," *Yale Law Journal,* 68: 405 (1959).

28. *U.S. v. Aloi, et al.* 77 Cr. 77 (E.D.N.Y., 1977).

29. Title 18 U.S.C. 1001. We may not be far from a prosecution for false statement of a university student who maintains eligibility for a federally subsidized educational loan by cheating on exams. A cooperative cheating effort in a fraternity might become a "conspiracy to defraud the United States." Title 18 U.S.C. 371.

30. "Sporkin the Enforcer," *Newsweek.* October 24, 1977, p. 94. Voices against the SEC's reliance on the power of negative publicity as punishment have been raised from both the defense and prosecution sides. Some argue that Sporkin is a paper tiger. "Why the SEC's enforcer is in over his head," *Business Week.* October 11, 1976, pp. 70; 73; 76.

31. Some of the criminal cases worked up by Los Angeles SEC investigators and federal prosecutors during this period included: Equity Funding, the most publicized corporate fraud of the decade; T. P. Richardson, one of the largest "third market" securities brokers in the country, for the biggest short-selling fraud in the history of SEC prosecutions; principals in All American Funds, in the first indictments under a section of the Investment Advisers Act of 1940 prohibiting fraud by an investment adviser; principals in Shamrock Mutual Fund, once rated the third most successful mutual fund of its size nationally and the first mutual fund ever forced into receivership, for the arrangement of kickbacks in return for the purchase of speculative securities; James Dondich, for an international investment fraud in the purchase of millions of tons of sugar, rice, and other commodities; Barry Marlin, for a real estate and commercial investment fraud which created a public loss estimated at more than $12 million. (Details and superlatives come from SEC Litigation Releases and from Annual Reports to the Attorney General of the U.S. Attorney's office for the Central District of California.)

32. According to an SEC staff lawyer who worked in the Los Angeles office during this period, Boltz insisted on running his own shop and resisted Sporkin's attempts to use regional resources for his own organizational needs. For example, a national SEC enforcement chief might try to motivate his staff by holding out the lure of desirable regional assignments such as a winter in Los Angeles rather than in Wisconsin. Boltz would resist when weaker regional administrators would not, and he argued openly with Sporkin at regional review meetings. From the commission's perspective, Boltz had acquired a controversial reputation from his work in Texas, and his selection to lead the West

was a strong confirmation by the commission leadership of his past performance. But the event that precipitated his assignment was the retirement of his predecessor—the natural process of attrition—not a formal change in SEC priorities.

33. Fred J. Cook, "Shaking the Bricks at the F.B.I." *New York Times Magazine*. March, 25, 1979, p. 31.

34. Jack Katz, "Legality and Equality: Plea Bargaining in the Prosecution of White-Collar and Common Crimes." *Law & Society Review* 13 (Winter 1979): 444.

35. See the various agency responses contained in appendices to a General Accounting Office report, "Federal Agencies Can, And Should, Do More to Combat Fraud in Government Programs," September 19, 1978. U.S. GAO Report to the Congress of the United States.

36. Paul Hoffman, *Tiger in the Court*. Chicago: Playboy Press, 1973, pp. 174-89.

37. Skolnick began working on the case in October 1972, after he "returned from a seven-month leave from the office which he had devoted to trying to get Edmund Muskie elected President." Aaron Latham, "Closing in on Agnew: The Prosecutors' Story." *New York,* Nov. 26, 1973, p. 54.

38. The natural history of the Lance case displayed the ability of low-level federal prosecutors, in this case assistant U.S. Attorney Jeffrey Bogart, to "make" major white-collar prosecutions without the leadership of their local U.S. Attorney, much less from the Justice Department. See L. J. Davis, "The Money Vanishes: The Case of Bert Lance and the Overdrawn Accounts." *Harper's*. September, 1979 (vol. 259, no. 1552), pp. 65-66.

39. Some observers, noting that John Mitchell's career had excruciating ironies, would say that the Justice Department earlier had been supportive in decisive ways. Mitchell's Justice Department pressed in 1970 for the passage of the "use immunity" statute which became instrumental in persuading witnesses to make many of the biggest cases, for example Agnew's. (But I do not believe the formal immunity statute was essential. Prosecutors previously had functional alternatives. The issue has been considered extremely debatable. For the Justice Department's view in the mid-1970s, see Richard L. Thornburgh, "Reconciling Effective Federal Prosecution and the Fifth Amendment," *Journal of Criminal Law,* 67 (June): 155-166, 1976). Mitchell responded generously to requests for staff increases from some offices that had made progress against political corruption, the most dramatic example being New Jersey which, according to tallies kept by the Executive Office for U.S. Attorneys, rose from 20 assistants in 1969 to 51 in 1971.

40. For the Southern District's history, I am drawing on a suggestion by Burke Marshall; an interview with Arthur Lyman, who was a white-collar crime section chief under Morgenthau in the early 1960s; and on Victor Navasky, "A Famous Prosecutor Talks About Crime," *New York Times Magazine.* February 15, 1970.

41. And, leaving the U.S. Attorney's office for an unsuccessful run as the Democratic candidate for Governor against Nelson Rockefeller in 1962, Morgenthau had had plenty of opportunity to publicize any strong views he may have had against "robber barons" and the corruption of the political process by private wealth.

42. "Natural": unproblematic to the participants; requiring no special explanation by way of unique personal perspective.

43. For Morgenthau's formulation, see his "Equal Justice and the Problem of White Collar Crime," *Conference Board Record.* August 1969, pp. 17-20.

44. Meyer's account of the pressure on him appeared in a delayed and partial form in "Politics Caused Him to Resign as U.S. Attorney, Meyer Says," Los Angeles *Times,* pp. 3; 22. January 19, 1972, part I.

45. Phillip Schrag, *Test of Loyalty*. New York: Simon and Schuster, 1974, p. 101.

46. Personal interview.

47. Frederick C. Mosher, *The GAO: The Quest for Accountability in American Government*. Boulder, Colorado: Westview Press, 1979, pp. 248-249.

48. Shils, E. A. 1965. "Charisma, Order, and Status." *American Sociological Review* 30 (April): 199-213; 1968. "Charisma," pp. 386-390 in *International Encyclopedia of the Social Sciences,* edited by D. Sills, Vol. 2. New York: Macmillan.

49. For a detailed description of possible criminal cases discovered by the Internal Revenue Service during the first 14 months following the effective date of the act and not disclosed to prosecutors specifically because of the act's disclosure limitations, see pp. 10 and 12 of "The Erosion of Law Enforcement Intelligence and its Impact on the Public Security," Hearing before the Subcommittee on Criminal Law and Procedure. Committee on the Judiciary, U.S. Senate, 95th Congress, 2d Session, Part 6A, Appendix, April 25, 1978. ("Five cases of possible bribery of Federal officials . . . fifteen cases of possible illegal political contributions by corporations . . . six cases of securities laws violations.")

50. "The new head of the General Services Administration Wednesday called his personnel 'all basically honest' and asserted that agency corruption was never as bad as reported. . . . Retired Navy Adm. Rowland G. Freeman III . . . was named by President Carter in March to succeed Jay Solomon, who had been criticized for his openness with the news media about the scandal." "GSA Fraud Overstated, New Agency Chief Says." Los Angeles *Times,* October 18, 1979, part I, p. 19.

51. "Budget restrictions will probably prohibit hirings to fill slots, a department spokesman said." "White-Collar Crime Targeted: Justice Dept. to Open 27 Units," *National Law Journal.* April 30, 1979, p. 2.

52. George P. Fletcher, "The Metamorphosis of Larceny," *Harvard Law Review* 89: 469, 1976.

8

HISTORICAL DEVELOPMENT OF
CONSUMER FRAUD LAW

JONATHAN A. SHELDON

GEORGE J. ZWEIBEL

A brief survey of the historical development of consumer
fraud law in England and later in the United States will place
in perspective modern consumer fraud approaches. Nevertheless,
the ensuing description is not a careful, scholarly treatise, but,
instead, a simplified and deliberately provocative sketch.

Because of the great incompleteness in primary sources and
the consequent lack of consensus among scholars, this historical
section cannot speak with the same authority as succeeding sections will about present day legal concepts. For example, sur-
viving case law from fourteenth century England comes disproportionately from selected records from the more sophisticated urban
tribunals, with little material, if any, from outlying districts.
Consequently, legal historians may take issue with some interpretations here,particularly since this section is summary historical
description aimed to provoke general readers into viewing present
day legal patterns with a broader perspective.

Most modern legislation was enacted to deal with flagrant
abuses, while permitting the underlying consumer-merchant relationship to remain one of caveat emptor, or "let the buyer beware."
But this notion of caveat emptor was fully articulated only after
the 18th century. Feudal English law contained an underlying concept of a "just" or sound price for a sound product. Even though
the majority of the population was excluded from the royal courts,
other mechanisms regulated the marketplace and enforced this principle of fair business dealings. The Commercial Revolution in the
fifteenth and sixteenth century saw the royal courts alter the common law to meet merchant needs, but notions of equity in the marketplace persisted.

Although various forces over the centuries would thwart in
various ways this ideal of a just price and a regulated market,
not until the development of stock speculation and futures markets
in the 19th century did the doctrine of caveat emptor fully replace
these earlier notions. Twentieth century consumer fraud legislation, with few exceptions, has not altered this fundamental principle of caveat emptor.

From Jonathan A. Sheldon and George J. Zweibel, "Historical Development of Consumer Fraud
Law," pp. 1-17 in *Survey of Consumer Fraud Law* (which was supported by a grant from the National
Institute of Law Enforcement and Criminal Justice, Law Enforcement Assistance Administration,
U.S. Department of Justice).

A. PRE-FEUDAL ENGLAND (900-1100)

The foundations of Anglo-American law date back to pre-feudal English "courts" where lord and vassals acting as prosecutor, "jury" and judge in one, gathered at the baron's banquet hall to pressure and discipline their weaker bretheren. These "manorial courts" kept few systematic records. Royal decrees, the "statutes" of the time, were only unevenly known or used.

B. THE ROYAL COURTS IN FEUDAL ENGLAND (1100-1400)

By the late eleventh century certain of these courts had developed into "royal" and other specialized courts. Still other courts grew from different sources until Feudal England presented litigants an array of forums that could adjudicate disputes. The royal courts left the most substantial written record and having the King's authority,were the most powerful in the land. Consequently,they are a good starting place to look at the development of consumer fraud law, before turning to the more numerous feudal courts and dispute resolution mechanisms that proved more influential in dealing with marketplace fraud as it affected most people.

The Crown used the royal courts to administer the realm, spell out the King's will (the "law"), punish misbehavior and make bargains for the exercise of preference. These courts thus merged traditional legislative, executive, and judicial functions, proving of great benefit to the Crown and the numerous officials representing the Crown. The courts kept the unruly nobility under constraint, but that nobility also found the courts invaluable in invoking the royal will and the royal army in their own cause. The courts also levied sizeable fines for "breach of the King's peace", allowing sheriffs and other Crown representatives to coerce significant payments from those too weak to resist collection efforts.

But the royal courts would not hear all disputes, but limited litigations to matters of special interest to the Crown, commonly real estate and other objects of value. By and large, the only individuals to sue in these courts were the nobility, certain well-to-do merchants with land holdings, and wealthy money lenders. Serfs and craftsmen might occasionally find themselves defendents, but their access to the royal courts were otherwise blocked. The courts adjudicated disputes of greatest concern to these wealthier classes who were able to bring actions-disputes over inheritance, mortgage contracts, collateral interests, other covenants, real estate bargains,and possession of land and certain valuable moveables.

A body of law slowly began to develop concerning these primarily realty issues. One might expect Crown representatives to make judicial decisions consistent with the Crown interest and other pressures applied. But the decisions were justified by reference to a preexisting local "practice", the so called

common law. Thus emerged a developing fiction that judges
were not making law so much as announcing an as yet incomplete-
ly articulated law. While other courts also utilized local or
"common" precedents, it was the royal courts that proceeded
most formally, and developed the most standardized body of law.
But even the common law in royal courts was not systematically
applied. Reporting was rudimentary, biased and otherwise spotty.
But the mystery of the common law added to the authority of the
early courts and elevated and complicated the law as a profession
for both bench and bar, adding to their power.

After the Norman Conquest, losers in the royal courts
began seeking exceptions from the court's ruling from the
Chancellor, the King's chief administrative agent. Later this
procedure became institutionalized in the Chancery Court, a
court of "equity" or extraordinary jurisdiction. It would
review actions of common law courts and hear some matters that
were not litigable at "law".

C. FEUDAL DISPUTE RESOLUTION OUTSIDE THE ROYAL COURTS (1100-1400)

Royal courts were generally unavailable for resolving con-
sumer-type fraud claims by the ordinary public unless the Crown
was somehow involved. But there were alternative methods to
resolve the times' marketplace disputes.

1. Informal Mechanisms

Most everyday private agreements between merchants and consumer buyers were sealed with a handshake in front of witnesses.
(More formal agreements involving noblemen and wealthy merchants
would be evidenced by sealed documents.) In the outlying hamlets,
self-help was used wherever possible to resolve simple marketplace
disputes. A rough sense of justice and a shared standard of moral
fairness, aided by sticks and neighbors, settled most disputes.
Defrauding itinerant merchants faced corporal punishment and
expulsion from town.

But over time, particularly in the larger cities, guilds
and town officials began to discourage such practices and point
to other dispute resolution mechanisms. Guilds preferred to discipline their own members, or present disputes during market days
to the chief officer of the Guild, the Portreeve (King's agent)
or an agent of the aristocrat who owned the town's charter.

An even older institution was the view of the frankpledge
where all men of the lower orders were organized in groups of
ten or twelve and were held responsible for each other's actions.
The emphasis was on preventing misconduct, not in remedying individually defrauded customers.

2. Local and Special Courts

Feudal England was dotted by numerous local and special
courts with diverse functions and characteristics that regulated

the conduct of a large portion of the population. These courts
and the law they interpreted differed in important ways from
each other and changed over time. But whatever their form, it
was these courts, not the royal courts, that affected most people's
marketplace dealings. Many of these courts evolved from old manorial and church courts and the town meeting, all dating back to pre-
feudal times.

Fines and some rough reformation of bargains were possible,
but methods of determining which party was in the right involved
primitive dispute mechanisms. Such earlier "trials" as wagers
of battle (where the two parties beat at each other with knives
or cudgels, the winner being declared the innocent party) or
trial by ordeal were probably outmoded by 1200. Instead a gentler
approach was used, called "a wager of law", the antecedent of the
jury system. Each party could call upon oath-helpers who would
swear to the truthfulness of their party's cause. If a predetermined number of oaths were brought forth, the defendent was acquitted. While the procedure varied, only citizens in good
standing could give oaths. Slaves, outlaws, non-conformists,
and outsiders were given short shrift by the "establishment"
who ran these courts -- the local Elders, Churchmen, burgers and
gentry knights.

3. Market Regulation and the Just Price

These informal dispute mechanisms and local courts were
part of a pervasive system of regulation that controlled feudal
England's limited and unsophistocated consumer transactions. Markets
were local because regional transportation was so bad it paid to
transport only luxury goods, fabrics, spices and jewelry. Famines
fifty miles from plenty were common enough. Goods were made to
order locally, with wholesaling virtually non-existent. Barter
was an important means of exchange. Local exchange values would
remain constant for many years, except briefly during catastrophes.

In this type of economy, it was possible for feudal society
to attempt to solve consumer fraud problems by extensive regulation of all aspects of the marketplace,including fixing the cost
of standard items at prices considered fair or just, not leaving
merchants to extract whatever price they could get in a free
market. It is unclear how successful feudal society was in this
monumental task of informal price and quality regulation, but
it is certain that several important institutions assisted in
the effort.

The Crown issued a number of Assizes or royal decrees requiring the appointment of local boards to set prices for various products such as bread and ale. These boards tried to punish cases of profiteering, often with corporal punishment such
as the pillory for bakers (who were usually men) and the dunking
stool for brewers (who were usually women). The Statutes of

Laborers in the mid-fourteenth century sought to fix labor prices which were threatening to sky-rocket as a result of the labor shortage brought about by The Black Death.

The Guilds were another feudal institution involved in price setting and quality standards. Towns living on commerce were usually run by merchant guilds which strictly regulated their membership and set standards for weights and measures and as to terms and conditions of sales, including prices. A craftsman could offer goods in most towns only after long apprenticeship, dues and election. Refusing to follow the rules got one expelled from the town and very nearly from society.

Whether the regulation was by guilds, the Crown, or others, it pervaded all aspects of sales. The way goods could be manufactured, displayed, weighed and measured, and sold were strictly controlled. To quote one commentator: "The object of the law was to insure to every good offered for sale a fair price, full measure, and good workmanship."* Fraud intervention approaches were based on publicity and prevention, not in remedying individually wronged customers.

Another source of rate regulation was the notion of a "just price". The concept was articulated by special merchant courts around 1200 to 1300. A sound price required sound goods. Goods had an intrinsic, just price, independent of their marketplace value determined by supply and demand. Goods should be sold at this fair price, not the marketplace price.

It is likely that this concept ante-dated its usage by merchant courts and more broadly applied to merchant-consumer relations. This would be consistent with the church supported doctrine that each thing had an intrinsic, relatively unvarying worth which was the sum of the cost of the labor and materials needed to make it. Aquinas and other church theoreticians saw a profound difference between wrongful trade carried on for profit and rightful trade which served public necessity. Profiteering beyond the just price or selling shoddy goods at quality prices was a sin at a time when the Church's influence was profound.

It is difficult to ascertain precisely how effective were feudal England's various attempts at setting a "just" price for goods and otherwise regulating the marketplace. Certainly they were not everywhere successful. Nevertheless, it is clear that these notions were widespread and provided an important standard for consumer transactions.

D. THE COMMERCIAL REVOLUTION (1400-1750)

During the commercial revolution, wealth shifted from the landed aristocrats to the merchant class, resulting in the royal courts beginning to involve themselves with merchants'

---

*Hamilton, Walter H., The Ancient Maxim Caveat Emptor, 15 Yale Law Journal 1133 (1931) disputes through specialized Courts Piepowder ("dusty feet" from the French, alluding to the itinerant merchants' griminess, so distinct from the noble litigant) which used a distinctly international breed of legal principles, called the Law Merchant. The Law Merchant was patterned after the law that grew up with Italian banking and Venetian trade and was very different than the Common law. In fact, most of the early merchants in England were not English, but foreigners. They used their own law in settling disputes, not English Common Law.

From about 1300 to 1500 the Law Merchant's development was largely limited to the Courts Piepowder in major trading towns. Thereafter, the royal courts began to seriously consider merchant litigants, and English jurists rapidly reformed the old common law precedents to meet the demands of the merchant class. The King recognized the new commercial law by royal decree.

The fifteenth and sixteenth century changes in the law resulted in altered and expanded causes of action that allowed defrauded buyers to seek legal redress in the royal courts. Three of these have special importance in the development of consumer fraud law.

Trespass on the Case for Warranty. This action developed from the old cause of action involving a trespass onto real property, and was abstracted to include invasions of individuals' other interests. It was used in the special circumstances when a seller more than just represented, but promised or warranted, that certain facts were true when they were not. Trespass on the Case for Warranty was very narrowly construed, with some cases failing to find a causable action if the merchant did not use the word "warrant" as in: "I warrant the following facts to be true."

Trespass on the Case in the Nature of Deceit. The limited nature of Trespass on the Case for Warranty gave impetus to the development, around 1450, of the action called Trespass on the Case in the Nature of Deceit. The action also borrowed elements from an old cause of action called Deceit involving misuse of legal process. The result was a cause of action that allowed damages for misrepresentation even if the seller did not "warrant" facts to be true. This action eventually was extended to even negligent misrepresentation.

Equity. Frauds which the law courts refused to recognize could still be actionable in the Chancery Courts in equity. Not only would equity utilize remedies not available at law - reformation or rescission of the contract, injunctive orders,

and other special rights beyond damages - but it would grant
relief even in innocent misrepresentation situations when the
misrepresenting party took advantage. Intent was not necessary
for the grant of relief from fraud.

The Commercial Revolution also challenged the notion of a
just price. The growth of markets and industry rapidly increased
the number of goods sold, their uses and quality. Difficulties
feudal England faced in regulating market transactions were
multiplied many times over. As the merchant class rose in power,
society also grew more sympathetic to a mercantile viewpoint,
ignoring earlier church doctrine that found activities performed
for profit sinful. These changes also coincided with a significant weakening of the central government and the church. The
extent to which these challenges succeeded in breaking down the
notion of a just price is unclear. Certainly the concept lived
on as an ideal standard, if not always followed.

E. DEVELOPMENT OF CAVEAT EMPTOR (1750-1900)

At least according to one legal historian, the medieval
concepts of a just price, a fair bargain and "a sound price
warranting a sound commodity" persisted as late as 1800. The
prices of many goods and services were settled, allowing juries
and judges to view contracts for their fairness independent of
the terms agreed to by the contracting parties.

In both England and America, juries and judges might not
enforce contracts if there was inadequate consideration. When
the selling price was greater than the supposed objective value
of the product, juries could refuse or reduce damages in actions
brought by sellers. Similarly, if a product did not measure up
to the standards its price implied, courts could enforce buyers'
implied warranty actions.

This doctrine of an independent standard of contractual
fairness apart from the original intent of the bargaining parties
conflicted with emerging nineteenth century commercial notions of
markets, speculation and business bargains. Merchants did not
want juries scrutinizing their business transactions but expected
a business bargain to be enforced. If the merchant received a
benefit in the bargain, he wanted to receive it if the contract
was later breached and his expected profits did not result.

Merchants at first sought alternative methods to enforce
their bargains, avoiding the courts' scrutiny of the contract
terms. Businessmen attempted to informally settle disputes
among themselves. Other matters were referred to a more
formal arbitration process. If court actions were necessary,
they attempted to bring them before merchant juries which

---

*Much of this section is based on M. Horwitz, "The Historical
Foundations of Modern Contract Law," 87 Harv. L. Rev. 917 (1974).
His article may be considered radical by some legal historians,
but it is included here because is is both provocative and documented.

might ignore common law doctrine. Another approach was the inclusion of penal bonds in agreements. While courts might still challenge the fairness of the penalty agreed upon, the bonds were usually enforced.

As the market economy spread and speculation became an important activity, courts began to alter traditional concepts to accomodate these new interests. From the end of the eighteenth century to the end of the nineteenth, changed economic conditions wrought a fundamental modification in contract law, resulting in the development of the concept of caveat emptor and the recognition of the sanctity of bargained for contracts.

Under the sanctity of contract doctrine, or will theory, as it is often called, parties are stuck with their bargains, fair or not. Courts will stop their scrutiny of a contract after determining that the parties reached an agreement. Finding agreement, the courts will enforce the bargain, however ill-balanced.

1. Speculative Markets Change Contract and Warranty Theories

The first turn-of-the-nineteenth century crack in the just price doctrine came when courts began recognizing expectation damages in stock and commodity speculations. Foreign to the just price concept, but essential to the operation of speculative markets, is the notion that a buyer be awarded damages if the seller breached an agreement to sell because the stock had subsequently gone up in value. As one leading commentator explains:

> Markets for future delivery of goods were difficult to explain within a theory of exchange based on giving and receiving equivalents in value. Future contracts for fungible commodities could only be understood in terms of a fluctuating conception of expected value radically different from the static notion that lay behind contracts for specific goods; a regime of markets and speculation was simply incompatible with a socially imposed standard of value. The rise of modern law of contract, then, was an outgrowth of an essentially pro-commercial attack on the theory of objective value which lay at the foundation of the eighteenth century's equitable idea of contract. Id. at 947.

In America, courts began awarding expectation damages in the 1790's in response to an active "futures" market in state securities. This speculation rapidly developed after the Revolutionary War in anticipation of the assumption of state debts by the new national government. The trend was facilitated by the existence of all-merchant juries.

Commodity markets developed somewhat slower and expectation damages for commodity speculation were not awarded until about 1820. Shortly thereafter, as other futures contracts became commonplace, the notion of a just price and fair exchange began to break down. In 1824, a sharply divided New York appellate court overruled one of the leading jurists of the time who refused to enforce a land contract because he found gross inadequacy of consideration. The appellate court countered:

> Every member of the Court must be well aware how much property is held by contract; that purchases are constantly made upon speculation; that the value of real estate is fluctuating...(there) exists an honest difference of opinion in regard to any bargain, as to its being a beneficial one, or not.... Seymour v. Delaney, 3 Con. 448 (N.Y. 1824).

Courts' attempts to accomodate the merchant class' use of the negotiable instrument further buried notions of fair bargains. Merchants convinced courts that promissory notes, to be effective, must allow subsequent holders to make free and clear of any defenses the debtor had against the original creditor. Commercial necessity must take precedence over any unfairness to individual debtors.

Old notions did not pass away quickly. In the 1820's commentators supporting the new theory still considered it the court's function to scrutinize contracts closely if the agreement appeared very unequal. The court would then look to see if one of the bargainers did not understand the contract, was oppressed or was unfairly treated.

By the 1840's the conflict between contracts based on an independent standard of fairness and those based on the bargainers' will was settled with the latter theory triumphant. Later developments would only articulate this basic will theory, voiding contracts under certain narrowly defined conditions such as fraud or total lack of consideration.

These developments in contract law paralleled the nineteenth century's limitation on implied warranties. Late into the eighteenth century both English and American courts held that "a sound price warrants a sound commodity." But in Seixas v Woods, a leading American case decided in 1804, the New York Supreme Court held that recovery could only be had from a merchant who had knowingly sold defective goods. The view spread to American states by the mid-nineteenth century. At the same time, English courts were also limiting the use of implied warranties.

2. Courts' Support of Commercial Interests Facilitates Change

In the space of 50 years, from the late 18th to the mid-19th centuries, the law's view of business transactions had been revolutionized. Courts, instead of insuring that bargains were fair and that a sound price warranted a sound product, blinked at all kinds of inequities, explaining their actions with the notions of caveat emptor and the sanctity of contracts.

While this change can be explained in large part by the law's responding to the demands of modern markets, it was also brought about by a significant shift in the sympathies of American courts. Eighteenth century American courts represented the interests of the small town, the farmer, and the small trader.

The will theory of contracts is evidence of how the courts in the following century became supporters of commercial interests. By enforcing unequal contracts resulting from merchants or consumers bargaining with merchants with superior power, skills, experience and resources, the courts were shaping the law to meet merchant interests and reinforcing existing social and economic inequalities.

But 19th century American courts went even further and used the will theory when it met the needs of the commercial interests but abandoned it when it did not. Courts held laborers strictly to the terms of their contracts, giving them no partial payment if they left before the full term of the contract; the same courts gave building contractors the fair value of their efforts even if the work was not completed. As described by one commentator:

> Although nineteenth century courts and doctrinal writers did not succeed in entirely destroying the ancient connection between contracts and natural justice, they were able to elaborate a system that allowed judges to pick and choose among those groups in the population that would be its beneficiaries. And, above all, they succeeded in creating a great intellectual divide between a system of formal rules—which they managed to identify exclusively with the "rule of law" —and those ancient precepts of morality and equity, which they were able to render suspect as subversive of "the rule of law" itself. Id.at 955, 956.

3. Actions for Fraud Limited

One final step toward the creation of the doctrine of caveat emptor was the narrowing of the common law action for fraud. The late eighteenth century action of Trespass on the Case in the Nature of Deceit was still presumed to reach both intentional and negligent misrepresentations. But as the doctrine of caveat emptor advanced on other fronts, the notion of deceit, or fraud, as it was alternatively called, became more and more difficult to prove. Eventually, before a court would find fraud, five elements had to be proved:

(1) a false representation, usually of fact;

(2) reliance on the representation by plaintiff;

(3) damage as a result of the reliance;

(4) defendant's knowledge of the falsity, called "scienter," and

(5) intentional misrepresentation seeking reliance.

The fifth element was not articulated until 1888 in the fraud case of Derry v. Peek, 14 A.C. 337. Until very recently, English courts refused to grant recovery for pecuniary loss where only negligent misrepresentation was involved. The same approach that purged the last vestiges of equitable price theory from the law's view of contracts can be seen in the articulation of the fourth and fifth elements of common law fraud.

American jurisdictions do not always embrace the scienter and intent elements; some states discard these elements and find sellers absolutely liable for their misrepresentations. Today in America the position has prevailed that negligent misrepresentation causing pecuniary harm is actionable. Scienter and intent may also be unnecessary in an action to rescind a contract or remedy a breach of warranty.

F. MODERN FRAUD APPROACHES (1900-Present)

By 1900 the doctrine of caveat emptor had replaced the "just price" concept. Defrauding merchants found courts ready to enforce their contracts no matter how unfair. Defrauded consumers, on the other hand, found little assistance but only numerous legal obstacles before them if they wished to bring actions for common law fraud or warranty.

Since 1900, various forms of state and federal legislation have, at least on their face, attempted to cure some of this imbalance. These statutes include the Federal Trade Commission Act and state statutes modeled after it, and numerous state occupational licensing acts. Other important categories of consumer fraud legislation are the thousands of statutes that directly prohibit or regulate specific practices and the Uniform Commercial Code's warranty sections. But these legislative attempts have not brought about a radical departure from the doctrine of caveat emptor, and, in fact, often reinforce it.

1. The Federal Trade Commission and Unfair and Deceptive Practices

One of the first such approaches was the creation of the Federal Trade Commission in 1914. The FTC was not created in response to outrages over consumer fraud but to turn-of-the-century concerns over monopolies. The new Commission was established to deal primarily with anti-trust issues. The Act passed in 1914 only prohibits "unfair methods of competition."

The courts immediately limited the scope of this rather vague and broad mandate. In FTC v. Gratz, 253 U.S. 421 (1920), the U.S. Supreme Court limited "unfair methods of competition" to acts previously considered opposed to good morals or against public policy, seeming to limit the FTC's jurisdiction to practices already considered unfair in 1914. The court further narrowed the FTC's scope in 1931 by deciding, in FTC v Raladam, 283 U.S. 643, that the Commission could only attack practices where competitors were injured, not where only consumers were harmed. The FTC Act, which at first glance seemed to include a broad and expansive consumer protection mandate, was whittled away by the courts until it only served to attack egregious anti-competitive conduct.

The Commission did not begin to take on a consumer protection function until the New Deal. A 1934 Supreme Court decision, FTC v. Keppel & Bros., 291 U.S. 304, overturned Gratz. Congress overturned Raladam in 1938 by enacting the Wheeler-Lee Amendment that authorized the FTC to prohibit not only "unfair methods of competition" but also "unfair and deceptive acts or practices." The Commission thus was given an independent consumer protection function, irrespective of a practice's anti-competitive effects.

Deception has proved a broad and evolving standard, allowing for much easier enforcement than common law fraud. Only a capacity to deceive a significant number of consumers need be shown. No proof of intent, actual deception or even actual damage is necessary.

This standard had been hailed as ending the days of caveat emptor. But, in fact, the Federal Trade Commission Act, even as amended, did little to alter merchant-consumer relations. Private individuals cannot sue under this liberal standard, and thus must rely on the FTC's own enforcement efforts. But commentators from Ralph Nader to the American Bar Association have recently criticized the FTC for its failure to take significant action to curtail fraud.

Two recent phenomena, spurred on by the consumer movement
of the late 60's and 70's, have somewhat altered this picture,
and have finally begun to dent caveat emptor's armor. One
is the reinvigoration of FTC enforcement assisted by recent
legislation that gives it expanded powers to police fraud
and redress injured consumer.

More importantly, every state but one has enacted
legislation modeled after the FTC Act, prohibiting unfair or
deceptive acts or practices, known as UDAP statutes. UDAP
statutes not only allow states to police deceptive practices,
but provide consumers with private rights of action, allowing
injured individuals to bring their own suits in court. In
forty-four states, defrauded consumers do not have to bring
common law fraud actions but can use the more liberal FTC
standard of deception.

2. Occupational Licensure

Occupational licensing is another 20th century legislative
innovation that on its face appears to provide protections
from consumer fraud. Numerous regulatory boards in all
states now license individual occupations, extensively
regulating who can enter occupations and how entrants can
conduct themselves.

In 1900, few occupations other than lawyers and doctors
were subject to state licensing. But the early twentieth
century saw literally scores of different occupations licensed.
North Carolina, for example, licensed 60 new occupations by
1938.

It would be convenient to report that this deluge of
occupational regulation was a reaction to the public's feeling
of powerlessness in light of caveat emptor. But, by and large,
occupational licensing resulted instead from the efforts of members of the occupation to be regulated. Their motives were to
restrict entry, reduce price competition, and consequently
increase profits. Another consideration was the desire of
members of an occupation to "professionalize" themselves, thus
adding to their stature in the community and, incidentally,
discouraging public scrutiny.

The appointment of a licensing board, comprised almost
entirely of industry members, was a small price to pay to
effectively preempt other efforts to impose stronger consumer
safeguards. The board, by channeling all consumer complaints
to it for informal industry members' resolution, effectively
insulates the occupation from individual litigation or state
prosecution.

Instead of undermining caveat emptor, occupational licensing may act to preserve it. Unlike the early English trade guilds, these boards do not insure that a sound price results in sound goods, but act more to preserve occupational privilege.

3. Criminal Statutes

A third form of twentieth century legislation altering the consumer-merchant relationship is the hundreds of state and federal statutes that prohibit specific forms of fraud, usually authorizing criminal fines or sentences as sanctions. Unlike the FTC Act that grew out of fears of monopolies, or occupational licensing that was based on merchants' desires to reduce competition, these statutes actually were reactions to public consumer fraud concerns.

The first area of business practices to be so regulated was advertising techniques. This is not surprising since aggressive mass advertising campaigns, being essentially recent phenomena, offered an easier target than business practices legitimized by their age. Nor does restricting advertising practices interfere with the merchant's ability to act as he chooses at the point of sale.

The first statutes to regulate advertising were called Printers' Ink Statutes, named after the advertising journal that, in 1911, drafted the model legislation upon which they were based. The model act prohibited "untrue, deceptive or misleading advertising" and provided misdemeanor penalties for violations. The model was soon adopted in most states.

The journal explained that the model law was based on the "recognition of the business world that the common law remedies were inadequate to restrain the excesses of advertising in an age of mass consumption." Another motive may have been to alleviate publishers' fears that they, not the advertisers, would be held liable for false advertising. The Printers' Ink Statutes, by exempting publishers from their scope, encourage publishers to be more liberal in allowing advertising to be printed. Whatever the reason for their passage, it is typical that the terms of the legislation were determined by the advertising community, not by consumers.

Mail fraud was another early legislative target. The Post Office enforced a series of statutes, passed early in the 20th century, that prohibited fraud in the use of the mails. Exaggeration or other mild misrepresentations short of fraud were not actionable.

Regulating fraud in the use of the mails, as with the Printers' Ink Statutes, did not interfere with point of sale

practices. Similarly, early FTC efforts against consumer
fraud patterned themselves after the Printers' Ink and mail
fraud statutes and were geared more to advertising misrepresentations than to underlying business practices.

Twentieth century consumer fraud legislation expanded
from this early regulation of advertising practices, and
began to prohibit specific point-of-sale and other fraudulent
selling techniques. As public attention focused on particular
sales abuses, statutes would be narrowly drafted to proscribe
the particular practice complained of. This legislative
strategy was consistent with the prevailing philosophy of
government regulation impinging as little as possible with
the free conduct of business.

This same guiding principle led states to minimize
legislation's impact on the consumer-merchant relationship
by allowing only state enforcement, with minimal criminal
fines or sentences as sanctions. Since criminal prosecutions
were difficult to bring, and were rarely brought against
white collar crime, only the most flagrantly abusive sellers
needed to concern themselves with fraud legislation.

Minor or unintentional violations or activity that
could be made to look unintnetional would never be challenged.
Even clearcut and serious violations were rarely prosecuted.
Aggrieved consumers had no viable private right of action,
and could only rely on infrequent government prosecutions.
Consumer restitution was not an available remedy in these
prosecutions.

These narrowly drawn statutes prohibiting specific
forms of fraud, and threatening criminal sanctions for
violations, gave the appearance of hard hitting reform for
publicly perceived abuses. But this appearance proved
largely illusory.

In fairness, criminal sanctions for narrowly drawn
violations was the period's primary law enforcement approach
for all types of anti-social behavior, not just consumer
fraud. But the important point to realize is that early
20th century consumer fraud law, by equating consumer fraud
with other crimes, was just reinforcing the doctrine of
caveat emptor. A strategy of giving consumers no added
rights in their day to day dealings with merchants, and
condoning all but the most flagrant business abuses, pre-
supposed that the previous century's doctrine of caveat
emptor, not earlier notions of fairness and justice in the
marketplace, should control 20th century consumer transactions.

4. Other Regulation

Public pressures earlier in this century for reform of
consumer abuses did not result only in criminal statutes.

Another option was the creation of government agencies to regulate industry practices. Unlike occupational licensing boards that were created by industry members to reduce entry and professionalize an occupation, these agencies were born out of public outcries for change. Even so, these regulatory boards have been criticized for their inactivity and for being dominated by the industries they regulate.

Insurance is a glaring example of how the industries to be regulated influenced legislators to enact a statutory scheme where government regulation would have a minimal impact. The insurance industry, concerned with federal efforts to curb insurance abuses, pushed the McCarren Ferguson Act through Congress. That bill preempted federal efforts in the insurance area where the states were already regulating the same practice. The insurance industry then proceeded to advocate the establishment of departments of insurance by state legislatures, departments whose functions were little more than to provide the appearance of state regulation, thereby preempting federal jurisdiction. The insurance industry had shaped its own regulation, taking it away from the federal government, and replacing it with 50 weaker state boards.

5. Warranty Law

A final important twentieth century legislative initiative against consumer abuses is the articulation of warranty laws. Before the nineteenth century, courts found various ways to enforce express and implied warranties. There were no clear distinctions between tort actions for misrepresentations and contract actions for breach of warranties. Actions such as Trespass on The Case for Warranty and Trespass on the Case in the Nature of Deceit provided vehicles to remedy most warranty-type problems. A sound price warranted sound goods. The nineteenth century brought a growing distinction between tort and warranty actions and limits on implied warranty actions. Fraud was moving in the direction where it was actionable only if the five elements including scienter and intent were proved. Warranty actions were beginning to be seen as derived from breaches of contracts in the sale of goods and were thus limited to where a contract could be shown. Caveat emptor conflicted with notions of implied warranties of merchantability.

The twentieth century eventually codified existing law first through the passage of the Uniform Sales Act and then the adoption of the Uniform Commercial Code. The UCC is a model state code that has recently been adopted in all states except Louisiana. The UCC does not focus on consumer protection issues. Instead, it is an attempt to provide uniform, predictable rules for dealings among merchants, not primarily between merchants and consumers. As such, it assumes that the two parties can bargain equally and arrive at proper arrangements as long as specific guidelines are set out.

The UCC describes when various express and implied
warranties are created and how breaches are remedied. But it
also sets out methods of waiving all of these warranties,
assuming that such waivers will be fairly bargained out
between merchants. In reality, when merchants deal with
consumers, almost all implied warranties are waived. Bargaining between consumers and merchants over warranties is rare
due to consumers' ignorance and inferior bargaining position.

6. Informal Dispute Mechanisms

Even though 20th century legislatures have adopted
numerous statutes impacting on consumer fraud, consumers are
still often left without legal remedy to rectify marketplace
abuses. In feudal England, buyers, also finding themselves
denied access to the courts, developed various informal
dispute resolution methods. Present day consumers find
themselves resorting to the same strategy.

Defrauded consumers in feudal England could deal with a
local merchant, call on the assistance of the local citizenry,
and rely on the underlying notion of a just price. Today,
consumers find themselves dealing with retailers, wholesalers
and manufactureres all of whom can be headquartered in other
states. The local citizenry is not organized around consumer
issues and the underlying legal doctrines are not sympathetic.

Nevertheless, several informal consumer strategies have
developed. A common approach is complaint handling and
mediation by Better Business Bureaus or other private agencies.
More aggressive steps include consumer pickets, boycotts and
demonstrations. Painting lemons on defective cars is one
example. Perhaps the most widespread consumer strategy is
to withhold payment, but present legal mechanisms give
merchants strong counter-measures.

9

CORPORATE CRIME
Issues in Research

MARSHALL B. CLINARD

PETER C. YEAGER

After many vicissitudes, the issue of corporate crime has at last become a real concern to the public, government, and criminologists. Opinion polls have shown that increasingly large proportions of the public have grave doubts about the honesty and integrity of major corporations in the United States (Walton, 1977: vii). Many federal regulatory agencies, including the Securities and Exchange Commission, Federal Trade Comission, Food and Drug Administration, Environmental Protection Agency, and others, as well as corresponding state agencies, have become more and more active in prosecuting the illegal behavior of large corporations, a trend indicated both in agencies' annual reports and in the increasing numbers of accounts printed in such major periodicals as the *Wall Street Journal.* In addition, while monetary penalties for corporate violations were minimal until relatively recently, Congress has significantly increased the penalties in a number of areas; for instance, the Federal Water Pollution Control Act provides for civil penalties of up to $10,000 per day, and criminal fines of up to $25,000 per dav of the violation (up to $50,000 for second convictions). That these penalties can mount up precipitously was demonstrated in 1976 when Allied Chemical Corporation was fined several million dollars in connection with discharges of the pesticide Kepone into Virginia's James River. Furthermore, the Department of

From Marshall B. Clinard and Peter C. Yeager, "Corporate Crime: Issues in Research," pp. 155-172 *Criminology: New Concerns.* Copyright 1979, American Society of Criminology.

Justice has been demanding ever stronger penalties. In one 1978 price-fixing case, for example, nine executives of various corporations were imprisoned (sentences of one or three months), more sentences issued in this case than was customary in past cases (*Wall Street Journal,* 1978: 11). In such price-fixing cases, fines of up to $1 million for the corporation and $100,000 for individuals can be imposed. The proposed Federal Criminal Code provides for general corporate penalties of up to $500,000. Some persons still maintain that these fines are not sufficiently severe in relation to the illgotten gains from corporate violations. However, corporations often lack ready cash and penalties often reduce profits. In addition, the possible widespread adverse publicity may seriously reduce the public's confidence in the corporation and thus benefit its competition.

It is generally agreed that the first empirical study to convince criminologists of the importance of research in this field was carried out by Sutherland (1949). His *White Collar Crime* dealt with the illegal behavior of 70 of the 200 largest U.S. nonfinancial corporations. Somewhat later Mannheim (1965: 470) suggested that if there were to be a Nobel Prize for criminology, certainly Sutherland would have been the foremost candidate for his work on white collar and corporate crime. During the 25 years following Sutherland's provocative work, however, there was little follow-up research, with only minimal study being carried out on illegal corporate behavior. Some articles and books have appeared, but most of them have been either of a rather general nature or limited to a few case studies, primarily of anitrust violations in the electrical industry or of selected regulatory agencies (cf. Geis, 1967; Turner, 1970). Only a relatively few quantitative research articles have appeared, and these have been narrow in scope, again dealing largely with antitrust violations (cf. Burton, 1966). This relative lack of research is significant; Sutherland's study is still the primary research on corporate crime. Thus, it continues to be widely cited, despite the facts that the data are old, the study is no longer relevant, the methodological procedures were weak, and little systematic attempt was made to analyze the data with the use of independent variables. Furthermore, the study covered only federal law violations by a small group of large corporations.

Although criminologists previously had paid lip service to the topic, largely it has been only since the mid-1970s that they have incorporated the area of corporate crime into the discipline and have begun to study it seriously. Probably the first basic book to include a chapter on corporate crime appeared in 1973 (Clinard and Quinney, 1973: ch. 8). Today textbooks conventionally include a chapter or lengthy discussion of this subject. Corporate crime first appeared as a separate topic at a professional society meeting at the 1975 session of the American Society of Criminology; in each subsequent year there has been a section on corporate crime, and such sections are now included in the meetings of the Society for the Study of Social Problems and the American Sociological Association. Articles on corporate crime are appearing more frequently in professional journals. Although only a few empirical investigations are currently underway, the interest is now substantial and research will undoubtedly increase rapidly.

REASONS FOR THE DEARTH OF RESEARCH

Many factors might be cited in explaining the paucity of research efforts involving corporate illegalities. One of the barriers to criminological research in this area is simply lack of experience and appropriate training. For criminologists trained in criminal law and accustomed to studying individual offenders, the study of corporate crime necessitates a significant retooling, involving familiarity with the concepts and research in the areas of political sociology, complex organizations, administrative law (e.g., the regulatory agencies), civil law, and economics. Corporate violations and their control occur in a complex political and economic environment, and most often involve administrative and civil sanctions to which criminologists generally have had limited exposure. Furthermore, most enforcement is carried out by state and federal regulatory agencies rather than by the courts, and criminologists have had little experience with such organizations. In the past, it was generally believed difficult to gain access to the enforcement data of regulatory agencies or court cases that involve corportions. Finally, limited funds have been available for research in this area, while resources have been plentiful for studies of ordinary crime, due partly to a lack of concern for research on illegal corporate behavior and partly to the fact that criminologists have felt unable to set up viable research projects. As a result, many criminologists have taken the easy path and continued to study conventional crime or, at best, small-scale consumer frauds.

SOCIAL FORCES AND
THE RECOGNITION OF CORPORATE CRIME

The growing recognition of corporate crime as an area for criminological research has largely been a natural response to various social forces. Particularly important has been the growth in public concern about corporate wrongdoings. Historically in the United States, major public concern has shifted from one type of crime to another, concentrating in turn on such areas as organized crime, "street crime," drug peddling, rape, and child abuse. Such changing concerns have greatly influenced how legislators and government enforcement agencies act with regard to certain behaviors, and have even influenced criminologists' choice of research topics.

In general terms, perhaps the central development promoting the growth of public and criminological concern with business crime has simply been the dramatic increase in the role and impact of major corporations in contemporary American society. Corporations such as Exxon, General Motors, IBM, and ITT are giant aggregations of wealth and political and social power, and their operations vitally influence the lives of virtually everyone "from the cradle to the grave."[1] The major corporations control the worklives—and hence the health and safety—of much of the population; have massive effects on prices (and therefore inflation), the quality of goods, and the unemployment rate; can manipulate public opinion through the use of mass media; palpably affect the environment and foreign relations; and, as the disclosures of recent years suggest, can jeopardize the democratic process with illegal political contributions. As Ralph Nader (1973: 79) noted—with only a touch of hyperbole—in connection with the difficulties, "Our states are no match for the resources and size of our great corporations; General Motors could *buy* Delaware . . . if DuPont were willing to sell it." The major corporations are the central institutions in our society. Little wonder that public and regulatory attention has turned increasingly toward them.

It is possible to identify some of the more specific social forces in American society which have contributed to what appears to be an almost sudden criminological interest and concern with corporate crime. They include certain highly publicized corporate violations, corporate irresponsibility and the growth of the consumer movement, increased environmental concern, reaction to the overconcentration on concern with lower class crimes and poverty problems, the black revolution and the prison reform movement, and the influence of conflict analysis and radical criminology.

1. The electrical conspiracy of the 1960s that involved most of the major electrical corporations in a highly secret and devious price-fixing operation received little publicity in the mass media (Dershowitz, 1961), even though it probably resulted in a greater loss than all burglaries committed during a single year (President's Commission on Law Enforcement

and Administration of Justice, 1967: 48). On the other hand, in recent years widespread publicity has been given to the Watergate crimes and the illegal political contributions by over 300 large corporations to the Nixon campaign, to the highly publicized role of ITT in heading off antitrust actions by a large contribution to the Republican National Convention, the political contribution of the Associated Milk Producers to obtain an increase in milk price supports, and the flagrant violations of the huge Equity Funding Corporation with its enormous losses. These cases particularly have led to the growth of public concern and increasing negative attitudes toward corporations, as shown in public opinion polls. In addition, many illegal actions of large corporations are being shifted to the front pages of daily newspapers from the less obvious financial pages. Now a few of these cases have even received wide publicity on nationally televised news broadcasts.

2. The widespread consumer movements were officially launched during the late 1960s with Ralph Nader's protest that the General Motors automobile, the Corvair, was "unsafe at any speed," and they were advanced by the subsequent research and widespread dissemination of over 50 studies done by Nader's group in other corporate areas. In recent years numerous consumer agencies have been created at federal and state levels, and laws designed to protect the buyer have resulted in greater liability of manufacturers for their widely distributed products. It has been estimated that by 1978 the federal government alone is annually receiving 10 million consumer complaints (Mouat, 1978). As a result of these public concerns various proposals have been presented for more drastic curbs on corporate power (Nader et al., 1972; Stone, 1975).

3. The growth of concern with the abuses to the environment culminated in the creation of the federal Environmental Protection Agency and numerous state and local level counterparts. Since corporations have been found to be major vio-

lators, widespread publicity has been given to cases of corporate air and water pollution, the use of harmful chemicals in manufacturing processes, and to other abuses of the natural environment.

4. During the 1960s governmental and private efforts were directed at the eradication of poverty, on the assumption that poverty was a necessary and sufficient condition for the commission of crimes. This overconcentration on poverty itself as an explanation of crime highlighted the inappropriateness of the application of this frame of reference to the unethical and illegal behavior of white collar groups and corporations.

5. Likewise during the 1960s, the black revolution and the prison reform movement called attention indirectly to the disproportionate representation of both blacks and poor in our prisons. Informed persons began asking what happened to the middle and upper class persons and the corporate executives who violated the law. The short sentences of a few months, or suspended sentences, given to Watergate offenders and to corporate offenders heightened the contrast between this leniency and the 10, 20, and even 50-year sentences given for burglary and robbery offenses. Today the threat of a criminal penalty against corporate executives is becoming a major governmental tool in the control of corporate violations.

6. Finally, the more static structural-functional approach to society taken by social scientists such as Talcott Parsons has been increasingly challenged by a Marxist or neo-Marxist interpretation in terms of class conflict. This approach has spread into the discipline as the radical or the new criminology, and has resulted in numerous publications, including those by Quinney, Chambliss, and Ian Taylor. Most of these works have pointed out the role of corporate abuses of power in a capitalist society and the relative immunity of the corporations from prosecution and penalties, particularly as compared to the lower and working class groups. Although their positions have often been overstated, they have had a salutary

effect in making criminologists question whether they have been class-biased in their research and other work. Criminologists have become aware that they have perhaps contributed to the public image of "the criminal" as a lower class person who commits the conventional crimes of larceny and burglary rather than the crimes of the corporate suites.

CORPORATE ETHICS AND LAW VIOLATIONS

A corporation exists to make profits; stockholders own stocks in a corporation with that same expectation. Social irresponsibility and unethical practices can flourish in such a setting. Unethical practices in turn set the stage for violations of law, as the practices within corporate settings often tend eventually to conflict with those values imposed by law (Quinney, 1964). Two anonymous surveys by large corporations of their managers, and those of other corporations, found that management feels under pressure to compromise personal ethics in order to achieve corporate goals. For example, "most managers believed that their peers would not refuse orders to market off-standard and possibly dangerous products" (Madden, 1977: 67; the surveys were commissioned by Pitney-Bowes Inc. and Uniroyal Corporation). This unethical behavior is justified primarily by the beliefs that if one has had good intentions one has behaved ethically, that what is workable is good, and that the marketing ethic is giving the customers what they want (Walton, 1977: 8-9). Corporate loyalty, carrying out the orders of someone else in management, and the desire to get ahead in salaries and bonuses are further justifications.

Ethical violations are of many types and are closely linked to corporate crime. (1) Exaggerated claims and misrepresentation of products have long been common sales practices. Advertising which is not necessarily illegal, but which is misleading, is widespread in newspapers, magazines, billboards, and on television. These practices have been termed advertising "puffing," such as "Ford gives you better ideas," "Breakfast of Champions," and "You can be sure if it's Westinghouse" (Preston, 1975). It is extremely difficult to distinguish "puffery" from illegal deception (Kintner, 1971). (2) The representation in the advertising media, particularly television, that the corporation is socially responsible and primarily interested in the general welfare instead of maximum profits, gives a false or "political" image and is unethical. (3) Harmful and unsafe products are frequently produced in the manufacture of autos, tires, appliances, children's toys, cosmetics, and drugs, and they are merchandised on the grounds that others are involved in selling such products or that it is an acceptable means of making a profit if the government does not make such production illegal. (4) Often virtually worthless products, such as foods and drugs—food items that lack nutritional qualities or over-the-counter drugs whose claimed effects have not been demonstrated—are marketed with assertions of their great values. Of the $780 billion spent by consumers in 1969, Senator Philip Hart estimated that about $200 billion had been expended on products of no value. (5) Manufacturers commonly refrain from developing or manufacturing cheaper products, withhold more efficient products from the market, or build obsolescence into their products. (6) Where there are no legal prohibitions, the physical environment is often disregarded and the country's natural resources exploited without adequate regard to either the resulting harmful effects or its possible effects on future generations. (7) The kickbacks or "gifts" given to purchasing agents are common practices which are only slightly different from pay-offs or the actual bribery of purchasers or officials, domestic or foreign. (8) Competitors are frequently spied upon, or their employees hired away from companies, in order to learn business secrets. (9) The possibility of future corporate employment is held open to employees of government agencies involved in regulating corporations. (10) Many corporations are operated to gain personal benefits for corporate management at the expense of the stockholders and the government, including expensive executive "perks." (11) Among further violations of ethics may be included the invasion of the privacy of employees, the firing of employees after years of service to save profits, and the lack of social responsibility to the community in which a corporation is operating.

Only a short step separates these unethical tactics from actual violations of the law. Many corporate practices which were formerly considered only unethical have now been made illegal and punished by government. Consequently, corporate crime today includes tax evasion such as false inventory values for tax purposes; unfair labor practices involving union rights, minimum wage regulations, working conditions, and overtime; violations of safety regulations concerning, for example, occupational safety and health; price-fixing to stabilize market prices and to eliminate competition; food and drug law violations; air and water pollution in violation of governmental standards; violation of energy regulations including rules on energy conservation; submission of false information for the sale of securities; false advertising and illegal rebates. It is doubtful that these practices would be approved by stockholders. Stone (1975: 82) has written as follows about such practices: "Even if management *had* made an express promise to its shareholders to 'maximize your profits' I am not persuaded that the ordinary person would interpret it to mean 'maximize *in every way you can possibly get away with,* even if that means polluting the environment, ignoring and breaking the law.' "

DIFFICULTIES IN
RESEARCHING CORPORATE CRIME

The first large-scale empirical study of corporate crime since Sutherland's work in 1949 is now being carried out by the authors and a research staff.[2] It involves a systematic analysis of federal and state actions (administrative, civil, and criminal) taken against the 624 largest U.S. corporations—industrial, wholesale, retail, and service—and their subsidiaries during 1975 and 1976. The difficulties encountered in this research partially explain the paucity of studies in the area of corporate crime, as well as the types of problems which should be anticipated by those who plan such research.

COMPLEXITY OF CORPORATIONS

The study of corporate wrongdoing cannot be likened to the investigation of burglars, embezzlers, or occupational criminals such as unscrupulous doctors who bilk welfare programs. Corporate crime is *organizational* crime which occurs in the context of complex and varied sets of structured relationships between boards of directors, executives, managers, and other employees on the one hand, and between parent corporation, corporate divisions, and subsidiaries on the other. Even with increased familiarity with the subtleties and varieties of corporate structure, the analyst working in this area will still face methodological difficulties stemming from the organizational nature of corporate phenomena. For instance, one sort of analytical problem which often arises is the difficulty in legally determining exactly where, and by whom, in the corporate structure the decision to violate has been made. For those interested in studying the *processes* underlying illegal corporate behavior, this problem requires carefully done qualitative investigations of selected cases. Such research involves the study of administrative agency and court documents and transcripts, as well as (ideally) interviews with regulatory and corporate personnel involved in the case.

Corporate complexity provides other methodological challenges to the quantitative researcher interested in the structural and economic correlates of business crime. One such problem is product diversification. Many corporations are huge conglomerates with annual sales that often total in the billions of dollars, and which are derived from a number of varied product lines. While such corporations may have a "main line" of business, they derive significant portions of their income from activities quite remote from their central product. For instance, International Telephone & Telegraph owns the Sheraton Hotel Corporation as well as business concerns in a variety of other fields, while Greyhound, noted nationally for its bus service, owns Armour and Company, a major meatpacker. Consequently, the researcher desiring to study violations by type of industry faces classification difficulties. One may choose to classify corporations by primary industry as assigned by investor's services. However, in this era of growing diversification and merger, some such classification may not be unambiguous, and the researcher should be aware of any limitations of its use for the corporate sample being analyzed.

Finally, the question of corporate subsidiaries can prove troublesome. Large corporations often have many subsidiaries in numerous product lines; in fact, in our sample we estimate that the 624 parent corporations own in the neighborhood of 9000 subsidiaries, 110 of which have annual sales of $300 million (the lowest figure in our corporation sample) or more, and 28 of which sell more than a billion dollars worth annually. In the attempt to compile the violations records of corporations, one would ideally include all violations of all subsidiaries. In a study the size we have undertaken, this is not practical, especially since violations of subsidiaries are often not reported with the name of the parent corporation. Consequently, we have chosen to focus on those wholly owned subsidiaries with at least $300 million in annual sales.

DATA DIFFICULTIES

Despite the severe limitations of the *Uniform Crime Reports*, there exists no equivalent report for the study of corporate crime. For the foreseeable future, the researcher himself must gather the data. Obviously, an equivalent of crimes reported to the police is not possible, except perhaps in the area of consumer complaints. In addition, investigations of corporations undertaken by authorities are difficult to obtain in many cases, simply because the records are often not publicly available unless violations have been revealed. Generally, the researcher must deal with enforcement actions initiated against companies (roughly the equivalent of arrests or prosecutions) and actions completed (equivalent to convictions). Such data are not easily available for studies such as ours. In order to compensate for deficiencies in completeness and comprehensiveness in any one source, we are relying on four main sources of data, some of which would not have been publicly available prior to the Freedom of Information Act of 1974:

(1) Data obtained directly from federal agencies on enforcement actions taken against the corporations in our sample.

(2) Law service reports (principally those of Commerce Clearing House and the Bureau of National Affairs) which give decisions involving corporation cases in such areas as antitrust, consumer product safety, and environmental pollution.

(3) Annual corporation financial reports (Forms 10-K) prepared for the SEC, which include a section on legal proceedings initiated against the firms.

(4) A computer printout of abstracts of enforcement proceedings involving corporations which have been reported in the *New York Times, The Wall Street Journal* and the leading trade journals.

In our attempt to study comprehensively the violations policed by more than 25 federal agencies and numerous state agencies, it is obviously not reasonable to expect a complete data set. First, government data on corporate violations vary in accessibility; some agency data are readily available on computers or through printed materials, while other data are kept only by date or case number or are available only in regional or district offices. Furthermore, data are generally kept in forms more useful for agency operational use than for outside research purposes. An example of such a situation is provided by the Department of the Interior's Mining Enforcement and Safety Administration which regulates mining safety conditions; though on computer, its approximately 90,000 cases a year covering over 15,000 mines are listed by name of mine rather than by parent corporation. Second, some violations data cannot be made public, even under the Freedom of Information Act. Such is the case for tax actions taken by the Internal Revenue Service except when, as seldom happens, the enforcement proceeding goes to appeal. Third, informal enforcement actions (as opposed to the formal administrative and judicial proceedings) are often difficult to collect as they are not always reported by district or regional agencies. Finally, the reporting of federal court cases in the *Federal Supplement* is not complete, and is left to the discretion of the individual courts.

Besides varying degrees of completeness, law service reports are somewhat difficult to use in that they are designed for the lawyer and businessman rather than for the sociologist. One practical problem which results is that the researcher must often read rather lengthy case reports to extract fundamental information on such variables as the violation, its date of occurrence, the penalty, among others. In addition, some such information may be missing from the account. Case material in 10-K reports to the SEC is also incomplete. The SEC requirement is that corporations report legal actions which may significantly affect their financial positions. With this system, minor violations can be expected to be seriously underreported. Finally, there is the problem of editorial selectivity in newspapers and other periodicals.

SANCTIONS

A major factor inhibiting research into corporate legal violations has been that criminologists' training has seldom included administrative and civil law and procedure.[3] Though the use of criminal sanctions in corporate cases is increasing, the bulk of enforcement actions are taken administratively by the many regulatory agencies. Research dealing with the enforcement behavior of numerous agencies requires knowing the natures of, and differences between, a wide range of possible sanctions, including warning letters, regulatory letters, notices of violation, administrative consent orders, court consent decrees, corrective action plans, recalls, seizures, injunctions, divestiture, class actions, contempt proceedings, and the like. Furthermore, it is necessary to be familiar with the administrative procedures of the various agencies, so that one is able to know, for example, when an administrative action has been finalized (cf. the differences between provisional and final consent orders). Moreover, each governmental agency often has its own unique set of enforcement actions and procedures, and the researcher often needs to contact the agency to clarify particulars.

SELECTED ANALYTICAL HURDLES

Research on corporate crime involves several analytical difficulties. One problem is comparing and ranking the relative seriousness of sanctions, even within a given type of sanction. The same ranking problem applies to assessing the absolute and relative seriousness of the various violations. Is a price-fixing scheme more harmful than fouling the environment or marketing untested or unsafe goods? And, within a single regulatory area (trade regulation), is an illegal merger affecting commerce in five northwestern states more serious than a false advertising campaign conducted nationally for a single product? And are strict liability offenses such as oil spills in any way comparable to corporate offenses in which individual or group blame is assessed? These are only a few of the questions with which a researcher in this area must grapple.

The seriousness question is significant in an additional direction. How many violations need a corporation tally before it is said to represent a serious crime problem? (Similarly, how much aggregate corporate criminality consititutes a national problem?) For example, Sutherland (1949) felt that his reported average of 14 government sanctions per corporation over an average period of 45 years constituted a serious corporate crime problem. However, it is difficult to make such a numerical determination of seriousness when a corporation has perhaps 50 to 100 subsidiaries, sales in the billions of dollars, a wide variety of product lines, and is subject to the control of a large number of state and federal agencies and a proliferating body of regulations, legislation, and case law.

OBJECTIVITY

A major difficulty encountered in doing research in the area of corporate crime is the maintenance of objectivity and the avoidance of moral judgments about corporate illegalities. This scientific canon is often violated by criminologists working in this field, in contrast to the field of conventional crime where the burglar, or other type of offender, is seldom morally condemned. One possible explanation for the differences in maintaining objectivity lies in the liberal political and economic views of many social scientists and criminologists who are doing such research. These views often lead to biased attitudes and research concerning corporations. In addition, social scientists are probably more sensitive than laymen to the ramifying social harm done by unethical and illegal corporate conduct.

CONCLUSIONS

This partial catalogue of problems is not meant to discourage research. Quite the contrary. Our experience indicates that while the difficulties are real, they are not only tractable but also provide stimulating challenges to the inventive analyst interested in the issue of corporate crime. Further research experience and familiarity with the data will doubt-lessly produce more refined studies, as old limitations are over-come and new barriers confronted. Furthermore, it is im-perative that criminology include this increasingly significant matter in its theoretical and applied work if sense is to be made of the "crime problem" and beginnings made toward its significant reduction. Writers in such areas as law, administra-tive science, and economics have, to a limited extent, studied corporate illegalities from the viewpoints of their respective specialties. It remains to study the nature and extent of corporate criminality and to construct integrated sociological explanations, joining such traditional criminological concerns as criteria for sanctioning and deterrence with such concepts as power and structural constraint in interorganizational relationships.

NOTES

1. The annual sales of many of the individual corporations exceed the gross national products of most nations in the world; they also surpass the general revenues of most of the states and cities in the United States (Nader, 1973: 90-93).

2. A pilot study in 1976 was supported by the University of Wisconsin—Madison Research Committee. The present study is supported by a 21-month grant (begin-ning in September, 1977) provided by the Law Enforcement Assistance Administra-tion of the U.S. Department of Justice. The senior author is the project director; the junior author is senior research assistant.

3. It is imperative that this deficiency be corrected in the academic training of graduate students in criminology.

REFERENCES

BURTON, J. F., Jr. (1966) "An economic analysis of Sherman Act criminal cases," in J. M. Clabault and J. F. Burton, Jr. (eds.) Sherman Act Indictments 1955-1965: A Legal and Economic Analysis. New York: Federal Legal Publications.

CLINARD, M. B. and R. QUINNEY (1973) "Corporate criminal behavior," ch. 8 in M. B. Clinard and R. Quinney (eds.) Criminal Behavior Systems: A Typology (rev. ed.). New York: Holt, Rinehart & Winston.

DERSHOWITZ, A. J. (1961) "Increasing community control over corporate crime—a problem in the law of sanctions." Yale Law J. 71 (December): 280-306.

GEIS, G. (1967) "White collar crime: the heavy electrical equipment anti-trust cases of 1961," pp. 139-151 in M. B. Clinard and R. Quinney (eds.) Criminal Behavior Systems: A Typology. New York: Holt, Rinehart & Winston.

KINTNER, E. W. (1971) A Primer on the Law of Deceptive Practices. New York: Macmillan.

MADDEN, C. (1977) "Forces which influence ethical behavior," pp. 31-78 in C. C. Walton (ed.) The Ethics of Corporate Conduct. Englewood Cliffs, NJ: Prentice Hall.

MANNHEIM, H. (1965) Comparative Criminology. Boston: Houghton Mifflin.

MOUAT, L. (1978) "Consumers on the march." Christian Sci. Monitor (January 27)

NADER, R. (1973) "The case for federal chartering," pp. 67-93 in R. Nader and M. J Green (eds.) Corporate Power in America. New York: Grossman.

——— M. J. GREEN, and J. SELIGMAN (1972) Taming the Giant Corporation New York: Norton.

President's Commission on Law Enforcement and Administration of Justice (1967) The Challenge of Crime in a Free Society. Washington, DC: Government Printing Office.

PRESTON, I. (1975) The Great American Blow-Up: Puffery in Advertising and Selling. Madison: Univ. of Wisconsin Press.

QUINNEY, R. (1964) "The study of white collar crime: toward a reorientation in theory and research." J. of Criminal Law, Criminology and Police Sci. 55 (June): 208-214.

STONE, C. (1975) Where the Law Ends: The Social Control of Corporate Behavior. New York: Harper & Row.

SUTHERLAND, E. H. (1949) White Collar Crime. New York: Holt, Rinehart & Winston.

TURNER, J. S. (1970) The Chemical Feast. New York: Grossman.

Wall Street Journal (1978) "Stiff penalties for price-fixing levied by court." February 6.

WALTON, C. [ed.] (1977) The Ethics of Corporate Conduct. Englewood Cliffs, NJ: Prentice-Hall.

10

CORPORATE CRISIS
The Overseas Payment Problem

EDWARD D. HERLIHY
THEODORE A. LEVINE

This Article discusses the problem of questionable corporate overseas payments which has surfaced over the past few years. It attempts to define the magnitude of the problem and explore its causes. Further, it outlines the various responses to the problem, both governmental and private, giving particular emphasis to the actions taken by the Securities and Exchange Commission, the one body which has been in the forefront in trying to structure a response to the problem pursuant to its responsibilities under the federal securities laws.

"Not perhaps since the robber baron era and certainly not since the 1930's—when New York Stock Exchange President Richard Whitney was convicted of stock theft and utility mogul Samuel Insull escaped prosecution by fleeing abroad dressed as a woman—has America witnessed such an epidemic of corporate corruption."[1]

INTRODUCTION

Throughout much of history, corruption has been no stranger to money dealings between businessmen, politicians, and others. The trail of Watergate, however, has led to revelations of foreign and domestic bribes, kickbacks, political payoffs, and other questionable

---

* The Securities and Exchange Commission, as a matter of policy, disclaims responsibility for any private publication by any of its members or employees. The views expressed herein are those of the authors, and do not necessarily reflect the views of the SEC or its staff.

** Branch Chief, Division of Enforcement, Securities and Exchange Commission; B.A., Hobart College (1969); J.D., George Washington University National Law Center (1972).

*** Assistant Director, Division of Enforcement, Securities and Exchange Commission; B.A., Rutgers University (1966); J.D., George Washington University National Law Center (1969). The authors gratefully acknowledge the invaluable contribution and assistance of David Winslow and Frank Howard, students of the Georgetown University Law Center.

[1] Green & Nader, *What to Do About Corporate Corruption*, Wall Street Journal, Mar. 12, 1976, at 8, col. 4.

From Edward D. Herlihy and Theodore A. Levine, "Corporate Crisis: The Overseas Payment Problem," 18(3) *Law and Policy in International Business* 547-568 (1976). Copyright 1976 by Law and Policy in International Business.

financial transactions involving U.S. and foreign corporations to an unprecedented extent and degree. These transactions have been facilitated by elaborate methods of concealment, including the fal-. sification of records and the structuring of fictitious transactions, which are generally lumped under the rubric of "management fraud."

The complexity and variety of the cases involving management fraud have perplexed observers. On a daily basis, new revelations of corporate misconduct, at home and abroad, are made. Although there is no distinct model or prototype, several factors typically are present, including the involvement of corporate management, the falsification of corporate books and records, the accumulation of secret pools of corporate funds or the diversion of funds from the corporate entity, and the illegality of the conduct involved.[2]

BACKGROUND

Scope and Magnitude of the Problem

A consideration of the purpose of the transaction, the form and source of the payment, and how the payment is accounted for and transferred to the recipients, is essential to an understanding of the nature of overseas payoff practices. Not every type of transaction can be discussed in this Article, and it is almost certain that new types will be revealed constantly in the course of ongoing investigations. However, an examination of some of the recently disclosed practices sufficiently reveals the general pattern of corporate activities in this area.

1. *Purpose of the Payments*

A wide variety of "business" reasons have been advanced to justify illicit payments. These reasons have included: the protection of an oil company's exploration rights;[3] the collection of past due

---

[2] It is critical to note that not all transactions involve illegal conduct. Some of the conduct might be described as "improper" or "questionable." For example, where a company makes a legal political contribution in a foreign country, but in order to conceal the identity of the recipient of the contribution and the amount paid, it falsifies its accounting records, the conduct is improper although not illegal. A payment from a hidden slush fund also is not illegal. The payments that are the focus of the present discussion are those that appear to have been of questionable legality under the laws of the foreign country in which the payments were made.

[3] REPORT OF THE SPECIAL COMMITTEE TO THE BOARD OF DIRECTORS OF ASHLAND OIL, INC., vol. 1, at 122–23 (June 26, 1975) ($190,000 paid by Ashland to two government officials in Gabon) [hereinafter cited as ASHLAND REPORT].

receivables for products sold to government agencies;[4] the provision of essential governmental services, including the protection of the company's produce;[5] the promotion of international and foreign air travel;[6] the acquisition of permission for a subsidiary to install or continue to operate certain equipment that was available for lease to third parties;[7] the guarantee of the personal protection of a subsidiary's employees while working in remote locations;[8] the reduction of a tax assessment;[9] the settlement of a tax liability;[10] and the acquisition of rights in an oil exploration and production venture.[11] A more unusual example involved the retention of a former Belgium statesman, Paul-Henri Spaak, as a director of International Telephone and Telegraph Corp. (ITT). ITT's European headquarters are located in a particularly attractive section of Brussels, and it has been alleged that it was Spaak's aid that enabled ITT to build its large headquarters complex in the area despite considerable local opposition.[12]

---

[4] SEC CURRENT REPORT, Form 8–K, Baxter Laboratories, Comm'n File No. 1–4448, at 3 (Feb. 1976) ($136,000 paid to officials in three countries and smaller payments made in three other countries by Baxter "to favorably influence government action") [hereinafter cited as Baxter 8–K].

[5] SEC CURRENT REPORT, Form 8–K, Castle & Cooke, Inc., Comm'n File No. 1–4445, at 1 (Dec. 1975) (payments amounting to $80,000 a year disbursed in Latin America and accounted for as "First cost of Fruit")[hereinafter cited as Castle & Cooke 8–K]; *cf.* Complaint at 4, SEC v. United Brands Co., Civil No. 75–0509 (D.D.C. filed Apr. 9, 1975).

[6] SEC REGISTRATION STATEMENT, Form S–7, Braniff International Corp., Comm'n File No. 2–49,583, at 11 (July 8, 1975) (payments to travel agents, tour groups, and promoters) [hereinafter cited as Braniff S–7].

[7] SEC CURRENT REPORT, Form 8–K, Rollins, Inc., Comm'n File No. 1–4422, at 1 (Jan. 1976) ($117,000 paid in one foreign country between 1971 and 1975) [hereinafter cited as Rollins 8–K].

[8] SEC CURRENT REPORT, Form 8–K, Amendment No. 1, Tenneco, Inc., Comm'n File No. 1–4101, at 2 (Jan. 1976) ($500,000 paid to military personnel) [hereinafter cited as Tenneco 8–K].

[9] Complaint at 3, SEC v. United Brands Co., Civil No. 75–0509 (D.D.C., filed Apr. 9, 1975); SEC REGISTRATION STATEMENT, Form S–7, Amendment No. 1, Smith International, Inc., Comm'n File No. 2–55,627, at 20 (Mar. 1976) ($13,349 payment) [hereinafter cited as Smith S–7].

[10] SEC CURRENT REPORT, Form 8–K, Dresser Industries, Inc., Comm'n File No. 2–55,410, at 21 (Jan. 1976) ($24,000 paid by a foreign subsidiary).

[11] SEC CURRENT REPORT, Form 8–K, Standard Oil Co., Comm'n File No. 1–170–2, exhibit 1, at 4 (Dec. 1975) (unknown portion of $218,000 paid to consultant channeled to government personnel) [hereinafter cited as Standard Oil 8–K].

[12] Egan, *Global Payoff Survey*, Washington Post, June 22, 1975, § F, at 1, col. 1 (discussing Thompson-CSF sales contract with the Lebanese government, which was effected by an administrative decision that was influenced by a bribe to a general in the Lebanese army).

It is possible to distill four basic reasons for which overseas corporate payments have been made: (1) to procure or maintain business and corporate activities; (2) to evade the payment of foreign taxes; (3) to prevent potential government interference with corporate operations; and (4) to affect or expedite ministerial matters at the lower levels of foreign governments. These reasons are by no means exclusive; they can, and often do, overlap. Affecting ministerial decisionmaking, for example, is closely related to the procurement of contracts, since it is often the administrative decision of a foreign official that results in the award of a contract.[13]

The procurement or maintenance of contracts for the sale of its products or services is a primary and legitimate concern of a multinational corporation. The manner in which such contracts occasionally are procured, however, is where the problem of bribes and questionable payments generally arises. For example, in August 1975, the Lockheed Aircraft Corp. (Lockheed) publicly conceded that it had paid officials and political organizations overseas at least $22 million in the preceding 5 1/2 years to help secure lucrative sales contracts.[14] As a part of its effort, Lockheed paid approximately $2 million through intermediaries to politicians in Japan primarily to help sell the company's L-1011 TriStar jets to All Nippon Airways,[15] and $7 million was paid to Yoshio Kodama, described as the leader of a pro-military political faction, also ostensibly for the purpose of promoting sales to All Nippon Airways.[16] Notably, U.S. corporations are not alone in relying on payments to foreign officials to procure contracts. In 1968, for example, a French corporation, Thompson-CSF, was implicated in the bribery of the then commander in chief of the Lebanese armed forces to consummate the sale of ground-to-air missiles to the Lebanese government.[17]

United Brands Company's (United Brands) activities in Honduras provide an example of the use of illicit payments to avoid foreign tax liabilities. United Brands has admitted paying a $1.25

---

[13] *Id.*

[14] Sansweet, *Crisis at Lockheed*, Wall Street Journal, Feb. 13, 1976, at 1, col. 6.

[15] Landauer, *Damage to Governments Friendly to U.S. Is Seen in Disclosure of Lockheed Bribes*, Wall Street Journal, Feb. 9, 1976, at 7, col. 1.

[16] Landauer, *Lockheed Aid to Militarist Japan Faction Blasted in Senate Study of Multinationals*, Wall Street Journal, Feb. 5, 1976, at 5, col. 1.

[17] Egan, *supra* note 12.

million bribe to a high government official in Honduras to obtain a reduction of the export tax imposed on bananas.[18]

Sometimes, payments to prevent interference with ongoing or potential corporate operations are mistakenly considered to be "better business" strategy because they involve less risk to the corporation than not paying. For example, Northrop Corp. (Northrop) decided to pay $450,000 through an agent, Triad Financial Establishment, to two Saudi Arabian generals to prevent their interference with the sale of jet fighters to the Saudi Arabian government.[19] Gulf Oil Corp. (Gulf Oil) also acceded to requests for payments to prevent interference with its corporate activities in Korea by paying $3 million in 1970 to the Democratic Republican Party of Korea (President Park's political party).[20]

Finally, there are payments to low-level government officials, such as tax assessors, police officials, customs inspectors, appointments secretaries, and immigration officials. These payments often are made in order to expedite ministerial activities which, due to bureaucratic red tape and slow-moving officials, impede corporate activities. For example, United Brands made a payment in Italy reportedly to ensure that there would be no delay in unloading 15,000 tons of bananas, which otherwise would have constituted a worthless cargo of rotting fruit shipped all the way from Central America.[21] Some payments are made to affect a ministerial decision itself, such as where Minnesota Mining and Manufacturing Co. (3M) paid $52,000 to a foreign customs official to avoid "charges of irregularities relating to customs matters."[22]

Of course, the purposes of some payments often overlap. In a deal involving a stock purchase agreement with Union Carbide, Ashland Oil Inc. (Ashland) was to be the successor in interest to certain oil concessions granted to Union Carbide by the government of Gabon. Subsequent to the execution of the agreement,

---

[18] *See* Wall Street Journal, Apr. 9, 1975, at 1, col. 6.

[19] REPORT TO THE BOARD OF DIRECTORS OF NORTHROP CORPORATION ON THE SPECIAL INVESTIGATION OF THE EXECUTIVE COMMITTEE 20 (July 16, 1975) [hereinafter cited as NORTHROP REPORT].

[20] REPORT OF THE SPECIAL REVIEW COMMITTEE OF THE BOARD OF DIRECTORS OF GULF OIL CORPORATION 101 (Dec. 30, 1975) [hereinafter cited as GULF REPORT].

[21] Maidenberg, *New Rules, Harsh Life in Bananas*, N.Y. Times, May 11, 1975, § 3, at 9, col. 6.

[22] REPORT OF THE SPECIAL AGENT TO THE BOARD OF DIRECTORS OF 3M COMPANY, app. 21, at 69 (Oct. 29, 1975) [hereinafter cited as 3M REPORT].

however, Ashland was informed of "certain outstanding obligations" of Union Carbide to two high government officials in Gabon
which had to be satisfied before transfer of the permits to Ashland.[23] Consequently, Ashland paid $190,000 to the officials in
order to secure exploration permits relating to the oil concessions.[24] This incident may be viewed in two ways: first, as a payment to influence an administrative decision; or secondly, as a
payment to prevent interference with the corporation's business
activities, since Ashland could have refrained from paying and
sought to achieve the transfer of the permits through legal chan-
nels by contesting its responsibility for Union Carbide's "obligations."

In almost all cases of overseas corporate payments, a specific
business benefit is sought, and a foreign government official is
involved, either directly or indirectly. Some foreign payments,
those intended to influence the outcome of a public election for
example, are more political than business in nature. By far the
largest such payment was made by Exxon's Italian subsidiary, Esso
Italiana, which funneled a total of $46 million into various Italian
political parties to "help bring about a political environment favorable to Esso Italiana's business interests."[25]

Gulf Oil has disclosed that it made $10.3 million available for
gifts, entertainment, or other expenses related to political activity
in the United States and abroad.[26] Ashland paid $125,000 to can-
didates for election in Canada.[27] Standard Oil Co. reported that an
Italian subsidiary had made "legal" political contributions between
1970 and 1973 totalling $617,000 and that another $35,700 had
been paid to various political parties in Canada.[28] American Home
Products Corp. paid $38,000 to political candidates in five foreign
countries,[29] and Cities Service Co. (Cities Service) disclosed that it
had made $30,000 available to a foreign subsidiary for "political

---

[23] Ashland Report, *supra* note 3, at 122–23.

[24] *Id.*

[25] SEC Registration Statement, Form S–7, Exxon Corp., Comm'n File No. 2–54,661, at
29–30 (Sept. 25, 1975) [hereinafter cited as Exxon S–7].

[26] Gulf Report, *supra* note 20, at 218.

[27] Ashland Report, *supra* note 3, vol. 1, at 93 (reporting that contributions were not
illegal).

[28] Standard Oil 8–K, *supra* note 11, exhibit 1, at 2–3.

[29] SEC Current Report, Form 8–K, American Home Products Corp., Comm'n File No.
1–1225, at 4 (Feb. 1976) [hereinafter cited as American Home Products 8–K].

purposes."[30] Castle & Cooke, Inc. (Castle & Cooke) made two "legal" political contributions of $15,000 each in an undisclosed foreign country.[31] Merck & Co. (Merck) disclosed that it had made "legal" political contributions in two foreign countries,[32] and Rockwell International Corp. reported having made contributions totalling $8,300 to Canadian political candidates.[33]

Other questionable activities that have come to light as a result of the Commission's enforcement actions or voluntary disclosures include: an annual payment of $13,000 to a foreign legislator;[34] a payment of $15,000 to a foreign lobbyist, which was paid against an invoice dated 3 months prior to its receipt;[35] a failure to report all profits and income for tax purposes, possibly in violation of foreign tax and exchange requirements;[36] the violation of the United States Grain Standards Act and the United States Warehouse Act;[37] an investment of $25,000 in a U.S. firm in which foreign governmental employees had an interest;[38] a payment of $330,000 in scholarship grants to a foreign country;[39] and a payment of $86,000 to 16 foreign government personnel and their families for travel and other expenses.[40]

2. *Form of Payment*

Improper and illegal corporate payments have involved both cash and non-cash transactions. Among the most notable cash payments are the payments totalling $4 million paid by Gulf Oil to the political party of South Korean President Park,[41] and the $1.25 million bribe paid to high government officials of Honduras by

---

[30] SEC CURRENT REPORT, Form 8–K, Cities Service Co., Comm'n File No. 1–1093, at 1 (Sept. 1975) [hereinafter cited as Cities Service 8–K].

[31] Castle & Cooke 8–K, *supra* note 5, at 3.

[32] SEC CURRENT REPORT, Form 8–K, Merck & Co., Comm'n File No. 1–3305, at 2 (Dec. 1975).

[33] SEC CURRENT REPORT, Form 8–K, Amendment No. 1, Rockwell International Corp., Comm'n File No. 1–1035, at 3 (Dec. 1975).

[34] Exxon S–7, *supra* note 25, at 32 (legality of payment not disclosed).

[35] Cities Service 8–K, *supra* note 30, at 2 (purpose of payment not disclosed).

[36] SEC CURRENT REPORT, Form 10–K, Pacific Vegetable Oil, Comm'n File No. 0–1773, at 1–1A (Oct. 14, 1975).

[37] SEC CURRENT REPORT, Form 8–K, Cook Industries, Inc., Comm'n File No. 1–5936, at 6 (Nov. 1975).

[38] Tenneco 8–K, *supra* note 8, at 2.

[39] *Id.*

[40] Standard Oil 8–K, *supra* note 11, exhibit 1, at 5.

[41] GULF REPORT, *supra* note 20, at 101.

United Brands.[42] Non-cash payments have taken a wide variety of forms. For example, Tenneco revealed that it made "payoffs" by investing in firms in which their foreign national consultants had interests,[43] and Gulf Oil provided the former president of Bolivia with a helicopter for his personal use.[44] There have been a multitude of other forms of payments including entertainment,[45] gifts,[46] and in some cases contributions to local welfare or charitable organizations.[47]

Many corporations have established secret "slush funds" from which payments can be made in the United States and abroad. This method has the advantage of avoiding the necessity of accounting for individual payments in the books of the company. A wide variety of strategies have been employed in channeling cash into the funds. Both Ashland[48] and Gulf Oil[49] diverted cash through foreign subsidiaries and back to secret funds in the United States. Ashland's transfers were reflected falsely in its corporate books as advances to foreign subsidiaries and withdrawals for exploration and production.[50] Gulf Oil also characterized the withdrawals as subsidiary expenses.[51]

A foreign subsidiary of Cities Service generated a $600,000 fund through "rebates" from brokers and suppliers that were unaccounted for in its books.[52] Burroughs Corp. generated cash for its secret fund by making withdrawals from a foreign subsidiary after submitting fictitious invoices containing inflated sales prices to the subsidiary, thereby offsetting the amounts withdrawn.[53] Braniff

---

[42] Complaint at 3, SEC v. United Brands Co., Civil No. 75–0509 (D.D.C., filed Apr. 9, 1975); Wall Street Journal, July 10, 1975, at 2, col. 2.

[43] Braaten, *Tenneco Discloses Payments*, Washington Star, Feb. 15, 1976, § A, at 1, col. 6.

[44] GULF REPORT, *supra* note 20, at 167.

[45] *Id.* at 106; *see* INVESTOR RESPONSIBILITY RESEARCH CENTER, INC., THE CORPORATE WATERGATE 66 (Oct. 1975) [hereinafter cited as INVESTOR RESPONSIBILITY REPORT].

[46] ASHLAND REPORT, *supra* note 3, vol. 1, at 132–33 ($2,500 wedding gift to an informal advisor of King Idris of Libya and a $7,500 "goodwill" gift to a Libyan government official).

[47] Egan, *supra* note 12 (reporting complaints by U.S. businessmen in the Philippines about requests to contribute to Mrs. Marcos' favorite charities accompanied by implied threats of sanctions for refusals).

[48] ASHLAND REPORT, *supra* note 3.

[49] GULF REPORT, *supra* note 20.

[50] ASHLAND REPORT, *supra* note 3.

[51] GULF REPORT, *supra* note 20.

[52] SEC REGISTRATION STATEMENT, Form S–7, Amendment No. 2, Cities Service Co., Comm'n File No. 2–54,016, at 28 (Sept. 30, 1975) [hereinafter cited as Cities Service S–7].

[53] SEC CURRENT REPORT, Form 8–K, Burroughs Corp., Comm'n File No. 1–145, at 1 (Jan. 1975) [hereinafter cited as Burroughs 8–K].

International generated a fund by selling unaccounted-for air travel tickets over a period of several years,[54] while Tenneco established and maintained its slush fund by annual cash contributions from high level executives.[55] Whittaker Corp. revealed that it had made payments of approximately $75,000 annually over a period of several years by placing money into an unrecorded cash fund and falsely describing the payments as commissions.[56]

Several companies have admitted making payments from secret bank accounts. For example, Goodyear Tire and Rubber Co. maintained an account using funds derived from volume discounts offered by vendors to foreign subsidiaries on purchases of materials from those vendors.[57] Funds from this account were periodically withdrawn for political contributions in the United States.[58] An undisclosed foreign subsidiary of Standard Oil maintained a secret bank account primarily by using rebates on foreign exchange commissions and interest from other disbursements from the account which were made "for the subsidiary's business purposes."[59] Exxon's wholly-owned Italian subsidiary maintained 40 secret bank accounts in Italy, from which unauthorized commercial payments of $10 million and unauthorized political contributions of $19 million were made.[60]

The techniques used to conceal the generation or diversion of funds also vary greatly. When the funds have been generated and diverted in a transaction such as the overbilling and rebating technique, there is no need for any further accounting procedure because the funds are completely off the books after the payment of the bill. When the payoff expenses come directly from existing and accounted for corporate funds, the expenses are often accounted for under a variety of false or misleading financial head-

---

[54] Braniff S–7, *supra* note 6, at 11 (at least 3,600 tickets valued at $750,000 were sold).

[55] Tenneco 8–K, *supra* note 8, at 3 (about 20 executives contributed $2,000 each beginning in 1966 or 1967).

[56] Wall Street Journal, Feb. 6, 1976, at 8, col. 2.

[57] SEC PROXY STATEMENT, Goodyear Tire & Rubber Co., Comm'n File No. 1–1927, at 7–8 (Mar. 3, 1975).

[58] *Id.* at 8 (amounts totaled $522,000, $260,000 of which was transferred to the United States for political contributions, including $40,000 to the Committee to Re-Elect the President, President Nixon's 1972 campaign committee).

[59] Standard Oil 8–K, *supra* note 11, exhibit 1, at 4 (after 1970, amounts totaled $206,000; after the account was closed in March 1975, $240,000 of the balance was transferred to the United States in violation of the foreign country's exchange regulations).

[60] Exxon S–7, *supra* note 25, at 29–30.

ings. For example, many of Gulf Oil's routine payments to customs officials of the Korean government were accounted for as "entertainment expenses."[61] Some of its political contributions in Italy were made to newspaper publishers controlled by political parties who provided the company with invoices for "newspaper journalistic services." The payments were recorded in Gulf Oil's corporate books as "publicity and promotion expenses."[62] Ashland used a scheme whereby money was transferred from an American corporate bank account to a foreign bank account, and accounted for in the United States as advances to the corporation's foreign subsidiaries or operating divisions. The same funds were then withdrawn in cash from the foreign account and returned to the corporate headquarters in the United States, and recorded in the books of the foreign subsidiary as exploration and production costs.[63] Once the funds had been drawn in cash, no further accounting was necessary, and they remained in the safe at Ashland's corporate headquarters.[64]

Another method of diverting corporate funds entails the use of agents or consultants. Many corporate disclosures have revealed exorbitant consulting fee arrangements with foreign nationals. The problem with such arrangements lies in trying to determine how much money has actually passed through the sales agents or the various companies to foreign government officials. There are two principal aspects of this problem: First, it is difficult, if not impossible, to obtain complete disclosure of a foreign national's business dealings as a sales agent or consultant, since he is neither under the complete control of the corporation nor subject to the jurisdiction of U.S. laws compelling disclosure; secondly, most of the involved corporations inadequately document the particular services rendered, or whether the services were commensurate with the amount paid.[65] Illustrative of this type of arrangement is Lockheed's disguising of $1.4 million in Italian payoffs to political parties and officials as payments under consulting agreements with

---

[61] GULF REPORT, *supra* note 20, at 107.

[62] *Id.* at 130.

[63] ASHLAND REPORT, *supra* note 3, vol. 1, at 75.

[64] *Id.*

[65] Statement of Roderick Hills, Chairman of the SEC, Before the Subcomm. on Priorities and Economy in Government of the Joint Economic Comm., Jan. 14, 1976, at 3.

sales agents.[66] Standard Oil,[67] Smith International,[68] and Public Service Co. of New Mexico[69] all reported employing consultants as conduits through which payoffs may have been channeled to various government personnel. Northrop used a system whereby a foreign consultant was retained for a period of several years, during which time the consultant overbilled Northrop. The excessive cash payments, approximately $376,000, in turn were rebated to a Northrop executive and director in the United States.[70] These payments were reflected in Northrop's books and tax returns as consultant fees, while the rebated cash and its subsequent disbursement were left unrecorded.[71] Tenneco disclosed that it had contractual arrangements to pay $12 million in consulting fees upon the completion of certain transactions.[72]

The use of numbered bank accounts in Switzerland and Liechtenstein has been quite common. For example, Lockheed was found to have paid millions of dollars in agents' fees for the sale of Lockheed aircraft to South Africa, Nigeria, and Spain to accounts in Liechtenstein and Switzerland.[73] Cities Service channeled payments via an intermediary through a Swiss bank account,[74] while Castle & Cooke disbursed corporate funds through a special account of a subsidiary labelled "First Cost of Fruit."[75] Merck channeled some payments through personal bank accounts of its overseas employees and recorded the payments as ordinary business expenses.[76]

The method of payment often is for the benefit of the recipient, but it also may be to the corporation's advantage to conceal a payment. Actually, there appear to be a number of reasons for using hidden bank accounts: to avoid the necessity of having to pay taxes on the amount concealed; to avoid criminal penalties relating

---

[66] Landauer, *supra* note 16, col. 2.

[67] Standard Oil 8–K, *supra* note 11, at 3–4.

[68] Smith S–7, *supra* note 9, at 20 (consultant paid $13,349 to unidentified government officials).

[69] SEC REGISTRATION STATEMENT, Form S–7, Public Service Co. of New Mexico, Comm'n File No. 2–54,489, at 24 (Sept. 24, 1975) ($9,656 paid to consultant who "may have had some connection" with an unsuccessful candidate for the U.S. Senate).

[70] NORTHROP REPORT, *supra* note 19, at 45–46.

[71] *Id.*

[72] Tenneco 8–K, *supra* note 8, at 2 (reporting efforts to void agreements).

[73] Halloran, *Payoffs Cost Lockheed $1 Billion Sale to Japan*, Washington Star, Feb. 11, 1976, § A, at 1, col. 2.

[74] Cities Service S–7, *supra* note 52, at 27.

[75] Castle & Cooke 8–K, *supra* note 5.

[76] SEC CURRENT REPORT, Form 8–K, Merck & Co., at 2 (Feb. 1976).

to the receipt or payment of funds; the existence of unstable political conditions in the recipient's home country and the consequential need for money in case of emigration; the existence of unstable currency conditions in the recipient's home country; and a desire to avoid public reaction.

The above description of methods used by corporations to conceal improper payments is not exhaustive. As a final example, Standard Oil devised a scheme to make payments to a foreign state-owned enterprise by increasing the sales price on its products sold to the enterprise by 2 percent and then making available to employees of the enterprise an amount equivalent to the increase.[77]

Causes of Improper Corporate Activity

As a part of an analysis of corporate misconduct, it is crucial to explore the forces and causes that have led to widespread bribery, kickbacks, and other questionable transactions in the international business community; namely, the pressures that make these corporate practices so-called "accepted business practice." Some of the reasons behind the practices are attributable solely to the foreign countries themselves—their cultural and socio–economic traditions, and their political structures. However, some of the reasons also stem from cultural attitudes and behavior within the United States.

Initially, the obvious factor of varying customs and mores around the world must be considered. Part of the current furor within the United States over recently revealed corrupt corporate practices derives from concepts of morality that are prevalent in American society but not necessarily in societies of many other countries. It must be recognized that in other countries, especially those with cultural traditions that are not a part of the heritage of the United States, such as most of the countries of the Mideast, Africa, and, to a lesser extent, Latin America, there have evolved methods and attitudes of doing business that are different from what has come to be publicly regarded as acceptable in the United States.

Historically, the Asian and African cultures have functioned with a type of economy that is different from that found in most Western cultures. Instead of a free market economy that functions

---

[77] Standard Oil 8–K, *supra* note 11, exhibit 1, at 5 ($16,700 credited to the enterprise's account in 1974 without being recorded as a liability on the books of the foreign subsidiary).

through price and quality competition, there has evolved a tradition of intricate tribal and oligarchic arrangements of social connections, family relations, and reciprocal obligations, lubricated by many forms of tribute.[78] In Japan, *On*, a custom that permeates and influences Japanese business relationships, requires that all favors be repaid, often in the form of cash.[79] The impact of this custom is that there are no moral qualms concerning the payment or receipt of such "returned favors." In fact, the failure to make such payments may even result in a loss of face.[80]

In countries such as Saudi Arabia, the need for a person with influence is more visible and freely admitted than in the United States and other Western countries.[81] Bribery and influence-peddling is certainly not alien to Western culture, however, as the revelations of enormous political payments in Italy and the United States demonstrate. The point is that what is normal and accepted business practice in some foreign countries may offend American ethnocentric views of business and morality. The revelations of corporate bribery in Japan and the Netherlands, among other developed countries, have resulted in substantial public outrage and incited investigations into the identities of the recipients,[82] and disclosures of illegal payments appear to have led to the replacement of the top government officials of at least one country, Honduras.[83]

Another aspect of this "other culture" approach to doing business and, in particular, one that partly explains the lack of political repercussions in the Mideast, is the social role of the sales agent. A recent Department of Defense memorandum discusses the historical beginnings and current role of the agent primarily in the Middle East.[84] The memorandum begins with the observation that

> [t]he Middle East, Far East and Latin America are areas of the world where an agent is generally required for the

---

[78] Gwirtzman, *Is Bribery Defensible?*, N.Y. Times, Oct. 5, 1975, § 6 (Magazine), at 102.

[79] TIME, Feb. 23, 1976, at 32.

[80] *Id.*

[81] *See* notes 84–88 *infra* and accompanying text.

[82] *See, e.g.*, Washington Star, Feb. 16, 1976, § A, at 4, col. 1; *id.*, Feb. 9, 1976, § A, at 5, col. 1.

[83] N.Y. Times, May 11, 1975, § 3, at 9, col. 5.

[84] *Hearings on the Activities of American Multinational Corporations Abroad Before the Subcomm. on International Economic Policy of the House Comm. on International Relations*, 94th Cong., 1st Sess. 100 (1975) [hereinafter cited as *House Hearings*].

successful completion of a commercial sale. In some areas of the Middle East it is a legal requirement to have a local agent before a proposal is considered. For the most part the Request for Quotations will request among other things, who the local agent is and without this information little or no serious consideration will be given to the contractor's response.[85]

The report goes on to state that although agents or concessionaries have existed since pre-Biblical times, their role became much more significant during the industrial revolution. At first, the local agent was retained primarily by the purchaser, who often did not have the "talent, facility or faculty to locate the equipment or product in a complex international market place."[86] However, as purchasers gradually became more familiar with the operations of the international market place, they began to use their own privately employed purchasing agents at a fixed salary, rather than pay an often excessive, percentage-basis "finder's fee"[87] to an outside agent. This change in the policy of purchasers precipitated a reversal of the role of the local agent who turned to selling on behalf of the supplier, often dealing with the same principals.

There are a variety of reasons for the use of a local agent, some of which are legitimate while others are more questionable. Among the many legitimate reasons for the use of local agents are: (1) the economic waste involved in setting up corporate sales offices in each potential customer country; (2) the very real need for a person who understands the "social, economic, political and traditional patterns of the country;"[88] and (3) the agent's "ability to interpret a government's requirements and circumstances to foreign businessmen, . . . [such as] identifying promising areas for sales, preparing proposals, making technical presentation, reporting on the decisionmaking process within the bureaucracy, participating in negotiations and meetings and assisting in implementing successful programs."[89] Other reasons for using agents include: a mistrust of

---

[85] *Id.*

[86] *Id.*

[87] *Id.*

[88] *Hearings Before the Subcomm. on Multinational Corporations of the Senate Comm. on Foreign Relations*, 94th Cong., 1st Sess., pt. 12, at 115 (1975) (statement of Richard W. Millar, Chairman of the Executive Committee of the Board of Directors, Northrop, Inc.) [hereinafter cited as *Senate Hearings*].

[89] *Id.*

foreigners on the part of some purchasers; the purchaser's preference to do business with a local agent in order to avoid dealing in a
foreign language; and the fact that the purchaser is often more at
ease with the local agent because of either a long-standing friendship or a continued course of business relationships.[90]

An alternative, or perhaps complementary, view of the agent's
role is "primarily that of influence peddler, that he knows who to
talk to and whose pocket to line, and in a particular country [how]
to get the job done."[91] The influence of an agent can range from
normal friendships or family ties between local agent and procur-
ing officer, to the payment of substantial sums of money to individuals in high government positions, with somewhat lesser
amounts paid to lower echelon government officials.[92] Thus, it
appears that the use of a local agent may serve legitimate, as well as
illegitimate, business purposes. Furthermore, it is apparent that the
use of a local agent is a business necessity in many countries. The
local agent's role—both legitimate and illegitimate—is shaped by a
particular culture as well as by other factors present in any business
transaction, and it continues to be a significant force that compli-
cates monitoring and influencing corporate behavior overseas.

The main problem with the use of local agents is how to ensure
that they are not used for illegitimate purposes, particularly as
conduits for payoffs to foreign officials. This problem is compounded by the size of the agent's fees. The dollar amount involved in the contracts being negotiated is often very high and the
agents usually work on a percentage-commission basis. As a result,
the size of their fees can be enormous. For example, Grumman
contracted to sell 80 F-14 Tomcat fighter planes for $2.2 billion to
Iran, and the fees which the company had originally contracted to
pay its "lobbyists" in connection with the sale were $28 million,
between 1 and 2 percent of the contract price. Adnan M.
Khashoggi, one of the most publicized of sales agents, attempted to
defend the size of agents' fees in general by first explaining the
legitimate business functions of agents such as himself, and then
comparing the fees to those of other businesses:

> Our compensation for our work for American com-
> panies may be large in amounts, but in terms of the

---

[90] *House Hearings, supra* note 84, at 101.
[91] *Senate Hearings, supra* note 88, at 133.
[92] *House Hearings, supra* note 84, at 101.

volume of business to be done under the contracts, it is
small indeed—often less than recommended by the Pentagon to American companies for their representatives all
over the world.

American real estate brokers and agents assembling
huge parcels of land in rural areas or cities with values in
the multi-millions receive as much as 10 percent for their
work.

Banks and investment houses may spend 30 to 90 days
arranging an $800,000,000 loan for a company and re-
ceive $8,000,000—1 percent—as a fee.[93]

He continued by pointing out that he sometimes must work 5 or
6 years to obtain a particular contract, and that if the contracts
are not obtained, he receives nothing for his "investment of money,
time, overhead, technical and managerial personnel, travel and so
on."[94] Nevertheless, Khashoggi requested Northrop to pay a total
of $450,000 to two Saudi generals to prevent their potential inter-
ference with Northrop's continued anticipated business with Saudi
Arabia. Northrop has admitted that the requests were made and
that it made the requested payments to Khashoggi, but it has
denied having direct knowledge as to whether the payments were
actually transferred to any official of the Saudi government.[95] No
investigations have begun and no public outcry has been heard in
Saudi Arabia as a result of these revelations. Iran, on the other
hand, has stepped into the transaction between Grumman and its
agents, and Grumman has agreed to pay the enormous commission
directly to the Iranian government.[96] These responses demonstrate
the existence of differing attitudes towards the propriety of the use
of sales agents even within the Mideast.

There are a number of other factors present in the international
business community that contribute to an atmosphere conducive to
the making of improper payments overseas. One is the low civil
service salaries paid in many foreign countries, and the consequential temptation to supplement income. For example, in the case of

---

[93] *Id.* app. .15, at 272–73 (statement of Adnan M. Khashoggi).

[94] *Id.*

[95] *Senate Hearings, supra* note 88, at 112 (testimony of Richard W. Millar). Khashoggi has
claimed that he pocketed the money to "punish" Northrop for thinking that the Saudis could
be bribed. TIME, Feb. 23, 1976, at 33.

[96] Washington Star, Feb. 10, 1976, § A, at 2, col. 5.

payments to expedite consideration of corporate matters by low-level bureaucrats, one commentator has stated that the speed with which these low-level bureaucrats apply themselves to a problem is in direct proportion to the amount paid by the particular corporate solicitor.[97] It has been observed further that "lubrication" to keep a particular corporation's documents on top of the bureaucrat's "get done today" basket is a normal procedure in many countries, and that such payments are a part of the "system by which those who use the services of the particular department of government share the payroll expense of those who labor within."[98]

For example, Gulf Oil maintained in Korea a special "off-the-books" account, entitled the "Gray Fund," from which payments were made primarily to individuals in agencies of the Korean government. According to the special report prepared by Gulf Oil, the fund was

> designed to ease access to government agencies with which Gulf had to deal in arranging appointments, obtaining permits and otherwise expediting Gulf's government business through the complexities of a tightly controlled and sometimes frustrating bureaucracy. It was a bureaucracy, at least in part, accustomed to and dependent upon gratuities to supplement the generally low salaries of the employees. Foreign companies, due to their language handicaps and unfamiliarity with the national customs, were especially faced with the expectation of such gratuities in Korea, but the practice was not confined to foreign enterprises (nor indeed is the practice confined to Korea).[99]

The recipients of payments can range from an appointments secretary, who is paid a small sum of money to arrange an urgent appointment with a high government official, to a customs official paid to avoid a potential claim of irregularities concerning corporate activities.[100] The size of the payment ordinarily is rather low—especially as compared to agents' commissions—thus, it is more difficult to detect their dollar amount or frequency. How-

[97] *Id.*, Feb. 6, 1976, § C, at 5, col. 2.
[98] *Id.*
[99] GULF REPORT, *supra* note 20, at 164.
[100] 3M REPORT, *supra* note 22, at 69 & app. 21.

ever, the existence of pressures for low-level bribes has apparently been a fact of business life in many foreign countries.

The pressure to provide supplemental income in return for services is not confined to low-level civil service workers. High-level government officials also desire to supplement their salaries and to create "retirement" funds. Due to the relatively unstable political structure in many foreign countries, a high government official's tenure in office often is of uncertain and frequently brief duration. Consequently, these individuals are strongly motivated to take advantage of every opportunity for personal enrichment in dealings with multinational corporations.[101] This situation has led to the use of bank accounts in Switzerland and Liechtenstein as the place of payment; thus, if political turmoil necessitates· departure from a particular country, the official will still have access to sufficient financial resources to tide him over.

Another factor that influences the making of payments is cultural and nationalistic bias. Some individuals in developing countries perceive themselves as having been exploited by the richer, usually Western, developed countries, and this perception has resulted in resentment of those countries and a determination to receive corporate payments as retribution. Even where such culturally-directed bias does not exist, there may be purely nationalistic tendencies that create pressures for payments from all foreign corporations.

Interwoven with political instability and cultural or national bias is the fear of nationalization. Although payments rarely are made for the express purpose of avoiding nationalization, corporate payments are made to maintain goodwill and to prevent interference with corporate activities. Thus, Gulf Oil contributed a helicopter to former Bolivian President Barrientos and paid cash to his political party to preserve stable relations in Bolivia,[102] and contributed $4 million to President Park of Korea and his political party in order to "continue profitable business without interference."[103] However, in Bolivia the payments appear ultimately to have been counter-productive. After Barrientos died in a helicopter crash and the existence of the contributions was revealed, Gulf Oil's holdings were nationalized, and the new regime threatened to

---

[101] Gwirtzman, *supra* note 78.
[102] GULF REPORT, *supra* note 20, at 164.
[103] *Id.* at 101, 103.

withhold $57 million still due in indemnification.[104] In any case, the real or imagined threat of nationalization exerts considerable pressure upon corporations in those particular industries, such as the oil industry, that have assets subject to potential expropriation in foreign countries, to make goodwill payments as a means of protecting their investments.

All of the above factors predominantly emanate from particular foreign countries, as opposed to those factors that are common to the international business community or to the American business community. There is probably only one factor that can be attributed vaguely to the international business community in general; namely, the pressure of worldwide competition between multinational corporations. This factor is one of the primary defenses of corporate bribery relied upon by U.S. corporations—if U.S. companies do not make the payments, then a foreign competitor will, resulting in a loss for domestic business.

French and British companies are described as being very aggressive in paying bribes when doing business outside of their own countries.[105] British business managers operate on an unspoken assumption when dealing with governments of developing countries: "[N]o substantial deal involving goods with a negotiated price can be concluded without the payment of bribes, 'payola,' or 'kickbacks.'"[106] These business persons know who receives the payments and how much each receives, because it would be un-businesslike if they were not sure the payments were reaching the "right" people.[107] The British government is concerned primarily with the promotion of exports, and not with the reformation of the business customs of foreign governments.[108] There is virtually no pressure to disclose or to stop these payments despite the fact that the Bank of England has a complete private record of virtually every bribe paid abroad.[109] A recent British article on Lockheed's present predicament observed, "Most businessmen selling capital goods abroad are surprised at the extent of the fuss being raised

---

[104] Griffith, *Payoff is Not "Accepted Practice,"* FORTUNE, Aug. 1974, at 124.

[105] Egan, *supra* note 12, at 2, col. 5.

[106] Nossiter, *A Part of Britain's Third World Business Deals,* Washington Post, Feb. 22, 1975, at 9, col. 1.

[107] *Id.*

[108] *Id.*

[109] *Id.* at col. 5.

over this question in the [United States]."[110] Some U.S. businessmen have argued that the persuasiveness of the overseas bribe by foreign business competitors, uninhibited by their own governments, often places U.S. corporations at a disadvantage in their sales efforts. For example, an American executive defending corporate conduct overseas summed up the competition rationale:

> Whatever your moral viewpoint may be, the fact is that if you are going to [do] business in those countries [where payments to government officials are common and an accepted method of doing business] and remain competitive, some such payments must be made.[111]

In a survey of 73 executives from a cross section of corporations, 52 percent of those answering a question on this topic of payments responded that "American companies operating abroad should adhere to American ethical standards," while 48 percent said they should adopt local standards, even if the standards sanction bribes or kickbacks.[112] During the hearings on overseas payments before the Senate Subcommittee on Multinational Corporations, the former president of Lockheed responded to Senator Church's characterization of overseas payments as "bribes" by saying, "We don't condone this. In our judgement it was the only way we could sell our product."[113]

There are, however, many U.S. corporations that strictly reject these practices and still survive economically in the international business community.[114] Of course, other factors, such as competing in industries where bribery is not necessary, or being an economically strong enterprise, may account for the continued survival of these companies in the international market.

It seems that certain industries are particularly prone to engage in overseas payments. Heavy capital goods industries, such as aerospace, arms, or those industries that are closely regulated by foreign government agencies, such as pharmaceutical companies, are subject to unusually heavy pressures for payoffs.[115] The

---

[110] *Id.* at 13, col. 3.

[111] Washington Star, Feb. 13, 1976, § A, at 3, col. 6.

[112] Washington Post, Feb. 13, 1976, § B, at 19, col. 1, and 21, col. 3.

[113] Washington Star, Feb. 7, 1976, § A, at 1, col. 5.

[114] N.Y. Times, Oct. 5, 1975, § 6 (Magazine), at 102.

[115] Washington Post, Feb. 13, 1976, § B, at 19, col. 1.

pressure upon aircraft manufacturers to make payoffs is especially intense because, unlike most industries, the sale of their products is not constant. Therefore, they must rely upon the procurement of one or two big contracts for the bulk of their revenues.[116] Oil companies also are subjected to tremendous pressures for payoffs, since their activities are so "vulnerable to unfavorable government action—expropriation, revocation of drilling concessions, tax increases, [and] price control."[117]

The final factor to be discussed is the influence of the profit motive in the context of a decision whether or not to make a payoff. How far it controls any corporate decision obviously depends on the degree and manner in which the responsible corporate decisionmaker reacts to the other previously mentioned factors. The reaction of the business community to the disclosure of particular acts of questionable corporate payments overseas reveals a great deal about the influence of the profit motive. Despite all the revelations of overseas payoffs by Northrop, its board of directors in November 1975 passed a resolution complimenting Thomas Jones [the president, chief executive officer, and, until recently, chairman of the board] and his subordinates for their excellent performance in the face of a challenging and adverse economic environment.[118] Jones was criticized mildly by the Northrop Executive Committee for certain errors of judgment in his dealings with consultants, and as a mild reprimand he was removed from his position as chairman of the board.[119] He subsequently was reinstated as chairman of the board, but was relieved as president.[120]

Similarly, at Ashland, despite reports of domestic and overseas payoffs on a large scale, the board of directors recommended against the firing of Orin Atkins (who was directly responsible for most of the payments) because the corporation's net income had grown from $31 million to $113 million since he had assumed control of the firm.[121] At Exxon's annual meeting in 1975, a resolution to require disclosure of the company's payments was defeated

---

[116] TIME, Feb. 23, 1976, at 31.
[117] *Id.*
[118] Washington Star, Feb. 6, 1976, § C, at 4, col. 8.
[119] *Id.*
[120] Wall Street Journal, Feb. 20, 1976, at 32, col. 1.
[121] Gwirtzman, *supra* note 78, at 101–02.

97 percent to 3 percent.[122] Also, at a stockholders' meeting of United Brands in 1975, after the disclosures regarding the Honduran bribes, the shareholders, who "seemed more interested in the company's profitability," apparently "applauded one speaker who said bribery was essential in doing business in many parts of the world."[123]

It certainly appears that there is some support for the use of overseas corporate payoffs when they are placed in the context of the continued or future profitability for a particular corporation. This is not to say that many corporations, business managers, and investors do not have different and often opposing attitudes concerning overseas payments. The point to be made is that the pressure for profits plays a significant role in creating a tolerant atmosphere conducive to bribery.

Despite the many pressures exerted upon U.S. businesses to make payments to foreign government officials, there are some U.S. companies that have not succumbed.[124] Paul Orrefice, President of Dow Chemical Company's domestic operations, spent 17 years in its international division and acknowledged that Dow employees had received demands for bribes, but stated that he was "100 percent sure no one in Dow has made one payment . . . . I would fire anyone who did."[125] Dow's policy of resistance has cost it some business opportunities, but its business has still continued very profitably.[126]

Another American company, Translinear, Inc., (Translinear) purportedly was forced to abandon a project in Haiti because of its firm conviction that to acquiesce to shakedown attempts would be bad business and unethical.[127] The president of Translinear, in support of the propriety of the decision to resist bribery, stressed that demands for payments are likely to multiply once a company indicates a willingness to comply.[128]

---

[122] *Id.* at 101.

[123] N.Y. Times, Aug. 19, 1975, at 51, col. 4.

[124] *See* Gwirtzman, *supra* note 78.

[125] Washington Post, Aug. 29, 1975, § D, at 6, col. 2.

[126] *Id.*

[127] Wall Street Journal, Mar. 3, 1976, at 3, col. 2.

[128] *Id.* In the opinion of the authors, the revelations of instances in which U.S. companies have been involved in bribes or other questionable payments have caused many adverse reactions overseas, with potentially or actually damaging results to business.

11

OPERATIONAL CODES AND BRIBERY

W. MICHAEL REISMAN

THE previous chapter documented the divergence, with regard to bribery, of myth system and operational code in three key sectors of contemporary life. There was no intention to suggest that all bribery was lawful or always lawful or that all bribery was the same. That is hardly the case. Bribery appears to flourish in certain social settings and not in others and to be viewed differently depending upon one's location and identities.[1] There are substantially different types of bribery, with different impacts on the larger social system in which they take place and different degrees of lawfulness. The operational code is a *normative* code. Like Plunkitt, it distinguishes between types of bribery, tolerating and even encouraging some while severely sanctioning others. There are three basic bribe varieties:[2] *transaction bribes, variance bribes,* and *outright purchases.* If the fact of the distinction is not edifying, it is sufficiently intriguing to warrant inquiry.

Transaction Bribes

A transaction bribe, or a TB, is a payment routinely and usually impersonally made to a public official to secure or accelerate the performance of his prescribed function. Examples of transaction bribes include the ten-dollar bill that an attorney probating a will in an American city may routinely

From W. Michael Reisman, "Operational Codes and Bribery," pp. 69-93; 214-230 *Folded Lies: Bribery, Crusades, and Reforms.* Copyright 1979 by The Free Press.

give to the clerk to accelerate the operation, or the bribe given to a customs official on the Mexican border to move things along more rapidly. There are a number of distinguishing characteristics here. First, the payment is made not to violate a substantive norm but rather to assure the performance of the official act with dispatch. The bribe to the probate clerk is not made to "cure" some critical defect in the will but simply to save the attorney a half hour or fifteen minutes in line.[3] The clerk's "shakedown" is based on his control over the time features of the process. He can move one will from the top to the bottom of the pile, he can putter through bureaucratic "mysteries" for twenty minutes and disappear into an office for another half hour, or, if fixed appropriately, probate you in less than five minutes. Similarly, the customs official's bribe secures speed, not a variance on the law. If the importer fails to get the signal, he may find it takes three days to clear customs. Hence the popular epithets "speed money," "grease money," "vigorish," and the like.

The transaction bribe is described—sometimes euphemistically, sometimes with a tone of resignation, sometimes with an almost bemused affection—as "taking care of" an official. There is a tendency among some informants to appraise the TB as quite innocuous and to assimilate it to the "tip" or gratuity voluntarily paid as a reward *post hoc* for the satisfactory performance of a task. Some TBs are like tips in amount yet some may be quite large, for example, the custom of a 5 percent "finder's fee" to a public official who arranges for a very large contract with his government. It would appear that key distinguishing aspects of the TB are ignored if it is viewed as no more than a *nunc pro tunc* tip in a seller's market. The TB is *collected* by a *public official,* and a sanction, though often mild, is imposed for nonpayment. Hence it affects perspectives about the probity and general task performance of officials and, most important in popular governments, superordinates the official at least in the performance of that task.

Second, the transaction bribe does not "buy" the official who pockets the bribe nor does it purchase a service different from that normatively prescribed. Time is, of course, an economic commodity. The accelerated performance of a task for one member of a class and not for others gives that member an edge and, at a certain point, begins to shade into quality. But this is a subtle point, pertinent only for some TBs and not always appreciated by those involved in the transaction. In this respect, the recipient of the transaction bribe is not corruptible in the broad acceptance of the term: he cannot be "bought" and he will not do "anything—for a price." Try to get the clerk to probate a defective will. Not only will he refuse but he is likely to be quite indignant. As in most conforming behavior, fear will be an element, for the clerk would become involved in acts over which he does not have exclusive control and that are, moreover, susceptible to review. But I believe that a critical element would be the clerk's rectitude; probating a will defective in formal require- ments would be wrong. Recipients of transaction bribes don't do that sort of thing. Responses such as these indicate that we are dealing not with a strictly economic event but with an event governed by a code sounding in many values beside wealth. The concrete result of a bribe may be the transforma- tion of a political or "nonmarket" situation into a market one in which time is sold, but the process introduces many other factors.

A transaction bribe can be corrupted into something else. For example, you may give the official four times what both of you know is the going rate for a particular transaction. If the official accepts, you have transformed the operation into a different type of bribe, perhaps a down payment on a variance bribe or an outright purchase, bribe types we will discuss shortly. But if you pay the going rate, you are paying for a service that is fungible—available to any member of the public on about the same terms.

Which brings us to the third characteristic of the trans- action bribe: it is a general service available to the public.

Though often effected surreptitiously, it is not secret but is discreet[4] in the sense in which we have used the term. Indeed, those who are rather unfamiliar with the operational code and know they are violating the myth system in tendering a bribe may be the ones insisting that the operation be done in almost exaggerated secrecy. A Latin American attorney remarked to me that he placed the equivalent of ten dollars, which one pays as "grease" in the passport office for passport and exit permits, in an envelope before he gave it to the clerk because, he observed with a certain self-derision, he is "overly refined." That ten dollars is divided up according to an operational tariff among all the functionaries in the office who play some role in processing the required document. There is no need to be surreptitious and, according to my informant, the clerk who takes the bribe, without being ostentatious about it, may distribute the shares quite openly.[5]

Compared to the substantial literature examining the social conditions of the types of bribery,[6] the material explaining where and why transaction bribery flourishes is quite scant. There are, as we have seen, certain features inherent in TBs: they are severable micro-acts, most often with the implicit penalty of delay for nonpayment of the bribe; the rather exclusive and effectively nonreviewable competence to impose the penalty is in the hands of the official soliciting the bribe; because the bribe does not affect the quality of the official service performed, the entire transaction is traceless. TBs tend to occur in routinized situations in which time is of recognized economic value, and the payments tend to be comparatively small.[7]

As far as I can tell, no one has undertaken the lugubrious task of actually detailing the extent of transaction bribery. To say that it is Eastern rather than Western or Latin American rather than North American might satisfy certain parochial demands but would be patently incorrect. In different societies there appear to be sectors in which TBs are acceptable according to an operational code and sectors in which they are not. The discovery of the social boundaries demarking bribal and nonbribal sectors is explored in chapter 5. But the actual extent of TB practices seems to vary according to the informant and, on inquiry, often according to what he views as a transaction bribe.

Some efforts have been made to account for the reasons that TBs flourish, but they are not always persuasive. I find the explanation of simple economics—that officials solicit these bribes to supplement low salaries—unsatisfactory. Many officials with unsatisfactory salaries apparently do not solicit TBs. The cultural explanation—for example, that TBs are solicited and paid in Indonesia for the performance of virtually every act because they are part of the culture—is like much functional anthropology, essentially truistic. Anything done anywhere is part of the culture; the examples we have used thus far should make clear that TBs, like toadstools, can pop up whenever it rains.[8] Factors such as professional esprit, structural features such as the distribution of a task among many individuals and departments rather than its concentration in one person or department, and the acuity of supervisory and control systems would appear to contribute to the low incidence of transaction bribery.

"Controllability," the relative ease and administrative cost of identifying and interdicting certain types of behavior, is probably as important a factor in decisions to criminalize certain conduct as is the degree of social harm of the conduct. We might hypothesize that the ease with which an activity can be deflected from its normative course and the ease of detection of the deflection are inversely proportional to the number of participants involved in it: the fewer people involved, the easier it is to cheat and the harder it is to discover the cheating. Compare fixing a game of jai alai to fixing a game of baseball. For obvious reasons, solo operations are more corruptible and less detectable, and TBs are often solo operations. Hence one reason they may be deemed tolerable is the comparative difficulty in arranging for the administrative control.

De minimis non curat praetor (The ruler does not bother with trifles). Because the threshold of criminalization can have a quantitative component, bureaucrats involved in transaction bribery may also have built-in incentives to keep the price low.[9] On the other hand, administrators who wish to control a pattern of transaction bribery may fractionate the activity among many different individuals and groups in the bureaucratic process, a technique that, Vaitsos reports, seems to have had some success in Latin American experience.[10] This technique will not be effective, we may assume, when the operational code tolerates TBs or when the bribers operate with determination and impunity. "Cornelius Vanderbilt and Daniel Drew each bribed New York's entire Common Council of Aldermen, including the infamous Boss Tweed, in their fight to control New York City's Harlem Railroad; they bribed the New York State legislature as well."[11] These bribes were probably of the variance rather than the transaction variety and the operation was facilitated by the prevailing environment of New York politics, where such exchanges seem to have been part of the operational code.

It is also difficult to assess exactly how deleterious, if at all, these bribes are on general public order.[12] Westerners, particularly of the middle classes, might assume that if the civil service presents itself as utterly incorruptible even though large numbers of officials do take transaction bribes, the practice will demean the image and lead to public cynicism and an erosion of expectations of authority. If, on the other hand, everyone assumes the prevalence of this type of petty corruption, it may have only the most minimal deleterious effect.[13] Where benefices are purchased in order to harvest TBs or are awarded by a monarch to key families and then transmitted intergenerationally, TBs may be said to be the very system itself. It would be incongruous to say that they are harming the system.

Another factor that can affect the level of harm is the price of the service: if it is beyond the means of certain strata, it "chills" rights to that service, that is, it effectively prevents its members from invoking the pertinent norms. It thus becomes an instrument of class reinforcement and discrimination,[14] performing a function roughly akin to the pricing of legal services in liberal democracies. But if its price is reasonable, the TB may actually facilitate invocation of a norm by a comparatively prepolitical stratum and is, thus, democratizing.[15] The economic position of the bureaucracy receiving TBs relative to that of the paying public may also be a factor. If the officials are patently underpaid, in terms of their class position, the bribes may be viewed as reasonable salary supplements and hence fair. If the bureaucratic TB-takers are popularly viewed as overpaid in terms of their class position, transaction bribes will be characterized as blood-sucking and are likely to exacerbate the latent and ever-present tensions between governing and governed, no matter how small the particular bribes may be. Under these circumstances, TBs could be rather deleterious to public order.

Variance Bribes

A second and generally more noxious type of illicit payment may be called the variance bribe. Here the briber pays not to facilitate or accelerate acts substantially in conformity with a norm but rather to secure the suspension or nonapplication of a norm to a case where the application would otherwise be appropriate. The transaction bribe is more difficult to track, for it involves no variance from the law, hence leaves few traces. A variance bribe can be tracked and thus is more dangerous and more expensive. Examples of variance bribes include

(1) payment to a customs officer, not to accelerate his performance of a lawful act but rather to allow the importation of goods that are legally prohibited;

(2) payment to a fire inspector to ignore violations of safety regulations and to certify a building as habitable;

(3) payments to an officer for a draft deferment, an early demobilization, or for a cushy assignment behind the lines.

You pay a variance bribe to make the system work for you. The payment is a bribe because a legal prescription in a particular instance is working against you and you want its operation suspended. This is a power and money-making opportunity for the official you address. In liberal democracies and market economies, politicians try to gain the political advantages of the variance bribe by enlarging their ambit of discretionary competence. For example, incumbents will defend a list of non-civil-service appointments,[16] the right to grant architectural contracts, insurance contracts on government buildings, the placing of public funds in bank accounts, and so on, for all of these decisions are discretionary. Since they are not subject to legal review, they can be used to pay off past debts or as down payments on immediate or future rewards from recipients. The more rigid the normative specification, the greater the tendency for variance bribes.

Variance bribes are often initiated by the briber to evade norms that are to be applied to a class of which he is a member. Hence they may be viewed as a much more serious departure from the law of the community than a transaction bribe. Insofar as law is viewed as a technique for securing an authorized pattern of production and distribution of values in a community, the VB frustrates the technique by and for those endowed with power and wealth. But the VB process may be complicated by other factors and may itself indicate an operational code commitment to special treatment for precisely those so endowed with power and wealth. VBs may be initiated by those in the control apparatus and become a form of extortion, as we will see shortly.

Consider a very white-collar example: a speeding ticket has been given to your son or daughter. Since this is a matter that may involve a police record, escalated insurance costs, and other unpleasantness, you "fix" it by a visit to your local committeeman. Depending on who you are or your relation to the political party represented by the committeeman, you may leave some money to "take care" of someone downtown, make a contribution to the party, or pay nothing, with the understanding that when you are contacted later, you will provide monetary or political support. The code covering this sort of variance can be quite complex and is not available to every violator. You may have to "plead" that your child is a good kid, that it is a first offense, and though some of this may be a skit that you and the committeeman act out to assuage your anxiety and to give a legal tone to what is in fact a fixing operation, part of it may involve registering the' fact that the child is not a rotten apple and that no social purpose would be served by imposing the legal sanctions.[17]

Some variance bribe contexts may take on transaction bribe characteristics. There are circumstances in which part of the legal apparatus initiates regulations you can escape only by payment of a bribe. Though you pay for what appears to be a variance, the process is so routinized that it almost amounts to a levy, which may even be deemed authorized under the operational code. Where the committeeman, for example, is an integral part of the traffic-fine decision process and police officers know that most tickets will be fixed, they will be much less restrained in resorting to that sanction; the sanction becomes a type of special tax or levy. In many commercial sectors, some argue that public regulation becomes a general form of shakedown. The regulatory code is cumbersome, they contend, and it is virtually impossible to comply with its many requirements and web of interlocking bureaucracies without self-bankruptcy. Hence the system requires variance bribes; shakedown and collection become major functions. Examples volunteered include building codes in some cities as well as customs and tax schemes in a number of developing countries.

A variance secured by a bribe need not involve a substantive violation of the law or of the operational code. Norms are often framed in general terms, appliers have a recognized ambit of discretion and it is expected that many factors will be taken into account in determining whether and how to apply them. Sometimes a variance is appropriate and available without a bribe, but bribery is quicker. In other cases the variance, though not available without a bribe, is generally deemed to be right in the circumstances. In cases such as these, the variance bribe takes on many of the characteristics of the transaction bribe.

But the real variance bribe, as its name suggests, involves a deviation from the proper application of the norm, accomplished surreptitiously, by illicit payment or by a money substitute. Two types of variance bribe can be distinguished. First, and more common, are those bribes that effectively suspend the proper application of an already prescribed or existing norm. Second are bribes intended to transform or change in an unlawful way, rather than merely to suspend, existing community norms.[18] Examples of the first type include paying meat inspectors not to inspect meat, or paying[19] grain inspectors to ignore or simply not to examine the discrepancies between the amount billed and the amount of grain actually shipped.[20] Other examples of the first type include bribes to legislators or other effective operators designed to ensure special treatment.[21] These payments, often exchanges of cash for political influence, circumvent or suspend the proper application of an entire range of prescriptions, ranging from the procedures for awarding of contracts[22] to the introduction of special bills[23] to the auditing of a company's tax return.[24]

The second type of variance bribe is characterized by the injection of bribery into the process of creating community norms. This occurs both domestically[25] and internationally.[26] When a multinational corporation bribes an official, whether directly or through a sales agent, in order to win a specific contract,[27] the corporation has suspended the existing commercial norm of fair competition. But when a multinational corporation bribes an official, whether directly or through a sales agent, in order to influence general legislation, the electoral process, or the entire constitutional order, we encounter the second type of variance.[28] Whether this type of payment is criminal will depend upon the local norms for legislation. These types of variance bribe are interrelated and the distinction between the two is sometimes unclear.[29]

In contrast to the transaction bribe, the variance bribe is a special product, not a fungible like a TB. As such it distorts the prescriptive program of the community in serious ways. In the short run, it is used to evade the application of norms to events for which they were designed. In the long run, variance bribes tend to reshape the general system in a process worth close attention.

Variance bribes begin as deviations from the prescribed norms of the community. They are secured by tendering a private favor or payment to the official charged with applying the law. The process of variance bribing may institutionalize itself over time and become a legitimate coordinate or even dominant process of authoritative decision. One example of this particular transformation is encountered in the development of equity jurisdiction alongside the common law courts in the English legal system. Though a review of this genealogy is irreverent, it is very instructive in the context of our discussion.

The Curia Regis, the King's Council, was the source of most of the decisions that developed the key institutions in the English system. One of the earliest institutions was the King's Bench, a network of courts that applied law according to a comparatively coherent and fixed code (derived in part from past judicial decisions). If the litigants were dissatisfied with the decisions of the King's Bench, they might turn to the king himself for a special discretionary justice that would set aside the accomplished (and later the anticipated) decision of the King's Bench. As more and more litigants sought variances from the decisions of the courts, the workload was shifted from the king to another official in the Curia Regis, the chancellor.

Now we may assume that the chancellor's dispensation of discretionary justice was given in return for a payment of some sort to the king's treasury or to the chancellor himself or, most plausibly, to both. In other words, the chancellor's was initially a system of variance bribes; indeed, a basic norm of this system was that certain variances could be purchased from the king himself. Over time, however, the chancellor's workload increased to the point where a bureaucracy for processing variance bribes was generated, ironically taking the form of a complementary system of tribunals alongside those of the common law courts. These chancery courts, whose origin was in a variance bribe system, gradually acquired a legitimacy no less than that of the king's original courts. Legitimization proceeded to the point where the bribe system was totally and openly integrated into the official system.[30] Those who take exception to the seamy origin of equity would do well to recall Freud's mordant observation that "neurotics and many others, too, take exception to the fact that *inter urinas et faeces nascimur. . . .*"

Initially, the chancery system outranked the common law courts. However, over time a system of coexistence and sharing of jurisdictions was established. Expectations crystallized, and both litigants and judges understood a rather complex code according to which some matters lay within the competence of the chancery courts while others lay within the competence of the common law courts. It was no longer accurate to say that one secured relief from common law courts through repairing to the chancery courts. Rather there were two systems of justice that interacted and overlapped to some extent but for the most part lived in accommodation.

The West African republic of Liberia[31] presents a variance bribe system that is authoritative but far less institutionalized and legitimized than common law and equity. For historical reasons that cannot be thoroughly explored here, Liberia's decision structure is made up of many comparatively autonomous components. Along the coast, an area quite influenced by Western European political traditions, one finds the system of courts and executive agencies roughly comparable to those found in the English and American legal system. But inland one encounters a system of tribal councils, often under the domination of a single figure, the chief. In Monrovia during the long administration of President Tubman, a type of equity jurisdiction developed. According to observers, many individuals who had the option of seeking the aid of the authorized courts or the official apparatus of government might nonetheless turn directly to President Tubman for a special type of justice—a discretionary justice rendered directly by the president. This justice was generally deemed to be superior, in terms of effective power, to the courts, though ironically it was a system of justice whose dictates were not deemed to survive the death of the president. Tubman justice may be viewed as a type of variance bribe system in its early stages.

If the Tubman system became institutionalized, we would begin to encounter a phenomenon roughly like that of the chancery- common law jurisdiction in England. There are similar examples in American cities where a certain allocation of jurisdiction is effected between the official apparatus—for example, the mayor's office—and the unofficial, effective apparatus—for example, the boss's machine.[32] An operator there could tell you for which matters you went to the boss and for which to the mayor, much as his ancestor could have told you when to repair to Rome and when to Constantinople.

A similar, although nonjudicial, example of the institutionalization of a variance bribe system is provided by the contemporary macro-political bribe. It is often thought that a bribe of, say, $1.1 million paid by an American aviation company to a foreign official is for the private account of the foreign official. Indeed, this may be the case, though it would seem implausible in most countries in which such bribes have been reported. In some countries a secondary structure of organization based upon party membership, political order, or, in some circumstances, tribal or kin-group membership overlays and interpenetrates the formal government at many points. Frequently the payment of the supplementary salaries from the general treasury of the party, the political order, or similar sources may be a reward for those who are members of these groups, a necessary cost-of-living increment in inflationary situations, or, as a result, a technique of internal control.[33] Funds for these supplemental salaries very often come from supplementary payments made by outsiders who seek special favors or variances from the government.

Consider the following example: an enterprising businessman in a small Latin American country would like to secure the exclusive dealership for an American automobile. He pays the equivalent of $100,000 to an official in the ministry of commerce and in return is granted the dealership for a period of twelve months. There is, of course, a regular license fee payable at a twelve month interval. The businessman must then regularly pay the official license fee as well as the supplementary $100,000 under-the-table bribe to the official on an annual basis.[34] The $100,000 paid to the official, we will often discover, is not for the private account of that official but is in fact transferred to party coffers or to the coffers of a smaller group that is using the government as a base of power. The money is thereupon divided up.

Many reported cases of very large bribes paid to individuals in developing countries would appear to be most plausibly construed as payments to mediators or operators; substantial parts of the funds are then distributed within the country and in some circumstances injected directly into the official apparatus of the government. They may well be reprehensible, but they are not *private* bribes paid to those individuals themselves, though agents can be expected to skim for themselves.[35] Skimming itself may be subject to a normative code that sets limits and indicates sanctions for excessive greed.[36]

In a formal sense the briber's scheme in the receiving country would seem to be wholly illegal. In fact it may be part of a thoroughly internalized operational code and indeed may itself be in the process of legitimization and incorporation into the general myth system. In many developing countries legislation in the early days of independence has been either mimetic of the metropolitan or promiscuously romantic. Even in the so-called developed countries, legislative ardor may exceed enforcement intentions or abilities. As a result, the laws themselves are or become unrealistic and inapplicable and almost demand a tempering and bending. For example, country X may provide salary limitations for high public officials that runaway inflation has made unrealistically low; everyone in the country who is politically aware recognizes that additional sums will be required. Such sums are usually provided by the political party of the high official.

The technique of payment of supplementary salaries gives the party a high degree of effective control over the official, for the power of the purse means that an official who is expelled from the party will find continued participation in government financially impossible. Funds for the payment of these supplementary salaries will regularly be gathered through contributions as well as through a secondary transaction or variance bribe system such as the one just described. Like all components of the operational code, the salary-supplement system is very susceptible to abuse. When all the rationalization is scraped away, it may be exposed as a mean and self-serving scheme: no more than an annuity plan or a get-rich scheme for party regulars or an instrument for maintaining vertical discipline.

Where the technique of variance bribes is integrated into the basic authority structure of the receiving state, it would be as perverse to construe the tendering of bribes there as unlawful as it would be to construe plea bargaining in the United States as unlawful. The practice may, of course, violate policies expressed in the local myth system or in some transcending code of values. The variance bribe can hardly be called socially progressive. If natural law, as Stammler put it, has a "variable content," popular welfare objectives might almost be characterized as a natural law demand of governments in this century. Theoretically, Robin Hoods of bribery may exist, but in relatively few cases will the VB system benefit broad strata of the population.

To say that bribery is lawful under the operational code is not to say that all aspects of bribery transactions are lawful. The secrecy with which bribery is accomplished creates multiple opportunities for ancillary delicts. Any system in which large sums are transferred under a skimpy record-keeping system invites skimming, diversion of a percentage of those funds by the transferring agent for his own account. I believe that the extent of skimming has been exaggerated. But even when it occurs, the mere fact that particular transactions may themselves be infected with illegality under either the operational code or the official myth system does not necessarily invalidate or render unlawful the entire transaction.

I suggest that most people would tend to treat as a lawful bribe one tendered to representatives of an institution who are well advanced in the process of institutionalizing a variance bribe system. The corollary of this criterion holds that bribes tendered at the earlier stages of the deterioration of an institution are likely to be viewed as unlawful insofar as the viewer internalized the values and the authority structures of the system undergoing deterioration; paradoxically, the viewer might even prefer the values of the new system on the horizon.

Harold Lasswell has hypothesized that effective power

tends to make itself more authoritative, and it appears that a variance bribe system that bureaucratizes will recruit, reward, and shape different personalities who may then seek respect and legitimacy even though this erodes the real economic commodity on which the variance bribe trades. Variance bribe systems institutionalize when

(1) They enjoy overt or tacit support at the pinnacle of the power process;
(2) the volume of variance business is large; and, as a result,
(3) a bureaucracy must be developed to process the volume.

In the absence of any of these elements, the variance bribe system will remain ancillary to the official decision-making system, acceptable, perhaps, under the operational code but not under the myth system.[37]

The legitimization of the variance bribery system thus paradoxically invites the development of a new variance bribe system.[38] Insofar as discrepancies in the distribution of authority and of effective power develop, additional variance systems will develop. We can hypothesize that the propensity for the institutionalization of variance bribe systems will increase in rough commensurance with the increasing discrepancy between authority and effective control; we might refer to this, for convenience, as *unauthorized change.* As a corollary, we can assume that the propensity for the institutionalization of VB systems

(1) will increase with the radical or discontinuous character of unauthorized change,
(2) will increase when the changes are initiated by a counterelite,
(3) will decrease when the changes are initiated by authoritative elites in accordance with authorized procedures.

Variance bribes, whatever their degree of institutionalization, perform a variety of social functions, some of which may be positive. V.O. Key suggests that this sort of bribery may achieve provisional accommodations between groups with dissimilar and incompatible moral codes:

> The stream of puritanism encounters powerful opposition from masses with different standards of behavior and from those who profit by catering to their tastes. Sentiment wavers. The newspapers and the churches "turn on the heat" occasionally. The community as a whole takes a hypocritical attitude. In this state of indecision and conflict the system of police graft makes possible prostitution, gambling and other practices. It serves in a way to "regulate" control, license and keep within bounds practices which are beyond the law. They cannot be controlled through the forms of law.[39]

Key also suggests, less persuasively, that such bribery may have facilitated or accelerated beneficial social changes.[40] This, however, would appear to be an accidental feature. The quality of the change depends, of course, on the preferences of the observer. VBs may also accelerate social dysfunctions if evaluated from a different set of social goals.

Those who want to believe that VBs are good for the system are Panglossian or are defining system only in terms of those elites actually involved in the variance bribery.[41] VBs are real violations. First, they violate the expectations of those people who believe in the laws that are being subverted. They also violate the basic rules of the market, which, in our civilization, are supposed to police quality and control price in the interests of consumers. But in circumstances in which the laws being violated are not related to market mechanisms, the noxious quality of VBs may be somewhat diminished.

If you are playing a variance bribe game, you ascribe utility to particular laws, not in terms of whether they contribute to community weal but whether they permit you to demand variance payoffs without impeding indispensable social and political functions. Hence the VBs should flourish where the salient laws were created for no other purpose than to generate a market for variances. For example, one informant claims that some safety regulations for elevators in a particular American city are, for all intents and purposes, unfulfillable. Even if compliance could be secured, scarcely any real increment of safety would result. Every elevator in town is in technical violation; when the inspector comes around he is paid to overlook it. (He will not overlook a real violation that does, in fact, jeopardize elevator riders.) The law in question may not have been created to generate a variance market, but that is its only function now.

In a larger organizational sense, the VB may, indeed, be said to perform a *homeostatic* function, easing social conflicts caused by rigidification of formal structures discrepant from the distribution of effective power. This can be viewed as a *positive* social function only from the most sterile organizational standpoint. The statement that an organization or a person survived tells us very little, for every entity always has some range of options for realizing a certain preference, each with a different cost-benefit constellation. Which options, with their unique costs, are rejected and why are the critical questions, from the standpoint of both organizational and moral theory. In this regard, one should note the very special costs of the variance bribe and why, paradoxically, an authoritative elite itself may encourage resort to it.

At one point in the Watergate affair, Richard Nixon is reported to have sighed, "Where will it all end?" The variance briber buys a service, but pays a larger and more continuing price than he may realize. The briber has done something often traceably unlawful, and at least one person in the official apparatus is privy to the fact; since the variance may have required the cooperation of other officials, the briber's actions may be known to quite a few people. The briber is, in some sense, a captive of the process he has subverted;[42] what he may have envisaged as a single transaction contains the kernel of a continuing association.[43] In general, he is likely to become reluctant to criticize corruption and may, in some circumstances, undergo general political paralysis.

From an elite perspective, anxiety is a preferred form of

social control, for it is economical and quiet. A ruling group may decide that it is in its own interests to encourage a degree of variance bribery, tracking and recording it, but not policing it. In India, for example, an informant reports that businessmen secure variances for private payment, only later to discover that the government knows this has been done; thereafter, the businessmen may be committed to support the government in monetary and other ways. Once this pattern is appreciated by businessmen, they will assume that their variance bribes are known to the government and behave accordingly. If the normative code and the bureaucracy are so complex as to require variance bribes in order to stay solvent, some strata may discover that there is virtually no evading this form of anxiety control.

In Iran I was told by a number of informants that the shah is believed to encourage bribery and corruption; but SAVAK, his secret police, keeps track of the corruption and leaks its activities. This knowledge thus becomes a subtle form of intimidation and police control.[44] A cognate and intriguing example is reported by Rebecca West in a study of treason and espionage. She observes that most non-Soviets who engage in espionage for the cause recruit themselves for "ideological" reasons; they do not seek monetary reward and are insulted when it is offered. Nonetheless the KGB's practice is to press payment, which may be intended as a potential instrument of blackmail if the volunteer should molt his ideology at a later stage.[45] The point is that where the transaction bribe may promote the sharing of power, the variance bribe may be used to paralyze political participation and to increase the concentration of power.[46]

The Outright Purchase

A third distinct type of bribery is the *outright purchase*, not of a service but of a servant. Here the objective is *not* to secure the performance of a particular act, but rather to acquire an employee who remains in place in an organization to which he appears to pay full loyalty while actually favoring the briber's conflicting interests. Every personality is a bundle of selves and no civil servant is without some loyalties to groups and individuals distinct from the official apparatus that employs him. The shift of loyalties is facilitated in modern society by the transitory character of loyalty itself: we are trained to generate intense but temporally limited loyalties to each of the series of "teams" we are members of through life.

OP does not refer to circumstances in which an official leans or tilts toward one faction in his exercise of discretion or perhaps leaks information to the press to aid or defeat a policy. Nor does it refer to the practice common in America and in some European systems according to which a civil servant or, let us say, a judge is appointed as and is known to be a machine or party man whose decisions are expected to reflect this loyalty and dependency. The outright purchase is a distinct concept, though it is blurred by the fact that it may be accomplished in a series of incremental and less visible operations, or through tacit promises of subsequent employment by the party with whom you are supposed to be at arm's length.

The term *conflict of interest* is often a euphemism for outright purchase bribes. In the United States, a public official's manifest loyalty is to the public. Where a public official works secretly for a special interest, whether a corporation, foreign country, or whatever, he has breached the public trust and can theoretically be severely sanctioned.[47] The current focus on conflicts of interest in the regulatory agencies and the legislative and executive branches of the United States government[48] is probably due to the uncertainty as to whether public officials are merely leaning or tilting toward one faction or special interest in a particular case, or whether some public officials may have actually sold themselves or have been purchased by special interests.

Though an outright purchase may be aided by ideological or kin ties, its core, regardless of prior conditions, is the surreptitious shift of service loyalty, for all or some purposes, to someone different from the manifest authority.[49]

The outright purchase is a widespread practice. Popular accounts of espionage have given currency to the official who is "turned," bought, or blackmailed into staying in place and from that position provides information or other services for his hidden principal or purchaser. Perhaps the most graphic account of the method of OP is supplied by Agee:

> Liaison officers [of the CIA] make money available to officers of the local service and it is expected that the local colleague will pocket some of the money even though it is supposed to be strictly for operations. The technique is to get the local police or intelligence officer used to a little extra cash so that not only will he be dependent on the station for equipment and professional guidance but also for personal financing.
>
> Security officers such as police are often among the poorest paid public servants and they are rarely known to refuse a gift. Little by little an officer of a local service is called upon to perform tasks not known to anyone else in his service, particularly his superiors. Gradually he begins to report on his own service and on politics within his own government. Eventually his first loyalty is to the CIA. After all, that is where the money comes from.[50]

Though the OP paradigm assumes distinct competing organizational structures, OP can occur within single organizations, in which organs, departments, even kin groups maintain comparatively discrete identifications. In the United States government, for example, the Joint Chiefs used an ensign assigned to a clerical position in the National Security Council to keep tabs on Henry Kissinger, then assistant for national security affairs. Informants have assured me that similar cases abound in corporations and even at the lower levels of commerce. A jobber, for example, may buy "into" a clerk in the employ of a distributor he uses with the expectation of receiving information, preferred treatment, or collaboration in stockroom thefts. By the same token, the outright purchase may be used by a government or a party to retain the loyalties of civil servants and politically relevant constituents in systems with minimal common identification and loyalty. In this country, machine politics is a control system that basically uses the outright purchase bribe.[51]

The utility of having a man "on the inside" hardly requires amplification,[52] but a word on the varying techniques of recruitment is necessary. In some settings, as Copeland asserts, the civil servant himself goes in search of a client.[53] Evelyn Waugh recounts the amusing case of one Wazir Ali Bey, who sold his information and loyalty, on an exclusive basis, of course, to every correspondent in Addis Ababa.[54] In other cases, as Agee has shown,[55] the client cultivates the official either by direct offer or, as we have seen, by somewhat more subtle techniques of entrapment.[56]

The consideration for services performed by an OP may vary from money and money equivalents[57] to promises of future indulgence, for example, a visa, a secure position in the company upon retirement from the government or the military, and the like.[58] Some OPs are recruited by threat and blackmail, but this involves techniques not considered in this essay.

Some patronage in American machine politics is an institutionalized system of outright purchase bribery, distinguished from some of the other examples only by the comparative openness with which it is conducted by politically relevant strata.[59] Favors are distributed by elites to officials and constituents as a means of creating and sustaining loyalties. Patronage is presumably necessary when (1) symbols alone will not generate sufficient loyalty, (2) spontaneous perceptions of common interest are low, and (3) coercion is deemed uneconomical or impractical. Patronage is the insider's bribe or outright purchase and it may be viewed by its practitioners as prophylactic to potential OPs from outsiders. Hence Boss Hague's apothegm that an honest man stays bought.

Machine politics is not always a nasty phrase in America; many who identify with the strata that benefited view machine practices with a certain nostalgic warmth.[60] In strict organizational terms, this system works, though it probably has an inherent inflationary dynamic.[61] Alas, it is a system with little potential for the authoritative control of power. A frightening current example is found in Idi Amin's regime in Uganda, a machine system in which supporters are created and sustained by pork, not from wealth accumulations of the state, the proverbial pork barrel, but from the living flesh of Leviathan.

Operational Distinctions

The Knapp Commission and the Nadjari operation in New York City distinguished early on between different violations of the myth system. The fact that judgeships were purchased was not corruption if the purchaser was seeking respect or opportunities for community service. But if he was buying a place at the bench to make money, he was corrupt. A cop who was taking the small bribes that many officers seemed to accept was distinguished from the one who was selling significant variances or providing information for the mob.[62] The small fry might be threatened with prosecution in order to make them cooperate in the investigation of the larger malefactors, but the small fry and their activities were not the major targets of the commission.[63] All bribery was, of course, illegal. Though it was not expressed, distinctions between lawful and unlawful bribery were being drawn, indicating that the community agents and the bribers shared some parts of an operational code.

It is interesting and revealing that in both SEC and Senate subcommittee confessionals the major sin corporations are admitting is transaction bribery or succumbing to extortion or whitemail. No one confesses variance bribes and *no one* confesses outright purchases. Perhaps our corporations are, as they claim, only TB bribers. But there are grounds for skepticism. Undoubtedly counsel have advised their clients that VBs and OPs may invite antitrust and criminal prosecutions, whereas TBs can be defended as no more than compliance with local standards and, in any case, are matters of limited materiality to investors. But I believe that the uniformity of self-characterization reveals a distinction drawn in the operational code: some bribery violates even the operational code.

TBs seem to have minimal effects on the working of the system. VBs do in fact change systems by aligning formal law with effective power. They also increase elite control by generating manageable anxiety. OPs undermine a system by penetration and infiltration. Of all the bribe categories, OPs require secrecy rather than discretion. And of all the categories, OPs elicit the most severe sanctions. In all this seamy behavior, they stand out as an ultimate betrayal and are most likely to be deemed unlawful under the operational code. But lawfulness, like beauty, is in the eye of the beholder and the normative content of his moral universe, a matter we have yet to consider.

1. For a general presentation of both the incidence and the evaluation of corrupt practices in various types of societies, see A.J. Heidenheimer, ed., *Political Corruption: Readings in Comparative Analysis* (1970), p. 24.

2. In a 1976 report to the U.N. General Assembly, the newly formed Commission on Transnational Corporations classified corrupt practices, including bribery, in the following general way: "In the international context the primary concern is focused on three types of corrupt practices: those involving improper participation by foreign interests in the political process, payments to public officials either directly or through middlemen, in order to obtain favourable decisions, and facilitative payments to achieve speedy action, which is not necessarily illegal." See United Nations Economic and Social Council, Report of the Secretary-General, "Transnational Corporations: Measures against Corrupt Practices of Transnational and Other Corporations, Their Intermediaries and Others Involved," E/5838/, June 11, 1976, p. 6. The commission has, for various reasons, decided to examine only those "payments to public officials either directly or through middlemen, in order to obtain favourable decisions."

In a 1977 report the Commission on Transnational Corporations further distinguished three types of illicit payments: expediting payments, decision-altering payments, and political contributions. See United Nations Economic and Social Council, Report of the Secretariat, "Corrupt Practices, Particularly Illicit Payments in International Commercial Transactions: Concepts and Issues Related to the Formulation of an International Agreement," E/AC.64/3, Jan. 20, 1977, pp. 8, 9. The second report is closer to the categorization I use, but "political payments" are not included here because they refer to the recipient rather than to the type of bribe.

Officials in Washington engaged in transnational bribery investigations have indicated considerably less interest in "facilitative" payments, or what are here called transaction bribes. This cannot be attributed to a reverence for the maxim "De minimis non curat lex," the law does not bother with trifles, for some TBs can be quite substantial. For further discussion, see T. Griffith, "Business

Morality Can Pay," *Los Angeles Times,* Aug. 24, 1975, pt. 8, pp. 1, 4.

3. There may be other, more subtle, reasons, such as the cementing of friendship for nonbusiness purposes, or even psychopathological reasons, such as the delight the briber may take in corrupting authority. For discussion of these aspects, see chapter 5.

4. See note 34 to chapter 1.

5. There is, to be sure, an economic distribution function to TBs, for the functionary who receives the bribe gets a "piece of the action": See D. Bayley, "The Effects of Corruption in a Developing Nation," *Western Political Quarterly* 19:4 (Dec. 1966), p. 727. The more business his clients have, the more he receives. But this does not mean that TBs are eufunctional, acting in some way as an incentive to better bureaucratic work. There is no reason to assume that TBs contribute to a qualitative amelioration of the performance of the bureaucratic function, for the bureaucrat, who has an effective monopoly of his service, has no incentive to do a better job in order to get more TBs.

6. See in general V.O. Key, "The Techniques of Political Graft in the United States" (Ph.D. dissertation, University of Chicago, 1934); and J. Gardiner & D. Olson, *Theft of the City* (1974).

7. In cases where public officials charge a standard percentage for the performance of their duty and their assistance is necessary for the successful completion of a large project, transaction bribes can become exceedingly large. I refer here not to those cases where a public official or sales agent uses influence to assist in the winning of a contract but to those instances where a contract, already awarded, still requires special assistance "in connection with importation of materials, customs, tax and other regulatory matters [as well as] for a general goodwill in connection with contracts." See *Wall Street Journal,* "GE Discloses Units Abroad Made $550,000 of Dubious Payments," Nov. 1, 1976, p. 18. This is apparently a common occurrence with multinational corporations where contracts and projects often run into millions of dollars. In such cases a six-figure transaction bribe, while seeming unreasonable, may be considered standard fare by all participants to the transaction. See P. Nehemkis, "Business Payoffs Abroad: Rhetoric and Reality," *California Management Review* 18 (Winter 1975), pp. 7-9.

8. Many societies use their own distinct expressions for the event I call transaction bribery. In Mexico, a TB is known as *mordida* (the bite); in Honduras, *pajada* (a piece of the action); in Brazil, *jeitinho* (the fix); in West Africa, *dash*; in France, *pot de vin* (jug of wine); *baksheesh* in the Middle East; *la bustarella* (little envelope) in Italy; *kumshaw* (literally, "thank you"), or tea money, in Japan and other Asian countries; and, of course, "a little grease" in the United States. For specific examples of these bribes in their home contexts, see Nehemkis, "Business Payoffs," pp. 7-9.

9. Another factor that may induce moderation in the prices set for TBs is the desire of the bureaucrat taking transaction bribes to avoid making the activity so lucrative that larger fish will either take it over or insist on providing "protection."

10. C.V. Vaitsos, *Intercountry Income Distribution and Transnational Enterprises* (1974), pp. 130-31.

11. C. Elias, *Fleecing the Lambs* (1971), p. 203.

12. Rather than speeding up the procedures, transaction bribes may produce the opposite effect. As the Santhanam committee noted: "Certain sections of the staff concerned are reported to have got into the habit of not doing anything in the matter till they are suitably persuaded. It was stated by a Secretary that even after an order had been passed, the fact of the passing of such an order is communicated to the persons concerned and the order itself is kept back till the unfortunate applicant has paid appropriate gratification to the subordinate concerned. Besides being a most objectionable corrupt practice, this custom of speed money has become one of the most serious causes of delay and inefficiency." See Report of the Committee on Prevention of Corruption, published by the Government of India, Ministry of Home Affairs, New Delhi, 1964, reprinted in United Nations Economic and Social Council, "Transnational Corporations," June 11, 1976, p. 7. In other words, the whole harm of TBs may be greater than the sum of its parts.

13. For an analytic discussion of this condition, see S. Huntington, "Modernization and Corruption," in *Political Order in Changing Societies* (1968), p. 59; for a description of a society where bribery is almost a behavioral norm, see E.C. Banfield, *The Moral Basis of a Backward Society* (1958), p. 85.

14. See United Nations Economic and Social Council Report E/AC.64/3 Jan. 20, 1977, p. 8, para. 30.

15. J.C. Scott, "Corruption, Machine Politics and Political Change," *American Political Science Review* 63:4 (1969), pp. 1142-59; Bayley, "The Effects of Corruption," pp. 719-32; Huntington, "Modernization and Corruption," pp. 59-71; Key, "Techniques of Political Graft," p. 52.

16. In regard to the appointment of appellate and district court judges, see J. Wooten, "Carter Establishes Merit Selection of Appellate Judges, but Yields to Senators on District Courts," *New York Times,* Feb. 18, 1977, p. A-28; and N. Miller, "The Merit System vs. Patronage," *Wall Street Journal,* Feb. 28, 1977, p. 14.

17. J. Gardiner, *Traffic and the Police: Variations in Law-Enforcement Policy* (1969), pp. 118-23; and *New York Times,* "L.I. Judge Guilty of Ticket Fixing," Dec. 17, 1976, p. B-2. Professor Davis opines that this sort of thing is an example of "injustice." But its persistence leads me to speculate on the existence of an "operational" norm. Se K. Culp Davis, *Discretionary Justice in Europe and America* (1976), pp. 1-2.

18. Every community and group with a recognized normative code is subject to the suspension or transformation of its code through the techniques of variance bribery. This needs to be clarified because many writers unduly restrict their discussion of this type of bribery to activities in the political arena. For a precise discussion of this point, see H.D. Lasswell, "Bribery," *Encyclopaedia of the Social Sciences* (1931), vol. 2, p. 690.

19. See S. Raab, "Payoffs to U.S. Meat Inspectors Are Found Common in City Area," *New York Times,* April 5, 1976, sec. C, p. 1; J. Kwitney, "Massive Indictment of Meat Inspectors Is Seen in New York," *Wall Street Journal,* Aug. 5, 1976, p. 7; and *Wall Street Journal,* "Federal Jury Charges 2 Defunct Meat Firms in Sales to Pentagon," Feb. 3, 1977, p. 11. If the meat inspectors were paid for speeding up the work and not for varying from substantive norms, these would be transaction bribes. Meat and grain inspection provide good examples of the gray areas between bribery and extortion, since their operations provide many opportunities for dilatory practices that can stimulate bribes.

20. See W. Robbins, "Inquiries into Grain Find New Data on Gratuities," *New York Times,* Aug. 4, 1976, p. 11; *Wall Street Journal,* "Inquiry into Scandal in Grain Inspection Spreads to 15 States," Aug. 3, 1976, p. 24; *Los Angeles Times,* "Grain Inspector Bribe Charges Called False," Aug. 6, 1976, pt. 1, p. 23; *Los Angeles Times,* "U.S. Sues Cook for $24 Million in Grain Scandal," Dec. 23, 1976, pt. 3, p. 9; and *Wall Street Journal,* "Cook Industries Inc. Sued for $23.9 Million by Justice Department," Dec. 23, 1976, p. 4.

21. See in general J. Gardiner & D. Olson, *Theft of the City,* (1974), chapter 4. Specific examples of bribes designed to suspend a norm and ensure special treatment include payoffs on the waterfront between union leaders and businessmen interested in "labor peace," avoiding the costs of strikes, and in price fixing. See *Wall Street Journal,* "United Brands Report Indicates Payoffs to Labor; High ILA Aide Is Indicted in New York on Charges of Racketeering Activity," Dec. 13, 1976, p. 8; L. Dembart, "U.S. Summons 350 in 2-Coast Inquiry on Pier Kickbacks," *New York Times,* Jan. 27, 1977, pp. 1, 70; *Wall Street Journal,* "U.S. Subpoenas Transway International; R.J. Reynolds Unit in Dock Crime Probe," Jan. 28, 1977, p. 4; and N. Gage, "Corruption Is Broad on the Waterfront, An Inquiry Indicates; 2 Grand Juries Hear Evidence; Federal Cases Reported to Involve 'Majority' of Longshoremen's Union Executive Council," *New York Times,* Feb. 7, 1977, pp. 1, 34. For an example of this type of variance bribe in the broadcasting industry, see *Wall Street Journal,* "FCC Hearings on 'Payola' and 'Plugola' by Broadcasters Planned for Early 1977," Dec. 24, 1976, p. 4; and in the New York City School System, see L. Buder, "Queens School Custodian Investigated on Kickbacks," *New York Times,* Feb. 11, 1977, p. B-3. A final example is supplied by Metromedia Inc.'s outdoor advertising division. Regular payments were made to domestic government employees in order to influence their decisions concerning the division's failure to comply fully with certain laws. See *Wall Street Journal,* "Metromedia Discloses Payoffs by Unit in U.S. to Government Aides," Jan. 14, 1977, p. 18. This type of variance bribe can, of course, occur in a transnational context. See A. Crittenden, "Business Bribery Abroad: A Deeply Etched Pattern," *New York Times,* Dec. 20, 1976, pp. D-1, D-3.

22. Most recent examples of this phenomenon include Brooklyn Democrat Frank Braso, who was convicted in 1974 of taking a bribe from a local trucking company, allegedly controlled by the Mafia, for which he had helped obtain a Post Office contract. And, four months later, another Brooklyn Democrat, Representative Bertram Podell, pleaded guilty to a charge that he had received money for helping a Florida airline win federal authorization to fly more profitable routes. See *Newsweek*, "Capitol Capers," June 14, 1976, p. 22. See also T. Robinson, "Graphic Arts Firms under Payoff Probe," *Washington Post*, Feb. 27, 1976, p. 1. In reference to shipping contracts, see W. Robbins, "Passman Is Said to Face Inquiry on Coercion of Aid Recipients," *New York Times*, July 11, 1976, sec. 1, pp. 1, 42; and related to the preceding article, see W. Robbins, "Agriculture Aides Queried in Inquiry Linked to Korea," *New York Times*, Nov. 1, 1976, p. 3. For a British caper of similar design, see B. Weinraub, "British Officer Linked to Bribes, Arrested in an Inquiry into Corrupt Arms Sales," *New York Times*, March 15, 1976, p. 7. In this account the officer allegedly fixed defense contracts, mostly for sale to Oman, by passing money to officials in the Ministry of Defence.

23. A recent example involved Representative Henry Helstoski, indicted for, among other things, soliciting and accepting bribes from aliens in the United States on whose behalf a congressman may introduce a special bill authorizing citizenship. Helstoski denies all charges. See R. Sullivan, "Helstoski Indicted by U.S. in Extortion on Alien Bills," *New York Times*, June 31, 1976, p. 41. Another recent example involved Massachusetts state senators Joseph J.C. DiCarlo, the Democratic majority leader, and Ronald C. MacKenzie, a ranking Republican. Both were indicted on eight counts of bribery and extortion following a two-year investigation. The indictments charged the two with conspiring to extort $40,000 from a New York management consultant firm for whitewashing a legislative report investigating a $3 million contract awarded to the firm. See *Los Angeles Times*, Aug. 13, 1976, pt. 1, p. 2.

24. Cyril Neiderberger, a former IRS auditor, was convicted for accepting "illegal gratuities" from the Gulf Oil Company. See *Wall Street Journal*, "Ex-IRS Aide Guilty of Letting Gulf Oil Pay for 4 Vacations," Feb. 28, 1977, p. 4. Gulf does not deny the gratuities

but comments that "there is no indication that any benefit to Gulf has been asked or received in connection with these actions." See *Wall Street Journal*, "Retired IRS Agent Indicted over Gratuity Gulf Oil Allegedly Paid," July 19, 1976, p. 2; *Wall Street Journal*, "Initial IRS Probe of Gulf Oil Slush Fund in '74 Was Incomplete, U.S. Aide Charges," Feb. 18, 1977, p. 10; *New York Times*, "Taking Gulf Favors Laid to I.R.S. Agent," Feb. 18, 1977, pp. D-1, D-11; and B. Calame, "Two Gulf Oil Aides Are under Scrutiny over Alleged Gifts to Ex-IRS Supervisor," *Wall Street Journal*, Feb. 10, 1977, p. 19. For details of a similar case, see *Wall Street Journal*, "Jeweler in New York Is Indicted for Gifts to Former IRS Agent," March 4, 1977, p. 3; and *New York Times*, "Head of Van Cleefs Charged with Gifts to I.R.S. Auditor," March 4, 1977, p. A-13.

25. Recent federal examples include the alleged bribe paid to then treasury secretary John Connally in 1971 for help in getting then president Nixon to increase federal milk price supports. See *Los Angeles Times*, "Witness in Connally Trial Gets Lecture, Probation in Milk Fund Bribe Allegations," Aug. 21, 1976, pt. 1, p. 6. A more recent federal example involves senators who changed their votes on the national no-fault auto insurance bill in March 1977 and received $5,000 each from a trial lawyers' political campaign committee. See M. Mintz, "Senators Change Votes, Get Funds: Two Switch on No-Fault Insurance, Receive Gifts from Lawyers' Group," *Los Angeles Times*, Aug. 30, 1976, pt. 1, p. 14. See also *Wall Street Journal*, "Six Are Fined, Jailed in Illinois Bribes Case over Concrete Trucks," Nov. 1, 1976, p. 10. For the medical profession's efforts at influencing legislation through bribery, see M. Seigel, "11 Podiatrists and 2 Crime Figures Indicted in Medicaid Bribery Plot," *New York Times*, Feb. 10, 1977, p. 43.

26. Thus Daniel Moynihan asserted that vote-buying occurs, albeit irregularly, on critical General Assembly resolutions. See K. Teltsch, "Moynihan Cites U.N. Vote-Buying, Says He Knew of Payments in Key Assembly Ballots," *New York Times*, May 30, 1976, p. 10. The American ambassador in Jamaica allegedly solicited $25,000 from the Aluminum Company of America, and apparently paid this money to Jamaican officials in order to gain support for an educational program that would explain to the citizens of Jamaica the advantages of permitting United States

investment in Jamaica. See R. Hershey, "U.S. Envoy Sought Gifts in Jamaica; Evidence Shows Ambassador Asked Alcoa for Money for Political Purposes," *New York Times,* July 16, 1976, p. 1; R. Hershey, "Alcoa Asserts a U.S. Envoy Solicited Payments Abroad," *New York Times,* July 15, 1976, p. 1. A final international example of the use of bribery in attempting to influence general community norms is supplied by the recent investigations of alleged bribes paid by South Korean businessmen, on behalf of the South Korean government, to American congressmen. See N. Horrock, "Inquiry to Korean Influence in U.S. Focuses on a List of 90 in Congress; Big Political Scandal Held Possible; Study Still in Early Stage," *New York Times* Oct. 28, 1976, p. 1; *Time* magazine, "Koreagate on Capitol Hill? Nov. 29, 1976, pp. 14, 19; R. Halloran, "Lobbying by Koreans Apparently Paid Off: 60 Congressmen Voting against Legislation Opposed by Seoul Got Some Form of Favor," *New York Times,* Dec. 6, 1976, p. 15; M. Tharp, "Far East Flap: Scandals Strain Links of South Korea, U.S.; Tension Worries Japan; Charges of Bribery, Bugging Could Undercut Alliance, Political Observers Fear; Business Ties Hold Firm," *Wall Street Journal,* Jan. 10, 1977, pp. 1, 10; and R. Halloran, "U.S. Envoy Said to Have Protested to Seoul on Lobby in Washington," *New York Times,* Feb. 3, 1977, p. 12. But see A. Marro, "Korea Lobby Is Reported Focusing on Two Ex-Congressmen," *New York Times,* March 28, 1977, pp. 1, 23; and *New York Times.* "Korean Watergate or Washout?" an editorial, March 29, 1977, p. 30.

27. In general, see *Time* magazine, "The Lockheed Mystery (*contd.*)," Sept. 13, 1976, pp. 31-32. More recently, see R. Halloran, "Lockheed Ex-Official Says Initiative in Bribe Cases Came from Japanese," *New York Times,* Dec. 20, 1976, p. A-8; M. Tharp, "Tanaka's Trial in Lockheed Payoff Case to Open Today before 3 Judges in Japan," *Wall Street Journal,* Jan. 27, 1977, p. 15; and *Wall Street Journal,* "Italian Panel Indicts Ex-Defense Officials in Lockheed Scandal," Jan. 31, 1977, p. 5. Another example is Northrop Corporation's bribe of $450,000 to two Saudi Arabian generals in 1972 and 1973 in order to secure aircraft contracts. See H. Watkins, "Effects of Aerospace Payoffs," *Los Angeles Times,* Feb. 15, 1976, pt. 6, pp. 1,4; and Nehemkis, "Business Payoffs," pp. 14-15. Other examples include Honeywell Bull and the stevedoring case men-

tioned in chapter 2. See C. Farnsworth, "Honeywell Bull: Episodes in Swiss Finance; After Being Defrauded, a Question of Bribes," *New York Times,* April 25, 1976, sec. F, p. 3; and R. Tomasson, "Stevedore Cited in $100,000 Bribe, Head of 5 Concerns Accused by Waterfront Commission," *New York Times,* May 10, 1976, p. 48. Many of the multinational corporate bribes disclosed during the past three years appear to be this form of variance bribe. See also the following articles for details of disclosures of further corporate payoffs: S. Hersh, "Hughes Aircraft Faces Allegations That It used Bribery in Indonesia," *New York Times,* Feb. 4, 1977, pp. 1, 14; D. Andelman, "Indonesia Opens Inquiry on Charge of Huge Payoffs in Satellite Project," *New York Times,* Feb. 4, 1977, p. A-1; *Wall Street Journal,* "SEC Complaint Says General Telephone Made a Questionable Payment in Iran," Jan. 28, 1977, pp. 2, 22; *Wall Street Journal,* "GTE Narrows List of South American Countries in Payoff," Feb. 8, 1977, p. 46; *Wall Street Journal,* "False Reporting Laid to American Hospital Supply; SEC Accuses Firm of Trying to Cover Up $4.6 Million of Saudi Arabia Payoffs," Dec. 30, 1977, p. 16; and *Wall Street Journal,* "Uniroyal Enjoined from Future Illegal Overseas Payments," Jan. 28, 1977, p. 2. This form of variance bribery has been exposed in the beer industry, in methods for awarding contracts and distributorships. The brewers were the first domestic industry to be investigated by the Securities and Exchange Commission; others may follow. See F. Klein, "Brewing Scandal: Beer Firms Are Target As Agencies Extend Bribery Probes to U.S.," *Wall Street Journal,* June 10, 1976, pp. 1, 22; R. Hershey, "S.E.C. Bribery Suit Names Emersons: Charge Is First Domestic One of Its Kind over Corporate Payments," *New York Times,* May 12, 1976, pp. 57, 69. See also E. Morgenthaler, "Bribery Build-up: How a Fraud Scheme & Steel Mill Arose Together in Indiana," *Wall Street Journal,* June 8, 1976, pp. 1, 16.

A statement by a member of the commercial fraternity distinguishing sharply between transaction bribes and variance bribes was made by a Budd Company spokesman in that company's formal disclosure of its practices in the United States and abroad. The spokesman said that payments were made "to induce them (officials) to expedite the performance of their routine duties" [transaction bribery] and "to obtain commercial advantages or to meet contractual obligations in a manner prohibited by local law [variance bribery]." See *Wall Street Journal,* "Budd Co. Discloses 'Improper Payments' in U.S. and Abroad," Nov. 8, 1976, p. 16.

28. The activities of virtually all oil companies in Italy are the best documented international case of this type of variance bribe. See in general G. Hodgson, "The Secret Power, Buying Italian Favours: The Role of BP and Shell," *Sunday Times* (London), April 11, 1976, p. 6; G. Hodgson, "Pay-off for the Oil Companies' Hand-outs: £500 Million," Sunday *Times* (London), April 18, 1976, p. 6. Other companies involved in this form of bribery include Gulf Oil in Korea, United Brands in Honduras, ITT in Chile and, of course, Exxon and Mobil Oil in Italy. For recent revelations on the ITT-Chile case, see *Los Angeles Times,* "500,000 Offer to Aid Allende Opponent Told," Dec. 25, 1976, pt. I, p. 10; G. Hovey, "Former U.S. Ambassador to Chile Charges Officials Lied on U.S. Role," *New York Times,* Jan. 12, 1977, p. A-9; and *Wall Street Journal,* "The Korry Case," Jan. 12, 1977, p. 14. For good coverage of these cases, see *Economist,* Intelligence Unit, "Bribery, Corruption, or Necessary Fees and Charges?" *Multinational Business,* no. 3 (1975), pp. 1-17; C. Flannery, "Multinational 'Payoffs' Abroad: International Repercussions and Domestic Liabilities," *Brooklyn Journal of International Law* 2:1 (1976), pp. 111-13; Nehemkis, "Business Payoffs," pp. 9-15. Nehemkis suggests that this form of corporate variance bribe does not elicit any attention in the United States because it is institutionalized domestically through lobbying. As we saw in chapter 2, transnational bribery designed to influence the creation of a specific community's or nation's general norms or legislation is a technique used by many agencies. See D. Binder, "More Heads of State Reported to Have Received C.I.A. Payments," *New York Times,* Feb. 19, 1977, p. 9; E. Behr, "CIA Reportedly Gave Israelis Millions While It Was Paying Jordan's Hussein," *Wall Street Journal,* Feb. 22, 1977, p. 2; and *Time* magazine, "Cutting Off the King's Dole," Feb. 28, 1977, p. 13.

29. In communities, organizations, or arenas where bribery is an accepted instrument of legislation, this characterization of bribery (that is, as a suspending of legislative norms) is inaccurate. Certainly bribery in the legislative process cannot imply a suspension of a norm if bribery itself, while not being a routine technique, is an accepted norm of legislative behavior.

30. We may hypothesize that any variance system in which effective elites receive rewards or otherwise secure gains will tend to institutionalize itself and routinize procedures as its workload increases. Over time, the variance character will become familiar and even authoritative. In the United States, for example, foreign states impleaded by our citizens for violations of private rights regularly turned to the Department of State and asked that "Suggestions of Immunity" be issued to the court seised of the case. These requests for variances increased in volume until the department found it necessary to develop an internal quasi-judicial procedure to respond to these claims for sovereign immunity.

31. P.A.Z. Banks, "Liberia: A Duality in the Law" (student paper, Yale Law School, 1975).

32. See J. Douglas, "Boss Tweed's Revenge," *Wall Street Journal,* June 30, 1976, p. 16. See also Key, "Techniques of Political Graft," pp. 51-52; Bayley, "The Effects of Corruption," p. 730. See in general J. Gardiner & D. Olson, *Theft of the City* (1974); A. Callow, *The City Boss in America* (1976); and L. Hershkowitz, *Tweed's New York* (1977).

33. A recent example of this phenomenon involves the Israeli government and the ruling Labor Party. For the Yadlin case, see *New York Times,* "Israeli Once Nominated for High Banking Position Is Indicted in Bribery," Dec. 14, 1976, p. 6; *New York Times,* "A Guilty Plea Shakes Israel's Ruling Party," Feb. 15, 1977, pp. 1, 4; *Wall Street Journal,* "Israeli Politician Discloses '73 Kickbacks to Labor Party, Implicates Rabin Aides," Feb. 15, 1977, p. 18; W. Farrell, "Israeli Labor Party Ponders Its Future; Disclosures on Kickback Money Add to Doubt about Outlook for Ruling Political Group," *New York Times,* Feb. 16, 1977, p. A-6; and W. Farrell, "Likud Bid to Check Israeli Labor Party's Funds Provokes Angry Debate and Shouts of Thieves!" *New York Times,* Feb. 17, 1977, p. 3. For the Ofer case, see *Time* magazine, "Suicide, Scandal and Political Chaos," Jan. 17, 1977, pp. 28, 29. For a rundown of a variety of Israeli government scandals, see p. 29 of this article. In addition, on the Ofer affair, see *New York Times,* "Week after Suicide Israel Halts Inquiry," Jan. 10, 1977, p. 8; and *Time* magazine, "Rabin on the Razor's Edge," March 7, 1977, pp. 32, 37.

34. The McCloy report on Gulf's bribe activities indicates that Western

bribers who entered into these arrangements abroad seemed to assume that bribe fees were either single payments or, if annual, were at a fixed price. In Korea, at least, it became clear that, from the bribe receiver's standpoint, the agreement regarding the bribe did not deal with the amount so much as with the commitment to continue to pay. Subsequent bribe requests might take account of factors such as inflation and windfall gains from the enterprise that could be "shared" through higher bribes. See, generally, J. McCloy, *The Great Gulf Oil Spill* (1976).

35. Agents skim in both national and transnational contexts. For skimming in regard to bank loans, see *Wall Street Journal,* "Two Former Aides of American City Bank Are Indicted," Dec. 28, 1976, p. 4; and *New York Times,* "Four Charged with Fraud in S.B.A. Loans by Banks," Jan. 12, 1977, p. D-3. For one case, among many, of transnational skimming, see R. Hershey, "$1.3 Million in Questionable Fees Cited by T.W.A. and Subsidiaries," *New York Times,* Feb. 9, 1977, p. D-1.

36. According to the *New York Times,* a Business International Report, "Questionable Corporate Payments Abroad," makes clear that some countries have unwritten codes stating which persons are "entitled" to receive irregular payments and setting out the proper amounts. If a "qualified" recipient requests too much, he risks a trip to jail. See A. Crittenden, "Business Bribery Abroad: A Deeply Etched Pattern," *New York Times,* Dec. 20, 1976, pp. D-1, D-3.

37. H.D. Lasswell & A. Kaplan, *Power and Society: A Framework for Political Inquiry* (1950).

38. Thus a legitimated variance bribe arrangement leads Russell Baker to the conclusion that legalization of bribery is a "sensible solution to a nasty problem." See R. Baker, "Passing the Buck," *New York Times,* March 30, 1976, p. 31.

39. Key, "Techniques of Political Graft," pp. 399-400.

40. See also M. Tolchin & S. Tolchin, *To the Victor: Political Patronage from the Clubhouse to the White House* (1971), p. 9.

41. See in this regard M. Goodman, "Does Political Corruption Really Help Economic Development?: Yucatan, Mexico," *Polity* 7:2 (Winter 1974), p. 143.

42. Ambrose Lindhorst, a Cincinnati lawyer, who spent twenty years

in local politics, warns prospective one-time bribers that once payoffs are initially made to policemen, building inspectors, and others, at "the curbstone level," there will be trouble. Once started, the practice never ends. Another veteran political worker, from Illinois, warns businessmen on state-level campaign contributions: "Stay away from anything that smacks of a trade-off. Do it once, and you'll do it forever, and it will get more costly." See *Business Week,* "Stiffer Rules for Business Ethics," March 30, 1974, p. 90.

In general, transnational bribers must be aware that investments secured by bribery are thereby made more subject to the caprice of a host government. If a political party in power is paid off, another party coming to power is likely to discover the arrangement and either up the ante or expropriate the holdings. Pertinent here are Gulf's experience in Bolivia—see J. McCloy, *The Great Gulf Oil Spill* (1976)—and Occidental Petroleum Company's experience in Venezuela—see *Wall Street Journal,* "Venezuelan Panel Assails Occidental, Urges No Compensation for Its Holdings," June 4, 1976, p. 7.

43. The relationship may become isonomic, that is, the briber may also have "captured" the official he has corrupted. As we will see, this really involves a distinct species of bribery, "the outright purchase."

44. See, generally, M. Zonis, *The Political Elite of Iran* (1971), pp. 101–103, 66–69, 305–306.

45. R. West, *The New Meaning of Treason* (1964). Students of the Soviet economy have suggested that a comparable function is performed by the USSR's highly structured market system and the centrally imposed *plan* or quota for each enterprise. It is impossible to fulfil the plan without committing severely sanctioned "economic crimes." Violations are detected by the control apparatus of the party that reaches into the factory itself and hence are accomplished with the knowledge and tacit collaboration of the local party watchdog. One consequence is that there is always fear and anxiety of exposure and punishment in the politically relevant managerial class, a fear that is periodically reinforced by well-publicized trials for economic crimes against the Soviet state. Anxiety-management results in submission. Professor Michael Libonati

remarks that "the system is less costly in terms of bodies than Stalinist purges, but no less effective."

46. See, in relation to the concentration of power through variance bribery, Key, "Techniques of Political Graft," pp. 50–52; and J. Scott, *Comparative Political Corruption* (1972), p. ix. Key's essay also deals with the use of bribery as a technique for retaining a position of power; see page 52.

47. But the chances of severe sanctioning for any public official for these infractions appear extremely low; see chapter 2. As *Newsweek* put it, "Like most other white-collar criminals, Congressmen spend little time behind bars." When a public official actually spends time in prison it does not, it seems, necessarily damage his public stature. But few congressmen have handled a prison sentence with the "flair of the late Rep. James Michael Curley of Massachusetts. Convicted on mail fraud charges, Curley spent six months in jail and had five brass bands waiting outside to trumpet his release in 1947. He then served out his fourth stint as Mayor of Boston—to which post he had been overwhelmingly elected while under indictment." See *Newsweek*, "Capitol Capers," June 14, 1976, p. 22. More recent examples of judicial deference to the operational codes of public officials are found in the Cunningham and Saypol cases. See D. Kleiman, "Keenan Will Appeal in Cunningham Case; Special Prosecutor Will Petition Court to Rescind the Dismissal of Indictment for Bribery," *New York Times*, Jan. 12, 1977, p. B-2; and idem, "Saypol Indictment Is Dismissed; Prosecutor Won't Appeal Ruling," *New York Times*, Jan. 18, 1977, p. 52.

48. See chapter 2 for examples of conflicting interests in the United States government. In particular, see A. Kneier, *Serving Two Masters: A Common Cause Study of Conflicts of Interest in the Executive Branch* (1976); and L. Reed, *Military Maneuvers: An Analysis of the Interchange of Personnel between Defense Contractors and the Department of Defense,* Council on Economic Priorities, New York (1975). See also L. Kohlmeier, "When Regulators Enlist with the Regulated," *New York Times,* Aug. 1, 1976, sec. 3, pp. 1, 2; W. Green, "Unlikely Alliance: Justice Agency, Law Firms Team Up to Oppose Lawyers' Ethics Plan on Regulatory Conflicts," *Wall Street Journal,* Aug. 11, 1976, p. 30; J. Finney, "Aid to Contractor by Currie Reported: Pentagon Official Cooperated on Missile Plan with Rockwell, Congressional Unit Says," *New York Times,* Oct. 15, 1976, p. A-9; N. Horrock, "Inquiry on Korean Influence in the U.S. Focuses on a List of 90 in Congress; Big Political Scandal Held Possible; Study Still in Early Stage," *New York Times,* Oct. 28, 1976, pp. 1, 12. Early in his administration, President Carter focused further attention on the issue of conflict of interests. For Carter's code of ethics, designed for his cabinet and top 2,000 political appointees, see *Congressional Quarterly Weekly Report* 35:2 (Jan. 8, 1977), pp. 52–53; *Los Angeles Times,* "Texts of Carter's Ethics and Conflict Rules," Jan. 5, 1977, pt. 2, p. 8; *Los Angeles Times* editorial, "Ethics: Breaking Fresh Ground," Jan. 5, 1977, pt. 2, p. 6; and D. Burnham, "G.A.O. Asks New Rules and Panel to Check on Conflicts of Interest," *New York Times,* March 1, 1977, p. 29.

49. The evaluation of the functional condition called conflict of interest in the United States may vary with culture and sector. One journalist noted that "the concept of conflict of interest for those holding positions in both government and business does not exist in France." See F. Lewis, "Business-Political Scandals Are Disillusioning French," *New York Times,* Jan. 10, 1977, p. 8.

50. P. Agee, *Inside the Company: CIA Diary* (1975). For details of a specific case involving similar techniques of outright purchase bribery, see R. Lindsey, "Alleged Soviet Spy Testifies He Was Blackmailed after Telling a Friend of C.I.A. 'Deception' of Australia," *New York Times,* April 27, 1977, p. A-16.

51. See D. Bell, "Crime and Mobility among Italian-Americans," in A.J. Heidenheimer, ed., *Political Corruption* (1970), pp. 159–66; H. Ford, "Municipal Corruption," *Political Science Quarterly* 19 (1904), pp. 673–86; J.Q. Wilson, "Corruption: The Shame of the States," 2 *Public Interest* (1966), pp. 28–38; A. Rogow & H.D. Lasswell, *Power, Corruption, and Rectitude* (1963), pp. 44–45; and Key, "Techniques of Political Graft," pp. 46–53.

52. For recent espionage cases, which were curtailed as a result of their disclosure, see *Los Angeles Times,* "Egypt Unmasks Double Agent Used in Israel," Dec. 25, 1976, pt. 1, p. 4; *Los Angeles Times,* "FBI Arrests Russian Emigrant as Spy," Jan. 8, 1977, pt. 1, p. 5; *Los Angeles Times,* "Ex-CIA Aide Accused of Bid to Sell Data to

Russia," Dec. 23, 1976, pt. 1, p. 12; *Los Angeles Times,* "CIA Data Seized in Arrest Described," Dec. 30, 1976, pt. 1, p. 23; *Time* magazine, "An Offer the Soviets Refused," Jan. 3, 1977, p. 53; and *Time* magazine, "From Russia with Lovers," Feb. 28, 1977, p. 32.

53. M. Copeland, *Without Cloak or Dagger: The Truth about the New Espionage* (1974), pp. 154–59.

54. P. Knightley, *The First Casualty: From the Crimea to Vietnam; The War Correspondent as Hero, Propagandist, and Myth Maker* (1975), p. 175.

55. Agee, *Inside the Company*; Key, "Techniques of Political Graft," p. 47.

56. The revelations of irregular activities between the South Korean government and certain United States congressmen and officials may bring to light recent examples of the old and "more subtle techniques of entrapment." See *Time* magazine, "Seoul Brother," Nov. 8, 1976, p. 27.

57. In the case of the United States government and the entire graphic arts industry in Washington, D.C., money equivalents ranged from lunches, dinners and Christmas presents to home furnishings, electronic sound-reproducing equipment, and lawn mowers. Of course there were large cash payments, and sex and whisky played their parts as well. See T. Robinson, "Graphic Arts Firms under Payoff Probe," *Washington Post,* Feb. 27, 1976, p. A-1.

58. See in general L. Kohlmeier, "When Regulators Enlist with the Regulated," *New York Times,* Aug. 1, 1976, sec. 3, pp. 1, 2; W. Green, "Unlikely Alliance: Justice Agency, Law Firms Team Up to Oppose Lawyers' Ethics Plan on Regulatory Conflicts," *Wall Street Journal,* Aug. 11, 1976, p. 30; and the saga of Dr. Malcolm Currie of the Pentagon discussed in chapter 2. See also J. Finney, "Rumsfeld Clears Pentagon Aide of Conflict of Interest in Missile Program; Eagleton Charges a 'Whitewash,' " *New York Times,* June 9, 1976, p. 9; J. Finney, "Aid to Contractor by Currie Reported; Pentagon Official Cooperated on Missile Plan with Rockwell, Congressional Unit Says," *New York Times,* Oct. 15, 1976, p. A-9; *Los Angeles Times,* "Official Resigns Defense Position," Jan. 6, 1977, pt. I, p. 10; and W. Rawls, "Ex-Pentagon Aide Joins Hughes Aircraft to Oversee Missile He Promoted," *New York Times,* Feb. 15, 1977,

p. 53. See also D. Burnham, "Ex-U.S. Controller Joins Bank Company; Took a Post with Concern That Owns Chicago First National Soon after Leaving Office," *New York Times,* Nov. 28, 1976, p. 27; B. Wolfe, "Corruption in Government Regulation, the Judge Who Made Oil Companies Richer," *New Haven Advocate,* Dec. 1, 1976, pp. 12, 13.

59. For a 1976 example of patronage in American machine politics, see M. Schumach, "Tammany Lives On in a Queens Club," *New York Times,* June 8, 1976, p. 35. For a classic discussion of patronage politics, see J. Douglas, "Boss Tweed's Revenge," *Wall Street Journal,* June 30, 1976, p. 16.

60. C. Rossiter, *Conservatism in America* (1962); see also L. Hershkowitz, *Tweed's New York: Another Look* (1977); and R. Butler & J. Driscoll, *Dock Walloper: The Story of "Big Dick" Butler* (1933).

61. Students of bribery have observed that machines tend to be mildly inflationary and that they flourish in economies in states of expansion. A concurrent condition may be the social changes and disintegrations of traditional loyalty units that may attend such expansion. See also J.C. Scott, "Corruption, Machine Politics, and Political Change," pp. 1154–59.

62. For a reference to this phenomenon, see S. Raab, "Corruption Charges against New York Police Decline," *New York Times,* Jan. 14, 1977, p. B-3.

63. For a case where a deputy inspector is suspected of being the "small fry," see L. Maitland, "Inspector Indicted in Inquiry on Police; Jury Studying Bribery in Harlem Cites McMahon for Perjury," *New York Times,* Feb. 23, 1977, pp. 1, 59; and idem, "Second Deputy Inspector Indicted by Jury Studying Bribery of Police," *New York Times,* March 9, 1977, p. B-2.

W. Michael Reisman is the author of Nullity and Revision and The Art of the Possible, *and coeditor of* Toward World Order and Human Dignity. *A Professor of Law at the Yale Law School, he is also a member of the Editorial Boards of the* American Journal of International Law *and the* Journal of Conflict Resolution *and has been a contributor to* The Nation, The New Republic, *and The New York* Times.

12

SECURITIES-RELATED CRIMES

AUGUST BEQUAI

The annual cost of securities-related crimes runs into the billions of dollars.[1] The total value of all stolen, missing, or counterfeit securities may run as high as $50 billion.[2] In 1974 a federal grand jury handed down a 24-count indictment charging the friend of a former United States President with conspiring to defraud one of the largest banks in the United States of $170 million.[3] That same year, federal investigators charged that an investment advisor had represented to his clients—reminiscent of the Middle Ages—that he would guarantee them high rates of return on their investments, because he had extrasensory perception.[4] It was also disclosed that a sixteen-year-old, who operated out of his bedroom in West Virginia, had been licensed as an investment advisor by the federal government.[5] A fifteen-year-old had been turned down only because he failed to forward a $150 application fee.[6]

Perhaps the most shocking news concerning the securities industry came in late August 1977. A federal report noted that the mayor of New York City, several officials, and a half dozen major financial institutions had misled investors in the offer, sale, and distribution of $4 billion of short-term city notes.[7] The investing public was not informed that the city might be unable to meet its financial obligations. Securities frauds present serious and extensive problems for law enforcement, in particular, and society as a whole.

Development of the Securities Industry

Financial frauds are not new, they can be traced back to ancient Egypt and Rome. In 1285 King Edward I of England gave the Court of Aldermen authority to police and regulate the growing brokerage industry in the City of London.[8] Prosecutions involving brokers were common before the year 1300.[9] During the sixteenth and seventeenth centuries, it was common for brokers and bankers to manipulate the prices of commodities and stocks. In 1697 Parliament enacted additional legislation to curb these abuses.[10]

The United States government, in an attempt to meet its war debts, issued $80 million in bonds in 1789.[11] Many of the states followed this example. In a short while, it became necessary to develop a forum in order to bring both buyers and sellers of securities together. In 1792 a group of New York stockbrokers met and signed the Buttonwood Tree Agreement, which

From August Bequai, "Securities-related crimes," pp. 17-31. Reprinted by permission of the publisher, from WHITE-COLLAR CRIME by August Bequai (Lexington, Mass.: Lexington Books, D. C. Heath and Company, Copyright 1978, D. C. Heath and Company).

established the New York Stock Exchange (NYSE).[12] This exchange initially dealt in government securities, and those of a few banks and insurance companies. The exchange had no offices, and the meetings were held in the streets. About the same time, a group of Philadelphia stockbrokers established an exchange in their own city. In 1817 the NYSE adopted a constitution; members had to buy their seats. By 1886 the daily volume topped the 1 million mark.[13]

The American Stock Exchange (AMEX), the second largest exchange in this country, was founded in the mid-nineteenth century.[14] The exchange was first known as the Curb Exchange, and its members gathered in the streets of downtown New York City and conducted business in the open air. In 1953 it adopted its present name. The AMEX and the NYSE, together, handle about 80 percent of all stock transactions in this country.

Today there are more than a dozen other exchanges, which are known as the regional exchanges. At one time, there were more than 100 such markets. Of these secondary exchanges, the Pacific and Midwest are the most prominent. Another important market, the Over-the-Counter (OTC), has grown in the last several years and handles more than 10,000 issues.[15] This is the key market for government securities. Brokerage firms doing business in this market are usually known as "wholesalers," and their dealers play a key role in the OTC. All trading in the securities of publicly held corporations takes place in one or more of these exchanges.

In 1852 the state of Massachusetts passed legislation to curb much of the abuse that had grown in the securities industry. Many other states also enacted legislation in this area by 1908. Three years later the state of Kansas passed the first of the blue-sky laws. These statutes were later adopted by the majority of the states. Presently, most states have adopted what has come to be known as the Uniform Sale of Securities Act, which imposes criminal penalties on anyone who engages in securities frauds.[16] Many states also provide for licensing of individuals who are employed in the securities industry, and some jurisdictions allocate funds to provide for policing and regulation of this industry within their borders.

October 26, 1929 is known as Black Tuesday in the securities industry, the day of the notorious stock market debacle. It was apparent to many that, in large part, the crash had been caused by the lack of adequate disclosure of the true finances of publicly held corporations. In response to public pressure, the federal government enacted a series of laws, beginning with the Securities Act of 1933 (1933 Act). The U.S. Congress also established the Securities and Exchange Commission (SEC) in 1934 to police this area. The SEC was given authority to enact necessary rules and regulations for the securities industry, and also to enforce those regulations. In terms of enforcement, the SEC can: (1) take civil action, (2) take administrative action, and (3) refer the matter for criminal prosecution to the

Justice Department. The exchanges also have policing units within them, referred to as the "self-regulators." The SEC and these self-regulators police an industry that includes more than 6000 broker-dealers,[17] that employs more than 200,000 individuals,[18] and has assets of more than $500 billion.[19]

Securities Laws

Both state and federal securities laws have as their objective the licensing of individuals who are employed in the securities industry and the registration of any offering or the issuance of a security. They also seek to curb, and punish, the use of any device, scheme, or artifice to defraud, obtain money or property by false representations, or engage in any securities fraud. At the federal level, the SEC has jurisdiction over any transactions that affect interstate or foreign commerce. The states have jurisdiction over only those transactions that occur within their borders.

The ruling body of the SEC is known as the *Commission*. It is a quasi-judicial organ, composed of five members. Only three of these may belong to the same political party. The chairman of this body is selected by the President, with the advice and consent of the Senate. The SEC contains a number of divisions, the chief one being the Enforcement Division. This unit is the policing and prosecutorial organ of the SEC. It investigates all violations of the federal securities laws and brings these to the attention of the Commission. With the approval of the latter, it can then take civil or administrative action, and may also refer the investigatory files to the Justice Department for criminal prosecution. There are also nine regional offices and a number of branch offices that assist the Division of Enforcement in its policing role.

Section 2(1) of the 1933 Act defines a *security* as being any note, stock, treasury stock, bond, debenture, evidence of indebtedness, certificate of interest or participation in any profit-sharing agreement, investment contract, or, in general, any interest or instrument known as a security. The U.S. Supreme Court has defined it as being any investment of money: (1) in a common enterprise, (2) with the expectation of receiving profits, and (3) solely from the efforts of the promoter or a third party.[20] The courts have given the term *security* an extremely broad definition. It encompasses almost every type of investment of money where the investor does not contribute his labor, but relies rather on that of the promoter. Thus stocks, bonds, and even orange groves can constitute a security.

The key federal securities statutes are the 1933 Act and Securities Exchange Act of 1934 (1934 Act). The objectives of the 1933 Act are to: (1) provide investors with material, financial, and other data pertaining to the securities that are offered for sale to the public at large, and (2) to prohibit deceit, misrepresentation, and other fraudulent acts in the sale (not purchase) of securities. Section 5 of the 1933 Act provides that a registration statement must be filed with the SEC by the issuer (the firm selling the security), setting forth financial data on the issuing firm. The securities may not be sold until the registration statement has become effective, which usually takes 20 days after the filing. Until the effective date, it is unlawful to sell these securities. The act provides for criminal penalties and fines—imprisonment of up to five years and/or fines of up to $5,000—for a willful violation of the act.

The Commission, if petitioned, may advance the effective date, but this is discretionary with that body. In the registration statement, the issuer should describe the business, properties, capital, and management of the firm. The financial statements are certified by an independent accounting firm, purportedly to ensure their authenticity. False and misleading statements made in the registration statements are a violation of Section 17 of the act. Such statements may also be in violation of Sections 11 and 12 of the act. The objective of the registration provisions is to provide accurate and fair information for the investor to be able to make an educated assessment of the securities being offered for sale.[21] The SEC does not pass on the merits, value, or business viability of the firm in question. Prosecutions under the 1933 Act have covered such areas as fraud in the sale of securities, touting of stock, failure to register securities distributed in interstate commerce, and filing of false registration statements with the SEC.[22]

The federal registration requirements apply to both domestic and foreign securities being offered to the public for sale. Failure to abide by these requirements can be prosecuted criminally under Section 24 of the 1933 Act or civilly under Section 22. Frauds involving the sale of securities are prosecuted in this fashion. However, not all securities need be registered with the SEC because of certain exemptions. Criminals, in an attempt to evade the federal securities laws, attempt to bring the offering within one of these exemptions and thus evade filing a registration statement. Many frauds have been committed by simply evading a filing through one of these exemptions.

Key among these exemptions are private offerings to a limited number of individuals or institutions, provided, however, that the buyers are familiar with the corporation and thus have no need for written information in the form of a registration. In addition, these securities must not be redistributed. Thus individuals and institutions not familiar with the workings of the firm and therefore in need of additional data in the form of a writing will not be the purchasers of these securities. This is in line with the intent of the federal securities laws—only firms that make disclosure will be allowed to sell their securities to the public.

Securities that are sold within a state, do not affect interstate or foreign commerce, and do not employ the mails in their sale need not be registered with the SEC. However, they may have to be registered with the appropriate state agency. A failure to do so could result in prosecution by the state.

An offering of securities not exceeding $500,000 in amount may also be exempted from registration under Regulation A offerings. A Regulation A firm must, nevertheless, file a notification statement with the appropriate SEC regional office and must use an offering circular that contains information on the company (although not as indepth as in registration situations). The objective is to make it easier for small firms to sell their stocks to the public and to avoid the burden of a deluge of red tape. This laxity, however, allows criminal elements to take advantage of these exemptions and perpetrate numerous frauds. By the time the government acts, it is too late. For example, several years ago a small New York firm sold securities via the Regulation A vehicle. The New York SEC regional office reviewed the notification statement the firm had filed with it and allowed it to go through. A superficial review of the statements the firm filed with that office made it easy for the officers of the firm to fabricate information relating to the company. When the investigators were finally made aware of the fraud, it was too late. Stockholders had lost their money.[23]

In 1934, in an attempt to further extend the disclosure requirements on firms, the federal government enacted the Securities Exchange Act of 1934 (1934 Act). This act makes it a felony, punishable by up to two years imprisonment and/or up to $10,000 in fines, for anyone to:

1. employ any device, scheme, or artifice to defraud;
2. make any untrue statement of a material fact, or omit to state a material fact in order to make the statement made, in the light of the circumstances under which they were made, not misleading; or
3. engage in any act, practice, or course of business which operates or would operate as a fraud or deceit upon any person, in connection with the purchase or sale of any security.[24]

The act makes it a crime to falsely make, or omit to make, statements that are of a material nature and necessary for the investing public to make an educated assessment of securities. It also covers both the purchase and sale of securities, whereas the 1933 Act only covers purchases. Material falsities filed with the SEC will be prosecuted under the act. Omissions of a material nature, such as a company failing to disclose large sums of money used to bribe either domestic or foreign officials, will also be in violation of the act.

Numerous securities frauds have been prosecuted under the 1934 Act. For example, the manipulation of the market in listed securities is a violation, as well as any fraud in either the purchase or sale of securities. The falsification of any filings, annual reports, or any registration statement is also a violation of the 1934 Act. The 1933 Act could possibly be employed here as well. False filings by members of the brokerage industry will also be in violation, along with trading in securities on "inside information" (to be covered later in the chapter).

There are several other securities acts that should be mentioned in any discussion of securities regulation. For example, the 1935 Act requires officers and controlling shareholders of registered public holding companies to report their ownership of securities; the 1940 Act covers the investment industry; and the 1940 Advisors Act covers investment advisors. Several other statutes have also been enacted. However, except for the 1933 and 1934 Acts, the other statutes play a minor enforcement role. Prosecutions under these other statutes, when combined, count for fewer than a dozen criminal prosecutions. Criminal cases brought under the 1933 and 1934 Acts account for the bulk of prosecutions for securities frauds.

Understanding the Corporate Animal

We have been conditioned to think of a corporation as an entity with its own personality and unique behavior. For example, some companies are known as "bad," while others have a reputation for being "good." Recently, one businessman proposed that we rehabilitate the bad ones, as if they were human and could be salvaged through therapy. There is, for example, the case of a large Buffalo-based corporation that operates in several foreign countries and in 39 states within this country.[25] It owns race tracks and professional sports teams and grosses more than $500 million annually. In 1972 a Los Angeles grand jury brought an indictment against the firm that resulted in a subsequent conviction. Five years later, the firm petitioned the President of the United States to pardon it. Prominent political figures also threw their weight behind this move. Lawyers for the company argued that it had radically altered its behavior and deserved leniency. It had, they said, changed its ways. The petition was denied.

Corporations, in the eyes of the law, are entities with legal rights, separate and distinct from those of the people who own or manage them. They are creatures of the police power of the state. Their charter, or articles of incorporation, gives them birth. They are usually classified as being either private or public. The former is established by private interest for the purpose of commerce of finance; the latter is established to serve a governmental need. A third type of corporate entity is the quasi-public one. This is usually a private interest serving a public need. Public utilities are examples of this type of corporation.

The formation of this artificial person is a simple matter. In most jurisdictions, three or more individuals may apply for a corporate charter and file proposed articles of incorporation with the state. The simplicity with which it can be established, and the legal identity of the corporate entity, offers felons a vehicle and veil behind which they can sometimes disguise their activities. The application lists the name of the proposed entity, its objectives, place of business, duration, officers, directors (at least three), incorporators, and capital stock. Most jurisdictions require that a corporate entity not commence doing business until at least $1000 has been received from the sale of its shares.

The corporate entity has a continuous life, regardless of who its stockholders are. It can borrow money or enter into contracts with other corporate entities or individuals. It can issue or endorse negotiable instruments, can transfer and purchase property, and can issue bonds and stock. Some corporations sell their securities to the public at large and do this through one of the exchanges already discussed. In the process, they file statements (registration) with the appropriate federal and/or state agencies.[26]

Corporations issue two types of stock: (1) common and (2) preferred. The former entitles a shareholder to one vote for each share owned. (The shareholder is also entitled to share in the profits of the firm in the form of dividends.) The latter category of stock has priority over common stock with respect to dividends. It may also have priority over common in the distribution of capital upon dissolution of the firm. Both common and preferred stock, in the case of publicly traded corporations, sell in one or more of the exchanges. The sale, purchase, offer, and other related matters in the instance of these publicly traded securities are controlled and dictated by both state blue-sky laws and the federal securities laws. The intent of these laws is to protect the public at large, which has limited or no knowledge of the corporate entity. Disclosure, to the investor, is a key factor in his decisionmaking. It is one's perception of the company and its finances that leads to investment in that firm's securities. Felons attempt to distort this perception through either the release of false information and/or the omission of material information.

Recently, one of the largest oil firms in this country was charged by the government with violating the federal securities laws. The firm had set up secret Swiss bank accounts and used these to funnel bribes to foreign political leaders.[27] A large car-rental firm disclosed that it had made more than $400,000 in questionable foreign payments.[28] In a separate case, the government accused an invention-promotional firm of evading the securities registration laws.[29] Several thousand investors had gone to this firm with their ideas. The firm, in turn, promised to evaluate, promote, and patent their ideas for a fee of $1000. These agreements were known as "development contracts." The government, however, maintained that the firm's agreements were securities and should have been registered with it.

The preceding cases illustrate one elemental truth of the business world: management and not the shareholders run the everyday affairs of a company. Large shareholders may have a stronger voice; but within a large corporate framework, the everyday affairs are too numerous and tedious for any one shareholder to deal with properly. Shareholders do have certain rights; they can inspect corporate books and records. However, because of the necessary technical know-how and the voluminous records involved in a large firm, the shareholder relies on what management tells him or her about the firm. It is precisely because of this that state and federal laws place such great stress on the disclosure of the firm's finances. A shareholder may sue, on behalf of the corporation, either management or its directors for damages caused by their wrongdoing. The shareholder's liabilities, however, are limited. He is not personally liable for the corporation's debts or wrongdoing. His risk is limited to the original capital he invested, although shareholders are the legal owners of the corporation. Management, with the growing complex nature of the business world, has assumed greater control and, in some instances, has perpetrated great abuse.

The management of a firm is entrusted, at least theoretically, to the board of directors. Board members are elected by the shareholders of the company. Many directors sit on several corporate boards, giving rise to legitimate fears that the confidential information they acquire in their duties as board members may be used for private investment purposes—buying based on inside information. The board of directors, especially where the directors are either the founders or large stockholders in a firm, can exercise great powers. Abuse is also a very real concern. For example, in the early 1970s, the board of a large firm made it an informal policy for the firm to show a steady 15 percent growth rate. Profit-and-loss records were altered; there was an attempt to dupe even the auditors of the firm.[30] In another case, one director and the chief executive officer of a firm were accused by government investigators of altering company records. The alteration was an attempt to disguise more than $4 million in illegal payments made to customers of the firm in order to obtain and retain their good will.[31] In a third case, former high company officials were accused by the government of altering, inflating, and creating fictitious sales and inventory to funnel millions of dollars of company money for their own personal benefit.[32]

In most organizations, the board of directors is the titular manager of the firm, and everyday affairs are actually conducted by management. The board usually delegates its managerial obligations to company officers. Some directors may also serve as high company officials. As agents of the company, officers are limited in their authority by the charter and bylaws of the company, as well as by the laws of agency. The board also issues instructions and supervises overall activities. However, with disclosures of managerial abuse in recent years, boards have come under increasing attack for having abandoned the firm to management. The relationship of company officials to the firm is a fiduciary one. They are liable, under law, for personal profits made at the expense of the firm; and they are also liable for willful or negligent actions that cause a loss to the firm. They are not, however, liable for everyday errors, provided there was no imprudent business conduct. The personality and everyday behavior of a firm must be accredited, in large part, to management's own conduct and also to that of the board of directors.

The personality and everyday behavior of a corporation reflects the relationship between management and its board; this relationship determines the corporation's course and fortune; management and the board set and implement policy. The stockholders, especially in large corporations, are innocent bystanders. They depend on the federal and state securities laws to ensure that their investments will not fall prey to fraud. Unfortunately, this has not been the case. Even the more sophisticated stockholders, as many recent frauds have demonstrated, can fall victim to securities-related crimes. Several years ago, investors lost more than $200 million to a massive securities fraud.[33] The chairman and president of the firm personally gained $10 million. Among those who lost their investments were many well-known financial institutions. The president of the firm was sentenced to one year imprisonment, but became eligible for parole within four months. He received no fines.

Categories of Offenses

Securities-related offenses take on various forms. One of the more common involves blue-sky law violations. States have their own securities laws that attempt to regulate the offer, sale, purchase, and registration of securities sold intrastate. These laws provide for both civil and criminal penalties.

Churning, a common abuse of stock brokers, involves short-term trading swings by brokers, especially when the client has given them discretionary powers over his account. The objective of churning is to generate huge commissions for the broker. The latter earns his livelihood through client commissions and thus has a vested interest in encouraging short-term buying and selling. The client, either relying on his broker's judgment and decisionmaking or else on his broker's advice, will participate in this without fully realizing the ultimate effect upon him. By the time he becomes aware of what is happening, he may have lost large sums of money and the broker will probably have gained huge commissions. Churning is a violation of the federal securities laws.

Unauthorized trading by brokers in a client's account is illegal. The broker, although not given power of attorney over a client's account, nevertheless takes the liberty to trade occasionally. Although a violation of law, brokers sometimes give the excuse that they acted on oral instructions from their clients. Since it is the broker's word against that of his client, prosecution is usually difficult.

Trading on inside information is another of the more common securities violations. Typically, a broker will use nonpublic information to an unfair advantage for himself or his clients over the other shareholders of the company. Trading on inside information may also involve company executives or directors who have access to confidential financial information. Based on such information, they may either buy or sell stock to their own advantage. The end result is that the public suffers not only a financial loss, but also a loss of confidence in the market place.

The classic insider-trading case involved the Texas Gulf Sulphur Company.[34] In November 1963, engineers for the company had drilled a test hole to determine if a certain area contained substantial amounts of copper and zinc. It was soon discovered that in fact large deposits lay buried in this region. No public announcement was made of the find. In 1964 additional tests were run, and there was further confirmation that in fact this area was rich in copper and zinc. While the information was still confidential and restricted to a small group within the company, some of its employees purchased additional shares in the company's stock. The SEC brought civil suit, and the court held that these purchases were illegal and in violation of the securities laws.[35] The court further added that all investors should have equal access to material information.[36] In essence, the court said that company officials (insiders) should not have an advantage over the public at large in the trading of company securities. The test of materiality is what an average investor would consider reasonably necessary to make a prudent decision on whether to buy or sell securities.[37]

Manipulation of stock is also a common offense. A broker who has a vested interest in a stock may make false or misleading statements to his clients or members of the general public, either directly or indirectly, with the objective of creating an artificial demand for the stock. He may be assisted by company officials, other brokers, or even members of the general financial community. The false information may be disseminated in the form of a press release, market analyst report, etc. The end result is that the stock is made to appear much more desirable than it really is. According to government investigators, one victim had been told by his broker that his stock would be "the next IBM." The victim invested and lost thousands of dollars. The firm was on the verge of bankruptcy and the broker wanted to unload his stock and that of his friends on an uninformed public.[38]

Boiler-room operations are also common in the securities industry. A number of manipulators will, through hard-sell tactics and a barrage of false or misleading information, induce members of the uninformed public to invest in unknown companies whose stock may be worth little, if anything. The buyer is led to believe that the company will do well. Once the manipulators unload the stock, the investor is left holding the bag.

One of the better known and more common securities frauds is the *Ponzi scheme*, named after Charles Ponzi who first initiated it in 1920. Ponzi's gimmick was Spanish postal reply coupons, which sold in Europe for 1 cent and could be redeemed in the United States for 10 cents. Ponzi promised investors a 50 percent return on their investment within a two-month period. More than 40,000 people invested more than $10 million in these Spanish postal coupons and waited for their enormous gains, as Ponzi had promised. No one bothered to check with the Spanish authorities if in fact such coupons had ever been issued and, if so, in what amounts. It was later learned that fewer than $1 million in these coupons had been issued by the Spanish government and that Ponzi had misled his investors. He was subsequently prosecuted and imprisoned.

Many years later, in the Commonwealth of Virginia, an employee of the Chesapeake & Potomac Telephone Company promised hundreds of investors 30 to 100 percent returns on their investments if they bought promissory notes in his European "industrial wine" scheme. A number of banks and prominent Virginia businessmen and political figures invested several million dollars in this "get rich quick" scheme. When investigators uncovered the fraud, some 400 investors had lost over $20 million.[39]

In a more recent case, more than 1000 airline pilots stand to lose as much as $40 million in a classic Ponzi scheme. The mastermind of this alleged fraud is a Los Angeles lawyer who promised large returns in tax-shelter ventures to thousands of investors.[40] The latter were barraged with telephone calls and mass mailings; many fell for the scheme.

In the early 1960s, American investors discovered off-shore banks. One of the better known off-shore bank frauds involved the notorious Bank of Sark. The bank was located on an English island, from which it took its name. Bank officials represented the bank as having assets of over $70 million. Bank of Sark certificates of deposit and letters of credit were widely sold to criminal elements, who in turn used them to defraud investors out of more than $40 million. The bank became a base of operation for organized crime figures. These phony letters of credit and certificates of deposit were used to acquire control of legitimate businesses.

Stolen and counterfeit securities run in the billions of dollars. In one New York brokerage firm, a well-organized ring was said to be stealing several million dollars worth of securities monthly.[41] One gang, when caught, was said to have more than $10 million in counterfeit securities in its possession.[42] Recently, a Pakistani citizen was indicted for using altered stock certificate specimens as collateral for bank loans.[43] The defendant would visit printers who had samples of stock certificates and ask to see some. He would then take the samples with him, telling the printers he wanted to review them with his associates. He would erase the word *specimen* and pass them on to unsuspecting bankers. In July 1977, the SEC initiated an experimental project—Autex—to gather and computerize information on stolen securities. The data bank would make this information available to banks and other financial institutions, hopefully to assist them in detecting stolen and counterfeit securities. The project, however, is too new for a present evaluation of its effectiveness to be made. Critics charge that the effort is too little and too late.

Banks and brokerage firms, however, have been reluctant to take any action to curb thefts and counterfeit operations that bilk them and the public of billions of dollars. (For many years, they were even opposed to project Autex.) A similar, privately funded system has been in operation for several years. The basis for resisting such projects is the holder-in-due-course doctrine. This law reinforces the reluctance to institute security measures because under this doctrine, one who takes an instrument (stocks or bonds) and who: (1) pays or gives something of value for it (a bank may give a loan for it if it holds it as collateral), (2) does so in good faith, and (3) has no notice that there is a claim on it by another party (the original owner of the securities) or any other defect in the instrument (that it is counterfeit) is not liable and is a holder in good stead. If the counterfeit or stolen instrument is discovered by another party, the bank or brokerage firm cannot be held liable, since it believed in good faith that the instrument was genuine. The problem is proving that the party did not have a good faith belief, that in fact it shut its eyes. Organized crime has wreaked havoc in this area.

Securities Cops

The SEC can take one or more of the following three actions against a violator of the securities laws: (1) administrative, (2) civil, and (3) criminal referral to the Justice Department. In the first instance, the defendant may be barred from the industry or suspended for a period of time. There are no fines or criminal penalties. For example, an investment advisor who used false or misleading advertising to induce the public to turn to his services was only censured by the SEC.[44] The defendant agreed to the action without admitting to the charges. Those who lost their money could not use the censure as an admission of guilt by the defendant in a court of law; in turn, the defendant escaped prolonged discovery and litigation.

In the area of civil action, more than 90 percent of all SEC cases result in consent agreements. The latter is a contract between the defendant and the government, whereby the former promises to abide by the law and the latter promises not to prosecute for the present violations. However, the defendant does not admit any guilt. If the defendant chooses to litigate the matter, the SEC may eventually obtain an injunction. The latter, however, is only an order to the defendant to cease and desist from further fraudulent activity. It is not retroactive, and many defendants keep the proceeds of their illicit activities.

Criminal referrals are rare, and criminal prosecutions are almost nonexistent. Fewer than 5 percent of all SEC investigations culminate in such prosecutions.[45] Criminal cases are extremely time consuming, litigation may be extensive, and it may be several years before a verdict is finally handed down. Further, the likelihood of imprisonment is only 21.5 percent, according to a study by the Bureau of National Affairs.[46] As a result, many investigators and prosecutors, when possible, take the consent-decree route. One federal prosecutor noted that, "it's not worth spending years on a case only to have the fellow walk out on probation." The truth of such a sentiment is self-evident.

The stock exchanges have their own private investigatory forces. These regulatory divisions are staffed by both attorneys and investigators. The NYSE spends several million dollars annually on regulatory activities, as does the AMEX.[47] These self-regulators are valuable policing tools and can be of assistance to federal law enforcement. For example, in one recent case, three brokerage firms were expelled by the National Association of Securities Dealers after it was found that they had violated the securities laws.

However, the self-regulators are seriously overworked; complaints are often registered that the SEC has failed to provide adequate support. From 1974 through 1976, the self-regulators referred more than 180 cases to the SEC for action; fewer than 1 out of 60 resulted in any court action.[48] The exchanges themselves suffer from a maze of bureaucratic red tape. Complaints involving member firms are referred to a committee, which acts as a quasi-judicial body. Its decisions can be appealed to the Board of Governors of the exchange. The process is time consuming, and cases can take several years before a final decision is handed down. The outcome may be a fine or suspension. Expulsion is rare and usually involves only extreme cases that should have been prosecuted criminally in the first place.

The securities enforcers are handicapped by a flood of red tape, as well as by the very complex nature of securities frauds. Further, a maze of antiquated rules and regulations invites criminal activity. For example, a thirteen-year-old can apply for registration as an investment advisor, and the SEC's staff can do little to keep him or her out. In addition, some sectors of the securities industry, in their attempts to curtail regulation, have castrated the normal law enforcement role that the securities enforcers can play. At present, the public is victimized for billions of dollars annually.

Notes

1. Chamber of Commerce of the United States, *White Collar Crime* (Washington, D.C.: Chamber of Commerce of the United States, 1974), p. 6.

2. Ibid., p. 48.

3. Public Citizens Staff Report, *White Collar Crime* (Washington, D.C.: Congress Watch, 1974), p. 10.

4. Jack Anderson, "Investment Advisers: Even Teenagers Get Licenses," *Washington Post*, August 15, 1976, p. C-7.

5. Ibid.

6. Ibid.

7. "SEC Weighs Action After Its Staff Accuses City, Banks of Hiding New York's Plight," *Wall Street Journal*, August 29, 1977, p. 2.

8. David E. Spray, ed., *The Principal Stock Exchanges of the World* (Washington, D.C.: International Economic Publishers, 1964), p. 16.

9. Ibid.

10. Ibid.

11. Ibid., p. 3.

12. Ibid., p. 4.

13. Ibid., p. 5.

14. Ibid., p. 21.

15. Ibid.; see also U.S., Securities and Exchange Commission, *Annual Report for 1975* (Washington, D.C.: Government Printing Office, 1975), pp. 76-78.

16. Ronald A. Anderson and Walter A. Kumpf, *Business Law* (Chicago, Ill.: Southwestern, 1967), p. 753.

17. U.S. Securities and Exchange Commission, *Annual Report for 1976* (Washington, D.C.: Government Printing Office, 1976), p. 180.

18. Ibid.

19. Ibid., p. 197.

20. *Securities and Exchange Commission* v. *Howey*, 328 U.S. 293 (1946).

21. Hill and Knowlton, Financial Relations Unit, *The SEC, the Stock Exchanges and Your Financial Public Relations* (New York: Hill & Knowlton, 1972), pp. 40-41.

22. Arthur F. Mathews and William P. Sullivan, "Criminal Liability for Violations of the Federal Securities Laws: The National Commission's Proposed Federal Criminal Code, S.1 and S.1400," *The American Criminal Law Rev.*XI (1973):883.

23. Based on my experience as a former federal prosecutor.

24. 17 C.F.R. sec. 240.10b-5, and 15 U.S.C. 78j(b).

25. Bill Richards, "Corporation Seeks Compassion," *Washington Post*, August 29, 1977, p. A-3.

26. For a review of the legal powers of a corporation, see Harry G.

Henn, *Handbook of the Law of Corporations and Other Business Enterprises* (St. Paul, Minn.: West, 1970), pp. 107-131.

27. John F. Berry, "SEC Charges Oil Firm with Hiding Foreign Revenues," *Washington Post*, May 4, 1977, p. C-1.

28. Ibid.

29. "SEC Cites Invention Promoters for $4 Million Fraud Scheme," *Washington Post*, August 9, 1977, p. D-8.

30. Based on my experiences while employed at the Securities and Exchange Commission.

31. "Arden-Mayfair, Two Aides Are Charged by SEC with Fraud and False Reporting," *Washington Post*, August 19, 1977, p. 34.

32. Based on my experiences while employed at the Securities and Exchange Commission.

33. Public Citizen Staff Report, *White Collar Crime* (Washington, D.C.: Congress Watch, 1974), pp. 11, 12.

34. Hill and Knowlton, Financial Relations Unit, *The SEC, the Stock Exchanges and Your Financial Public Relations*, pp. 9, 10.

35. Ibid., p. 11.

36. Ibid.

37. Ibid., p. 13

38. Based on my interviews with federal officials.

39. "Charles Ponzi's Legacy," *Business Week*, June 29, 1974, p. 61.

40. Jim Drinkhall, "Thousands of Investors Accuse California Man of Defrauding Them," *Wall Street Journal*, April 22, 1977, p. 1.

41. Chamber of Commerce of the United States, *White Collar Crime*, p. 48.

42. Ibid., p. 49.

43. "Pakistani Is Indicted for Securities Fraud Believed To Be Novel," *Wall Street Journal*, August 18, 1977, p. 26.

44. "Investment Adviser is Censured by SEC for Misleading Ads," *Wall Street Journal*, August 12, 1977, p. 4.

45. U.S. Securities and Exchange Commission, *Annual Report for 1975*, pp. 209, 210.

46. John A. Jenkins and Robert H. Rhode, *White Collar Justice Special Report* (Washington, D.C.: Bureau of National Affairs, 1976), p. 11.

47. John A. Jenkins, "Flood of Insider Trading Referrals to SEC Result in Trickle of Investigations, Lawsuits," *Bureau of National Affairs Securities Regulation & Law Reports*, July 20, 1977, p. A-4; and John A. Jenkins, "The Self-Regulators," *Bureau of National Affairs Securities Regulation & Law Reports*, April 20, 1977, pp. AA-8, AA-9.

48. Ibid.; see also, John A. Jenkins, "Securities Enforcement: A Growth Industry, the Critics," *Bureau of National Affairs Securities Regulation & Law Reports,* April 13, 1977, p. AA-1; and John A. Jenkins, "In Case of Corruption, Break Glass," *Student Lawyer* (November 1977): 39.

August Bequai is a partner with the firm of Reed, Bequai, Ross, & Burger. He is author of several books on computer crime including Computer Crime, White Collar Crime, *and* Organized Crime in the Computer Era *(all published by D.C. Heath). He is also a contributor to many publications on the subject of criminality.*

13

ORGANIZED CRIME AND ENTREPRENEURSHIP

DWIGHT C. SMITH, Jr.

Organized Crime Control: The Contemporary Scene

The modern era of organized crime control began in 1950, when a select Senate committee [1, p. 147] chaired by Estes Kefauver was persuaded to see an "elusive, shadowy, sinister organization" called Mafia as the integrating mechanism for nation-wide gambling activities. In the succeeding quarter century, law enforcement activities became rallying points for further revelations concerning secret criminal organizations. Early stratagems utilized traditional enforcement tactics that focused on solitary criminals. When organized crime did not disappear, attention was redirected at the presumed organization of organized crime. It was invisible, and thus impossible to measure. As organized crime activity began to appear more frequently, however, a sense of formidability and ominousness was soon attached to the invisible organization. Quantitative measures of size were later assigned to it, based largely on guesses of what ominousness "ought" to represent. Ultimately a sense of powerlessness in the face of such presumed strength led Robert Kennedy to write [2, p. 265] that "if we do not attack organized criminals, with weapons and techniques as effective as their own, they will destroy us".

A body of doctrine subsequently evolved through investigative reports and news accounts. There was little credible evidence to support it, but it achieved formal status through endorsement by the President's Crime Commission [3]. In essence, the doctrine charged that organized crime was the product of a secret Italian-American criminal conspiracy devised for the purpose of committing crimes and dedicated to an alien philosophy of social conduct. Its byproducts were corruption, lawlessness, dishonesty and immorality. The conspiratorial organization behind it exploited techniques of secrecy so successfully that well-meaning citizens were often duped into doubting its existence. Some

From Dwight C. Smith, Jr., "Organized Crime and Entrepreneurship," 6(2) *International Journal of Criminology and Penology* 161-177 (May 1978). Copyright 1978 reprinted with permission.

adherents to organized crime doctrine believed that its gross annual revenues exceeded $50 billion, with net profits alleged to be between $7 billion and $10 billion. The inner-core membership of its parent conspiracy was said to be limited — perhaps 5000 to 10 000 persons — but its total employment was believed to have exceeded 100 000 and its sophistication and diversification were presumed to rival that of General Motors.

If these assertions had been anywhere near accurate, American institutions would be faced with a powerful and ominous foe. Whether true or not, the doctrine was believed; and the Crime Commission [3, p. 16] urged a federal campaign to "destroy the power of organized crime groups". The Commission's recommended approach was based on the assumption that organized crime as a social menace would be erased if we could only eliminate the persons and organizations engaged in purveying its illegal products. The Commission's rhetoric was persuasive, and in 1968 and 1970 [4] Congress adopted the bulk of its organized crime control program.

There are reasons, as will be detailed below, for questioning these interpretations of organized criminality. But even within that context — and despite such superficial success signs as well-publicized arrests, convictions and long-term prison sentences — the subsequent campaign against organized crime may best be characterized as a significant social failure. The recent report of the Comptroller General [5] provides ample evidence for this conclusion. The root problem is not an inadequately-implemented strategy, however, but an incorrect premise. Though the phenomena we identify as organized crime are certainly real, they have been defined and circumscribed by an inadequate and misdirected set of concepts. Certain events — conveniently collected under the "Mafia" label — have been viewed as the criminal acts of a specified organization. On the presumption that acts labeled "crime" should be eliminated, public debate has then centred on two responses: decriminalization of some acts, or elimination of the perpetrators themselves. In some circumstances, such as the debate over legalized gambling, arguments for decriminalization have prevailed. Ordinarily, though, proponents of attrition have won the day. Faith in the effectiveness of an attrition strategy has rested on a belief that acts of crime are the sole responsibility of the perpetrator, and that as a consequence of removing him from society, the criminal acts would disappear.

From the beginning, however, there were dissenters from these doctrines. One of the earliest and most prominent was Daniel Bell [6], who challenged the Kefauver Committee's assumption that ethnicity signified the existence of a unique form of criminal methodology. In its place, Bell argued that one of the few routes of upward mobility open to new immigrants lay through a range of illegal, risky and potentially profitable businesses; and that the Kefauver group had observed little more than a new tide of Italians who had inherited the vice rackets that previous immigrants had used as stepping stones to wealth, influence and (for their progeny, at least) respectability. More recent studies [7, 8] have suggested that the earlier Mafia legendry in this country was based on a complete misreading of the Sicilian experience; others [9, 10] have called into question the validity of law enforcement's insistence upon the existence of a formal criminal hierarchy. Still other probings by scholars and investigative reporters [11, 12] have provided new strength to Daniel Bell's earlier argument by demonstrating the rise of non-Italian but ethnically-related criminal enterprises.

But converts from law-enforcement have been few. The most noticeable shift in thinking has been limited to the transfer of earlier ethnic assumptions of criminal methodology to new groups — i.e. Black or Puerto Rican or Cuban Mafias. The shift is cosmetic. "Ethnic succession" as Daniel Bell meant it might appeal to academics, but men faced with responsibility for crime control continue to find the alien conspiracy theory more persuasive. The Justice Department's reorganization of its organized crime control program might have been an implicit recognition that current stategies have faltered [13] but official policy remains mired in older precepts. Despite a growing array of challenges there is no evidence of serious, sustained efforts by the law-enforcement establishment (or its supporters) to look beyond those precepts, and to re-examine critically their underlying rationale.

Meanwhile, a growing body of observers (e.g. Moquin [14], Nelli [15], Plate [16]) have tried to improve upon the doctrines of organized crime control by restating them in the language of business. Their approach has its roots in an older art, that rose to prominence during Al Capone's heyday, of using business terms as an ironic or cynical way of describing illegal behavior that seemed uncomfortably close to the practices of legitimate businesses [17]. Newer uses of the business analogy have been more serious, but within existing theoretical limits have been only partially successful. Nevertheless, they reflect a desire for a more comprehensive framework for describing particular forms of illegal activity.

Needed: A Broader Focus on Illicit Enterprise

The underlying flaw in the Crime Commission's proposals was to assume that organized crime was more akin to such felonious activities as burglary and assault than to legal business activities. The immediate and practical effect of that assumption was to leave responsibility for understanding and controlling organized crime to the traditional agencies of criminal law enforcement. Beyond that, its more important consequence was to mold patterns of thought in such a way that organized crime would be understood as a distinct set of events, limited by the character of its perpetrators. The mold was so strong that dissenters from law enforcement's assertions formed their counter arguments within the same conceptual limits.

But organized criminal activities are not simply vice crimes; and they are not the consequences of a deeper criminal conspiracy. Nor are they just alternative avenues by which new ethnic groups obtain the wherewithal to join the mainstream of society. Though law violations are integral to their existence, their more important characteristics — from the standpoint of effective public policy — rest in the fact that they are entrepreneurial. Viewed apart from traditional assumptions about lower-class crime, the events we have called organized crime become a sub-set of a more widespread economic problem. They represent, in virtually every instance, an extension of a legitimate market spectrum into areas normally proscribed. Their separate strengths derive from the same fundamental considerations that govern entrepreneurship in the legitimate marketplace: a necessity to maintain and extend one's share of the market. The behavior patterns that have generally focused attention on criminality rather than entrepreneurship reflect the dynamics of the illicit marketplace. Organized crime theory was developed apart from such considerations, however; the appropriate behavior cues were misconstrued as evidence of criminal organizations because there was no adequate conceptualization of illicit enterprise by which they might alternatively be assessed.

I mean by "illicit enterprise" the extension of legitimate market activities into areas normally proscribed, for the pursuit of profit and in response to latent illicit demand. In this context, the loan shark is an entrepreneur in the banking industry; the drug or cigarette smuggler is a wholesaler and the fence a retailer; and the bribe-taker is a power broker. Public opinion has generally overlooked these connections, preferring to see the loan shark, smuggler, fence and briber as members of a criminal conspiracy that is explicable in its own terms without reference to banking, wholesaling, retailing or power brokering.

These observations reflect two fundamental assumptions: that the range of activity in any marketplace is continuous in character, from the very saintly to the most sinful; and that organizational concepts ordinarily applied only to legitimate businesses are applicable to that entire range of activity. These assumptions are not new. The concept of ranges in social behavior has been developed by Leslie Wilkins [18]. The concept of organizational dynamics (from which my second assumption flows) has been explored at length in contemporary business literature by James Thompson [19], though the underlying interpretation of criminal businesses operating in a criminal economy — the illicit end of the market spectrum — was first described in American criminological literature by Frederick Thrasher [20] in 1927 and John Landesco [21] in 1929.

With these assumptions as a base point and my earlier observations regarding loan sharks, smugglers, fences. bribers, and other entrepreneurs as horizon points, we can construct a generalized theory of illicit enterprise by which so-called "organized crime" incidents — as well as a much wider, and perhaps more significant, range of illicit behaviors — can be reinterpreted. It begins with a series of theorems drawn from conventional organization theory.

1. *The heart of any enterprise is its core technology, the technical functions by which it is able to create and dispose of its end product or services.* Technologies range widely in form, from the assembly line of the large

manufacturer to the double entry book-keeping processes of the banker and the professional knowledge and licensure of the lawyer or doctor; but whatever their forms, entrepreneurial behavior revolves around them.

2. *That core technology exists in a task environment, a set of external conditions that enable it to function, on the one hand* (by supplying it with raw materials and customers), *but simultaneously offer hazards to its continuance* (by providing competitors and regulators, each of which represent uncertainties in their own rights as well as being inhibiting forces on either suppliers or customers) [22]. The task environment represents conditions the entrepreneur does not directly control.

3. *The core technology of an enterprise works most efficiently when it is protected by some form of buffering* (inventory controls, market forecasts, etc.) *from the uncertainties of the task environment.* Since efficiency is likely to maximize profits, a major obligation of the entrepreneur is to see that such buffering takes place.

4. *The result of activity aimed at protection of the enterprise's technology is the creation of a territory, or domain: a set of claims staked out in terms of a range of products, population served, or services rendered.* As "domain" produces stability, efficiency and increased profits, the focus of the entrepreneur is consequently upon protecting and expanding his sense of domain in the face of contrary pressures from competitors or regulators and the potential for fluctuating levels of demand for his product or supply of his raw materials.

These conditions govern any enterprise, without respect to its technological processes or the nature of its product. Opportunities for initiating an enterprise, and the methods used in establishing its domain, may reflect differences in product or process but the basic entrepreneurial obligation remains the same. The current task environment of most enterprises is more complex than this, however, and for our purposes two other conditions are noteworthy for their relevance to illicit enterprise.

5. *In a complex market economy, task environments necessarily overlap, and multiple roles become the order of the day.* A corporation may be an enterprise in its own right, with suppliers, customers, competitors and regulators; at the same time it may be the customer of another enterprise (such as an independent market research or public relations firm). In turn, the enterprise of which it is the customer has its own competitors and regulators. The result of this overlapping is likely to be increasing ambiguity of roles within each enterprise.

6. *Though an increasing number of enterprises in a complex economy require significant capital investment for long-range viability, a large number of opportunities continue to exist for which modest or minimal investments are sufficient or for which necessary capital can easily be secured; in such circumstances, the commitment to entrepreneurial risk-taking may vary.* In traditional forms of enterprise the typical commitment may be full time; but there are increasing opportunities for seasonal, part-time, moonlighting, or even

one-time entrepreneurial activity, particularly for the individual normally viewed as an employee or hired professional elsewhere who is searching for supplemental income. The high school physical education instructor who runs the food concession at the town pool is a seasonal entrepreneur; the semi-retired steamfitter who makes a side income as the neighborhood plumber is a part-time entrepreneur; the police officer who drives a taxi during off-duty hours is a moonlighting entrepreneur; the college student who spends a festive weekend selling hot dogs on consignment may be a one-time entrepreneur. The nature of the less-than-full-time entrepreneurial commitment need not be associated with the entrepreneur's primary skill or profession, depending upon the particular requirements of both major and minor roles (note that in the moonlighting example above, the police officer might have utilized his primary skill as an off-duty security guard for a suburban shopping center); but regardless of association, opportunities for dual activities add further ambiguity to the entrepreneurial role.

There is obviously much more to be said about dynamic organizational behavior; these theorems merely touch the surface. The analyst of illicit enterprise will need more than this framework, and for that deeper level of understanding James Thompson's work is particularly instructive. Meanwhile, our six opening theorems introduce an interpretation of enterprise that is neutral on the question of legality. "Illicit enterprise" comes into focus as we move one more step into Thompson's concept of "technologies" and add to it the spectrum concept of Wilkins.

7. *If we think of organizational processes through which products or services are generated and marketed as "technologies", we can distinguish different market groupings of entrepreneurship, depending upon the nature of the technology and its end product.* Thompson differentiates three such technologies, while recognizing that they do not exhaust the possibilities: the *long-linked technology,* as when a cigarette manufacturer might direct a sequence of activities from tobacco growing to the case-lot distribution of packaged cigarettes; the *mediating technology,* as when bankers serve as middlemen in the transfer of funds between lenders and borrowers; and the *intensive technology,* as when a nursing home brings a variety of services to bear upon the needs of a patient. For our purposes, I would add a fourth to the list: the *service technology,* as when the Wells Fargo or Burns organization markets private security services. Using the ultimate product or service as the distinguishing characteristic, a series of "markets" can be established to group competitors without respect to the legality of their technological processes (i.e., smuggling *v.* legitimate importation) or their end products (i.e., usurous loans *v.* legitimate lines of credit). Note that in so doing it is important to label the marketplace in value-free terms, to enable the full legal-to-illegal spectrum to appear. This task will become clearer later, as we examine some specific markets.

8. *In each such market there are criteria by which the end product or service,*

and the process by which it is obtained or fabricated, can be categorized as legal or illegal. In banking, legitimacy has to do with the relationship between collateral, risk, and maximum rates of interest. In enforcement and protective services, it has to do with authority to use deadly force.

9. *With criteria of legitimacy as benchmarks, various forms of entrepreneurship can be ranked according to the degree of legitimacy or illicitness by which the business is conducted.* The progression of the spectrum may be easier to hypothesize than to find. Descriptions of permissible behavior on the legal side of the market may be written in ways that recognize limited, discrete options; processes of competition (or its control) may produce a voluntary or pragmatic limit to legal, above-the-table transactions; other conditions of the market (thin profit margins in an area of high volume sales, for example) may appear to collapse the spectrum into a single process for doing business within the law; and, in some markets, the criteria of legitimacy may be ambiguous, and may vary by location (as different standards of obscenity may affect the production and distribution of printed material).

10. *Entrepreneurship itself may also reflect a spectrum of legitimacy.* To some, the idea of producing an illegal product, or of producing a product in an illegal way, might never occur; to others, the thought alone might be offensive. From their perspective the premise of a continuum including illicit entrepreneurs would not be real. But there are other ways of doing business, buttressed by such mental processes as a fear of failure greater than a fear of illegality; a lack of respect for the niceties of the law; a high tolerance for rationalizing questionable behavior; a desire for profit at any cost; a principled disagreement with certain legal restrictions; or a contempt for the law and/or its minions. Specific motives are obviously difficult to classify and probably harder to measure, in either frequency or intensity; but the main purpose in noting them is not their quantification but a recognition that a spectrum of legitimacy for the market may be met by the willingness of entrepreneurs to spread themselves across it.

11. *Just as there is a spectrum of entrepreneurship, there is a spectrum of customers.* There are four major categories across that spectrum: the customer who has legitimate needs that are met legally; the customer with legitimate needs for whom the legal market is, for some reason, unresponsive; the customer with illicit needs who cannot risk dealing with the legitimate entrepreneur (who would need to keep business records that could subsequently be subpoenoed by an enforcement agency); and, at the end of the spectrum, the extortionist or pirate who is his own customer, intent simply upon capturing the domains of other entrepreneurs for their value to him.

12. *The meaning of "legality" limits the use of regulation in controlling the search for domain at the illicit end of the market.* Regulation as a device for defining the entrepreneurial rules of the game applies only to legal activities. The only regulatory response to illegality is suppression. If domain for the illicit entrepreneur is to be modified in any fashion other than such traditional

"headhunting", pressure must be applied elsewhere in the task environment. As a further complication to the role of regulation, we may note that in a political environment — which is .to say an environment that takes into account more than the direct power dynamics of the marketplace — regulation may be the only means for protecting social values that are not inherent to the market economy. Consumer protection, environmental protection and equal employment policies are three examples. The debate between their proponents and entrepreneurs who maintain that such regulation is inappropriate to market control adds a further level of ambiguity to the demarcation between legitimate and illicit enterprise.

13. *The strategy of conglomeration, as a mechanism for solving certain problems of domain, is applicable across the market spectrum.* In legitimate enterprises, conglomeration is a formal process of organization that enables a large enterprise to protect itself from sudden shifts in consumer tastes, or to obtain solid capitalization to finance new ventures, or otherwise to encourage profits while reducing (or spreading) costs and risks. A comparable process occurs among illicit enterprises, though for different reasons because the problems of domain are different (i.e., capitalization is likely to be less important than security against regulation), and with less formal results (since the absence of a legally constructed organization, through which a conglomeration would be formally recognized, is a condition of a wholly illicit business). Since any conglomerate leads to concentration of power across the economy generally, as distinct from monopoly concentration within a specific technology and marketplace, its appearance is important across the entrepreneurial spectrum.

The Junction of Theory and Reality: An Analytic Taxonomy

Our failure to recognize illicit enterprise has been due in large measure to the strength of the criminal label "Mafia" that, since 1946, has been increasingly intertwined with the law-enforcement based theory of organized crime. Though independent in origins, both label and theory have come to reinforce each other to a degree that has effectively inhibited any sustained interpretation of the activities in question as anything except criminal. My recent analysis of the role played by the "Mafia" label in American public opinion [23] has illustrated, however, that when the label is stripped from view the remaining evidence points strongly to a theory of illicit enterprise as a more comprehensive and convincing explanation than the theory of organized crime.

Whether one adheres to conventional doctrines or opts for illicit enterprise, the key question remains constant: does it effectively interpret reality? The objective in either case is a conceptual base on which public policy can be constructed and administered. Thus the immediate purpose of either "organized crime" (or "Mafia") or "illicit enterprise" is to facilitate the grouping of events into a comprehensible pattern of behavior. Each evokes a taxonomic process through which a series of possibilities can be evaluated and categorized; the end of the process is that central set of circumstances on which public action should be focused. The taxonomies emerging from both organized crime theory and illicit enterprise theory have been described elsewhere [23, pp. 16-21, 335-342; 24] but to put some substance on their abstractions, let us consider how the analyst uses them.

Figure 1 provides a schematic illustration of the logic by which the organized crime analyst proceeds. In practice, of course, he is not likely to be that formal. His major clue, and conscious starting point, is the basic "organized crime family" structure revealed to the world in 1963 by Joe Valachi and subsequently

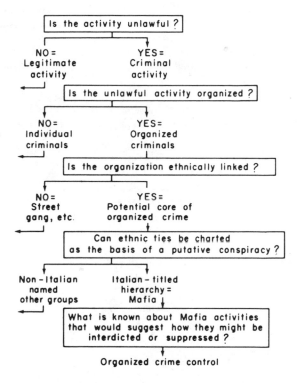

Fig. 1. The taxonomy of "organized crime" control.

endorsed by the Crime Commission. That structure focused on the roles of Boss, Underboss, and Caporegime. Though holding any of those positions would not in itself be a criminal matter, their formation of hierarchy and structure prepared the stage for a listing, at the bottom of the Crime Commission's chart [3, p. 9], of illegal things to do: gambling, narcotics, loansharking, labor racketeering, extortion, alcohol, and others. The analyst knows that not every gambler or extortioner — and certainly not every "other" lawbreaker — is a member of organized crime; but he can test a list of prospects against the organized crime taxonomy. Can each person in turn be linked to an "organized crime" act? Does he do it in an organized way, with others who share ethnic ties and act as if they are part of a larger conspiracy? If the answers are all Yes, the object of scrutiny belongs on that chart; if any answer is No, the analyst can move on to the next case.

The task is not really that simple in practice, and real decisions are seldom that structured. The analyst may be smarter than the Crime Commission chart, and may realize (consciously or not) that the real task is not to play rudimentary pigeonhole games but to try to discern whether, and how, a complex set of criminal activities are interrelated. He may have historic findings to build upon, and private information from informants or wiretaps; but however the evidence may have been assembled, his task may be described by the test outlined in Figure 2; which of these criminal types is part of the organized crime scene before me?

Corrupter

Enforcer / Muscleman / Underground policeman

Loan shark

Fence

Contraband importer

Contraband wholesaler

Contraband retailer:

Dope peddler
Numbers runner
Pornography store clerk

Truck hijacker

Car thief

Bank robber

Mugger

Burglar

Hotel thief

Fig. 2. Who is in organized crime.

The organized crime analyst begins by looking for evidence that a group of criminals are working together. As he looks jointly for criminal activity and signs of conspiratorial organization, he will be attempting to draw an imaginary line around some organized crime indicators that will correspond in a rough way to the Crime Commission's model. The list in Figure 2 represents an array of options from which an alternative set of "illegal activities" will be chosen. How will the analyst draw the imaginary line?

Conditions obviously vary, but it is common knowledge that corrupters and enforcers belong on any organized crime chart. Indeed, Cressey [25, pp. 322-324] made their joint presence a condition of organized crime. The loan shark traditionally has been linked with organized crime; and if by "importer" we mean the bootlegger or narcotics smuggler and by "wholesaler" we mean his domestic associates, then their "membership" is also likely. The fence may, by conventional wisdom, need approval of a Boss in order to function; but unless he also shares ethnic ties with the Boss, that endorsement does not guarantee the fence's inclusion in one of the "higher levels of sophistication" [26, pp. 18-30] by which organized crime is distinguished from lower level street gangs and burglary rings. The "retailers" are often linked with organized crime, especially when their products come from the importer and wholesaler, but they are generally considered to be on the fringes of a "family" at best. Once again, ethnic ties are likely to provide the litmus test. Truck hijacking and car theft may be linked with a crime family, particularly in more cosmopolitan districts, but the link is generally interpreted as an ad hoc venture into "ordinary" crime by a family member, not as a permanent component of organized crime. The robbers, muggers, burglars, and thieves at the bottom of the list may seem to be there only for effect; they are hardly ever associated with organized crime.

Notice how the selection process worked. In deciding where to draw the line around organized crime, the analyst looked for the directions in which a criminal organization might have expanded. The choice was among criminal roles; and the selection in each case was a matter of deciding which roles might be accorded particular significance because they were linked to organized crime.

The illicit enterprise analyst confronts the same list of criminal roles, but with a different perspective and a different evaluation. His taxonomic base is illustrated schematically in Figure 3; like the organized crime analyst, he must also proceed in a more direct and pragmatic way to sort his evidence. His test revolves around the same criminal activities; but as Figure 4 illustrates, the answers do not revolve around a mutually shared "family" relationship. Rather, each role is considered in its own terms as an entrepreneurial extension of a larger spectrum of legitimacy. The "extension of legitimate market activities into areas normally proscribed, for the pursuit of profit and in response to latent illicit demand", is thus revealed. A corrupter and a loan shark may find that there is mutual gain in working together, much as a legitimate nursing home operator may find it advantageous to hold an interest in a pharmacy; but note that for the illicit enterprise analyst the corrupter (or briber) has been replaced on the entrepreneurial spectrum by the bribe-taker. He exists because there are opportunities for power brokering that legitimate enterprises do not (or cannot) satisfy, and the loan shark is there because the regulations governing banking leave potential customers unserved. The fundamental relationship is horizontal in this schematic representation, in contrast to the vertical relationship of the organized crime test.

My schematic approach is sketchy, preliminary, and hypothetical. I do not presume to know all of the details that would be necessary to substantiate a

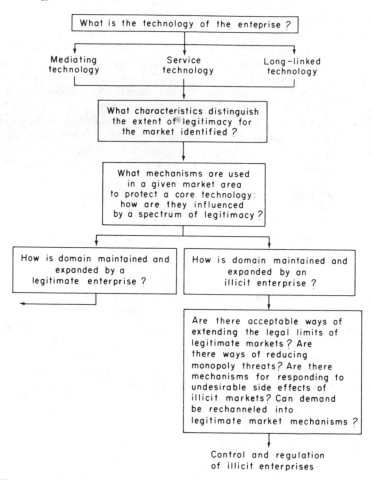

Fig. 3. The taxonomy of illicit enterprise.

complete analysis of even this limited a set of entrepreneurial technologies. It may be helpful, then, to look more closely at two of the technologies, to demonstrate that there is substance to a theory of illicit enterprise and not simply implied promises.

Consider first the mediating technology of power brokering. I have in mind a series of social mechanisms through which individuals or groups are able to exercise a "right" to governmental assistance or corporate acquiescence, or are able to obtain redress from a "wrong" application of government or corporate power. It is a mixed market, as some mechanisms are government agencies and others are private entrepreneurs. They would be ordered on a spectrum of

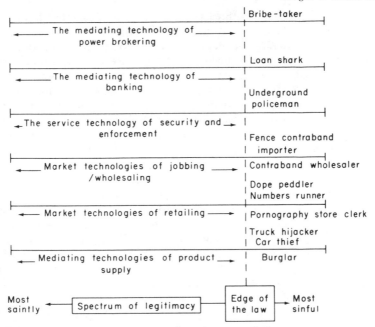

Fig. 4. What is illicit enterprise?

legitimacy by the degree of sanction supporting each one's actions in mediating aspirations. The most legitimate mechanism would be a civil claims court. It would be followed by various licensing bureaus which are less legitimate because their mediating activities can be appealed to the courts. The new role of government Ombudsman would be somewhere near courts and administrative agencies, but perhaps less sanctioned than either of them, (though to another observer the Ombudsman might be seen as a higher point in the sanctioned appeals structure). Below them and largely operating in the private sector are Expediters and, in some cities, the political machine's Precinct Captain. The normally sanctioned portion of the spectrum is almost closed at this point. Straddling the gray area between legitimacy and crime is the five-percenter of wartime fame; and rounding out the spectrum is the self-evidently illegal but apparently necessary bribe-taker.

The illicit enterprise analyst would take this list and ask what comprises the core technology of power brokering. A tentative answer might be that it consists of a knowledge of the rules and how to play the bureaucratic game, combined with "connections". What and Who one has to know, and How the rules work may depend on the enterpreneur's place on this spectrum. Each has a problem of domain; for the government agency or the court, however, competitive skill may be less important than legal authority. As the degree of sanction decreases, and as we move across the spectrum toward the bribe-taker, it seems clear that domain becomes increasingly dependent upon two factors: a continuing high level of frustration in customer dealings with the more legitimate mechanisms on the spectrum, and increasing use of corruption and co-optation by the entrepreneur who otherwise lacks legitimate, sanctioned entry to the market.

Consider also the service technology of security and enforcement, a series of mechanisms through which individuals or groups are able to obtain security of person or property, or are able to obtain enforcement of rights with respect to other persons or groups, or are able to provide (or have provided for them) mechanisms for regulating the conduct of other individuals or groups. It is also a mixed market, in which the spectrum of legitimacy is ordered by the degree of sanctions supporting each mechanism's scope of actions, exercise of force, and confining of persons. Highest sanctions go to the armed forces, followed by the federal criminal justice and regulatory agencies. As the scope of authority decreases across the spectrum, state (and then local) criminal justice and regulatory agencies appear. As a transition from government security agencies, the ad hoc police mechanism of the deputized posse would emerge, followed by commercial security agencies (Pinkerton, Brinks, Burns, Wackenhut and their less-evident competitors) and private police. At the edge of the gray area between legitimacy and crime are neighborhood action groups; below them are lynch mobs and other vigilante groups. At the end of the spectrum stands the illicit entrepreneur, the underground policeman (or Enforcer).

The core technology for the security and enforcement enterprise is simple: skill in the application of sanctions. This is more than a question of muscle. The clients of the underground policemen may wish sanctions to be applied to someone else who is vulnerable to legitimate enforcement agencies; his "application of sanctions" may be nothing more than turning the third party in. Any experienced large city detective will have a fund of illustrations available, under the general heading of "blowing the whistle".

As with power brokering, the problems of domain for legitimate governmental agencies lie primarily in the political arena, where scope of authority and legal sanctions are defined. Moving across the spectrum domain depends again on customer frustration *vis-a-vis* legitimate mechanisms. The story of Amerigo Bonasera, with which the *The Godfather* begins [27, pp. 11-12, 29-37] is a classic illustration [28]. Once the line of legitimacy has been passed, the illicit entrepreneur stays in business, and protects his domain, by an appropriate mix of threats of reprisal in one direction and the corruption of more highly sanctioned mechanisms in the other.

The technologies of power brokering and security are not simply classroom exercises. As the concept of illicit enterprise comes into sharper focus it becomes clear that they form the nucleus around which other illicit enterprises cluster. They are integrative mechanisms, providing the climate in which those other enterprises flourish. More importantly, however, as they are given the opportunity to enter market areas normally occupied by government agencies, they open the door for the successful illicit entrepreneur to exert a profound effect on community values. Rather than a frontal attack as the Crime Commission [3, p. 16] recommended, by a "full-scale commitment to destroy the power of organized crime groups", we might be better served by learning how to reduce the domain of the illicit power broker or enforcer. The key to that strategy is a deeper appreciation of a theory of illicit enterprise.

Toward Wider Horizons

Before dismissing the Crime Commission's organized crime theories entirely, we should look closely at the shape of its conclusions in relation to their origins. Bear in mind that the Commission had not intended to study organized crime. The topic was added to their agenda at the urging of the law enforcement community, whose spokesmen "knew" what the problem was and also "knew" what to do about it. The study thus reflected the natural bias of its proponents, which centered on three mistaken assumptions: that the significant variable in the events defined as "organized crime" was conspiratorial criminal behavior by Italians; that those events were limited in scope to the traditional vice crimes of gambling, narcotics, prostitution and bootlegging, plus loansharking and labor racketeering; and that remedies for them lay in suppression through a better use of police power.

In these circumstances, the Commission did the best it could. The natural predisposition of the law-enforcement approach tended toward two Utopian remedies: destruction of the Mafia/Cosa Nostra conspiracy and, as an obvious consequence, eradication of vice. The Commission avoided them both. The constitutional failure of the Smith Act was a clear signal that a Mafia — if there were one — could not be attacked directly; and common sense was proof enough that a vice-free community was an impractical goal. Instead, the Commission found a subtle middle ground and urged, in its call to arms, that the focus of organized crime control be the destruction of the *power* of organized crime groups. The justification for the Commission's call may sound Utopian in its own way, but it does get to the heart of the issue.

> Organized crime is not merely a few preying upon a few. In a very real sense it is dedicated to subverting not only American institutions, but the very decency and integrity that are the most cherished attributes of a free society. As the leaders of Cosa Nostra and their racketeering allies pursue their conspiracy unmolested, in open and continuous defiance of the law, they preach a sermon that all too many Americans heed: The government is for sale; lawlessness is the road to wealth; honesty is a pitfall and morality a trap for suckers [3, p. 24].

Decency and integrity are powerful ideas in a democracy, and the development of standards and goals by which to evaluate our preservation and protection of them would be a challenge for any commission. "The power of organized crime groups" may be a particularly apt touchstone for such a set of standards. But when the 1967 Crime Commission had finished its declaration, the limitations under which it had labored proved too strong. One question remained unanswered: Who are the preachers and who are their converts? Later revelations give us a new set of answers for which the Crime Commission was not prepared by an organized crime-centered agenda. Who says that government is for sale? Ask Gulf Oil. Who says lawlessness is the road to wealth? Ask Equity Funding. Who says honesty is a pitfall? Ask Lockheed and Prince Bernhard. Who says morality is a trap for suckers? Ask the operators of the Medicaid mills.

In this context, the wider conceptual opportunities of illicit enterprise theory are self-evident. The "infiltration of legitimate business" argument by which the law-enforcement community has long (and unsuccessfully) tried to win corporate and business support for its anti-Mafia campaign can be replaced by a wider appreciation of the entire market spectrum and a deeper analysis of the dynamics that nurture its illicit aspects. Its practical applications obviously remain to be proved; in the meantime, its invitation to further research and study is open.

Notes and References

1 U.S. Senate Special Committee to Investigate Organized Crime in Interstate Commerce. *Third interim report.* Washington, D.C., Government Printing Office. 1951.
2 R. F. Kennedy, *The Enemy Within.* New York, Harper. 1960.
3 President's Commission on Law Enforcement and Administration of Justice. *Task Force Report: Organized Crime.* Washington, D.C., Government Printing Office. 1967.
4 See Public Law 90-351, Omnibus crime control and safe streets act of 1968, esp. Title III; and Public Law 91-452, Organized crime control act of 1970, Title I-X.
5 Comptroller General of the United States. *War on Organized Crime Faltering-Federal Strike Forces Not Getting the Job Done.* Washington, D.C., Author. 1977.
6 D. Bell, Crime as an American way of life. *The Antioch Review* 1953, 13, 131-154.
7 A. Blok, *The Mafia of a Sicilian Village, 1860-1960.* New York, Harper & Row. 1969.
8 H. Hess, *Mafia and Mafiosi: The Structure of Power.* Farnborough, Saxon House. 1973.
9 J. Albini, *The American Mafia: Genesis of a Legend.* New York, Appleton-Century-Crofts. 1971.
10 F. A. J. Ianni with E. Reuss-Ianni, *A Family Business.* New York, Russell Sage Foundation. 1972.
11 F. A. J. Ianni, *Black Mafia.* New York, Simon & Schuster. 1974.
12 S. Raab, Top drug dealers named by police. *New York Times* 1975, 9 December, 1.
13 N. Gage, Justice agency shifting tactics, *New York Times* 1976, 10 February, 13.
14 W. Moquin (Ed.), *The American Way of Crime.* New York, Praeger. 1976.
15 H. S. Nelli. *The Business of Crime.* New York, Oxford University Press. 1976.
16 T. Plate, *Crime Pays!* New York, Simon & Schuster. 1975.
17 The ironic art form predates Capone, of course, as illustrated by John Gay's masterpice, *Beggar's Opera.*
18 L. T. Wilkins, *Social Deviance.* Englewood Cliffs, Prentice Hall. 1965.
19 J. D. Thompson, *Organizations in Action.* New York, McGraw-Hill. 1967.
20 F. M. Thrasher, *The Gang.* Chicago, University of Chicago Press. 1927.
21 J. Landesco, Organized crime in Chicago. Part III in Illinois Association for Criminal Justice, *Illinois Crime Survey.* Chicago, Author. 1929, pp. 865-1087.

22 Other circumstances, to be sure, may also affect the behavior of suppliers and customers. A union (as "supplier" of labor) may strike for reasons having little to do directly with the enterprise; customers may decline to purchase — as when a gasoline shortage or tight credit may influence automobile sales. I have ignored this level of complexity in the marketplace only for the purpose of simplifying the basic argument concerning illicit enterprise.

23 D. C. Smith, Jr., *The Mafia Mystique.* New York, Basic Books. 1975.

24 D. C. Smith, Jr., Illicit enterprise: the real world behind the stereotypes of organized crime. Paper presented at the 142nd annual meeting of the American Society for the Advancement of Science, Boston, 23 February 1976.

25 D. Cressey, *Theft of the Nation.* New York, Harper & Row. 1969.

26 Office of the Counsel to the Governor. *Combating Organized Crime.* Albany, New York. Author. 1966.

27 M. Puzo, *The Godfather.* New York, G. P. Putnam's Sons. 1969.

28 Film buffs will recall that Francis Ford Coppola pulled these two episodes together into an exceedingly powerful opening to the film version of Puzo's novel.

Dwight C. Smith, Jr. is Associate Professor in Criminal Justice at Rutgers—The State University. His current research interests are organized and white collar crime theory and criminal justice information systems. He is the author of Mafia Mystique *(New York: Basic Books, 1975) and coauthor with Richard Alba of "Organized crime and American life"* (Society, 1979).

14

FEDERAL INFLUENCE AND
URBAN POLICY ENTREPRENEURSHIP IN
THE LOCAL PROSECUTION OF ECONOMIC CRIME

MICHAEL A.BRINTNALL

ABSTRACT

In the early 1970's a score of local prosecutors around the United States instituted programs to address the problem of white collar crime and consumer fraud. This article analyzes this process of innovation as a form of policy entrepreneurship. The article concludes with consideration of key questions addressing the sources, character, and consequences of local policy entrepreneurship and the character of federal influence.

In the early 1970's, a score of local prosecutors around the United States instituted programs to address the problem of white collar crime and consumer fraud. These efforts were modest compared to the responses to street crime and other traditional matters; but the economic crime programs were nevertheless full time, sustained undertakings with demonstrable results. They represented the first serious programmatic commitment by the local prosecutor to the problem of economic crime in the United States.

The development of the programs is worth close examination. Economic crime, as white collar crime and consumer fraud will be called here, is an important and complex social issue. The emergence of a sustained public response to it alone is of great interest. But beyond this, the development of economic crime prosecution bureaus stands out as a major policy innovation at the local level. At a time when the capacity of local public officials to innovate, and even to govern, is in question, policy innovation of any sort at the local level is worth close inspection.

This article focuses on such a process of innovation as a form of policy entrepreneurship. Entrepreneurship can be defined as the actions of public officials, or of groups or

From Michael A. Brintnall, "Federal Influence and Urban Policy Entrepreneurship in the Local Prosecution of Economic Crime," 7(3) *Policy Studies Journal* 577-592 (Spring 1979). Copyright 1979, Policy Studies Organization.

individuals with easy access to public officials, to "seek new programs to put before the public, even though no appreciable part of the public is demanding them."[1]

Entrepreneurship by prosecuting attorneys in the creation of economic crime programs is of particular interest because it is based on the interplay of multiple influences--political, professional, fiscal, and federal. Paradoxically, the intersection of these multiple influences has increased rather than diminished the discretion of prosecuting attorneys to initiate and define the public need they will address, and establish which clientele they will serve.

LEADERSHIP AND CONSTRAINTS ON LEADERSHIP. One of the distinctions between what might be called the old study of urban politics, and the new study of urban public policy-making is that the former asked who governs, and the latter asks what are the constraints on governing. Most of the current studies of urban policies focus on the limitations confronting policy makers, e.g. from the federal system, from the class structure, from the bureaucracy, from pluralism in general, or from personal leadership style.[2] These studies of the capacities and boundaries of leadership have led to the generalization that the combination of the many individual factors impinging on urban leadership paralyzes the city.[3]

Another perspective has also developed, however, looking at the abilities of leaders to manipulate resources or combinations of resources to implement innovative policy. Russell Murphy has examined such a process in the New Haven antipoverty projects; Frank Levy and others noted it in Oakland, describing the resulting policy process as "Galbraithian politics" in which policy leaders have substantial influence over the demand for program services; Sarah Liebschutz has explored revenue sharing funds as a resource for policy innovation for elected officials; and Roger Cobb et al. have posed an "inside access" model of agenda building for analysis of policy development which occurs without the participation of the public.[4]

In most instances, these studies have shown policy leadership emerging because outside influence has provided external resources which leaders can use to act independently of the many other forces which constrain them. That is, influences can create discretion. The way this happens is intrinsically important to the study of policy making. But the study of discretion raises an immediate difficulty--how can we both understand the development of discretion, that is, relative independence in setting policy directions, and also find some basis for an understanding of the directions which resulting policy will take. This paper explores such a relationship between discretion and the direction of policy in the case of the formation of economic crime bureaus.

In these bureaus the interaction among multiple levels of influence has expanded the discretion of the prosecutor to initiate and direct policy, and has promoted successful entrepreneurship. This interaction has created what can be called "avoidance initiatives" for local prosecutors dealing with economic crime. Combinations of local and national resources and the diffuse, non-intense public support of economic crime programs, interact to provide prosecutors discretion to develop programs without the need for support from any single strong constituency, and to shift the program focus freely to avoid any forms of intense opposition. The forms of opposition which the prosecutors avoided indirectly serve to set the program directions, because of the elimination of alternatives.

This paper explores how such politics have worked in economic crime policymaking by prosecutors, and some of the important implications of their interaction. It will look first briefly at what economic crime bureaus are and what they do, and then at the influences on their development--the local political setting, national program funds, professional role identity, and the specific characteristics of the "political climate" of the policy issue involved.

THE NATURE OF ECONOMIC CRIME BUREAUS. This study is based on research in local prosecutors' offices in fifteen large counties around the United States. Each of the sites studied was participating in a project managed by the National District Attorneys Association (NDAA) to demonstrate and improve the capabilities of local prosecutors to address economic crime.

Economic crime investigation and prosecution has not generally been considered a major part of the local prosecutor's repertoire. It has traditionally been handled on an ad hoc basis and most often left to the U.S. Attorney and to specialized regulatory agencies. Yet, in each of these fifteen sites, in the early 1970's, prosecuting attorneys established new bureaus to handle economic crime, with full time, regularly assigned staff. These bureaus developed a systematic program of operations which became a local policy system, reflecting "an interrelated set of events which return upon themselves to complete and renew a cycle of activities."[5] Each bureau developed regular working relationships with other investigative agencies, courts, police, and even other bureaus within its office. Maintaining relationships with these other segments of the policy arena influenced decisions about caseloads as much as the character of individual cases being pursued.[6]

On the average in a month, a bureau would employ five attorneys, eight investigators, informally handle citizen complaints involving over $40,000 in disputed consumer and investor transactions, and return over $6,000 to victims in formal court ordered restitution. Surprisingly, contrary to the expectations of many, these bureaus consistently responded formally and informally to the needs of victims usually ignored by the legal system, such as minorities and the elderly.[7]

Yet by no means were all of the bureaus similar in approach or structure. Significant differences emerged among them. Four sites were selected for intensive analysis, based on variation in their responses to two key policy differences --emphasis on major criminal prosecution and emphasis on consumer complaint handling. Thus one bureau stressed only major prosecutions, another only consumer complaint handling, and the other two had different mixes of both.

The following exchange between two prosecutors (one of them is not in these case studies) at an economic crime prosecution planning conference, illustrates the differences:[8]

[District Attorney 1]: The most important thing
is to develop major cases with major impact
rather than to try to solve peoples' individual
problems, in order to use resources more effectively. This way you can create an atmosphere
of deterrence and local impact.

[District Attorney 2, in response]: I don't want
to lose sight of the individual victim who loses
a life savings or suffers in some other way
because of a focus of the major fraud case. There
are other forums and agencies which can handle
major cases, but those agencies calling themselves
consumer protectors have not helped the little
guy.

The four sites studied cannot be identified because of assurances of anonymity made at the time of the research.

The sites were visited repeatedly during 1974 and 1975.
Office staff and informants in the communities were interviewed, and investigative and prosecutive records were studied
in depth. A major source of information was a comparative data
system, the Uniform Economic Crime Reporting System, which
recorded the nature and outcome of each investigation and prosecution for all offices in a standardized format for an
evaluation of the NDAA project.[9]

ECONOMIC CRIME POLICY AS INNOVATION. The directions innovations took in the bureaus can be examined in terms of three
broad themes:

   -the ambiguity of the economic crime issue itself;

   -local politics and the interactions with other segments
    of the local governmental sector;

   -extra-local factors, such as the national program men-
    tioned above, funds from the Law Enforcement Assistance
    Administration, and professional standards felt by
    prosecuting attorneys, and more importantly, by their
    staff.

A key relationship among these themes can be stated:
local forces create boundaries on innovation; extra-local
forces create possibilities. To understand this, it is necessary first to look at each theme individually, and then to
examine them in interaction.

AMBIGUITY. Economic crime is ambiguous. It is ill-defined
and hard to detect. Little tradition surrounds the local
prosecutor's role in addressing economic crime. Short of
the sensational case any prosecuting attorney will milk for
the publicity, no one really expects or demands the prosecuting attorney to take a systematic approach to economic
crime, and few could recognize it if he did.

Furthermore, no one really agrees on what economic crime
is in the first place. Prosecutors, and the legal profession,
have perhaps been somewhat more in agreement about what economic crime is than the academic profession, but not much.

Some scholars have defined economic crimes as those committed in the course of occupations, usually by upper class
or high social status business men.[10] Another defines them
as "illegal acts committed by nonphysical means and by concealment or guile" for business or personal advantage.[11] Much
wrangling has taken place in the literature over whether an
economic crime is a violation of pre-existing criminal law,
or whether it is an action that "ought" to be considered criminal, but is not by the legal doctrine or the legal system, for
various reasons such as the influence of the offender.[12]

This ambiguity about the definition is usually resolved
in practice by reliance on imprecise, vernacular description--
unfairness, deception, exploitation in economic transactions;
and colorful language--bait and switch advertising, Ponzi and
pyramid schemes, "sweetheart" contracts, check kiting, or
medical quackery.[13] Use of this language does not just illuminate the problem, but allows the prosecuting attorney to play
some light tricks--defining or redefining his program by
choosing among definitions as necessary.

Thus, the very ambiguity of the policy problem weakens
the potential for specific constituent or interest groups to
place strong demands on the prosecuting attorney, because the
prosecutor can control public definition of the issue while
the broad diffuse support the prosecuting attorney can expect
for action in response to "economic crime" is not lessened.

LOCAL POLITICS. The discretion which local prosecutors derived
from the ambiguity surrounding the economic crime issue, and
from other factors discussed below, was exercised in almost
every site to minimize the potential of opposition from strong
local interests, rather than to maximize support from any
particular group. Programs were insulated from local politics
and interests; program differences among the sites do not vary
in any predictable way in relationship to various indicators
of political culture or interest group structure, contrary to
what Wilson, Jacobs, or Levin have found in other legal system
issues.[14] One explanation of this is that few mechanisms
exist by which local politics can influence economic crime
policy. To understand this, it is necessary to examine the
various ways prosecutors are usually made accountable or are
influenced locally: the election of prosecutors, relations
with the judiciary, and interest group behavior.

Selection of Prosecutors. In his study of styles of policing,
James Q. Wilson found "the most important way in which political culture affects police behavior is through the choice of
police administrator and the molding of expectations that
govern his role."[15] In the case of economic crime programs,
the "prosecutive administrator" is elected rather than
appointed, and campaigns on the basis of unrelated issues such
as response to street crime, regulation of public morality,
and the appropriateness of plea-bargaining. Only one of the
prosecutors studied here introduced his plans for an economic
crime bureau as a campaign item, and his opponent declined to
make it an issue.

Judiciary. While the judiciary can, from time-to-time, have
an important effect on economic crime bureaus, judges rarely
have had a systematic effect, contrary to circumstances in
traditional crime areas. Economic crime bureaus have a

relatively low caseload, and there is thus both limited
opportunity for judicial influence to develop, and increased
possibility for economic crime bureau attorneys to shop for
supportive judges. Bureaus also have greater alternative
resources for disposition of cases than do traditional crime
bureaus and thus are less dependent on the judiciary. And
they have developed expertise in an area of law unfamiliar to
most local judges. While this latter fact, I was told, is
usually unimpressive to the judiciary in responding to individual cases, particularly in the lower, misdemeanor courts,
it places the prosecutor in an altered position vis-a-vis the
courts when routine interaction does develop. The limited
interaction with the judiciary after economic crime programs
develop provides little opportunity for judicial influence on
policy development.

Interest Groups. Political structure may be unrelated to
policy development in economic crime bureaus because the
values served by particular political systems are not germane
to the nature of economic crime programs in the first place.
Herbert Jacob and Kenneth Vines, for example, have observed
that "while criminal proceedings appear to be closely linked
with a community's political machinery, civil proceedings
appears to reflect its interest group structure."[16] In this
respect, white collar criminal proceedings involving disputes
arising from economic transactions, may be perceived and
treated locally as essentially civil proceedings, regardless
of the actual remedy the prosecutor uses.

    Yet, interest groups too are generally absent. Two
kinds of interest groups might be expected to have an interest
in bureau policy--business oriented groups concerned about the
intervention of the prosecutor into economic relationships;
and private associations or social service agencies concerned
about the consumer or the victim. No evidence was unearthed in
the case studies indicating that business groups lobbied the
prosecuting attorney or his staff directly, in any significant
manner. In most of the counties, business "self-regulatory"
groups such as the Local Association of Swimming Pool Contractors and the like existed and made gestures to work with
the prosecuting attorneys office in self-regulation but to no
apparent consequence.

    Available evidence suggests that, rather, business
lobbying is carried out at the state legislature, seeking
favorable changes in substantive law, except for occasional
unsuccessful efforts by business to get prosecutors to handle
bad check cases.[17] After all, in the age of consumerism, how
could a business risk exposure of a compromising attempt at
influence.

    Non-business associations and social service associations
also had little direct contact with prosecutors. In the case
studies, no community organizations were found to have lobbied
for the consumer interest as a factor in the formation of
economic crime bureaus, or to have altered directions of any
programs. In fact, consumerism and economic crime have generally been found not to be a good local organizing issue at
all.[18]

Risk Avoidance. Not all elements of insulation of economic
crime bureau practice from local politics is specific to

economic crime itself. Prosecutors have intentionally insulated their programs as well. From this perspective, local
politics and interest group activity does have an indirect
influence on policy formation, through the creation of boundaries or regions of risk across which the prosecutor will not
move.

Two forms of risk avoidance are evident. The first is
general to all bureaus--the insulation of the resource base
for the bureau. The second is idiosyncratic--depending on
local circumstances.

Resources. Each of the prosecutors adopted some means
of insulating the budget sources for the bureaus from outside
control or influence--e.g., by drawing funds from within the
office without seeking an outside increased budget appropria-
tion, or by a long term state administered federal grant.
This budgetary insulation was never directed toward any
specific opponent, but was in response to uncertainties about
the impact of the bureaus in their early years, before they
had their own record to stand on. Surprisingly the federally
funded NDAA program in which each bureau participated was not
an important source of such resources; prosecutors often saw
these funds as too unstable and risking too many entanglements
to rely on.

Idiosyncracies. Other patterns of insulation of bureau
activity differed in each site. Each prosecutor adopted his
own peculiar risk avoidance strategy. In one site, the prosecuting attorney said that although he has never been lobbied
directly by business interests regarding his consumer protection program, "some of the business interests are scared of
the consumer protection issue and it could work against me" if
raised in a political campaign. (He has never been opposed
in a campaign, and thus has been spared the reality of this
anticipated conflict.) Office policies regarding the bureau
have been correspondingly conservative.

In another, the prosecutor also anticipated business
opposition, and took steps to demonstrate the beneficial
aspects of bureau operations to the business community by
giving high priority to an initial prosecution involving
lumber dealers defrauding local developers and building contractors, and to show that the bulk of his resources would be
devoted to criminal violations rather than to consumer protection. Once the first criminal case was won, it became much
more difficult for opposing interests to resist the bureau.
A "mystique of criminal prosecution," once a big case was won,
served in general to insulate the prosecutor from criticism.[19]

In the third site, the bureau was created in the wake of
a grand jury investigation and prosecution for corruption of
the prosecutor's predecessor. In that climate, the new prosecuting attorney was reluctant to break a local tradition by
creating his own independent investigatory force, because of
potential partisan opposition to seeming aggrandizement. He
chose instead to legitimate his bureau's actions by working
through existing investigatory agencies, and adjusting his
policies accordingly.

The fourth site is an exception to risk avoidance strategies. The prosecuting attorney knew he had the political

resources to endure business opposition. In fact, there are
indications he believed that by blatantly ignoring business
opposition he would actually increase his effective resources.
His economic crime bureau policies are not, consequently,
adapted to avoiding potential local opposition, but to
maximizing his support.

Consequences. In three of the four sites, the policy directions were shaped by the avoidance of opposition, before that
opposition was manifest. Such risk avoidance is not a complete
explanation of the policy, but is an important piece of the
picture. To use intertwined metaphors from statistics and
business, the prosecuting attorney has more degrees of freedom
in setting performance directions than are satisfied by situational factors such as interest group influence. There are
many equally acceptable ways the prosecuting attorney can
address the economic crime problem, and seek a clientele.
Many of these are inherently as satisfactory as others. The
prosecuting attorney faces little competition from other local
agencies or groups in addressing economic crime and thus is
not constrained by "market" forces to a particular style.
Avoiding potential opposition is one of the ways the prosecutor
reduces these degrees of freedom.

A remark by W. Ross Ashby on communications theory
illustrates this:

> The fundamental principle of decision on a finite
> quantity of information may be expressed thus:
> Use all that you know to shrink the range of pos-
> sibilities to their minimum; after that, do as
> you please. [20]

Of course, "doing as you please" is an overstatement here.
The boundaries of the policy space are real and important,
reflecting values and interests of other segments of the local
government and media elite through exposure, resources, and
ideology. But the important point is that rather than extending
traditional commitments and orientations, the prosecutor uses
the economic crime bureau to acquire resources and to achieve
goals not available to him under politics and policies as
usual. The specific directions of this entrepreneurship tend
to be set by extra-local forces, to which I will now turn.

EXTRA-LOCAL INFLUENCES ON POLICY ENTREPRENEURSHIP. It is well
known that local policy entrepreneurship is significantly influenced by factors outside of the community, notably by policies
and resources of the national government. This influence is
most often analyzed in terms of specific loci of extra-local
influence dominating local policy directions. But extra-local
influences may function in a different way. Extra-local factors may combine to set boundaries on local action, and to
augment discretion within those boundaries. This can be
observed in economic crime bureaus.

Three areas of extra-local influence stand out in the
case of economic crime bureaus:

-program resources from the national government, and the
National District Attorneys Association, including
funds, ideas, communications, and prestige;

-professional role identity among prosecutors as a group,
particularly in their role as lawyers;

-the favorable political climate of national consumer
protection politics for discretionary action at the
local level.

Though none alone had a dominant effect on local operations,
together these forms of influence were important in creating
opportunities in the areas in which local prosecutors exercised discretion. They deserve brief individual note.

National Program Resources. Federal funds and policies have
played a major role in economic crime bureau development, but
have not been translated into domination of policies of the
bureaus. Federal funds influence the intercession of the
National District Attorneys Association. This has worked
primarily in three ways.

First, most federal funds used in economic crime bureaus
came from state allocations of the LEAA block grant program,
in which the local prosecutors themselves took the initiative
to insert economic crime program categories. The availability
of these block grants also weakened the influence of nation-
wide discretionary funds funneled through the National District
Attorneys Association.

Second, LEAA has provided its national, discretionary
funds for economic crime programs with characteristic lack
of direction. For example, when a consortium of local prosecutors approached the LEAA in 1974 for support for an economic crime project, the LEAA resolved internal debate over
whether or not the project was a law enforcement program, and
thus within its purview, by the Solomonic gesture of authorizing
the entire proposed program but providing only one-half of the
requested funds. Only after the project gained favorable
national publicity and enthusiastic support of a wider audience
of prosecutors did the LEAA increase funding. Full approval
and funds were then given to a second year of the project
before the first year evaluation report, required by LEAA, had
even been completed.[21]

Third, federal influence was weakened because federal
monies were passed through a national project office which
was an arm of the National District Attorneys Association.
The operation of this Project Center is a fascinating story in
its own right.[22] It is important here only to note that this
center operated largely to mirror local interests rather than
to enforce national goals.

The Economic Crime Project Center operated with no significant basis of power, other than the cooperation of its member
offices. While it ostensibly controlled disbursement of
national discretionary funds to participating offices for
hiring additional staff, the Project Center acquired little
leverage from their use. Its one attempt to discipline an
office by discontinuing funding met with opposition from
influential prosecuting attorneys within NDAA, and funds were
quietly restored some time later.

Consequently, rather than enforcing direct compliance
with its objectives, the Economic Crime Project capitalized
on the existing enthusiasm within the participating offices
to develop a sense of allegiance to the project which could
then be transferred into support for specific program objectives as they developed. The intraproject "esprit de corps"

which comprised the Project's main resource was built up by
emphasizing as much direct interaction among the bureaus as
possible, holding quarterly conferences, formulating common
guidelines for action, such as liaison with federal and state
agencies, and encouraging direct working cooperation among
the bureaus.

The Economic Crime Project in this way intensified and to
some degree standardized local actions, but did not particularly alter their directions--except to strengthen professional role definitions among the prosecutors and thus to
encourage actions consistent with those roles, as discussed
below. Extra-local influence of money and program coordination can in this way be considered important primarily for
the ways it interacted with other influences involved.

Professional Role Identity. A second form of extra-local
influence of tremendous importance, often taken for granted
in study of public policy, is the professional role identities of the officials involved. Professional identity is
often a centralizing force, breaking down local influences.
It operated in such a manner in economic crime bureaus.
Professional norms and traditions in this case operated to
favor formally efficient and complex prosecutions characterized
by technical attributes of the case as much as by the prosecutive target. The implicit model was usually that of the U.S.
Attorney. The Economic Crime Project Center, in its search for
ways to coordinate fifteen disparate offices, symbolized and
operationalized this professional model, reinforcing the tendencies toward complex prosecution in local bureaus, and discouraging other approaches. In this way, it countered
localistic policy choices of the prosecuting attorneys.

As with federal resources, the federal prosecutive model
influenced local program initiative, but did not control its
outcome. Through the mechanism of the national project, the
federal prosecutive model reinforced that part of the local
prosecutor's professional identity which inclined him away
from direct responsiveness to various local constituencies,
and toward a more independent, professionally inclined policy
orientation. Federal influence created the potential for
local policy discretion, by legitimating alternatives to
strictly locally oriented political action.

Consumer Protection Politics. Mass support or opposition for
local policies often emerges on the basis of how those policies are defined in national politics, rather than in the
locality. This is especially likely to happen when the politics involve diffuse and passive support--allowing extensive
definition of the issue by elites who become involved with it.

Consumer protection is such an issue, and has had an
extensive impact on economic crime policy making by district
attorneys. Consumer protection nationally has evoked a
passive form of politics in the U.S., in which action is led
by a small group of activists making a career out of full or
part time involvement. Consumer protection policies are elite
defined, though widely supported.[23] The resulting pattern of
diffuse support is ripe for exploitation by policy entrepreneurs, such as the prosecuting attorneys studied here.

The effect of consumer politics on prosecutors is compounded by the legacy of recent social welfare policy. The consumer movement has been influenced by recent national social welfare programs, e.g. the War on Poverty, which has focused attention on the legal and consumer needs of the poor; has stressed procedural remedies, such as improved service delivery, over substantive remedies, such as new legislation, and stimulated greater local efforts in responding to many consumer needs.

The interaction of a national agenda of consumer protection and social welfare programs strengthens the discretion of the prosecuting attorney and counteracts the influence of professional norms by justifying a service approach as well as a prosecutive orientation.

It is in the face of this nationally derived issue context which local economic crime policy emerged--economic crime bureaus at the local level were created by prosecutors responding to an issue created outside of the boundaries of the local community served. Local constituencies, when they have appeared for these programs, have appeared in response to the way the prosecutor has defined the economic crime issue. As the prosecuting attorney in one county said, in discussing the balance in his office between handling citizen complaints and prosecuting major cases: "we can increase or decrease the public response almost at will--we can put out information that we have a very efficient means of taking complaints--as soon as we publicize that complaints go up."

CONCLUSIONS. The politics of "avoidance initiative" generally adopted by local prosecuting attorneys in the creation of economic crime bureaus takes place because of the options created by the interaction of several extra-local forms of influence. Multiple levels of influence simultaneously constrain and augment discretion--through the establishment of boundaries to policy directions, and the supplying of resources to support initiatives by local prosecuting attorneys within those boundaries.

These processes are unusual. Individually, the components of local and extra-local influence observed as important in the economic crime policy process are common-place in other policy areas--the absence of clear national goals; the importance of national issues in framing an issue context in which local politics emerge; the segmented nature of the local elite structure. But the way these factors come together for economic crime policy is uncommon and made more unusual by additional factors not discussed above, such as the requirement that local prosecutors be attorneys, the tension between the elected and the professional role orientation of the prosecutor,[24] and the abstruse nature of economic crime law and technical lore.

In spite of this singularity of detail, the questions raised by these economic crime policy processes are of very broad applicability, however, and in conclusion I wish to discuss some of these implications, as an agenda for future work. Three key questions addressing the sources, character, and consequences of entrepreneurship, deriving from the above work, are the following:

-whether innovative behavior is motivated by electoral/ organizational interests of policy entrepreneurs, or by some generalized sense of ideological interest.

-whether innovative behavior results in dramatic,
non-incremental changes, or in conservative innovation which is not truly new;

-who benefits from policy entrepreneurship.

In particular, in exploring these questions, I am interested
in the character of federal influence--which in the case of
economic crime plays an important role in terms not only of
its presence but of its character.

Motives. Why does the urban political entrepreneur innovate?
One can address this question in several ways--assuming for
example that interest in innovation is generally high, but
routinely blocked by other political forces; or that interest
in innovation is related to a more general interest in personal or organizational gain, and materializes when opportunities for such gain are apparent. Paul Peterson and J.
David Greenstone explore the implications of these alternatives at some length. They contrast an electoral/organiza-
tional interest model, in which a decision maker's choice of
political strategies is based on the possibilities for electoral
advancement or organizational maintenance, with an ideological
model, in which decision makers, notably elected officials,
will act on the basis of their ideological attitudes, broadly
defined. They conclude that "ideology motivates behavior when
its relevance to current political issues is perceived."[25]
Three salient political issues in which ideological motivation
appeared relevant to Greenstone and Peterson were "racial roles
encompassing black-white relationships, class roles encompassing
employer-employee relationships, and the authority roles that
encompass the relationships of citizens and officials in the
American regime."

In short, innovative behavior by public officials can be
identified even when the immediate electoral/organizational
interest calculus comes up short. Such activity need not be
construed necessarily as altruistic, but rather as a different
kind of self-interested behavior arising when action becomes
relevant at all. In the case of economic crime bureaus, local
prosecutor's actions cannot be explained solely on the basis
of electoral/organizational interest calculations, except to
the degree that their actions would not undermine their short-
term support. Much of the impetus for their bureaus, and
especially for the variety among economic bureau programs, can
more adequately be ascribed to achievement of ideological
self-interest.[26]

Furthermore, the initiative and audience for this ideological achievement derived not from local politics or local
demands, but from the federal arena which created a national
forum for expression of such self-interest. Federal influence,
in other words, may induce a form of ideologically oriented
policy innovation by supplying resources and context by which
policy entrepreneurs can express an ideological bent which
has previously been submerged in more fundamental electoral/
organizational interest battles. In fact such interest may be
viewed as efforts by local officials to atone or compensate
for more hackneyed and self-maintenance or enhancement oriented
approaches to bread and butter electoral issues.

Character. A second way of looking at this issue is in terms
of the character of policy change which results from entrepreneurship. While entrepreneurship implies innovation, some
evidence suggests that such innovation will not deviate much
from community norms or expectations. Sarah Liebschutz
examined such a "familiarity" norm in her study of general
revenue sharing as a political resource for local officials.[27]
"Voters must have some awareness of programs before they can
perceive benefits from the allocation of revenue funds for
them." Indeed, her study concluded that in those sites in
which shared revenue was used for innovative projects, the
results were nonetheless not a "novelty" for the community,
e.g. an addition to the town hall.

Such conservative innovation may indeed flow as a general
rule from entrepreneurship dominated by electoral interest
calculations. In the case of economic crime bureaus, however,
the innovation was far less conservative--involving policy
decisions which were not generally accepted or tested in terms
of "community acceptability or familiarity" at the local level.
While this may indeed suggest an alternative self-interest
calculation on the part of prosecutors, it may also simply
reflect the consequences of an alternative kind of "familiarity"
--one linked indirectly to the local decision maker through the
federal arena. The diffuseness of consumer protection politics
--in which the issue is never well defined or linked with specific practices--makes any sort of local action legitimate
whether it is a conservative adjustment to past practices, or
a dramatic innovation. Such diffuseness is not a characteristic of all federally influenced policies, but when it does
occur, is likely to be a product of politics played out at a
remote arena from the local system.

Outcome. Finally, we can ask what difference does entrepreneurial politics make. Who is likely to benefit, and in what
way. Again the federal influence plays a major role in understanding local policy. One cannot explain differences in the
policy consequences of economic crime programs in terms of
local factors alone. Federal influence comes in to play first
of all through the insulation of local prosecutors from a need
to rely on local resources, second from the ambivalence by
which the issue becomes defined at all, and third of course
by the fact that federal legitimation of policy alternatives
implies boundaries outside of which local entrepreneurship is
unlikely to survive.

The consumer protection/social service heritage of one
strand of federal issue identification led to a component of
local programs providing particularistic rewards to local
consumers. The professional/prosecutive heritage of the other
strand of federal issue identification, however, took some of
this away. The prosecutor can rely on public "familiarity"
with the consumer protection heritage to build support for
his bureau, in order to carry out, often, a very different
kind of policy reflecting professional interests.

It can be shown that as major criminal prosecutions
increase, within and between bureaus, use of those sanctions
for cases involving consumers decreases.[28] Attention in general to individual clients is withdrawn, as the bureau turns
to professionally more interesting "cases." In turn this disparity between clients and cases tends to result in an altered

class distribution of rewards, since more interesting cases tend to be those with greatest dollar loss.[29]

Federal influence has abetted this outcome in two ways. The diffuseness of consumer protection politics creates a climate of support for the local programs, without creating strong expectations about what those programs do. The competing federal role model for local prosecutors--as professional attorneys handling cases rather than serving clients-- provides the setting for local prosecutors to direct their energies toward these interesting cases, while building on the support engendered by the quite different idea of consumer protection.

In sum, the question of who benefits cannot be answered until more is known about the ways groups benefit. One can suggest that the more diffuse and the more pluralistic the federal influence in local policy entrepreneurship, the more such policy will disengage from a direct response to local interests.[30]

NOTES

[1] J. Tobin and W. A. Wallis, Welfare Programs: An Economic Appraisal (Washington, D.C.: American Enterprise Institute for Public Policy, 1968), p. 42.

[2] Martha Derthick, New Towns In-Town (Washington, D.C.: The Urban Institute, 1972); Isaac Balbus, Dialectics of Legal Repression (New York: Russell Sage Foundation, 1973); Michael Lipsky, "Toward a Theory of Street-level Bureaucracy," in Willis Hawley and Michael Lipsky, Theoretical Perspectives on Urban Politics (Englewood Cliffs: Prentice-Hall, 1976); Jeffrey Pressman and Aaron Wildavsky, Implementation (Berkeley: University of California Press, 1973); Martha Weinberg, Managing the State (Cambridge: MIT Press, 1977).

[3] Douglas Yates, The Ungovernable City (Cambridge: MIT Press, 1977); Theodore Lowi, "Machine Politics--Old and New," The Public Interest, 9 (Fall 1967), pp. 83-92.

[4] Russell Murphy, Political Entrepreneurs and Urban Poverty (Lexington, Mass.: D.C. Heath and Company, 1971); Frank Levy et al., Urban Outcomes (Berkeley: University of California Press, 1974); Sarah Liebschutz, "General Revenue Sharing as a Political Resource for Local Officials," in Public Policy Making in a Federal System, ed. by Charles O. Jones and Robert D. Thomas (Beverly Hills: Sage Publications, Inc., 1976); Roger Cobb et al., "Agenda Building as a Comparative Political Process," American Political Science Review, LXX, 1 (March, 1976), pp. 126-138.

[5] Daniel Katz and Robert L. Kahn, The Social Psychology of Organizations (New York: John Wiley and Sons, 1966), ch. 2.

[6] See in general Michael A. Brintnall, "The Allocation of Services in the Local Prosecution of Economic Crime" (unpublished Ph.D. Dissertation, Massachusetts Institute of Technology, 1977).

[7] Michael Brintnall and Herbert Edelhertz, "Prosecutive Responses to Different Categories of White-Collar Crime," paper presented to the American Society of Criminology, Atlanta, November, 1977.

[8] Cited in Brintnall, note 6 above, p. 21.

[9]Further information on the Economic Crime Project and UECRS can be found in Herbert Edelhertz, "The N.D.A.A. Economic Crime Project, Structures, Goals, and Operations," paper delivered at the annual meeting of the North Central Sociological Association, Columbus, Ohio, May 6, 1975; Battelle Law and Justice Study Center, Research and Evaluation Report on the Second Year of the Economic Crime Project (Seattle: 1975).

[10]Edwin Sutherland, White Collar Crime (New York: Dryden Press, 1949).

[11]Herbert Edelhertz, The Nature, Impact and Prosecution of White-Collar Crime (Washington, D.C.: Government Printing Office, 1970).

[12]The conventional argument is summarized in Marshall B. Clinard, "Crime: White Collar Crime," International Encyclopedia of the Social Sciences, 2nd ed.; see also Harold E. Pepinsky, "From White Collar Crime to Exploitation: Redefinition of a Field," The Journal of Criminal Law and Criminology 64, no. 2 (1974).

[13]For a glossary of these terms, see Herbert Edelhertz et al., The Investigation of White Collar Crime, A Manual for Law Enforcement (Washington, D.C.: U.S. Government Printing Office, 1977), Appendix C.

[14]Brintnall, note 6 above; Martin A. Levin, "Urban Politics and Judicial Behavior," in Rough Justice, ed. by John Robertson (Boston: Little, Brown and Company, 1974), pp. 192-209; James Eisenstein, "Counsel for the United States: An Empirical Analysis of the Office of the United States Attorney" (unpublished Ph.D. dissertation, Yale University, 1968), p. III-3; Herbert Jacob and Kenneth Vines, "The Role of the Judiciary in American State Politics," in Judicial Decision-Making, ed. by Glendon Schubert (New York: The Free Press, 1963), pp. 250-251.

[15]James Q. Wilson, Varieties of Police Behavior (New York: Atheneum, 1973), p. 233.

[16]Jacob and Vines, note 14 above, p. 250.

[17]From private interviews by the author with prosecutors and staffs in 15 sites.

[18]Lawrence Grossman, "Program Action Issues and Action Organizing Tasks," in Readings in Community Organization Practice, ed. by Ralph M. Kramer and Harry Specht (Englewood Cliffs: Prentice-Hall, Inc., 1969), pp. 314-323; also see the theoretical treatment, applicable to consumer issues, in J. D. Thompson, Organizations in Action (New York: McGraw-Hill Book Co., 1967), p. 31.

[19]The "mystique of criminal prosecution" is an analogue to the "myth of rights" discussed by Stuart Scheingold, The Politics of Rights (New Haven: Yale University Press, 1974).

[20]W. Ross Ashby, "Letter to the Editor," Science 169, no. 3933 (May 15, 1970), p. 777.

[21]For a fuller discussion of this see Michael A. Brintnall, "Problems of the Evaluation of the Economic Crime Project," paper delivered at the annual meeting of the North Central Sociological Association, Columbus, Ohio, May 6, 1975.

[22]Brintnall, note 21 above.

[23]Peter H. Rossi and Richard A. Berk, "Local Political Leadership and Popular Discontent in the Ghetto," Annals of the American Academy of Political and Social Sciences 391 (September, 1970), p. 126; Mark Nadel, The Politics of Consumer Protection (Indianapolis: Bobbs-Merrill Company, 1971).

[24]See the discussion of this in: Lief Carter, The Limits of Order (Lexington, Mass.: D.C. Heath and Co., 1974).

[25]Paul E. Peterson and J. David Greenstone, "Two Competing Models of the Policy-Making Process: The Community Action Controversy as an Empirical Test," in Theoretical Perspectives on Urban Politics, ed. by Willis D. Hawley and Michael Lipsky (Englewood Cliffs, N.J.: Prentice-Hall, Inc., 1976), p. 94 and passim. Following quote is on p. 72.

[26]Brintnall, dissertation, note 6 above, chapters 8 and 9.

[27]Liebschutz, note 4 above.

[28]Brintnall, dissertation, note 6 above, chapter 8.

[29]Roger Cobb et al., in their inside access model of agenda building, suggest that the result will generally be to reflect the status interests of the group making or influencing decisions. See note 4 above.

[30]For similar conclusions in quite different settings see: Richard A. Cloward and Irwin Epstein, "Private Social Welfare's Disengagement from the Poor: The Case of Family Adjustment Agencies," in Social Welfare Institutions, ed. by Mayer N. Zald (New York: John Wiley and Sons, Inc., 1965), pp. 623-44; and Philippe Nonet, Administrative Justice: Advocacy and Change in a Government Agency (New York: Russell Sage Foundation, 1969).

Michael Brintnall is Assistant Professor of Political Science at Brown University and a member of the faculty of the Urban Studies Program. He is the author of "Police and white collar crime" in Fred Meyer and Ralph Baker (eds.), Determinants of Law Enforcement Policies *(Lexington, MA: Lexington Press, 1979). He is the coauthor (with Ezra Stotland) of a forthcoming study of deterrence in home repair fraud in the Sage* Criminal Justice System Annuals *(Vol. 13). His research interests include urban public policy making, politics of local justice, evaluation research, and bureaucratic influences on policy.*

Part III:

VIOLENCE

People of widely differing political persuasions and opposing social philosophies would readily agree that criminal violence is but a tiny part of the general problem of violence in our time. Wars, instances of genocide, human destruction resulting from political upheavals, and the brutal governmental oppression prevalent in countless nations are all either with us or are vivid memories. No one can overlook the fact that the amount of death and injury resulting from accidents, negligence, neglect, and the corruption of the environment by the industrial process exceeds by many times that caused by criminals. Still, it is clear that for many Americans—and probably for many Europeans and Asians, too— fear of the kind of assault described by John Conrad at the beginning of his article is typically more salient. Perhaps we feel resigned toward great catastrophes. Perhaps we accept the death of 50,000 annually in automobile accidents because they were not killed "on purpose." But perhaps the reason for the special dread of a mugging—a dread quite disproportionate to our chance of experiencing it—is because it, unlike catastrophes and accidents, continuously threatens to undermine a basic assumption of our daily existence: namely, that we can live next to one another as strangers in safety.

Incongruous though it may seem in the face of the vast amount of violence this century has produced and borne, our civilization differs from the civilizations of other ages in encouraging this assumption; most people now appear to have accepted the practical and moral necessity of peace in their day-to-day lives. We expect safety abroad, even though we do not always anticipate finding it. True, we are fascinated by the sight of violence, but we regard this interest as prurient. Above all, we find resorting to violence in face-to-face relations—except, perhaps, when deliberately staged for this purpose—to be a sign of immaturity or "lower class culture." It is an insufferable insult to the union of self and society that such a basic presupposition about the nature of existence could be put to the ultimate test by a youngster whose aimless life has brought him, "Saturday-night special" in hand, into a totally unpredictable chance encounter with his victim. To die in an airplane crash, to be burned in an apartment fire, to be born with withered limbs because of thalidomide poisoning, or to have one's spine severed by a Viet Cong mine are all more bearable. But to be a victim of a criminal assault, it appears, is unbearable because it is quintessentially evil: It strikes at the very basis of what we have in mind as being human with each other.

In the chapter entitled "Fear" from his honest and humane book, Charles Silberman provides materials suggesting such an interpretation. Putting Erving

Goffman's work on public order to good use, Silberman implies that crime, both in contemplation and aftermath, undermines our sense of the world as a place where what we do can have an effect because it challenges our sense of others as civilized persons. It is not only personal confrontation with criminals, Silberman proposes, that engenders this sort of response but invasion of the spaces and things in which ourselves are invested also engenders it.

The pages by Silberman convey something of and about the experiences of victims; Leonard Berkowitz attempts an interpretation of the motives of certain assailants. He takes issue with the "subculture-of-violence" thesis. Based on evidence obtained from interviews with British convicts, he argues that many assailants are motivated by feelings of rage rather than acting from a conscious desire to meet subcultural standards of conduct. Two comments on Berkowitz's article are also included, the three together presenting an illuminating illustration of the value and difficulty of discussing the motivational background of assaultive acts. When they are compared with Silberman's account, all three suggest how differently assaultive acts may appear from the standpoints of victims and assaulters.[1] Both Toch and Curtis are restive with Berkowitz's interpretation of the subculture-of-violence thesis, a thesis also of concern to John Conrad.[2] Both think Berkowitz's findings may not be incompatible with properly interpreted subculture-of-violence view. Toch notes, further, that understanding motives is, at best, a risky business, perhaps subject in the end to preferences among frameworks for conceiving the dynamics of human action. Curtis apparently concurs and shows his preference for frameworks that do not scant "external influences," as, presumably, those employed by psychologists like Berkowitz are wont to do.

John Conrad's essay, prepared especially for this volume, incisively summarizes what is known, or thought to be known, about the sources of criminal violence. He concludes that although further research may articulate these sources more clearly and finely, it is unlikely to result in proposals that will permit much reduction in violence by the criminal justice system at any cost many of us would be willing to bear. Ted Gurr, on the basis of quite different data, implies the same conclusion, suggesting that "the criminal law, police, courts, and prisons together can only restrain common crime if they reinforce underlying social forces that are moving in the same direction." Neither appears to believe that this is now the case.

Gurr pulls together and attempts to interpret existing data on trends in violent crime in Europe and America. The data show that, over the course of time until recently, the overall trend has been downward. Though it doubtless provides small if any comfort to current victims, and though the knowledge of the overall trend even if widely dispersed would arguably not reduce fear, it, as well as the relative and rapid rise in crime since the 1950s, stands in need of interpretation. Gurr presents some tentative explanations for these trends. It is scarcely surprising, given the complexity of the events to be explained and the recency of acquisition of this knowledge, that his explanations leave us with a somewhat less than satisfactory hope that the normal working of "social gravitation" will assure that whatever has gone up has to come down.[3]

Dane Archer and Rosemary Gartner also provide quantitative data on violent crime trends, although they address different questions than Gurr. In part, their article serves to make more familiar the sorts of efforts to develop archives of quantitative data that are proceeding apace. The Comparative Crime Data File discussed in the article appears to be a particularly inventive and potentially useful archive that will help answer a host of methodological and substantive questions. Archer and Gartner provide tentative answers to one of each. "Poor" crime indicators, they suggest, may be more useful for trend analysis than previously believed. Further, large cities may *always* have had higher homicide rates than the average rates of the nations of which they are parts—but city homicide rates generally have *not* increased as these cities have grown in population over time.[4] Put differently, the *absolute* size of cities appears to have less to do with their crime rates than sometimes supposed; the crucial size variable appears to be entirely *relative* to the cities' surrounds. One might also infer from these data that context-bound features of cities and their countrysides strongly affect their crime rates and keep them, as it were, closely related to each other.

The final article in this section, by Peter Scharf and his associates, draws attention to the function of violence in the administration of criminal justice. They deal with discretionary acts by policemen and point to the value of training programs in the development of more considerate and less rigid decisions on the part of officers faced with situations in which deadly force may be used. Their consideration of the "moral development" of policemen is novel and suggests one of the ways that modern developmental psychology may contribute to understanding, and perhaps to modification, of the criminal justice process, if only by clarifying what we can and cannot expect from the sort of brief training experience mounted by Scharf and his colleagues. Obviously violence by and against police is not the only issue of violence in the administration of criminal justice, although it is currently among the most debated. Violence in penal institutions and the death penalty are two obvious other instances.

The articles by Conrad, by Gurr, and by Archer and Gartner, especially, all leave us with the sense that changes in rates of violent crime have had little to do with changes in the criminal justice system. Lynn Curtis, reflecting on the implications of Berkowitz's findings, suggests that future changes in rates will have equally little to do with what he abhors as "the continued Vietnamization of the criminal justice system." Whether, in light of Silberman's speculations about the meaning of violent crime to its potential and actual victims, "continued Vietnamization," if it occurs, will serve to reduce fear about violent crime is, we think, equally questionable. One could entertain precisely the opposite conclusion: "more men, more equipment, more incursions, and swift and sure punishment to deter a nonwhite enemy whose psychology the white power brokers of this nation presume to understand," noted by Curtis, may serve to exacerbate fears "warranted by neither the facts at hand nor the canons of scientific inference."

NOTES

1. It should be noted, of course, that Berkowitz did not interview persons engaged in robbery. Silberman's account is substantially based on the responses of robbery ("mugging") victims. For an account that reduces this difference, see Robert Lejeune, "The Management of a Mugging," 6(2) *Urban Life* 123-148 (1977).

2. Ambivalence toward the thesis deserved emphasis. A seminal notion in modern studies of criminal violence, it is nowhere more sharply criticized than in Ruth Kornhauser's *Social Sources of Delinquency: An Appraisal of Analytic Models*. Chicago: University of Chicago Press, 1978, esp. pp. 186-189, from which a selection was published in the first volume of the *Yearbook*. Part of the difficulty, surely, lies in insufficient analysis of the implications of a strong conception of "culture." In a strong sense, a "culture" or "subculture" indicates something more than a differential propensity to engage in certain actions if conditions are right, and then to justify, or deny shame about, these actions. A strong idea of culture indicates putting a special value on such actions as ends in themselves or as means to an end and actively promoting this value.

3. A few scholars have "known" about the reduction in crime rates for some time, of course. A neglected example is Paul Reiwald, a European criminologist who celebrated the conquest of peace some 35 years ago in *Eroberung des Friedens*. (Zurich: Europa Verlag, 1944.) Writing in the midst of World War II, Reiwald treated as established the fact that violence had been banned from personal relations and that violent crime had been brought to an irreducible minimum. As Gurr's article shows, rates of violent crime did go down until the 1950s.

4. Archer and Gartner, as well as Gurr, note that Japan provides exceptions for generalizations otherwise apparently quite widely applicable. Japan is rapidly becoming the criminologist's counterpart to the gamesman's "south." Stephen Potter notes somewhere that whenever a generalization is offered, the proper gamesman always parries with the remark: All right, but what about the south?

CURING THE AMERICAN DISEASE
The Violent Predator on the Unsafe Streets

JOHN P. CONRAD

I

This incident happened in San Francisco on a spring evening in 1979. Dr. and Mrs. H— and another couple, the J—'s, had planned a Saturday dinner together at a restaurant, to be followed by a concert. The J—'s were to pick up the H—'s in their car; they were late, and in their hurry Dr. H— forgot his wallet. No problem, J— said when Dr. H— commented ruefully on his penniless situation; he had enough cash for all four.

The evening was enjoyed as planned. On the way back to Russian Hill, the H—'s decided that they would like to walk back to their apartment and asked to be let out. Strolling contentedly down a quiet residential street, they were suddenly accosted by a young black man who ordered them to stop and give him their money. Dr. H— protested that he had no money at all. The command was repeated. Dr. H— turned out his empty pockets. The robber fired his handgun. Dr. H— fell, shot in the upper abdomen. A woman who had heard the commotion from her bedroom window called an ambulance. Dr. H— survived the attack. The robber fled; so far as I know, he has yet to be apprehended.

In spite of impressions to the contrary, events of this kind are not commonplace in American cities. Most American never have personal knowledge of armed robberies, and not many are perpetrated in middle-class residential districts. Less-affluent neighborhoods are less fortunate. Victim surveys consistently show that the victims of violent crime are far more frequently black than white. Dr. H—'s assailant, we may be fairly sure, had not limited his depredations to comfortable white neighborhoods. Fear of him and of people like him pervades the inner city at night, but actual victims are few.

It is a staple of criminal justice discourse that the fear of violent crime destroys the trust on which the sense of community is built. Although even more wanton violence is frequent in many other countries, and although it is by no means new in the United States, American are not yet resigned to enduring it. It is supposed that an efficient system of criminal justice, enlightened, perhaps, by the discoveries of social science, would reduce to a tolerable level the hazards of the city streets. This belief animated Congress in the passing of the Omnibus Crime Control and Safe Streets Act of 1968, which brought the Law Enforcement Assistance Administration into being. More good things have ensued from this legislation than LEAA has received credit for, but the reduction of violent crime has not, so far, been one of them.

The federal interest in improving urban criminal justice has included provision for a huge expansion of criminology. An inconspicuous backwater of the social sciences hardly more than a decade ago, the number of its practitioners has now vastly increased. Research flourishes as never before, and much of interest and value has been extracted from data whisked through the computers. But it is now time to concede that empiricism has made very little headway in creating a new basis for preventing and controlling the violence that brought LEAA into being. Our understanding of the principles that should be observed in the management of the police, the courts, and the prisons has increased, and the training of personnel in every branch of criminal justice has been improved, as anyone with a long familiarity with the system can attest. Unfortunately, we have not succeeded at all in diverting potential robbers from violating the law. The rates of violent crime fluctuate independently of any influences that can be credited to the contributions of social science.

An empiricist myself, I will not allow that our work has been futile. Gradually, we are arriving at a consensus as to what should be done with the violent felon once he has fallen into the hands of the law. If personnel can be found to do what ought to be done, and if money can be found to enable them to do it, criminal justice in America need not be the clumsy and inept system that we now maintain. But although we can expect that the system will become more efficient in the performance of its functions and more humane in its treatment of the criminals it arrests, convicts, and locks up, we have little reason to expect that it will become significantly more effective in the prevention of crime and the control of criminals. Great discoveries toward these ends are not to be foreseen; we are most unlikely to break through to a new and happy state of enlightenment. We should continue our research for reasons that I hope to make plain later in this essay, but criminologists will never be acclaimed for wonderful changes in the rates of violence that we study so assiduously. If fewer citizens are subjected to the experience that Dr. H— and his wife survived, it will be because of remedies discovered for the insidious social pathology that afflicts modern America, not because the study of crime has evolved a solution to prevent it. Criminologists' have no difficulty in saying what needs to be done, but our polity lacks both the will and the program for doing it.

An inventory of the state of our knowledge and understanding of violent crime can be compressed into ten propositions of major significance. It will be seen that they do not lend themselves to the formulation of novel policy that promises dramatic changes of criminal justice for the better. Instead, they tend to establish boundaries around what it is possible to do.

In considering the brief inventory that follows, I have attempted a summary of what we know about criminal violence that can be used in making laws and policy. Each of the ten propositions to be presented has corollaries of importance, most of which I will not discuss. It is enough for my purposes here to sketch what we seem to know with a view to coming to conclusions about the extent to which increased knowledge may be expected to diminish violent crime. To proceed:

(1) There is a subculture of violence which is socially situated in the working class and the underclass. The idea of the subculture first came to the attention of criminologists in the work of Albert K. Cohen, whose *Delinquent Boys* concentrates on the sharing of variant norms among young men and boys.[1] The theory was adopted by Wolfgang and Ferracuti, whose *Subculture of Violence* is still the classic theoretical discourse on the cultural determinants of violent crime.[2] Their definitional statement sets an acceptable boundary for any discussion of the notion:

> A subculture implies that there are value judgements or a social value system which is apart from and a part of a larger or central value system. From the viewpoint of this larger, dominant culture, the values of the subculture set the latter apart and prevent total integration, occasionally causing open or covert conflicts. The dominant culture may directly or indirectly promote this apartness, of course, and the degree of reciprocal integration may vary, but whatever the reason for the difference, normative isolation and solidarity of the subculture result. There are shared values that are learned, adopted, and even exhibited by participants in the subculture, and that differ in quantity and quality from those of the dominant culture.[3]

The authors proceeded to a set of propositions describing the distinctive elements of a subculture of violence. The gist of these statements is that the subculture must interlock with the dominant culture, although its norms legitimate and require the use of violence for specific occasions. Not all participants in such a subculture will be overtly violent; situations requiring violent responses will not happen with any regularity in the lives of those committed to its norms. The authors stress that there must be a transmission of favorable attitudes toward the exercise of violence, but the existence of a subculture does not require that all its participants must partake of its values, or express these values in action. Necesarily psychological factors must be taken into account in considering the extent to which participants will differ in violent actions. Differing proneness to rage, hostility, and aggression must be expected among the members of any society, regardless of the norms that may legitimate or proscribe violence.[4]

Having gone so far with their conceptualization, the authors were cautious in accounting for it.[5] They limited their discussion of the origins of the violent subculture to the suggestion that there were probably many different ways in which subcultures germinate and thrive. Without empirical support for a bolder formulation, they left their theory in this incomplete form. They did not attempt to trace the beginnings and the mutagenesis of the subculture. They went on to a pair of speculations about social intervention with such subcultures, neither of which now seems helpful. The first proposal was:

> Predictable and positive prevention of additional crimes of violence is possible by social action that is designed (a) to disperse, disrupt, and disorganize the representatives of the subculture of violence, and at the same time (b) to effect changes in the system.[6]

Measures for accomplishing these ends are left to the reader's imagination. Despite the wide circulation and frequent and favorable citation of the theory of the subculture of violence this recommendation has yet to be translated into a program for action. We need not look far for the reasons for dismissing the idea as impractical. Relatively small subcultures such as the Italian Red Brigade or the Irish Revolutionary Army have carefully organized themselves to be as invulnerable as possible to disruption and dispersion, and it is becoming apparent that any change in the system short of their demands will be unacceptable. To a lesser degree, the same is true of organized crime groups in this country. Uncertainties regarding the organization and structure of the American "Mafia"—if it exists in the tightly hierarchial form that some observers suppose—show how difficult it will be to act on the Wolfgang-Ferracuti recommendation when we are not sure what it is we are to disrupt and disperse.

At an even more intractable level, we have to face the vast subculture of violence to be encountered in the American inner city. It is not clear from the authors' analysis that they have in mind the application of their theory to black or Hispanic urban phenomena. Surely it would be slanderous to suppose that all inner-city blacks or Hispanics are committed to a subculture that accounts for the high incidence of violent crimes in their communities. But it is incontestable that the rates of violent crime are very high in cities with populous concentrations of these minorities. Adherence to the prevailing values of the dominant culture is certainly general in these communities; unless this were the case most American cities would be uninhabitable. But inspection of the violent crime rates reported in the Uniform Crime Reports or in the victimization surveys prepared under the joint auspices of the Law Enforcement Assistance Administration and the Bureau of the Census indicates all too clearly that there is a tragic association between violence and minority status in this country. The subcultural determinants are easy to conjecture. Communities of chronically unemployed people who perceive themselves as the victims of discrimination will develop norms that are significantly different from those of the dominant culture. Adversity and deprivation will loosen the consensus against violence and often will motivate it. These processes are obvious, of course, and they are facilitated by the separation of minority communities from the dominant society.

A suggestion of the power of this influence is contained in Curtis's *Criminal Violence*.[7] In his analysis of the incidence of violent crime in major American cities, Curtis found that if socioeconomic status is held constant, there is no significant correlation between rates of violence and the percentage of the population that is black in poor sections of Boston, Atlanta, and San Francisco. But in Chicago and Philadelphia this correlation is significant. To Curtis this finding from an admittedly exploratory study suggested that there is some connection between the very large concentrations of blacks in inner cities and disproportionate rates of violent crime. Curtis's data indicate that a population of 500,000 may be the critical level.

Much more work must be done with this straw in the wind before it can be turned into an explanatory hypothesis. However, its superficial plausibility is suggestive and ominous. It does not call for a high flight of imagination to infer that as a poor black population increases in volume individuals living in it create a subculture that is influenced by the dominant culture in inverse proportion to its numbers. If this is true, the dimension of numbers becomes a critical element in the study of any subculture, particularly the subculture of violence.

Whether Curtis's preliminary hypothesis is confirmed or not, the usefulness of this approach to the understanding of violent crime is obviously great, even if neither criminologist nor policy maker can think of ways to take advantage of the knowledge gained. A subculture whose participants number in the hundreds of thousands is not to be dispersed or disrupted. If Wolfgang and Ferracuti's recommendation for change in the system is to be followed, the essential change must be a solution to the unemployment of youth. That has yet to be contrived, despite general acknowledgment of its urgency.

Wolfgang and Ferracuti present as their second recommendation a comparably difficult set of prescriptions:

> Therapy in correctional institutions is most effective with assaultive offenders from a subculture of violence if (a) the offenders are not permitted to retain their collective and supportive homogeneity in prison; (b) values contrary to the subculture of violence are infused into their personality structure and into the prison social system with clarity and commitment by the therapists; (c) these inmates are brought to the point of anomic anxiety; and (d) they are not returned to the subculture of origin.[8]

No one can doubt that significant positive results would be achieved if it were in the power of prison authorities to accomplish a program of this kind. But even step (a) has proved next to impossible. Jacobs's account of gang activities at Stateville vividly shows how stubborn is the homogeneity of street groups.[9] Where the power of social control by a coercive authority falls so far short of its goal, it must not be supposed that values contrary to the subculture of violence will be successfully infused, anomic anxiety will be achieved, or released prisoners will be prevented from returning to the subculture that held them in allegiance while they were confined.

So far the idea of a subculture has produced little or nothing of practical value for the prevention and control of violent crime by the police, courts, or corrections. Perhaps its ineffectiveness must be attributed to its assumptions. The dominant culture cannot possibly change the subculture by unilateral measures of its own. Small cohesive subcultures like the Irish Republican Army will modify their murderous ways only by the gradual realization that they are ineffectual in the achievement of their goals. The hope must be that negotiation can then take place which will defuse the ideology that requires violence. The fostering of alternate political movements which reach goals consistent with those of such a subculture as the IRA without the repellent violence to which the subculture is committed will assist greatly in bringing about this remote objective.

Likewise, the violence that festers in the inner cities of America cannot possibly be dissolved by the measures suggested by Wolfgang and Ferracuti. No matter how heavy the hand with which the police powers are exercised, it cannot be heavy enough to bring about the dispersion, disruption, and disorganization proposed. If there is a solution to the inner-city subculture of violence, it must be found in the inner city itself. It will help if the economy can find productive places for the thousands of unemployed black young men and women who must find alternatives to crime. But leadership of the inner-city culture must be acceptable to the inner city itself. It will have to be magnetic indeed to draw young people away from the values so heedlessly thrust on them by the dominant culture.

This consideration of the Wolfgang-Ferracuti hypothesis of a subculture of violence leads to the conclusion that, if it can be confirmed, it is of no practical use. The proponents' recommendations for putting into effect policies derived from the theory are clearly not feasible under the most favorable of circumstances. It is almost axiomatic that circumstances are seldom if ever favorable for programming improved control of crime.

It is difficult to suppress the question of whether the idea of a subculture of violence has sufficient validity to be a useful concept. I have already noted that the majority of those in the social classes from which the subculture of violence is supposed to emanate are neither violent nor accepting of the values that support violence. To suppose that there is some underlying predisposition to violence in the disadvantaged social classes which erupts only in a minority, a small minority, in these strata of our society borders on mysticism. Evidence for the existence of such a subculture is scanty and strung together with conjectures. Kornhauser puts it this way:

> One searches throughout Wolfgang and Ferracuti's book for the few pages that present any evidence of a subculture in which violence may be valued. The "evidence" finally unearthed consists of the recital of a few statistics and allusion to a few studies, all of which merely record frequencies of violent behavior. Homicide is most common [among] poor, black, young urban males. Child-rearing studies show the lower socioeconomic strata more often resort to physical punishment of their children, who are said to be more likely also to settle disputes with their fists. And that is all. While the authors concede that no culture could ever value in-group violence, they assert with aplomb that a subculture can do just that.[10]

The Wolfgang-Ferracuti concept fails because it is absurd to postulate a culture as distinguished by one phenomenon of behavior. This defect should be apparent from their own definition of the term "subculture" as quoted at the outset of this section. Violence has many differing origins, functions, and meanings. A youthful gangster protecting his turf in the inner city uses violence for far different purposes from the Irish Republican Army guerrilla planting a time bomb. It does not increase our understanding of violence or of those who perpetrate it to refer to a subcultural origin, even if such an origin could be intelligibly defined.

It is undeniably true that social disorganization is a process which differentially affects the social classes in any society. One of the major features of the process is the erosion of social control, and a symptom of that condition is the violation of those norms expressed in the criminal law. Much better to study these processes and the forces that may retard or accelerate them than to suppose that we can identify a subculture whose principal feature is a commitment to violence. The processes that have produced violence have also produced many other social pathologies which are also destructive but which cause less fear in the comfortable classes.

(2) There is an overrepresentation of blacks among both violent offenders and their victims. It is important to note that no other minority is so prone to violence or so afflicted with it as the blacks. Attempts to explain away the data produced by police statistics and victim surveys are futile evasions of stubborn and unwelcome facts. Criminological literature dealing with this topic has been sparse. It has fallen to Charles Silberman, a careful journalist, to bring out the disagreeable association between blackness and violent crime.[11] His data are by no means as rigorous as a strict social scientist would like, but few social scientists, strict or otherwise, have ventured to chart this thicket.

Noting that in New York City Puerto Rican and black populations are roughly comparable in size, but that Puerto Ricans are significantly poorer than blacks (the median Puerto Rican income being 20 percent lower than the median black income), Silberman suggests that if violent crime is merely the function of poverty and social class, the incidence of violent crime among Puerto Ricans should be at least as high, if not higher than among blacks. But police data for 1970-1972 show that 63 percent of the arrests for violent crime were of blacks, whereas 15.3 percent of those arrested were Hispanic. Similar data were marshaled for a comparison of violence among California blacks with that among Chicanos.

It is not possible to devise a statistical solvent for the inevitable inference from these crude data. To attribute these disparities to a racist system of criminal justice is to propose that the animus of the police against blacks exceeds by far their prejudice against Puerto Ricans or Chicanos and that the police are allowed to overlook the most serious categories of crimes when committed by persons of any race but blacks. On the contrary, it is often and credibly argued that the police are likely to overlook crimes of the utmost gravity when commited by blacks against blacks. Exact measurements in matters of this kind are never possible. If there were a rough parity in the data of black crime and Hispanic crime, we might attribute high rates of violence to the factors common to both minorities: excessively rapid urbanization, welfare poverty, lack of economic opportunity, and similar factors that have affected dislocated populations plunged into our metropolitan melting pots. That rough parity does not exist. The reasons for the extraordinary rates of black crime must be sought in the black experience itself, uniquely different from the experience of any other minority in America.

The obvious need not be labored. Violence and race are associated. Depending on one's predilection for theoretical refinement, many explanations of this association lie ready to hand, but the cure is elusive. It depends on the accomplishment of immense changes in our urban economic arrangements. Black unemployment must be seen as destructive not only to those who must endure it but also to the whole community. The dilapidated slums in which the black poor stagnate in fury or apathy, depending on their susceptibility to illusions, must become as intolerable to the comfortable as they are to those who live in them. The slum schools must be transformed from custodial facilities into oases of hope for the disadvantaged young.

The magnitude of the changes that must be made has baffled all who have honestly confronted them. But crime and misery are inextricably associated. We shall not be substantially relieved of the former until there has been an abatement of the latter. The misery of the black poor is of a different order from the miseries that other Americans face. The violence exploding in our ghettos must be read as signals of the urgency of social justice.

(3) Recidivist offenders commit a disproportionate share of violent crimes. The classic birth cohort study of Wolfgang, Figlio, and Sellin is by now too well known to require a summary here.[12] It provides the first and most convincing empirical proof of what most police have thought they always knew: Repetitive criminals commit far more than their share of serious crimes. It will be recalled that Wolfgang and his associates defined those members of their cohort who had more than four violations as *chronic recidivists.* These boys constituted 18 percent of the delinquents identified in the cohort. They committed more than 51 percent of all the recorded offenses charged against the whole cohort. Using the Sellin-Wolfgang scale of offense seriousness,[13] it was found that not only do chronic offenders commit more crimes than less persistent offenders but the crimes they commit are significantly more serious.

A more recent study of violent juveniles in Columbus, Ohio, arrived at a similar finding.[14] In a cohort of 811 persons arrested once or more often for index violent offenses, it was found that 33.6 percent were chronic recidivists. This group was responsible for 44.8 percent of the violent offenses committed by the whole cohort.

No similar study of adult violent criminals has yet been completed. Preliminary findings from another Columbus investigation with which I have been associated appear to lead to a similar conclusion.[15] This project traced the careers of about 1600 persons arrested for the commission of index violent crimes in the period 1950-1975. There is no doubt that the recidivists committed a disproportionate share of all the violent offenses recorded for the sample—and of the nonviolent offenses, too. The well-known Rand studies[16] carried out by Greenwood and Petersillia, although based on self-reported data, lead to the conclusion that chronic or "intensive" offenders are responsible for an enormous number of crimes, although it is not clear how many of these crimes were violent.[17]

The true outlines of the dilemma of sanctions for serious crime are now apparent. Incarceration of juvenile offenders, and almost certainly of adults, too, confirms the recidivist in his criminal career. Those who return to crime will return more quickly after each release from custodial control. On the other hand, considerations of incapacitation and deterrence (to which I shall presently come) seem to require increasing severity which can only be expressed in long periods of imprisonment. It is not difficult to project a plausible set of alternative sanctions for property offenders. They are not likely to improve their behavior in the long run when subjected to systematic supervision in the community, but we can expect that the harm they do will endanger no one's life or limb. The risk presented by a violent offender is of a different order. If he is a first offender charged with a violent crime, the circumstances must be very favorable if he is to be released to surveillance in the community. If he is a recidivist, realism compels the recognition that the risk of another crime, while far from a certainty, is sufficient to rule out any such disposition, even though it must be expected that his return to crime after release from prison will be rapid, though not necessarily violent

Further research may lead to a more hopeful balance of these conflicting considerations. But it is unlikely that we can escape the unattractive dilemma presented by the research accumulated so far. We cannot lock up enough offenders for long enough to protect the community from them, but in locking them up at all we confirm them in long and active criminal careers.

(4) Prediction of a violent offense is insufficiently effective to improve on mere chance. Many writers in the popular literature of criminal justice criticism have argued that if we cannot reform criminals, we can at least incapacitate them.[18] This utilitarian objective has attracted the teleologically minded since the time of Jeremy Bentham,[19] and its logic is airtight, if exceedingly simple. A convicted criminal cannot harm anyone but his guards and his fellow prisoners so long as he is kept in prison. It follows that if we select for incarceration those criminals who present the most serious dangers to society we will reduce the number of crimes they can commit during their careers. I shall explore this notion further in section 5, below.

To ascribe dangerousness to a criminal is to make a prediction about him. It is important therefore to examine the status of the prediction of criminality, especially violent criminality, after years of exhaustive and ingenious statistical work. There can hardly be a full-fledged criminologist who is unfamiliar with the contributions of the long list of distinguished social scientists who have given years of their attention to this problem; in a modest way, it has been for criminology what Fermat's last theorem still is to mathematicians. The list is long and the work it represents is surely important. The concentration of minds like Sam Bass Warner, Ernest Burgess, Lloyd Ohlin, Daniel Glaser, Hermann Mannheim and Leslie Wilkins, Don Gottfredson, Frances Simon, Ernst Wenk, and James Robison—to list only some of the most persistent and ingenious— brought into focus for them many issues to which they subsequently turned with more fruitful consequences. That statistical prediction has its uses for the conduct of research cannot be doubted. Its usefulness is zero for the purpose of forecasting the commission of a violent crime by a particular offender. We do not have any reason to suppose that our predictive powers will dramatically improve. Without a valid or reliable method of predicting danger, which we cannot conceivably have at a level remotely approaching certainty, there are only two possible bases for a policy of incapacitation. We can rely on intuition exercised by the sentencing authority, recognizing that there are many honest differences in intuition that will flaw the appearance of justice. Or we can declare that any class of violent offenders for whom the risk of further violence exceeds some established level—perhaps 30 percent—constitutes an unacceptable hazard to the community and therefore may be incarcerated for an extended period. In the next section I shall return to the grave implications of any such policy.

The prediction of recidivism has arrived at some certainties. The base expectancy methods created by Mannheim, Wilkins, and Gottfredson, and for many years in irregular use in California, could forecast with nearly absolute certainty the nonrecidivism of some occasional offenders, as, for example, men and women who had committed crimes of passion. They could also identify the equally certain recidivists, usually petty thieves who had few alternatives to crime if they were to maintain their preferred style of life. Between were offenders falling into groups whose chances hung in various balances—40-60, 50-50, 60-40, and so on. Not only were these probabilities indefinite and incapable of refinement as to any individual falling into groups whose chances were so defined, but it was impossible to formulate a prediction as to if or when any such individual would commit a crime of violence.

A further objection, not often mentioned in the literature, is that all predictions about recidivism must be made from experience with men released from prison who have had an opportunity to commit crimes. As to those who are not released, or who are retained for periods extending into their dotage, or nearly so, the prediction is foregone—made by the judge or the paroling authority who decided to continue their retention in custody.

But the most formidable objection to the use of prediction methods in deciding how violent offenders shall be sentenced turns on the ineffectiveness of all known means of predicting the commission of a violent crime by any particular person. In his elegant review of the uses of prisons, Norval Morris contributed an assessment of the empirical status of parole prediction on the use of the concept to determine dangerousness.[20] For a full understanding of Morris's position, the reader must turn to his book; I must be content with a brief summary of a wonderfully compressed argument.

Morris relied primarily on the work of Wenk, Robison, and Smith for this demonstration that it is impossible to predict a violent crime with sufficient reliability to allow its use in sentencing practice.[21] That study, based on California data, led to a finding that predictions of violent crime as to felons to be released on parole would be wrong in 86 to 95 percent of the cases. The somewhat better results claimed by Kozol, Boucher, and Garofalo still produced an unacceptable percentage of false-positive predictions—i.e., predictions of violent behavior that were not realized in fact.[22] That study is open to the same objection I have made above; we must face the certainty that relatively few of the predictors' unfavorable predictions were tested in the community. Indeed, we must suppose that the 49 individuals who were predicted to commit a violent act must have been considered by those who released them as persons who had a better chance of postrelease success than those who were retained in custody. It is at least probable, if not subject to demonstration, that if all the persons who might be considered dangerous were released, the proportion of false-positives in that total would fall drastically. Empirical proof of this or any similar proposition is most unlikely.

Finally, some light is shed on the false-positive problem by work recently published by the Columbus group in which I have played a part.[23] In that work, we examined the known criminal careers of 164 individuals arrested and charged in Columbus in 1966 for the commission of violent crimes. We made the hypothetical supposition that all these violent offenders, only 21 of whom served sentences of five years or more, were sentenced to uniform terms of five years in prison. Tracing all the arrest histories for these individuals, we found that only 9, or fewer than 5.5 percent of the cohort studied, were reconvicted for a violent crime. No policy of incapacitation could be based on predictions as inefficient as that.

Morris divided the methods of prediction into three types: intuitive, categoric, and anamnestic. His finding that there is no empirical evidence that any of these kinds of prediction is reliable in the prediction of a violent act is convincingly demonstrated by the research available. There is no research that gives us reason to believe that as to the prediction of a violent crime—rather than the commission of *any* crime—results better than those approaching mere chance can be produced.

Elsewhere, I have argued that there can never be a practical method for the prediction of violent acts.[24] I hold that the prediction of any future event depends on regularities characteristic of natural processes in the physical environment. A violent act cannot be said to be the consequence of any such natural process. It is the consequence of the convergence of many forces, some natural, but most of them social. The randomness of such situations is irremediable, and any attempt to predict such convergence will inevitably produce more false-positives than true.

(5) A policy of incapacitation for the purpose of reducing the incidence of violent crime cannot succeed without incurring enormous economic and human costs. Nothing can be expected from the manipulation of crime statistics that will make possible a system capable of predicting the violent behavior of any person to be sentenced. But predictive methods have never been of much interest to legislators and judges, let alone to the general public. What does seem reasonable is the notion that locking up criminals for longer periods of time should bring about some relief from the dread of crime.

The simplest way of achieving this goal would be to make statutory changes as to the sentences to be imposed on certain classes of criminals to be defined in the law. Legislatures are prone to make such changes with just such an aim at times when public alarm about crime puts them under pressure to take action on the crime problem. To add substantially to a minimum sentence for a class of crimes certainly proclaims a heightened disapproval and provides whatever satisfaction there may be in increasing the gravity of the consequences for those criminals who are caught. Common sense suggests that, in addition, greater stringency should reduce crime by reducing the population of criminals free to commit it.

This supposition is true enough, but the reduction cannot be very great, and the costs are so enormous that the systematic application of such a policy would radically transform both the criminal justice system and society as a whole. The demonstration of this proposition depends on a simple method of research which will produce well defined conclusions from which orderly speculations can be made.

In a study which my colleagues and I have published recently, the potentiality of augmented severity for the reduction of violent crime was tested.[25] With access to the records of the Court of Common Pleas of Franklin County, Ohio—the county in which Columbus is situated—we decided on a series of statistical experiments. There were 342 adults arrested in 1973 and charged with the commission of 638 violent crimes. From the Uniform Crime Reports for that year, we found that 2892 crimes of violence were reported to the police departments of Franklin County. The question for which we sought an approximate answer was: *How many of those 2892 crimes might have been prevented had each offender who had previously been found guilty of any felony been sentenced to a flat five-year term in prison?*

Putting values on our certainties was easy enough. Of the 342 adults who were arrested, 63 (18.4 percent) had had a felony conviction during the previous five years. They were charged with 111 counts of violent crime, or 3.8 percent of the 2892 crimes committed in 1973. The remaining 279 persons arrested could not have been prevented from committing their 1973 crimes because they were first offenders in that year, or, in a few cases, persons who had committed their last previous felony before 1968.

There were also 126 juveniles who were charged with 154 violent offenses in 1973. Of that number, 33 had had previous charges at the felony level since 1968 and, had they been committed to five years of confinement, the 35 offenses with which they were charged could also have been prevented.

The total of 111 adult charges and 34 juvenile charges constitutes about 5 percent of the 2892 violent crimes of 1973, all that could have been certainly prevented by the imposition of a five-year sentence on the occasion when the criminal justice system had its chance to restrain them. Clearly, more crimes would have been prevented, but after all the data had been manipulated for all they were worth, the final answer is shrouded in the "dark figure of crime," the crimes for which the police were unable to make a clearance. Mixing as much information as we could with our speculations, we arrived at the conclusion that the percentage of violent crimes that the known recidivists could have committed in 1973 lay between 25 and 35 percent.[26] It follows that any policy of incapacitation that provided for a five-year sentence for any felony could not have prevented 65 to 75 percent of the violent crimes committed.

The experiment was deliberately set at a draconian level of sentencing. No court in the land has ever imposed uniform five-year sentences for all felonies, nor has any legislature considered such a statute. Our calculation was intended to find out how many crimes could have been prevented even at this extreme. The answer is that a not inconsiderable number could have been prevented, but the cost would have been prohibitive. To commit the criminal justice system to such a policy would require the state of Ohio to increase its prison population from about 9000 to about 42,000 at least, and quite possibly more if extrapolations are made from the 1972 figures on which that estimate was based. For Ohio, the economic cost would have to be based on the addition of about 30,000 cells to its present dilapidated prison structures at costs which could not be less than $50,000 per cell, or a total investment of $1.5 billion. The human costs of a system in which the net was spread so wide to catch so many of the poor, black, and disadvantaged would be impossible to estimate, but it would begin with a pervading sense of injustice, angering the poor and troubling the comfortable.

Less severe sanctions would result in much less prevention. A three-year sentence for any felony would prevent about 11 percent of the crimes to be ascribed to adults, but it would result in increasing the prison population to about 29,000. Limiting the mandatory term to a five-year sentence for a violent felony would have prevented only 16 of the 2892 violent offenses; even if this figure is quadrupled, to allow for crimes committed by persons arrested but not charged, less than 2 percent of the 1973 crimes of violence would have been prevented.

This set of conclusions does not touch the propriety of severe and incapacitating sentences administered to individual violent offenders whose past record and future prospects indicate to the common sense of the judge or the parole board that prudence dictates such dispositions. On this point, Morris's conservatism in limiting sanctions to just desert collides with the recognition that even though risks cannot be mathematically computed they can be estimated by a review of the past and a consideration of the future. As to the justice of such a decision, social science must be silent; though it can be said that the prediction of a third violent act by an offender who has committed two will be incorrect at least

50 percent of the time, it must be conceded that a person who presents a risk of future violence at such a level differs sufficiently from the general population to justify his restraint.

No discussion of incapacitation policies and studies would be complete without mention of the exhaustive review commissioned by the National Academy of Sciences and carried out under the direction of Blumstein, Cohen, and Nagin.[27] The review conducted by these scholars was based on a half-dozen studies in which various data, some real, some hypothetical, were subjected to mathematical model-building processes. Assumptions were made about the rate of commission of uncleared crimes and the rates of recidivism, all tending to show so much variation from each other as to demonstrate that an incapacitation policy based on categoric prediction is not now possible. Although these writers scrupulously refrain from the conclusion that such a policy can never be created (they have many recommendations for further research), it seems most unlikely to me that further light from this pattern of research will eventually shine on a solid basis for categoric incapacitation. By its very nature, justice depends on the wise use of discretion. That exercise must always provide for the uses of informed intuition.

(6) There is no empirical evidence to support any proposition concerning the deterrence of violent crime. In common with members of all cultures affected by utilitarian thought, Americans are persistent teleologists. It is quite generally believed that the criminal law should deter potential offenders from deciding to commit a crime. It follows from this view of the law that if crime is increasing the remedy is an increase in the penalties meted out by the courts. Reviewing their own behavior with respect to driving motor vehicles or preparing an income tax return, most people reason that robbers, rapists, and other violent men and women will make their decisions about proceeding with a crime in light of their expectations of arrest and of the probable sanction to be imposed. The possibility of such a calculus was first introduced by Jeremy Bentham in the late eighteenth century, and it has permeated thought about criminal justice ever since.

It was not always thus. For Immanuel Kant and most continental moral philosophers before and since, it was simply wrong to subordinate a man's fate to the objectives of the law. For Kant, a punishment should be imposed

> only on the ground that [the criminal] has committed a crime; for a human being can never be manipulated merely as a means to the purposes of someone else and can never be confused with the objects of the Law. . . . The law concerning punishment is a categorical imperative, and woe to him who rummages around in the winding paths of a theory of happiness looking for some advantage to be gained by releasing the criminal from punishment or by reducing the amount of it.[28]

Kant's view of criminal justice was strictly retributionist, allowing judges to settle penalties by no other criteria than the nature and gravity of the crime itself. His application of the retributive principle was stringent indeed, and few would wish to revive the *lex talionis* in the form prescribed in Kant's *General Theory of Justice.* But the principles prescribed by Kant are the same that animate von

Hirsch and his colleagues in their report on the purposes of incarceration, *Doing Justice*.[29] The idea of the just desert as the basis for punishment releases the criminal law from the obligation to rummage around in the winding paths of utilitarianism.

Until criminal justice is relieved of its teleological burdens, research on deterrence can be justified to scholar and public alike as necessary to judgments about the value of measures designed to reduce the rate of crime by adjusting police activity and criminal sentences. Of all domains of criminological research, the study of general deterrence must be the most conceptually intricate. To begin with, it is obvious that there is no direct empirical means for determining the number of persons who might commit a crime but who decide not to because of their estimate of the probability of arrest and the severity of the punishment that would be inflicted. Only indirect means can provide clues about the influence of the negative incentives of the criminal law on the incidence of crime in general or specific crimes which might be studied individually. Economists set considerable store on mathematical models transplanted from the market, apparently believing that economic man and criminal man have a close family resemblance. Palmer's comprehensive review of the literature describes the methodology and recapitulates the results, but encourages no practical application.[30] Subsequent to that review, Nagin's long and detailed summary of the literature on deterrence provides an unrivaled perspective of the achievements and potentialities of research on general deterrence.[31] Readers interested in informing themselves about these ingenious and difficult studies must consult Nagin's admirably clear but compressed article; its recapitulation here will not be attempted.

Nagin's conclusion, however, deserves attention for its refreshingly candid realism. After noting that his review has drawn on over 20 published studies completed in less than a decade of intense effort, Nagin writes:

> The empirical evidence is still not sufficient for providing a rigorous confirmation of the existence of a deterrent effect. Perhaps more important, the evidence is woefully inadequate for providing a good estimate of the magnitude of whatever effect may exist. . . .

> This is in stark contrast to some of the presentations in public discussion that have unequivocally concluded that sanctions deter and that have made sweeping suggestions that sanctioning practices be changed to take advantage of the presumed deterrent effect. Certainly, most people will agree that increasing sanctions will deter crime somewhat, but the critical question is, By how much? There is still considerable uncertainty over whether that effect is trivial (even if statistically detectable) or profound. Any unequivocal policy recommendation is simply not supported by the evidence.[32]

Leaving aside for the moment the feasibility of more research on the deterrent effect of police efficiency and sanctioning severity, it is appropriate to inquire as to how the criminologist would expect the policy maker to act on unequivocal evidence if it could somehow be collected and confirmed. If the deterrent effect is trivial, it is obvious that even the firmest of utilitarians will concede that one of the pillars of his philosophy has crumbled. If, on the other hand, it is discovered that the deterrent effect is "profound" numerous questions will arise as to what to do with it. It is unlikely, to say the least, that deterrence operates in identical fashion for all crimes. A heavy fine and the certain prospect of having one's car towed away will deter most motorists from illegal parking. Empirical evidence of this proposition is readily obtainable, and policy on illegal parking can take it into account, although in this case the need for research for the confirmation of policy is questionable.

As to the violent crimes, the situation is likely to differ from community to community and from crime to crime. Assuming that the deterrent effect is significantly but differentially profound for each offense and from place to place, how is the law to be changed? How profound an effect would justify increasing police patrols by some large percentage, when the empirical evidence so far shows that increasing patrol activity has little or no value in reducing crime?[33] To what extent must we increase our already heavy sentencing policy to take advantage of a profound deterrent effect? Is it to be believed that the demonstration of a deterrent effect in a statistical table would induce the police to be more zealous in their detection of crimes against the person or the prosecutor to be more remorseless in his determination to obtain convictions of violent offenders?

Questions such as these would have to be asked if a working party were about to embark on a straightforward, methodologically simple program of research to assess the value of the deterrent effect. But the difficulties in the way of arriving at any answer at any level of confidence for the question of general deterrence are so formidable as to be considered insuperable. Nagin lists some of them. The establishment of crime rates depends on the reporting of crimes to the police, which always results in gross understatements. The reporting of the sanctions imposed is even more inaccurate. Victimization surveys and police reports may roughly establish the volume of crime for limited purposes, but systematic records of dispositions have never been kept by any statistical agency, and are not now being kept. It is impossible to establish valid ratios between the numbers of crimes committed and the number of arrests made, or the number of arrests to the number of convictions to say nothing at all of the number of the various possible dispositions to the number of convictions. These are soluble problems— at least in principle—but any work done with data now available must be wildly speculative, useful only as a private exercise in model-building.

(7) Violent criminal careers tend to be extinguished at age 35-40. The Columbus study of violent careers is the prime source of empirical evidence of this statement, and, at this writing, it has not yet been published.[34] However, in a study of nearly 1600 careers that included one or more violent crime, my colleagues and I found that the number of violent offenses committed after age 35 dropped sharply from that shown in previous age-groups. After age 40 the number was negligible; most of that group were persons who had committed crimes of passion.

This finding merely confirms another fact that the police have always thought they knew. Criminals in general and violent criminals especially "burn out" as they approach middle age. Why this is so may still be debated, and the data my colleagues and I have collected do not shed light on the reasons for extinction of violent careers. Some writers have attributed the termination of criminal careers to the processes of maturation and in doing so come close to a tautology: If the termination of a criminal career is attributable to maturation and if the evidence of maturation is the termination of criminal behavior, our understanding has not been increased.

What is of practical importance is the recognition that incarceration of violent offenders past the age of 40 serves no purpose as to their intimidation or incapacitation. If sanctioning policy is determined by the intention to incapacitate the offender, the value of incapacitation past the later thirties or the early forties is slight. Likewise, it must be redundant to intimidate an offender whose advancing years are probably intimidating him already. For the retributivist these questions are irrelevant; punishment must be carried out according to just desert rather than with reference to lessened inclination to commit crime.

There is much more that ought to be known about the natural history of a criminal career. Our reliance on arrest records and prison files allows us little insight into what happens to an offender after his exit from the career of crime. Most confirmed violent offenders spend so many of their adult years in the abnormal circumstances of confinement that their capability for a normal social and economic life is seriously reduced. Sentencing policy for the violent offender who is approaching middle age should allow for preparations that will at least give him an alternative to thievery.

(8) *There is little evidence that biological or genetic influences are significantly related to the incidence of violent crime.* The demolition of the Lombrosian hypothesis did not dissuade those who are inclined to think in Lombrosian terms. While the crudities of Lombroso's notions would attract no thoughtful person today, the eagerness with which some greeted the discovery of the XYY chromosome anomaly as a determinant of violent crime shows that Lombrosianism dies hard. Citizens who believe themselves to be normal want to put as much distance as they can between themselves and those who must be considered dangerous. If the dangerous are truly different from the rest of humanity, then the rest of us are unlikely to become dangerous and those who are can justifiably be treated differently.

If they really exist, the biological substrates of violent behavior have not yet been demonstrated to be innate. That traumatic events and disease can bring about chronic conditions that dispose the individual to violence cannot be doubted.[35] Most physicians and surely all forensic psychiatrists are familiar with conditions of these kinds. What is lacking is any research on their prevalence. We simply do not know how much violent crime can be attributed to brain abnormalities. We do know that many such conditions can be relieved with psychoactive drugs and others can be dealt with, at some risk—many would say unacceptable risks—of irreversible damage. Because some especially horrifying crimes of violence can be traced to brain abnormalities, it is to the general advantage to pursue further research into the origins, the natural course, and the treatment of these grave conditions. It is troubling to observe that in the present state of knowledge treatment for some otherwise hopeless conditions cannot be administered because of the impossibility of obtaining informed consent from a patient who is inaccessible to information by the very nature of his mental situation.

There is no reason to believe that the incidence of violent crime is largely affected by these brain conditions, even though it is credible that they cause some of the most serious crimes of all. What is much more troubling is the ancient puzzle of psychopathy. Psychiatric theory has made little headway with the definition of the term, the etiology of the disease, or the standards for therapy since the term was first introduced in the nineteenth century. The textbook symptoms are vague, usually impossible to subject to strict verification, and tend to circularity.[36] It is not too much to say that for some clinicians the principal objective symptom of psychopathy is a criminal record. A canon of treatment is not to be found, and not much successful research leading to an appropriate therapy has been reported. Some success has been indicated in the administration of imipramine and similar medications, but research has not advanced to the point that treatment is standard or its potential verified.[37]

In spite of the chronic conceptual disarray of the study of psychopathy, few who have been exposed to large numbers of offenders doubt that the symptoms so offhandedly listed by Cleckley[38] are characteristics of criminals. Indeed, the recent work of Yochelson and Samenow is largely an elaboration of Cleckley's clinical symptomatology.[39] What is lacking is an understanding of its etiology and a basis for classifying its subtypes. Many of the symptoms attributed to the condition have a good deal more to do with the cultural influences bearing on persons with long experience of criminal behavior and its consequences. The necessary and sufficient connections between the condition and any kind of violent crime have yet to be convincingly demonstrated.

(9) There are no predictably effective rehabilitative treatments for violent offenders. Leaving out of our consideration the offender whose violence is a solitary incident in an otherwise law-abiding lifetime, the repetitively violent criminal is a sufficiently unusual individual to justify the assumption that something must be wrong with him. Whatever that may be, no one has arrived at a generalization that leads to a successful treatment rationale. As I have suggested above, there is an empirically established correlation between the approach of middle age and the extinction of a career of violence. The prevalent notion that rehabilitative programs do not "work" has led to some confessions of futility, and psychotherapeutic procedures for imprisoned offenders of any kind are no longer as prevalent as they were ten and twenty years ago.

Offenders who persist in violence in prison are usually, almost invariably, consigned to administrative segregation where, with some adjustment to allow for due process in response to federal court rulings, they are kept for long periods of time. The effects of such protracted isolation from the main prison community are thought by many to make a bad condition worse, whereas others, particularly their custodians, see no alternative if the safety of the prison is to be maintained. But whatever the truth of the matter may be, there has never been a serious assessment of these effects. What is certain is that for these unusual criminals no coherent attempt has been made to modify their behavior pattern in any fundamental way. Psychiatric contact with them is cursory, usually limited to the administration of sedatives to the excited.

But most violent offenders are tractable enough when sent to prison. Their rate of recidivism is lower than that of property offenders—much lower in the case of murderers and rapists—and it must be assumed that for many the processes of intimidation have deterred them from further offending, together with the effects of aging, as mentioned already. Does this bleak inference indicate that efforts to change behavior by various forms of psychotherapy are futile or redundant? I think such a conclusion is blocked by a volume of anecdotal evidence which cannot be disregarded. There are far too many examples of extraordinarily violent individuals who have been exposed to situations that were intended to be therapeutic and for whom the results were positive. The prediction of success in psychotherapy is far from infallible, and it is not likely to improve in accuracy. Its positive benefits can seldom suffice to offset the misadventures and adverse conditions of ordinary living. But it is one of the few positive offerings at the disposal of the correctional apparatus, and its cost is modest in comparison with money spent on maintaining a prisoner in his cell. We do well to encourage it, even if the benefits are uncertain and sometimes difficult to discern.

Certain disappointment awaits those who think that rehabilitation should become a "technology" capable of delivering recipes for transforming violent criminals into productive citizens. Anthony Burgess's *A Clockwork Orange* is rooted in the bad theory of aversive treatment, not in successful application. I doubt that any responsible clinician who has undertaken to treat violent criminals has seriously believed that such a system was feasible. But if by "rehabilitation" we mean that imagination can contrive an environment in which new choices can be made by troubled men and women so that they can discover for themselves new ways of living, then some fragments of evidence exist to indicate that modest successes may lie in this direction. It is a route that has been infrequently traveled. It deserves the initiative of the social inventor.

(10) There is no evidence of a deterrent effect resulting from the imposition of capital punishment. There are only two justifications for the execution of criminals. One is the retributive argument, eloquently stated by Immanuel Kant:

> If, however, he has committed murder, he must die. In this case there is no substitute that will satisfy the requirements of legal justice. There is no sameness of kind between death and remaining alive even under the most miserable of conditions, and consequently there is also no equality between the crime and

retribution unless the criminal is judicially condemned and put to death. . . . Even if a civil society were to dissolve itself by common agreement of all its members . . . the last murderer remaining in prison must first be executed, so that everyone will duly receive what his actions are worth and so that the bloodguilt thereof will not be fixed on the people because they failed to insist on carrying out the punishment; for if they fail to do so, they may be regarded as accomplices in this public violation of legal justice.[40]

The most loyal Kantian is uncomfortable with this famous passage. Like all retributivists, Kant sought a principle for scaling punishments. He thought he had found it by making the punishment fit the crime as closely as possible. In the nearly two centuries since the publication of his *Metaphysical Elements of Justice,* there has been a drift away from Kant's uncompromising position. Even persisting advocates of capital punishment, as, for example, Ernest van den Haag,[41] will not go so far in their demands for its revival. For the more contemporary version of retributivism, given its most articulate expression in von Hirsch's *Doing Justice,*[42] the infliction of certain but limited consequences appears to satisfy the requirements of a more lenient age.

Decisions about the morality of sentencing criminals are arguable only on moral grounds. Both advocates and opponents of capital punishment have hoped that the consideration of deterrence—abhorrent to Kant—might provide an empirical basis for settling the issue. The work of Sellin[43] in comparing abolitionist and retentionist states convinces the convinced abolitionist and leaves the retentionist as dubious as ever. Walker suggests an analogy to tuberculosis,

> which is easy to reduce when [its prevalence] is high but not at all easy to reduce beyond a certain low level. Although it sounds a paradoxical hypothesis, it is by no means unlikely that capital punishment is a more effective deterrent in countries with high murder rates.[44]

The hypothesis is not tested, nor does Walker propose a method for investigating this proposition further.

Recently Ehrlich, an econometrician, has formulated an elaborate theory of the interaction of offense and defense in the case of homicide in which he presumed that criminal man resembles economic man in that "offenders respond to incentives." This theory is tested by statistical techniques leading to the conclusion that capital punishment does indeed deter potential murderers from committing homicide. His conclusion is already famous:

> In fact, the empirical analysis suggests that on the average the tradeoff between the execution of an offender and the lives of potential victims it might have saved was of the order of magnitude of 1 for 8 for the period 1933-1967 in the United States.[45]

Reviewing Ehrlich's article, Klein et al. considered that his findings

> simply are not sufficiently powerful, robust, or tested at this stage to warrant use in such an important case. They are as fragile as the most tentative of econometric estimates of parameters, and we know full well how uncertain such results are under

extrapolation. It is not that Ehrlich's estimates are demonstrably wrong; it is merely that they are too uncertain and must, at best, be interpreted as tentative at this stage.[46]

But the panel commissioned by the National Academy of Sciences to consider the present state of research and knowledge on deterrence and incapacitation concluded that certainty in this matter is not to be had:

> Any policy use of scientific evidence on capital punishment will require extremely severe standards of proof. The non-experimental research to which the study of the deterrent effects of capital punishment is necessarily limited certainly will be unable to meet these standards of proof. Thus the Panel considers that research on this topic is not likely to produce findings that will or should have much influence on policy-makers.[47]

With this conclusion I must heartily agree. We are left with Kant's inplacable retributivism as the only way to justify capital punishment. Given the continuities in the evolution of criminal justice, none of which was foreseen by Kant, it is unlikely that the stoutest retentionist will advocate a return to that great philosopher's *lex talionis*.

III

This recital of the principal accomplishments of criminological investigations of violent crime resolves most of the outstanding problems confronting the criminal justice system. Research probably cannot shed much more light than we now have on the issues of crime in an apparently static society.

A statement like that cannot fail to unsettle those who are accustomed to hear at the conclusion of such an article that there is a need for much more research to clear away ignorance or to introduce more precision in our fund of knowledge. I will not deny that more research is needed, but as to the ten propositions in my inventory additional investments in research will not produce a foundation for major changes in policy.

The connections among poverty, race, and violence are irrefutably established. Enough career studies have been done to show the inability of the criminal justice system to moderate the recidivism of the violent criminal. There is strong evidence that intervention merely accelerates it. There is cold comfort to be found in the fact that advancing years extinguish violent careers between the ages of 35 and 40. Hopes that longer periods of incarceration will reduce the crime rate can be realized only at the expense of incapacitating many who would commit no crime at all if left free, and at an economic cost transcending by far our present investments in criminal justice. We have no evidence to show that increased police, or more severe sanctions, will deter violent criminals more than they are now deterred. Rehabilitation is occasional, unpredictable, and worth continuing to attempt, if only on the moral ground of offering prisoners and others under control a realistic hope of change. Continued psychiatric research may uncover conditions for which treatment may provide relief, but it is hardly to be expected that violent crime will be significantly reduced as a result. Finally, it is unlikely that the deterrent effect of capital punishment can be proved at a level of confidence justifying its retention on that ground.

Two conclusions emerge. First, it is improbable that the criminal justice system can improve much on its present performance, if it is to be measured by the reduction of crime. That does not say that much cannot be done to improve every element of the system. Both in efficiency and in humane treatment of the citizens it is there to serve, it is often clumsy, unimaginative, and bound by meaningless form. But is not going to catch many more criminals than it does, nor is it able to increase the number it controls without prodigal waste of lives and funds.

Second, as long as relations are as infected with interracial and interclass hostility in a static if not a contracting economy, there is little reason to expect that violent crime will abate. As matters stand now, violent crime occurs in a society that is saturated with violence. The news that Americans read and see on television titillates curiosity and anesthetizes sympathy without adding to understanding. Every day we guard ourselves against the dangers of great machines and speeding vehicles whose power to destroy the momentarily careless is obvious. Children in school are exposed to apprentice muggers in locker-rooms; the old and feeble in our crowded cities cower in their homes, fearful of predatory intruders. Our games and entertainments reflect our excitement at the sights and sounds of pain. We live in a nation obsesses by violence; little wonder that much of our violence is criminal.

Declamations against this abstraction, this well-defined consequence of a malfunctioning social system, are so frequent that it is impossible to find new words and phrases to express them. It is hard to make deliberate changes in a system that has maintained democracy for so long, that has made its citizens so free and prosperous, and has treated so many of them so fairly. But our vitality is being drained by fear. We turn to the police, the courts, and the prisons for protection at enormous social and economic costs and risk the withering of liberty. To no avail. Criminal violence increases and no amount of casuistry can explain away the ominous statistics.

We are not unique in these respects. We can congratulate ourselves that we have so far been spared the perverted doctrines of organized terrorism. So far we have enjoyed the immense differences between police conduct in an open society and the unrestrained violence of the police in the closed society of communist and fascist dictatorships. But there are other countries in which the incidence of violence is trivial, hardly enough to constitute a problem for study. Comfortable Americans incline to sniff at the boredom said to prevail in such countries as New Zealand, Sweden, and Switzerland, but those who do are not those who have been shot down on the streets by thugs expressing their frustration on the discovery of the empty pockets of their victims. The statistics of violence are desiccated numbers arranged in columns and rows, with totals at the bottom and percentages at the sides. In form they resemble the data of property crimes or of bank deposits or freightcar loadings. Whether one is a citizen reading the quarterly score of murders, rapes, and assaults in his or her city, or a criminologist pondering the trends, it is too easy to overlook the guns and knives that caused these numbers and the blood and death that they represent. Surely, we think, there must be some adjustment in the criminal justice system to which these numbers will respond.

What can be done, if the criminal justice system can do no more than process the culprits into appropriate dispositions and, perhaps, compensate their victims? We have not yet plotted a route to a society of social justice. Even if we wished for such a result, we cannot transform the United States into a new Switzerland. We have behind us the almost archaic remains of the New Deal and the ruins of the Great Society. It is easy to make a virtue out of not trying any more in hopes that the Invisible Hand of the free market will come to our rescue. No thoughtful criminologist can be comfortable with such a prescription. Too much crime can be traced to black discontent and white inability to make adequate room for blacks in the whole society.

The problem was foreseen by Alexis de Tocqueville, a century and a half ago:

> There is a natural prejudice that prompts men to despise whoever has been their inferior long after he has become their equal; and the real inequality that is produced by fortune or by law is always succeeded by an imaginary inequality that is implanted in the manners of the people. Among the ancients this secondary consequence of slavery had a natural limit; for the freedman bore so entire a resemblance to those born free that it soon became impossible to distinguish him from them.

> The greatest difficulty in antiquity was that of altering the law; among the moderns it is that of altering the customs . . . the real obstacles begin where those of the ancients left off. This arose from the circumstances that . . . the abstract and transient fact of slavery is fatally united with the physical and permanent fact of color. . . . Thus the Negro transmits the eternal mark of his ignominy to all his descendants, and although the law may abolish slavery, God alone can abolish the traces of its existence.[48]

I think we have done better than Tocqueville prophesied. He foresaw no possibility of an intermingling of the races, or of even the appearance of equality, except at the level of freedom before the law. He also foresaw the eventuality of great race wars as blacks strove to relieve their oppression, and instead we have witnessed a civil rights movement which, although it has not realized all its aims, has substantially added to the dignity and the opportunities of blacks in a society that once seemed mostly closed. For the black middle class, there is still an element of precariousness that their white peers do not share, even though the quality of life for all in this decade has taken on a quality of uncertainty and insecurity of which we had once hoped to rid ourselves.

For the black underclass, subsisting on welfare, the sense of ignominy that Tocqueville foresaw among the descendants of the slaves is alive and devouring. In his introduction to Fanon's *The Wretched of the Earth,* Jean-Paul Sartre put the matter brutally, although he was not referring to the American situation but rather to the misdeeds of his countrymen in Africa:

> During the last century, the middle classes looked on the workers as covetous creatures, made lawless by their greedy desires, but they took care to include these great brutes in their own species, or at least considered that they were free men— that is to say, free to sell their own labor. In France, as in England, humanism claimed to be a universal.
>
> In the case of forced labor, it is quite the contrary. There is no contract, there must be intimidation and this oppression grows. Our soldiers [reject] the humanism of the mother country . . . since none may enslave, rob, or kill his fellow man without committing a crime, they lay down the principle that the native is not one of our fellow men. Our striking power has been given the mission of changing this abstract certainty into reality: the order is given to reduce the inhabitants of the annexed country to the level of superior monkeys to justify the settler's treatment of them as beasts of burden.[49]

The oppression of the black underclass in America has some of the same texture. The black poor cannot be used because they are inferior, violent, untrained, or undependable, or all these adjectives. To justify our enslavement of them, and later our discriminant oppression of them, white Americans persuaded themselves that blacks were innately inferior, to be used when needed as beasts of burden, and to be put out of sight when such beasts were no longer needed—as is more and more the case in a technological age. The statisticians of unemployment do not even count as unemployed those persons who are not actively seeking work. The redundancy of young single blacks does not count in the perspective of the economist as the equivalent of the unemployment of the head of a family. Our indifference to the fate of these justifiably angry young men and women has direct consequences, one of which is the incidence of violent crime, to which I have referred at several points in this essay. It is not a new observation. It has been uttered on many occasions by many social philosophers and scientists. No one listens; it has to be said again, but this time with the added emphasis that we do not have any choice at all between justice for the whole black community and the degeneration of our cities into a quasi-anarchy in which only violence can protect us from the violent.

Sartre's unsparing rhetoric was a preface to the tocsin of Frantz Fanon. In the *Wretched of the Earth,* Fanon did not hesitate to justify violent crime when it is committed against the colonialist.

> It's a waste of breath to say that such-and-such a hero is a thief, a scoundrel, or a reprobate. If the act for which he is prosecuted . . . is an act exclusively directed against a colonialist person or colonialist property, the demarcation line is definite and manifest.[50]

These passionate utterances were heard far away from France and Africa. In the event, as France withdrew from its African colonies, violence continued, but it was more intertribal than interracial. Except in southern Africa, little is heard about terrorism directed against whites. There is no love lost between the races in any part of Africa, but for most of the continent Fanon's apocalyptic vision has faded into the chronic anxieties and pains of the developing nations, blocked from affluence, or even adequate subsistence, by forces far more subtle than an occupying power.

America is not a developing nation, and the anxieties and pains we confront find expression in many ways other than the heavy incidence of violent crime. Our economy does not work well, especially for those who are excluded from career participation, as for example the welfare underclass. The traditions of rugged individualism of which our forefathers were so proud are inapplicable to men and women in that class. No one can be sturdy and independent, or even a fully realized person when he is a lifelong though able-bodied dependent on public charity.

The answers to this problem of creating an economy capable of providing for all are beyond the competence of a criminologist. We can remind whoever will listen that criminal violence responds marginally, if at all, to the efforts of the criminal justice system to control it. It is a dependent variable, but it does not measure the effectiveness of a police innovation in patrolling or the deterrence exercised by long terms in prison. It does measure our ability to achieve a society of justice, freedom, and opportunity. The evidence to be found in our technical reports is that we are not making perceptible progress toward that end.

NOTES

1. Albert K. Cohen. *Delinquent Boys*. New York: Free Press, 1955.

2. Marvin E. Wolfgang and Franco Ferracuti. *The Subculture of Violence*. London: Tavistock, 1967.

3. Ibid., p. 99.

4. Ibid., pp. 158-161. Wolfgang and Ferracuti advanced seven propositions in formal style; I have attempted to compress them without misrepresentation.

5. Ibid., p. 163.

6. Ibid., p. 315.

7. Lynn A. Curtis. *Criminal Violence*. Lexington, MA: D. C. Heath, 1974, pp. 150-151.

8. Wolfgang and Ferracuti, op. cit. at note 2, p. 315.

9. James B. Jacobs. *Stateville: The Penitentiary in Mass Society*. Chicago: University of Chicago Press, 1977.

10. Ruth Rosner Kornhauser. *Social Sources of Delinquency: An Appraisal of Analytic Methods*. Chicago: University of Chicago Press, 1978, p. 187.

11. Charles L. Silberman. *Criminal Violence, Criminal Justice*. New York: Random House, 1978, pp. 117-123.

12. Marvin E. Wolfgang, Robert M. Figlio, and Thorsten Sellin. *Delinquency in a Birth Cohort*. Chicago: University of Chicago Press, 1972, pp. 88-105.

13. Thorsten Sellin and Marvin E. Wolfgang. *The Measurement of Delinquency*. New York: John Wiley, 1964.

14. Donna Martin Hamparian, Richard Schuster, Simon Dinitz, and John P. Conrad. *The Violent Few*, Lexington, MA: D. C. Heath, 1978.

15. Simon Dinitz, John P. Conrad, and Stuart Miller. *The Career of Violence*. Lexington, MA: D. C. Heath, 1980 (forthcoming).

16. Peter W. Greenwood. *Rand Research on Criminal Careers.* Santa Monica, CA: Rand Corporation, 1979.

17. Joan Petersillia, Peter W. Greenwood, and Marvin Lavin. *Criminal Careers of Habitual Offenders.* Santa Monica, CA: Rand Corporation, 1977.

18. See James Q. Wilson. *Thinking About Crime.* New York: Basic Books, 1975, pp. 200-201. Wilson's advocacy of incapacitation is qualified, cautious, and practical; he bases his position on the research of Shlomo and Reuel Shinnar. "A simplified model for estimating the effects of the criminal justice system on the control of crime." At the time of the publication of Wilson's book, this article was unpublished. It has since been published in *Law and Society Review* 9:4 (1975) pp. 581-611. This analysis of a perplexing problem has been critically reviewed by Jacqueline Cohen in Alfred Blumstein, Jacqueline Cohen, and Daniel Nagin (editors). *Deterrence and Incapacitation: Estimating the Effects of Criminal Sanctions on Crime Rates.* Washington, DC: National Academy of Sciences, 1978, pp. 196-198.

19. John P. Conrad. "Things are not what they seem: the ontology of criminal justice." *Toledo Law Review* 10 (Winter 1979) pp. 334-369.

20. Norval Morris. *The Future of Imprisonment.* Chicago: University of Chicago Press, 1974, pp. 62-73.

21. Ernst Wenk, James Robison, and Gerald Smith. "Can violence be predicted?" *Crime and Delinquency* 18 (1972) pp. 393-402.

22. Harry L. Kozol, Richard J. Boucher, and Ralph F. Garofalo. "Diagnosis and treatment of dangerousness." *Crime and Delinquency* 18 (1972) pp. 371-392.

23. Stephan Van Dine, John P. Conrad, and Simon Dinitz. *Restraining the Wicked.* Lexington, MA: D. C. Heath, 1978, pp. 99-114.

24. John P. Conrad and Simon Dinitz. *In Fear of Each Other.* Lexington, MA: D. C. Heath, 1978, pp. 1-11.

25. Van Dine et al., op. cit. at note 23.

26. Ibid, p. 122.

27. Blumstein et al., op. cit. at note 18, pp. 187-243.

28. Immanuel Kant. *The Metaphysical Elements of Justice.* Translated by John Ladd. New York: Library of Liberal Arts, 1965, p. 100.

29. Andrew von Hirsch. *Doing Justice: The Choice of Punishments.* New York: Hill & Wang, 1976.

30. Jan Palmer. "Economic analyses of the deterrent effect of punishment." *Journal of Research in Crime and Delinquency* 14:1 (n.d.) pp. 4-21.

31. Blumstein et al., op. cit. at note 18 pp. 95-139.

32. Ibid., pp. 135-136.

33. G. Kelling, T. Pate, D. Dieckman, and C. E. Brown. *The Kansas City Preventive Patrol Experiment.* Washington, DC: Police Foundation, 1974.

34. Dinitz et al., op. cit. at note 15.

35. Vernon H. Mark and Frank R. Ervin. *Violence and the Brain.* New York: Harper & Row, 1970.

36. Hervey Cleckley. *The Mask of Sanity.* St. Louis: Mosby, 1950, pp. 363-400. Cleckley proposed sixteen clinical signs of psychopathy, beginning with "1. Superficial charm and good intelligence" and ending with "16. Failure to allow any life plan." It is not too much to say that this clinical generalization is fairly typical of most texts.

37. In Simon Dinitz, Russell R. Dynes, and Alfred C. Clarke (editors). *Deviance Studies in Definition, Management and Treatment.* Second Edition. Oxford: Oxford University Press, 1975, p. 457.

38. Cleckley, op. cit. at note 36.

39. Samuel Yochelson and Stanton E. Samenow. *The Criminal Personality.* New York: Jason Aronson, 1976 and 1977.

40. Kant, op. cit. at note 28, p. 102.

41. Ernest van den Haag. *Punishing Criminals: Concerning a Very Old and Painful Question.* New York: Basic Books, 1975.

42. Von Hirsch, op cit. at note 29, pp. 67-83.
43. Thorsten Sellin. *The Death Penalty*. Philadelphia: American Law Institute, 1959, p. 34.
44. Nigel Walker. *Sentencing in a Rational Society*. London: Penguin, 1969, p. 61.
45. In Blumstein et al., op. cit. at note 18, p. 359.
46. Klein et al., in Blumstein et al., op. cit. at note 18, p. 358.
47. Blumstein et al., op. cit. at note 18, p. 63.
48. Alexis de Tocqueville. *Democracy in America*. New York: Knopf, 1945.
49. In Frantz Fanon. *The Wretched of the Earth*. New York: Grove, 1963, pp. 14-15.
50. Ibid., p. 69.

15

FEAR

CHARLES E. SILBERMAN

Men come together in cities in order to live; they remain together in order to live the good life.

— ARISTOTLE

One of the bargains men make with one another in order to maintain their sanity is to share an illusion that they are safe even when the physical evidence in the world around them does not seem to warrant that conclusion.

— KAI T. ERIKSON, *Everything in Its Path*

"Every time I'm mugged, I feel like I'm that much less of a person."

— STATEMENT OF A MUGGING VICTIM

I

All over the United States, people worry about criminal violence. According to public opinion polls, two Americans in five—in large cities, one in two—are afraid to go out alone at night. Fear is more intense among black Americans than among whites, and among women than among men. The elderly are the most fearful of all; barricaded behind multiple locks, they often go hungry rather than risk the perils of a walk to the market and back.

These fears are grounded in a harsh reality: since the early 1960s, the United States has been in the grip of a crime wave of epic proportions. According to the Federal Bureau of Investigation's *Uniform Crime Reports*, the chance of being the victim of a major violent crime such as murder, rape, robbery, or aggravated assault nearly tripled between 1960 and 1976; so did the probability of being the victim of a serious property crime, such as burglary, purse-

From Charles E. Silberman, "Fear," pp. 3-20; 456-457 in Criminal Violence, Criminal Justice. Copyright 1978 by Charles E. Silberman and reprinted by permission of Random House.

snatching, or auto theft. The wave may have crested—crime rates have been relatively stable since the mid-1970s—but criminal violence remains extraordinarily high. If recent rates continue, at least three Americans in every hundred will be the victim of a violent crime this year, and one household in ten will be burglarized.

In some ways, the crime statistics understate the magnitude of the change that has occurred, for they say nothing about the nature of the crimes themselves. Murder, for example, used to be thought of mainly as a crime of passion—an outgrowth of quarrels between husbands and wives, lovers, neighbors, or other relatives and friends. In fact, most murders still involve victims and offenders who know one another, but since the early 1960s murder at the hand of a stranger has increased nearly twice as fast as murder by relatives, friends, and acquaintances. (Much of the latter increase involves killings growing out of rivalries between drug dealers and youth gangs.) In Chicago, for which detailed figures are available, the number of murders of the classic crime-of-passion variety rose 31 percent between 1965 and 1973; in that same period, murders by strangers—"stranger homicides," as criminologists call them—more than tripled.[1]

Rape has been changing in a similar direction. In 1967, people known to the victim—estranged husbands and lovers, other relatives and friends, and casual acquaintances—were responsible for nearly half the rapes that occurred. (Some studies put the proportion even higher.) In 1975, two-thirds of all rape victims were attacked by strangers, with such attacks accounting for virtually the entire 140 percent increase in the number of reported rapes since the mid-1960s.

On the other hand, robbery—taking money or property from another person by force or the threat of force—has always been a crime committed predominantly by strangers. The chances of being robbed have more than tripled since the early 1960s, a larger increase than that registered for any other major crime. Robbers are more violent than they used to be: nowadays, one robbery victim in three is injured, compared to the 1967 ratio of one in five. Although firm figures are hard to come by, it would appear that robbery killings have increased four- or fivefold since the early 1960s, accounting for perhaps half the growth in stranger homicides.[2]

The most disturbing aspect of the growth in "street crime" is the turn toward viciousness, as well as violence, on the part of many young criminals. A lawyer who was a public defender noted for her devotion to her clients' interests, as well as for her legal ability, speaks of "a terrifying generation of kids" that emerged during the late 1960s and early '70s. When she began practicing, she told me, adolescents and young men charged with robbery had, at worst, pushed or shoved a pedestrian or storekeeper to steal money or merchandise; members of the new generation kill, maim, and injure without reason or remorse.

It would be an exaggeration to call viciousness the rule, but it is far from exceptional. The day I began revising this chapter for publication, the mother of a good friend—a frail (and frail-looking) woman in her seventies—was thrown to the sidewalk in the course of a mugging; she sustained a fractured hip and collarbone and will have to use a cane or "walker" for the rest of her days. During an earlier stage of my research, an acquaintance who was moonlighting as a cabdriver was held up by two passengers. After they had taken all his money—my acquaintance put up no resistance—one of the robbers shot him through the right hand, shattering a bone, severing a nerve, and leaving him with life-long pain; several operations later, he still has difficulty using his hand with the agility needed in the craft on which his livelihood depends. (Fortunately, my own family has escaped violent crime until now; but my home was burglarized, as was my son and daughter-in-law's, while I was writing this book.)

For a long time, criminologists, among others, tried to pooh-pooh talk about a rise in street crime, pointing out that the *Uniform Crime Reports* provide only a crude measure of the number of crimes committed each year.* But the increase has been too large, and conforms too closely to people's day-to-day experience, to be dismissed as a statistical illusion. The fact is that criminal violence has become a universal, not just an American, phenomenon. Once crime-free nations, such as England, Sweden, West Germany, the Netherlands, and France, as well as more turbulent countries, such as Italy, are now plagued with an epidemic of murder, kidnapping, robbery, and other forms of crime and violence—some of it politically inspired, all of it criminal in intent and consequence. (Within the United States, crime has increased more rapidly in suburbs and small cities than in large cities.) Wherever one turns—in virtually every free nation except Japan—people are worried about "crime in the streets." As Sir Leon Radzinowicz, director of Oxford University's Institute of Criminology, has written, "No national characteristic,

* For an analysis of the problems involved in measuring crime, see Appendix.

no political regime, no system of law, police, justice, punishment, treatment, or even terror has rendered a country exempt from crime."[3]

Nor does any national characteristic render a country immune to the corrosive effects of crime. Criminal violence is debasing the quality of life in American cities and suburbs. Quite apart from the physical injuries and financial losses incurred, fear of crime is destroying the network of relationships on which urban and suburban life depends. Anger over crime is debasing the quality of American politics as well: witness the fact that the preeminent issue in the 1977 mayoral election in New York City was the death penalty, something over which the mayor has no control whatsoever. The issue was injected by the winning candidate as a way of shedding his previous image as a liberal. (The friend whose mother was robbed and injured told me, only half jokingly, "A liberal is someone who has not yet been mugged.") What is at stake is not liberalism or conservatism as such, but the ability to think clearly about what can (and what cannot) be done to reduce criminal violence, and at what cost. In any society beset by violence, there is a danger that people's desire for safety and order may override every other consideration; the United States has avoided that mistake so far.

II

Why are people as afraid as they are? The answer cannot lie in the number of violent crimes alone; from an actuarial standpoint, street crime is a lot less dangerous than riding in an automobile, working around the house, going swimming, or any number of other activities in which Americans engage without apparent concern. The chances of being killed in an automobile accident are ten times greater than those of being murdered by a stranger, and the risk of death from a fall—slipping in the shower, say, or tumbling from a ladder—are three times as great.

Accidents also cause far more nonfatal injuries than do violent crimes. More than 5 million people were injured as a result of automobile accidents in 1973 and some 24 million people were hurt in accidents at home—about 4 million of them seriously enough to suffer a temporary or permanent disability. By contrast, fewer than 400,000 robbery victims were injured, and about 550,000 people were hurt in incidents of aggravated assault. Yet radio and television newscasts are not filled with accident reports, as they are with crime news; people do not sit around their living rooms trading stories about the latest home or auto accident, as they do about the latest crime; nor has any candidate for high office promised to wage war on accidents or restore safety to our highways and homes.

In fact, it is perfectly rational for Americans to be more concerned about street crime than about accidents, or, for that matter, about white-collar crime. Violence at the hand of a stranger is far more frightening than a comparable injury incurred in an automobile accident or fall; burglary evokes a sense of loss that transcends the dollar amount involved. The reasons have a great deal to do with the nature of fear and the factors that produce it. From a physiological standpoint, what we call fear is a series of complex changes in the endocrine system that alerts us to danger and makes it possible for us to respond effectively, whether we choose to attack or to flee. The first stage—the one we associate most closely with fear or tension—prepares the entire body for fight or flight: the heart rate and systolic blood pressure go up; blood flow through the brain and the skeletal muscles increases by as much as 100 percent; digestion is impaired; and so on. The second stage provides the capacity for rapid aggression or retreat; the third for a slower, more sustained response.

Thus fear serves as a kind of early warning system. The hormonal changes involved also make it possible for us to respond to danger at a higher level of efficiency, as anyone who has been in combat or has faced other emergencies knows from experience. When life or reputation or honor are at stake, we achieve feats of speed, strength, and endurance—not to mention imagination and intellectual clarity—that we never thought possible, and that in fact we cannot attain under ordinary circumstances.

But as most of us also know from experience, fear can be counterproductive as well. The same hormonal changes that alert us to danger and make it possible to perform herculean feats get in the way of normal behavior. If stress continues too long without being resolved, it leads to illness or pathological behavior. If the danger is so great that it overwhelms us, or so sudden that the early warning system, i.e., the first stage of hormonal change, is by-passed, we may become literally paralyzed with fear. The vulgar metaphors of extreme fear accurately describe the physiological processes; loss of control over the bladder and sphincter are common phenomena.

What this means, as the sociologist Erving Goffman writes, is that people exhibit two basic modes of activity: "They go about their business grazing, gazing, mothering, digesting, building, resting, playing, placidly attending to easily managed matters at hand. Or, fully mobilized, a fury of intent, alarmed, they get ready to attack or to stalk or to flee."[4] We can do one or the other; we cannot do both at the same time—at any rate, not for very long.

How, then, do we guard against danger while going about our normal activities? "By a wonder of adaptation," as Goffman puts it, people have "a very pretty capacity for dissociated vigilance" which enables us to monitor the environment out of the corner of the eye while concentrating on the task at hand. Sights, sounds, smells, and a host of other subtle cues give us a continuous reading of the environment. When that reading conveys a hint of danger, we take an unconscious closer look and may return to our task with just a microsecond's confirmation that things are in order; if that second look suggests that something is awry, our full attention is mobilized immediately.*

For this process to work, we have to know what to fear; we have to learn to distinguish cues that signal real danger from those that can be ignored, at least temporarily, without incurring too much risk. If a warning system is too sensitive—if it produces full mobilization at the merest hint of a danger—people so "protected" would live in a constant state of frenzy and thus would be unable to do all the other things, besides defending themselves, that are essential for survival. Too little sensitivity would be equally fatal.

Human beings tend to equate strange with dangerous; the most common early warning signal of approaching danger is the sight of a stranger. Hence armies post sentries; frightened people use watchdogs. In tightly knit urban communities, as Jane Jacobs has described in sensitive detail, people are always watching the street, and an extraordinary network of communication announces the presence of strangers as soon as they appear.[5] (In some German and Polish neighborhoods in Milwaukee, a stranger driving through the streets is enough to trigger several calls to the police.)

Life in metropolitan areas thus involves a startling paradox: we fear strangers more than anything else, and yet we live our lives among strangers. Every time we take a walk, ride a subway or bus,

---

* Police develop this capacity to an unusual degree. Experienced officers can operate a patrol car, listen to the police radio, and carry on a conversation with a partner while they simultaneously monitor the streets, sidewalks, and alleys, picking up cues that are invisible to the civilian.

shop in a supermarket or department store, enter an office building lobby or elevator, work in a factory or large office, or attend a ball game or the movies, we are surrounded by strangers. The potential for fear is as immense as it is unavoidable.

We cope with this paradox in a number of ways. The equation whereby strange means dangerous has an obverse, in which familiar means safe. The longer something is present in the environment without causing harm, the more favorably we regard it and the warmer our feelings are likely to be. People who live near a glue factory become oblivious to the smell; city dwellers come to love the noise, often finding it hard to sleep in the countryside because of the unaccustomed quiet. In psychological experiments, people who were shown nonsense syllables and Chinese ideograms for a second time judged them "good" as opposed to "bad" in comparison with other nonsense syllables and ideograms they were shown, later on, for the first time. The more often people were shown photographs of strangers, the warmer their feelings became toward them.

In cities, familiarity breeds a sense of security. People who know that they have to be on guard in a strange neighborhood, especially at night, feel more secure in their own neighborhood and come to believe that they have a moral right to count on its being safe. This tendency helps explain a phenomenon that has puzzled social scientists: the fact that people's assessment of the safety of the neighborhood in which they live seems to bear little relationship to the actual level of crime there. In one survey, 60 percent of those queried considered their own neighborhoods to be safer than the rest of the community in which they lived; only 14 percent thought their neighborhood was more dangerous. What was striking was that people felt this way no matter how much crime there was in their neighborhood: in Washington, D.C., precincts with crime rates well above the average for the city, only 20 percent of respondents thought the risks of being assaulted were greater in their neighborhood than in other parts of the city.[6]

This same phenomenon makes crime a terribly bewildering, as well as fear-evoking, event when it is experienced on one's own turf. "Casual conversations with urban citizens or regular reading of the newspapers in recent years would indicate that many, if not most, inner-city residents live with the fatalistic expectation that sooner or later they will be mugged," Robert LeJeune and Nicholas Alex write in their richly informative study of the experiences of mugging victims. "But closer examination reveals that most of these fear-

assuming that people beyond this range—whether in front or behind —can be ignored. As other people enter the scanning range, they are glanced at briefly and then ignored if their distance, speed, and direction imply that neither party has to change course to avoid a collision. When people have been checked out in this manner, Goffman writes, they can be allowed to come quite close without evoking concern. Moreover, pedestrians ignore oncomers who are separated from them by other people; thus someone may walk in dense traffic and be completely unconcerned about people just a few feet away.[8]

While one person is checking out those who come into his range in this manner, others are checking him out in the same way; none of them is aware, except in the vaguest sense, that this is what they are doing. And the process can become much more complicated. If an initial body check indicates that the pedestrian and a stranger are on a collision course, or if the stranger's course is not clear, an individual may follow one of a number of procedures. "He can ostentatiously take or hold a course, waiting to do this until he can be sure that the other is checking him out," Goffman writes. "If he wants to be still more careful, he can engage in a 'checked-body-check'; after he has given a course indication, he can make sure the signal has been picked up by the other, either by meeting the other's eye (although not for engagement) or by noting the other's direction or vision, in either case establishing that his own course gesture has not likely been overlooked. In brief, he can check up on the other's eye check on him, the assumption being that the other can be relied on to act safely providing only that he has perceived the situation."

This process of unconscious mutual accommodation is even more complex when traffic is heavy. If pedestrian A is walking behind pedestrian B, A not only accommodates to the movements B makes to avoid colliding with pedestrian C; he frequently will adjust his movement to what he *assumes* B is about to do to avoid C. And when these adjustments are not possible—for example, if a narrow path has been cut through heavy snow or around a construction site or other obstacle—one of several other adjustments comes into play automatically. As Goffman observes, "City streets, even in times that defame them, provide a setting where mutual trust is routinely displayed between strangers."

This kind of voluntary coordination usually works because, under ordinary circumstances, no one has much to gain from violating

laden accounts are not associated with a corresponding mental frame necessary to develop the appropriate precautionary behavior."[7]

To the contrary, the mugging victims studied by LeJeune and Alex had all assumed before they were mugged that however dangerous *other* neighborhoods might be, they were reasonably safe from attack in their own. "I never felt afraid," said one victim, a widowed secretary. "Well, I'm not willing to say that I wasn't afraid at all," she added. "Everybody has a little bit of a feeling of fear." What she meant, it turned out, was that she had always been afraid of the neighborhood in which her daughter lived. "Because I heard things of that neighborhood—and it wasn't safe. I heard of people being mugged. And there I didn't feel secure." Her own neighborhood was something else again. As she explained, "Here I wasn't afraid. . . . In my neighborhood there are police cars, there are people walking. How can anybody be afraid? . . . And on *my* block—I'm not going to be afraid on Post Avenue."

But city dwellers rarely stay cooped up in their own neighborhood; most adults have to venture elsewhere to go to work, to shop, to visit relatives and friends, or to use the cultural and entertainment facilities that make cities cities. When we enter any environment, whether familiar or strange, we automatically take a quick "reading" or "sounding" in order to decide whether to be on guard or not. If things are as they should be, if appearances are normal, we can be off guard; we can concentrate on the task at hand, confident of our ability to predict what will happen from the cues we pick up out of the corner of the eye. The result is the sense of safety that comes from feeling in control of one's own fate. For if we can predict danger in advance, we can avoid it—if only by retreating in time to some safer haven.

The process is extraordinarily fragile. We can predict danger only if the subtle cues on which we depend—for example, people's dress or attitude or demeanor—are accurate, which is to say, only if things are as they appear. Ultimately, the whole fabric of urban life is based on trust: trust that others will act predictably, in accordance with generally accepted rules of behavior, and that they will not take advantage of that trust. For life to go on in public places—in city streets, building lobbies, elevators, and hallways— people must put themselves in other people's hands.

Consider the elaborate etiquette pedestrians employ to avoid bumping into one another. The American pedestrian maintains a scanning or check-out range of about three or four sidewalk squares,

the rules. At the same time, the fact that coordination is required provides a standing invitation to gamesmanship, and adolescents often pick up the challenge. When gaining face is important, the psychological payoff from violating the rules—staring someone down, for example, or maintaining a course that requires the other person to step aside—may be large. Under the system of racial etiquette that prevailed in the South until fairly recently, blacks were required to step aside—into a muddy street, if need be—in order to let whites (*any* whites) go past with full possession of the sidewalk. Equally important, eye contact with whites was prohibited as another means of symbolizing white superiority and black inferiority; for a black man to eye a white woman was to invite a lynching.[9]

It is not surprising that some members of the present generation of black adolescents find delight in reversing the old conventions—for example, walking four or five abreast so that white pedestrians have to stand aside, or conversing in the street in a group so that a white driver backing his car out of his driveway has to wait until the youngsters choose to move. As accompaniments to these triumphs of reverse gamesmanship, there may be eye contact as well, in the form of a long, hate-filled glare.

Encounters of this sort are discomforting, for they show how fragile the social order really is—how dependent it is (and always has been) on acceptance of the rules by people who never have had much reason to accept them. "It has always been the case that the orderly life of a group contained many more points of weakness than its opponents ever exploited," Goffman writes, and a breakdown in what we consider civility or decorum exposes those weaknesses.

III

Crime does more than expose the weakness in social relationships; it undermines the social order itself, by destroying the assumptions on which it is based. The need to assume that familiar environments are safe is so great that until they have become victims themselves, many people rationalize that newspaper and television accounts of crime are greatly exaggerated. "This kind of thing happens on television, but not in real life," a college student exclaimed after she and a friend had been held up on the Ellipse, an area adjacent to the White House. (Although the two students were not injured, a migrant worker sitting on a nearby bench was shot in the face and blinded when he told the robbers—correctly—that he had no money.) "You just don't shoot someone in the back like in a Western movie," a young woman who had been shot and seriously injured in a D.C. robbery attempt told a Washington *Post* reporter.

Even when they admit that crime does occur, people comfort themselves with the assumption that it won't happen to them—in much the same way that we assume our own immortality, or our invulnerability to earthquake or flood.* It is only in retrospect, as LeJeune and Alex explain, that victims realize they should have been more aware of their own vulnerability. "Of course the conditions have been getting worse and worse," one of their respondents observed. "Uh, someone thinks that accidents happen to other people but they don't happen to me. Then when it did happen I was very upset because I didn't think it could happen to me."[11]

The need to feel safe is so powerful that people routinely misread cues that should signal danger. They may simply delay responding to a stranger, to give him a chance to explain or apologize; intuitive knowledge of this tendency on the part of pickpockets, assassins, and saboteurs makes it possible for them to carry out their mission.[12] People also may redefine a danger signal as a normal event—for example, by assuming that a mugger is merely panhandling or playing a practical joke. Consider these explanations by three of LeJeune and Alex's respondents:

"I was walking down the street. Four young men approached me. I say, 'Oh, cut this fooling out.' And then they put their hands in my pocket."

"When I got into the elevator I felt a hand, you know, and I thought the fellow was joking. But then I started feeling the pain. He was very strong. It was no joke."

Similarly, a victim may perceive a threatening stranger as a friendly neighbor who forgot his keys:

"I thought: it's one of my neighbors waving to me not to close the door. He must have forgotten his key. Just then somebody grabbed me in the back of the neck and held my head in both his arms."

* "In this respect, as in many others, the man of prehistoric age survives unchanged in our unconscious," Sigmund Freud wrote. "Thus, our unconscious does not believe in its own death; it behaves as if immortal. . . ." We really believe that " 'Nothing can happen to me.' On the other hand, for strangers and for enemies, we do acknowledge death. . . ."[10]

Or the victim may interpret a robber's demand for money as a request for a loan:

> "When we started getting off the elevator he turned around and he said: 'Give me ten dollars.' I thought he wanted to borrow ten dollars. He said, 'I don't want any trouble. Give me ten dollars.' And I looked him up and down, and I see he has a knife in his hand. So I didn't let myself get knifed. I gave him the ten dollars and he got off."[13]

People *need* to be able to make sense out of their environment; otherwise, life would be intolerable. To "live with fear," as victims call it—to be suspicious of every sound and every person—converts the most elementary and routine aspects of life into an exercise in terror. It is to avoid such terror that people who have not been victimized (and some who have) interpret threatening gestures and events in terms that are more understandable and comfortable.

Thus the emotional impact of being attacked by a stranger transcends the incident itself; it reaches a primordial layer of fear unlike anything evoked by an equally damaging encounter with an automobile or other inanimate object, or even by a crime that does not involve a direct encounter with another person. A criminal attack is disorienting as well, evoking traumatic reactions similar to those the sociologist Kai T. Erikson found among the survivors of the Buffalo Creek Flood.* Victims of criminal violence, like victims of earthquake or flood, develop what Erikson describes as "a sense of vulnerability, a feeling that one has lost a certain natural immunity to misfortune, a growing conviction, even, that the world is no longer a safe place to be." Because they previously had underestimated the peril in which they lived, the survivors of a disaster lose confidence in their ability to monitor their environment; as a result, they live in constant fear that something terrible will happen again.[14]

Crime victims are affected in much the same way; the inability to tell friend from foe—the sense that they no longer know how to monitor their environment—can turn the most ordinary encounter into a nightmare. Until the attack in which he was blinded, James Martin, a nineteen-year-old former handyman, never worried about

---

* On February 26, 1976, 132 million gallons of mud and debris broke through a faulty mining company dam in Buffalo Creek, West Virginia, killing 125 and leaving 4,000 of the hollow's 5,000 residents homeless.

crime. In the Washington, D.C., ghetto where he lived, talk about crime was a constant, but Martin recalls, "I never paid any attention . . . I felt safe. I thought people would look at me and say, 'the dude ain't got nothing.' " He was wrong. The men who held him up at a bus stop were enraged when Martin told them he had only $6 on his person; they knocked him down, beat his head against the sidewalk, then smashed a soda bottle on the curb and rammed the jagged edge into his right eye, completely destroying his vision. Although the robbers were convicted and imprisoned, Martin found that there was no way he could continue to live in Washington. Afraid to go out alone and equally afraid to stay home, he could not sleep, either, for fear his assailants would break out of prison and return to attack him again. He and his family moved back home to a small town in North Carolina, to live in a trailer on his mother-in-law's farm.[15]

This sense of vulnerability and fear seems to be a universal feeling, regardless of whether the person attacked is injured or not. Instead of familiar environments being automatically defined as safe, they now are perceived as uniformly dangerous because of the victim's inability to rely on the old cues. Asked whether being mugged had changed their outlook on life in any way, respondents in LeJeune and Alex's survey replied as follows:

"I am just so much more frightened wherever I turn, and it seems as though the entire city has turned into an incredible jungle. . . . It's incredible that I think that way, that I feel that way; it's so unlike me."

"Yes. It's made the city more of a jungle to me. Yes it has. And I haven't got too long to retire. And where I had really thought I would stay in the city, you believe it, I'll get out."

"Well it has. I mean I don't feel free, like to do things. You feel you like to go to the movies or something. You don't feel you could do it. You always fear that there's somebody, uh, even if you go to the movies and you're safe—you're inside—coming out you'll always have that fear, of my God, somebody's passing or something."

The worst fear is felt in the area in which the person was attacked, particularly if it is his own neighborhood. "I've been living here for three and a half years, and I've never had any real fear of it," a mugging victim who decided to move out of her neighborhood told LeJeune and Alex. "It's like it's my home. I know the block. I recognize people. It's all very familiar to me. Now it's become very unfamiliar to me, very threatening, very, very much like a jungle. I trust nobody. You know, I'm constantly looking around me. . . . I will never walk on *that* block again."

The most disorienting aspect of all is the senselessness of the whole experience, which shatters victims' belief that cause and effect have some relationship. They no longer can view the world as a rational, hence predictable, place over which they have some control. "The thing that bothers me, and always will, is why they shot me," says Sally Ann Morris, a twenty-six-year-old woman badly injured in a holdup attempt. "I didn't pose any threat to them; I was running away. . . ."[16] Tommy Lee Harris, a sixty-two-year-old man who was badly beaten by two young muggers after he had given them all his money, says in obvious bewilderment, "I don't know why it happened; I didn't know the men." After beating Harris to the ground, breaking four ribs, the muggers put him in the trunk of his own car, which they proceeded to drive away. Harris' life was saved when a policeman saw the muggers run through a red light and pursued them in his patrol car.[17]

The victim's bewilderment is compounded by the realization of how large a role coincidence and chance had played. For the first week after the shooting, Ms. Morris blamed the friend who had been with her at the time:

> "I thought why couldn't it have been him, he could have taken it better. Why me?" she recalls. "Isn't that just terrible to think like that? . . . And then I spent a long time thinking: if it had just taken longer to park, or if we had gone down another street. . . ."

The discovery that life is irrational and unpredictable makes victims feel completely impotent. This, in turn, exacerbates their fear: whether or not we feel in control of a situation directly affects the way we respond to it. Indeed, psychological experiments indicate that fear is substantially reduced if people merely *believe* they have some control over a stimulus, even if their response has no effect. One such experiment, described to the forty students who participated as a study of "reaction time," was conducted at the State University of New York at Stony Brook. The students were given a series of electric shocks lasting six seconds each, after which they were divided into two groups. One group was told that if they pulled a switch rapidly enough, they could reduce the shock they received from six to three seconds; the other group was told that they would receive three-second shocks no matter what they did. In fact, both groups received shocks of the same duration—three seconds. But the members of the first group, who believed that their actions could reduce the shock, showed far less stress as measured by galvanic skin reactions than did the members of the second group.[18]

Thus accidents are far less terrifying than crime because they do not create the sense of impotence evoked by crime. "You can't slip in the shower unless you're *in* the shower," the psychologist Martin E. P. Seligman points out, and "You can't get into an automobile smash-up unless you're riding in an automobile." One can take precautions, moveover, that extend the sense of control over one's environment and fate—using a skidproof rubber mat in the shower, checking a ladder to make sure it is steady, swimming in the ocean only if a lifeguard is on duty and the surf and undertow are not too strong, and keeping a careful eye out for other drivers and pedestrians.

In some of these situations, such as driving a car, people know in advance that they must be vigilant. And the automobile itself acts as a kind of armor or shield, protecting both driver and passenger from the invasion of self that interpersonal crime involves. Indeed, when riding in an automobile, people usually behave as if they were invisible to other drivers and passengers—which in a psychic sense they are—and as if the other drivers and passengers were invisible to them. It is only young children, who have not yet been socialized into highway etiquette, who make eye contact with people in other cars. The rest of us display what Goffman calls "civil inattention" to others when we drive or walk in public.

In violent crime, there is a direct intrusion on the self that produces anger and shame, in addition to fear. "My whole life has been invaded, violated—and not just by the act itself," says a forty-seven-year-old woman who was raped in her apartment. "It didn't happen just to me but to my husband and children." The rape totally shattered her sense of self, leaving her with a feeling of having been defiled, of being "stained and different," that, ten months later, her husband's love and understanding had not been able to overcome. "She says, 'You don't want anything to do with me because I am so dirty,'" the husband reports, and the wife wonders if she can ever put her life together again. "There have been times when I wish [the rapist] had killed me—it would have been kinder. . . . It was as though there were something lacking in dignity in still being alive." At times, to be sure, she feels a glimmer of hope: "I know that somehow we will work it out. . . ." But she adds: "I have changed and the world has changed. I don't see things the way I used to." In the best of moods, in fact, she is besieged by fear, afraid to go out alone and afraid to stay home, obsessed, as so many victims are, that the attacker will come back to seek revenge on her or on her two younger children.[19]

Although the sense of shame and defilement is most evident (and most understandable) in instances of rape, robbery and assault victims have similar, if less intense reactions. Our sense of self is bound up with our ability to control the personal space in which we live. As administrators of prisons and concentration camps well know, stripping people of their clothes serves to strip them of the normal defenses of their egos, leaving them far more compliant and docile. Victims of muggings, robberies, and assaults also experience a diminishment in their ego defenses. Male victims feel stripped of some portion of their masculinity as well; hence they often display a compulsive need to explain why it was impossible for them to resist or prevail. This need is strongest of all in men who have been the victims of homosexual rape.

Crimes such as homicide and rape deprive both victims and their relatives of the protective mantle of privacy, converting their intensely private agony and pain into public experiences. "It's impossible for somebody who hasn't been through it to understand the difference between a father dying of natural causes and being murdered," the married daughter of a murdered Bronx pharmacist told a New York *Post* reporter a year after the event. "If I had to name one thing that I hate [the murderer] for the most, it is that he made my father's death—which you should have to cope with privately— a very public thing."[20]

Burglary, too, evokes considerable fear, even though there is no confrontation with a stranger. For one thing, burglary victims are highly conscious of the fact that there might have been a confrontation had they come home earlier, hence they often are afraid to be home alone. Children whose homes have been burglarized sometimes need psychiatric help to cope with the fear.

More important, forced entry into one's home is an invasion of the self, for our homes are part of the personal space in which we live. We express our individuality in the way we furnish and decorate, and in the artifacts we collect; we may view some of our possessions in a casual manner, but others are invested with layers of meaning that bear no relationship to their monetary value. I can still feel the rage that overcame me when I discovered that the person who had burglarized my home had taken a set of cuff-links and studs worn by my father on his wedding day. The fact that they were covered by insurance was irrelevant; their value lay in their power to evoke my father's physical presence seventeen years after his death. I remember, too, the enormous relief my wife and I felt when we discovered that the burglar had been interrupted before he had a chance to take the candlesticks my mother had used to usher in the Sabbath every week of her life.

Because our homes are psychological extensions of our selves, burglary victims often describe their pain in terms strikingly similar to those used by victims of rape—and in a symbolic sense burglary victims *have* been violated. The saying that one's home is a sanctuary is no mere epigram; it expresses a profound psychological truth. One of the oldest and most sacred principles of Anglo-Saxon law held that no matter how humble a person's cottage might be, not even the King could enter without his consent. The principle is recognized, after a fashion, by totalitarian regimes. The dramatic symbol of totalitarianism is the harsh knock on the door in the middle of the night; as Goffman points out, the fact that even storm troopers knock implies their acknowledgment of the territorial rights of the residents. It is not too much to conclude that crime threatens the social order in much the same way as does totalitarianism.

In the United States, because of the abnormally low base from which the crime wave of the 1960s and early '70s began, the upsurge in criminal violence has been even more traumatic than otherwise might have been the case. Americans who came of age during the 1930s, '40s, and '50s had their general outlook and expectations shaped by an atypical, perhaps unique, period of American history. During their formative years, crime rates were stable or declining, and the level of domestic violence was unusually low. Never having experienced the crime and violence that had characterized American life for a century or more, this generation of Americans—the generation from which most governmental and other opinion leaders are drawn—came to take a low level of crime for granted.

For people over the age of thirty-five, therefore, the upsurge in crime that began in the early 1960s appeared to be a radical departure from the norm, a departure that shattered their expectations of what urban and suburban life was like. The trauma was

384   *Criminology Review Yearbook*

exacerbated by the growing sense that the whole world was getting out of joint, for the explosive increase in crime was accompanied by a number of other disorienting social changes—for example, a general decline in civility, in deference to authority, and in religious and patriotic observance. But this is getting ahead of the story.

Notes

1. *Fear*

1. For Chicago, see Richard Block, "Homicide in Chicago: A Nine-Year Study (1965–1973)," *Journal of Crime and Criminology*, Vol. 66, No. 4 (December, 1976), pp. 496–510; Block and Franklin E. Zimring, "Homicide in Chicago, 1965–1970," *Journal of Research in Crime and Delinquency*, Vol. 10, No. 1 (January, 1973), pp. 1–112. On homicide trends generally, see Lynn A. Curtis, *Criminal Violence* (Lexington, Mass.: D. C. Heath & Co., 1974), esp. Ch. 3; A. Joan Klebba, *Mortality Trends for Homicide, by Age, Color, and Sex: United States, 1960–1972* (Rockville, Md.: National Center for Health Statistics, undated, mimeo). I have updated Curtis' analysis of trends in stranger homicide through use of the FBI's *Uniform Crime Reports.*
2. The discussion of crime trends is based on my own analysis of data contained in the following sources: Donald J. Mulvihill and Melvin M. Tumin, with Curtis, *Crimes of Violence*, A Staff Report to the National Commission on the Causes and Prevention of Violence, Vol. 11, Ch. 5 (Washington, D.C.: U.S. Government Printing Office, 1969); J. Edgar Hoover, *Crime in the United States: Uniform Crime Reports, 1967* (Washington, D.C.: U.S. Government Printing Office, 1968); Clarence M. Kelley, *Crime in the United States, 1975 (Uniform Crime Reports)*, and Kelley, *Crime in the United States, 1976 (Uniform Crime Reports)* (Washington, D.C.: U.S. Government Printing Office, 1976 and 1977); *Criminal Victimization in the United States, 1973*, A National Crime Panel Survey Report (U.S. Government Printing Office, 1976); *Criminal Victimization in the United States: A Comparison of 1973 and 1974 Findings*, A National Crime Panel Survey Report (U.S. Government Printing Office, 1976); *Criminal Victimization in the United States: A Comparison of 1974 and 1975 Findings*, A National Crime Panel Survey Report (U.S. Government Printing Office, 1977). See also Curtis, *Criminal Violence*, Ch. 3.
3. Leon Radzinowicz and Joan King, *The Growth of Crime* (New York: Basic Books, Inc., 1977), p. 3. On the growth of crime throughout the world, see also Ted Robert Gurr, "Contemporary Crime in Historical Perspective: A Comparative Study of London, Stockholm, and Sydney,"

Annals of the American Academy of Political and Social Science, Vol. 434 (November, 1977), pp. 114–36; Gurr, *Rogues, Rebels, and Reformers: A Political History of Urban Crime and Conflict* (Beverly Hills, Calif.: Sage Publications, 1976); Marshall B. Clinard and Daniel J. Abbott, *Crime in Developing Countries* (New York: John Wiley & Sons, 1973).

4. Erving Goffman, *Relations in Public* (New York: Harper Colophon Books, 1971), p. 238.

5. Jane Jacobs, *The Death and Life of Great American Cities* (New York: Random House, Inc., 1961).

6. Jennie McIntyre, "Public Attitudes Toward Crime and Law Enforcement," *Annals of the American Academy of Political and Social Science*, Vol. 374 (November, 1967), pp. 38–39. See also *Crimes and Victims: A Report on the Dayton–San Jose Pilot Survey of Victimization* (Washington, D.C.: U.S. Department of Justice, Law Enforcement Assistance Administration, 1974), Table 13.

7. Robert LeJeune and Nicholas Alex, "On Being Mugged: The Event and Its Aftermath," *Urban Life and Culture*, Vol. 2, No. 3 (October, 1973), reprinted in *The Aldine Crime and Justice Annual, 1973* (Chicago, Ill.: Aldine Publishing Co., 1974), pp. 161–89.

8. Goffman, *Relations in Public*, pp. 11–12.

9. For a discussion of the complex rules governing eye contact in human society, see Michael Argyle, "The Laws of Looking," *Human Nature*, Vol. 1, No. 1 (January, 1978), pp. 32–40.

10. Sigmund Freud, "Thoughts on War and Death," in Freud, *On War, Sex, and Neurosis*, reprinted in Richard D. Donnelly et al., *Criminal Law* (New York: The Free Press, 1962), p. 347.

11. LeJeune and Alex, "On Being Mugged," p. 171.

12. Goffman, *Relations in Public*, pp. 265ff. On pickpockets, see David W. Maurer, *Whiz Mob* (Gainesville, Fla.: American Dialect Society, November, 1955), esp. Ch. 5.

13. LeJeune and Alex, "On Being Mugged," pp. 167–69.

14. Kai T. Erikson, *Everything in Its Path* (New York: Simon & Schuster, 1976), p. 234.

15. John Saar, "Attack at Bus Stop Wrecks Man's Life, Denies Ambition," Washington *Post* (March 9, 1975).

16. Ron Shaffer, "Tormented Gun Victim Asks Why," Washington *Post* (November 29, 1975).

17. Shaffer and Alfred E. Lewis, "You Go Out . . . and Might Not Get Back," Washington *Post* (August 23, 1975).

18. Maggie Scarf, "The Anatomy of Fear," *New York Times Magazine* (June 16, 1974), pp. 18–20.

19. John Saar, "Rape Victim's Memories Haunt Her," Washington *Post* (April 20, 1975).

20. Barry Cunningham, "Murder Victim's Family: One Year Later," New York *Post* (September 12, 1974), p. 54.

Charles E. Silberman is the author of Crisis in the Classroom, Crisis in Black and White, The Myths of Automation, *and* The Open Classroom Reader *(all published by Random House). His most recent book is* Criminal Violence, Criminal Justice.

16

IS CRIMINAL VIOLENCE NORMATIVE BEHAVIOR?
Hostile and Instrumental Aggression in Violent Incidents

LEONARD BERKOWITZ

Analyses of criminal violence often fail to draw the important distinction between angry and instrumental aggression. The former is directed mainly toward the injury of the intended target, whereas the latter is instrumental to attaining another goal such as social approval. Various conceptions, including the subculture of violence idea, assume that many violent acts are instrumental aggression, although they may actually be, in large part, angry outbursts intended primarily to hurt rather than to gain approval. Interviews with sixty-five white British violent offenders are used to document this thesis. The role of ego threats is also discussed.

Many behavioral scientists assume that aggression, the intentional injury of another, is often (but not always) carried out in an attempt to get social rewards and is frequently reinforced primarily by other people's approval (see Bandura, 1973). The display of aggression is thus supposedly controlled largely by anticipations of benefits from others. One of the problems with this conception is that it does not adequately recognize the different kinds of aggression. It especially fails to draw the important distinction between hostile and instrumental aggression (see Feshbach, 1964). In the latter case, although the actor attempts to hurt someone, he wants more than the injury of his victim. His aggression is actually only instrumental to the attainment of a more important goal, such as money or social status. Hostile aggression, on the other hand, is governed chiefly by anticipations of the actions' injurious outcomes. The aggressor's major aim in this instance, usually when he is angry, is to harm

LEONARD BERKOWITZ: Vilas Research Professor in Psychology, University of Wisconsin, Madison.

This research could not have been possible without the fine cooperation and assistance of many people. Professor Nigel Walker and his colleagues at the Cambridge University Institute of Criminology provided me with encouragement and facilities and also established the initial contacts. Mr. Will Knapp and Mr. Warren A. Young, also of the Institute of Criminology, conducted the interviews with great ability and dedication (Will Knapp did most of this work), and I am especially grateful to them. I am also indebted to Mr. Ralph Skrine and his associates at the Home Office Prison Department and the governors and staff at the various penal institutions we visited for their cooperation and suggestions. Ms. Randie Margolis was responsible for the coding of the interview transcripts and contributed valuable suggestions for the analysis of the data.

or perhaps even to destroy his victim. This type of violent behavior is reinforced when the attacker learns that he has inflicted what he regards as an appropriate level of pain (Swart and Berkowitz, 1976).

Our present thesis rests on this simple distinction. Many analyses of criminal violence essentially view violent offenses as typically instrumental actions, whereas we hold that a good many (but not all) of these incidents are better understood as hostile aggression.

The notion of a subculture of violence is one variation of this overemphasis upon instrumental aggression carried out for social rewards. This formulation was initially advanced to explain group differences in homicide rates (Wolfgang, 1959), but it has now been extended to cover the broad spectrum of antisocial aggression (Wolfgang and Ferracuti, 1967). Put simply, it contends that a pervasive set of values, assumptions, and expectations is directly responsible for much of the high incidence of homicides and assaults in violent groups. This belief system presumably first defines certain encounters as provocations, so that the individuals in these groups are relatively easily angered, and then prescribes aggression as the appropriate response. According to Wolfgang (1959:189), "Quick resort to physical combat as a measure of daring, courage, or defense of status appears to be a cultural expectation, especially for lower socioeconomic class males of both races." Thus, the men living in this subculture of violence presumably attack others mainly because they believe they are expected to do so. If they have been provoked, the only way they can receive the respect and approval they desire from the bystanders is to lash out at the offending party. A failure to strike might bring punishment in the form of a decline in the onlookers' regard for them. As Wolfgang and Ferracuti (1967:160) put it, "The juvenile who fails to live up to the conflict gang's requirements is pushed outside the group. The adult male who does not defend his honor or his female companion will be socially emasculated. The 'coward' is forced to move out of the territory, to find new friends and make new alliances."

This type of analysis is now widely accepted by students of criminal violence (e.g., Clinard, 1974; Gibbons, 1973; Schur, 1969). Disregarding what may be an unwarranted generalization from youthful gangs to adults, they attribute many of the assaults committed by low-SES men to the values and expectations these people have acquired in their subculture of violence, and to their striving for the social rewards that violence would presumably bring them (Short, 1974; Short and Strodtbeck, 1965).[1] The reasoning seems to be some-

---

1. The conception of conflict gangs held by many writers may also be overdrawn or even incorrect in important respects. Short has argued that few conflict-oriented street gangs are the cohesive, tightly knit groups that they are often said to be. Interestingly, Short's observations of the aggression displayed by gang members indicate that this violence is rarely impelled by normative influences. His analysis of the group processes involved in gang behavior gives much greater weight to status threats as a determinant of aggression.

what oversimplified: If the men are not mentally ill, their aggression must be "an appropriate form of behavior in a fairly wide variety of situations" (Schur, 1969:129). For this school of thought the action apparently has to be one or the other, either neurotic or psychotic conduct on the one hand or conformity to the norms of a particular group on the other.

However, as popular as this conception is, there are growing doubts as to whether it can serve as an adequate general theory of illegal aggression. For one thing, it is now increasingly recognized, as Wolfgang and Ferracuti had acknowledged, that much of the reasoning is quite circular. The proponents explain group differences in violence by positing subcultural values; they then use these same differences in aggressive behavior as evidence that the groups do have different values. As a matter of fact, when researchers explicitly ask about these attitudes and values, they find that the expected group differences do not exist in any clearcut fashion (Baker and Ball, 1969; Erlanger, 1974a, 1974b).

There is some doubt whether American violent offenders typically subscribe to the values of toughness and machismo, as the subculture thesis contends (Ball-Rokeach, 1973). But even if these values are pervasive in certain groups, they might only lower restraints against aggression rather than actually impel fighting. The aggression is not necessarily carried out because onlookers advocate such behavior. Some ethnic or racial or low-income groups could have a relatively high rate of violence because of the frequent frustrations to which they have been exposed and because of a damaged self-concept. They might be spurred to attack the one who had provoked them by their anger rather than by their belief that they have to strike their antagonist if they want the approval of their friends and acquaintances. Nor is their aggression necessarily reinforced only by any social benefits they might have gathered. Angry people want to hurt, and they are gratified when they have injured their victim sufficiently.

The present investigation was a preliminary attempt to ascertain the motives behind the aggressive actions displayed by a number of violent criminals. We interviewed a sample of British men who had been convicted for assaulting another male, focusing our questions primarily on the aggressive incident. The offenders' explanations of why they had injured the victim were of particular interest to us. Had they wanted the approval of the bystanders? Did they believe their friends and acquaintances expected them to punish the person who had provoked them? Affirmative answers to these questions would suggest that they had acted aggressively in the hope of social rewards, and could also indicate that they had complied with a group standard. These men had a history of violence. Were their assaults normative in the sense that these actions were prescribed by the subculture of violence in which these people lived? Our failure to obtain any such indications that their aggression was normative behavior obviously would not mean that normative considerations are never operative in criminal conduct. We cannot disprove the subcultural thesis. Other people, such as members of youthful conflict gangs, might attack someone because their groups call for aggression in certain situations. Even our respondents might believe that there are occasions when they have to hit a person who had insulted them if they are to look good to their friends and acquaintances. However, the absence of evidence of normative influences in a substantial proportion of our cases would suggest that many violent offenses are not simply the result of the aggressors' adherence to their groups' expectations. They could have attacked someone because of anger and without even thinking of what others wanted or expected them to do.

PROCEDURE

Our sample consists of sixty-five white males between the ages of eighteen and forty-three, with the modal category (37 percent) being in the late twenties. They were chosen because (1) they had been found guilty of inflicting either "actual" or "grievous" bodily harm (2) on another male (3) but not in the course of a robbery. As we would expect from other research into violent offenders, the men were overwhelmingly from the working class. Forty-two percent had fathers who were skilled workers, while most of the others had fathers who were either semiskilled or unskilled. (Seventeen percent did not provide any information about their fathers.) Their own occupational status was commensurate with their background: About one-third were skilled, while 56 percent were divided equally between the two lowest socioeconomic levels, and the rest had no occupation or were still in school. (Sixty percent of the group said they were employed at the time of their conviction.) Furthermore, most of the men had terminated their formal education at fifteen, which was standard for their social status.

They also tended to be persistent troublemakers. The great majority (83 percent) had been convicted of another crime before their last offense, and over half the sample admitted to anywhere between six and twenty-seven earlier convictions. In two-thirds of the cases, at least one of the prior convictions was for violence. Following the latest conviction (the focus of our interview), 84 percent were sent to jail, where they were interviewed, while the remaining eleven cases had received noncustodial sentences.

Needless to say, we cannot claim that the sample is representative of British violent criminals or even of men jailed for assaulting others. Yet it does appear that these people, by and large, are not too different in important respects from many other violent offenders. At the very least, they are relatively violent men even if they do not faithfully mirror the characteristics of all assaultive criminals. It is meaningful to ask whether their aggression was normative behavior for their particular groups. Was their violence instrumental to the attainment of their peers' approval or at least to the avoidance of disapproval for violating their group's expectations?

The jailed men were incarcerated in seven institutions in or relatively close to East Anglia in England. Each inmate meeting our criteria was informed of the interviews by a member of the prison staff. If he agreed to participate in the research,[2] the inmate was taken to the interview room where he met one of the two interviewers who told him of the study. (The study was described as a nongovernmental investigation into "what produces violence so that there is trouble with the law.") After assuring the subject of complete anonymity and promising that no one outside the project would be able to identify who said what, the interviewer asked whether the conversation could be tape recorded "for research purposes." All inmate subjects agreed to this. The other eleven men were contacted individually by letter after they had been sentenced. If they agreed to cooperate in the study, a meeting was scheduled at the respondent's convenience, usually in his home. Again, the interview was tape recorded with the respondent's consent. The interviews were relatively structured in that the questioning was guided by a prearranged schedule. However, since we were unsure at first of how cooperative the men would be, we decided to allow the conversation some free rein in order to keep it fairly natural. Unfortunately, this meant that every respondent did not answer each and every question; consequently, we do not have quantitative data for all sixty-five men for each item.

As in any interview study of this sort, we cannot be certain that the answers were always accurate or, for that matter, that the men even tried to be entirely truthful. Our candid impression is that they were usually straightforward. But even if they distorted their replies on occasion, seeking to put the best face on their behavior, how did they attempt to justify their actions? Any self-serving answers to our questions could also tell us what they think are the important values and ideals guiding social conduct.

Two independent judges read each transcript of the interviews after several days of training and did two types of coding. First, the respondents' replies to each question were categorized into one of several possible response classes. (For most items, there were three to five such response classes.) The two judges had a very acceptable degree of agreement in doing this; over all sixty-five cases they were in accord 80 percent or more times for twenty-seven out of the thirty-six questions, with the median agreement over all items being 85 percent. In addition, the judges also counted the frequency of twenty-five different ideas whenever they were expressed during the interview (e.g., idea 7, wants to hurt someone; idea 8, wants to protect or enhance reputation as tough or strong). For all but one of these (idea 2, engaging in violence, hurting another physically), the coders had an average difference of less than one, and the mean difference for that notion was less than two. Whatever the level of agreement, however, the judges also discussed every discrepancy and then recorded for analysis whatever response they agreed upon.

---

2. The prison officials did not inform us how many refused to be interviewed, but we gathered that this was only a very small number. Most of the respondents apparently welcomed the interview as a change in their routine. We did not pursue this matter since our sample obviously is not representative of the prison population.

FINDINGS

The Context

At the beginning of each interview, the respondents were asked to describe in their own words the incident that had led to their most recent arrest. They were then questioned in some detail about what had happened. In most instances, the incident had occurred some time earlier: 23 percent of the cases had arisen less than six months earlier; for 29 percent, the event had taken place one to two years before; and for 12 percent, more than two years had passed.

Troublesome though this time interval might be, there are some indications that the incidents in which our men were involved might not be glaringly different from many of the violent encounters in British or American urban areas. We have already noted that the offenders tended to be relatively young, typically less than thirty years of age, and only about 8 percent were thirty-five or older. A survey of violent offenses in London obtained much the same pattern (Sparks, 1974). Then, too, the assaults were most likely to take place on the weekends (51 percent), a pattern which has also been found in American cities such as Philadelphia (Wolfgang, 1959) and St. Louis (Pittman and Handy, 1964). Eighty-four percent of the incidents occurred at night. As is also common in the United States (see Wolfgang and Ferracuti, 1967), the assaults might have been alcohol related since 85 percent said they had been drinking just before the event occurred and 14 percent reported being drunk. Unlike the pattern usually seen for homicides, however, the victim was most often a complete stranger (51 percent) or a slight acquaintance (17 percent). Only 28 percent of the offenders indicated that they had attacked a relative or someone who was well known to them. On the other hand, they usually were acquainted with the other people around them at the time (about two-thirds of the cases). Much more often than not, these were men; only 15 percent of the respondents said they were in the company of wives or girlfriends.

The Incident and Reactions to It

The incident was more likely (one-quarter of the cases) to have grown out of an argument than to be the result of any other factor. Relatively few (9 percent) of the respondents said the other person had insulted or physically attacked them at the start. Interestingly, the second most frequent cause was a friend's need for assistance (17 percent). The quarrel, or whatever it was, then increased in intensity until the fight broke out. Most of the respondents claimed they did not strike first. About half of our sample said the brawl actually began when the antagonist had attacked, while only 20 percent indicated that the adversary had not gotten in the first blow.

The Desire to Hurt. This precipitating event produced two major reactions, as is shown in Table 1. About 41 percent of those asked this question ("Think

Table 1. What the Respondents Said
They Wanted to Do upon Being Provoked

Answers	%	N
Wanted to hurt other	30.8	20
Wanted safety, security, or to be left alone	21.5	14
Wanted to protect or enhance reputation	0	0
Wanted approval from people other than victim	0	0
Other	13.8	9
Didn't think	7.7	5
Question not asked	26.2	17

back to the moment you did it [i.e., hit the other person]. What had you wanted to do? What did you want to accomplish?") said their initial response was to want to hurt their opponent. They were furious and strove to attack the man who had provoked them. Their internal stimulation, their anger, propelled their aggression. Again and again, the offenders described their behavior as driven, almost compulsive, in nature. A twenty-seven-year-old man with previous arrests for burglary as well as violence talked about a fight he had gotten into with several policemen after they had stopped him for reckless driving. He claimed they immediately started to goad him on so that he lost his temper.

> Interviewer: How much were you trying to hurt him?
> Respondent: If I could have, if the [other] police hadn't grabbed me, I wouldn't have stopped. I would have carried on till I'd really hurt him. . . .
> Interviewer: At the time did it strike you what other people would think of what you were doing?
> Respondent: I didn't care.
> Interviewer: And you didn't care about the other policemen there or . . .
> Respondent: No, I didn't care. They'd got me in that much of a state I'd have had a go at them as well, you know. That's the way it was.

The case of a man with fifteen previous convictions, fourteen of them for violence, gives us yet another—although perhaps extreme—example of a rage-driven assault. The incident had started innocently enough. He had called a police ambulance, he said, when he saw a dead man in a car parked on his street. A patrol car pulled up soon after he telephoned but just then an old woman living nearby also found the body and began to scream. The respondent described what happened:

> Straight away he [the policeman] said, "What's the game?" I says, "It's the guy in the car. He's O.D. so I thought I'd phone an ambulance. . . ." He [the policeman] just started off. This woman across the road was shouting,

and he turned round and said, "Come on, get in the car." Well, I had no shoes on, no shirt on, 'cus I was sitting down with my old woman watching telly, minding me own blinking business, and he said, "Get in the car." Well, first I walked over to the car. Then I thought, "Well, fuck it." Just got on me back then. . . . He said, "Get in the car." I said, "What for?" He said, "You're under arrest." . . . "What for? You tell me first and I'll get in." It went on like that. He said, "Head down," and shoved me head in the door. I said, "Fuck you." That was it, just elbowed him, brought him over me shoulder, and stamped him with me foot. Then this other Panda [patrol] car pulled up, sergeant in it, so I thought, "Well, I'm done anyway. They know me. It's no good fucking disappearing." So I slammed the fuck out of him. [Just then a police car arrived with reinforcements.] When I see the van I got the machete out of the kitchen and jumped into 'em and went the whole fucking hog. . . . [He fought eight policemen in all, cutting only two of them because the others kept out of reach.]

Admittedly, this is an unusual example. However, our impression is that it differs from most of the other cases in degree rather than in kind. This person's self-control might have been relatively weak, but a good many of the people we interviewed seemed to lack strong inhibitions against aggression. He evidently was also quick to become extremely angry, but again, many of our offenders also had a very low boiling point. Later in the interview the man described himself in a way that could also apply to quite a few of the others: "When someone annoys me, I freak completely. I don't see people. I don't see nobody. I simply go blank."

This last point has to be qualified somewhat. Our men do not always explode into uncontrolled violence on being provoked. Even when they feel compelled to attack the antagonist, they can hold themselves back at times and limit how much injury they do in line with the constraints of reality—*if reality intervenes soon enough, before the aggression has accelerated.* Here is someone who had beaten up his wife's lover with his fists. (He too had a record of arrests, including some for violence.)

Yeah, well I'll tell you something, what I was going to do. There was a bottle there, a wine bottle. Right. Well, I broke the bottle [but] I thought, "No you don't. I ain't going to use this. . . ." I thought, "If I use the bottle, I'll probably kill him.". . . So I threw the bottle away and I just set about the geezer.

The Desire for Security. The second most common desire (exhibited by 29 percent of those asked the question) was for security or self-protection. A twenty-four-year-old man with eleven previous convictions for a variety of offenses including violence maintained that this is what he had wanted.

It wasn't a matter of hurting them. It was just a matter of protecting myself. . . . I wasn't sure if the man had a gun. I just wanted to get them. I was just lashing out to get them out of the way so I could back out and get out.

Other Possible Benefits. Not one of the men stated that they had sought approval or wanted to maintain a reputation when they reacted to the instigation. The respondents were told to think back to the time just before they had struck their opponent and were asked about any onlookers who might have been present: "At that moment, were you thinking that what you did might make you look good or bad to this person (these people)?" They were also asked about any others who might hear about the incident: "As far as you can remember, did you think at that time that people besides those present would learn what you did in this situation? What would these people have expected you to do?" Many of the men replied as did the two offenders quoted earlier who had fought the policemen: They usually did not care what others thought. Our extremely violent case, the man who had attacked eight police with a machete, pictured himself as oblivious to the views of others even when he refused to fight someone who had annoyed him.

> I've walked out of the pub rather than actually kick his brains out. Other people turn round and say you're better doing that, you know. But I don't worry about what people think. It's just me, the way I react. It's me own mind. I don't care about other people.

He did value some people's good opinions, and especially wanted to please his girlfriend. But he didn't fight to get their approval.

After the respondents had described their first reactions, in all but fifteen cases they were then specifically asked whether they had attempted to injure someone during the fight. ("Were you trying to hurt anyone?") Fifty-two percent of those replying said yes, while the rest denied having made such an attempt. Whatever they sought to do, they ended up injuring their opponent, often because they were skilled and experienced battlers. In vivid contrast to the American situation, they typically used only their own hands, feet, and head to do this (60 percent of the cases), or an object that happened to be available (9 percent). Fewer than 20 percent employed a knife or gun. Undoubtedly, because of their previous successes in fighting, if they had considered the possible outcome of the battle at all before it began, they expected to win. When asked, "At the time [of the fight], were you thinking that you would win?" over 60 percent of those queried said yes. No one in the sample had anticipated losing. But much like the men we have just quoted, a good proportion said they had not thought about the outcome in one way or another (38 percent of the people who had been asked this question). They just struck out at their opponent in fury. As one of the offenders put it when asked whether he ever thought about losing the fight he was in, "No, I never had it in my mind. I just had it in my mind to hit him."

Ideas Expressed during Interview. The tallies of the men's ideas during the course of the interview add further detail to the picture we have been developing here. Their aggression, as they saw it, was a response to someone else's action, not something they initiated all by themselves. Only 11 percent of the respondents referred to an attack on another person in the absence of a provocation. Much more often, they pictured themselves as having been provoked and then trying to restrain themselves. The entire sample spoke at least once about attempting to hold themselves back when they were aroused, and 57 percent indicated they sometimes just walked away from the person who was bothering them. But, as we noted before, this effort at self-control was not always successful: Many of the men (82 percent) also talked one or more times about losing their temper or flying into a rage. Violence ensued.

This idea count also gives us some clues as to what the men wanted to do by hitting the victim. Here again we see that they were not seeking social approval. Ninety-seven percent of the respondents *never* mentioned wanting or expecting approval for their aggression. On the other hand, some were a bit concerned about maintaining a reputation as tough and strong: While 63 percent did not bring up this notion at all, 36 percent of the sample indicated such a desire a few times. But even these latter cases did not appear to burst into violence mainly because of their concern with a reputation for toughness. One of the offenders, a thirty-year-old man with quite a few convictions for assaults (including the use of weapons), talked about his reputation for fighting. In a show of candor he said he tried to live up to other people's conception of him. "I suppose it's just showing off in a way, isn't it? Letting them know that you're still around. . . ." Yet, with all of his concern for his public image, he often got into fights without thinking of his reputation at all.

> At the time I'm not thinking that at all, you know. It's afterwards I think this all out, but at the time I don't stop to think. At the time it seems the natural thing to do or the right thing to do.

Another one of our sample who also spoke about not wanting to be disgraced in front of his mates [friends] described one of his violent outbursts, an attempted murder, in similar terms. This man had been "brought up rough" by his parents, and especially by his father who had been in prison. He had started scrapping as a young boy, he said, and now had a string of convictions for various violent crimes. But when the interviewer asked him whether he had attacked his opponent on this particular occasion because he thought he would look bad if he did not do anything, he answered, "No, I didn't think nothing like that. Just done it on the spur of the moment."

Security was somewhat more important than a reputation, judging from the frequency with which this idea was expressed. Forty percent said they had wanted safety or security or to be left alone. But most often (45 percent of the cases) they said they had sought to hurt someone. We certainly should not be surprised at this. The goal of angry aggression is to inflict injury, and an angry person usually wants to hurt the one who has provoked the anger. He is rewarded when he believes he has accomplished this purpose.

The Role of the Self-Concept

Our observations clearly suggest that the offenders' aggression was by no means always an attempt to restore their pride or build up their self-esteem. Relatively few of the men (only 12 percent of the sample) indicated they had struck their opponent in order to get self-satisfaction. This is not to say that their actions were unaffected by their images of themselves. In various ways they reported that they were often easily angered by threats to their self-esteem. Our impression is that their egos were fragile indeed. One of our previously cited cases, the man who had been "brought up rough" by his exconvict father, manifested this when he said he was touched off by "anybody trying to be a big mouth" or anybody "putting on a front, . . . trying to create an image for themselves which they haven't got." He apparently felt that he was being put down whenever someone else attempted to enhance his own worth.

This ego fragility can also be seen in the men's experience with insults. A fairly high proportion (58 percent of those asked) told us, in response to the question, "Have you ever been insulted by another man?" that other people had tried to humiliate them either very often or occasionally, and only 15 percent denied ever having been deliberately insulted. The men readily developed situations in which they thought their pride was at stake. They were quick to see themselves as challenged and frequently interpreted someone else's remarks as belittling them, even if (as in the above example) the other person was only boasting or insisting on his own viewpoint in an argument. They felt called upon to prove themselves again and again, to others and to themselves.

The crucial point here is that the challenge, the perceived threat to their self-concept, often infuriated these men and stimulated them to lash out impulsively at the antagonist, especially if they had been drinking. This is also indicated by the men's answers to the series of questions about insults. Thirty of the men were asked, "How would most of the men you know act if they were insulted?" Fifty-three percent believed that "most men" would react with a violent counterattack. But this was not necessarily because a violent response was prescribed by their social group. The reaction was modal but not normative. Recall that few of the respondents were concerned about their reputation or sought approval from others for being tough. In the case of violent responses to an insult, only a small proportion (21 percent) thought such a violent reaction was desirable. At the back of their minds they realized that violence could lead to trouble. Not surprisingly, then, fully 73 percent of the sample said one or more times during the interview that they thought their fighting might get them into some difficulty or might even bring punishment.

This very pattern was described by one of the offenders, a man who had been arrested and convicted six times, including at least three times for violence. At the end of the interview, when he was asked how violence usually arose in his experience, he answered:

> I think usually it will start where you have got more than one feller. . . .
> You have had a drink. It's just that you've had a drink. Stimulation. And

'er, you've had an argument, and you get into a position where you can't back down. In my case, rather than talk about it, I automatically strike out like, you know. I know that. I can think of the times when I've said to myself, "It won't happen again," but I don't seem to be able to control it. As I say, I've got to be in that sort of situation where I've had a drink. I'm never on me own. It's usually when I'm with somebody else. . . . It usually arises out of something trivial. Someone says something or you bump into someone. . . .

Seen from a distance, the incident sparking the fight was often a trivial one. But our man did not regard it as such at the time. The other person's action, however minor, had threatened his picture of himself and he could not back down before the challenge. His temper exploded and, unable to restrain himself, he hit his opponent.

DISCUSSION

Obviously, the observations reported here have to be regarded with caution. We certainly cannot say that the respondents were representative of all violent offenders in the United Kingdom or even of all those jailed for violent offenses in the East Anglia area. In a sense, this study is akin to the investigations of juvenile gangs in which the adolescents interviewed were not necessarily representative of all gang members in the United States or even in their particular city. Yet for all of their sampling problems, these studies have yielded hypotheses that have stimulated and guided other research into other groups. The present sample may also furnish some leads to be pursued in later investigations.

If we accept these reports at face value, then, we have the picture of a number of men who were infuriated by what they regarded as a threat to their self-esteem, who then struck out at their antagonist in rage, wanting more than anything else to hurt him. Their intense anger had apparently stimulated the attack on the offending party, not a desire to look good to their peers or the bystanders around them. They could restrain themselves on occasion—if their wives or girlfriends were present or if they thought they were sure to receive a severe beating. Quite often, however, they did not think of the consequences. They were concerned only with the present. Their goal was to hurt, and whatever injury they inflicted was the immediate reinforcement that maintained their aggressiveness.

This is not to say that the victim's pain was all they desired or the only reward that sustained their violence. Aggression, like much of human conduct, is carried out for many reasons, and a variety of events can maintain this behavior. The fighting could conceivably be reinforced at times by the approval of their friends and acquaintances even when the offenders were angry. However, our interviews suggest that social rewards were not particularly important in either bringing about or reinforcing the aggression displayed by many of the men in this sample. If anything, pride appears to be far more significant than direct external benefits. Wounded pride certainly seems to enrage them, and in some cases they might have hit their antagonist in an attempt to restore their self-esteem (Toch, 1969).[3] Quite a few of the offenders told how they did not want to back down before a challenge, a challenge that was either blatantly open (as in an insult) or only implicit (as in an argument). Much like a cavalier in the time of the Stuarts or perhaps even the stereotypic hero in the stories of the Old West, they felt they had to stand up to the threat. They had to return word for word, insult for insult, blow for blow, but this was for their own self-approval rather than the approval of others. As the interchange mounted in intensity, some of them could have lashed out at their opponent in order to assert their dominance or master the other person or perhaps even to enhance their self-image. Nonetheless, in many instances the violence was an impulsive outburst stimulated by strong anger. This is a familiar theme in the interviews. Many of the violent men indicated that their aggression accelerated rapidly as their anger flared. Their violence was driven more by the stimulation of internal rage than by the hope of external benefits.

REFERENCES

BAKER, R. K., and S. J. BALL
  1969 "The Actual World of Violence." In *Violence and the Media,* Vol. 9: 341–362. Staff report to the National Commission on the Causes and Prevention of Violence. Washington, D.C.: U.S. Govt. Printing Office.
BALL-ROKEACH, S. J.
  1973 "Values and Violence: A Test of the Subculture of Violence Thesis." *American Sociological Review* 38: 736–749.
BANDURA, A.
  1973 *Aggression: A Social Learning Analysis.* Englewood Cliffs, N.J.: Prentice-Hall.
CLINARD, M. B.
  1974 *Sociology of Deviant Behavior,* 4th ed. New York: Holt, Rinehart and Winston.
ERLANGER, H. S.
  1974a "Social Class and Corporal Punishment in Child Rearing: A Reassessment." *American Sociological Review* 39: 68–85.
  1974b "The Empirical Status of the Subculture of Violence Thesis." *Social Problems* 22: 280–292.

3. Toch's important study of imprisoned violent men, which contributed both directly and indirectly to our own research, also highlights the role of ego threats. Many of the people in his sample also reported becoming enraged by the threats to their self-concepts that they detected all too readily. However, Toch assumes that their violent reactions were often an attempt to defend or restore their images of themselves where we suggest that a good deal of this violence was actually only an impulsive outburst stimulated by the men's anger.

FESHBACH, S.
 1964   "The Function of Aggression and the Regulation of Aggressive Drive." *Psychological Review* 71: 257–272.

GIBBONS, D. C.
 1973   *Society, Crime and Criminal Careers,* 2d ed. Englewood Cliffs, N.J.: Prentice-Hall.

PITTMAN, D. J., and W. HANDY
 1964   "Patterns in Criminal Aggravated Assault." *Journal of Criminal Law, Criminology and Police Science* 53: 462–470.

SCHUR, E. M.
 1969   *Our Criminal Society.* Englewood Cliffs, N.J.: Prentice-Hall.

SHORT, J. F., JR., and F. L. STRODTBECK
 1965   *Group Processes and Gang Delinquency.* Chicago: University of Chicago Press.

SHORT, J. R., JR.
 1974   "Collective Behavior, Crime and Delinquency." In *Handbook of Criminology,* D. Glaser, ed. Chicago: Rand McNally.

SPARKS, R.
 1974   "Criminal Victimization in Three London Areas." Unpublished manuscript. Cambridge University Institute of Technology.

SWART, C., and L. BERKOWITZ
 1976   "The Effects of a Stimulus Associated with a Victim's Pain on Later Aggression." *Journal of Personality and Social Psychology* 33: 623–631.

TOCH, H.
 1969   *Violent Man: An Inquiry into the Psychology of Violence.* Chicago: Aldine.

WOLFGANG, M. E.
 1959   *Patterns in Criminal Homicide.* Philadelphia: University of Pennsylvania Press.

WOLFGANG, M. E., and F. FERRACUTI
 1967   *The Subculture of Violence: Towards an Integrated Theory in Criminology.* London: Tavistock.

Leonard Berkowitz is Vilas Research Professor in Psychology, University of Wisconsin. He is the editor of Advances in Experimental Social Psychology *(Volumes 1-12, published by Academic Press, 1964-1979). His research specialties are determinants of aggression, influence of media violence, and determinants of helpfulness.*

17

NORMATIVELY HOSTILE, PURPOSEFULLY HOSTILE, OR DISINHIBITEDLY BLOODY ANGRY?

HANS TOCH

Dichotomous distinctions are useful in describing extremes, but they lose their credibility when we turn to the midrange of humanity. Such is the fate of the concepts "instrumental" and "hostile" aggression (Feshbach, 1970). The first term helps us to understand the work of loyal employees of Murder, Inc.; the second seems apt in characterizing unmitigated bullies, for whom the medium (victimization) is its intended message.

But garden variety violent behavior is complex and overdetermined, and it can usually be described either in terms of hostile or instrumental components. Bandura, for example, suggests that "since, in all instances, the behavior is instrumental in producing certain desired outcomes, be they pain, approval, status, or material gain, it is more meaningful to differentiate aggressive behaviors in terms of their functional value rather than whether or not they are instrumental" (Bandura, in press). Berkowitz agrees with Bandura's rejection of either/or characterizations of violence, but he prefers to highlight hostility (disinhibition) as the dominant theme of aggression (Berkowitz, supra).

My mind concurs with Bandura, but my heart belongs *to some extent* to Berkowitz. This is the case because I find Berkowitz's views valuable as a corrective to simplistic translations of dominant (subcultural) theories of violent conduct. I say "simplistic translations" because Berkowitz's darts are less aptly aimed at Wolfgang et al. than they are at young instructors in Sociology 101 who think of "norm" and "value" literally, and who evoke images of hoodlums pummelling old ladies to secure commendations from peers, or who see violence transmitted through conversations such as "When someone adversely mentions your mother, it is incumbent on you to coldly and dispassionately. . . ." Lest I be accused of disciplinary parochialism, let me add that such conceptual translations are not confined to sociologists. A recent effort to apply Rokeach's value inventory as a test of subcultural theory (Ball-Rokeach, 1973), for example, presupposes that such theory sees violent behavior stemming from generic norms (intellectually subscribed to) about violence. It is significant that, when Wolfgang and Ferracuti *themselves* set out to test their views, they used a number of projective instruments, which were designed to

From Hans Toch, "Normatively Hostile, Purposefully Hostile, or Disinhibitedly Bloody Angry?" 15(2) *Journal of Research in Crime and Delinquency* 162-165 (1978). Copyright 1978 by the National Council on Crime and Delinquency.

tap unconscious reactions to violence-related perceptual stimuli (Ferracuti and Wolfgang, 1973).[1]

The relationship between the violent offender and the norms of his reference groups can obviously be highly variable. Some youths are overconformists, and some (who are just as other-directed) use violence to "prove" their independence.[2] Normative influence can also vary in kind. Some of us respond to monothematic pressures, while others of us are subject to cross-pressures. Finally, there are some situations that call for normative behavior (what Redl calls the "playing of the peer cassette") and others that do not. A youth may thus let an insult pass in a deserted alley, but he cannot afford to do so when he is surrounded by the ladies' auxiliary of his street gang. Berkowitz's own data contain rich illustrations of contextual variability. In two-thirds of Berkowitz's incidents, for example, he tells us that the perpetrators "were acquainted with the other people around them at the time"; Berkowitz notes that "some [aggressors] were a bit concerned about maintaining their reputation as tough and strong," and that more than half thought that "most men" would have reacted violently if they were similarly provoked. What Berkowitz emphasizes is that at the point of wielding the knife or bottle or whatever, few men were concerned with public opinion. At this juncture, the men tell us that they were monomoniacally committed to the task at hand, which was inflicting lacerations and concussions. But the aggressors also tell us that they felt they had been attacked and victimized, that their honor was impugned, and that *this* interpersonal situation—as opposed to other situations they had encountered —justified the lifting of their self-controls and the opening of their floodgates of unmitigated hostility.

Berkowitz's informants did not characterize themselves as throwing random tantrums or as picking convenient targets for satisfying catharses (such statements, one hastens to add, *are* on occasion made, in interviews, by violent offenders, but fortunately they are rare). In not responding this way, the men reflected their view of "appropriate" contextual forces defining the occasions for their violence—forces that *are* reconcilable with subcultural theory—at

---

1. In their original statement, Wolfgang and Ferracuti (1967) proposed the use of psychophysical methods to test their theory. Since this approach sounds implausible and the projective approach proved less than useful, alternate procedures for confirming the subcultural hypothesis remain to be invented by some ingenious partisan of the theory.

2. In a sense, this can involve a norm that is antagonistic and one that is affirmative. In Berkowitz's self-styled "unusual" example (which is not so unusual), we have a case in point: "[The constable] said, 'Get in the car.' I said, 'What for? . . . You tell me first and I'll get in.' It went on like that." The norm has to do with the obligation of legitimate authority to document its instructions with a rationale. Violence, incidentally, could have been prevented if the officer had been somewhat sensitive to this norm. And this probably means an officer who did not carry violence-promotive norms of his own, such as "No one has the right to question Representatives of the Law."

least with some readings of it. The theory stipulates that norms must be internalized by subcultural members. This means that peers do not have to be there, encouraging the aggressor to aggress; it means that it is unnecessary for the aggressor to reminisce about whence he derived his criteria of honor or his indexes of self-esteem. What is necessary is that the offender's perspective about unforgivable affronts should be more compatible with the criteria that are prevalent in his neighborhood than with reactions fashionable in other parts of town. About such perspectives, we lack systematic data. What we have are impressionistic observations of codes of honor undergirding vendettas in Sardinia and fist fights among Philadelphia or Chicago street gang members, and these observations are compatible with the subcultural hypothesis.

I am not denigrating—nor do I wish to denigrate—Berkowitz's documentation of the role of unleashed rage in violent conduct. An excessively rationalistic or sociologistic view of violence is a gross caricature. By the same token, a full-blooded (no pun) perspective of violence requires keeping in mind the discoveries of sociologists and of social learning theorists (Bandura, 1973), so as to avoid regression to a stripped-down frustration-aggression model which ignores the dramatic fact that even dedicated violent offenders explode in a restricted range of situations, which (to them) have violence-promotive connotations (Toch, 1969).

To be sure, there are the personal motives, purposes, and functions of violence, which our quote from Bandura has summarized. This issue is one that the subcultural perspective does not illuminate; the theory admits that some persons are more apt to internalize subcultural norms than others; it even accommodates the possibility that violent men may exceed subcultural prescriptions or may adopt them overeagerly. The theory tells us little about the connotations attached to subcultural norms by the prodigious violence-practitioner who, by virtue of his violence-virtuosity, is unrepresentative of his own subculture.

As much as it hurts me to admit it, I believe that psychological interpretations of violent people's motives are clinical judgments, and that they reflect predilections for dynamic constructs that are matters of taste. Feshbach and I, for example, have a fondness for the concept of self-esteem, which is not shared by Berkowitz and others. Berkowitz, on the other hand, finds it useful to focus on the phenomenology of impulse release, which appeals to me but not to Bandura, who finds cognitive concepts more useful than he does images of boilers, valves, and unleashed impulses.

What is most important, however, is that all of us (including the subculturists) are apt to welcome first-hand descriptions of violence which highlight pressures and motives operating in real-life aggression. Here Leonard Berkowitz has done us a remarkable favor. In his move from ingenious laboratory studies of aggression to sensitive interviews in the gaols of not-so-merrie England, Berkowitz has added to our repository of portraits of significant violent acts, which enrich our understanding. It is a tribute to Berkowitz that any students of violence, of whatever persuasion, can find his portraits suggestive. Berkowitz has enriched our thinking, and greater tribute hath no man in the enterprise to which we subscribe.

REFERENCES

BALL-ROKEACH, S. J.
 1973 "Values and Violence: A Test of the Subculture of Violence Thesis." *American Sociological Review* 38: 736–750.
BANDURA, A.
 1973 *Aggression: A Social Learning Analysis.* Englewood Cliffs, N.J.: Prentice-Hall.
 In   "The Social Learning Perspective: Mechanisms of Aggression." In *The*
 Press *Psychology of Crime and Criminal Justice,* H. Toch, ed. New York: Holt, Rinehart and Winston.
FERRACUTI, F., and M. WOLFGANG
 1973 *Psychological Testing of the Subculture of Violence.* Rome, Italy: Bulzoni.
FESHBACH, S.
 1970 "Aggression." In *Carmichael's Manual of Child Psychology,* Vol. 2, P. H. Mussen, ed. New York: Wiley.
TOCH, H.
 1969 *Violent Men: An Inquiry into the Psychology of Violence.* Chicago: Aldine.
WOLFGANG, M., and F. FERRACUTI
 1967 *The Subculture of Violence: Towards an Integrated Theory of Criminology.* London: Tavistock.

Hans Toch is Professor in Department of Psychology at the State University of New York at Buffalo. He is the author of Psychology of Crime and Criminal Justice, Men in Crisis, *and the forthcoming* The Therapeutic Community in Prison.

18

VIOLENCE, PERSONALITY, DETERRENCE, AND CULTURE

LYNN A. CURTIS

Professor Berkowitz's article raises in my mind some conceptual, empirical, and policy questions.

For the most part, I am thinking about homicide and assault, the two crimes most associated with a culture of violence in present-day urban America.

CONCEPTUAL OBSERVATIONS

Berkowitz believes that the notion of a culture of violence is one of several theories which place too great an emphasis on instrumental aggression. Instrumental aggression involves the seeking of social rewards—especially the approval of other people, or at least the avoidance of their disapproval.

The culture of violence has been presented in a number of different ways. Some, I believe, are not based mainly on violence as a means of gaining the approval of others.

My own work (1974, 1975) illustrates this point of view. I have looked at how poor, young American males adapt to structural inequalities, institutional racism, and blocked economic opportunities. One convenient paradigm is that presented by Lee Rainwater (1970):

White cupidity
creates
structural conditions highly inimical to social adaptation
to which nonwhite minorities adapt
by
social and personal responses which
serve to sustain the individual in his punishing world
but which
also generate aggressiveness toward the self and others
which results in
suffering directly inflicted by nonwhite
minorities on themselves and on others

We must begin, I believe, with individual personalities. Some people who are young, poor, and male find that there are fewer obstacles to expressing themselves in American society through physical toughness than through material

From Lynn A. Curtis, "Violence, Personality, Deterrence, and Culture," 15(2) *Journal of Research in Crime and Delinquency* 166-171 (1978). Copyright 1978 by the National Council on Crime and Delinquency.

success. We do not know much about why some adapt to the inner-city environment in this way and why others do not. Careful investigations, such as those by Hans Toch (1969), must conclude that different individuals have different instigators and inhibitors to violence, in spite of common circumstances.

One critical—and relatively unexplored—personality variable may be verbal manipulative ability. The most sophisticated street pimps are said to use violence only as a last resort in keeping their women under control. However, less verbally skilled pimps are said to place greater reliance on physical means of maintaining control. This may be generalizable to young, poor males in many different situations—where lack of verbal skill leaves by default only force and toughness (e.g., Milner and Milner, 1972).

Persons may develop these responses on their own, or they may learn them from others, especially in inner-city ghettos and slums. This is part of the socialization experience. Such learning can be the basis for sharing values that teach how masculinity is expressed by physical toughness. These values can be the basis of what can loosely be called a culture of violence.

Consider how this applies to the most frequently reported context of homicide and assault—an ostensibly trivial altercation between two young, poor males. An acceptance of physical toughness and its associated values by one or both parties can increase the probability that (1) conflicts will begin and (2) they will then escalate in physical intensity. The first probability reflects a brittle defensiveness and a reiteration of the significance of expressive, physical manliness in word and action. These can generate heated standoffs in situations that persons not accepting violence-related values might find trivial. Once a conflict has been initiated, the second probability is raised by the precedent of violent conflict resolution learned through past socialization experience.

I do not see such recourse to violence as a constant or intense search for external approval—although peer acceptance is reinforcing and, in this sense, the masculine image generated is a reward. To me, such recourse to violence is more a means of adapting and coping that is shared by some individuals through values and behaviors. There is a common understanding of violence as self-approval (Berkowitz's term), rather than a shared need for confirmation by others.

Berkowitz's men tend to show internal rage, almost compulsive aggression, low boiling points, and limited self-control. The implication is that these are "inner" characteristics, independent of external influences. I would argue that they might be a combination of "inner" characteristics and learned values and behavior.

In this way, I believe that Berkowitz's work can be integrated into a version of the culture of violence thesis, rather than used as an argument against it. Berkowitz's work is valuable as a tool in helping relate personality variables to cultural variables. Such linkages have been lacking in most work on the idea of a culture of violence.

EMPIRICAL OBSERVATIONS

This speculation should not displace the necessity for testing more directly the culture of violence theories. Empirical proof by defenders of the thesis has not been forthcoming.

Yet it is equally true that the work of critics is seriously flawed. This has not been brought to light in most debates over the theory. I wish to do so here.

Professor Berkowitz refers to the works of Ball-Rokeach (1973) and Erlanger (1972, 1974a, 1974b). Elsewhere, I have detailed the many problems with Ball-Rokeach's measures of values (Curtis, 1975). Using the Rokeach Value Survey, which she describes as "particularly well suited" to measure values related to a "macho" lifestyle, Ball-Rokeach finds little support for the Wolfgang-Ferracuti version (1967) of the culture of violence thesis. The value of this survey is questionable.

Robinson and Shaver (1973) have noted that Rokeach does not say how the initial set of values was selected and then modified into the final instrument of eighteen "terminal" and eighteen "instrumental" values. In turn, it is difficult to follow how Ball-Rokeach selected a subset of these values and labeled them indicators of "macho" lifestyles.

The fundamental question is one of validity. There is a need to validate empirically (e.g., through factor or cluster analysis) the appropriateness of parameters derived from the literature. Ball-Rokeach seems to pluck out certain parameters in a relatively ad hoc way from a questionable instrument and label them "macho" without any thought of empirical verification of their validity.

Ball-Rokeach bases part of her criticism on a sample of inmates. Armed robbers are classified as "violent" and unarmed robbers as "nonviolent." Thus, Ball-Rokeach seems unaware of the greater frequency of injury in unarmed than in armed robbery, which has been demonstrated in several studies. Nor does she recognize the possibility, raised in other research, that unarmed robbers may associate with violent cultural values more frequently than armed robbers. It can therefore be argued that her procedure misclassifies the two sets of robbers, consequently yielding invalid scores for her "degree of participation in violence" index when the so-called violent group is compared with the nonviolent one (Curtis, 1975).

There is much more that is misguided about Ball-Rokeach's work, and Erlanger has helped point this out. His own criticism of the culture of violence is more thoughtful and analytically rigorous. Yet, here too, many questions can be raised. Again, I draw upon my more detailed examination (Curtis, 1975) to demonstrate flaws in Erlanger's research.

For example, Erlanger places heavy reliance on a household sample in presenting empirical evidence unsupportive of the culture of violence. Yet there is good reason to believe that the most intense violence-related patterns are carried by "streetcorner" men and boys often not attached to households, or, if they are, rarely at home. Further, in assessing a culture of violence in terms of participant observation and other field studies, Erlanger says that many well-known investigations, such as those of Liebow (1967) and Suttles (1968), make little or no mention of violence. Yet, curiously, Erlanger does not refer to the well-known participant observations, at least equal in number, that do. The studies by Hannerz (1969), Rainwater (1970), and Hippler (1974) are obvious examples.

More definitive work is necessary. In the meantime, a careful summary and criticism of empirical findings, pro and con, are very much needed.

POLICY OBSERVATIONS

Professor Berkowitz's work is useful in cautioning against the positions of conservatives who call for a policy of deterrence as the major strategy against crime. These writers make the critical assumption that offenders act "rationally" and so will reconsider potential crime if its costs are raised sufficiently. For example, James Q. Wilson (1975) argues that, "If the expected cost of crime goes up without a corresponding increase in the expected benefits, then the would-be criminal—unless he or she is among that small fraction of criminals who are utterly irrational—engages in less crime."

Yet, as Berkowitz's pursuit of noninstrumental violence helps suggest, a continuum of "rational" to "irrational" behavior does not really fit behavioral reality. Such academic descriptions do not capture the personality factors, events, precipitating forces, motives, perceptions, and decisions underlying much of the homicide and assault perpetrated. This thinking has only limited relevance to street values and ghetto experiences in the United States.

Although homicide and assault are the most serious crimes, Wilson disregards them by saying that he is interested in "predatory street crime," which is largely theft. But even here research findings are equivocal. Wilson demonstrates the same limitations as does Ball-Rokeach. He does not seem to realize that most theft is committed by relatively unsophisticated and unprofessional offenders, who often act in unplanned and ostensibly random ways. They not only will rob persons who do not have money but will fight back; they usually are young; and they tend not to carry weapons. These persons use physical force and inflict injury more often than the minority of robbers who are Wilsonian cost-effective professionals.

To be sure, there are studies by economists that show a statistically significant, but weak, negative association between certainty and severity of punishment, on the one hand, and crime rates, on the other. To a limited but statistically significant degree, more punishment is associated with less crime and less punishment with more crime. Yet this situation does not necessarily prove that punishment deters crime. An equally plausible inference is that crime deters punishment; that is, as more crime overwhelms the police, the courts, and the prisons, it becomes less likely that criminals will be caught and jailed.

This is not to argue that the criminal justice system is ineffective in deterring certain offenders from committing certain crimes in certain situations. Any doubter need only observe the increase in crime during police strikes and slowdowns. The point is that, from what is known, we cannot confidently predict that more severe and more certain punishment will greatly affect rates of violent crime. Much of the work on deterrence is based on untested assumptions or invalid generalizations made from limited statistics.

The net effect of the deterrence philosophy and its inaccurate behavioral assumption is to provide a rationale for the continued Vietnamization of the criminal justice system—more men, more equipment, more incursions, and swift and sure punishment to deter a nonwhite enemy whose psychology the white power brokers of this nation presume to understand. This overall tone is warranted by neither the facts at hand nor the canons of scientific inference.

CONCLUSIONS

I do not, finally, want to be labeled as an inflexible advocate of the notion of a culture of violence. I interpret culture as a critical variable, but one that is intervening between the ultimate determinants—the structural inequalities—and the behavioral outcomes of violent crime. Policy intervention should concentrate on the structural conditions. A change in these will, in time, cause a change in the cultural adaptations.

REFERENCES

BALL-ROKEACH, S.
   1973   "Values and Violence: A Test of the Subculture of Violence Thesis." *American Sociological Review* 38: 736–750.
CURTIS, L.
   1974   *Criminal Violence.* Lexington, Mass.: Lexington Books.
   1975   *Violence, Race and Culture.* Lexington, Mass.: Lexington Books.
ERLANGER, H. S.
   1972   "An Empirical Critique of Theories of Interpersonal Violence." Paper presented at the 67th Annual Meeting, American Sociological Association. New Orleans, La. (Aug. 28).
   1974a "The Empirical Status of the Violence of Culture Thesis." *Social Problems* 22: 280–292.
   1974b "Social Class and Corporal Punishment in Child Rearing: A Reassessment." *American Sociological Review* 39: 68–85.
HANNERZ, U.
   1969   *Soulside.* New York: Columbia University Press.
HIPPLER, A.
   1974   *Hunter's Point.* New York: Basic Books.
LIEBOW, E.
   1967   *Talley's Corner.* Boston: Little, Brown.

MILNER, C., and R. MILNER
   1972   *Black Players.* Boston: Little, Brown.
RAINWATER, L.
   1970   *Behind Ghetto Walls.* Chicago: Aldine.
ROBINSON, J., and P. SHAVER
   1973   *Measures of Social Psychological Attitudes.* Ann Arbor: University of Michigan.
SUTTLES, G.
   1968   *The Social Order of the Slum.* Chicago: University of Chicago Press.
TOCH, H.
   1969   *Violent Men.* Chicago: Aldine.
WILSON, J. Q.
   1975   *Thinking about Crime.* New York: Basic Books.
WOLFGANG, M., and F. FERRACUTI
   1967   *The Subculture of Violence: Towards an Integrated Theory of Criminology.* London: Tavistock.

Lynn A. Curtis is Urban Policy Advisor to HUD Secretary Patricia Roberts Harris on her personal staff and Executive Director of the Interagency Urban and Regional Policy Group that developed the President's National Urban Policy. He is the author of five books and over 50 articles and speeches on criminology.

19

ON THE HISTORY OF VIOLENT CRIME
IN EUROPE AND AMERICA

TED ROBERT GURR

Great social and demographic changes seem to work profound changes on patterns of crime. This is especially true of the most personally threatening kinds of offenses: murder and assault, robbery and rape. Looking back at the historical traces of crime and crime control in Western societies, we can dimly see the shapes of tidal waves of violent crime, many decades apart, which far overshadow the short-run ebbs and flows described as "crime waves" by contemporary journalists and officials. In the United States one of these tidal waves may have crested in the 1970s, as Wesley Skogan argues in the next chapter, but its passing—if indeed it does pass—will leave in its wake a persisting debate about its origins and profound anxiety about the future among crime-scared Americans. What I shall try to do in this chapter is interpret America's experience of violent crime by comparison with what has happened in other Western societies in the recent and more distant past. The historical and comparative record should help dispel the notion that America's contemporary social problems, along with her tattered virtues, are somehow unique. And while this record does not point to unambiguous explanations for rising crime, it does suggest that some common-sense explanations are more plausible than others.

England is the chief source of American legal codes and institutions of criminal justice, so we shall begin there.

THE ENGLISH EXPERIENCE

Crimes against persons and property leave victims, not statistical records. The court records on which most historical analysis relies are a gauge of the success of victims, witnesses, and constables in bringing offenders to justice, not a direct measure of the extent of crime. Some variations in the records may be due to quirks of official procedures or to changing law and judicial practice. Still, most historians are reasonably confident that court records of the most serious offenses correlate with

AUTHOR'S NOTE: *The author is Payson S. Wild Professor of political science at Northwestern University. His many books and monographs include* Why Men Rebel, *which won the Woodrow Wilson Prize as the best book in political science of 1970, and* Rogues, Rebels, and Reformers: A Political History of Urban Crime and Conflict *(Sage Publications, 1976).*

the true incidence of crime. They also conclude that when courts record large changes over time in the volume of serious offenses brought to trial, they usually are responding to real changes in the extent of crime.[1]

A recent study of some remarkably complete thirteenth-century records shows convincingly that murderous brawls and violent deaths at the hands of robbers were everyday occurrences in medieval England. The annual murder rates ranged from 10 to 25 per 100,000 population in rural counties—with the average nearer the higher figure than the lower one. The comparable rate for England and Wales now is 1.97 per 100,000 (in 1974) while in the United States it is 9.77 (1974). One remarkable feature of medieval homicide, from our perspective, is that it was most common in villages and isolated farmsteads. The homicide rates in the small cities of Bristol and London were lower by half, just the opposite of our contemporary pattern of crime-ridden cities and orderly towns and countryside.[2]

By almost all accounts the medieval period in all Europe was a violent and brutal age whose chronicles and letters, as Given remarks, are "filled with stories of murder and rapine."[3] In fact his data for England suggest that homicide rates were increasing during the thirteenth century. But then the view is clouded over and nearly 400 years pass before we find another longitudinal study. Beattie has traced the incidence of crime from 1660 to 1800 through the court records of two English counties, rural Sussex and suburban Surrey, which includes London south of the Thames. In this era crimes against persons and property were considerably more numerous in urban parishes than rural ones, judging by numbers of indictments per 100,000 population. Trends were also somewhat different between town and country, suggesting that different socioeconomic forces were at work. But one general pattern stands out. From 1660 to c. 1720 the trend in indictments for serious crimes held steady or declined in both counties. Then, between the 1720s and the 1760s, came a series of sharp but temporary increases, some of them as great as 400 percent: the peaks in urban assault occurred in the 1720s, 1730s, and again in the 1760s; in rural assault in the 1730s; in property crime in the 1740s and 1750s. After these peaks the rates declined for a generation or more, only to begin a sharp across-the-board rise just before 1800.[4] Beattie's study ends here at the threshold of the modern era. Concern about crime in nineteenth-century England was now centered in the cities, above all in London. The disorderly metropolis was the crucible in which present-day English and American policies and institutions of criminal justice were forged.

By the 1820s London was Europe's largest city, the commercial and political hub of the world's most prosperous society and greatest empire. It was also a dangerous, crime-ridden place. Professional robbers and receivers flourished in neighborhoods where it was worth a prosperous man's life and possessions to venture at night. Thousands of street urchins lived by petty theft during the day and slept in the noisome alleyways and courtyards. A contemporary writer summed up London's squalor and disorder when he denounced the city as "the infernal wen."[5]

The criminal laws designed to control the rampant crime of Georgian England had a harsh bite. The death penalty was specified for more than 200 offenses, on the widely accepted principle that severe punishment was an effective deterrent. But no centralized, professional police force existed to catch offenders. Constables, professional "thief-takers," and private citizens hailed petty offenders before magistrates who were seldom trained in law and were often venal. The judges who heard serious cases had neither the legal discretion nor the inclination to be lenient. The defendant's hopes rested with the reluctance of many a jury to convict in capital cases, or the mercy of the crown in commuting his death sentence to transportation to the Australian penal colonies. Such prisons as existed aimed neither to punish nor rehabilitate. Gaols (the Americans spelled it "jails") held debtors and those waiting to be tried or executed; the bridewells put vagrants and other petty offenders to forced labor for the profit of their officials.

Between the 1820s and the 1870s this hodgepodge was transformed into a modern system of criminal justice. A series of parliamentary acts overhauled the criminal law, penalties were prescribed in proportion to the seriousness of the offense, the death penalty was abolished for all crimes except murder and treason. London's patchwork police services of river police and Bow Street runners, constables and parish watchmen, were replaced in 1829 by the centralized Metropolitan Police. The courts were improved. Beginning in the 1850s, child thieves were committed to new reformatories and kept there long enough to receive basic education and work training. Adult offenders were sentenced to long terms in the new convict prisons, where discipline was harsh and rehabilitation piously sought through hard, monotonous labor.

The zeal of London's new "bobbies" showed up at first in increased arrests and convictions. But by the 1850s common crime seemed on the decline and by the end of Queen Victoria's reign in 1901, the city was thought by the English and visiting continentals alike to be one of the most orderly in all Europe. The official statistics suggest to social historians that the trend continued till the late 1920s, when the conviction rate for all indictable (serious) offenses was one-ninth of the eighteen-forties level. Police statistics on known offenses and arrests, first published in 1869, are especially convincing. Known serious offenses fell by an average of 10 percent per decade for 60 years thereafter. The arrest rate for all offenses, serious and petty ones, was down by a ratio of three to one despite a steady increase in the absolute and proportional size of the Metropolitan Police force. Data on convictions show assault down by a ratio of five to one, total theft by four to one, robbery by more than ten to one. Burglary was the only serious offense to go against the trends, thanks to the activities of a small cadre of professional housebreakers who became increasingly successful at eluding the police.[6]

London was the bellwether for all England and Wales. Professional police forces on the London model were established throughout the country by mid-century. Court reform and the new prison system operated nationwide. The incidence of crime may have reached its peak as early as the 1820s, but the peak in official action, as registered by numbers of trials and convictions, occurred in the 1840s. Thereafter all the national indicators of crime and punishment declined steadily, parallel to those of the Metropolitan Police district.

Serious crime reached it lowest recorded ebb in London late in the 1920s. During the Great Depression which followed, burglary thrived while the war years from 1940 to 1945 saw sharp increases in murder, assault, and robbery. In 1945-1946 the ranks of the Metropolitan Police were expanded from their wartime low, and returning veterans, who were responsible for at least part of the crime problem, soon found their ways into jobs or prisons. So serious crime subsided after 1946, but only for a few years. Early in the 1950s an inexorable increase began. In the 25 years after 1950 indictable offenses known to police in London grew by 450 percent, with the nastiest kinds of crimes increasing most sharply. From 1950 to 1974 murders were up 300 percent, rape by 600 percent, assault by 900 percent, and robbery by 1,200 percent. In this period as in the nineteenth century, London led the way for all England and Wales. Countrywide crime rates were lower but the rates of increase were very much the same.

The evidence sketched above points to three great surges of violent crime in England, roughly a century apart. They crested in the mid-1700s, in the 1830s and 1840s, and perhaps in the 1970s. Figure 13.1 shows London's incidence of higher-court convictions for murder and assault from the 1830s, when they averaged 12 per year per 100,000 people, to the 1920s, when they were less than 2 per 100,000. It also shows the sharp increase in murder and manslaughter known to police which began c. 1955 and reached 18 per 100,000 by 1974. Assaults known to police are literally off the graph. In 1950 they were reported at the rate of 13 per 100,000, by 1974 they exceeded 120 per 100,000. This does not mean that the 1970s were more violent in London than the 1830s, since far more offenses come to police attention than ever culminate in convictions. The national trends since 1945 in crimes against persons and serious theft are shown in Figure 13.3. The lowest recorded rate in the 30-year period is set at 1.00 so that each increase of one unit on the vertical axis represents an increase of 100 percent in the rate of crime.

The recent peaks in English crime are so dramatic that they obscure a much longer-term trend which is of equal or greater importance. It is the decline in violent crime, which is evident from the homicide rates summarized in Table 13.1. Homicide rates were three times higher in the thirteenth century than the seventeenth, three times higher in the seventeenth century than the nineteenth, and in London they were twice as high in the early nineteenth century as they are now. The decline in homicide has been particularly great in the towns and rural areas. And though Londoners today are more murderous than in the recent past, the metropolis remains a far safer place than it was in earlier centuries.

This brief survey of the English historical evidence suggests two patterns in need of explanation: the long-run decline in interpersonal violence, and the short-run peaks in serious crimes against persons and property. A plausible one-word explanation for the decline in homicide is "civilization" and all that it implies about the restraint of aggressive impulses and the acceptance of humanistic values. By their own accounts medieval people were easily angered to the point of violence and enmeshed in a culture which accepted, even glorified many forms of brutality and violence. The progress of Western civilization has been marked by increasing internal and external controls on the show of violence. People are socialized to control and displace anger. Norms of conduct in almost all organized activity stress nonviolent means of accomplishing goals. Interpersonal violence within the community and nation is prohibited and punished in almost all circumstances. None of this was true of medieval society, in England or on the Continent, and the changes occurred gradually and selectively. The process contributed not only to the decline in homicide but the decline and ultimate abandonment of executions in most Western

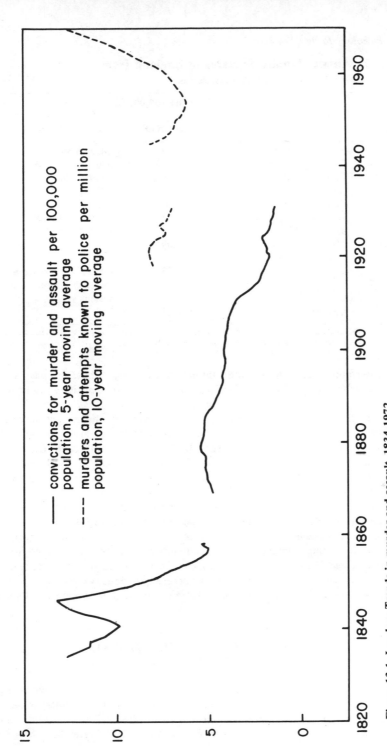

Figure 13.1: London: Trends in murder and assault, 1834-1972

Source: work cited in note 6, pp. 371-372.

415

Table 13.1: Annual Homicide Rates in England from the 13th to the 20th Centuries

Date	Locale	Rate per 100,000 Population[a]	Source
c. 1250	5 rural counties	c. 20	Given, note 2
c. 1200	London	c. 12	ibid.
1663-65	Surrey County (incl. S. London)	6.1	Beattie, note 4
1722-24	Surrey County	2.3	ibid.
1821-30	England and Wales excluding Middlesex	1.48	*British Sessional Papers,* various years
1821-30	Middlesex County (incl. most of London)	2.09	ibid.
1921-30	London	0.73[a]	*Report of the Commissioner of Police. . . .* various years
1966-72	London	1.29[a]	ibid.

a. Rates before 1900 are calculated from committals to trial for murder and manslaughter; rates after 1900 are calculated from cases known to police. Known offenses and committals are only approximately comparable.

societies, the end of slavery and the brutalization of wage labor, the passing of corporal punishment in schools and prisons, and many other positive features of contemporary life that are often taken for granted.[7]

How far does this cultural explanation go toward explaining changing crime rates? It is plausible to apply it to all crimes in which force and violence are used, including assault, rape, armed robbery, and vandalism. But it is scarcely applicable to property crimes without violence, and in fact there is reason to think that offenses like burglary, fraud, and petty theft march to different music: they seem to vary with economic necessity and opportunity.[8]

The cultural explanation for the declining trend in homicidal violence does not explain the episodic increases in serious crimes in English history. It is trivial to say that they occurred because the civilizing constraints on aggression were temporarily relaxed, just as it is superficial to attribute contemporary crime in the United States to "permissiveness." The questions are which of many constraints have eased, on whom, and why. Before suggesting answers to these questions, we review evidence for the occurrence of major crime waves elsewhere, beginning with the United States.

PERSPECTIVES ON THE HISTORY OF CRIME IN AMERICA

Studies of crime's patterns and trends in the United States as a whole have always been hindered by the lack of good, comparable data. Even in the 1960s, some 30 years after the FBI began compiling and publishing the annual Uniform Crime Reports, criminologists were of the opinion that the United States had the least reliable crime data of all Western societies.[9] The key reason is not political malfeasance or bureaucratic ineptitude—though those factors have played a part—but rather the localized character of policing and criminal justice administration in the United States. There are sharp differences among cities and regions in police efficiency, procedures, and statistical recording practices. Only gradually and grudgingly has the reporting of data on offenses known to police and arrests become more uniform across the country. And even now there is no regular, comprehensive reporting on criminal indictments and convictions in the United States, though the English have compiled such data since 1805.

The history of crime in the United States has been most thoroughly studied in cities where urban police and court records exist in greatest depth and detail. We know most about crime trends in Massachusetts, especially Boston and Salem, beginning in the 1820s. The general trend traced by data on arrests is summarized by Roger Lane: "serious crime in metropolitan Boston has declined sharply between the middle of the 19th century and the middle of the 20th." The decline is most pronounced with respect to murder and assault. Boston's murder arrest rate peaked above 7.0 per 100,000 c. 1860 and was less than 2.0 in 1950, as shown in Figure 13.2. The arrest rate for assault declined by a 4 to 1 ratio over the same period. Other offenses show different trends. Rape steadily increased over the century, perhaps because victims became more willing to report offenses. Burglaries and robberies decreased raggedly during the latter part of the nineteenth century but jumped sharply during the First World War and the Great Depression. Moreover the rate of arrests for petty offenses moved pronouncedly upwards from the 1840s onward, almost entirely because of increasing drunk and disorderly arrests. Drunkenness was a dire problem in nineteenth-century American cities, as it was in much of Europe. Tolerated at first, it gained increasing attention from the temperance movement and the police. The rise of professional policing and the decline of serious crime both helped city police in Boston and elsewhere give greater attention to controlling public drunkenness.[10]

Boston's trend of declining serious crime from the 1860s to the 1950s parallels the century of improving public order in London and all England and Wales. Moreover it was accompanied by similar reforms in the criminal justice system, especially the professionalization and expansion of the Boston police. But what the decline actually represents, as we have seen in England, is the ebb from a great wave of crime. The peak in England occurred in the 1830s and 1840s; in Boston and other American cities the upsurge began in the 1850s and crested in the 1870s. In both societies the onset of the waves precedes the introduction of comprehensive systems of recording crime data, so the precise timing, magnitude, and composition of the increase is difficult to ascertain. But the converging evidence of different American studies is convincing about the fact of the wave. Ferdinand's study of Boston begins in 1849, and virtually every arrest indicator he uses shows two sharp increases after 1849, the first peaking in 1855-1859 and the second around 1870, with a lull during or immediately after the Civil War years (see Figure 13.2). The overall rate of increase in arrests for major crime in the 20 years after 1849 was roughly 300 percent.[11] Another study of Boston which uses arrests for property offenses pushes our knowledge back to the 1820s: low crime rates in 1849 were not a fluke but seemingly the result of a gradual decline in property crime that had been underway for a generation.[12] In a parallel study of Salem, Massachusetts, Ferdinand found that assault rates and serious offenses generally went sharply upward in the 1860s and 1870s before begining the now familiar irregular, long-term decline. Powell reports a similar rise in crimes against the person in Buffalo, New York, beginning in the 1850s and peaking out c. 1870.[13] Two other cities whose early arrest data show a rise beginning in the 1850s are New York and New Orleans.[14] In fact I have found no historical study of American crime for this period whose evidence traces any other pattern, though of all the scholars cited only Powell regards the wave as in any way exceptional or worth explaining.[15]

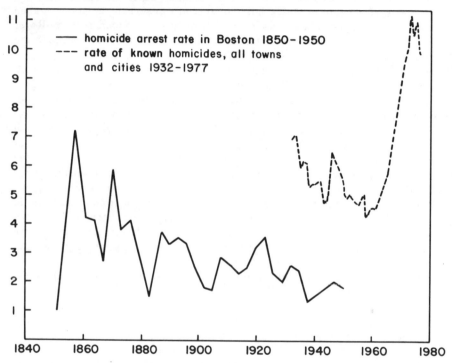

Figure 13.2: Urban homicide trends in the United States per 100,000 population

Sources: Boston: Theodore N. Ferdinand, article cited in note 8, p. 372; all cities: FBI Uniform Crime Reports.

The gradual ebb in urban American crime from 1870 to 1940 is more evident in studies which begin in 1850 than those which begin at the turn of the twentieth century. In the 1920s many Americans were convinced that a crime wave was in progress because, just before the First World War, serious offenses against persons and property began to increase and continued upward until the onset of the Great Depression. The reversal is evident in a number of the city studies cited above and is most clearly documented in a study by Sutherland and Gehlke which spans the period from 1900 to 1930. In five major cities they find that homicide, robbery, and burglary arrests all increased from 1910 to the late 1920s by as much as 500 percent. But they are skeptical about the persistence of the trend and critical of journalistically inspired emotionalism about crime rates.[16] In retrospect, their contention that the crest had passed before 1930 was correct. A later study of Chicago from 1919 to 1939 by Willbach shows that arrest rates for crimes against persons peaked in 1927 followed by a 3:1 decline in the next twelve years. The same author's careful study of New York during this period gives similar results.[17] And the FBI's Uniform Crime Report show that for the country as a whole the period from 1933 to 1940 was one of declining crime.

After 1940 serious crime in the United States followed trends similar to those in England. Personal and property crime both edged up during the Second World War, reaching a plateau in the late 1940s. (In England they declined after the war; in the United States they merely leveled off.) The renewed upward trend which has inspired so much contemporary controversy, fear, and "law and order" crime policies began early in the 1950s. Property crime rates moved up first; the combined rate of known burglaries and armed robberies quadrupled between 1950 and 1974. Crimes against persons did not turn sharply upward until after 1960. The trend in urban murder rates from 1932 to 1977 is compared with Boston's historical record in Figure 13.2. Not much can be made of the difference between Boston and other cities because known offenses and arrests are not precisely comparable. More important is the evidence that the urban murder rate increased by 250 percent between the late 1950s and 1973, the year which marks the apparent peak in violent crime.

The American historical evidence is too shallow to allow us to determine whether there is a long-term secular trend of declining interpersonal violence analogous to England's 700-year trend of falling murder rates. But the evidence of periodic waves of serious crime in both countries is unmistakable. Their most recent crime waves coincided with one another, but historically they did not, which suggests that if the waves have common causes or dynamics, they can operate in ways unique to one society *and* simultaneously among them. Before explanations are considered, we will look for evidence of similar crime trends and waves in crime in other Western societies.

CRIME IN OTHER WESTERN SOCIETIES

England's experience of successful crime control in the nineteenth and early twentieth centuries has parallels in other Western countries. In New South Wales, at literally the opposite end of the earth, colonial officials followed England's lead in reforming criminal justice and the police during the second and third quarters of the nineteenth century, and indicators of serious crime fell by ratios of ten to one and more. Since Australia's crime problems were imported from England in the form of transported convicts, it is scarcely surprising that crime rates fell when the convict population declined simultaneously with the introduction of more rational and humane treatment of offenders.[18] It is more surprising to find in Stockholm—a far smaller city in a very different society—a long-run pattern precisely like that of England and New South Wales. High rates of serious crime and the reforming impulse coincided in Sweden in the second quarter of the nineteenth century and the results were much the same. In the century between the 1840s and the 1930s the rate of convictions for crimes against persons in Stockholm declined by a ratio of about four to one and thefts by five to one. Moreover the most serious offenses declined more sharply than the less serious ones.[19]

Elsewhere in Europe crime trends were rather different. In France, the national rate of convictions for serious property crimes declined irregularly from the 1820s to the early 1960s, with temporary increases during and after the Franco-Prussian War of 1870-1871 and the First and Second World Wars. The rate of serious offenses against the person did not decline, however. Conviction rates for murder and grave assaults were as high in the 1920s as the 1820s, and as low in the 1860s as the 1950s. On the other hand, trials for petty assaults increased throughout the nineteenth century, probably because of increased official attention, not real changes in interpersonal violence.[20] In Germany, which did not become a unitary state until 1871, the property and personal crime rates moved gradually upward from 1882 until just before the onset of the First World War.[21] One consequence of military defeat and demobilization in postwar Germany and the remnants of the Austro-Hungarian Empire was a massive wave of personal and property crime, which subsided later in the 1920s.[22] We remarked above the postwar increase in crime in France, but it was of far lesser magnitude than in Germanic Europe.

The countries most affected by the Second World War also had short-lived "crime waves" during the war and its immediate aftermath, but everywhere the effects were temporary. The most remarkable postwar phenomenon is the near-universality of rising crime in Western societies during the 1960s and early 1970s. The British and North American experience is in no way unique. The late 1940s and early 1950s marked the low ebb of common crime in virtually every English-speaking country. Thereafter the trends were consistently upward. Some data on known offenses in five countries are given in Table 13.2. The rates of offense are quite different in any given year but not too much should be made of the differences since national crime-counting systems differ. Trends within each country are more realiably assessed than absolute differences among them. The trends can be reliably compared and in these countries all of them are strongly positive. In the United States homicides and assaults together increased at an average of 12 percent per year for a generation. Elsewhere the 1950s rates for these offenses were initially lower but the increases have been swifter. The rising trends in theft have been sustained just as long, and averaged between 8 and 14 percent per annum from 1950 to the 1970s. Moreover the most serious forms of property crime—robbery and burglary—rose about twice as rapidly as total theft in all these societies. Ireland seems the most favored country in this comparison. Its relatively low volume of crime may be credited to its Gaelic culture, religious traditionalism, or simply its small urban population. But these conditions did not inhibit the Irish from emulating the growing Anglo-American fondness for mayhem and theft during the 1960s.

Scandinavia provides another set of evidence, with Stockholm serving as a historical laboratory. Unlike London, the Great Depression of the 1930s had little effect on the Swedish capital's crime rates. During wartime, crime in neutral Stockholm rose and then subsided—until about 1950. Since then virtually every category of offense against persons and property has skyrocketed. These are some

Table 13.2: Crime Trends in English-Speaking Countries since 1950

Known Murder and Assaults per 100,000 population

	1950	c.1960	1970s[a]	Average Annual Increase
England and Wales	13.0	32.4	144.3	40%
London	13.0	26.2	123.5	35%
United States	58.0	91.2	237.4	12%
New South Wales	no data	15.5	21.7	4%
Canada	no data	158.2	436.0	13%
Republic of Ireland	5.9	13.7	38.3	24%

Known Theft per 100,000 Population

	1950	c.1960	1970s[a]	Average Annual Increase
England and Wales	847	1,317	3,659	13%
London	1,056	1,942	3,624	10%
United States	1,108	1,786	5,002	14%
New South Wales	no data	604	1,467	14%
Canada	no data	1,408	3,883	13%
Republic of Ireland	346	472	1,065	9%

a. Data for 1974 except England and Wales (1975), United States (1976), New South Wales (1970), and Ireland (1973).

20-year increases in crimes known to police: murder and murder attempts, 600 percent; assault and battery, more than 300 percent; rape and attempted rape, 300 percent; "crimes inflicting damage" (i.e., vandalism), 500 percent; all theft, 350 percent; robberies alone, 1,000 percent; fraud and embezzlement, 700 percent. In 1971, there was one theft reported to police for every eleven inhabitants of the city, which can be compared with 1974 figures of one per 20 Londoners, and one per 18 New Yorkers. In fairness to Stockholmers, they are more likely to report thefts to their trusted police than are cynical New Yorkers. The point remains that the Swedish welfare and criminal justice policies, which reformers credited for the historical improvement in public order, have not inhibited the contemporary rise of urban crime.

Stockholm represents in most severe form a criminal malaise that affected all of Scandinavia. Some comparative data are shown on Table 13.3. At the national level, crimes against persons started up later and more slowly than in Stockholm or the English-speaking countries, but there is no mistaking the presence of an escalating trend. The same is true of property crime. Moreover, we find in Scandinavia a phenomenon familiar from the English-speaking countries: the most serious property offenses have increased far more steeply than common theft. In Sweden, from 1950 to 1974, known theft increased by a multiple of three while the rarer offense of robbery grew tenfold. In Finland, from 1961 to 1973, the proportional increases were: all theft, 275 percent; robbery, 720 percent.

In the heartland of Western Europe that portrait of crime is significantly different in one major respect. There are no long-term increases in murder and assault in the

Table 13.3: Crime Trends in Scandinavian Countries since 1950

Known Assault and Murders per 100,000 Population

	1950	c.1960	1970s[a]	Average Annual Increase
Denmark	41.2	39.2	66.7	2%
Finland	no data	127.9	282.0	9%
Norway	no data	52.4	91.8	5%
Sweden	115.7	126.4	260.7	5%
Stockholm	90.7	266.5	403.2	16%

Known Theft per 100,000 Population

	1950	c.1960	1970s[a]	Average Annual Increase
Denmark	1,922	2,332	4,868	6%
Finland	no data	886	2,850	15%
Norway	no data	748	1,740	9%
Sweden	1,568	2,726	4,958	9%
Stockholm	1,933	4,250	8,215	15%

a. Data 1974-75 except Stockholm (1971).

continental democracies. Congratulations are premature, though, since Germany and France both began to move up in the late 1960s, too recently to certify the existence of an enduring trend. Property crime on the Continent is more of a piece with the English and Scandinavian experience. Theft rates began to rise later, sometime between 1955 and 1965, depending on the country. Since then the official statistics document steadily rising trends into the mid-1970s—with the sole exception of Switzerland, where theft rates have held essentially steady since 1945. These generalization about the continental countries neatly encompass Israel's experience as well.[23]

From the Marxist-Leninist point of view, this evidence of the rising tide of disorder in Western societies is the harbinger of capitalism's long-awaited collapse. The Eastern European commentators who offer this interpretation no doubt are uncomfortably aware that their own societies are suffering a similar affliction. How serious it is neither we nor they can say, since the European Communist states have not published sufficient statistical information to determine the trends.[24]

There is finally the case of Japan, an industrialized democratic society which has had unparalleled success in reducing crime rates—serious crime most of all—during the last two decades. Since 1955, Japan's murder and assault rates have both been halved. Simple theft has been reduced by about a quarter, known white-collar crime has been reduced to one-fifth its former levels, while the robbery rate is scarcely one-tenth of what it was in 1949-1950.

This pattern of change duplicates what happened in England, Sweden, and Australia between the 1840s and the 1920s: as public order improved, serious offenses declined more rapidly than petty ones. And it is the reverse of what has happened in contemporary Western societies, in which serious property crime has increased far faster than petty offenses.

These contrasts and images imply that a fairly high level of petty theft is endemic to prosperous societies, but that serious crime is not. Japan is a case in point. It is a capitalistic society which has had extraordinary success in reducing the incidence of murder, assault, and robbery. The improvement has been a sustained one—some 25 years in duration—and it has taken place in a society undergoing the rapid social and economic changes that elsewhere are assumed to be criminogenic.[25]

EXPLANATIONS OF CRIME

There are many hotly debated explanations of criminal behavior. Some blame the individual: the "criminal" is genetically or morally flawed. At the other end of the spectrum, officials are blamed: they selectively label certain acts deviant and those who engage in them criminal, for whom the stigma becomes a self-fulfilling prophecy.[26]

We want to explain, not individual behavior, but rather the periodic waves of serious crime which punctuate the history of many Western societies. Most explanations are specific to particular societies and periods. Many of them echo prevailing conservative, liberal, or radical views of society. The liberal explanations of rising crime in contemporary English-speaking societies are especially numerous. Substantial social and economic inequalities exist in all these societies, despite their general prosperity. Everywhere the penal system is harshly criticized because prisons are "schools for crime" which brutalize offenders rather than rehabilitating them. The police are often accused of corruption and a heavy-handed disregard for civil liberties. Add to this the special explanations preferred by social analysts confronted with rising crime in particular countries. Britain? Class tensions in a static economy. The United States? An angry black under class, its hopes stirred by promises of a Great Society which never arrived. Ireland? Modernization is eroding traditional acceptance of poverty and authority. Australia? Merely beery, exuberant youths challenging unpopular police.

If there is any universal truth to these kinds of conventional liberal wisdom about the social origins of crime, the Scandinavian countries surely should be more favored than some of the English-speaking nations. They are ethnically homogenous and their social ethos is strongly egalitarian. Their cities are free of slums and their social services are among the best in the world. Economically they have prospered since the end of the Second World War and have had low unemployment. Their police are widely respected, justice is ordinarily even-handed and efficient. Rehabilitation is the central aim of their penal system. But we have already seen that crime in Scandinavia has risen at rates comparable to those of English-speaking societies. Egalitarianism and social well-being may account for their lesser rates of increase in violent crime. They have not inhibited the growth of serious or petty theft in the least.

In pop and radical sociology it has been fashionable to blame rising crime rates on intensified policing and more thorough crime-reporting systems. Contemporary examples of both can be found: there are wide fluctuations in police attention to "victimless" crimes like prostitution and drug abuse, while changes in reporting systems produce abrupt discontinuities in crime statistics.[27] But neither explanation accounts for persistent trends up or down in the rate of common crime. If this explanation for the rising tide of theft and assault were to be taken seriously, we would have to suppose that the police forces of almost every Western society began a sustained expansion in manpower, detection, and crime reporting in the 1950s and 1960s. In none of our city or country studies is there evidence of such changes. These reforms occurred in European societies in the nineteenth century, not in the midtwentieth century, and they coincided with falling rates of common crime, not increasing ones. Also, common crimes come to police attention through reports of private citizens. If rising crime rates in Western societies were due mainly to more conscientious reporting by citizens, the increases would consist disproportionately of petty offenses. But the opposite is the case: serious offenses have increased much more than petty ones.[28]

The "better policing" explanation of rising rates of serious crime since 1950 is largely a myth. It is naive to think that crime statistics depict precisely the real incidence of crime because many victims, especially in high-crime areas, think it is useless to report their losses. But there is little doubt that the long-term trends common to most Western societies reflect real changes in social behavior of large magnitude. This is the social issue most in need of explanation, not the vagaries of police behavior.

The historical circumstances of great crime waves should help us distinguish between plausible and implausible, general and idiosyncratic explanations. Three kinds of social forces seem to be at work. One is modernization, the process by which Western societies were transformed from predominantly rural, agricultural societies into their present industrial, urban shape. Such transitions can be criminogenic if they disrupt traditional patterns of life and thought without replacing them with effective alternatives. And this is evidently what happened to some but not all the rural migrants to European cities in their early stages of growth. The more modern and urban a society becomes, however, the greater its capacity to absorb rural people without criminogenic effect. Modern cities which offer immigrants real economic opportunities, within the framework of a formal network of social control exercised by schools, associations, police, and courts, are not likely to have high rates of crime among immigrants. In fact the immigrants may have less opportunity for crime than in impoverished rural areas. The point is that industrialization and urbanization have complex effects on crime rates. If there is a general pattern—the empirical evidence is sparse and ambiguous—it is a rise in urban crime in the earliest stages of modernization followed by a decline once the process is in full swing.[29]

Modernization is a gradual process, not one that is likely of itself to create a single tidal wave of disorder. The connection between warfare and crime waves is much more precise. In fact, war is the single most obvious correlate of all the great historical waves of crime in England and the United States. A mideighteenth-century wave of crime coincided with Britain's involvement in a succession of wars from 1739 (war with Spain) to 1763 (the end of the Seven Year's War). The upsurge of crime in the early nineteenth century began while Britain was enmeshed in the Napoleonic wars, from 1793 to 1815, and continued through the long and severe economic depression which followed the war's end. Sweden also was involved in the

Napoleonic wars, which may help account for Stockholm's high crime rates in the early nineteenth century. In the United States the peak of urban crime in the 1860s and 1870s coincides with the social and political upheavals of the Civil War. We noted above the great increase in crime which followed Germany and Austria's defeat in the First World War. Lesser crime waves coincided with and followed both world wars in Britain, the United States, and most of the continental democracies.

There are various explanations for the widely observed correlation between war and crime. It has been attributed to wartime social disorganization, postwar economic dislocation, the maladjustment of returned veterans, and also to the legitimation of violence: "some members of a warring society are influenced by the 'model' of officially approved wartime killing and destruction." Archer and Gartner have compared the homicide rates of a large number of nations which participated in one or both world wars and find that the "legitimation of violence" explanation is most consistent with the evidence.[30] Powell offers a somewhat different interpretation of high crime during the American Civil War period, saying that it was due most fundamentally to the collapse of the institutional order. He argues that "The war marked the triumph of industrial capitalism over agrarian and commercial forms of organization," the consequence of which was "extreme disorganization, or anomie . . . . The abnormally high crime rate is but one symptom of the pervasive chaos of the period. However, as the social system began to stabilize in the mid-70s, the crime rate dropped."[31]

A third basic factor that directly influences the extent of both personal and property crime is the size of the youthful population. All records of crime in Western societies, now and in the past, show that young males are disproportionately represented among offenders. If their relative numbers are high in a society or a city, its crime rates are likely to be higher than in societies or cities with older populations. And if the relative number of young males increases substantially in a short time, so will crime. Such changes have occurred periodically in Western societies, often as a consequence of socioeconomic change or war. A population boom was underway in England during the first half of the 19th century thanks to better nutrition and higher birth rates. Concurrently it became the practice of many English rural families to send their adolescent children to the cities to fend for themselves.[32] As a result there was a remarkably high proportion of young males in London's population. In 1841 males aged 15 to 29 made up 13.5 percent of the city's population, a proportion never surpassed from 1821 to the present. The comparable percentages during the low crime years of the early 1920s and early 1950s were 11.5 percent and 9.1 percent, respectively.[33]

The explosion in youth crime in the 1960s and 1970s is closely linked to the profound changes in the age structure in the United States, Britain, and most other Western societies. Birth rates declined to their lowest recorded point in most Western societies during the Great Depression of the 1930s. Then, in the immediate aftermath of the Second World War, they soared upward. In the United States the "silent generation" of 1950s college students might better be called the "small generation" because its members were little more than half as numerous as the college-age population of the late 1960s. The shape and timing of the "age bulge" differ among Western societies and so do their postwar crime trends. The countries which had early and large baby booms, like England and the United States, had early and rapid increases in crime rates, as shown in Figures 13.3 and 13.4. In England and Wales the correspondence between the changing size of the youth population and changing crime rates is particularly striking for property crime. In the United States the correspondence since 1955 is equally close. Germany and Austria (not shown on graphs) provide a marked contrast. They had baby "boomlets" which began later, after economic recovery set in during the 1950s, and were smaller. Their crime rates turned up later and much less sharply. In Japan, however, no correlation is apparent between declining crime rates and changes in the size of the youth population. The latter remained virtually constant from 1946 through 1971.[34]

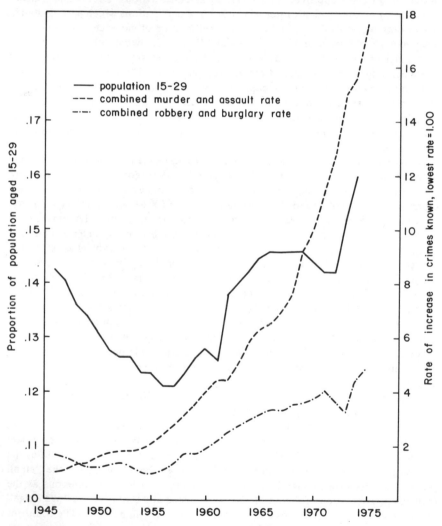

Figure 13.3: Youth population and crime in England and Wales, 1946-1975

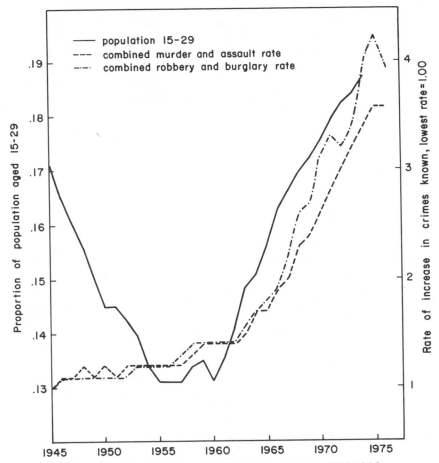

Figure 13.4: Youth population and crime in the United States, 1945-1976

It is not entirely convincing to attribute crime increases of 300 or 500 percent to 50 percent increases in the size of the youthful population. Presumably there are other social forces at work which encouraged a growing proportion of contemporary youths to resort to mayhem and theft. We have seen that international and civil war seem to legitimate interpersonal violence. The 1960s was the decade of revolutionary wars and counterinsurgency, which were glorified, villified, and above all amplified by the media. It was also an era in which politicians and officials publicized their deadly fantasies of nuclear incineration. The mass media saturated a whole generation with violent entertainment. It is plausible to argue that the 1960s saw a significant reversal in the long secular tendency toward restraining and condemning violence. And the people most susceptible to this new tolerance for violence were young people.

Value change in the 1960s went beyond a greater tolerance for interpersonal aggression. Distinctive new "postindustrial" values were articulated on university campuses during the 1960s and soon echoed by young people throughout Western societies. By emphasizing peace, toleration, and social progress they provided an antidote to the public celebration of violence. They also turned attention away from material concerns and celebrated personal liberation and development.[35] But there were distortions of these positive values which were socially more corrosive. The most corrosive form of this alternative ethic might be called aggressive hedonism, which is equally a perversion of traditional Western humanism and of postindustrial values. At its core is a belief that almost any means are justified in the pursuit of personal satisfactions. It resembles a mutation of Western materialism, stripped of its work ethic and generalized from material satisfactions to social and sexual ones. Moreover it often coexists with a sense of resentment against large, impersonal organizations, or indeed any external source of authority that might restrain people from "doing their own thing."

This discussion has come a long way from the consideration of crime waves. The strands can be brought together by concluding that each great wave of violent crime is caused by a distinctive combination of basic social forces. Some crime waves follow from fundamental social dislocation, as a result of which large segments of a population are torn lose from the social fabric. They may be migrants, demobilized veterans, or a growing population of young people for whom there is no social or economic niche. The most devastating episodes of public disorder, though, seem to occur when these kinds of social crises coincide with changes in values. Violent conflict among and within nations seems to legitimate interpersonal violence. I have suggested that the contemporary crime wave which pervades Western societies may be a fallout from a shift toward postindustrial values among college-educated youths of the 1960s and 1970s.

Nowhere in this discussion have major changes in crime been attributed to the police, courts, or prisons. Historically, reform in these institutions was thought to be responsible for the nineteenth-century improvement of public order in European societies like England and Sweden. Yet the same institutions, policies, and practices which evolved during the century of improving public order are essentially the same as those which are now unable to control rising crime. The answer to this apparent paradox is that the criminal law, police, courts, and prisons together can only restrain common crime if they reinforce underlying social forces that are moving in the same direction. These institutions and their policies were effective in turn-of-the-century societies dominated by a self-confident middle class convinced that prosperity in this life and salvation in the next could be achieved through piety, honesty, and hard work. All authorities spoke with the same voice. The institutions of public order were effective because they reinforced the dominant view. They did not merely punish those who transgressed. They were missionaries to the under class, informing them of the moral order through arrest, trial, and imprisonment.

Today, no self-confident consensus on standards of behavior is to be found in most of Western society. There are many self-proclaimed authorities offering may alternatives. Where a solid foundation of social support is lacking, the police, courts, and prisons drift. At worst, the police adopt a siege mentality, hostile to society and offenders alike. The courts devise expedients, such as plea bargaining, which serve administrative efficiency at the expense of both justice and public safety. And the prisons become warehouses which, like the gaols and workhouses of early nineteenth-century England, keep the offender out of circulation for a little while, but only inadvertently punish or rehabilitate him.

There are correctives to crime waves. Uprooted people may be incorporated in the matrix of new institutions or renovated old ones. Traditional values which condemn theft and interpersonal violence may reassert themselves. New values adopted by alienated people, caught between new life ways and old ones, may constrain harmful social behavior in ways even more effective than old values. Methodism is credited with just such effects among the new urban working class of nineteenth-century England, for example. If the Western crime wave of the 1960s does continue to ebb, it will be partly because the invisible hand of hedonism has dictated that an unprecedented proportion of young adults in North America and Europe forego having the children who would become the potential criminals and victims of the 1980s. And the recession in crime may be due in part to a reaffirmation of older moral values and a retreat from the individual freedom and diversity of behavior which flowered in the 1960s. Whatever the reasons, all historical evidence suggests that crime, like economic growth and population size, has finite limits. Call it a law of social gravitation: what goes up beyond supportable limits will eventually come down.

NOTES

General: This chapter is based on research supported by the Center for Studies of Crime and Delinquency of the U.S. Public Health Service and by the German Marshall Fund of the United States. Thanks are due to Tina Peterson for surveying historical studies of crime trends and to Eric Monkkonen for his comments on an earlier draft. The chapter incorporates portions of the author's article, "The Criminal Ethos," which appeared in *The Center Magazine*, 11 (January-February 1978): 74-79.

1. For an evaluation of the reliability of nineteenth-century English crime statistics, see V.A.C. Gatrell and T.B. Hadden, "Criminal Statistics and their Interpretation," in E.A. Wrigley, ed., *Nineteenth-Century Society* (Cambridge: The University Press, 1972): 336-396. A general discussion of the interpretations of different kinds of crime data is Ted Robert Gurr, *Rogues, Rebels, and Reformers: A Political History of Urban Crime and Conflict* (Beverly Hills: Sage Publications, 1976), Ch. 2.

2. James Buchanan Given, *Society and Homicide in Thirteenth-Century England* (Stanford: Stanford University Press, 1977). The records of homicides in thirteenth-century England are probably as accurate as those of any other period before the twentieth century because of strong incentives for local people to report them to the king's justices and equally compelling penalties for failing to do so. The rates' imprecision is due to the lack of accurate population data.

3. Ibid., 35.

4. J.M. Beattie, "The Pattern of Crime in England 1660-1800," *Past and Present*, 62 (February 1974): 47-95.

5. The epithet was applied by the journalist and radical reformer William Cobbett. For a detailed protrayal of the city in this era, see Francis Sheppard, *London, 1808-1870: The Infernal Wen* (London: Secker and Warburg, 1971).

6. This sketch is drawn from David Peirce, Peter N. Grabosky, and Ted Robert Gurr, "London: The Politics of Crime and Conflict, 1800 to the 1970s," in Ted Robert Gurr, Peter

N. Grabosky, and Richard C. Hula, *The Politics of Crime and Conflict: A Comparative History of Four Cities* (Beverly Hills: Sage Publications, 1977), Part II.

7. Given, op. cit., Ch. 1, surveys evidence on the medieval attitudes toward violence. Some evidence for the moderating effect of Enlightenment thought on criminal justice policies is reviewed in Gurr, *Rogues, Rebels, and Reformers*, Ch. II.5. See especially, Norbert Elias, *The Civilizing Process: The History of Manners* (New York: Urizen, 1978—original ed. 1939), 191-205.

8. Many trend and correlation studies show that in the eighteenth, nineteenth, and early twentieth centuries property crime tended to increase during hard times. But from c. 1925 onward in both England and the United States, the pattern is reversed: the greater economic prosperity, the more property crime. Among the studies which report such findings are Gatrell and Hadden, op. cit., 363-376; Theodore N. Ferdinand, "The Criminal Patterns of Boston Since 1849," *American Journal of Sociology* 73 (July 1967): 688-698; Leroy C. Gould, "The Changing Structure of Property Crime in an Affluent Society," *Social Forces*, 48 (September 1969): 50-60; and M. Harvey Brenner, "Effects of the Economy on Criminal Behavior and the Administration of Criminal Justice: A Multinational Study," paper presented to the Conference on Economic Crisis and Crime, United Nations Social Defence Research Institute, Rome, 1975. The last study uses national data for the United States, Canada, England and Wales, and Scotland. Also see Dorothy Swaine Thomas, *Social Aspects of the Business Cycle* (London: Routledge, 1925).

9. Many scholars, officials, and journalists have criticized American crime statistics; see the following chapter by Wesley Skogan. A comprehensive appraisal is Ch. 2, "American Criminal Statistics: An Explanation and Appraisal," in Donald Mulvihill and Melvin Tumin, *Crimes of Violence, Report to the National Commission on the Causes and Prevention of Violence*, Vol. 11 (Washington, D.C.: U.S. Government Printing Office, 1969). For evidence of the politically inspired manipulation of crime statistics in American cities c. 1970, see David Seidman and Michael Couzens, "Getting the Crime Rate Down: Political Pressure and Crime Reporting," *Law and Society* (spring 1974): 457-493.

10. The principal studies of crime in Boston are Sam Bass Warner, *Crime and Criminal Statistics in Boston* (Cambridge: Harvard University Press, 1934); Ferdinand, op. cit.; and Roger Lane, *Policing the City: Boston, 1822-1885* (Cambridge, Mass.: Harvard University Press, 1967). The quotation is from Roger Lane, "Urbanization and Criminal Violence in the 19th Century: Massachusetts as a Test Case," in Hugh Davis Graham and Ted Robert Gurr, eds., *Violence in America: Historical and Comparative Perspectives* (various eds., 1969), Ch. 12, 470 in the Praeger edition

11. Ferdinand, op. cit.

12. Charles Tilly et al., "How Policing Affected the Visibility of Crime in Nineteenth-Century Europe and America," (Ann Arbor: Center for Research on Social Organization, University of Michigan, n.d. [1975]), unpublished ms.

13. Theodore N. Ferdinand, "Politics, the Police, and Arresting Policies in Salem, Massachusetts Since the Civil War," *Social Problems*, 19 (spring 1972): 572-588; Elwin H. Powell, "Crime as a Function of Anomie," *Journal of Criminal Law, Criminology, and Police Science*, 57 (June 1966): 161-171.

14. Tilly et al., op. cit.

15. Powell, op. cit. His interpretation of crime as a consequence of social dislocations is most fully developed in Powell, *The Design of Discord: Studies of Anomie: Suicide, Urban Society, War* (New York: Oxford University Press, 1970), Part 2.

16. Edwin H. Sutherland and C.E. Gehlke, "Crime and Punishment," in *Recent Social Trends in the United States*, Report of the President's Research Committee on Social Trends (New York: McGraw-Hill, 1933).

17. Harry Willbach, "The Trend of Crime in New York City," *Journal of Criminal Law and Criminology*, 29 (1938): 62-75; and "The.Trend of Crime in Chicago," *Journal of Criminal Law and Criminology*, 31 (1941): 720-727.

18. Peter N. Grabosky, *Sydney in Ferment: Crime, Dissent, and Official Reaction, 1788-1973* (Canberra: Australian National University Press, 1978).

19. See Peter N. Grabosky, Leif Persson, and Sven Sperlings, "Stockholm: The Politics of Crime and Conflict, 1750 to the 1970s," in Gurr, Grabosky, and Hula, op. cit., Part III.

20. Arthur MacDonald, "Criminal Statistics in Germany, France, and England," *Journal of Criminal Law and Criminology*, 1 (1910): 59-70; Abdul Qaiyum Lodhi and Charles Tilly, "Urbanization, Crime, and Collective Violence in 19th-Century France," *American Journal of Sociology*, 79 (September 1973): 296-318.

21. MacDonald, op. cit.; Vincent E. McHale and Eric A. Johnson, "Urbanization, Industrialization, and Crime in Imperial Germany, Parts I and II," *Social Science History*, 1 (fall 1976): 45-78; 1 (winter 1977): 210-247.

22. Among the most detailed studies ever made of war's impact on crime are F. Exner, *Krieg und Kriminalitaet in Oesterreich* (New Haven, Conn.: Yale University Press, 1927); and M. Liepmann, *Krieg und Kriminalitaet in Deutschland* (Stuttgart: Deutsche Verlags Anstalt, 1930).

23. The foregoing data on postwar crime rates are from Ted Robert Gurr, "Crime Trends in Modern Democracies since 1945," *International Annals of Criminology*, 16 (1977): 41-85.

24. For evaluations of contemporary problems of crime in European Communist states, see Valery Chalidze, *Criminal Russia: Essays on Crime in the Soviet Union* (New York: Random House, 1977); and Ivan Volgyes, ed., *Social Deviance in Eastern Europe* (Boulder, Colorado: Westview, 1978).

25. A recent study which helps account for the Japanese success in dealing with crime is David Bayley, *Forces of Order: Police Behavior in Japan and the United States* (Berkeley: University of California Press, 1976).

26. A recent survey of theories of criminal behavior is Gwynn Nettler, *Explaining Crime* (New York: McGraw-Hill, 1974).

27. For interpretations of crime data as indicators of official behavior see, for example, Clayton A. Hartjen, *Crime and Criminalization* (New York: Praeger, 1974); and Austin Turk, *Criminality and Legal Order* (Skokie, Ill.: Rand-McNally, 1969). A historical study of San Francisco which tests this approach is Eric Monkkonen, "Toward a Dynamic Theory of Crime and the Police: A Criminal Justice System Perspective," *Historical Methods Newsletter*, 10 (fall 1977): 157-165.

28. A more detailed discussion of the relative importance of changing social behavior and changing policies in accounting from crime trends is Ted Robert Gurr, "Contemporary Crime in Historical Perspective: A Comparative Study of London, Stockholm and Sydney," *Annals of the American Academy of Political and Social Science*, 434 (November 1977): 126-134.

29. For historical evidence on the complex relationship between urban growth and crime, see, for example, Lodhi and Tilly, op. cit.; McHale and Johnson, op. cit.; and Powell, *Design of Discord*, Part 2.

30. Dane Archer and Rosemary Gartner, "Violent Acts and Violent Times: A Comparative Approach to Postwar Homicide Rates," *American Sociological Review*, 41 (December 1976): 937-963, quotation 943.

31. Powell, "Crime as a Function of Anomie," 169.

32. John R. Gillis, *Youth and History: Tradition and Change in European Age Relations 1770-Present* (New York and London: Academic Press, 1974), Ch. 2.

33. Decennial data on the youthful proportion of the London population from 1801 to 1971 are given in David Peirce, Peter N. Grabosky, and Ted Robert Gurr, "London: The Politics of Crime and Conflict, 1800 to the 1970's," in Gurr, Grabosky, and Hula, op. cit., 43.

34. These comparisons and Figures 13.3 and 13.4 are based on crime and demographic data gathered and analyzed by the author.

35. The most detailed empirical study of postindustrial values in Western societies is Ronald Inglehart, *The Silent Revolution: Changing Values and Political Styles Among Western Publics* (Princeton: Princeton University Press, 1977). Gillis, op. cit., Ch. 5, discusses the changes in youth subculture during the 1950s and 1960s in historical perspective. A contemporary analysis is Herbert Moller, "Youth as a Force in the Modern World," *Comparative Studies in Society and History*, 10 (April 1968): 237-260.

20

HOMICIDE IN 110 NATIONS
The Development of the Comparative Crime Data File

DANE ARCHER

ROSEMARY GARTNER

For a number of historical reasons research on the causes of crime has tended to be unfortunately insular and even ethnocentric. For example, almost all systematic research on the social, economic, and cultural origins of homicide has been done with respect to the experiences of single societies (18). While these investigations of an individual society are of great descriptive value, they do not by themselves result in general explanations and theories. In addition, researchers interested in homicide rates have lavished repeated attention on the data of a handful of nations — e.g., the U.S. and Great Britain — and neglected the inspection of a heterogeneous range of societies.

The reason for this narrow and culturally biased approach has not been lack of interest. The need for a truly comparative approach to crime has long been acknowledged (Sellin and Wolfgang, 1964 ;

(*) This project and the development of the 110-Nation Comparative Crime Data File were supported by NIMH Grant Number MH 27427 from the Center for Studies of Crime and Delinquency, and by a Guggenheim Fellowship to the first author. Responsibility for the findings and interpretations in this paper belongs, of course, to the authors alone.

(18) Some important exceptions are the following works : Straus (M.) and Straus (J.), « Suicide, homicide, and social structure in Ceÿlon », *American journal of sociology*, 1953, 58, 461-469 ; Verkko (V.), Survey of current practice in criminal statistics, *Transactions of the Westermark Society*, 1956, 5-33 ; Wolfgang (M.E.), « International crime statistics : A proposal »,*Journal of Criminal law, Criminology, and Police Science*, 1967, 58, 65-69 ; *Wolfgang* (M.E.) and Ferracuti (F.), *The Subculture of Violence*, New York, Tavistock, 1967 ; Clinard (M.B.) and Abbott (D.J.), *Crime and Developing Countries : A Comparative Perspective*, New York, Wiley, 1973 ; Newman (G.), *Comparative Deviance : Perception and Law in Six Cultures*, New York, Elsevier, 1976 ; Gurr (T.R.), Grabosky (P.N.), and Hula (R.C.), *The Politics of Crime and Conflict : A comparative History of Four Cities*, Beverly Hills, Sage Publications, 1977.

From Dane Archer and Rosemary Gartner, "Homicide In 110 Nations: The Development Of The Comparative Crime Data File," 16(1 & 2) *International Annals of Criminology* 109-139(1977). Copyright 1977 by the Societe Internationale de Criminologie.

Mannheim, 1965 ; Wolfgang, 1967 ; and Mulvihill and Tumin, 1969) and even researchers working with the data of single nations have underlined the importance of cross-national investigations. Although cross-national comparisons are always fraught with a number of methodological problems, the primary obstacle to such comparative research has been a dearth of information. In the past, the social sciences have not had available adequate historical (or « time series ») data on rates of homicide in a large number of societies.

Without such a cross-national data base, rigorous comparative research has not been possible on a large scale. As a result, our understanding of the causes of homicide and other offenses remains, at best, provincial and primitive and, at worst, simply wrong. Illustrations of this problem are not hard to find.

For example, sociologists have for a long time suspected that wars might somehow produce a postwar increase in homicide rates (e.g., Sorokin, 1928 : 340-344). However, in the absence of historical, cross-national data on homicide rates, efforts to research this question have been limited to isolated case studies — often as limited as the case of a single nation after a single war (19). For example, the eminent criminologist Herman Mannheim published an entire book on this question (Mannheim, 1941). The book was based on the only crime data readily available to Mannheim — rates for England. On the strength of the English experience after World War I, Mannheim concluded that wars do not produce postwar « waves » of homicide. Recent comparative research, however, indicates that Mannheim was almost certainly wrong — i.e., he was misled by studying a single nation's experience which turned out to be idiosyncratic (Archer and Gartner, 1976).

A second example concerns an apparent paradox of current interest to many sociologists. Based on cross-sectional comparisons of the homicide rates of large and small U.S. cities, sociologists have repeatedly demonstrated taht larger cities have dramatically higher homicide rates than smaller cities (e.g. Wolfgang, 1968). However, there is almost no longitudinal or historical research on whether a given city's homicide rate grows as its population increases (20). Without such evidence,

---

(19) An important exception was the early study by Sellin (T.) : « Is murder increasing in Europe ? » *The Annals of the American Academy of Political and Social Science*, 1926, 126, 29-34. Sellin compared the post-WW I homicide rate changes in five belligerent nations and four non-belligerent nations.

(20) The few exceptions have generated considerable interest precisely because they have not found general increases in crime rates with populations growth — e.g., Lane (R.), « Urbanization and criminal violence in the 19th century : Massachusetts as a test case ». In Graham (H.D.) and Gurr (T.R.) (Eds.), *Violence in America : Historical and Comparative Perspectives,* Washington. U. S. Government Printing Office, 1969, 359-370.

of course, it is difficult to explain or understand the relatively higher homicide rates observed in large cities. The reason for our continued ignorance on this question is, again, the unavailability of historical data on homicide. What one would like to have to answer this question is a cross-national file of historical homicide data for large cities in several societies.

A third example can be drawn from the area of social policy. Many legislative issues in the Justice area involve an assumption that proposed changes in law are likely to affect homicides rates — e.g., gun control laws, temporary periods of « amnesty » for the surrender of illegal or unregistered weapons, and death penalty legislation. Here again, however, the poverty of available cross-national data has made comprehensive research impossible. There has been essentially no systematic research on how changes in gun ownership in other societies have affected their homicide rates, and also little recent research on how changes in death penalty legislation have affected homicide rates in other societies. This near absence of rigorous comparative research on the effect of death penalty legislation is particularly conspicuous since a great deal of deterrence research has been done using American offense rates (e.g., Gibbs, 1975).

These three examples are, unfortunately, only a few of the important questions which remain unresearched and unanswered because the necessary time series data on homicide rates have not been available for a large sample of nations and cities. There are many other areas where the empirical foundations of existing theory about homicide are embarrassingly provincial. For example, little is known about how fluctuations in unemployment or other economic indicators affect homicide rates. There have been a small number of American studies — including the classic study by Henry and Short (1954) — but virtually no attempts to explore this question using the evidence of other societies (21). This omission in the literature is particularly unfortunate, since there are recent indications that fluctuations in unemployment and other economic variables have important societal consequences in terms of individual behavior (e.g., Brenner, 1973).

In all these areas, our knowledge of the social origins of homicide is lamentably culture-bound. Without historical homicide data from a large number of societies, there have been no opportunities to explore the causes of this violent offense in a range of cultures, or even to attempt more modest replications of findings based primarily or exclusively on American data.

---

(21) A well-known exception is the work of Radzinowicz — e. g., « Economic pressures ». IN Radzinowicz (L.) and Wolfgang (M.E.) (Eds), *Crime and Justice. The Criminal in Society*, New York, Basic Books, 1971, vol. 1. 420-442.

These constraints on empirical research have had predictable consequences for social theories about the origins of crime. The poverty of existing resources for comparative homicide research have created a climate in which nation-bound and ungeneralizable theory have flourished. A casual reading of many texts on crime or the sociology of violence reveals several propositions about homicide which appear to be readily disconfirmable by the experience of other societies. Perhaps even worse, it is easy for a reader of these texts to form an impression that homicide and other offenses do not exist outside the United States — since so many conclusions appear to rest rather precariously on American data alone. In summary, the absence of readily examinable homicide data for large numbers of societies has retarded the development of general theories about the social origins of homicide.

The 110-Nation Comparative Crime Data File (CCDF).

The major obstacle to generalizable research on the social origins of homicide has been the absence of a dependent variable. For this reason, beginning in 1972, we undertook the creation of an archive of crime rate data which had both comparative breadth and historical depth. After several years of intensive data collection, we have assembled a 110-nation Comparative Crime Data File (CCDF) with time series rates of five offenses for the period 1900-1970. These five offenses are homicide, assault, robbery, theft, and rape. In addition to the data series for 110 nations, the CCDF also includes series for 44 major international cities as well.

The principle sources for the creation of this massive comparative file have been : (1) correspondence with national and metropolitan governmental sources in essentially all societies in the world : (2) examination of documents and annual reports of those nations which have published data on their annual incidence of various offenses ; and (3) correspondence with other record-keeping agencies.

The time series in the CCDF begin in the year 1900, although many of the nations in the file did not begin maintaining crime data until much later. For example, the so-called « developing » nations generally have data in the CCDF only for relatively recent periods. In addition, the records for some nations contain interruptions due to national emergencies and bureaucratic lapses. These factors mean that for any given year or period, the CCDF has effective data for fewer than 110 nations and fewer than 44 cities.

As part of the collection of the 110-nation CCDF, we have reviewed the available literature on possible sources of unreliability and invalidity in official crime data. The implications of these concerns for comparative research with the CCDF have been discussed elsewhere, and efforts have been made to identify research designs which minimize these problems (Archer and Gartner, 1976). For example, the most conservative design using the CCDF is one which : (1) examines homicide rather than other offenses ; (2) examines only longitudinal trends within each of several societies and eschews cross-sectional comparisons of absolute offense rate levels across several societies ; and (3) uses some kind of data quality control procedure to take into account the variable validity of the different offense indicators (e.g., offenses known versus arrests) which are present for various nations in the CCDF.

With these methodological precautions, the CCDF makes it possible to investigate the effects upon offense rates of a great number of possible antecedent variables. In addition, the CCDF can maximize the comparative rigor of homicide research by maximizing a researcher's chances of identifying both internationally general relationships and also relationships which hold only for certain types of societies.

As one goal of the CCDF project, the entire data archive will be published as a resource for the cross-national investigations of other researchers. Before making the data base available, of course, it will be necessary to include a number of methodological guidelines, caveats, and safeguards. As just a single example, it will be necessary to alert potential users to when (and in what way) an apparently continuous data series in the CCDF actually conceals a measure change. Each methodological aspect of the CCDF will be discussed along with the relative merits of various potential solutions. In the case of a measure change, for example, two alternative solutions might be (1) to smooth the series by estimating the measure change discontinuity and adjusting either the pre- or post-change series ; or (2) simply to treat the two parts of the series as separable cases or replications. Either decision, of course, requires the researcher to make a number of unique assumptions. When the CCDF data base is published, it will include a detailed methodological guide intended to inform potential users of the CCDF about the relative merits of a wide variety of research decisions and designs and their attendant assumptions.

The long-term goal of the CCDF project is to make possible a comprehensive assessment of whether, and to what degree, trends in homicide rates follow lawful and explicable patterns. Faced with a nearly infinite list of potential antecedent variables, we have chosen to treat in greatest detail the following four classes of potential social origins of homicide : (1) short-term *societal events* (e.g., recessions, wars, etc.) ; (2) long-term *social-changes* (e.g., urbanization, unemployment rate fluctuations, etc.) ; (3) relatively durable aspects of *social structure* (e.g., resource concentration or distribution, type of national economic organization, etc.) ; and (4) discrete changes in *policy an law* (e.g. gun control legislation, changes in courtroom evidentiary procedures, death penalty abolition or restoration, etc.) (22). A study on the effects of one of these antecedents, wars, has already been published (Archer and Gartner, 1976).

The 110-nation CCDF makes possible for the first time a genuinely international approach to the study of homicide, and work toward this demanding objective has just begun. It is our hope that empirical research drawing upon the CCDF will provide the historical and comparative basis for truly general theories about the social origins of homicide. The rest of this paper reports two of the initial findings made possible by this massive new data archive. One of these is a methodological question ; the second concerns a substantive question of both classic and current concern to sociologists.

Study I : A Methodological Observation on Different Homicide Indicators.

A classic concern of social scientists working crime data has been the relative merits of different indicators of the « real » rate of an offense. For an offense like homicide, for example, different jurisdictions (e.g., countries, or states and cities in the same country) could conceivably report one or more of the following indicators : offenses known to the police. arrests, indictments, pleas entered in court, convictions, incarcerations, or even figures on the local prison population as of a certain date.

Since these various indicators reflect phases of the legal system which are increasingly more remote from the original offense, they obviously suffer from a progressive attrition of numbers. Different indicators, therefore, report different fractions of the « real » rate. As a result, it is manifestly unwarranted to compare two jurisdictions on the *absolute level* of their offense rates if they report different indicators of this offense. The invalidity of primitive cross-sectional research designs of this kind is extremely well-known. although they are occasionally still published.

It has been established for some time that the most accurate or « valid » indicator of homicide and other crimes is the number of offenses known to the police (Sellin, 1931 ; Ferdinand, 1967 ; Mulvihill and Tumin, 1969 ; Clinard and Abbott, 1973, Hindelang, 1974). This fact has direct implications for cross-sectional research designs. The researcher interested in comparing the absolute homicide rates of different nations. therefore. will probably choose the relatively conser-

---

(22) In addition, we are working on a number of analyses internal to the CCDF data set itself. For example, we are using the time series in the file to learn whether the trends of various offenses are collinear, or whether there are factors of offenses which vary together over time. Finally, we are using the CCDF to the try to resolve a number of mothodological issues — one of which is discussed below.

vative procedure of limiting comparisons to nations using only this optimal indicators (23).

For almost generations of social scientists, as a result, it has been a point of dogma to consider only one indicator — the number of offenses known — as valid for research purposes. Although this methodological purism is quite reasonable on a *prima facie* basis, it is by contemporary standards somewhat uncritical and unsophisticated (24).

It is important to remember that the preference for the « offenses known » indicator evolved in the context of *cross-sectional* comparisons of absolute crime rates in different jurisdictions.

One of the major advances in social science epistemology in recent years has been to contrast the causal power of cross-sectional and longitudinal research designs (e.g., Lieberson and Hansen, 1974). It now seems clear that these two different methods can address the same question and yet emerge with unrelated (or even opposite) conclusions about the relationship between two variables. since only a longitudinal design can include a temporal relationship between the variables, this design is inherently superior to a cross-sectional design.

The difference between these two research designs can be illustrated with an example to be discussed in greater detail below. For example, suppose a researcher is interested in the relationship between city size and homicide rates. There are two obvious designs by which this question can be addressed. A cross-sectional design would involve a comparison (with appropriate concern for the consistency of offense definition and recording, etc.) of the homicide rates of large and small cities. A longitudinal design, by contrast, would involve a study of how the annual homicide rates of one or more cities have changed as they have grown in size. In the case of city size and homicide rates, as discussed below, these two designs in fact reach two different conclusions. The essential difference between the two designs is that only the longitudinal design has a historical dimension.

---

(23) In actual research, however, this precaution is only of limited value. There are many hazards to cross-sectional comparisons of the offense rates of different nations, and limiting comparisons to only nations with the best indicator is necessary but insufficient. The comparative researcher must also minimize the effect of other artifacts — e.g., national differences in the definition of an offense, national differences in statistical accuracy such as underreporting, etc. Although the validity of cross-sectional comparisons of homicide rates is jeopardized by many potential artifacts, we continue to believe that prudent comparisons of this kind are possible.

(24) For example, in comparisons involving large numbers of nations, the presence of different types of indicators can be resolved using a data quality control procedure (Naroll, 1962 ; Archer and Gartner, 1976).

Since the preference for the « offenses known » indicator dates from a period dominated by cross-sectional research designs, it is important to reassess the quality of different types of indicators for the more powerful longitudinal designs. If a « poor » indicator (e.g., homicide convictions) bears a consistent relationship to a « good » indicator (homicide offenses known), then either indicator would be an equally valid indicator of the trend of a nation's homicide rate. For example, if a nation's number of homicide convictions are a stable fraction — e.g., 40 % — of the nation's number of homicide offenses known, then the two indicators are equally valuable in longitudinal studies of national homicide trends (25).

Since longitudinal designs seem certain to dominate future comparative research on crime rates, it is very important to determine whether good and poor homicide indicators do — in fact — have a stable relationship over time. If different indicators can be shown to be collinear, then they are of equal quality as measures of national homicide trends.

An empirical answer to this question requires redundant homicide data for several societies — i.e. more than one indicator over a reasonably long interval. The CCDF has data of this kind for 14 nations. A measure change is involved for two of these nations, so the total number of discrete cases is 16. Table 1 shows the correlations between good and imperfect indicators over time in these 16 cases (26). The table also indicates the period over which the comparison is being made, and the exact types of indicators being compared.

The evidence in Table 1 is extremely persuasive for the usefulness of even poor indicators as measures of trends. For the 16 cases in Table 1, good and poor indicators are strongly collinear. In fact, the *lowest* median correlation across all cases in Table 1 is. 85-a figure considerably above the reliabilities of most measures in sociology and psychology. The remaining correlations among indicators in Table 1 are even higher.

This means that poor indicators are in most cases a consistent fraction of good indicators. As a result, good and poor indicators are generally interchangeable as measures of a nation's offense rate trend. In cases where a researcher has available a good (offenses known)

---

(25) Even if this fraction is not perfectly stable, a resarcher may be protected from spurious results. If fluctuations in this fraction are random or « benign », the most likely consequence is a reduction or « attenuation » in the researcher's chances of finding a significant relationship between the homicide series and some other variable. The error, therefore, is likely to have conservative consequences.

(26) This data was first presented in a paper read at the 1975 annual meeting of the Society for the Study of Social Problems.

TABLE I

Correlations between good and imperfect indicators of the same offense for 16 cases from the 110-Nation Comparative Crime Data File.

NATION	YEARS	INDICATORS	CORRELATION BETWEEN TWO INDICATORS FOR EACH OFFENSE
Australia	1964-1972	(1) Crimes known (2) Crimes cleared	Murder and Man-slaughter 1.00_1 Assault 1.00_1 Rape .98 Robbery .96
Canada	1919-1943	(1) Offenses known (2) Convictions	Offenses against the person ; murder, manslaughter and assault .90 Offenses against property with violence; robbery and burglary .93 Offenses against property without violence ; theft .94
Canada	1952-1967	(1) Charges (2) Convictions	Homicide .82 Assault .96 Robbery 1.00_1 Theft .93 Offenses against women .98
Denmark	1933-1947	(1) Crimes known (2) Crimes cleared	Homicide .95 Assault .96 Rape .90 Robbery .91 Theft .97
Denmark	1948-1959	(1) Crimes known (2) Crimes cleared	Homicide .92 Assault .92 Robbery .91 Theft .87 Rape .81
Finland	1913-1924	(1) Offenses reported (2) Prosecutions	Homicide .84
		(1) Offenses reported (2) Convictions	Homicide .74

Ireland	1961-1964	(1) Crimes known (2) Court cases	Murder	.85
			Manslaughter	1.00₁
			Assault	1.00₁
			Indecent assaults against females	.99
			Robbery	1.00₁
			Burglary and housebreaking	.99
			Offenses against property without violence	.41
Kenya	1964-1968	(1) Crimes known (2) Arrests	Homicide	.79
			Robbery	.11
			Theft	.93
		(1) Crimes known (2) Convictions	Homicide	.94
			Robbery	-.59
			Theft	.85
Mexico	1966-1972	(1) Cases presented (2) Convictions	Homicide	.73
			Assault	.81
			Rape	.65
			Robbery	.89
Netherlands ...	1949-1972	(1) Final sentences (2) Crimes known	Murder and manslaughter; crimes against life	.77
			Assault	.79
			Robbery, theft and housebreaking	.41
New Zealand ..	1920-1954	(1) Offenses known	All offenses	.96
	1956-1971	(2) Offenses cleared	All offenses	.98
Norway	1957-1970	(1) Offenses known (2) Persons proceeded against	Homicide	.42
			Assault	.92
			Robbery-theft	.97
			Rape	.42
Sweden	1959-1966	(1) Offenses reported (2) Offenses cleared	Homicide	.89
			Robbery	.86
			Burglary	.48
			Rape	.82
Tanzania	1962-1972	(1) Crimes known (2) Convictions	Murder and manslaughter	-.60
			Assault	-.52
			Robbery	.74
			Theft	-.39
Thaïland	1945-1962	(1) Crimes known (2) Convictions	All offenses	1.00₁

| U. S. . . . . | 1933-1971 | (1) UCR murder and non-negligent manslaughter (2) Rates of death caused by homicides, vital statistics of US2. | Homicide | .85 |

MEDIAN CORRELATION ACROSS ALL CASES :

Homicide, murder and manslaughter	.85
Rape	.86
Assault	.92
Robbery, property offenses with violence	.90
Theft	
All offenses (3 cases)	.98

1 correlation is .995 or greater.
2 Vital statistics section of U.S. Statistical Abstract.

time series, of course, he or she does not need to use other indicators as measures of trends. But the analysis of Table 1 suggests that in the absence of offenses known data, a researcher would be justified in using other indicators as measures of rate trends (27).

In practice, a researcher with the luxury of data on a large number of nations is able to confirm the implications of Table 1 to his or her own satisfaction. If different nations in the sample use different indicators, the researcher can use a data quality control procedure — i.e., he or she can analyze the data in successive waves. Nations with data on offenses known can be analyzed in one wave, and nations with other indicators can be analyzed in a separate wave.

The strongly collinear relationships among indicators in Table 1 prompt us to make the following prediction : in longitudinal studies using large numbers of nations, analyses of nations with good indicators will agree with analyses of nations with poor indicators. Al-

(27) The impressive collinearity in Table 1 applies to studies of national *trends* in offense rates. In studies where researchers wish to detrend an offense rate time series, and study only the detrended residuals, Table 1 does not of course tell us anything about the relationship between the detrended residuals of good and poor indicators. This issue is also, however, an empirical question and is easily investigable using the CCDF. We are grateful to Marc Lieberman for this observation.

though work with the CCDF is still in its early stages, this prediction is supported by the work already completed.

For example, Archer and Gartner (1976) used a data quality control procedure in their study of how wars affect postwar homicide rates. The nations with good indicators were analyzed separately from nations with other indicators — and the results of these two analyses did not differ (Archer and Gartner, 1976, p. 951). This finding supports our expectation that longitudinal studies of national homicide rates — whether of the number of offenses known or of other indicators — will reach identical conclusions. The conclusions of longitudinal research designs, therefore, are not dependent on the type of indicator maintained by the nations in the studies.

In summary, the infatuation of two generations of social scientists with the offenses known indicator may have been overstated and indiscriminate. The indispensability of this indicator in cross-sectional designs remains unquestioned. But the evidence reported here indicates that longitudinal designs do not require this indicator. In fact, this analysis reveals that several different indicators are equally valid as measures of a nation's homicide rate trend.

Comparative researchers are justified, therefore, in performing longitudinal research which includes nations with data on offenses known as well as nations with other indicators. As a conservative device, of course, researchers can still elect to use a data quality control procedure. This procedure, in effect, constitutes a « replication » using the two different types of indicators in separates waves.

Study II : City Size, City Growth, and Homicide Rates.

Although urban crime has been a central concern of several social sciences for a long time, it remains poorly understood. Despite several generations of urban theory and descriptive research, explanations of urban crime are still beclouded by controversy and apparently contradictory research findings (28).

Cities have long been regarded as centers of crime and violence. This unfavorable reputation is at least as old as the Bible. For example, in Ezekial (7.23), one of the explanations God is said to have given for his wrath is that « the land is full of bloody crimes and the city is full of violence ». Over succeeding centuries, many writers have contrasted the immorality of cities with the innocence and purity of rural life. In some of these accounts, the city is described as seducing

---

(28) The classic and recent literature on urban rates of crime and violence are reviewed in some detail in Archer, Gartner, Akert, and Lockwood (1977). Only the central themes of this literature are indicated here.

its new arrivals into a life of crime. For example, Adam Smith wrote that a man of « low moral character » could be constrained to behave properly in a village environment, « but as soon as he comes into a great city he is sunk in obscurity and darkness... and he is very likely to... abandon himself to every sort of low profligacy and vice » (quoted in Mannheim, 1965 : 545).

This image of the city has been extremely influential in the history of sociology and, with some refinement, constitutes today the dominant theory about crime in cities. In sociology, this perspective is particularly identified with Durkheim and Wirth. In *The Division of Labor in Society* (1933), Durkheim suggested that the « common conscience » is diluted as a city grows in size :

...local opinion weighs less heavily upon each of us, and as the general opinion of society cannot replace its predecessor, not being able to watch closely the conduct of its citizens, the collective surveillance is irretrievably loosened, the common conscience loses its authority and individual variability grows (p. 300).

Wirth (1940) accepted this view of cities and discussed the mechanisms by which cities dissolved traditional forms of social control. According to Wirth, the effects of cities included an increase in residential mobility, isolation, and anonymity as well as a breakdown of kinship ties and other informal sources of social control.

In addition to this Durkheim-Wirth view of the city as a place where traditional social controls are minimized and anonymity is maximized, no fewer than six additional theoretical explanations have appeared in the literature on urban crime. These six hypotheses can be stated in abbreviated form as follows : (1) cities foster the development of criminal subcultures ; (2) cities produce class, cultural, and racial conflict as a function of greater population heterogeneity ; (3) cities increase criminal opportunities because of population size and the large numbers of commercial establishments ; (4) cities have relatively impersonal police-civilian relations which lead to rigid law enforcement practices and therefore arrest rates which are inflated compared to those of non-urban areas ; (5) the age and sex composition of cities have been altered by the arrival of immigrants (from rural areas, other nations, etc.) who are predominantly young males ; and even (6) the possibility that the population density of cities might by itself increase the likehood of pathological behavior.

Unfortunately, empirical evidence has not matched the richness and variety of this theoretical banquet. Despite the existence of at least seven quite plausible theoretical explanations, the available evidence on urban homicide rates and their social origins is both parochial and paradoxical.

Much of the empirical confusion concerning urban homicide derives from a collision between cross-sectional and longitudinal approaches to this area. The two approaches imply questions which are radically different. The cross-sectional approach asks whether there are homicide rate implications of *city size* at any one moment in time ; the longitudinal approach asks whether there are any implications of *city growth* over time.

At least until recently, the cross-sectional approach dominated research on urban homicide. This research has been based primarily on American data, and has produced results which are as consistent as they are striking (29). For example, Wolfgang (1968) and Clinard (1974) analyzed offense rates for American cities of various sizes and found impressively higher homicide rates in large cities than in small cities.

The vividness of this cross-sectional finding with American data must be seen to be fully appreciated. We have replicated this well-known finding, using the most recent data available and also smoothing over five years to reduce the effects of short-term idiosyncracies. Using the FBI's Uniform Crime Reports, we aggregated the mean rates of murder and non-negligent manslaughter for cities of various size categories over the period 1971-75. The results of this analysis produce a cross-sectional picture of the homicide rates in American cities of various sizes, and this relationship is graphed using a semi-log scale in Figure 1.

Figure 1 : *City Size and homicide Rates in the U.S. : 1971-1975*

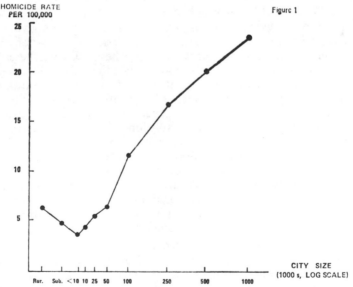

(a) Source : Adapted from the FBI's Uniform Grime Reports, 1971-75. Rates shown are the means of the five-year period 1971-1975.

(29) This cross-sectional question has also been addressed using some data from other nations by Szabo, 1960 ; Mannheim, 1965 ; and Tarniquet, 1968.

The strength of the relationship in Figure 1 indicates why this finding is one of the most widely accepted tenets of urban sociology. For cities alone (i.e., excluding rural and suburban areas), the relationship between city size and homicide rates is monotonic and approximately logarithmic. The relationship is monotonic in that each city size category has a homicide rate higher than all smaller size categories and lower than all larger size categories. The relationship is logarithmic in that the most dramatic differences in homicide rates occur among the smaller city size categories — for more populous cities, it takes much larger city size differences to produce comparable differences in urban homicide rates.

In an earlier publication, we have called this cross-sectional result a « logarithmic J-curve » because of the shape of the graph in figure 1 (Archer, Gartner, Akert, and Lockwood, 1977). The graph is J-curve rather than linear because rural areas have homicide rates which are actually higher than the rates for smaller cities.

This finding is quite provocative, since it seems intuitively more plausible to expect rural homicide rates to be lower than all urban rates. In fact, none of the seven theoretical models summarized earlier can explain the finding that rural homicide rates exceed the rates of small cities and are as high, in fact, as the rates of cities with populations between 50,000 and 100,000. The ecology of homicide is clearly multivariate in nature, and rural homicides cannot be understood without the introduction of other theoretical variables which are, at present, unidentified.

By itself, the cross-sectional approach represented in Figure 1 seems straightforward and — except for the unexpectedly high homicide rates in rural areas — quite compatible with any of the seven theoretical explanations listed earlier. All seven theoretical models predict greater homicide rates in large cities, although for different reasons, and the cross-sectional evidence appears to support this prediction. This finding only becomes a paradox when longitudinal evidence is examined.

The relationship shown in Figure 1 has led many researchers to the quite reasonable expectation that this effect of city size might have implications for city growth as well. If it is true that the homicide rates of large cities exceed those of small cities, it seems reasonable to expect the homicide rates of a city to soar as the city grows from small to large. A few longitudinal studies of this question have been made, however, and the results of these inquiries constitute the other half of the paradox of cities and homicide. These few longitudinal studies are paradoxical precisely because they have *not* found the reasonable and the expected — i.e., they have not found that individual cities experience homicide rate increases as they grow in population size.

Threee of these longitudinal studies have examined cities over a period of roughly one century. For example, Powel (1966) studied Buffallo between 1854 and 1956; Ferdinand (1967) studied Boston from 1849 to 1951 ; and Lane (1969) studied both Boston and Massachusetts generally from the mid-19th to the mid-20th Century. These three studies of American city growth found a consistent decline in murder and other serious crime rates, despite the population gains of these cities during the century studied (30).

There have also been some historical studies of entire societies. Although studies at this level of aggregation bear only imperfectly upon our question, they appear to support analyses done at the city level. For example, Lodhi and Tilly (1973) studied records of crimes against the person in 19th Century France and found that the rate of these offenses fluctuated mildly over time but had no discernible trend.

This, then, is the paradox of cities and homicide rates : why do large cities currently have higher homicide rates than small cities, if there is no evidence of increasing homicide rates as a city grows ? The cross-sectional evidence on city size and homicide seems at first to suggest that cities must grow to some absolute size (e.g., 100,000 persons) before having a high homicide rate. But this apparently reasonable proposition is contradicted by the longitudinal evidence which shows that cities do not in fact show homicide rate increases as they grow. In short, if larger cities currently have higher homicide rates than small cities, how did they get these high rates — if not by growing in population size ?

Using the wealth of 20th Century data series in the 110-nation CCDF, we have attempted a new interpretation of this apparently paradoxical relationship between cities and homicide rates. Our approach has been to try to provide answers to three conceptually separable questions which, we believe, provide the key to this paradox.

The first two of these questions address the cross-national generalizability of the two sides of the paradox as we have described them, and the third attempts a synthesis of these findings. The three questions are : (1) Since much of the cross-sectional evidence has

---

(30) An important recent work in this area is by Gurr, Grabovsky, and Hula (1977). These authors studied « common » crimes (offenses against persons and property combined) in four international cities and found a decreasing trend in this aggregate index until 1930 and an increase after. Again, these results run counter to any expectations that offense rates should increase systematically with urban population growth.

depended on American data, is it generally true — in a comparative or cross-nation sense — that big cities have high homicide rates ? (2) Does comparative longitudinal evidence support the tentative indications that urban homicide rates do not necessarily increase as a city grows in population size over time ? And (3) can these two designs be combined in some way to provide a historical picture of the dynamic relationship between the homicide rates of large, growing cities and those of non-urban areas over time ?

1. — City Rates and Other Rates (A Cross-Sectional Question)

As shown by the logarithmic J-curve in Figure 1, there is no question that large U.S. cities have atypically high homicide rates. But in a heterogeneous society like the U. S., this finding could well be due to factors other then the size of cities *per se* — e.g., the homicide rate differences could easily be due to the social and economic differences between rural and large urban areas, etc. For this reason, a comparative researcher might well ask if the finding in Figure 1 can be replicated cross-nationally.

The CCDF provides an opportunity to assess the replicability of this finding, although the test is somewhat indirect. In addition to aggregate data for entire nations, the CCDF includes offense data for 44 major international cities — cities which are either the largest city or one of the largest cities in their societies. This feature of the CCDF data archive makes it possible to compare homicide rates in each of these major cities with the national homicide rate of the corresponding society.

If these two rates differ, it will be a conservative test of the relationship between city size and homicide rates for two reasons : (1) the national homicide rate obviously includes the rate of the city and this artifact will diminish the observed difference between the two rates, and (2) the national homicide rate reflects both rural areas and other urban areas, in addition to the major international city itself. The effects of these two artifacts is conservative. Differences will only be observed if the homicide rate of the major city differs from the aggregate homicide rate for all national sectors combined — rural areas, small cities, other large cities, and the major international city itself.

Since the CCDF generally contains data for only a single major city in a given country, however, it is not at present possible to test for the fine gradations of city size categories shown in Figure 1. The test will only contrast the homicide rates of very large cities and the aggregate rates of the corresponding nations.

This comparative, cross-sectional test is shown in table 2 (31). In order to smooth the effects of erratic annual fluctuations, the rates shown in Table 2 are in general the averages of the most recent five-year period in the CCDF : 1966-1970.

TABLE 2

Primate City Homicide Rates and National Rates : A Cross-Sectional Comparison (a).

City Homicide Rate Lower than National Rate (n=6)		City Homicide Rate Higher than National Rate (n = 18)	
Homicide rate (b)		Homicide Rate	
1. Guyana (1966-70)	6.18	1. Australia (1966-70)	1.28
Georgetown	5.21	Sydney	1.57
2. Japan (1966-70)	2.23	2. Austria (1966-70)	.73
Tokyo	1.78	Vienna	.89
3. Kenya (1964-68)	5.67	3. Belgium (1965-69)	.29
Nairobi	5.27	Brussels	.45
4. Panama (1966-70)	11.07	4. Finland (1966-70)	.35
Panama City	4.96	Helsinki	.65
5. Sri Lanka (1966-70)	6.09	5. France (1966-70)	.45
Colombo City	5.59	Paris	.61
6. Turkey (1966-70)	9.65	6. India (1966-70)	2.72
Istanbul	4.84	Bombay	2.85
		7. Ireland (1966-70)	.34
		Dublin	.35
		8. Mexico (1962, 66, 67, 72)	13.24
		Mexico City	13.34
		9. Netherlands (1966-70)	.50
		Amsterdam	1.23
		10. New Zealand (1966-70)	.16
		Wellington	2.32
		11. Northern Ireland (1964-68 c)	.20
		Belfast	.35
		12. Philippines (1966-70)	7.98
		Manila	23.86
		13. Rhodesia (1966-70)	5.33
		Salisbury	7.20
		14. Scotland (1966-70)	.78
		Glasgow	1.56

---

31 Although it is tempting to try to make direct homicide rate comparisons across the international cities and across the nations shown in Table 2, such comparisons are hazardous without a careful inspection of the CCDF from which these data are drawn. Although the same indicator (e.g., offenses known) was used *within* each pair in Table 2, not all pairs used the same indicator. In addition, national idiosyncracies in homicide classification and definition make cross-national comparisons of absolute homicide rates far from uncomplicated.

15. Spain (1964-68)	.49
Madrid	.56
16. Sudan (1961-64,68)	5.67
Khartoum	30.25
17. Trinidad & Tobago (66-70)	14.00
Port-of-Spain	15.31
18. United States (1966-70)	6.62
New York City	11.54

Median Country Rate :	6.14	Median Country Rate :	.76
Median City Rate :	5.09	Median City Rate :	1.57

(a) Because of national idiosyncrasies in definition and reporting, the reader is cautioned against making direct cross-national comparisons of homicide rate levels. As explained in the text, this is not a problem for urban-national comparisons within the same society.

(b) Source for all data is the 110-Nation Comparative Crime Rate File. Homicide rates are given in offenses per 100,000 population. In order to smooth the effect of annual fluctuations, the rates are the means of the years shown. The difference in rates between nations and cities is conservative for two reasons : (1) the national rate includes the urban rate, and (2) the national rate also includes other urban areas (i. e., the national rates aggregate both urban and rural areas).

(c) The period 1966-70 also shows Belfast as having a higher homicide rate. This period was not used in this analysis, however, because Northern Ireland's most recent political violence began in 1969.

Even though the CCDF contains crime data for 44 international cities, several of these cities could not be included in Table 2 for one of two reasons : (1) one (or both) of the city and nation time series were not available in the CCDF for the period 1966-1970 ; or (2) even if both series were available for this period, the city reported a different homicide indicator than was available for the entire nation. However, appropriate city-nation comparisons could be made for 24 cases.

In general, the cross-sectional analysis in Table 2 indicates that the homicide rates of primate cities exceed the rates of nations as a whole. This was true for 75 % (18 out of 24) of the pairs of cities and nations. As discussed earlier, it should be noted that the differences in Table 2 understate the actual differences between large city rates and non-urban rates — because the national rate actually includes the major city rate and the rates of other cities as well as the rates of non-urban areas.

The exceptional cases are often provocative in comparative research, and it is interesting to speculate about the six exceptional cases in Table 2. Are these six cases qualitatively similar, and are they in some way unlike the societies which constitute the majority pattern in Table 2 ? Although *post hoc* interpretations require more art than system, it does seem that the two types of outcomes in Table 2 might be related to national levels of « development », industrialization, etc. Five of the six exceptional cases are « pre-industrial » societies. Perhaps homicide rates in these societies are in some way qualitatively unique — e.g., kinship feuds, revenge killings, etc., which might characterize rural areas more than the less traditional urban areas in these nations (32).

However, even this explanation for the exceptional cases has an exception. Japan is the only heavily industrial nation in which the large city, Tokyo, has a lower homicide rate than the national average. Despite the presence of a clear majority pattern in Table 2, and also a not outrageous explanation for the exceptional cases, Japan stands out as an anomaly. Why is Tokyo, alone of the major cities in heavily industrial nations, characterized by a homicide rate below the national average ? Comparative research is both a search for cross-national generalizations and also a quest for unique cases, of course, and we intend to discuss this and other unusual cases in a later publication.

With these exceptions, then, the comparative evidence in Table 2 is in rough agreement with cross-sectional evidence for the U.S. — in both cases, large cities have homicide rates higher than their national averages. It is also interesting that although all the cities in Table 2 are large cities, there is obviously great variation among the homicide rates of these cities-just as there is great variation among the rates of the nations themselves. This variance indicates that absolute city size does not correspond in any direct way to the absolute magnitude of a city's homicide rate — i.e., cities of 500,000 people do not necessarily have a homicide rate of, say, 17 per 100,000 people.

This suggests the intriguing possibility that large cities have homicide rates which are unusually high *only in terms of the overall homicide rates of their societies.* An international city, therefore, can have a homicide rate which is remarkably low (when compared to other large cities worldwide) but which is still a high rate for this specific society. This pattern can be illustrated using two of the cases in Table 2. Both Paris and New York City had over 7,000,000

---

(32) Alternate explanations are not difficult to find. In terms of the Durkheim-Wirth hypothesis discussed earlier, for example, it might be that major cities involve a weakening of kinship and community ties in developed societies but not in developing nations. Perhaps developing societies have lower rates of mobility, or perhaps people moving to cities in developing societies move with intact families rather than alone. Developed societies might also have greater controls over rural homicides — e.g., decentralized law enforcement which reduces blood feuds, marauding gangs, etc.

inhabitants for the period 1966-70. But as Table 2 indicates, these two cities have dramatically different homicide rates. In both cases, however, the homicide rate of the city is higher than the rate of the entire society.

If this observation is well-founded, the relationship between city size and homicide rates is *relative* rather than absolute — i.e., there is no formula relating specific homicide rates to specific city sizes. Sociologists are unlikely, therefore, to identify a theoretical model which can predict an international city's homicide rate purely from its population. On the basis of the evidence in Table 2, it seems much more promising to pursue theories which try to explain why the homicide rates of large cities appear to be anchored to — and yet higher then — the corresponding national rates. Other evidence for this « nation-anchored » hypothesis of urban homicide rates will be discussed below.

2. — Homicide Rates in Growing Cities (A Longitudinal Question)

As discussed above, the historical half of the paradox has been the observation that a few specific cities — chiefly Buffalo and Boston — have not experienced homicide rate increases as they have grown in size. Since the experience of a handful of cities could easily be idiosyncratic, it seems important to test the cross-national generalizability of this observation as well.

In order to provide a rough test of this longitudinal question for the international cities in the CCDF, a simple zero-order correlation was calculated between : (1) the city's population, and (2) the city's homicide rate. Since almost all the cities increased continuously in population during this period (33), this correlation provides a crude index of the homicide trend during this period. A positive correlation indicates homicide rate increases during this period ; a zero correlation indicates essentially no change ; and a negative correlation indicates homicide rate decreases.

Some of the 44 international cities in the CCDF have data points which are too few in number or too scattered to permit calculation of this trend. However, it is possible to produce 34 correlations, each one roughly analogous to the single-city studies of Buffalo and Boston discussed earlier. Since fewer than 100 years were available for these 34 cities, however, our analysis is not as deep as these previous case studies. This analysis is much broader, however, in that it examines 34 cities in 28 countries. The results of this analysis are shown in table 3.

---

(33) Two of the very few cities to decline in population or show discontinuous growth are Belfast and Glasgow.

TABLE 3

Homicide Rates and Population Size for Primate Cities : A Longitudinal Analysis (a).

CITY	Correlation Between City Population and City Homicide Rate (b)	Number of Years in the Analysis	Significance
New York (c)	.98	8	.001
Istanbul	.88	19	.001
Manila	.79	23	.001
Ouezon City (d)	.64	8	.090
Calcutta	.51	16	.044
New York (c)	.47	12	.121
Panama City	.45	11	.167
Salisbury (d)	.41	22	.058
Port-of-Spain	.38	25	.061
Johannesburg	.33	10	.360
Georgetown	.27	18	.273
Sydney	.27	40	.090
Ouezon City	.26	11	.437
Wellington	.16	17	.542
Colombo	.15	74	.198
Khartoum	.13	13	.683
Amsterdam	.02	43	.911
Port-of-Spain (d) .	-.04	25	.851
Mexico City	-.13	12	.697
Dublin	-.15	47	.315
Brussels	-.17	27	.409
Oslo	-.18	14	.541
Salisbury	-.21	22	.361
Munich	-.26	28	.181
Vienna	-.32	21	.155

Montevideo	-.36	31	.045
Glasgow	-.38	72	.001
Paris	-.45	39	.004
Nairobi	-.50	21	.022
Belfast	-.54	52	.001
Madrid	-.57	16	.021
Tokyo	-.57	73	.001
Helsinki	-.58	43	.001
Bombay	-.66	16	.005
Median r :	-.01		

(a) Source : the 110-Nation Comparative Crime Data File. This analysis tests for the presence of any linear relationship between changes in population size and changes in homicide rates for these primate cities.

(b) Since most of these cities have grown consistently over time, the correlations are easily interpreted. A positive correlation means that the city's homicide rate has increased over time ; a zero r indicates no consistent change in homicide rate ; and a negative r means that the city's homicide rate has decreased over time.

(c) New York City appears twice because a change in recording procedures created two series : one before 1966 and one after.

(d) Indicates that a rate for « murder » was used for this city other rates are homicide rates.

As Table 3 clearly indicates, there is no universal or general relationship between city growth and changes in absolute homicide rates. The correlations range from a low of — .66 (for Bombay) to a high of .98 (for New York City), and the 34 cases are evenly divided into 17 positive r's and 17 negative r's. This broad scatter is responsible for the fact that the median correlation in Table 3 is essentially zero (-.01).

The inconsistency of these 34 longitudinal analyses suggests that there is no invariant tendency for the homicide rates of large cities to increase as these cities grow in size. Table 3 shows that homicide rates are just as likely to decrease with city growth as they are to increase.

Even though the time periods reflected in Table 3 are shorter than the century-long studies of individual American cities cited earlier, several cities in Table 3 have data for more than 50 years. This variance in time periods can be used for a kind of data quality control procedure. If one limits the comparison to the four cities with 50 or more years of data, for example, the median correlation is still only -.46. Even for cities with a half-century or more of data, therefore, there is still no strong evidence that homicide rates increase with city growth.

It is possible, of course, that the near-zero median in Table 3 conceals some lawful differences among different types of societies. There might be two different outcomes of population growth. Thirteen of the 34 correlations in Table 3 are, in fact, significant at the .05 level, and this considerably exceeds the 1.7 cities (five per cent of 34) one would expect to reach significance by chance alone. This does support the idea that Table 3 might reflect two radically different outcome patterns.

Although the fit is not perfect, there does seem to be some typological order to the scatter of Table 3. Cities in « developing » nations seem to be over-represented among the positive correlations — i.e., major cities in developing nations may be more likely than other cities to experience increasing homicide rates as they grow. This purely speculative typology does not, of course, alter the general lack of a consistent pattern in Table 3.

In passing, it is also interesting to speculate about the different conclusions which would have resulted from independent studies of single cities — i.e., without benefit of the CCDF. For example, a researcher examining 20th Century data for Tokyo would have concluded that homicide rates declined with city growth ; a different researcher studying data for Amsterdam would have found no relationship between the variables of population growth and homicide rates ; but a third researcher doing a case study of Manila would have found homicide rate increases with city growth and would have concluded that previous researchers were wrong. The unique strength of the CCDF for sociological research on homicide rates is that it can maximize a researcher's view of the range of possible outcomes across several societies and also indicate whether any general pattern occurs. In this case, the CCDF data in Table 3 demonstrates that city growth can have an extremely wide range of implications for homicide rates and that, in general, there is no evidence that cities and homicide rates grow together.

Seven of the international cities in Table 3 have essentially uninterrupted homicide data for the entire period 1926-1970. These seven cities are Amsterdam, Belfast, Colombo City, Dublin, Glasgow, Helsinki, and Tokyo. The homicide rates of these seven cities can be reprensented, therefore, by a median rate for each year. This median rate reflects the same seven cities for each year in this period and the graph of this median rate over time therefore has an interpretable slope. The median rate for these seven cities between 1926 and 1970 is shown in Figure 2.

Figure 2 : *Trends in Primate City Homicide Rates,* 1926-1970 *(a)*

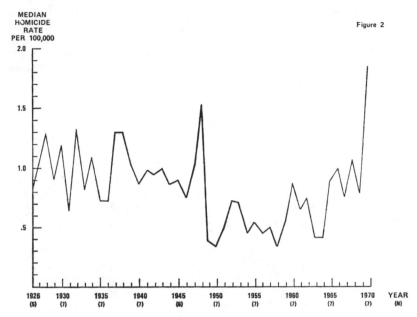

(a) Source : The 110-Nation Comparative Crime Data File. The cities in this trend line are Amsterdam, Belfast, Colombo city, Dublin, Glasgow, Helsinki, and Tokyo. These seven cities have essentially uninterrupted homicide data for this entire period.

✴✴

Just as Table 3 provided evidence that urban homicide rates do not in general increase with city growth, Figure 2 indicates that these seven international cities do not show any consistent increase in homicide rates over time. The slope of the graph in Figure 2 is essentially zero (-.006) — i.e., there is no evidence of progressively higher homicide rates over time. A city's population growth, therefore, does not appear to have any consistent implications for the city's homicide rate.

This completes the generalizability test of the second half of the paradox. Based on an examination of the CCDF, it does seem to be generally true that both : (1) cross-sectionally, large cities appear to have homicide rates which are atypically high for their respective societies ; and also (2) longitudinally, there is no consistent tendency toward elevated homicide rates as a city grows in size. The third phase of our analysis attempts a modest resolution of this apparent paradox.

3. — **Urban and Non-Urban Rates Over Time**

The cross-sectional evidence in Table 2 shows that, at a given moment in time, the homicide rates of large international cities generally exceed their national averages. Table 3 and Figure 2, on the other hand, both show that there is no general tendency for urban homicide rates to increase as cities grow. The paradoxical question remains, therefore, how did large cities acquire high homicide rates if not by growing to a certain population size ?

We propose to answer this question by extending the time « window » in Table 2 backwards in time. Specifically, we propose to use the historical depth of the CCDF to ask whether major international cities have *always* had homicide rates which are high relative to their societal averages. If urban homicide rates have always exceeded national rates — despite the tremendous changes in urban size over time — then the atypically high homicide rates must be attributed to certain urban characteristics rather than others.

We have used the method of controlled comparison to provide this test of the historical relationship between urban and national rates. Because of missing data or incomparable indicators, only the period 1926-1970 could be included. For each of these years, the median homicide rate of the international cities can be compared to the median rate of the corresponding societies. This is a controlled comparison strategy since each national rate acts as a paired « control » for each urban rate — i.e., a city is only included in the median for a given year if its corresponding national rate is also available for that year. This controlled comparison prevents any bias due to the partial entry (e. g., only for the median urban rate) of homicide data from a society with unusually high or low homicide rates.

The historical relationship between the homicide rates of international cities and the rates of entire nations is shown in Figure 3. The number of pairs (each pair consists of one city and one nation) in the analysis is indicated at five-year intervals.

The most striking pattern in Figure 3 is that international cities have consistently had homicide rates higher than their national averages. The gap between the solid and broken lines in Figure 3 is a conservative index of urban-national differences. It is conservative, again, because the dotted line actually includes the rate of the solid line, and it also includes the rates of other large and small cities as well. The difference between the two lines in Figure 3 is perhaps particularly impressive because these international cities were much smaller — in terms of absolute populations — at the beginning of this period than they are now.

Figure 3 : *Primate City Homicide Rates and National Homicide Rates :*

A Longitudinal Comparison (a).

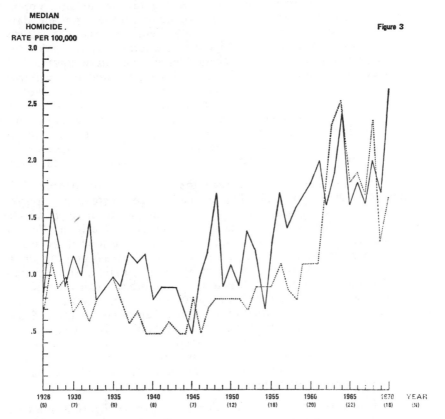

(a) Source : The 110-Nation Comparative Crime Data File. The solid line shows the median homicide rate of primate cities for each year ; the broken line shows the median rate of the corresponding nations. The number of pairs (each pair is one city and one nation) in the analysis is indicated at five-year intervals.

**
**

The median homicide rates in Figure 3 show that the main finding of Table 2 (that primate cities have homicide rates anchored to, but higher than, their national averages for 1966-70) could be « replicated » for any period between 1926 and 1970. If anything,

Figure 3 shows that the effect of city size was even more pronounced earlier in this century than during the period (1966-70 (34).

The consistent difference reflected in Figure 3 is our most important longitudinal finding. Although we do not have homicide data reaching back into the 18th and 19th Centuries, the consistently higher rates of the cities in Figure 3 encourage us to make the following extrapolation : In general, large cities have always had homicide rates higher than their national averages, and this was true even when these cities were much smaller than they are today. Even in 1926, the first year in Figure 3, these international cities were still more « urban » than their societies as a whole. We are suggesting, therefore, that it is the relative size of « large » cities at any moment in time — rather than their absolute population in thousands — which is responsible for their consistently higher homicide rates.

The high rates of urban areas, therefore, must be attributed to variables *other than* their absolute population size. There are, of course, many other urban characteristics which could elevate urban homicide rates. Even when these international cities were much smaller in absolute terms, for example, they were still characterized by many urban characteristics : in-migration from rural areas, housing on a basis other than kinship, heterogeneity of population, stratification into rich and poor areas, etc. It is to these and other urban variables — variables which are not linked firmly to any specific city size — that we must look for an explanation of high urban homicide rates. Some combination of these urban characteristics apparently acts to inflate or exaggerate the general level of homicide in a society. Although urban rates are « anchored » near their national rates, therefore, they have consistently exceeded them — at least for the time period we have been able to examine.

A final caveat should be mentioned concerning Figure 3. Because different data points in Figure 3 reflect a different combination of cases — depending on the availability of city and nation data in any given year — the slope of these lines is not meaningful. Since different cities and nations are included in different periods of the table, the lines cannot provide an indication of trends for either cities or nations over time.

Our investigation of the paradoxical relationship between cities and homicide rates can be summarized as follows : (1) Homicide rates and city size are strongly and monotonically related. for U. S.

---

(34) A plausible interpretation for the narrowing of this gap after 1960 is suggested by the exceptional cases in Table 2. After roughly 1960, developing nations are increasingly represented in the CCDF, and Table 2 suggests that developing nations may not have the same relationship between city size and homicide as is found in developed nations.

cities, by a « logarithmic J-curve » — with the interesting exception that rural homicide rates exceed the rates of small cities ; (2) This cross-sectional result is also true cross-nationally — the homicide rates of large cities exceed their national homicide rates between 1966 and 1970 ; (3) However, longitudinal analysis shows that the homicide rates of international cities generally have not increased as these cities have grown in population over time ; and (4) The explanation for this apparent paradox is that homicide rates of international cities have consistently exceeded national homicide rates — even when these cities were much smaller in absolute size than they are now.

The key to interpreting the paradox of urban homicide rates, we believe, is the observation that the rates of major international cities have consistently exceeded their national rates. The determinant of a city's homicide rate therefore, is not the absolute size of the city, but its size *relative* to its contemporary society. Even small cities can have relatively high homicide rates, if at any moment in history they are « urban » by local national standards. With some exceptions, any city more urban than its national environment is likely to have a homicide rate which exceeds its national average. The relative nature of this relationship, we believe, is the answer to the paradoxical question of why large cities have high homicide rates which do not grow higher as the cities grow larger.

The CCDF : An Agenda for Comparative Research and Theory.

The two studies described above illustrate the potential contributions of the 110-nation Comparative Crime Data File, although they tap this potential only lightly to address two extremely concrete questions.

The methodological study establishes, we believe, the appropriateness of using any of a range of indicators as estimates of trends in national homicide rates — i. e., it no longer seems necessary to restrict longitudinal homicide research to the « offenses known » indicator. This study also illustrates how various data quality control procedures can be incorporated in research designs, given a data archive as massive as the CCDF.

The substantive study attempts to resolve the apparent paradox of urban homicide rates. Cross-national urban data from the CCDF show that large cities do have atypically high homicide rates, but also that there is no evidence that homicide rates increase as these cities grow in population over time. The explanation of this apparent contradiction between cross-sectional and longitudinal findings appears to be the *relative* population size, rather than the absolute size, of cities. Our analyisis shows that cities have consistently had atypically high homicide rates, even when these cities were only a fraction of their current size. While it is true that cities have high homicide rates, therefore, these rates can only be attributed to urban characteristics other than population size.

It is our long-term hope that the CCDF will contribute to the empirical foundations of a genuinely international understanding of homicide. We believe this massive data resource can assist realization of this goal in two ways. This archive can help researchers to discover those patterns which generalize across boundaries of nation states and time periods, and also to identify exceptional cases where specific national and urban characteristics outweigh or even reverse these general patterns. An extensive program of this kind of cross-national empirical research is clearly indispensable if we are ever to see a truly general theory of the social origins of homicide.

REFERENCES

ARCHER (D.) and GARTNER (R.), « Violent acts and violent times : A comparative approach to postwar homicide rates ». *American Sociological Review*, 1976. 41. 937-963.

ARCHER (D.). GARTNER (R.). AKERT (R.) and LOCKWOOD (T.). « Cities and homicide : A new look at an old paradox ». (« Tomasson (R.) (ed.). *Comparative Studies in Sociology*. Volume 1 (in press), 1977.

BRENNER (M.H.). *Mental Illness and the Economy*, Cambridge. Harvard University Press. 1973.

CLINARD (M.B.). *Sociology of Deviant Behavior*, New York, Holt, Rinehart and Winston. 1974.

CLINARD (M.B.) and ABBOTT (D.J.). *Crime in Developing Countries, A Comparative Approach*, New York, Wiley, 1973.

DURKHEIM (E.), *The Division of labor in Society* New York. The Free Press. 1933 (Translated by G. Simpson).

FERDINAND (T.). « The criminal patterns of Boston since 1849 », *American Journal of Sociology* 1967. 73 : 84-99.

GIBBS (J.P.). *Crime, Punishment, and Deterrence*, New York, Elsevier, 1975.

GURR (T.R.). GRABOSKI (P.N.) and HULA (R.C.), *The Politics of Crime and Conflict : A Comparative History of Four Cities*, Beverly Hills and London. SAGE Publications, 1977.

HENRY (A.F.) and SHORT (J.F. Jr.) *Suicide and Homicide : Some Economic, Sociological, and Psychological Aspects of Aggression*, Glencoe, Free Press. 1954.

HINDELANG (J.J.), « The uniform Crime Reports revisited ». *Journal of Criminal Justice* 1974, 2 : 1-17.

LANE (R.), « Urbanization and criminal violence in the 19th century : Massachusetts as a test case », IN Graham (H.D.) and Gurr (T.R.) (eds), *The History of Violence in America,* Washington, D.C., U. S. Government Printing Office, 1969, 468-484.

LIEBERSON (S.) and HANSEN (L.K.), « National development, mother tongue diversity, and the comparative study of nations », *American Sociological Review,* 1974, 39 : 523-541.

LODHI (A.Q.) and TILLY (C.), « Urbanization, crime and collective violence in 19th century France », *American Journal of Sociology,* 1973, 79 : 296-318.

MANNHEIM (H.), *War and Crime,* London, Watts, 1941.

MANNHEIM (H.) *Comparative Criminology,* London, Routledge and Kegan Paul, 1965.

MULVIHILL (D.J.) and TUMIN (M.M.) (co-directors) *Crimes of Violence,* National Commission on the Causes and Prevention of Violence, Vols, 11, 12, 13. Washington, D.C., U.S. Government Printing Office, 1969.

NAROLL (R.), *Data quality control : A new Research Technique,* New York, Free Press, 1962.

NEWMAN (G.), *Comparative Deviance : Perception and Law in Six Cultures,* New York, Elsevier, 1976.

POWELL (E.), « Crime as a function of anomie ». *Journal of Criminal Law, Criminology and Police Science,* 1966, 57 : 161-171.

RADZINOWICZ (L.), « Economic pressures ». IN Radzinowicz (L.) and Wolfgang (M.E.) (eds), *Crime and Justice : The Criminal in Society,* New York, Basic Books, 1971, Vol. 1, 420-442.

SELLIN (T.), « Is murder increasing in Europe ? », *The Annals of the American Academy of Political and Social Science,* 1926, 126 : 29-34.

SELLIN (T.), « The basis of a crime index ». *Journal of Criminal Law and Criminology,* 1931, 22 : 335-56.

SELLIN (T.) and WOLFGANG (M.E.). *The measurement of Delinquency,* New York, John Wiley and Sons, 1964.

SOROKIN (P.), *Contemporary Sociology theories,* New York, Harper, 1928.

STRAUS (M.) and STRAUS (J.), « Suicide, homicide, and social structure in Ceylon », *American Journal of Sociology,* 1953 58, 461-469.

SZABO (D.), *Crimes et Villes,* Louvain, Université Catholique, 1960.

TARNIQUET (H.), « Crime in the Rapidly Industrializing Urban Environment », *Revue Internationale de Criminologie et de Police Technique,* 1968, 22 (1) : 49-58.

VERKKO (V.), « Survey of current practice in criminal statistics ». *Transactions of the Westermarck Society,* 1956, 3 : 5-33.

WIRTH (L.), « Urbanism as a way of life ». *American journal of Sociology,* 1940, 743-755.

WOLFGANG (M.), « International crime statistics : a proposal », *Journal of Criminal law, Criminology and Police Science,* 1967, 58 : 65-9, « Urban crime », IN Wilson (J.Q.) (ed.), *The Metropolitan Enigma, Cambridge, Mass, Harvard University Press,* 1968, 245-281.

WOLFGANG (M.) and FERRACUTI (F.). *The Subculture of Violence,* New York, Tavistock, 1967.

21

DEADLY FORCE
The Moral Reasoning and Education of Police Officers Faced with the Option of Lethal Legal Violence

PETER SCHARF   ROD LINNINGER

DAVE MARRERO   RON BAKER

CHRIS RICE

INTRODUCTION. This paper offers an analysis of police responses to hypothetical dilemmas about the use of deadly force. We will also present a brief description of officer response to use of deadly force dilemmas and describe a training intervention designed to heighten officer awareness of the dilemmas implicit in the use of a potentially lethal weapon. Im many cities this topic is a critical one for police administrators, scholars and the public. At once there have been numerous incidents where police officers have shot innocent bystanders presuming them to be dangerous and armed felons. On the other hand there have been similar incidents where police officers have been killed in situations where they might have been saved had they effectively used their weapons in time.

Critical to any understanding of the police officer's assessment of the "deadly force" dilemma is a theory of legal decision-making. One approach to legal decision-making is found in Kohlberg's (1977) theory of moral judgment. Kohlberg's theory posits six stages of moral development, evolving sequentially in all societies. Each moral stage contains a qualitatively discreet conception of the relationship of law to individual and society. A correlation between Kohlberg's moral stages and legal reasoning has been empirically documented in a recent study of legal socialization (Tapp and Kohlberg, 1974).

Stage one is the stage of punishment and obedience. Stage two orients to instrumental hedonism. Stage three offers what we call the good boy/girl orientation. At stage four, there is a shift toward fixed definitions of law and society. Stage five is a legalistic-contract orientation. Law becomes the agreed upon contract among social equals with duties of stage and individual clearly defined and regulated. At stage six, Kohlberg argues that there is a rational basis for ethical decision-making where the law is repository for broader ethical principles.

The developmental theory of legal decision-making offers a unique perspective towards the problem of police decisionmaking. It suggests that democratic social reasoning represents a cognitive process not attained by all individuals. Kohlberg, for example, estimates that less than 10 percent of the American adult citizenry attain the Stage 5 level of reasoning necessary to fully understand the moral principles underlying institutional law. This implies that many police officers lower than Stage 5 may not fully understand the moral logic necessary to implement many legal statutes.

From Peter Scharf et al., "Deadly Force: The Moral Reasoning and Education of Police Officers Faced with the Option of Lethal Legal Violence," 7(Special Issue) *Policy Studies Journal* 450-454 (Special Issue 1978). Copyright 1978, Policy Studies Organization.

Two hypotheses were posited for the purposes of this study:

1. That there would be an association between stage of moral reasoning and the decision on a hypothetical use of force dilemma.
2. That officers would show increases in moral maturity on standard and police dilemmas during a twelve week training seminar dealing with difficult discretionary decisions.

SUBJECTS. Twenty-four police officers were randomly selected from two California police departments. The sample included eighteen patrolmen, four sergeants, and two lieutenants. The officers ranged in experience from six months to twenty-seven years of duty. Exactly half of the group possessed a college degree, and the mean age was thirty years.

INSTRUMENTS. An interview schedule including moral dilemmas from police and non-police situations was developed for this study. The standard dilemmas were those developed by Kohlberg and were carefully normed in terms of rating procedures. A police dilemma was developed by the authors; it asked officers to decide if it was right to shoot a suspect who was holding a hostage in a convenience store if it was 50 percent probable that he could kill the perpetrator without harm to the suspect and 30 percent probable that if he did not shoot, the perpetrator would shoot the hostage.

RESULTS. Descriptive analysis revealed an apparent association between moral stage and decision on the "shooting dilemma."

TABLE 1

	Shoot	Not Shoot
Postconventional (Stage 4/5 and 5)	0	5
Conventional (Stage 3 and 4)	5	9
Preconventional (Stage 2 and 3)	4	1
Total Responses	9	15

Most Stage 2 officers in our sample tended to view the hostage dilemma as a problem of personal authority and control; many of the Stage 2 officers showed a strong concern with power and domination:

I go into a situation and attempt to show control. I am king of this roost. I am going to show everyone who is boss. I first get control, then I decide what to do...I try to get them to respect my uniform--to know that I am the law!

Among these Stage 2 officers there was typically a greater consideration of the risk to their own life than that of the hostage (Question: "What would you consider in deciding whether to shoot?"):

It would depend whether or not he fired at me. That's the first thing...If he shoots at me and misses--he's a dead man.

The fourteen Stage 3 and 4 officers demonstrated quite different reasoning processes from those observed in the pre-conventional subjects. While the preconventional police officers were concerned with concrete consequences to them-selves or others, the conventionally reasoning subjects showed a far greater concern with the procedural legality of particu-lar actions. For example, one officer suggested that the penal code's sanctions defined his obligations in the shooting situ-ation. What is right is defined by what is legally permissible rather than a specifically moral assessment:

I'd be more inclined to shoot than not shoot. Like, there was a guy who had fifty-six arrests. Given that kind of background, I think the law would back me up in shooting....

The Stage 5 officers: (there were no Stage 6 officers in our study) officers demonstrated a quite different perspective from that seen in either preconventional or conventionally reasoning officers. These officers suggested that while taking a life would be justified under certain circumstances, it must be regarded as a last "in extremis" strategy. One officer characteristically suggested:

Taking a life must be the ultimate thing. It's like playing God. I would never shoot unless a life were in imminent danger. Shooting for property makes no sense at all. We don't have capital punishment for theft. The important thing is saving the life.

This analysis of the officer interviews tentatively sup-ported our hypothesis that the process of decision-making would be related to the outcome of the hypothetical decision.

The perspective we have offered here suggests a focus upon the moral reasoning of police officers as a clue to their be-havior in shooting situations. If our hypothesis regarding moral judgement and shooting behavior were to be confirmed in real life as opposed to hypothetical situations several policy alternatives seem to follow.

First, officers who possess the critical intellectual capacities necessary to resolve complex decisions might be selected in larger numbers by law enforcement agencies. Another strategy involves the ongoing moral and legal education of law enforcement personnel. This second approach received a brief test in a twelve week dilemma training course conducted by the authors. Dilemma situations involving, for example, the harassment of known felons, "overreaction" by officers to citizen provocation, as well as "shooting" situations, were discussed in a similar manner focusing upon both the legal as well as strategic issues relevant to the case. Additionally, elaborate training simulations were created in which the officers were placed into potential shooting situations analogous to situations which might be faced in the "line of duty." In one simulation for example, officers were given an order to report to a building where they met a "neighbor," actually a plainclothes officer, who was reporting a (family disturbance). Upon entering the building, the officers found a psychotic husband with a knife at the throat of his panicky wife (both, in reality, police officers). During a "debriefing session utilizing video-tapes of the simulation, the moral, legal and strategic elements of the case were discussed in small groups. We hypothesized that it might be possible to both stimulate moral maturity gains among the officers involved in both standard and police moral dilemmas. Interviews were administered and scored following procedures described by Kohlberg, to ten police officers selected at random.

RESULTS. Analysis of moral change during the course of the intervention revealed complex results. Non-significant change was found in the responses to the standard Kohlberg dilemma. This is understandable due to the high average age of the subjects and the short duration of the intervention 36 contact hours.

Significant change was found in terms of the shift in responses to the police dilemma. This was theoretically interesting as it suggests a form of what Piaget calls horizontal decalage: change in the application of an existing cognitive or moral capacity. Thus, several of the officers who did not change in terms of moral judgment did change in their responses to the police dilemma. This implies that while we were not able to alter the moral reasoning capacity of officers we were able to encourage them to apply their available moral capacities to the police situations.

TABLE 2

CHANGE IN MORAL REASONING AS A RESULT
OF A 36 HOUR TRAINING INTERVENTION

	Pre	Post
Standard Moral Maturity Index	n = 333	n = 335
	n.s. T = 0.722 (DF=9)	
Police "Shooting" Dilemmas	n = 320	n = 366
	T = 2.102 (DF=9)	

CONCLUSIONS. The approach described here offers a new conception of law enforcement education. Instead of simply training in techniques and the rules of law enforcement, we have attempted to create a training program focusing on the process of legal decision-making. If in future replications we find that it is possible to alter officer moral reasoning through such a "case method" program, it would appear that a new form of law enforcement education is possible, an education which would focus on the process of legal reasoning rather than simply on legal roles and police strategy. Our approach seeks not only to encourage philosophic reflection by officers as well as the application of philosophy to the practical problems of police work. While still in a pilot phase we hope our program proves suggestive for those committed to the selection and training of a police force appropriate for a democratic society.

REFERENCES

Banton, M. The Policeman in the Community. London: Tavistock, 1964.

Barker, B. M. "Police discretion and the principle of legality." Criminal Law Quarterly 8 (1966): 400–407.

Kohlberg, Lawrence. "Cognitive-developmental approach to moral education." In Peter Scharf, Readings in Moral Education. Minneapolis, Minnesota: Winston Press, 1977.

LaFave, Walter. Arrest: The Decision to Take a Suspect into Custody. Boston: Little, Brown and Co., 1965.

Muir, William K. Police: Street Corner Politicians. Chicago: University of Chicago Press, 1972.

Reiss, A. J. Police and the Public. New Haven: Yale University Press, 1971.

Scharf, Peter, and Hickey, Joseph. "Inmates' conception of legal justice." Criminal Justice and Behavior III (2) (July 1976).

Skolnick, Jerome. Justice Without Trial: Law Enforcement in a Democratic Society. New York: John Wiley and Sons, Inc., 1966.

Tapp, June. "Legal socialization: Strategies in ethical legality." Stanford Law Review 29 (1974): 1–74.

Peter Scharf is Assistant Professor at University of California, Irvine. He is author of the recently published book Towards a Just Correctional System *(San Francisco: Jossey-Bass). He is currently project director to study police deadly force.*

Part IV:

ECOLOGY

Ecological variables have occupied an enduring, respectable, but rather inconspicuous place in modern criminology. Ecologically speaking, their location has been closer to the periphery than to the center—except, perhaps, when Robert Park's students were trying to determine the spatial distribution of evil in the city of Chicago nearly half a century ago. This is unfortunate, we think, because an ecological approach to crime and criminal justice, more than many other approaches, contains the possibility of counteracting the profound tendency among theorizers and practitioners to locate the causes of crime in the "evil minds" of individuals. We shall return to this thought below, though we cannot undertake to demonstrate the claim.

The subject matter of ecology is capable of being defined with, for the social sciences, rather unusual precision. It deals with the relationships between behavioral complexes, crime, and criminal justice in our case and the environment within which these activities take place. Inevitably, of course, although the core of the ecological endeavor can be defined rather clearly, its boundaries are diffuse. It is not always possible to say precisely, for example, whether some element belongs to the situated complex or to its situation. Thus, the role of the neutral bystander to crime encompasses, at one end, the unwitting accomplice and, at the other, the vicarious victim; and as witnesses, bystanders function both as components of the justice process and as part of the environment affected by and affecting its operations. Further, past uncertainties concerning the scope of ecology have been magnified by certain recent developments. The term *ecology* has come to express our solicitude for the integrity of the environment. Accordingly, the inherited ecological problematics, which were overwhelmingly concerned with environmental determinants and their effects on the distribution, frequency, and character of criminality (and, to a lesser extent, crime control), are coming to be augmented by studies dealing with the impact of crime and its control on the environment.

A great deal of ecological study is dedicated to either actuarial or cartographic description. Much of this is instructive, sophisticated, sensitive to change, and of potential value for crime control planning and administration.[1] Another area of work consists of city planning and architectural design dedicated to the enhancement of the quality of urban life, with greater or lesser emphasis on crime control.[2] But the aspirations that fueled the work of the Chicago School during the 1920s have not been abandoned. Although the hope that the incidence of crime would be explainable through the kind of mapping represented by the well-known "concentric zone theory" is no longer entertained, the hope that such studies will lead to more powerful theories remains.

The modern approach to area analysis generally involves the use of highly complex mathematical techniques of data analysis; the following articles by the Brantinghams and by Richard Block provide excellent examples. Both articles tend to confirm the belief, developed by earlier ecologists, that the boundaries of "neighborhoods" divided by class and race, particularly, are the areas of high crime rates. While older findings of this sort did not lend themselves readily to use by city planners—such boundaries being treated as a "natural" fact of life to a considerable extent—the Brantinghams attempt to present their findings in a manner that might increase such use. They point to the possibility of establishing "neighborhoods" in ways that would minimize the observed effects.

Urban ecology has never completely disregarded the moral aspects of the environment, but it concentrated on the study of its physical character. To speak of an area as "deteriorating" involves a social judgment, but it is a judgment about the physical state of buildings, roads, and other facilities. Recent work, however, has directed attention to the moral and social environment in an unmediated sense. Leon Sheleff's powerful book on the bystander, from which we reprint a chapter, forcefully reminds us about the fact, and its importance, that we are all bystanders in each others' lives, a fact that appears to receive much more deliberate attention in the way we conduct our affairs in practice than it has in social science inquiry. Sheleff is mainly concerned with bystanders' reactions to crimes they witness. He also discusses, however, some of the ways in which people's activities could be organized to lessen the risk of crime.

Attention to persons as bystanders requires the analysis of the environment along temporal as well as spatial dimensions. An analysis of places in terms of what characteristically goes on in them at various times, and how that influences the likelihood and nature of crime in those places, is attempted in the fascinating article by Cohen and Felson. It is unfortunate that criminologists pay so little attention to rhythm, tempo, and timing of routine activities in structuring crime. After all, it is common knowledge that experienced offenders plan their activities with careful consideration of these factors. "Casing a joint" means precisely finding opportunities for "hits" within the normal stream of social time.[3] There is little doubt that, in part, this neglect reflects dogged adherence to etiological theories involving individualistically working irrational factors.

The final two articles in this section deal with the impact of crime on the environment. It should be noted that what is being identified as an effect of crime may not be the effect of crime itself, but the effect of the social awareness of its existence—which may be based on fact. Elsewhere in this volume, Garofalo presents evidence showing the fear of crime and withdrawal from activity based on fear is primarily a function of age and sex, rather than experience with or factual knowledge of crime. However, Mario Rizzo's article illustrates an attempt to assess the effect of crime on residential property values by a method that relates reported crimes to housing costs, while carefully controlling a number of factors that are known to influence the latter. The final article, by Steven Balkin, is actually no more than a brief allusion to a seemingly farfetched consequence, namely, crime's impact on energy policies. Balkin lightly, but deftly, touches some aspects of the problem. One can, without much intellectual effort, add to his list the energy that goes into attempts to prevent crime in the forms of lighting, alarms, and patrols; and the energy it takes to keep prisons, jails, and all the other facilities occupied by the functionaries of the criminal justice establishment lit, heated, and generally functioning; and a great many more such things. The cost of crime, as Rizzo also argues, is far greater than the figures generated by focusing on its obvious targets.

The ecological problem in criminology does not involve a single, unified approach or an internally consistent complex of problematics. It also does not seem likely that the ecological perspective will ever provide the basis for a particular theory of crime.[4] Instead, it presents a fund of information, thought, and analysis that counterbalances all monothematic tendencies within criminology, but especially the view that sees crime as a function of deeply immanent psychological forces within the soul of the criminal which move him or her in the direction of targets without regard for time, place, or circumstance. And it does not really matter much whether in such theorizing the determining factors are thought to be deeply embedded instinctual factors (of the sort the sociobiologists write about), complicated affective complexes (so dear to psychologists and psychiatrists), or rational responsiveness to incentives (of the sort economists emphasize).

Academicians are not the only persons concerned with crime whose views are challenged by ecology. People who make it their business to fight crime may be amused by the observation that a desire for privacy, or a penchant for surrounding oneself with expensive and easily portable enjoyables, virtually designs the conditions most favorable for crime, especially if the location of comfort and wealth is combined with a schedule of activities that causes these objects to be unattended for a good deal of time. But they would be less amused by insistence that the existence of crime ought to be understood and crime control strategies designed *in important part* on the basis of such considerations. The prevailing view is that crime is caused by an evil mind, and the inclusion of any other factor in its serious explanation is seen as a moral compromise. The notion of "evil mind" may appear in a different terminology, but under the verbal disguise that various secular theories of causation and control provide, it remains as strong as ever.

NOTES

1. See, for example, Keith D. Harries, *The Geography of Crime and Justice.* New York: McGraw-Hill, 1974.

2. See Oscar Newman, *Defensible Space*. New York: Macmillan, 1972.

3. For a fine description of "casing," see Peter Letkemann, *Crime As Work*. Englewood Cliffs, NJ: Prentice-Hall, 1973.

4. At the same time, the strong resemblances between the theories developed by Cohen and Felson, on the one hand, and Hindelang and his associates, on the other hand, in their contributions to this volume should be noted. Both emphasize time, place, and circumstances in generating crime. Since both conceive of crime as a complex event requiring a conjunction of actors with their environments, the resemblances are suggestive of the general direction in which an ecological perspective (which would seem to require this conception of crime) pushes theorists. Similarly, those taking an ecological approach to crime control are moved to thinking about the ways time, places, and circumstances affect criminal opportunities.

22

RESIDENTIAL BURGLARY AND URBAN FORM

PATRICIA L. BRANTINGHAM
PAUL J. BRANTINGHAM

Urban planning has a strong spatial element: it is concerned with ordering and influencing the distribution of human activity. Planners often manipulate land-use controls to effect specific social and economic goals. One prominent social goal, crime reduction, has rarely been considered by planners. This neglect is probably rooted in a general lack of knowledge of the relationship between land-use patterns and crime. If certain crimes could be shown to be related to specific land-use patterns, planners might be able to consider crime reduction along with other goals during the urban planning process. This paper will begin to explore the relationship between crime and land-use patterns by looking at one crime, residential burglary, in one American city, Tallahassee, Florida.[1] It will be shown that in Tallahassee there is a strong relationship between the patterns of residential development and the patterns of residential burglary. Set theory and point-set topology will be the principal tools used to examine the land use and crime patterns.

The common ground on which urban planning and criminology meet is found in the work of the urban ecologists of the Chicago School of Sociology. Park and Burgess (1925) and their colleagues introduced the concepts of biological ecology into the study of city structure and social behaviour. Two principal concepts have survived the general criticism of their analogies to biology: the concentric zone theory of urban form which postulated a simple, universal urban model; and the concept of the urban 'natural area', which was a smaller unit of city structure, a segment of a particular zone formed by topographical or cultural barriers, or both.

Park and Burgess' zonal hypothesis became the starting point for a major avenue of criminological enquiry. Shaw and McKay (1969) examined the spatial distribution of the residences of delinquent children in Chicago and other American cities, demonstrating that the homes of delinquent children were spatially distributed in general conformance with the zonal model: the highest rates occurred in the central circle formed by the CBD and the 'zone of transition' and successively lower rates occurred in each successive outer ring.

While early replication studies gave strong support to Shaw and McKay's findings, (e.g., White, 1932; Lottier, 1938; see the extensive list of supportive studies cited in Shaw and McKay, 1969, 12-13) from the planning standpoint, these studies present two

Patricia L. Brantingham is at the Department of Urban and Regional Planning, Florida State University, and Paul J. Brantingham is at the School of Criminology, Florida State University.

[1] Tallahassee is the capital of the State of Florida. It is located in the northern part of the state and is surrounded by rural, agricultural land. As of the 1970 Census, Tallahassee had a population of over 71,000. Twenty-nine per cent of the population was black. The average owner-occupied house cost $19,400 and the average monthly rent was $96. The major industries in Tallahassee are government and education.

problems. First, they tell the planner where criminals live, but they tell him very little about where crimes occur. The spatial descriptions of crime which have been done suggest that crime occurrence patterning may be very different from offender residence patterning and that the spatial patterning of individual sorts of crime such as assault or burglary or bicycle theft may be very different from each other. (White, 1932; Schmid, 1960a and b). Recent works by Jeffery (1971) and Newman (1972) show how knowledge of crime patterning permits the architect to abate some crime problems through building design and suggest the possibility of general urban crime control planning. Second, the level of areal aggregation at which ecology of crime studies have been conducted—square miles, or more recently, census tract or political ward—is so large that the complex socio-spatial structure of the city is obscured. Spatial regularities in the occurrence of crime may be hidden or the association of crime with land-use patterns may be lost because the units of the urban structure are smaller than the units of aggregation or because the areal unit—the census tract most commonly—does not conform to the spatial dimensions of the natural area (Schmid, 1960b, 656; Slatin, 1969). This second problem is particularly acute because the great contribution of the ecological studies of crime and criminal residence has been to focus attention on the natural areas or neighbourhoods of the city and to suggest that the transitional zones between neighbourhoods may be of greatest criminological importance.

The problem of producing information on the spatial patterning of crime which will be useful to urban planners takes on several aspects. First a technique for modelling the natural socio-spatial neighbourhoods of an urban area, built up from small areal units, must be developed. Second, crime occurrence data must be gathered and accurately mapped. Third, informed analysis of the spatial patterning of crime in relation to the urban model must be carried out. Fortunately, new methods of data collection and reporting undertaken by the United States Census Bureau in the 1970 census combined with new geocoding computer techniques developed through the census use study make such an undertaking feasible. The ways in which we tackled these problems are described in the Methodological Appendix at the end of this article.

Modelling Urban Form

The approach to modelling urban form which we chose was to construct small areal units—neighbourhoods—from individual city blocks, then to construct larger areal units from the neighbourhoods, and so on until a full model of the city was achieved. We chose this approach because it best preserves the small socio-spatial units which were of criminological interest, the neighbourhoods.

The concept of neighbourhood, of course, is one of the most problematic in social science. It has both spatial and social interaction aspects and these aspects are by no means necessarily congruent. The concept of neighbourhood used here will concentrate on the spatial aspect and will be similar to socio-spatial concepts developed by the American planner Kevin Lynch in his seminal work *The Image of the City* (1960) and by the British psychologist Terrence Lee.

Lynch advanced the concept of the 'district' as one of the principal perceptual building blocks of the city. He defined a district as 'an area of homogeneous character, recognized by clues which are continuous throughout the district and discontinuous elsewhere' (Lynch, 1960, 103). It was a relatively large sub-unit of the city which could be identified by visual characteristics.

The neighbourhood concept used in this paper can be as strong as Lynch's district, but it also includes weak differences between adjacent areas. The important quality of a residential neighbourhood is internal homogeneity or continuity of characteristics across adjacent blocks. Similarities between adjacent city blocks produce perceptual units or neighbourhoods.

Neighbourhoods as conceived here may be rather small and may be characterised by many variables: the socio-economic characteristics of the residents; the cultural or ethnic characteristics of the residents; the housing type and cost; the architectural and design variation, and areas may be more similar on one characteristic than on another. Consider an apartment area of a city with two sub-areas, one dominated by Italian-Americans and the other dominated by German-Americans. At one level, housing type, this is a homogenous neighbourhood. At a different level, this spatial area contains two neighbourhoods dominated by two different cultural groups. Each level of description defines a neighbourhood for some specific but different planning purpose. Generally, the perceptual distinctiveness of a neighbourhood increases as the number of similar characteristics increases. In this sense, the neighbourhoods constructed in this paper will resemble Lee's 'homogeneous neighbourhood' defined by boundaries which '. . . are set by a gradient in the size, price or condition of the houses and the kind of people who live in them'. And in which,

'The most pervading social relationship . . . is one of "mutual awareness", a largely cognitive interaction which none the less has an important place in the neighbourhood schema and which probably exerts social control although no overt interaction takes place' (Lee, 1968, 250).

The Spatial Patterning of a Crime

As discussed above, the work of the criminological ecologists is unsatisfactory from the planner's perspective because it says very little about where crime occurs. Such studies have also been criticised by criminologists for lumping crime data together under generic descriptions such as 'delinquency' or 'felony' when it is both rationally and empirically the case that such diverse legal classifications as murder, burglary or narcotics possession are behaviourally distinct. A recent trend in criminological research has been to focus on an individual legal category such as robbery (Conklin, 1972) or burglary (Ferdinand, 1970; Conklin and Bittner, 1973; Scarr, 1973). This study has focussed on a single crime because useful planning information seems more likely to be generated.

Residential burglary was selected as the crime for study for several reasons. *A priori*, burglary should, more than most crimes, exhibit a spatial distribution related to land-use patterning because it is a crime against real property: the breaking and entering of a dwelling house with the intent to commit some further crime therein. Burglary is also a crime of significant public interest. It is by far the most frequently occurring of the seven serious crimes included in the Uniform Crime Reports index offences (Federal Bureau of Investigation, 1972, 61). It also appears to be the crime most feared and resented by the American public (Conklin and Bittner, 1973, 207). Finally, burglary is a crime

which police have remarkably little success in solving (Federal Bureau of Investigation, 1972, 21; Florida Department of Law Enforcement, 1972, 31) and is therefore a crime for which small preventive gains through prevention planning can pay large real world dividends.

The crime data for this study were all residential burglaries known to the police of the City of Tallahassee during the calendar year 1970. The burglaries were geocoded to the city block on which they occurred (as designated by the Census Bureau so as to be spatially comparable with other block level census data) and mapped using the GRIDS line printer mapping system. Raw incidence patterning showed heavy concentrations around the two universities located in Tallahassee (Florida State University and Florida Agricultural and Mechanical University) and in some other locations. Burglary rates were then calculated to show the intensity of burglary as a function of 100 dwelling units per block according to the rationale advanced by Boggs (1964, 1966) and Scarr (1973, 22). The rates were also mapped using GRIDS.

Neither map revealed consistent and easily interpretable visual patterns. There appears to be a ring of high incidence round the two universities, but the rate pattern is exceptionally complex with high, medium, and low rates intermixed. High rate blocks seem to form no clear pattern. Burglaries did not seem to pile up along major traffic arteries. There were distinct clusters of high rate blocks on two heavily travelled roads, Meridian Road and Jackson Bluff Road, but there were also clusters in low traffic areas. High rates cluster in some rich, white districts and in some poor black districts; but low rates also cluster in similar districts. Indeed, without an interpretive tool such as the neighbourhood sets and without the hint from criminological ecologists that it is the zones of transition where different neighbourhoods border on one another that are of interest, one might be tempted to conclude that there is no meaningful patterning to the rates.

Very few prior studies have attempted to ascertain whether burglary exhibits meaningful spatial patterning. Lottier (1938) found a gradient pattern in chain store burglaries, but no gradient pattern for residential burglaries when he plotted offence data across zones radiating out 25 miles from Detroit city hall for 1932-34. Schmid (1937) using census tracts and concentric zones failed to find any gradient in the spatial distribution of residential burglaries in Minneapolis-St Paul in 1933-36, but in a later study of Seattle (1960b) found gradients for residential burglary for 1940-41 and for 1949-51. Ferdinand (1970) mapped all residential burglaries known to police in Auburn, Massachusetts, in 1969, by street address. He found no spatial patterning, but his spatial analysis was informal.

The most ambitious study of the patterning of burglary to date was recently completed by Harry Scarr (1973) for the Law Enforcement Assistance Administration. Scarr studied residential and commercial burglary in Washington, D.C., and in two adjacent suburban counties: Fairfax County, Virginia; and Prince George's County, Maryland. He studied burglary, burglary victims, burglars and methods of burglarising. He used official police statistics, victimisation reports gathered by his own researchers, and 1970 census data. His study was massive. Among other things, he tried to uncover temporal and spatial patterning and tried to demonstrate that burglars perceive certain areas as 'good' targets. He concluded that it was not possible to distinguish high and low burglary rate areas by social indicators in suburban areas, but that social indicators could be used to locate high rate urban areas.

As the unit of analysis was large, it was not possible to distinguish the social characteristics which foster burglars (theoretically popular characteristics include poverty, broken homes, and low educational level) from the physical characteristics which separate 'good targets' from 'bad targets'.

Ultimately, Scarr's study is aspatial. The data for one census tract are not spatially related to the data from any other tract. It might be the case, for instance, that burglaries occur at high frequency where tracts with many apartments are adjacent to tracts with single family homes. Traditional statistical analysis, such as Scarr used, makes it possible to uncover characteristics of independent areas, but interaction between areas is not easily examined. In fact, if there is a lack of independence between observations, then one of the basic assumptions of most statistical analyses is not met.

This problem in Scarr's study, inherent in the use of census tract as a unit of spatial analysis, is minimised by the set construction used in this paper. Small, relatively homogeneous units (blocks) are joined together to produce larger units. Within-unit variation is reduced substantially. In essence, the set construction can be used to restructure census (and other types of data) into homogeneous units of analysis. Use of the neighbourhood sets allowed us to analyse the spatial patterning of the burglary rates which seemed so chaotically distributed to eyeball analysis. In analysing the burglary rates, we were particularly interested to see whether there were any consistent differentials in rates between blocks identified as interior to a particular neighbourhood set and blocks identified as border blocks. On the basis of the 'zone of transition' tradition in criminological ecology and on the basis of suggestive findings elsewhere in criminological literature (e.g., Tobias, 1972, 132-134; Komesar, 1973) we hypothesised that border blocks would exhibit significantly higher burglary rates than interior blocks.

Results

When the crime rates by block were compared with the location of the blocks in the neighbourhood sets, the hypothesised structure emerged: blocks which were in the border areas had higher burglary rates than blocks which were in the interior of the neighbourhood sets.

For the simple topology created for average rent per block, the pattern is as shown in Table 1. For each group of sets, as the permitted inter-block variation decreases, the interior blocks have a lower burglary rate than the border blocks. The pattern

Table 1

Average Rent Topology: Mean Burglary Rate

	Sets with 30% inter-block variation	Sets with 20% inter-block variation	Sets with 10% inter-block variation
Interior blocks	1·616 (n = 141)	1·396 (n = 116)	1·197 (n = 106)
Border blocks	3·348 (n = 909)	3·329 (n = 930)	3·331 (n = 940)

'is even more striking when we examine what happens to interior blocks as the permitted variation decreases from 30 per cent to 20 per cent and then to 10 per cent.

Interior blocks in the 30 per cent variation sets have a mean rate of 1·616 (see Table 2). When these blocks are decomposed into border and interior blocks

topology is 0·739 (n = 118), but for the border blocks the mean is 3·146 (n = 928).

The topology created for percentage single family dwellings produced similar results. Once again sets were created at the 30 per cent, 20 per cent, and 10 per cent inter-block variation levels. Table 3 presents the results. For each group of sets, the interior

Table 2

Mean Burglary Rate for Border and Interior Blocks as the Neighbourhood Sets Decompose

Sets created by:

30% inter-block variation	Border blocks (3·348)	Interior blocks (1·616)		
20% inter-block variation	Border blocks (3·348)	Border blocks (2·634)	Interior blocks (1·396)	
10% inter-block variation	Border blocks (3·348)	Border blocks (2·634)	Border blocks (3·511)	Interior blocks (1·197)

Table 3

Percentage Single Family Topology: Mean Burglary Rate

	Sets with 30% inter-block variation	Sets with 20% inter-block variation	Sets with 10% inter-block variation
Interior blocks	0·841 (n = 148)	0·631 (n = 112)	0·715 (n = 84)
Border blocks	3·489 (n = 898)	3·412 (n = 934)	3·324 (n = 962)

in the 20 per cent variation sets, the blocks which are interior in both sets have a mean rate of 1·396, but the blocks which become border blocks in the 20 per cent variation sets have a mean rate of 2·634. Similarly, when the 20 per cent variation sets are decomposed into sets with 10 per cent inter-block variation, the interior blocks at the 20 per cent level which have a mean rate of 1·396 are divided into interior blocks with a mean rate of 1·197 and border blocks with a mean rate of 3·511.

The other simple topologies produced similarly interesting results. A topology was created for percentage small apartments. Three types of sets were created: (1) sets with 30 per cent inter-block variation; (2) sets with 20 per cent inter-block variation; and (3) sets with 10 per cent inter-block variation. The different inter-block variations produced exactly the same sets, so results from only one type of set will be presented. The mean burglary rate for interior blocks in the small apartment

US—12/3 L

blocks had lower burglary rates than the border blocks.

A product topology was created using sets generated in the average rent topology, the percentage small apartment topology and the percentage single family dwellings topology. The sets created by allowing a 20 per cent inter-block variation were used. The results are shown in Table 4. The pattern is clear. As the sets in the product topology intersect, those blocks which are border blocks in one or more groups of sets have higher burglary rates than the blocks which are interior in all three groups of sets.

The blocks which are border blocks in all three simple topologies have a mean rate of 3·605. The blocks which are interior in all three simple topologies have a mean rate of only 0·820. Even more surprisingly, blocks which were interior in the average rent topology and had a mean rate of 1·396 decompose into two groups of blocks in the percentage

Table 4

Mean Burglary Rate for the Product Topology

Average rent sets

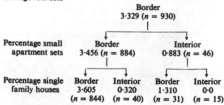

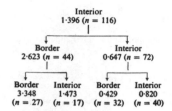

small apartment topology with a mean of 2·623 for the border blocks and a mean of only 0·647 for the interior blocks. These border blocks, in turn, decompose into border and interior blocks in the percentage single family topology. The mean rate for border blocks at this lowest level is 3·348 and for interior blocks is 1·473. The blocks in the sharp boundary areas between neighbourhood sets in the product topology have higher mean burglary rates than the less sharp boundaries or the interior blocks.

The topology for percentage large apartment (over ten units) presented technical difficilties. The computer programme which created the sets is still experimental and is not as efficient as it eventually might be, therefore core limitations in the CDC 6500 made it impossible to directly create these sets in a manner which would be compatible with the other sets.

The basis sets for the percentage small apartment were used to create sets of blocks based on the variable percentage large apartment. The value for percentage large apartments was calculated by subtracting the percentage small apartment and percentage single family from 100. The border and interior designations were taken from the set construction for the variable percentage small apartment.

Table 5

Mean Rate for Percentage Large Apartment Sets

	Interior	Border
Mean rate	0·206	4·431
	($n = 27$)	($n = 619$)

There was a substantial difference between the rate for border and interior blocks (see Table 5). The mean rate was then calculated for those blocks which were over 50 per cent large apartments. The mean

rate for border blocks jumped to 7·363 ($n = 174$) and the mean rate for interior blocks dropped to zero ($n = 23$). When the calculation was restricted further to blocks which were over 80 per cent large apartments, the mean rate for boundary blocks increased to 8·344 ($n = 132$) and the mean rate for interior blocks, of course, remained zero.

The percentage black and average cost sets did not produce such interesting results. For the sets created by allowing a 30 per cent inter-block variation in average cost of housing, the mean rate for border blocks was 3·236 and for interior blocks the rate was 2·423. But when the 30 per cent variation sets were decomposed into 25 per cent variation sets the mean rate for the interior blocks was 2·547 ($n = 145$) and the rate for the border blocks was only 0·926 ($n = 12$). The percentage black sets were created allowing a 50 per cent inter-block variation and a 30 per cent inter-block variation. The interior blocks with a 50 per cent variation had a mean rate of 0·648 ($n = 239$). For the 30 per cent variation sets, the interior blocks decomposed into border blocks and interior blocks. The interior blocks had a mean rate of 0·555 ($n = 94$) while the border blocks had a rate of 1·044 ($n = 261$). These were not very large differences.

Generally, however, the results were quite satisfying. The mean rate for interior blocks was almost always lower than the mean rate for border blocks. The burglars of Tallahassee do seem to pick targets in border areas more often than in interior areas of neighbourhoods. When the dimensions of a neighbourhood are defined in tentative fashion through product topology, the pattern becomes stronger still. The burglary rates are much higher in the border blocks, in the zones of transition from one neighbourhood to another, than in the interiors of neighbourhoods.

Conclusions and Speculations

The neighbourhood construction in this research produces a type of natural area. Burglaries are shown to occur at high rates on the borders of these natural areas and at much lower rates in the interiors of these natural areas. Thus a spatial distribution of burglary which might prove useful to planners has been uncovered. The 'good target' areas are neighbourhood borders, the 'safe' areas are neighbourhood interiors. This suggests that it might be possible to reduce the burglary incidence by controlling the size and shape of neighbourhoods. Fig. 1 presents

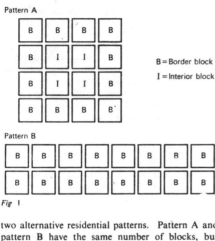

Pattern A

B = Border block
I = Interior block

Pattern B

Fig 1

two alternative residential patterns. Pattern A and pattern B have the same number of blocks, but pattern B has no interior blocks. In fact, Tallahassee has such a corridor neighbourhood and it has a very high burglary rate. Pattern A has four interior blocks which should be relatively safe from burglars. Generally, long, narrow, or sector-shaped areas have more boundary blocks than circular or square-shaped areas.

Border areas can also be reduced by making the transition from one type area to another gradual. If blocks which are 20-30 per cent apartment are adjacent to blocks which are 30-40 per cent apartment, they may form one neighbourhood where the transition is gradual. Fig. 2 illustrates the point.

There is a very large difference between the percentage of apartments in the left-most and right-most clusters of Fig. 2, but the transition from the 20 per cent block cluster to the 40 per cent block cluster is gradual. For any fixed inter-block variation greater than 10 per cent, the blocks would form just one neighbourhood set. There would be no border blocks on the joining edges.

Percent apartment by block cluster

| 20% | 22% | 24% | 26% | 28% | 30% | 32% | 34% | 36% | 38% | 40% |

Fig. 2.

Some obvious limitations to what we have said ought to be mentioned as a prelude to a few speculations. The neighbourhood set construction in this paper is a tentative first step at building an accurate model of neighbourhoods. The development of the model is incomplete: many improvements and extentions are in order. Non-residential land uses should be added to the sets as should social dimensions. The sharpest sorts of borders may be those between residential and commercial land uses, or those between social use or characteristic dimensions not included in these simple sets. Second, this research reveals a general spatial pattern but does not investigate the specific characteristics of individual high rate neighbourhoods or border areas (or low rate neighbourhoods or interiors). Such investigation might produce even more useful planning information. It might be the case that it is borders between multi-family and single family dwellings which produce the high rates, or in the Gold Coast—Slum tradition (Zorbaugh, 1929; Komesar, 1973) it might be the borders between high income and low income areas which produce the very highest burglary rates. Third, the fact that the spatial pattern is generalised in Tallahassee, of course, does not guarantee that it will appear elsewhere (though we expect that future research will show that it does occur in other cities). Fourth, the spatial patterning of burglary should not be used to infer anything about expected spatial patterning of different classes of criminal behaviour such as murder or robbery or drunk driving. We would expect that the spatial patterning of different sorts of crime would be quite different from the spatial patterning of burglary. Obviously, future research should improve the neighbourhood model, replicate the burglary study in other cities and map the spatial distribution of other crimes.

Having properly qualified and cautioned our research, we close with a speculation about why such a spatial patterning of residential burglary might occur.   Recent research into target choice and general behaviour patterns amongst burglars (Shover, 1972; Reppetto, 1973; Scarr, 1973) suggests that burglars spend considerable time in selecting target structures to burglarise and can be put off particular sorts of high 'take' targets by environmental cues of both blatant and subtle character.   Reppetto's research on burglars and burglaries in Boston, in particular, suggests that implicit perceptual cues are important in target choice.   Black burglars tend to be reluctant to 'work' the white suburbs and tend to burglarise centre city public housing projects despite the fact that they identify white suburbia as the part of the metropolis likely to provide high 'takes' and despite a capacity for wide ranging mobility.   White burglars tend to be reluctant to 'work' the inner-city housing projects.   In both cases, the reluctance is apparently rooted in a fear of standing out as a suspicious stranger.   As burglars become more experienced and more skilled, they tend to lose this concern and to concentrate on learning where good potential 'takes' are located, then on learning to fit into the perceptual requirements of that location (Reppetto, 1973; Scarr, 1973, 67-72).   Oscar Newman's recent book *Defensible Space* (1972) explored how architectural variations in buildings or housing complexes can help or hinder the residents in identifying 'strangers' who are potential criminals. His efforts to enhance the social identification process through architectural change, and thereby reduce the crime rates in particular public housing projects point in the same direction as the studies of burglars' target choice.

The social identification mechanism Newman is concerned to foster, and which apparently is important to burglars in target choice, may well work on a larger scale than individual building or building clusters.   To the extent that Lee's (1968) 'homogeneous neighbourhood' or Lynch's (1960) 'district' concept reasonably coincides with our neighbourhood sets, we would speculate that a dual perceptual process on the part of burglars and residents might account for the spatial patterning we found.   As Lee points out (1968, 250), the crucial interactive relationship between the residents of a homogeneous neigh-

bourhood is that of 'mutual awareness' rather than the overt interactive process of 'neighbouring'. Residents of a homogeneous neighbourhood are likely to have implicit perceptions of routine behavioural patterns amongst neighbours whose names might not be known, and on the part of appropriately present non-residents (e.g., milkmen, postmen, police).   We would speculate that this sort of perceptual awareness would be strongest on the interior of the neighbourhood and weakest on the borders where perceived strangers straying from bordering neighbourhoods might be most common and hence least likely to challenge.   Similarly, burglars might well perceive the relative social anonymity available to them in border areas and select targets in border areas rather than interiors.   (Of course, the skilled professional burglar who was prepared to invest the necessary time in developing a perceptual protective coloration might easily penetrate to the interiors of neighbourhoods in search of high 'takes'.)

We have no strong evidence for the validity of our speculation, of course.   Still, it does seem to produce a nice fit linking the recent research of criminologists to Newman's findings and to our findings on the spatial patterning of burglary in Tallahassee.   To the extent that future research supports this speculation, it has strong planning implications.

Methodological Appendix

Mathematical Building Blocks

Set theory and point-set topology provide the theoretical concepts used in constructing our models of residential neighbourhoods.   Several general definitions are necessary before the neighbourhood model can be presented.

First, the definition of a topological space: *A topological space, T, is defined as follows: Let X be a set of objects called points of X.   A topology in X is a non-empty collection of subsets of X.   The open sets in the topology satisfy the following conditions: (1) the null (empty) set is an element of the topology; (2) if $x_1, x_2, \ldots, x_n \ldots$ are in the topology then their union is also in the topology; and (3) if $x_1 \ldots x_n$ are elements of the topology then their intersection is in the topology* (Kelly, 1955; Hu, 1964).   The open sets are the building blocks of the topology.   The operations of unions and intersections on open sets in the topology produce interesting structures.   The interesting structures, however, are not limited to unions and intersections, but space does not permit the exploration of more complex structures in this paper.

Second, an important concept in topology is that of a *basis*. *A basis is a subcollection of the topology such that every open set in the topology is in the union of the sets in the basis.* Consider the two-dimensional plane (*R²*). The natural topology for this space can be constructed by taking the unions of circles of various radii. The infinite number of circles which can be drawn in *R²* form the basis. The open sets are the unions of circles.

In constructing the neighbourhood topology, the basis sets were created first. To conform to perceptual concepts of neighbourhood, the basis sets were structured as clusters of contiguous city blocks which had internal homogeneity or continuity from block to block. Block level census data from the 1970 United States Census for Tallahassee, Florida, were used to create the sets because they were readily available and because they represented a sufficiently small unit of spatial aggregation to permit construction of relatively fine sets which conform to intuitive feelings of neighbourhood. Alternative spatial groupings of census data for Tallahassee, block groups and census tracts, were considered too large to reveal the shading of one neighbourhood into another. Block face or individual plot data, which would have provided finer basis sets, are not provided by the United States Bureau of the Census and the limited resources available prohibited their collection.

Six block level census variables were used: average cost of housing; average rent; percentage white/percentage black; percentage single family dwellings; percentage small apartment block dwellings (two to nine apartments in the structure); and percentage large apartment block dwellings (ten or more apartments in the structure). A different topology was created for each variable. In each topology a basis set was the set of all contiguous block clusters such that the inter-block variation of the variable of interest was less than some fixed percentage.

Within each topology many sets can be constructed as the inter-block variation is allowed to increase or decrease. Consider the example of the basis set constructed from the census block variable 'average cost of housing'. Suppose the variation from block to block is limited to 25 per cent. Contiguous blocks will be added to a set as long as the variation along the joining block face or edge does not exceed 25 per

cent of the average cost of housing in the continuous block with the highest cost of housing. For example, if two contiguous blocks had average housing costs of $7,000 and $10,000, then they would not belong to the same set since the maximum allowed inter-block variation is 25 per cent of $10,000 or $2,500. The actual difference in this example is $3,000. If, however, the actual values for the two blocks were $9,000 and $10,000, they would belong to the same set.

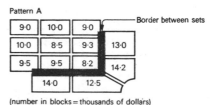

Pattern A

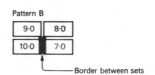

(number in blocks = thousands of dollars)

Pattern B

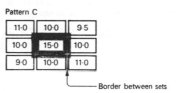

Pattern C

Fig. 3.

The basis sets constructed in this topology can produce interesting patterns. Fig. 3 shows three interesting patterns. In pattern A, the set grows outward in a relatively uniform pattern. A border develops when the variation in the cost of housing exceeds the permitted 25 per cent. In pattern B, the set turns in upon itself. There is a permitted variation from $10,000 to $9,000 to $8,000 to $7,000, but the variation turns downward, producing an unallowable variation between the block with an average housing cost of $7,000 and the block with an average housing cost of $10,000. A border then separates the set from itself. In pattern C, a ring of contiguous blocks which fall within the permitted variation surround one block which falls outside the allowed range. Of course, the patterns described here are only examples, many other structures are possible.

Each clustering of blocks which fall within the permitted range of variation forms a set. The range of variation, obviously, need not be fixed at 25 per cent, it could be fixed at any point from zero to infinity. The family of sets, as the fixed variation moves from zero to infinity, form the basis for the topology.

As the permitted variation increases or decreases, the shape of the neighbourhood emerges. A set constructed from a 30 per cent inter-block variation will contain sets constructed from a 20 per cent inter-block variation. These in turn will contain sets constructed from a 10 per cent variation. Every block which is a border block for a fixed inter-block variation will also be a border for sets constructed on smaller inter-block variations. That is, if a block is a border for a set constructed allowing 30 per cent inter-block variation, then it will be a border block for sets constructed allowing 20 per cent or 10 per cent variation. But border blocks for the smaller variation sets will not necessarily be border blocks for larger variation sets. Many patterns of borders could develop: the border blocks could be the same for many changes in the permitted variation (Fig. 4).

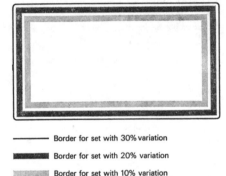

—————— Border for set with 30% variation

▬▬▬▬ Border for set with 20% variation

▨▨▨▨ Border for set with 10% variation

Fig. 4.

This pattern would show a high level of block to block continuity or homogeneity within the area and a sharp break with adjacent areas. Many new

border blocks could be created as the inter-block variation decreases. This pattern (Fig. 5) suggests less homogeneity or block to block continuity.

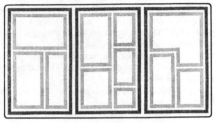

Fig. 5.

There is less perceptual continuity in an area where there is large inter-block variation. New border blocks could be introduced on one side of the set and not on the other (Fig. 6) as the variation decreases. This pattern represents a strong, sharp border on one edge of the residential area and a weaker border on another edge.

Fig. 6.

What has been described above is a simple topology, only one variable being considered. A similar logical construction can be used to create topologies for the other census variables under consideration. The simple topologies can be considered simultaneously by looking at the product topology. The product topology is the topological technique which is similar to multivariate techniques in statistics. In the product topology, the open sets in the simple topologies can be considered simultaneously. Once again, the interesting structures are produced by what happens to the basis sets as the permitted variations increase or decrease. In a residential area the basis sets may follow the same pattern for each of the component topologies. Within a residential area a block may be a border block for several variables and many changes in permitted variation. Such an area would have a high level of internal block to block continuity for several characteristics and sharp borders with adjacent areas. Such an area would also have a high degree of perceptual distinctiveness. If the border blocks change for each variable and for changes in permitted variation, then there are no sharp borders between adjacent areas. As was noted when examining simple topologies, any pattern between these two extremes is possible.

Ideally, in constructing neighbourhood sets the inter-block variation should range over a wide interval, producing many sets until a clear urban structure emerges. Also ideally, a plotter mapping system should be developed to graphically represent the sets in three-dimensional plots. With a mapping system it would be possible to 'see' how one neighbourhood shaded into another or where borders are sharp and distinct. Since such a mapping system does not exist and computer resources were limited, it was necessary to limit the number of sets created. For each of the census variables used, one to three collections of basis sets were generated using different interblock variations. (Computer programmes were written for use on the CDC 6500 computer to create the neighbourhood sets using census data and geocoding base files from the Census Bureau.) See Table 6.

Table 6

Variables and Permitted Variations Used To Create Neighbourhood Sets

Variable	Percentage inter-block variation		
Average cost of housing	30	25	—
Average rent	30	20	10
Percentage single family	30	20	10
Percentage small apartments (2-9 units)	30	20	10
Percentage large apartments (10 or more units)	—	20	—
Percentage black	50	30	—

Even with these limited runs, the complexity of the neighbourhood structures was evident. The largest set contained 315 blocks in a cluster; the smallest set contained one block. As the permitted inter-block variation decreased, the largest set also decreased in size. For the topology constructed with the single variable percentage single family, for instance, the largest set decreased from 315 to 87 contiguous blocks. For the percentage black topology, the largest set decreased from 150 blocks to 135 blocks. As the sets decomposed as the permitted variation decreased, many of the patterns described above did indeed appear. A large set in the percentage single family topology had a sharp border on one side and a fuzzy border on the other. The two large sets in the percentage black topology remained about the same size as the inter-block variation decreased from 50 per cent to 30 per cent. Both these sets had sharp borders with adjacent areas. For each variation used, many small sets (one to five block clusters) were generated. There were many areas in Tallahassee where the pattern of urban development was highly varied and where the homogenous areas were quite small.

Without an adequate graphics system, it proved impossible to develop a workable pictorial representation of the residential complexity of Tallahassee. It was possible, however, to use the model within the computer. Each block in Tallahassee was filed as a record indicating its characteristic as a member of each of the generated topologies (i.e., a listing of all sets to which it belonged and its position as a border block or an interior block in each set.) The model was then used as a tool to analyse the spatial distribution of one specific crime, residential burglary.

REFERENCES

Boggs, S. L. (1964)
The Ecology of Crime Occurrence in St. Louis: A Reconceptualization of Crime Rates and Patterns. St Louis: Washington University (Unpublished Ph.D. dissertation).
Boggs, S. L. (1966)
Urban crime patterns. *American Sociological Review,* 30, 899-908.
Bordua, D. J. (1958)
Juvenile delinquency and 'anomie': an attempt at replication. *Social Problems,* 6, 230-238.
Cartwright, D. S. (1969)
Ecological variables. In Borgatta, E. F. and Bohrnstedt, G. W.: *Sociological Methodology 1969.* San Francisco: Jossey-Bass.
Chilton, R. J. (1964)
Continuity in delinquency area research: a comparison of studies for Baltimore, Detroit and Indianapolis. *American Sociological Review,* 29, 71-83.
Conklin, J. E. (1972)
Robbery and the Criminal Justice System. Philadelphia: Lippincott.
Conklin, J. E. and Bittner, E. (1973)
Burglary in a suburb. *Criminology,* 11, 206-232.
Department of Law Enforcement, State of Florida (1972)
Crime in Florida: 1972 Annual Report. Tallahassee: F.D.L.E.
Federal Bureau of Investigation (1972)
Uniform Crime Reports for the United States—1972. Washington: United States Government Printing Office.

Ferdinand, T. N. (1970)
Burglary in Auburn, Massachusetts. Boston: Northeastern University (mimeo).
Ferdinand, T. N. (1972)
Burglary in Auburn, Massachusetts: 1960-1969. In Adler, F. and Mueller, G. O. W.: *Politics, Crime and the International Scene: An International Focus,* 287-301. San Juan, Puerto Rico: North-South Center Press.
Gordon, R. A. (1967)
Issues in the ecological study of delinquency. *American Sociological Review,* 32, 927-944.
Harris, C. D. and Ullman, E. L. (1945)
The nature of cities. *Annals of the American Academy of Political and Social Science,* 242, 7-17.
Hoyt, H. (1939)
The Structure and Growth of Residential Neighbourhoods in American Cities. Washington: United States Government Printing Office.
Hu, S. T. (1964)
Elements of General Topology. San Francisco: Holden-Day.
Jeffery, C. R. (1971)
Crime Prevention Through Environmental Design. Beverly Hills and London: Sage Publications.
Kelley, J. L. (1955)
General Topology. Princeton: Van Nostrand.
Komesar, N. K. (1973)
A theoretical and empirical study of victims of crime. *Journal of Legal Studies,* 2, 301-321.
Lander, B. (1954)
Towards an Understanding of Juvenile Delinquency. New York: Columbia University Press.
Lee, T. R. (1968)
Urban neighbourhood as a socio-spatial scheme. *Human Relations,* 21, 241-267.
Lottier, S. (1938)
Distribution of Criminal Offenses in Metropolitan Regions. *Journal of Criminal Law and Criminology,* 29, 37-50.
Lynch, K. (1960)
The Image of the City. Cambridge, Mass.: M.I.T. Press.
Morris, T. (1957)
The Criminal Area: A Study in Social Ecology. London: London: Routledge & Kegan Paul.
Murdie, R. A. (1969)
The Factorial Ecology of Toronto: 1951-1961. Chicago: Dept. of Geography, University of Chicago. (Research Paper No. 116.)
Newman, O. (1972)
Defensible Space: Crime Prevention Through Urban Design. New York: Macmillan.

Park, R. E. and Burgess, E. W. (1925)
The City. Chicago: Chicago University Press.
Polk, K. (1967)
Urban social areas and delinquency. *Social Problems,* 14, 320-325.
Quinney, R. (1964)
Crime, delinquency and social areas. *Journal of Research in Crime and Delinquency,* 1, 149-154.
Reppetto, T. A. (1973)
Age, race and drug use as determinants in criminal behaviour among burglary offenders. Paper read at annual meetings of the American Society of Criminology, New York.
Robson, B. T. (1969)
Urban Analysis: A Study of City Structure with Special Reference to Sunderland. Cambridge University Press.
Rosen, L. and Turner, S. H. (1967)
An evaluation of the Lander approach to the ecology of delinquency. *Social Problems,* 15, 189-200.
Scarr, H. A. (1973)
Patterns of Burglary (2nd ed.). Washington: United States Government Printing Office.
Schmid, C. F. (1937)
Social Saga of Two Cities. Minneapolis: Minneapolis Council of Social Agencies.
Schmid, C. F. (1960a)
Urban crime areas: Part I. *American Sociological Review,* 25, 527-542.
Schmid, C. F. (1960b)
Urban crime areas: Part II. *American Sociological Review,* 25, 655-678.
Shaw, C. R. and McKay, H. (1969)
Juvenile Delinquency and Urban Areas (2nd ed.). Chicago: Chicago University Press.
Shover, N. (1972)
Structures and careers in burglary. *Journal of Criminal Law, Criminology and Police Science,* 63, 540-549.
Slatin, G. T. (1969)
Ecological analysis of delinquency: aggregation effects. *American Sociological Review,* 34, 894-907.
Tobias, J. J. (1972)
Urban Crime in Victorian England. New York: Schocken Books.
Wallis, C. P. and Maliphant, R. (1967)
Delinquent areas in the County of London: Ecological factors. *British Journal of Criminology,* 7, 250-284.
White, C. R. (1932)
The relation of felonies to environmental factors in Indianapolis. *Social Forces,* 10, 498-509.
Zorbaugh, H. W. (1929)
The Gold Coast and the Slum. Chicago: Chicago University Press.

23

COMMUNITY, ENVIRONMENT, AND
VIOLENT CRIME

RICHARD BLOCK

Urban dwellers have known for many years, at least since the Renaissance, that some neighborhoods are more dangerous than others. The newcomer to a city is often told which neighborhoods are safe, which are dangerous at night, and which should be avoided altogether. To many suburbanites and nonurban dwellers, the whole city is defined as dangerous. Although communities believed to be dangerous may not be overrun with crime, and although suburban communities may not always be crime-free, folk wisdom often does reflect real crime counts. Thus, it is not surprising that included among

AUTHOR'S NOTE: *The research reported in the paper was completed at the Center for Studies in Criminal Justice of the University of Chicago Law School. This study was supported by PHS Research Grant No. 1R01MH27575, NIMH (Center for Studies of Crime and Delinquency) and by grants from the Ford Foundation. It could not have been completed without the help and cooperation of the Chicago Police Department's Superintendent James Rochford, Deputy Superintendent Michael Spiotto, and Homicide Division Commander Joseph Di Leonardi. I would like to thank Franklin Zimring for his constant help, patience, and advice. Thanks go to all my assistants on this project, especially Ruth (O'Brien) Perrin and Nancy Haverfield, and to Ronald Gilbert for his computer assistance.*

From Richard Block, "Community, Environment, and Violent Crime," 17(1) *Criminology: An Interdisciplinary Journal* 46-57 (May 1979). Copyright 1979, American Society of Criminology.

the earliest research on criminal behavior were studies of the geographic distribution of urban crime (Levin and Lindesmith, 1937). This research predated even that of physical anthropologists, such as Lombroso. From this early start research has proceeded fitfully. In the United States the work of the Chicago School in the 1920s and 1930s was a good beginning and in many ways served as a basis for current research in the geographic distribution of urban crime (Shaw and McKay, 1972). Between World War II and the beginning of large-scale funding of criminological research in the mid-1960s, geographic research concentrated on census tract variation in crime and used factor analysis or multiple regression (Shevky and Bell, 1955; Boggs, 1965; Ebert and Schwirian, 1968; Chilton, 1964).

From the mid-1960s to the present, both geographers and criminologists have developed increasingly sophisticated research methods for analyzing spatial distributions of crime. Among these are isoline analysis, models of spatial distance of victim and offender and crime site, and increasingly precise methods for differentiating and factoring areas of high and low crime (Curtis, 1975; Harries, 1974; Pyle, 1974; Capone, 1975; Reppetto, 1974).

The research presented here is a reflection of all these traditions of criminological analysis. Using data based upon records of the Chicago Police Department, community area variation in the distribution of violent crime and correlates of that variation are analyzed.

With the cooperation of the Chicago Police Department, the Center for Studies in Criminal Justice was able to obtain detailed and complete codings of all homicides in 1974 and large samples of robbery and aggravated assault in 1975. Coded information included a description of the crime, demographic information for victim and offender, and the crime's location (Block, 1977). This location was later recoded into census tracts and aggregated into 76 community areas as uniformly defined by the early Chicago School and the 1970 census (Hunter, 1976). After coding was completed, information was grouped by census tract and community area. Thus, for each area census data, crime rate, and crime characteristic data (e.g., percentage of robberies with guns) were available. The aggregated community area file forms the base of the analysis presented here. Community areas were chosen as units of analysis because of the inclusion of data on crime characteristics. Even with large samples, most census tracts had no— or only a few—violent crimes. These low crime tracts distorted analysis of the correlation of crime characteristics and crimes. Larger aggregation units reduced this problem.

The definition of most variables used in this analysis is straightforward. A few need explanation. All rates of crime are logged because of their nonlinear nature. Robberies and aggravated assault rates are projected for an entire year, and community areas in which no cases of a violent crime occurred were set to a value of 0. Although technically incorrect, this decision had little statistical effect. The variable "proximity" consists of the ratio of families earning more than three times poverty level to those earning 75% or less. This type of measure is usually taken as an indicator of income disparity. In terms of crime analysis, however, it can be more properly thought of as an indicator of spatial proximity of middle-class and poor.

The evidence and findings of this paper should be viewed with great caution. Inherent in the data and methodology are the following problems:

- Some findings may be unique to Chicago or to Chicago in the mid-1970s.
- Census data were collected in 1970, crime data in 1974 and 1975. The character of a few community areas may have changed.
- The crime data are based upon police records. Crimes not reported to the police and events which were downgraded or not accepted as crimes by the police are excluded. This bias seems to be related to the seriousness of a crime. Police and victim survey data tend to converge for more serious crimes (Block, 1979).

- This analysis is subject to both ecologically false interpretation and to overinterpretation due to the tendency for ecological correlations to be higher than individual correlations.
- The interpretation of all findings are post hoc and should therefore be retested.

ANALYSIS OF DATA

Explanations of area variation in rates of violent crime are usually cultural, subcultural, or economic (Miller, 1958; Wolfgang and Ferracuti, 1967). Thus, high rates of violence in Houston are said to reflect a frontier tradition and a heritage of quick and easy justice (Lundsgarde, 1977). High rates of violence in the South are said to represent either a tradition of violence (Gastil, 1971) or the presence of vast rural poverty among both whites and blacks (Loftin and Hill, 1974).

In any study of violence in the United States race is always an important variable. Rates of both victimization and offense are consistently higher for blacks than for whites (Wolfgang, 1958; Brearley, 1932). These differences are explained by economics, by frustration and aggression resulting from the prejudiced and discriminatory nature of American society, or by southernness and the relative recency of black emigration to urban areas.

In Chicago, community areas which are predominantly black have higher rates of violence than those which are predominantly white. The 16 community areas with a 75% or larger black population have a logged homicide rate of 3.92 (51 per 100,000) while the 47 community areas with fewer than 25% black population have a logged homicide rate of 1.77 (6 per 100,000). It is not surprising that virtually all victims in black communities are black and those in white communities are white. Chicago is an extremely segregated city.

Still, as seen in Table 1, for Chicago's community areas, racial composition is not the strongest zero-order correlate of crime

TABLE 1
Pearson Correlation Violent Crime Rates With Demographic and Crime Characteristics of Community Areas

| | Natural Log Rate Per 100,000 Pop | | |
	Homicide	Robbery	Aggravated Assault
Proximity	.75**	.61**	.62**
Perc. Black	.69**	.52**	.47**
Perc. South	.74**	.57**	.58**
Perc. Old	-.35**	-.12	-.18
Perc. H.S. Educ	-.65**	-.54**	-.60**
Perc. 75% Pov	.64**	.46**	.48**
Perc. 300% Pov	-.67**	-.48**	-.55**
Room Density	-.02	-.24	-.13
Perc. 16-21 Unemp	.72**	.53**	.52**
Perc. Fem. Head	.63**	.48**	.49**
Perc. No. Fam	.29*	.39**	.33*
Perc. Stable	-.47**	-.50**	-.40**
Perc. Rob. Gun	.03	-.06	-.22
Perc. Rob. Out	.09	.18	.21
Perc. Rob. Mul. Off.	-.05	-.04	.05
Perc. Rob. Resis	-.01	.02	.20
Perc. Rob. Inj	-.04	.05	.26
Perc. Rob. Teen Off.	-.01	-.20	-.11
Perc. Homi. Rob	.22	.21	.22
Perc. Homi. Unk	.11	.25	-.14
Perc. Homi. Gun	.36*	.36**	.25
Perc. Homi. Out	-.01	-.21	-.12
Perc. Homi. Teen	-.06	-.15	-.31*
Perc. Ass. Unpro	.25	.23	-.37**
Perc. Ass. Unk	-.07	-.04	-.21
Perc. Ass. Gun	.27*	.22	.45**
Perc. Ass. Dead	.01	.06	-.02
Perc. Ass. Teen	-.28*	-.16	-.39**
Perc. Ass. Out	-.01	-.04	.16
Lg. Nat. Homi	1.00	.70	.64**
Lg. Nat. Rob	.70**	1.00	.54**
Lg. Nat. Ass	.64**	.54**	1.00

*p < .01
**p < .001

rates.[1] Two variables are consistently more strongly related to violent crime rates—percentage of residents from the South and residential proximity of poor and middle-class families. Percentage of residents who are black and percentage who are southern immigrants are very strongly correlated. Initially only one of these variables was included in the analysis. But the meaning of the two variables is different in predominantly white and predominantly black neighborhoods. In predominantly black neighborhoods percentage southern is negatively correlated with poverty (−0.43), while in predominantly white neighborhoods the correlation is positive (poverty 0.76). In black neighborhoods southernness is related to stable residential patterns, while in white neighborhoods it is related to unstable patterns. The emigration of southern whites to Chicago is a more recent phenomenon than that of southern blacks. Thus, the differential meaning of southernness in white and black communities in Chicago probably accounts for the slightly stronger correlation of percentage southern born and crime rates than percentage black.

Residential proximity of poor and middle-class families is also strongly correlated with racial composition (0.62) and percentage southern born (0.67). Yet neither correlation is so strong as to entirely explain variation in residential proximity. And residential proximity is more strongly correlated to crime rates than either of the other two variables.

What is the meaning of close residential proximity of poor and middle-class families? Ulf Hannerz and others have noted that a particular problem for middle-class blacks is their close residential proximity to poorer community members (Hannerz, 1969). This close residential pattern mostly stems from discriminatory housing patterns and results in clashing and conflictual life styles. This economically based proximity conflict might result in higher crime rates in any community regardless of whether or not the neighborhood were predominantly white or black. Crime rates are high and fear is great in communities in which the middle class has not created a buffer to keep out the poor (Silver, 1967).

A second explanation of the correlation of crime rates and residential proximity is that proximity may merely reflect the combined effects of neighborhood racial and income composition. It is known that poor neighborhoods and communities which are predominantly black have higher crime rates than those which are predominantly white. A variable which combines both correlates of crime may be more strongly related to crime rates than either variable alone. Both explanations of the strong correlation of residential proximity and violent crime rates are probably correct.

Given the high correlation of many of the independent variables under analysis, bivariate analysis is insufficient for understanding the relationship between community area and crime rate variables. In Table 2 a multiple regression analysis is presented for three logged crime rates. In this table additional variance explained by the inclusion of each variable and its standardized Beta weight is included for each independent variable. Each regression equation is limited to five steps.

It is clear that neighborhoods in which poor and middle-class families live in close proximity are likely to have higher crime rates than other neighborhoods. More than half the neighborhood variance in homicide rates and close to 40% of the variance in robbery and aggravated assault rates are explained by variation in residential proximity. The mean homicide rate for community areas above the median in proximity was 3.48; for those below the median it was 1.58.

Only percentage of residents southern born also enters into all three equations, and it explains relatively little of the variance in either robbery or aggravated assault rates. About 10% of the variance in robbery rates is accounted for by the percentage of homicides with unknown assailants. Individual level analysis indicates that most homicides with unknown assailants probably result from robberies. Thus, a high percentage of homicides with unknown assailants is probably a result of a high robbery rate with death as a potential outcome of any act of violent crime. No other variable entered these equations either strongly or consistently.

Residential proximity of the poor and middle class so dominate the initial regression analysis that it was decided to replicate the multiple regression for community areas above and below the median for class proximity. Given the high percentage of variance already explained by proximity, it is not surprising that there is little variance left to explain. This is

TABLE 2
Multiple Regression Violent Crime with Community Area Characteristics

Natural Log Homicide Rate Per 100,000 Pop.		
Variable	R^2 Change	Beta
Proximity	.56	.42
Perc. South	.10	.42
Perc. Stable	.05	-.18
Perc. Homi. Uk. Off.	.02	.18
Perc. Rob Teen Off.	.01	.09
Total R^2	.73	

Natural Log Robbery Rate Per 100,000 Pop.		
Proximity	.37	.41
Perc. Homi. Uk. Off.	.10	.56
Perc. Homi. Teen Off.	.11	-.34
Perc. South	.04	.32
Perc. Homi. Outside	.04	.22
Total R^2	.66	

Natural Log Aggravated Assault Rate Per 100,000 Pop.		
Proximity	.39	.30
Perc. Rob. Inj.	.08	.32
Perc. Ass. Unprov.	.06	.28
Perc. South	.06	.34
Perc. No. Family	.04	.21
Total R^2	.63	

especially true in high proximity neighborhoods. In these neighborhoods the mean logged homicide rate was 3.48 (32.5), and the standard deviation was 0.73. The mean logged homicide rate for low proximity neighborhoods was 1.58 (4.9) more than two standard deviations below that for high proximity neighborhoods.

Given the large difference in crime rates, it is not surprising that crime rate regression equations for high proximity neighborhoods are almost completely different from those for low proximity neighborhoods. For high proximity neighborhoods, percentage of residents southern born is strongly related to rates of robbery and homicides. This variation may reflect both southernness and racial segregation in these neighborhoods.

Gun use during robberies is negatively related to both homicide and robbery rates. As the percentage of robberies using guns increases, the rate of violence declines. These results seem to contradict common sense. At an individual level both police data and victim survey data indicate a positive relationship between gun use and the probability of a robber's success. Additionally, gun use in robbery is positively correlated with death while negatively correlated with injury.

The negative relationship between gun use and rates of robbery and homicide at a *community* level, however, may be explained by some of the correlates of gun use in robbery. Both at an individual and community level, gun use is positively related to commercial robberies. Street crimes are less likely to involve gun use than commercial crimes. If neighborhoods with many street crimes are different from those with many commercial crimes, then the negative relationship of gun use in robbery and rates of robbery may be explained. On the other hand, the correlation could be interpreted to depict a dominance of fear in high-crime communities. If there are fewer robberies in communities where the percentage of gun robberies is high, it may mean that fear of gun use has resulted in a reduction of crime or that robbery is so frequent that only armed robberies are reported to the police.

The range of variation of crime rates in low proximity neighborhoods is much larger than in high proximity communities. Demographic variables related to violent crime rates are similar to those found in earlier research. And rates of violent crime seem to be dominated by robbery and pseudo-robbery indicators. Thus, rates of both robbery and homicide are positively correlated with youth unemployment, while robbery and aggravated assault rates are negatively correlated with family stability.

As previously noted, the percentage of homicides with unknown offenders is strongly related to the percentage of homicides which results from robberies. Thus, in low proximity neighborhoods, this variable is positively correlated with rates of robbery and homicide. However, percentage of homicide offenders unknown is negatively correlated with rates of aggravated assault. probably this reflects a high rate of robbery relative to assaults in some low proximity communities.

Percentage of assaults resulting from unprovoked attacks enter the aggravated assault equation first. Communities with a high probability of random violence have higher overall rates of aggravated assault. Probably this reflects a high rate of community stability and assault is negative, it is positive in the regression equation. The data available for analysis could provide no explanations for variation in random violence prevalence or the positive Beta of stability and aggravated assault.

While the matrix of variables entering regression equations to explain variation in crime rates in neighborhoods with high and low proximity of poor and middle-class residents is clearly different, and sometimes confusing, it should be remembered that proximity explains more of the variation in crime rates than any other variable.

Does the strength of the relationship between proximity of poor and middle-class residents and rates of violent crime invalidate the known relationships between race, southern migrant status, or economic conditions and criminal violence?

I think not. The power of proximity of residence to explain crime rates probably comes from its relationship to both the unequal distribution of income in some neighborhoods and the racial composition of communities. Proximity represents two aspects of racial discrimination—the extreme racial segregation of housing units in Chicago and the lack of housing choices for blacks. Most violent crime in Chicago, including robbery, is between members of the same race. Rates of violence against blacks are far higher than against whites. Much of this difference probably reflects the burden of discrimination of black people in a northern urban community.

NOTE

1. A complete copy of this matrix can be obtained from the author.

REFERENCES

BLOCK, R. (1977) Violent Crime: Environment, Interaction and Death. Lexington, MA: Lexington Books.

———— and C. BLOCK (1979) A Look in the Black Box: The Transformation of Robbery Incidents into Official Robbery Statistics. Paper delivered at the convention of the American Sociological Association, Boston, August 1979.

BOOGS, S. (1965) "Urban crime patterns." Amer. Soc. Rev. 30 (December).

BREARLEY, H. C. (1932) Homicide in the United States. Chapel Hill: University of North Carolina Press.

CAPONE, D. and W. NICHOLS (1975) "Urban structure and criminal mobility." Paper presented at the 27th annual meeting of the American Society of Criminology, Toronto, Canada.

CHILTON, R. J. (1964) "Continuity in delinquency area research: a comparison of studies for Baltimore, Detroit, and Indianapolis." Amer. Soc. Rev. 29 (February): 71-83.

CURTIS, L. (1975) Criminal Violence: National Patterns and Behavior. Lexington, MA: Lexington Books.

EBERT, P. and K. SCHWIRIAN (1968) "Metropolitan crime rates and relative deprivation." Criminologia 5 (February): 43-52.

FLEISHER, B. (1956) The Economics of Delinquency. Chicago: Quadrangle.

GASTIL, R. D. (1971) "Homicide and a regional culture of violence." Amer. Soc. Rev. 36: 412-427.

HANNERZ, U. (1969) Soulside. New York: Columbia University Press.

HARRIES, K. (1974) The Geography of Crime and Justice. New York: McGraw-Hill.

HUNTER, A. (1976) Symbolic Communities. Chicago: University of Chicago Press.

LEVIN, Y. and A. LINDESMITH (1937) "English ecology and criminology of the past century." J. of Criminal Law and Criminology 27 (March): 801-816.

LOFTIN, C. and R. H. HILL (1974) "Regional subculture and homicide: an examination of the Gastil-Hackney thesis." Amer. Soc. Rev. 39 (October): 714-725.

LUNDSGARDE, H. P. (1977) Murder in Space City. New York: Oxford University Press.

MILLER, W. (1958) "Lower class culture as a generating milieu of gang delinquency." J. of Social Issues 14: 5-19.

PYLE, G. (1974) The Spatial Dynamics of Crime. Chicago: University of Chicago Press.

REPPETTO, D. (1974) Residential Crime. Cambridge, MA: Ballinger.

SHAW, C. and H. D. McKAY (1972) Juvenile Delinquency and Urban Areas. Chicago: University of Chicago Press.

SHEVKY, E. and W. BELL (1955) Social Area Analyses. Standard, CA: Stanford University Press.

SILVER, A. (1967) "The demand of order in civil society," pp. 1-24 in David Bordua (ed.) The Police: Six Sociological Essays. New York: John Wiley.

WOLFGANG, M. E. (1958) Patterns in Criminal Homicide. Philadelphia: University of Pennsylvania Press.

——— and F. FERACUTI (1967) The Subculture of Violence: Towards an Integrated Theory in Criminology. London: Tavistock.

Richard Block is Associate Professor in the Sociology Department at Loyola University of Chicago. He is the author of Violent Crime *(Lexington, MA: D.C. Heath, 1977). His areas of research are violent crime and analyzing patterns of crime cross-nationally.*

24

THE CRIMINAL TRIAD
LEON SHELEFF

Of all the bystander situations, the one that has probably caused the most concern has been in connection with crime. It was a crime—the Genovese incident—which touched off the original public reaction and academic involvement; it is crime in general—far more than disasters or accidents—that affects people's perceptions and feelings about their society. Disasters, for all the traumatic impact, are exceptional circumstances, which happen fortuitously, and may never impinge directly on a particular individual or community at all. Accidents are admittedly more prevalent, but do not normally induce fear or pose a threatening situation. Crime, on the other hand, is not only endemic in society, but the fear of being victimized looms large, and the awareness of crime as a major and troublesome social problem is pervasive.

Yet, despite the growing interest in the bystander in general, and despite the extended work that criminologists have been devoting in recent years to the position of the victim of a crime, only minimal research has been oriented to the role of the bystander in crime. The spate of social psychology research into bystander activity has dealt with the crime situation only peripherally; nearly all the laboratory and the field projects deal with noncriminal situations.

When the research does not relate to crime as such, it is not possible, in most cases, to extrapolate to a criminal situation. In the work of the Piliavins and Rodin, as discussed in chapter 2,[1] it would be interesting to know whether the widespread positive response to the plight of a person collapsing in a subway train would have been replicated had the passengers been confronted with a crime, particularly a crime of violence. One variable that they did examine—an inebriated person collapsing in contrast to someone sober—did show clear differences in the responses of bystanders. In the research project of a person falling off a ladder[2] and crying out in pain for help, it would be interesting to know if the basically positive response recorded for the staged fall would have been replicated for a staged crime.

Research on Criminal Situations

Latané and Darley specifically relate to the fact that there are unique aspects of a crime which make extrapolation inapplicable. Even so, their own research involves only a few examples of a crime—for instance the theft from a grocery store in the presence of witnesses.[3] In their preparatory remarks to the research they note that, generally, crime is differentiated from other stress situations, mainly because an individual bystander may be harmed by the culprit.

> A villain represents a danger not only to the victim, but to anybody who is rash enough to interfere with him. A single individual may be reluctant to tangle with a villain. If it comes to physical violence, his odds are at best equal. At worst, the villain will be armed and vicious. Undeterred from crime he may be undeterred from physical violence as well.[4]

Recently some initial attempts have been made to probe more deeply into the specific nature of bystander behavior in criminal situations. In cases where the work has been in the tradition of staged real-life situations, often serious problems arise in setting up the research in a meaningful manner so as to resemble real situations. On the one hand there is a possibility that the action will be perceived to be staged, and the subjects will ignore what is happening. On the other hand there is a danger of an overzealous response where the act is carried out too vividly. The research by Shotland and Straw[5] gives evidence of both situations. In one simulated incident over 40 percent of the subjects claimed that they realized that the action was staged. In another situation, the acting was so real that three subjects took measures for their own self-protection and two nearby workers who had been informed beforehand of what was about to take place tried nevertheless to intervene.

The researchers had taken care to ensure there were confederates available to avoid any unforeseen escalation of the violence, a task that was facilitated by the fact that the violence enacted took place in a building on a university campus and not in a downtown street.

This research focused partly around the specific variable of the reaction to an altercation between a male and a female. In earlier research Barofsky and his colleagues[6] had found that there was a tendency for males not to go to the rescue of a female who was being assaulted; they attributed this reluctance to the vicarious sexual and/or hostile gratification that the bystanders were deriving from the action.

In the experiment by Shotland and Straw a contrast was made between two situations—in one case the altercation was between a male and a female who were ostensibly strangers; in the other case, between a married couple. In this latter situation there was a marked trend to interpret the violence as an internal quarrel in which outsiders should not intervene.

Other reactions recorded for both situations pointed out the importance of competence to act. In many instances the subjects proceeded slowly toward the scene of the assault, clearly uncertain as to exactly what they should do; some stated afterwards that they were hopeful that their appearance on the scene would be sufficient to halt the attack. Two subjects who took firm steps to intervene directly had specialized competence which they were intent on activating; one had studied martial arts, the other, a female student, had recently been at a lecture where advice had been given as to how to repulse an assailant.

In their article Shotland and Straw discuss also the ethical and practical aspects of doing such research. Before the research was undertaken they had discussed the advisability of undertaking it with a number of their colleagues who had favored the research; after each incident they had spoken to the subjects to assess their reactions, which were positive, many of them stating that they had no objection to being exposed to the artificially induced stress.

Both the Barofsky and Shotland projects took place in a building on a university campus. Far more complicated are staged muggings in a downtown street or in a subway train.

The kind of problems that this research poses is exemplified by the opposition encountered by Stewart and Cannon[7] in their attempt to stage a theft on the streets, even though there was no violence used and due precautions were taken to ensure the safety of all concerned. They had also consulted with the police and business organizations, who had supported their endeavors and expressed their opinion that the research could be of much value. Nevertheless when the public became aware of the research there was an outcry, and the local press mounted a barrage of criticism against it, as a result of which the project was abandoned.

Other simulated crimes have involved shoplifting. Gelfland and her colleagues[8] encountered an initial problem in that only 28 percent of their interviewees noticed the theft; of these, a little over a quarter reported it.

Bickman has focused on the degree to which a casual prior contact between the bystander and the victim or the wrongdoer might affect the response. He found[9] that there was a greater tendency to report when the bystander had, immediately prior to the shoplifting attempt, been treated in a pleasant manner by a sales clerk. On the other hand, the prior behavior of the wrongdoer seemed to have no effect on the subsequent reaction of the bystander.[10] In one interaction the wrongdoer had made a friendly remark, and in the other he had behaved rudely. No marked differences were noted in the tendency to report the theft, and the researchers conclude that revenge is not a factor in the bystander's considerations.

A novel approach has been followed by Geis, Huston, and their associates.[11] Utilizing the Good Samaritan Compensation Scheme in California, they have interviewed bystanders who, after being injured in the course of their intervention, subsequently made an application to the compensation board to be recompensed for the harm caused them. This is a unique project, presenting a methodical analysis of bystander behavior, in conditions generally of violent crime.

In presenting their work they stress the fact that laboratory research can never adequately replicate the kinds of perilous conditions that confront Samaritans. Their research indicates, as already noted in chapter 2, that the motivations and the considerations of the intervening bystander may be very different from those of the bystanders in the laboratory research. They note the confidence of the intervenors, their anger, and their concern, as well as a certain recklessness and adventurousness.

They argue that because of the impossibility of fully replicating a real-life situation and particularly its dangers, researchers often come to inaccurate conclusions about intervenors.

The need for pursuing this line of research—follow-up interviews of intervening bystanders—is highly desirable, but the use of the victim compensation program as the source of interviewees has obvious limitations, dealing mainly with crimes in which there was an element of violence, and only with those bystanders who helped, were injured, and then sought compensation.

Another important and unique line of research has been that adopted by Pecar in his studies of crime in Yugoslavia.[12] In the course of analyzing the nature of criminal-victim relationships in homicide along the lines originally laid down by Wolfgang,[13] Pecar noted that the interaction between these two principal parties to the crime was often influenced to a significant degree by the behavior of third parties—whom Pecar terms "involved bystanders." In many instances it was their behavior in the initial stages that served to precipitate or to provoke the crime. Whereas Wolfgang in his study had made a notable contribution to victimology by empirically showing that in many murder cases the victims bore major responsibility for the interaction preceding and leading up to the crime (it was they who tended to be drunk, who escalated a verbal argument into physical violence, who refused to be calmed), Pecar showed that by extending the investigation of the pertinent interaction it could be seen that in many cases the basis for the crime was laid in some prior provocation by a third person, who subsequently assumed only a minor role as a bystander. In some instances he provides examples of homicides committed within the home in which the original provocations which led to the final act of violence were initiated by a member of the family who was neither victim nor wrongdoer but whose behavior touched off a more violent interaction between other members. Pecar argues convincingly that if the aim of victimology is to expand our awareness of crime as an interactive phenomenon then there is a need to investigate also the role of the involved bystander in crime, not only for possible prevention but also for possible precipitation.

Pecar seems to have touched on a major unexplored area of criminological and victimological research, but so far there has been no follow-up to his pioneering approach.

While the California experiment deals with the role of the bystander as a Good Samaritan in trying to prevent crime, and the Yugoslavian research deals with the "involved bystander" as a precipitant agent in causing the crime, a third area remains the most elusive—the behavior of bystanders who are witness to actual criminal cases but fail to intervene. There seem to be few means of resolving this problem, for such bystanders are by the very nature of their inaction not easily accessible to the researcher.

Newspaper Reports

Meanwhile, given the paucity of criminological knowledge at this stage, it would seem useful to gain some kind of idea—admittedly selective and not entirely reliable—of the nature and dimensions of bystander behavior in criminal situations from sources such as the mass media and impressionistic recollections of those involved in law enforcement and criminal justice administration. No conclusions can be drawn on the basis of such facts, but useful leads for further research might easily be found.

While it is true that often it is the unusual and sensational case that attracts particular attention by the mass media, or that remains etched in the memory, it should not be forgotten that many social scientists have pointed out that the extreme or unusual case may serve to clarify aspects of human behavior. While the cases reported in the paper may be atypical they do indicate the broad lines of possible behavioral responses that could be subjected to further in-depth investigation.

It is also advisable to take note of the type of responses that attract public attention, because, just as in the case of the Genovese murder, they have a cumulative effect on the manner in which the general public regard the problems of crime and anticipated bystander behavior.

Thus, for instance, one story in a widely circulated magazine[14] describes the heroic action of two teenagers who chased after a robber, one of the two being killed in the process; the article then details the subsequent reaction of the survivor to the incident; the guilt at the death of his close friend; the harrowing experience of the hours immediately after the murder, where, instead of being given the emotional support that he so badly needed, he was subjected to a lengthy interrogation for several hours, including a visit to the scenes of the robbery and the murder; the tension of giving evidence in court where he spent an unpleasant hour on the witness stand being cross-examined by the defense attorney; the depressed state that he was in for many months afterwards, including the development of a stammer.

Both the youths were rewarded for the action (the dead friend posthumously), but the overall impression of the article is of the regret of the survivor at having become involved, his retroactive wisdom that had he known that the robber was armed he would never have intervened, and his resolve never to become involved again. "Does it pay to be a hero?" is the rhetorical question underlying the theme of the story.

On the other hand a newspaper report[15] tells of other Good Samaritans who had no regrets as to their action, despite the fact that they had themselves suffered serious and permanent injury. In one case a woman had been involved in a shoot-out between a gunman and two policemen. She had grabbed the gunman's arms, deflecting the bullet, and thereby possibly saving the lives of the policemen. However, she had herself been hit by a police bullet, and had been paralyzed from the waist down. On being awarded a prize for her bravery, she had stressed that, despite her injury, she had no regrets, and had merely done what was necessary under the circumstances.

This particular victim is an example of a special group of victims—small in number, but awesome in the implications—of bystanders killed or maimed in the course of a shoot-out between police and criminals. Sometimes this even occurs merely by the unhappy circumstance of their fortuitous presence in the vicinity, without any active intervention on their part at all. Tappan notes that, on some occasions, the bystander may actually be a victim of incorrect identification by the police, who open fire in the mistaken belief that they are confronted by a criminal.[16] Sometimes the bystander falls prey to the criminal's error. Wolfgang[17] noted in his study of homicide in Philadelphia that six out of 550 victims in his sample were bystanders, having no connection with either the criminal or the intended victim.

Yet most cases of harm to bystanders probably result from their involvement as a result of their own volition, in a desire to express tangibly their role of good citizenship.[18] In some instances the intervention is a calculated risk, as a violent response may be anticipated, such as in the case of an armed robbery. In these cases the robbers are ostentatiously armed, explicitly warn against trying to thwart them, have planned their campaign thoroughly, and have undertaken clear risks with the intention of brooking no interference with their operation. In other cases relatively innocuous incidents have serious repercussions for the unsuspecting Good Samaritan.

In one incident,[19] a young sixteen-year-old high-school student joined in a chase after two bicycle thieves and captured them. While helping to surround and hold the thieves in anticipation of the arrival of the police, the youth was suddenly attacked by one of the thieves, who stabbed him in the body, delivering a fatal wound. The dead youth was described as quiet and scholarly; his motivation for helping to apprehend the criminals may well have been the fact that two weeks earlier he too had been the victim of a bicycle theft.

The facts of this case touch on a potentially important point for future research—the degree to which prior victimization might be an important factor affecting bystander response. In their ongoing research, Geis and Huston[20] have found that a significant number of involved bystanders had previously been victims themselves and are at present probing this aspect further. There are obviously important implications for the extent to which empathy with a victim is a major consideration for a bystander.

Incidents of physical harm, occasionally fatal, or of conscious risk-taking behavior, are extreme examples of bystander intervention. However, in the realm of crime it is not only such precarious situations for bystanders that are of importance—it is also the nature of bystander behavior in other, less threatening, situations which constitute a problem of major proportions; for the capacity to ensure public security and confidence through efficient and equitable law enforcement and judicial administration is, to a large extent, a function of the willingness of people—victims and bystanders—to report crime to the police and to make themselves available to give evidence in a subsequent criminal trial.

There is growing evidence of a general dissatisfaction with the existing position; there are references in the mass media to the reluctance of people to cooperate with the police and the prosecution, because of the inconveniences imposed on them subsequently; of police interrogation, of giving evidence before a grand jury or preliminary investigation, and finally of testifying in court.

The Criminal Justice System

In the 1930s Sellin[21] had addressed himself to the problem and suggested a number of reasons that might influence people's reluctance to report a crime, including inconvenience of reporting to the police and then testifying in court, the force of public opinion which may not favor the enforcement of certain laws, indifference or ignorance, or personally knowing the wrongdoers and being reluctant to incriminate them.

A pertinent factor sometimes is the attitude toward, and the interaction with, the police; and the perceptions that people have as to the efficiency and fairness with which the police operate. Where there is little hope that the police will succeed in resolving the case, or where there is little prospect that the police will respond promptly to an emergency, people may ignore them altogether.

The police have for some time been aware of the importance of negative reactions and some police forces have set up special police-community associations to improve the image of the police and the nature of their relationship with the community. Where positive relations exist, there will be a far greater propensity to assist the police and to keep them informed as to suspicious activities.[22]

Another factor is the problem of the bystander as witness in the criminal justice system. Law books give detailed reports of the intricate rules of evidence and procedure; sometimes specialized guide books are written on the art of cross-examination.[23] Yet very rarely are the specific perspective and problems of the witness presented.

Here, too, however, there are incipient indications of growing awareness of the problem, and a recognition of the need to seek a solution, lest the criminal justice system be rendered impotent. A number of writers have, in the last few years, begun addressing themselves to the human aspect of testifying in court, trying to set out the factors militating against full citizen cooperation, while seeking means of making the system more efficient and responsive to citizen's needs.

The accumulated dissatisfaction at the treatment generally accorded by-standers is finally being accorded some attention, with attempts being made to assess the overall damage done to the system because of unpleasant experiences of witnesses, all imperceptibly eroding public support and, in specific cases, adversely affecting the bystander's future response to a criminal situation.

It is clearly difficult to show with any degree of certainty the nature of the impact that such general, often inchoate, dissatisfaction with the operation of the criminal justice system has on bystanders. It is not possible to know how many bystanders ignore the pleas for help of a victim because of their rapid analysis of the consequent inconveniences of court appearances.

Yet the awareness, whether clearly perceived or only dimly sensed, of the many impositions that a bystander may be subjected to as a witness, is surely partly responsible for the reluctance of bystanders to become involved, perhaps most noticeably in situations where the crime itself does not entail any sacrificial or risk-taking action. Thus, although the concept of the altruistic bystander conjures up the idea primarily of aid extended to a victim in stress circum-stances—and much of the research has been focused on such situations—the actual concern for another's plight and the altruistic action in support may be tested under other, far less critical, circumstances. Though less discussed in the literature, the willingness of people to help victims and report criminal activities and suspicious acts to the police in nonemergency situations is also an important feature of bystander behavior.

Ash[24] has set out many of the problems liable to be encountered by witnesses in the course of their involvement with the criminal justice system, noting in particular that injudicious treatment of witnesses "has a deleterious impact on the prevention and deterrence of crime . . . [discouraging] countless numbers of witnesses in our criminal justice system from ever 'getting involved' again, that is from reporting a crime, from cooperating with investigative efforts, and from providing testimony crucial to conviction."[25]

Ash describes the series of annoyances a witness is liable to encounter at the hands of an indifferent bureaucratic structure that shows little concern for the witnesses as they suffer through continuances of a trial to a later date or long, tedious waits before being called to give evidence. Where fees are allowed for court appearances these constitute no more than token recompense for lost earnings; and even then, many courts do not bother to apprise the witnesses of their rights in this regard.

After generally describing the hardships of the witness, Ash notes that "nowhere is there hard data on witnesses in criminal cases. This absence is part of a larger pattern of blindness and neglect. In a real sense, our system does not 'see' witnesses in their human dimension. Consequently we are neglectful of their interest and problems."[26] In fact, Ash argues that the additional rights accorded to the accused in recent times have often led to further problems for witnesses, for instance, often causing them to repeat their evidence on a number of occasions; he argues that the judges never considered the impact on witnesses of their decisions extending the rights of the accused.

Banfield and Anderson,[27] in an empirical investigation of the operation of one jurisdiction, have come to similar conclusions. They remark upon the casual and informal manner in which judges accede to defense lawyers' requests for continuances, and argue that some continuances are requested as part of a strategy to wear out the witnesses in the hope that they may fail to appear again. Lawyers, they stress, often insist on all the witnesses being present for all hearings.

Penegar has also noted that the inefficient operation of the criminal justice system "could quite conceivably have detrimental effects on the rate of crime. Seen as a form of communication between the system and the general public, particularly potential violators, the syndrome of delay tells these audiences in effect that crime and its participants are not really urgent public business."[28] Thus witnesses—not just bystanders but even the victim—become resentful of wasted time and lose interest in the trial, and there is constant slippage, in which nonappearance by witnesses, after several wasted days, leads to the case being dismissed.

Komesar,[29] in discussing specifically the victims of crime, attempted to assess the real costs of being victimized, pointing out that such costs were not limited to the pecuniary loss for damages inflicted or goods stolen. A full and true accounting of the price of crime, or more accurately, the price of victimization, must include factors such as the inconvenience of a whole series of subsequent activities—reporting the crime to the police, informing the insurance of the loss or damage, visits to the doctor for treatment, time spent in searching for a replacement of the goods stolen or damaged, backlog in work, and general pain and suffering.

Similar analysis could be made of the secondary losses sustained by the bystander/witness. The most obvious loss would be, as already noted, the time spent waiting to give evidence—at the police station, in discussion with the prosecutor, in the courtroom—often aggravated by the fact that the witness is kept waiting while behind-the-scenes negotiations take place for plea-bargaining, so that the evidence may, finally, not even be required.

Recently a major attempt was made by Cannavale and Falcon[30] to probe empirically the various dimensions of the problem of witnesses. In a novel research project witnesses were questioned as to their attitudes to the court system and the reasons for any dissatisfaction that they might have felt; finally a number of possible solutions were offered for making the system more responsive to the needs of the witnesses, and for facilitating future cooperation in efforts at crime prevention.

They note that prosecutors are often aware of the problems of witnesses, attributing the lack of cooperation by witnesses to some of their difficulty in winning a conviction. Yet, they are unable to offer reasonable remedies for a situation that troubles them. In their book, Cannavale and Falcon argue that a substantive change could be achieved by a consistent effort to introduce better management techniques into the criminal justice system. In their view greater consideration for the very real human problems of the witnesses is the key to ensuring witness cooperation.

They have set out a detailed list of improvements that could be instituted in order to make the court appearance a more pleasant experience. These relate to such issues as allaying the witnesses' apprehensions of reprisals from the defendants or their friends and family, the preparation of guidelines for witnesses, adequate witness fees and efficient payment procedures, prompt notification to witnesses of delays, counseling for reluctant witnesses, and obtaining feedback from witnesses through follow-up interviews to learn of their experience as witnesses in order to detect weaknesses in the existing facilities and procedures and to improve them.[31]

Ash also suggests that there is a need for witness liaison and support squads to represent the interests of witnesses, to make any necessary representation on their behalf, and in general to "act as advocate for legitimately aggrieved witnesses who themselves may be too timid or inarticulate to complain."[32] He suggests also that such an agency might even handle more prosaic details of witness concerns such as having witnesses on telephone standby or arranging for transport to and from the court for handicapped and elderly witnesses, or babysitting services where necessary. In addition he adds that there is a need to give more attention to the provision of better facilities in the court buildings, including free coffee, reading material, television, and gymnastic facilities.

Ash himself is dubious as to the possibility of most of these ideas being introduced, because of the extremely limited lobbying power of the witnesses, who constitute an amorphous group, which is constantly changing, having little contact among themselves, each believing that their own personal experiences are somehow unique and not likely to be repeated, rarely realizing how widespread the negative phenomena encountered are.

Most of the discussion by Ash and by Cannavale and Falcon revolves around the technical issues of court appearances; they only touch marginally upon the problems of actually testifying in court. Here, too, serious problems confront witnesses and should be given due consideration in any attempt to improve their position and to encourage their participation in the criminal justice system.

Marshall[33] has set out the wide range of problems confronting a witness when appearing in the unusual atmosphere of a courtroom. Little consideration is given to the very real psychological difficulties involved in perception of the event, memory, recall, and the capacity to recount the event lucidly. The legal fraternity has only marginal knowledge of these problems, and only in isolated instances is an attempt made to bridge the gap between the strict legal rules of evidence and procedure, and the practical problems that witnesses face in trying to describe what they remember.

Frank,[34] an American judge, has been particularly critical of the judicial system, since it accentuates what he calls the fight theory, based on adversary competition, and not the truth theory, based on a systematic piecing together of the actual facts. The consequences of accentuating the competitive aspects of the trial as opposed to a more objective and cautious search for the truth are that witnesses are caught up in a struggle in which they really have no part. In cross-examination they may be exposed to the verbal onslaughts of the lawyer, who has all the advantages afforded by the rules of evidence.

Outside the courtroom other problems may occur, and the witness may be subjected to threats by the accused or his friends and family. In some exceptional circumstances the witness may be held in custody as a material witness until after completing evidence.[35] Sheleff and Shichor[36] have outlined these and other aspects of witness behavior, suggesting that often the bystander/witness may end up by becoming the victimized party.

Crime Prevention in the Community

However important the need to improve the situation of bystanders in terms of their exposure to the police and the courts, the real issue of bystander involvement will nevertheless more likely be resolved in the community. At the practical level, probably most effort has been expended at this level, much of it out of a growing realization that direct concerted efforts on the part of the community provide the best protection and there is thus a need to foster a willingness to cooperate both among the members of a community and between the community as such and the police.

Sometimes frustration and anger lead to spontaneous reactions on the part of the public. In the early 1970s a number of reports appeared in the mass media of instances where angry bystanders had responded to a crime, not merely to protect the victim but also to vent their rage at the criminal.[37] It was noted then that it was quite possible that perceptions of the breakdown of law and order were leading, as often occurs, to vigilantism, in which enraged citizens would protect themselves by immediate lynch-type law.[38]

The possibility of overzealous reactions by concerned and enraged citizens is a recurring and troubling phenomenon. A recent analysis of violence in America[39] contained a presentation of the semilegitimized expression of violence in the form of vigilantism, posses, and lynching, often providing no more than a thin cover for the expression of deeper political and ideological beliefs.

In some instances official bodies have shown a reluctance to encourage too much citizen involvement in crime prevention, in the knowledge that such encouragement might lead to abuses. The United Nations Social Defense group has gone on record with its concern at the fact that in some countries citizen contributions to crime prevention often escalate into serious infringements of the suspected criminals' rights, with immediate lynch justice being meted out.[40]

On the other hand, there are also attempts being made to channel these sorts of citizen concerns into acceptable activities. In many cities special citizen groups are set up to serve as an auxiliary force, fulfilling various protective functions in the community.

Washnis, in a recent survey of citizen involvement in crime protection,[41] prefaces his book with the statement that police officials and criminologists believe that organized citizen involvement is essential if crime is to be contained and if there are to be any real possibilities of substantially reducing the crime rate. He writes that "out of necessity the general public has been stimulated to assist undermanned, overtaxed, and often non-community oriented police forces in the development of healthy and secure communities."[42] He adds though that "considerable uncertainty exists about the extent to which the public should be involved, about what the public is capable of doing, and about the degree to which public participation can affect the reduction of crime and fear."[43]

Washnis discusses the various kinds of programs that have been instituted and critically analyzes their effectiveness. The most widespread is probably the block association. Washnis describes the major considerations which led to their establishment, including the "fear of crime, dissatisfaction with law enforcement and the criminal justice system, and the desperate feeling by some citizens that they have to get actively involved in order to force crime down."[44] Any efforts of this nature often have a cumulative effect; the knowledge that the citizens of a particular neighborhood are sufficiently concerned to set up a protection association often evokes greater concern on the part of the police for the welfare of that neighborhood. In fact, one of the major aims of block associations is to seek closer communication and contacts between the community and the police. In cities where there has been a determined effort to activate the populace, the number of block associations may even run into the thousands, as in large cities such as New York or Los Angeles.

The block association is usually set up as a response to increased concern with rising crime rates, and the ensuing apprehensions that people have. Among the major functions of the association is to act as "eyes and ears" for what is happening on the block, to encourage citizens to be prepared to report crime and to be witnesses at the subsequent trial, to work in cooperation with the police, to lobby for better police service, to educate the public about the basic crime prevention techniques, and to provide aid to the victims of crime.

Care is taken to avoid any use of violence, and in particular to prevent the development of an aura of vigilantism. Stress is placed on neighborly interaction, where neighbors come to accept responsibility for watching over each other's homes, and to commit themselves to call the police should they see any suspicious activity in the neighborhood. Generally it is made clear that the members of the block association are not expected to intervene personally against a criminal, but are trained in the most efficient and rapid means of calling the police. Often use is made of ear-splitting whistles, sirens, or horns when help is urgently required. On hearing their high, piercing sound, other neighbors are expected to take appropriate action—calling the police, switching on lights, or adding their own noise to the din to help attract attention, and to frighten the would-be criminals. A further activity is community walks, in which two or more people will walk through the neighborhood, generally in the evenings at times considered high-risk for crime, ever on the alert for any untoward activity in the vicinity. In some cases, mobile patrols may be used, using cars that may also be equipped with citizens-band radios for rapid communication. Although almost no academic research has been done on these activities, police statistics indicate that often there is a marked drop in the crime rate.

Apart from the reduction in the crime rate and the sense of security afforded, often a qualitative transformation takes place in the community with the block association acting as a catalyst for further positive social interaction.

> In regard to developing a sense of community, block associations have been one of the most effective ways of bringing people together. In city after city, the majority of block members report that they had never known most of their neighbors and that only through the block club coffee sessions and regular meetings and the door-to-door contact had they really gotten to know each other and to appreciate mutual problems. In many cases, prior to block organizing, even neighbors next door to each other communicated infrequently. Crime prevention provided the motivation to get together and block association offered the mechanism for doing it. The simple factor of adults and youth knowing each other has helped to reduce fear. Familiarity has developed friendly attitudes and an increased concern for ones neighborhood.[45]

Outside of the neighborhood, special citywide programs are sometimes set up, with occupation often being the link. Thus, the specific problems facing night-shift employees have, in some cases, led to a special service being instituted for their benefit. The Service Employees Union, which represents mainly cleaning women, many of whom work at night, has set up a special body in New York—the Maintenance Employees Night Protection Alert Cooperation—to help such employees, many of them older women who travel to and from work in the night hours. One of the features of the work of the Cooperation is the institution of a buddy system, whereby members travel to and from work together, thereby radically reducing the chance of becoming a mugging victim.

An interesting means of using citizen resources is the taxi patrol. Civilian Radio Taxi Patrol has also been set up in New York, in which taxi drivers voluntarily commit themselves to informing their dispatchers of any emergency situations, with the dispatcher then passing on the information to the police (or any other relevant authority such as hospital or fire department). The idea for such extensive use of readily available facilities was originally put forward by a taxi owner in New York who had been disturbed by the Genovese case and wished to make some positive contribution to avoid such happenings in the future.

As the program has grown, drivers have been given special training and have discussed techniques for effectively helping to combat crime. For instance, one of their policies is to wait until passengers get safely inside their houses before pulling away.[46] Even without an official organization, instances have been increasing where people with CB radios have used them to submit a report of a crime, accident, or suspicious activity, often in situations where, without radio, the particular person may not have bothered, or been able, to report.

This is not the only circumstance in which specialized knowledge and/or facilities may be conducive to helping behavior. The papers often carry reports of bystanders utilizing their training in first aid or in self-defense techniques to provide critically needed help under emergency conditions. It would seem that as concern for rising crime grows, so is there a greater enrollment in such courses.[47]

Both at the local and at the national level, there are increasing instances of clinics or organizations being set up to cater to the needs of special classes of victims. Both professionals and volunteers may offer their services, thereby finding a means of providing constant aid to those in need. In some cases, where there are considerations of anonymity or distance, the help may be offered through telephone calls. In Britain, there is a national organization known as The Samaritans, with some 17,000 volunteers, linked in 150 centers, who are available at any time to talk on the telephone to people in need of help, advice, or just simple human communication.[48]

Yet, in the final analysis, all these and similar attempts to provide a greater degree of protection by mutual responsibility and readiness are really hinting at a far deeper phenomenon. Block associations are basically ex post facto attempts to recreate a spirit of community—in the realization that only such a spirit can guarantee that intricate and delicate web of human community which turns a random and loose conglomeration of people living in proximity with each other into a meaningful relationship based on personal acquaintance, common interests, and mutual trust.

The Urban Environment

Recently a number of urban planners, architects, social scientists, and criminologists have been researching the correlation between the human environment and social problems. As Jeffery has argued, "The way we design our urban environment determines the crime rate and type of crime to a great extent." He goes on to bemoan the fact that till recently "we have never considered crime prevention an integral part of urban planning." He argues that manipulating the environment to prevent crime "offers new avenues of thought and development for those who are attempting to thread their way effectively and sensitively between two undesirable extremes–high crime rates . . . and a police state, besieged mentality, fortress society response."[49]

In essence this approach seeks a physical structure which will be naturally conducive to the kinds of protection artificially supplied by organizations such as the block associations. It raises the possibility of designing buildings and neighborhoods, even in dense urban centers of population, in such a way as to encourage maximum interaction among neighbors, and constant surveillance of persons and property.

Newman,[50] an architect, has been a dominant figure in this approach. He has stressed the correlation between certain types of housing development (for example, high-rise apartments) and a high crime rate, and has argued that the best means of curbing the crime rate is to restructure the environment in which we live in such a way as to provide the sense of community, which generally characterized nonurban settlements. According to Newman,

> we are witnessing a breakdown of the social mechanism that once kept crime in check and gave direction and support to police activity. The small-town environments, rural or urban, which once framed and enforced their own moral codes, have virtually disappeared. We have become strangers sharing the largest collective habitats in human history.
>
> In our society there are few instances of shared beliefs of values among physical neighbors. Although this heterogeneity may be intellectually desirable, it has crippled our ability to agree on the action required to maintain the social framework necessary to our continued survival. . . . It is clear to almost all researchers in crime prevention that the issue hangs on the inability of communities to come together in joint action. The physical environment we have been building in our cities for the past twenty-five years actually prevents such amity and discourages the pursuit of a collective action.[51]

Newman claims that the key to reversal of these trends is to change the physical environment. He sees the need for a clearly defined area–outside of the hidden privacy of the home, but also beyond the exposed and open nature of the public domain–that will "belong" to the immediate inhabitants, where they will have security, and from which outsiders will be excluded. Any intruders into such an area will likely be asked to explain and justify their presence.

Newman suggests the concept of "defensible space" as a "model for residential environments which inhibits crime by creating the physical expression of a social fabric that defends itself."[52] He explains that defensible space is a surrogate term for the range of mechanisms—real and symbolic barriers, strongly defined areas of influence, and improved opportunities for surveillance—that combine to bring an environment under the control of its residents. A *defensible space* is a living residential environment which can be employed by inhabitants for the enhancement of their lives, while providing security for their families, neighbors and friends. . . .

The public areas of a multi-family residential environment devoid of defensible space can make the act of going from street to apartment equivalent to running the gauntlet. The fear and uncertainty generated by living in such an environment can slowly eat away and eventually destroy the security and the sanctity of the apartment unit itself. On the other hand, by grouping dwelling units to reinforce associations of mutual benefit; by delineating paths of movement; by defining areas of activity for particular users through their juxtaposition with internal living areas; and by providing for natural opportunities for visual surveillance, architects can create a clear understanding of function of a space, and who its users are and ought to be. This, in turn, can lead residents of all income levels to adopt extremely potent territorial attitudes and policing measure which act as strong deterrents to potential criminals.[53]

Newman's idea is to create a gradual transition from private into public areas through the use of what he calls semiprivate and semipublic areas allowing for maximum surveillance from the private areas into the semiprivate and semipublic areas, through judicious positioning of the various spaces, the use of large windows, and so on. Newman claims that, in buildings which approximate to these standards, there is a lower crime rate, a greater sense of security, and a greater willingness to be active as a bystander.

Newman's analysis is focused mainly on the specific housing area; other writers have adopted a broader perspective of the total neighborhood. Writing before Newman, Jacobs has described how to make the cities attractive and safe for its citizens.[54] Whereas Newman describes how the immediate housing area, semiprivate and semipublic, can be made safer by facilitating interaction among the residents and by subtle exclusion of strangers, Jacobs focuses on the public areas and shows how these too could be made safer by increasing the voluntary surveillance of people who live and work in the neighborhood. "Where city streets are being properly used they fulfil certain 'self-government functions' . . . to weave webs of public surveillance and thus to protect strangers as well as themselves: to grow networks of small-scale, everyday public life and thus of trust and social controls; and to help assimilate children into reasonably responsible and tolerant city life."[55]

She claims that the best way to ensure the security of citizens is to create conditions which will lead to as much activity as possible in the streets at all times. The prevention of crime will flow not so much from police patroling but from a vital community in which all regular users of the streets recognize that they constitute the "eyes and ears" of the community—sensitive to any nuances of change, alert to any lurking dangers, prepared to become personally involved. Like Newman she feels that the environmental structure is of prime importance, and calls for thoughtful planning in which due consideration is given to the human aspects and the way in which urban settings can best facilitate social interaction.

There is clearly a need to delve much deeper into all the ramifications of the criminal triad, and of the overall impact that knowledge of, and fear of, crime has for people. This is an aspect of crime that has been far removed from the concerns of most criminologists. Even within victimology the focus has tended to remain on the immediate interaction between criminal and victim. Yet the key factor differentiating crime from other wrongdoing is that it is presumed to cause harm to the society at large. From this perspective it behooves us to measure the nature of that harm.

The 1967 President's Commission on Crime noted the impact that a high crime rate has on people's perceptions of the community, and how it affects their daily behavior—the involvement in the life of the community; the willingness to move about freely, particularly at night; the transitory nature of people's life as they search for safer areas.

Conklin[56] is one of the few criminologists who have devoted a full study to the subject. He warns against the danger of excessive personal precautions against crime, which might become pathological. People may get trapped in houses that they have barred too effectively; guns, bought for protection, may go off suddenly, killing innocent people. Sometimes the very efforts made to secure personal protection may hinder the efforts at a community interaction of the type described by Jacobs. In setting up protective devices, barriers also become erected that hinder easy and natural contacts among neighbors.

The French sociologist Durkheim,[57] in a theoretical presentation that has had much influence on modern criminological thinking, claimed that crime, in reasonable proportions, might serve a functional purpose in helping to integrate the community as it united against criminal outsiders. This is a theme that has been used by other writers who see conflict as being an important integrative force in society.[58] Conklin, however, takes issue with Durkheim and suggests that "crime often drives people apart by creating distrust and suspicion."[59]

The consequences of crime are in fact varied. A community's resilience is often severely tested. While the desire to ensure one's own personal security is understandable, the best protection is probably vouchsafed when community bonds are strengthened, and neighbors provide mutual assurances of support.

Notes

1. See Irving M. Piliavin, Judith Rodin, and Jane Allyn Piliavin, "Good Samaritanism: An Underground Phenomenon?" *Journal of Personality and*

Social Psychology, 1972, *24*, pp. 392-400; and J.A. Piliavin and I.M. Piliavin, "Effects of Blood on Reactions to a Victim," *Journal of Personality and Social Psychology*, 1972, *23*, pp. 353-361.

2. See discussion in chapter 2 of research by Russell D. Clark and Larry E. Word, "Why Don't Bystanders Help? Because of Ambiguity?" *Journal of Personality and Social Psychology*, 1972, *24*, pp. 392-400.

3. See Bibb Latané and John Darley, *The Unresponsive Bystander: Why Doesn't He Help?* (New York: Appleton-Century-Crofts, 1970), chapter 8, "The Bystander and the Thief," pp. 69-78.

4. Ibid., p. 69.

5. R. Lance Shotland and Margaret K. Straw, "Bystander Response to an Assault: When a Man Attacks a Woman," *Journal of Personality and Social Psychology*, 1976, *34*, pp. 990-999.

6. G. Borofsky, G. Stoll, and L. Meese, "Sex Differences in Bystander Reactions to Physical Assault," *Journal of Experimental Social Psychology*, 1971, *7*, pp. 313-318.

7. John E. Stewart and Daniel A. Cannon, "Effects of Perpetrator Status and Bystander Commitment on Responses to a Simulated Crime," *Journal of Police Science and Administration*, 1977, *5*, p. 318.

8. Donna M. Gelfland, Donald P. Walder, Patrice Hartman, and Brent Page, "Who Reports Shoplifters?—A Field-Experimental Study," *Journal of Personality and Social Psychology*, 1973, *25*, pp. 276-285.

9. Leonard Bickman, "Attitude toward Authority and the Reporting of a Crime," *Sociometry*, 1976, *39*, pp. 76-82.

10. Leonard Bickman and Susan K. Green, "Is Revenge Sweet? The Effect of Attitude toward a Thief on Crime Reporting," *Criminal Justice and Behavior*, 1975, *2*, pp. 101-112.

11. Ted L. Huston, Gilbert Geis, Richard Wright, and Thomas Garrett, "Good Samaritans as Crime Victims," In E. Viano, ed., *Crimes, Victim and Society* (Leiden: Sitjhoff International, 1976).

12. See Janez Pecar, "Involved Bystanders: Examination of a Neglected Aspect of Criminology and Victimology," *International Journal of Contemporary Sociology*, 1972, *9*, p. 81. See also "Involved Bystanders—Victimological Aspects," *Rev. Kriminalist. Kriminol., 22*, p. 172, indexed in *Abstracts in Criminology, 12*, p. 76.

13. Marvin E. Wolfgang, *Patterns in Criminal Homicide* (Philadelphia: University of Pennsylvania Press, 1958).

14. Theodor Irwin, "A 16-Year-Old Boy Asks: Does It Pay to Be a Hero?" *Parade*, October 19, 1975, p. 28.

15. John Barbour, "To Samaritans Scars are Minor," *Los Angeles Times*, June 26, 1977, p. 1.

16. See Paul W. Tappan, *Crime, Justice and Correction* (New York: McGraw-Hill, 1960), p. 286.

17. Wolfgang, p. 209.

18. See, for instance, the editorial "Citizens Against Crime," *New York Times*, June 20, 1973, which relates three occasions within a week in which bystanders in New York took an active part in preventing street crimes. The paper notes "a gratifying re-emergence of public co-operation with police efforts to combat crime."

19. Joseph P. Treaster, "Two Young Bike Thieves Kill Youth Who Chased Them," *New York Times, 23*, July 1974.

20. Personal communication from Gilbert Geis and Ted Huston.

21. Thorsten Sellin, *Research Memorandum on Crime in the Depression* (New York: Science Research Council, 1937), pp. 69-70.

22. See Terry Eisenberg, Robert H. Fosen, and Albert S. Glickman, *Police-Community Behavior Patterns* (New York: Praeger, 1973). For a specific experimental program, involving a demilitarized uniform, more in keeping with civilian modes of dress, see James H. Tenzel and Victor Cizanckas, "The Uniform Experiment," *Journal of Police Science and Administration*, 1973, *1*, p. 421.

23. See, for example, Francis Wellman, *The Art of Cross-Examination* (Garden City: Garden City Books, 1948).

24. Michael Ash, "On Witnesses: A Radical Critique of Criminal Court Procedures," *Notre Dame Lawyer*, 1972, *48*, pp. 386-425.

25. Ibid., p. 388.

26. Ibid., p. 399.

27. Laura Banfield and C. David Anderson, "Continuances in the Cook County Criminal Court," *University of Chicago Law Review*, 1968, *35*, p. 261.

28. Kenneth L. Penegar, "Appraising the System of Criminal Law, Its Processes and Administration," *North Carolina Law Review*, 1968, *47*, pp. 69-157.

29. Neil K. Komesar, "A Theoretical Empirical Study of Victims of Crime," *Journal of Legal Studies*, 1973, *2*, pp. 301-322.

30. Frank J. Cannavale, Jr., and William Falcon, *Witness Cooperation: With a Handbook of Witness Management* (Lexington, Mass.: Lexington Books, 1976).

31. Ibid., part II, chapters 2 and 3.

32. Ash, p. 413.

33. James Marshall, *Law and Psychology in Conflict* (Indianapolis: Bobbs-Merrill, 1966).

34. Jerome Frank, *Courts on Trial* (Princeton: Princeton University Press, 1969).

35. See Ronald L. Carlson, "Jailing the Innocent: The Plight of the Material Witness," *Iowa Law Review*, 1969, *55*, p. 1; comment, "Pre-trial Detention of Witnesses," *University of Pennsylvania Law Review*, 1969, *117*, p. 700.

36. Leon S. Sheleff and David Shichor, "Victimological Aspects of Bystander Involvement," *Crime and Delinquency*, (forthcoming).

37. For a number of such instances see William L. Claiborne, "New Yorkers Fight Back: The Tilt toward Vigilantism," *New York*, 1974, pp. 49-53.

38. See Gary T. Marx and Dane Archer, "The Urban Vigilante," *Psychology Today*, January 1973, p. 45.

39. See Richard Brown, "The American Vigilante Tradition," in Hugh Graham and Ted Guss, eds., *Violence in America* (New York: Bantam, 1969). For further discussion of vigilantism and related phenomena, see next chapter.

40. Report, "Preparatory Meeting of Experts in Social Defense (African Region) for the Fourth United Nations Congress on the Prevention of Crime and the Treatment of Offenders," *International Review of Criminal Policy*, no. 27, 1969.

41. George Washnis, *Citizen Involvement in Crime Prevention* (Lexington, Mass.: Lexington Books, 1976).

42. Ibid., p. 1.

43. Ibid.

44. Ibid., p. 7.

45. Ibid., p. 9.

46. For details of various programs, see ibid., chapter 5, "Special Crime Prevention Projects," pp. 69-90.

47. For excellent concise advice on how to act in a wide range of conceivable emergencies, both in order to save oneself and to rescue others, see Anthony Greenback, *The Book of Survival* (New York: Harper and Row, 1967).

48. See C. Varah, *The Samaritans in the 70's* (London: Constable, 1973). For a critical review of their work, see Julian Bell, "The Samaritan Concept of Befriending," *British Journal of Social Work*, 1975, pp. 413-422. Bell argues that by offering to befriend strangers in need, there is a debasement of the traditional notion of friendship. For general discussion of helping programs see L.A. Hoff, *People in Crisis* (Reading, Mass.: Addison-Wesley, 1978).

49. C. Ray Jeffery, *Crime Prevention through Environmental Design* (Beverly Hills: Sage [second edition], 1977), p. 343.

50. Oscar Newman, *Defensible Space: Crime Prevention through Urban Design* (New York: Macmillan, 1972).

51. Ibid., pp. 1-2.

52. Ibid., p. 3.

53. Ibid., pp. 3-4.

54. Jane Jacobs, *The Death and Life of Great American Cities* (New York: Random House, 1961).

55. Ibid., p. 119.

56. John E. Conklin, *The Impact of Crime* (New York: Macmillan, 1975).

57. Emile Durkheim, *The Rules of Sociological Method* (New York: The Free Press, 1938).

58. See Lewis Coser, *The Functions of Social Conflict* (Glencoe, Illinois: The Free Press, 1956).

59. Conklin, p. 68.

Leon Sheleff is Senior Lecturer in the Institute of Criminology and Criminal Law and in the Department of Sociology at Tel-Aviv University. He is author of Generations Apart *(New York: McGraw-Hill, 1980). His research interest is in the study of capital punishment, particularly as it affects political crimes.*

25

SOCIAL CHANGE AND CRIME RATE TRENDS
A Routine Activity Approach

LAWRENCE E. COHEN

MARCUS FELSON

In this paper we present a "routine activity approach" for analyzing crime rate trends and cycles. Rather than emphasizing the characteristics of offenders, with this approach we concentrate upon the circumstances in which they carry out predatory criminal acts. Most criminal acts require convergence in space and time of *likely offenders, suitable targets* and the *absence of capable guardians* against crime. Human ecological theory facilitates an investigation into the way in which social structure produces this convergence, hence allowing illegal activities to feed upon the legal activities of everyday life. In particular, we hypothesize that the dispersion of activities away from households and families increases the opportunity for crime and thus generates higher crime rates. A variety of data is presented in support of the hypothesis, which helps explain crime rate trends in the United States 1947–1974 as a byproduct of changes in such variables as labor force participation and single-adult households.

INTRODUCTION

In its summary report the National Commission on the Causes and Prevention of Violence (1969: xxxvii) presents an important sociological paradox:

Why, we must ask, have urban violent crime rates increased substantially during the past decade when the conditions that are supposed to cause violent crime have not worsened—have, indeed, generally improved?

The Bureau of the Census, in its latest report on trends in social and economic conditions in metropolitan areas, states that most "indicators of well-being point toward progress in the cities since 1960." Thus, for example, the proportion of blacks in cities who completed high school rose from 43 percent in 1960 to 61 percent in 1968; unemployment rates dropped significantly between 1959 and 1967 and the median family income of blacks in cities increased from 61 percent to 68 percent of the median white family income during the same period. Also during the same period the number of persons living below the legally-defined poverty level in cities declined from 11.3 million to 8.3 million.

Despite the general continuation of these trends in social and economic conditions in the United States, the *Uniform Crime Report* (FBI, 1975:49) indicates that between 1960 and 1975 reported rates of robbery, aggravated assault, forcible rape and homicide increased by 263%, 164%, 174%, and 188%, respectively. Similar property crime rate increases reported during this same period[1] (e.g., 200% for burglary rate) suggest that the paradox noted by the Violence Commission applies to nonviolent offenses as well.

* Address all communications to: Lawrence E. Cohen; Department of Sociology; University of Illinois; Urbana, IL 61801.

For their comments, we thank David J. Bordua, Ross M. Stolzenberg, Christopher S. Dunn, Kenneth C. Land, Robert Schoen, Amos Hawley, and an anonymous reviewer. Funding for this study was provided by these United States Government grants: National Institute for Mental Health 1-R01-MH31117-01;National Science Foundation, SOC-77-13261; and United States Army RI/DAHC 19-76-G-0016. The authors' name order is purely alphabetical.

[1] Though official data severely underestimate crime, they at least provide a rough indicator of trends over time in the volume of several major felonies. The possibility that these data also reflect trends in rates at which offenses are reported to the police has motivated extensive victimology research (see Nettler, 1974; and Hindelang, 1976, for a review). This work consistently finds that seriousness of offense is the strongest determinant of citizen reporting to law enforcement officials (Skogan, 1976: 145; Hindelang, 1976: 401). Hence the upward trend in official crime rates since 1960 in the U.S. may reflect increases in *both* the volume and seriousness of offenses. Though disaggregating these two components may not be feasible, one may wish to interpret observed trends as generated largely by both.

In the present paper we consider these paradoxical trends in crime rates in terms of changes in the "routine activities" of everyday life. We believe the structure of such activities influences criminal opportunity and therefore affects trends in a class of crimes we refer to as *direct-contact predatory violations*. Predatory violations are defined here as illegal acts in which "someone definitely and intentionally takes or damages the person or property of another" (Glaser, 1971:4). Further, this analysis is confined to those predatory violations involving direct physical contact between at least one offender and at least one person or object which that offender attempts to take or damage.

We argue that structural changes in routine activity patterns can influence crime rates by affecting the convergence in space and time of the three minimal elements of direct-contact predatory violations: (1) motivated offenders, (2) suitable targets, and (3) the absence of capable guardians against a violation. We further argue that the lack of any one of these elements is sufficient to prevent the successful completion of a direct-contact predatory crime, and that the convergence in time and space of suitable targets and the absence of capable guardians may even lead to large increases in crime rates without necessarily requiring any increase in the structural conditions that motivate individuals to engage in crime. That is, if the proportion of motivated offenders or even suitable targets were to remain stable in a community, changes in routine activities could nonetheless alter the likelihood of their convergence in space and time, thereby creating more opportunities for crimes to occur. Control therefore becomes critical. If controls through routine activities were to decrease, illegal predatory activities could then be likely to increase. In the process of developing this explanation and evaluating its consistency with existing data, we relate our approach to classical human ecological concepts and to several earlier studies.

The Structure of Criminal Activity

Sociological knowledge of how community structure generates illegal acts has made little progress since Shaw and McKay and their colleagues (1929) published their pathbreaking work, *Delinquency Areas*. Variations in crime rates over space long have been recognized (e.g., see Guerry, 1833; Quètelet, 1842), and current evidence indicates that the pattern of these relationships within metropolitan communities has persisted (Reiss, 1976). Although most spatial research is quite useful for describing crime rate patterns and providing post hoc explanations, these works seldom consider—conceptually or empirically—the fundamental human ecological character of illegal acts as *events* which occur at specific locations in *space* and *time*, involving specific persons and/or objects. These and related concepts can help us to develop an extension of the human ecological analysis to the problem of explaining changes in crime rates over time. Unlike many criminological inquiries, we do not examine why individuals or groups are inclined criminally, but rather we take criminal inclination as given and examine the manner in which the spatio-temporal organization of social activities helps people to translate their criminal inclinations into action. Criminal violations are treated here as routine activities which share many attributes of, and are interdependent with, other routine activities. This interdependence between the structure of illegal activities and the organization of everyday sustenance activities leads us to consider certain concepts from human ecological literature.

Selected Concepts from Hawley's Human Ecological Theory

While criminologists traditionally have concentrated on the *spatial* analysis of crime rates within metropolitan communities, they seldom have considered the *temporal* interdependence of these acts. In his classic theory of human ecology, Amos Hawley (1950) treats the community not simply as a unit of territory but rather as an organization of symbiotic and commensalistic relationships as human activities are performed over both space and time.

Hawley identified three important temporal components of community structure: (1) *rhythm*, the regular periodicity with which events occur, as with the rhythm of travel activity; (2) *tempo*, the number of events per unit of time, such as the number of criminal violations per day on a given street; and (3) *timing*, the coordination among different activities which are more or less interdependent, such as the coordination of an offender's rhythms with those of a victim (Hawley, 1950:289; the examples are ours). These components of temporal organization, often neglected in criminological research, prove useful in analyzing how illegal tasks are performed—a utility which becomes more apparent after noting the spatio-temporal requirements of illegal activities.

The Minimal Elements of Direct-Contact Predatory Violations

As we previously stated, despite their great diversity, direct-contact predatory violations share some important requirements which facilitate analysis of their structure. Each successfully completed violation minimally requires an *offender* with both criminal inclinations and the ability to carry out those inclinations, a person or object providing a *suitable target* for the offender, and *absence of guardians* capable of preventing violations. We emphasize that the lack of any one of these elements normally is sufficient to prevent such violations from occurring.[2] Though guardianship is implicit in everyday life, it usually is marked by the absence of violations; hence it is easy to overlook. While police action is analyzed widely, guardianship by ordinary citizens of one another and of property as they go about routine activities may be one of the most neglected elements in sociological research on crime, especially since it links seemingly unre-

lated social roles and relationships to the occurrence or absence of illegal acts.

The conjunction of these minimal elements can be used to assess how social structure may affect the tempo of each type of violation. That is, the probability that a violation will occur at any specific time and place might be taken as a function of the convergence of likely offenders and suitable targets in the absence of capable guardians. Through consideration of how trends and fluctuations in social conditions affect the frequency of this convergence of criminogenic circumstances, an explanation of temporal trends in crime rates can be constructed.

The Ecological Nature of Illegal Acts

This ecological analysis of direct-contact predatory violations is intended to be more than metaphorical. In the context of such violations, people, gaining and losing sustenance, struggle among themselves for property, safety, territorial hegemony, sexual outlet, physical control, and sometimes for survival itself. The interdependence between offenders and victims can be viewed as a predatory relationship between functionally dissimilar individuals or groups. Since predatory violations fail to yield any net gain in sustenance for the larger community, they can only be sustained by feeding upon other activities. As offenders cooperate to increase their efficiency at predatory violations and as potential victims organize their resistance to these violations, both groups apply the symbiotic principle to improve their sustenance position. On the other hand, potential victims of predatory crime may take evasive actions which encourage offenders to pursue targets other than their own. Since illegal activities must feed upon other activities, the spatial and temporal structure of routine legal activities should play an important role in determining the location, type and quantity of illegal acts occurring in a given community or society. Moreover, one can analyze how the structure of community organization as well as the level of technology in a society provide the circumstances under which crime can thrive. For example, technology and organization

---

[2] The analytical distinction between target and guardian is not important in those cases where a personal target engages in self-protection from direct-contact predatory violations. We leave open for the present the question of whether a guardian is effective or ineffective in all situations. We also allow that various guardians may primarily supervise offenders, targets or both. These are questions for future examination.

affect the capacity of persons with criminal inclinations to overcome their targets, as well as affecting the ability of guardians to contend with potential offenders by using whatever protective tools, weapons and skills they have at their disposal. Many technological advances designed for legitimate purposes—including the automobile, small power tools, hunting weapons, highways, telephones, etc.— may enable offenders to carry out their own work more effectively or may assist people in protecting their own or someone else's person or property.

Not only do routine legitimate activities often provide the wherewithal to commit offenses or to guard against others who do so, but they also provide offenders with suitable targets. Target suitability is likely to reflect such things as value (i.e., the material or symbolic desirability of a personal or property target for offenders), physical visibility, access, and the inertia of a target against illegal treatment by offenders (including the weight, size, and attached or locked features of property inhibiting its illegal removal and the physical capacity of personal victims to resist attackers with or without weapons). Routine production activities probably affect the suitability of consumer goods for illegal removal by determining their value and weight. Daily activities may affect the location of property and personal targets in visible and accessible places at particular times. These activities also may cause people to have on hand objects that can be used as weapons for criminal acts or self-protection or to be preoccupied with tasks which reduce their capacity to discourage or resist offenders.

While little is known about conditions that affect the convergence of potential offenders, targets and guardians, this is a potentially rich source of propositions about crime rates. For example, daily work activities separate many people from those they trust and the property they value. Routine activities also bring together at various times of day or night persons of different background, sometimes in the presence of facilities, tools or weapons which influence the commission or avoidance of illegal acts. Hence, the timing of work, schooling and leisure may be of central importance for explaining crime rates.

The ideas presented so far are not new, but they frequently are overlooked in the theoretical literature on crime. Although an investigation of the literature uncovers significant examples of descriptive and practical data related to the routine activities upon which illegal behavior feeds, these data seldom are treated within an analytical framework. The next section reviews some of this literature.

RELATION OF THE ROUTINE ACTIVITY APPROACH TO EXTANT STUDIES

A major advantage of the routine activity approach presented here is that it helps assemble some diverse and previously unconnected criminological analyses into a single substantive framework. This framework also serves to link illegal and legal activities, as illustrated by a few examples of descriptive accounts of criminal activity.

Descriptive Analyses

There are several descriptive analyses of criminal acts in criminological literature. For example, Thomas Reppetto's (1974) study, *Residential Crime*, considers how residents supervise their neighborhoods and streets and limit access of possible offenders. He also considers how distance of households from the central city reduces risks of criminal victimization. Reppetto's evidence—consisting of criminal justice records, observations of comparative features of geographic areas, victimization survey data and offender interviews—indicates that offenders are very likely to use burglary tools and to have at least minimal technical skills, that physical characteristics of dwellings affect their victimization rates, that the rhythms of residential crime rate patterns are marked (often related to travel and work patterns of residents), and that visibility of potential sites of crime affects the risk that crimes will occur there. Similar findings are reported by Pope's (1977a; 1977b) study of burglary in California and by Scarr's (1972) study of burglary in and around the District of Columbia. In addition, many studies report that architectural and environmental design as well as community crime programs serve to decrease target suitability and increase capable guardianship (see, for example, Newman, 1973; Jeffery, 1971; Washnis, 1976), while many biographical or autobiographical descriptions of illegal activities note that lawbreakers take into account the nature of property and/or the structure of human activities as they go about their illegal work (see, e.g., Chambliss, 1972; Klockars, 1974; Sutherland, 1937; Letkemann, 1973; Jackson, 1969; Martin, 1952; Maurer, 1964; Cameron, 1964; Williamson, 1968).

Evidence that the spatio-temporal organization of society affects patterns of crime can be found in several sources. Strong variations in specific predatory crime rates from hour to hour, day to day, and month to month are reported often (e.g., Wolfgang, 1958; Amir, 1971; Reppetto, 1974; Scarr, 1972; FBI, 1975; 1976), and these variations appear to correspond to the various tempos of the related legitimate activities upon which they feed. Also at a microsociological level, Short and Strodtbeck (1965: chaps. 5 and 11) describe opportunities for violent confrontations of gang boys and other community residents which arise in the context of community leisure patterns, such as "quarter parties" in black communities, and the importance, in the calculus of decision making employed by participants in such episodes, of low probabilities of legal intervention. In addition, a wealth of empirical evidence indicates strong spatial variations over community areas in crime and delinquency rates[3] (for an excellent discussion and re-

view of the literature on ecological studies of crimes, see Wilks, 1967). Recently, Albert Reiss (1976) has argued convincingly that these spatial variations (despite some claims to the contrary) have been supported consistently by both official and unofficial sources of data. Reiss further cites victimization studies which indicate that offenders are very likely to select targets not far from their own residence (see USDJ, 1974a; 1974b; 1974c).

Macrolevel Analyses of Crime Trends and Cycles

Although details about how crime occurs are intrinsically interesting, the important analytical task is to learn from these details how illegal activities carve their niche within the larger system of activities. This task is not an easy one. For example, attempts by Bonger (1916), Durkheim (1951; 1966), Henry and Short (1954), and Fleisher (1966) to link the rate of illegal activities to the economic condition of a society have not been completely successful. Empirical tests of the relationships postulated in the above studies have produced inconsistent results which some observers view as an indication that the level of crime is not related systematically to the economic conditions of a society (Mansfield et al., 1974: 463; Cohen and Felson, 1979).

It is possible that the wrong economic and social factors have been employed in these macro studies of crime. Other researchers have provided stimulating alternative descriptions of how social change affects the criminal opportunity structure, thereby influencing crime rates in particular societies. For example, at the beginning of the nineteenth century, Patrick Colquhoun (1800) presented a detailed, lucid description and analysis of crime in the London metropolitan area and suggestions for its control. He assembled substantial evidence that London was experiencing a massive crime wave attributable to a great increment in the assemblage and

[3] One such ecological study by Sarah Boggs (1965) presents some similar ideas in distinguishing *familiarity* of offenders with their targets and *profitability* of targets as two elements of crime occurrence. Boggs's work stands apart from much research on the ecology of crime in its consideration of crime occurrence rates separately from offender rates. The former consist of the number of offenses committed in a given area per number of suitable targets within that area (as estimated by various indicators). The latter considers the residence of offenders in computing the number of offenders per unit of population. Boggs examines the correlations between crime occurrence rates and offender rates for several offenses in St. Louis and shows that the two are often independent. It appears from her analysis that *both* target and offender characteristics play a central role in the location of illegal activity.

movement of valuable goods through its ports and terminals.

A similar examination of crime in the period of the English industrial expansion was carried out by a modern historian, J. J. Tobias (1967), whose work on the history of crime in nineteenth century England is perhaps the most comprehensive effort to isolate those elements of social change affecting crime in an expanding industrial nation. Tobias details how far-reaching changes in transportation, currency, technology, commerce, merchandising, poverty, housing, and the like, had tremendous repercussions on the amount and type of illegal activities committed in the nineteenth century. His thesis is that structural transformations either facilitated or impeded the opportunities to engage in illegal activities. In one of the few empirical studies of how recent social change affects the opportunity structure for crime in the United States, Leroy Gould (1969) demonstrated that the increase in the circulation of money and the availability of automobiles between 1921 and 1965 apparently led to an increase in the rate of bank robberies and auto thefts, respectively. Gould's data suggest that these relationships are due more to the abundance of opportunities to perpetrate the crimes than to short-term fluctuations in economic activities.

Although the sociological and historical studies cited in this section have provided some useful *empirical* generalizations and important insights into the incidence of crime, it is fair to say that they have not articulated systematically the *theoretical* linkages between routine legal activities and illegal endeavors. Thus, these studies cannot explain how changes in the larger social structure generate changes in the opportunity to engage in predatory crime and hence account for crime rate trends.[4]

To do so requires a conceptual framework such as that sketched in the preceding section. Before attempting to demonstrate the feasibility of this approach with macrolevel data, we examine available microlevel data for its consistency with the major assumptions of this approach.

Microlevel Assumptions of the Routine Activity Approach

The theoretical approach taken here specifies that crime rate trends in the post-World War II United States are related to patterns of what we have called routine activities. We define these as any recurrent and prevalent activities which provide for basic population and individual needs, whatever their biological or cultural origins. Thus routine activities would include formalized work, as well as the provision of standard food, shelter, sexual outlet, leisure, social interaction, learning and childrearing. These activities may go well beyond the minimal levels needed to prevent a population's extinction, so long as their prevalence and recurrence makes them a part of everyday life.

Routine activities may occur (1) at home, (2) in jobs away from home, and (3) in other activities away from home. The latter may involve primarily household members or others. We shall argue that, since World War II, the United States has experienced a major shift of routine activities away from the first category into the, remaining ones, especially those nonhousehold activities involving nonhousehold members. In particular, we shall argue that this shift in the structure of routine activities increases the probability that motivated offenders will converge in space and time with suitable targets in the absence of capable guardians, hence contributing to significant increases in the

---

[4] The concept of the opportunity for crime contained in the above research and in this study differs considerably from the traditional sociological usage of the *differential opportunity* concept. For example, Cloward and Ohlin (1960) employed this term in discussing how legitimate and illegitimate opportunities affect the resolution of adjustment problems leading to gang delinquency. From their viewpoint, this resolution depends upon the kind of social support for one or another type of illegitimate activity that is given at different points in the social structure (Cloward and Ohlin, 1960: 151). Rather than circumstantial determinants of crime, they use differential opportunity to emphasize structural features which motivate offenders to perpetrate certain types of crimes. Cloward and Ohlin are largely silent on the interaction of this motivation with target suitability and guardianship as this interaction influences crime rates.

direct-contact predatory crime rates over these years.

If the routine activity approach is valid, then we should expect to find evidence for a number of empirical relationships regarding the nature and distribution of predatory violations. For example, we would expect routine activities performed within or near the home and among family or other primary groups to entail lower risk of criminal victimization because they enhance guardianship capabilities. We should also expect that routine daily activities affect the location of property and personal targets in visible and accessible places at particular times, thereby influencing their risk of victimization. Furthermore, by determining their size and weight and in some cases their value, routine production activities should affect the suitability of consumer goods for illegal removal. Finally, if the routine activity approach is useful for explaining the paradox presented earlier, we should find that the circulation of people and property, the size and weight of consumer items etc., will parallel changes in crime rate trends for the post-World War II United States.

The veracity of the routine activity approach can be assessed by analyses of both microlevel and macrolevel interdependencies of human activities. While consistency at the former level may appear noncontroversial, or even obvious, one nonetheless needs to show that the approach does not contradict existing data before proceeding to investigate the latter level.

EMPIRICAL ASSESSMENT

Circumstances and Location of Offenses

The routine activity approach specifies that household and family activities entail lower risk of criminal victimization than nonhousehold-nonfamily activities, despite the problems in measuring the former.[5]

---

[5] Recent research indicates the existence of substantial quantities of family violence which remains outside of UCR data (see annotated bibliography of family violence in Lystad, 1974). While we cannot rule out the likelihood that much family violence is concealed from victimization surveys, the latter capture information absent from police data and still

National estimates from large-scale government victimization surveys in 1973 and 1974 support this generalization (see methodological information in Hindelang et al., 1976: Appendix 6). Table 1 presents several incident-victimization rates per 100,000 population ages 12 and older. Clearly, the rates in Panels A and B are far lower at or near home than elsewhere and far lower among relatives than others. The data indicate that risk of victimization varies directly with social distance between offender and victim. Panel C of this table indicates, furthermore, that risk of lone victimization far exceeds the risk of victimization for groups. These relationships are strengthened by considering time budget evidence that, on the average, Americans spend 16.26 hours per day at home, 1.38 hours on streets, in parks, etc., and 6.36 hours in other places (Szalai, 1972:795). Panel D of Table 1 presents our estimates of victimization per billion person-hours spent in such locations.[6] For example, personal larceny

---

indicate that nonfamily members are usually much more dangerous than family members are to each other (see text). Also, when family violence leads to death, its suppression becomes quite difficult. The murder circumstances data indicate that about two-thirds of killings involve nonrelatives. Without denying the evidence that the level of family violence is far greater than police reports would indicate, available data also suggest that time spent in family activities within households incurs less risk of victimization than many alternative activities in other places. In addition, many of the most common offenses (such as robbery and burglary) always have been recognized as usually involving nonfamily members.

[6] Billion person-hours can easily be conceptualized as 1,000,000 persons spending 1,000 hours each (or about 42 days) in a given location (Szalai, 1972:795). Fox obtained these data from a 1966 time budget study in 44 American cities. The study was carried out by the Survey Research Center, the University of Michigan. We combined four subsamples in computing our figures. We combined activities into three locations, as follows: (1) at or just outside home; (2) at another's home, restaurants or bars, or indoor leisure; (3) in streets, parks, or outdoor leisure. Our computing formula was

$$Q = [(R \div 10^5) \div (A \cdot 365)] \cdot 10^9,$$

where Q is the risk per billion person-hours; R is the victimization rate, reported per 10^5 persons in Hindelang et al. (1976: Table 318); A is the hours spent per location calculated from Szalai (1972: 795); 365 is the multiplier to cover a year's exposure to risk; and 10^9 converts risk per person-hour to billion person-hours.

Table 1. Incident-Specific Risk Rates for Rape. Robbery. Assault and Personal Larceny with Contact, United States, 1974

A.*		Rape	Robbery	Assault	Personal Larceny with Contact	Total
PLACE OF	In or near home	63	129	572	75	839
RESIDENCE	Elsewhere	119	584	1,897	1,010	3,610
B.*						
VICTIM-	(Lone Offender)					
OFFENDER	Relative	7	13	158	5	183
RELATIONSHIP	Well Known	23	30	333	30	416
	Casual Acquaintance	11	26	308	25	370
	Don't Know/Sight Only	106	227	888	616	1,837
	(Multiple Offender)					
	Any known	10***	68	252	43	373
	All strangers	25***	349	530	366	1,270
C.*						
NUMBER	one	179	647	2,116	1,062	4,004
OF	Two	3	47	257	19	326
VICTIMS	Three	0	13	53	3	09
	Four Plus	0	6	43	1	50
D.**						
LOCATION AND	Home, Stranger	61	147	345	103	654
RELATIONSHIP	Home, Nonstranger	45	74	620	22	761
(sole	Street, Stranger	1,370	7,743	15,684	7,802	32,460
offender	Street, Nonstranger	179	735	5,777	496	7,167
only)	Elsewhere, Stranger	129	513	1,934	2,455	4,988
	Elsewhere, Nonstranger	47	155	1,544	99	1,874

   * Calculated from Handelang et al., 1977: Tables 3.16, 3.18, 3.27, 3.28. Rates are per 100,000 persons ages 12 and over.
   ** See fn. 6 for source. Rates are per billion person-hours in stated locations.
   *** Based on white data only due to lack of suitable sample size for nonwhites as victims of rape with multiple offenders.

rates (with contact) are 350 times higher at the hands of strangers in streets than at the hands of nonstrangers at home. Separate computations from 1973 victimization data (USDJ, 1976: Table 48) indicate that there were two motor vehicle thefts per million vehicle-hours parked at or near home, 55 per million vehicle-hours in streets, parks, playgrounds, school grounds or parking lots, and 12 per million vehicle-hours elsewhere. While the direction of these relationships is not surprising, their magnitudes should be noted. It appears that risk of criminal victimization varies dramatically among the circumstances and locations in which people place themselves and their property.

Target Suitability

Another assumption of the routine activity approach is that target suitability influences the occurrence of direct-contact predatory violations. Though we lack data to disaggregate all major components of target suitability (i.e., value, visibility, accessibility and inertia), together they imply that expensive and movable durables, such as vehicles and electronic appliances, have the highest risk of illegal removal.

As a specific case in point, we compared the 1975 composition of stolen property reported in the Uniform Crime Report (FBI, 1976: Tables 26–7) with national data on personal consumer expenditures for goods (CEA, 1976: Tables 13–16) and to appliance industry estimates of the value of shipments the same year (*Merchandising Week*, 1976). We calculated that $26.44 in motor vehicles and parts were stolen for each $100 of these goods consumed in 1975, while $6.82 worth of electronic appliances were stolen per $100 consumed. Though these estimates are subject to error in citizen and police estimation, what is important here is their size relative to other rates. For example, only

8¢ worth of nondurables and 12¢ worth of furniture and nonelectronic household durables were stolen per $100 of each category consumed, the motor vehicle risk being, respectively, 330 and 220 times as great. Though we lack data on the "stocks" of goods subject to risk, these "flow" data clearly support our assumption that vehicles and electronic appliances are greatly overrepresented in thefts.

The 1976 Buying Guide issue of *Consumer Reports* (1975) indicates why electronic appliances are an excellent retail value for a thief. For example, a Panasonic car tape player is worth $30 per lb., and a Phillips phonograph cartridge is valued at over $5,000 per lb., while large appliances such as refrigerators and washing machines are only worth $1 to $3 per lb. Not surprisingly, burglary data for the District of Columbia in 1969 (Scarr, 1972: Table 9) indicate that home entertainment items alone constituted nearly four times as many stolen items as clothing, food, drugs, liquor, and tobacco combined and nearly eight times as many stolen items as office supplies and equipment. In addition, 69% of national thefts classified in 1975 (FBI, 1976: Tables 1, 26) involve automobiles, their parts or accessories, and thefts from automobiles or thefts of bicycles. Yet radio and television sets plus electronic components and accessories totaled only 0.10% of the total truckload tonnage terminated in 1973 by intercity motor carriers, while passenger cars, motor vehicle parts and accessories, motorcycles, bicycles, and their parts, totaled only 5.5% of the 410 million truckload tons terminated (ICC, 1974). Clearly, portable and movable durables are reported stolen in great disproportion to their share of the value and weight of goods circulating in the United States.

Family Activities and Crime Rates

One would expect that persons living in single-adult households and those employed outside the home are less obligated to confine their time to family activities within households. From a routine activity perspective, these persons and their households should have higher rates of predatory criminal victimization. We also expect that adolescents and young adults who are perhaps more likely to engage in peer group activities rather than family activities will have higher rates of criminal victimization. Finally, married persons should have lower rates than others. Tables 2 and 3 largely confirm these expectations (with the exception of personal larceny with contact). Examining these tables, we note that victimization rates appear to be related inversely to age and are lower for persons in "less active" statuses (e.g., keeping house, unable to work, retired) and persons in intact marriages. A notable exception is indicated in Table 2, where persons unable to work appear more likely to be victimized by rape, robbery and personal larceny with contact than are other "inactive persons." Unemployed persons also have unusually high rates of victimization. However, these rates are consistent with the routine activity approach offered here: the high rates of victimization suffered by the unemployed may reflect their residential proximity to high concentrations of potential offenders as well as their age and racial composition, while handicapped persons have high risk of personal victimization because they are less able to resist motivated offenders. Nonetheless, persons who keep house have noticeably lower rates of victimization than those who are employed, unemployed, in school or in the armed forces.

As Table 3 indicates, burglary and robbery victimization rates are about twice as high for persons living in single-adult households as for other persons in each age group examined. Other victimization data (USDJ, 1976: Table 21) indicate that, while household victimization rates tend to vary directly with household size, larger households have lower rates per person. For example, the total household victimization rates (including burglary, household larceny, and motor vehicle theft) per 1,000 households were 168 for single-person households and 326 for households containing six or more persons. Hence, six people distributed over six single-person households experience an average of 1,008 household victimizations, more than three times as many as

Table 2. Selected Status-Specific Personal Victimization Rates for the United States (per 100,000 Persons in Each Category)

Variables and Sources	Victim Category	Rape	Robbery	Assault	Personal Larceny with Contact	Personal Larceny without Contact
A. AGE	12–15	147	1,267	3,848	311	16,355
(Source:	16–19	248	1,127	5,411	370	15,606
Hindelang, et al., 1977:	20–24	209	1,072	4,829	337	14,295
Table 310, 1974	25–34	135	703	3,023	263	10,354
rates	35–49	21	547	1,515	256	7,667
	50–64	33	411	731	347	4,588
	65+	20	388	492	344	1,845
B. MAJOR	(Male 16+)					
ACTIVITY OF	Armed Forces	—	1,388	4,153	118	16,274
VICTIM	Employed	—	807	3,285	252	10,318
(Source:	Unemployed	—	2,179	7,984	594	15,905
Hindelang, et al., 1977:	Keep house	—	0	2,475	463	3,998
Table 313, 1974	In school	—	1,362	5,984	493	17,133
rates)	Unable to work	—	1,520	2,556	623	3,648
	Retired	—	578	662	205	2,080
	(Female 16+					
	Keep house	116	271	978	285	4,433
	Employed	156	529	1,576	355	9,419
	Unemployed	798	772	5,065	461	12,338
	In School	417	430	2,035	298	12,810
	Unable to work	287	842	741	326	1,003
	Retired	120	172	438	831	1,571
C. MARITAL STATUS	(Male 12+)					
(Source: USDJ:	Never Married	—	1,800	5,870	450	16,450
1977, Table 5,	Married	—	550	2,170	170	7,660
1973 rates)	Separated/Divorced	—	2,270	5,640	1,040	12,960
	Widowed	—	1,150	1,500	—	4,120
	(Female 12+)					
	Never Married	360	580	2,560	400	12,880
	Married	70	270	910	220	6,570
	Separated/Divorced	540	1,090	4,560	640	9,130
	Widowed	—	450	590	480	2,460

Line indicates too few offenses for accurate estimates of rate. However, rates in these cells are usually small.

one six-person household. Moreover, age of household head has a strong relationship to a household's victimization rate for these crimes. For households headed

Table 3. Robbery-Burglary Victimization Rates by Ages and Number of Adults in Household, 1974 and 1976 General Social Survey

Age	Number of Adults in Household		
	One	Two or More	Ratio
18–35	0.200 (140)	0.095 (985)	2.11
36–55	0.161 (112)	0.079 (826)	2.04
56 and over	0.107 (262)	0.061 (640)	1.76
All Ages	0.144 (514)	0.081 (2451)	1.78

(Numbers in parentheses are the base for computing risk rates.)

Source: Calculated from 1974 and 1976 General Social Survey, National Opinion Research Center, University of Chicago.

by persons under 20, the motor vehicle theft rate is nine times as high, and the burglary and household larceny rates four times as high as those for households headed by persons 65 and over (USDJ, 1976: Table 9).

While the data presented in this section were not collected originally for the purpose of testing the routine activity approach, our efforts to rework them for these purposes have proven fruitful. The routine activity approach is consistent with the data examined and, in addition, helps to accommodate within a rather simple and coherent analytical framework certain findings which, though not necessarily new, might otherwise be attributed only "descriptive" significance. In the next section, we examine macrosocial trends as they relate to trends in crime rates.

CHANGING TRENDS IN ROUTINE ACTIVITY STRUCTURE AND PARALLEL TRENDS IN CRIME RATES

The main thesis presented here is that the dramatic increase in the reported crime rates in the U.S. since 1960 is linked to changes in the routine activity structure of American society and to a corresponding increase in target suitability and decrease in guardian presence. If such a thesis has validity, then we should be able to identify these social trends and show how they relate to predatory criminal victimization rates.

Trends in Human Activity Patterns

The decade 1960–1970 experienced noteworthy trends in the activities of the American population. For example, the percent of the population consisting of female college students increased 118% (USBC, 1975: Table 225). Married female labor force participant rates increased 31% (USBC, 1975: Table 563), while the percent of the population living as primary individuals increased by 34% (USBC, 1975: Table 51; see also Kobrin, 1976). We gain some further insight into changing routine activity patterns by comparing hourly data for 1960 and 1971 on households *unattended* by persons ages 14 or over when U.S. census interviewers first called (see Table 4). These data suggest that the proportion of households unattended at 8 A.M. increased by almost half between 1960 and 1971. One also finds increases in rates of out-of-town travel, which provides greater opportunity for both daytime and nighttime burglary of residences. Between 1960 and 1970, there was a 72% increase in state and national park visits per capita (USBC, 1975), an 144% increase in the percent of plant workers eligible for three weeks vacation (BLS, 1975: Table 116), and an 184% increase in overseas travellers per 100,000 population (USBC, 1975: Table 366). The National Travel Survey, conducted as part of the U.S. Census Bureau's Census of Transportation, confirms the general

Table 4. Proportion of Households Unattended by Anyone 14 Years Old or Over by Time of Day during First Visit by Census Bureau Interviewer, 1960 and 1971

Time of day	1960 Census	November, 1971 Current Pop. Survey	Percent Change
8:00– 8:59 a.m.	29%	43	+48.9%
9:00– 9:59 a.m.	29	44	+58
10:00–10:59 a.m.	31	42	+36
11:00–11:59 a.m.	32	41	+28
12:00–12:59 p.m.	32	41	+28
1:00– 1:59 p.m.	31	43	+39
2:00– 2:59 p.m.	33	43	+30
3:00– 3:59 p.m.	30	33	+10
4:00– 4:59 p.m.	28	30	+ 7
5:00– 5:59 p.m.	22	26	+18
6:00– 6:59 p.m.	22	25	+14
7:00– 7:50 p.m.	20	29	+45
8:00– 8:59 p.m.	24	22	– 8

Source: Calculated from USBC (1973b: Table A).

trends, tallying an 81% increase in the number of vacations taken by Americans from 1967 to 1972, a five-year period (USBC, 1973a: Introduction).

The dispersion of activities away from households appears to be a major recent social change. Although this decade also experienced an important 31% increase in the percent of the population ages 15–24, age structure change was only one of many social trends occurring during the period, especially trends in the circulation of people and property in American society.[7]

The importance of the changing activity structure is underscored by taking a brief look at demographic changes between the years 1970 and 1975, a period of continuing crime rate increments. Most of the recent changes in age structure relevant to crime rates already had occurred by 1970; indeed, the proportion of the population ages 15–24 increased by only 6% between 1970 and 1975, compared with a 15% increase during the five years 1965 to 1970. On the other hand, major changes in the structure of routine activities continued

---

[7] While the more sophisticated treatments of the topic have varied somewhat in their findings, most recent studies attempting to link crime rate increases to the changing age structure of the American population have found that the latter account for a relatively limited proportion of the general crime trend (see, for example, Sagi and Wellford, 1968; Ferdinand, 1970; and Wellford, 1973).

during these years. For example, in only five years, the estimated proportion of the population consisting of husband-present, married women in the labor force households increased by 11%, while the estimated number of non-husband-wife households per 100,000 population increased from 9,150 to 11,420, a 25% increase (USBC, 1976: Tables 50, 276; USBC, 1970–1975). At the same time, the percent of population enrolled in higher education increased 16% between 1970 and 1975.

Related Property Trends and Their Relation to Human Activity Patterns

Many of the activity trends mentioned above normally involve significant investments in durable goods. For example, the dispersion of population across relatively more households (especially non-husband-wife households) enlarges the market for durable goods such as television sets and automobiles. Women participating in the labor force and both men and women enrolled in college provide a market for automobiles. Both work and travel often involve the purchase of major movable or portable durables and their use away from home.

Considerable data are available which indicate that sales of consumer goods changed dramatically between 1960 and 1970 (as did their size and weight), hence providing more suitable property available for theft. For example, during this decade, constant-dollar personal consumer expenditures in the United States for motor vehicles and parts increased by 71%, while constant-dollar expenditures for other durables increased by 105% (calculated from CEA, 1976: Table B-16). In addition, electronic household appliances and small houseware shipments increased from 56.2 to 119.7 million units (*Electrical Merchandising Week*, 1964; *Merchandising Week*, 1973). During the same decade, appliance imports increased in value by 681% (USBC, 1975: Table 1368).

This same period appears to have spawned a revolution in small durable product design which further feeds the opportunity for crime to occur. Relevant data from the 1960 and 1970 Sears catalogs

on the weight of many consumer durable goods were examined. Sears is the nation's largest retailer and its policy of purchasing and relabeling standard manufactured goods makes its catalogs a good source of data on widely merchandised consumer goods. The lightest television listed for sale in 1960 weighed 38 lbs., compared with 15 lbs. for 1970. Thus, the lightest televisions were 2½ times as heavy in 1960 as 1970. Similar trends are observed for dozens of other goods listed in the Sears catalog. Data from *Consumer Reports Buying Guide*, published in December of 1959 and 1969, show similar changes for radios, record players, slide projectors, tape recorders, televisions, toasters and many other goods. Hence, major declines in weight between 1960 and 1970 were quite significant for these and other goods, which suggests that the consumer goods market may be producing many more targets suitable for theft. In general, one finds rapid growth in property suitable for illegal removal and in household and individual exposure to attack during the years 1960–1975.

Related Trends in Business Establishments

Of course, as households and individuals increased their ownership of small durables, businesses also increased the value of the merchandise which they transport and sell as well as the money involved in these transactions. Yet the Census of Business conducted in 1958, 1963, 1967, and 1972 indicate that the number of wholesale, retail, service, and public warehouse establishments (including establishments owned by large organizations) was a nearly constant ratio of one for every 16 persons in the United States. Since more goods and money were distributed over a relatively fixed number of business establishments, the tempo of business activity per establishment apparently was increasing. At the same time, the percent of the population employed as sales clerks or salesmen in retail trade declined from 1.48% to 1.27%, between 1960 and 1970, a-14.7% decline (USBC, 1975: Table 589).

Though both business and personal

property increased, the changing pace of activities appears to have exposed the latter to greater relative risk of attack, whether at home or elsewhere, due to the dispersion of goods among many more households, while concentrating goods in business establishments. However, merchandise in retail establishments with heavy volume and few employees to guard it probably is exposed to major increments in risk of illegal removal than is most other business property.

Composition of Crime Trends

If these changes in the circulation of people and property are in fact related to crime trends, the *composition* of the latter should reflect this. We expect relatively greater increases in personal and household victimization as compared with most business victimizations, while shoplifting should increase more rapidly than other types of thefts from businesses. We expect personal offenses at the hands of strangers to manifest greater increases than such offenses at the hands of nonstrangers. Finally, residential burglary rates should increase more in daytime than nighttime.

The available time series on the composition of offenses confirm these expectations. For example, Table 5 shows that commercial burglaries declined from 60% to 36% of the total, while daytime residential burglaries increased from 16% to 33%. Unlike the other crimes against business, shoplifting increased its share. Though we lack trend data on the circumstances of other violent offenses, murder data confirm our expectations. Between 1963 and 1975, felon-type murders increased from 17% to 32% of the total. Compared with a 47% increase in the rate of relative killings in this period, we calculated a 294% increase in the murder rate at the hands of known or suspected felon types.

Thus the trends in the composition of recorded crime rates appear to be highly consistent with the activity structure trends noted earlier. In the next section we apply the routine activity approach in order to model crime rate trends and social change in the post-World War II United States.

Table 5. Offense Analysis Trends for Robbery, Burglary, Larceny and Murder; United States, 1960–1975

A. ROBBERIES[a]	1960	1965	1970	
Highway Robbery	52.6	57.0	59.8	
Residential Robbery	8.0	10.1	13.1	
Commercial Robbery	39.4	32.9	27.1	
Totals	100.0	100.0	100.0	
B. BURGLARIES	1960	1965	1970	1975
Residential	15.6	24.5	31.7	33.2
Residential Nighttime	24.4	25.2	25.8	30.5
Commercial	60.0	50.2	42.5	36.3
Totals	100.0	99.9	100.0	100.0
C. LARCENIES	1960	1965	1970	1975
Shoplifting	6.0	7.8	9.2	11.3
Other	94.0	92.2	90.8	88.7
Totals	100.0	100.0	100.0	100.0
D. MURDERS	1963	1965	1970	1975
Relative Killings	31.0	31.0	23.3	22.4
Romance, Arguments[b]	51.0	48.0	47.9	45.2
Felon Types[c]	17.0	21.0	28.8	32.4
Totals	100.0	100.0	100.0	100.0

Source: Offense Analysis from UCR, various years.

[a] Excluding miscellaneous robberies. The 1975 distribution omitted due to apparent instability of post-1970 data.

[b] Includes romantic triangles, lovers' quarrels and arguments.

[c] Includes both known and suspected felon types.

THE RELATIONSHIP OF THE HOUSEHOLD ACTIVITY RATIO TO FIVE ANNUAL OFFICIAL INDEX CRIME RATES IN THE UNITED STATES, 1947–1974

In this section, we test the hypothesis that aggregate official crime rate trends in the United States vary directly over time with the dispersion of activities away from family and household. The limitations of annual time series data do not allow construction of direct measures of changes in hourly activity patterns, or -quantities, qualities and movements of exact stocks of household durable goods, but the Current Population Survey does provide related time series on labor force and household structure. From these data, we calculate annually (beginning in 1947) a household activity ratio by adding the number of married, husband-present female labor force participants (source: BLS, 1975: Table 5) to the number of non-husband-wife households (source: USBC, 1947–1976), dividing this sum by the total number of households in the U.S. (source: USBC, 1947–1976). This calculation provides an estimate of the proportion of American households in year t expected to be most highly exposed to risk of personal and property victimization due to the dispersion of their activities away from family and household and/or their likelihood of owning extra sets of durables subject to high risk of attack. Hence, the household activity ratio should vary directly with official index crime rates.

Our empirical goal in this section is to test this relationship, with controls for those variables which other researchers have linked empirically to crime rate trends in the United States. Since various researchers have found such trends to increase with the proportion of the population in teen and young adult years (Fox, 1976; Land and Felson, 1976; Sagi and Wellford, 1968; Wellford, 1973), we include the population ages 15–24 per 100,000 resident population in year t as our first control variable (source: USBC, various years). Others (e.g., Brenner, 1976a; 1976b) have found unemployment rates to vary directly with official crime rates over time, although this relationship elsewhere has been shown to be empirically questionable (see Mansfield et al., 1974: 463; Cohen and Felson, 1979). Thus, as our second, control variable, we take the standard annual unemployment rate (per 100 persons ages 16 and over) as a measure of the business cycle (source: BLS, 1975).

Four of the five crime rates that we utilize here (forcible rape, aggravated assault, robbery and burglary) are taken from FBI estimates of offenses per 100,000 U.S. population (as revised and reported in OMB, 1973). We exclude larceny-theft due to a major definitional change in 1960 and auto theft due to excessive multicollinearity in the analysis.[8] For our homicide indicator we employ the

homicide mortality rate taken from the vital statistics data collected by the Bureau of the Census (various years). The latter rate has the advantage of being collected separately from the standard crime reporting system and is thought to contain less measurement error (see Bowers and Pierce, 1975). Hence, this analysis of official index crime rates includes three violent offenses (homicide, forcible rape, and aggravated assault), one property offense (burglary), and one offense which involves both the removal of property and the threat of violence (robbery). The analysis thus includes one offense thought to have relatively low reporting reliability (forcible rape), one thought to have relatively high reliability (homicide), and three others having relatively intermediate levels of reporting quality (Ennis, 1967).

Since official crime rates in year t are likely to reflect some accumulation of criminal opportunity and inclinations over several years, one should not expect these rates to respond solely to the level of the independent variables for year t. A useful model of cumulative social change in circumstances such as this is the difference equation, which can be estimated in two forms (see Goldberg, 1958). One form takes the first difference $(y_t - y_{t-1})$ as the dependent variable—in this case, the change in the official crime rate per 100,000 population between year $t-1$ and year t. Alternatively, one can estimate the difference equation in autoregressive form by taking the official crime rate in year t as a function of the exogenous predictors plus the official crime rate in year $t - 1$ on the right-hand side of the equation. (See Land, 1978, for a review of these and other methods and for references to related literature.) Both forms are estimable with ordinary least squares methods, which we employ for the years 1947 through 1974. The N is 28 years for all but the homicide rate, for which publication lags reduce our N to 26.

Even if a positive relationship between the household activity ratio and the official crime rates is observed, with controls for age and unemployment, we are open to the charge that this may be a spurious consequence of autocorrelation of disturbances, that is, the possibility that residu-

---

[8] The auto theft rate lagged one year correlated quite strongly with the predictor variables. This multicollinearity impaired our difference equation analysis, although we again found consistently positive coefficients for the household activity ratio. We were able to remove autocorrelation by logging all variables and including the unemployment as a control, but do not report these equations.

als are systematically related for nearby time points. While spurious relationships are a risk one also takes in cross-sectional regression analysis, time-series analysts have devised a variety of methods for monitoring and adjusting for spuriousness due to this autocorrelation, including the Durbin and Watson (1951) statistic, Durbin's h statistic (Durbin, 1970), the Griliches (1967) criterion, as well as Cochrane and Orcutt (1949) corrections. We employ (but do not report in detail) these methods to check for the likelihood that the observed relationship is spurious. (See Land, 1978, for a review of such tests and the related literature on their applicability and robustness; see Theil, 1971, for a methodological review.)

Findings

Our time-series analysis for the years 1947–1974 consistently revealed positive and statistically significant relationships between the household activity ratio and each official crime rate change. Whichever official crime rate is employed, this finding occurs—whether we take the first difference for each crime rate as exogenous or estimate the equation in autoregressive form (with the lagged dependent variable on the right-hand side of the equation), whether we include or exclude the unemployment variable; whether we take the current scales of variables or convert them to natural log values; whether we employ the age structure variable as described or alter the ages examined (e.g., 14–24, 15–19, etc.). In short, the relationship is positive and significant in each case.

Before calculating the difference equations, we regressed each crime rate in year t on the three independent variables for year t. This ordinary structural equation also produced consistent positive and significant coefficients for the routine activity coefficient, the total variance explained ranges from 84% to 97%. However, the Durbin-Watson statistics for these equations indicated high risk of autocorrelation, which is hardly surprising since they ignore lagged effects. Reestimated equations taking first differences as endogenous reduced the risk of autocorre-

lation significantly (and also reduced variance explained to between 35% and 77%). These equations also consistently produce significant positive coefficients for the household activity variable. When unemployment is included in these equations, its coefficients are all negative and near zero.

The top panel of Table 6 presents regression estimates of first differences for five official crime rates, with the age structure and household activity variables in year t as the only predictors. Again, the household activity coefficients are consistently positive, with t ratios always significant with a one-tailed test. Except for the aggravated assault equation, the household activity variable has a t ratio and standardized coefficient greater than that of the age structure variable. The standardized coefficients for the household activity variable range from .42 to .72, while the age structure coefficients are consistently positive. In general, the household activity variable is a stronger predictor of official crime rate trends than the age structure.

The equations in the top panel of Table 6 generally have lower variance explained but also lower risk of autocorrelation of disturbances than those reported above. For all five equations, the Durbin-Watson statistic allows acceptance of the null hypothesis that autocorrelation is absent at the 1% level. A 5% level (which *increases* the likelihood of proving the statistic nonzero) allows us neither to accept nor reject the null hypothesis that autocorrelation is absent in the homicide and robbery equations.

Though autocorrelation has not been proven to exist in these five equations, risk may be sufficient in two to motivate further efforts at equation estimation (see bottom panel of Table 6). We estimated the equations in autoregressive form to see if the risk abates. Since the Durbin-Watson statistic was not designed for evaluating autocorrelation in these equations, we calculated Durbin's h, a statistic specifically designed for equations estimated with a lagged dependent variable (Durbin, 1970), and recently found to be robust for small samples (Maddala and Rao, 1973). This statistic allows ac-

Table 6. Regression Equations for First Differences in Five Index Crime Rates and Sensitivity Analyses, the United States, 1947–1974

FIRST DIFFERENCE FORM	(1) Nonnegligent Homicide	(2) Forcible Rape	(3) Aggravated Assault	(4) Robbery	(5) Burglary
Constant	-2.3632	-4.8591	-32.0507	-43.8838	-221.2303
t ratio	.3502	5.3679	7.6567	3.4497	3.7229
Proportion 15–24 (t)					
Standardized	.1667	.1425	.4941	.2320	.1952
Unstandardized	3.2190	6.4685	132.1072	116.7742	486.0806
t ratio	1.0695	.7505	3.3147	.9642	.8591
Household Activity Ratio (t)					
Standardized	.7162	.6713	.4377	.4242	.5106
Unstandardized	4.0676	8.9743	34.4658	62.8834	374.4746
t ratio	4.5959	3.5356	2.9364	1.7629	2.2474
Multiple R² Adjusted	.6791	.5850	.7442	.3335	.4058
Degrees of Freedom	23	25	25	25	25
Durbin-Watson Value	2.5455	2.3388	2.3446	1.4548	1.7641
1% test	Accept	Accept	Accept	Accept	Accept
5% test	Uncertain	Accept	Accept	Uncertain	Accept
AUTOREGRESSIVE FORM					
Multiple R² Adjusted	.9823	.9888	.9961	.9768	.9859
Durbin's h	-1.3751	-.7487	.9709	1.5490	1.1445
–1% test	Accept	Accept	Accept	Accept	Accept
–5% test	Accept	Accept	Accept	Accept	Accept
Griliches Criterion					
Cochrane-Orcutt Correction.					
Effect upon Household Activity	Minimal	Minimal	Minimal	Minimal	Minimal
Unemployment Rate as Control.					
Effect Upon Household Activity	Minimal	Minimal	Minimal	Minimal	Minimal

ceptance of the null hypothesis (at both 1% and 5% levels) that autocorrelation is absent for all five equations. Application of the Griliches (1967) criterion further allows acceptance of each equation as manifesting distributing lags rather than serial correlation. We also employed the Cochrane-Orcutt (1949) iterative procedure to calculate a correction estimate for any autocorrelation present. The resulting correction for the household activity coefficient proves minimal in all five cases. Finally, we calculated each of the above equations for natural log values of the relevant variables, finding again that the household activity coefficient was consistently positive and statistically significant and the risk of autocorrelation reduced still further.

The positive and significant relationship between the household activity variable and the official crime rates is robust and appears to hold for both macro- and microlevel data; it explains five crime rate trends, as well as the changing composition of official crime rates reported in Table 5. These results suggest that routine activities may indeed provide the opportunity for many illegal activities to occur.

DISCUSSION

In our judgment many conventional theories of crime (the adequacy of which usually is evaluated by cross-sectional data, or no data at all) have difficulty accounting for the annual changes in crime rate trends in the post-World War II United States. These theories may prove useful in explaining crime trends during other periods, within specific communities, or in particular subgroups of the population. Longitudinal aggregate data for the United States, however, indicate that the trends for many of the presumed causal variables in these theoretical structures are in a direction opposite to those hypothesized to be the causes of crime. For example, during the decade 1960– 1970, the percent of the population below the low-income level declined 44% and the unemployment rate declined 186%. Central city population as a share of the whole population declined slightly, while the

percent of foreign stock declined 0.1%, etc. (see USBC, 1975: 654, 19, 39).

On the other hand, the convergence in time and space of three elements (motivated offenders, suitable targets, and the absence of capable guardians) appears useful for understanding crime rate trends. The lack of any of these elements is sufficient to prevent the occurrence of a successful direct-contact predatory crime. The convergence in time and space of suitable targets and the absence of capable guardians can lead to large increases in crime rates without any increase or change in the structural conditions that motivate individuals to engage in crime. Presumably, had the social indicators of the variables hypothesized to be the causes of crime in conventional theories changed in the direction of favoring increased crime in the post-World War II United States, the increases in crime rates likely would have been even more staggering than those which were observed. In any event, it is our belief that criminologists have underemphasized the importance of the convergence of suitable targets and the absence of capable guardians in explaining recent increases in the crime rate. Furthermore, the effects of the convergence in time and space of these elements may be multiplicative rather than additive. That is, their convergence by a fixed percentage may produce increases in crime rates far greater than that fixed percentage, demonstrating how some relatively modest social trends can contribute to some relatively large changes in crime rate trends. The fact that logged variables improved our equations (moving Durbin-Watson values closer to "ideal" levels) lends support to the argument that such an interaction occurs.

Those few investigations of cross-sectional data which include household indicators produce results similar to ours. For example, Roncek (1975) and Choldin and Roncek (1976) report on block-level data for San Diego, Cleveland and Peoria and indicate that the proportion of a block's households which are primary individual households consistently offers the best or nearly the best predictor of a block's crime rate. This relationship persisted after they controlled for numerous social variables, including race, density, age and poverty. Thus the association between household structure and risk of criminal victimization has been observed in individual-level and block-level cross-sectional data, as well as aggregate national time-series data.

Without denying the importance of factors motivating offenders to engage in crime, we have focused specific attention upon violations themselves and the prerequisites for their occurrence. However, the routine activity approach might in the future be applied to the analysis of offenders and their inclinations as well. For example, the structure of primary group activity may affect the likelihood that cultural transmission or social control of criminal inclinations will occur, while the structure of the community may affect the tempo of criminogenic peer group activity. We also may expect that circumstances favorable for carrying out violations contribute to criminal inclinations in the long run by rewarding these inclinations.

We further suggest that the routine activity framework may prove useful in explaining why the criminal justice system, the community and the family have appeared so ineffective in exerting social control since 1960. Substantial increases in the opportunity to carry out predatory violations may have undermined society's mechanisms for social control. For example, it may be difficult for institutions seeking to increase the certainty, celerity and severity of punishment to compete with structural changes resulting in vast increases in the certainty, celerity and value of rewards to be gained from illegal predatory acts.

It is ironic that the very factors which increase the opportunity to enjoy the benefits of life also may increase the opportunity for predatory violations. For example, automobiles provide freedom of movement to offenders as well as average citizens and offer vulnerable targets for theft. College enrollment, female labor force participation, urbanization, suburbanization, vacations and new electronic durables provide various opportunities to escape the confines of the household while they increase the risk of predatory

victimization. Indeed, the opportunity for predatory crime appears to be enmeshed in the opportunity structure for legitimate activities to such an extent that it might be very difficult to root out substantial amounts of crime without modifying much of our way of life. Rather than assuming that predatory crime is simply an indicator of social breakdown, one might take it as a byproduct of freedom and prosperity as they manifest themselves in the routine activities of everyday life.

REFERENCES

Amir, Menachem
1971 Patterns of Forcible Rape. Chicago: University of Chicago Press.

Boggs, Sarah
1965 "Urban crime patterns." American Sociological Review 30:899–905.

Bonger, W. A.
1916 Criminality and Economic Conditions. Boston: Little, Brown.

Bowers, W. J. and Glen L. Pierce
1975 "The illusion of deterrence of Isaac Ehrlich's research on capital punishment." Yale Law Journal 85:187–208.

Brenner, Harvey
1976a Estimating the Social Costs of National Economic Policy: Implications for Mental and Physical Health and Criminal Aggression. Paper no. 5, Joint Economic Committee, Congress of the United States. Washington, D.C.: U.S. Government Printing Office.
1976b Effects of the National Economy on Criminal Aggression II. Final Report to National Institute of Mental Health. Contract #282-76-0355FS.

Bureau of Labor Statistics (BLS)
1975 Handbook of Labor Statistics 1975—Reference Edition. Washington, D.C.: U.S. Government Printing Office.

Cameron, Mary Owen
1964 The Booster and the Snitch. New York: Free Press.

Chambliss, William J.
1972 Boxman: A Professional Thief's Journey. New York: Harper and Row.

Choldin, Harvey M. and Dennis W. Roncek
1976 "Density, population potential and pathology: a block-level analysis." Public Data Use 4:19–30.

Cloward, Richard and Lloyd Ohlin
1960 Delinquency and Opportunity. New York: Free Press.

Cochrane, D., and G. H. Orcutt
1949 "Application of least squares regression to relationships containing autocorrelated error terms." Journal of the American Statistical Association 44:32–61.

Cohen, Lawrence E. and Marcus Felson
1979 "On estimating the social costs of national economic policy: a critical examination of the Brenner study." Social Indicators Research. In press.

Colquhoun, Patrick
1800 Treatise on the Police of the Metropolis. London: Baldwin.

Consumer Reports Buying Guide
1959 Consumer Reports (December). Mt. Vernon: Consumers Union.
1969 Consumer Reports (December). Mt. Vernon: Consumers Union.
1975 Consumer Reports (December). Mt. Vernon: Consumers Union.

Council of Economic Advisors (CEA)
1976 The Economic Report of the President. Washington, D.C.: U.S. Government Printing Office.

Durbin, J.
1970 Testing for serial correlation when least squares regressors are lagged dependent variables." Econometrica 38:410–21.

Durbin, J., and G. S. Watson
1951 "Testing for serial correlation in least squares regression. II." Biometrika 38:159–78.

Durkheim, Emile
1951 Suicide: A Study in Sociology. New York: Free Press.
1966 The Division of Labor in Society. New York: Free Press.

Electrical Merchandising Week
1964 Statistical and Marketing Report (January). New York: Billboard Publications.

Ennis, Philip H.
1967 "Criminal victimization in the U.S.: a report of a national survey, field surveys II." The President's Commission on Law Enforcement and the Administration of Justice. Washington, D.C.: U.S. Government Printing Office.

Federal Bureau of Investigation (FBI)
1975 Crime in the U.S.: Uniform Crime Report. Washington, D.C.: U.S. Government Printing Office.
1976 Crime in the U.S.: Uniform Crime Report. Washington, D.C.: U.S. Government Printing Office.

Ferdinand, Theodore N.
1970 "Demographic shifts and criminality." British Journal of Criminology 10:169–75.

Fleisher, Belton M.
1966 The Economics of Delinquency. Chicago: Quadrangle.

Fox, James A.
1976 An Econometric Analysis of Crime Data. Ph.D. dissertation, Department of Sociology, University of Pennsylvania. Ann Arbor: University Microfilms.

Glaser, Daniel
1971 Social Deviance. Chicago: Markham.

Goldberg, Samuel
1958 Introduction to Difference Equations. New York: Wiley.

Gould, Leroy
1969 "The changing structure of property crime in an affluent society." Social Forces 48:50–9.

Griliches, Z.
1967 "Distributed lags: a survey." Econometrica 35:16–49.

Guerry, A. M.
1833 "Essai sur la statistique morale de la France." Westminister Review 18:357.

Hawley, Amos
1950 Human Ecology: A Theory of Community Structure. New York: Ronald.

Henry, A. F., and J. F. Short
1954 Suicide and Homicide. New York: Free Press.

Hindelang, Michael J.
1976 Criminal Victimization in Eight American Cities: A Descriptive Analysis of Common Theft and Assault. Cambridge: Ballinger.

Hindelang, Michael J., Christopher S. Dunn, Paul Sutton and Alison L. Aumick
1976 Sourcebook of Criminal Justice Statistics—1975. U.S. Dept. of Justice, Law Enforcement Assistance Administration. Washington, D.C.: U.S. Government Printing Office.
1977 Sourcebook of Criminal Justice Statistics—1976. U.S. Dept. of Justice, Law Enforcement Assistance Administration. Washington, D.C.: U.S. Government Printing Office.

Interstate Commerce Commission (ICC)
1974 Annual Report: Freight Commodity Statistics of Class I Motor Carriers of Property Operative in Intercity Service. Washington, D.C.: U.S. Government Printing Office.

Jackson, Bruce
1969 A Thief's Primer. New York: Macmillan.

Jeffery, C. R.
1971 Crime Prevention Through Environmental Design. Beverly Hills: Sage.

Klockars, Carl B.
1974 The Professional Fence. New York: Free Press.

Kobrin, Frances E.
1976 "The primary individual and the family: changes in living arrangements in the U.S. since 1940." Journal of Marriage and the Family 38:233–9.

Land, Kenneth C.
1978 "Modelling macro social change." Paper presented at annual meeting of the American Sociological Association, San Francisco.

Land, Kenneth C. and Marcus Felson
1976 "A general framework for building dynamic macro social indicator models: including an analysis of changes in crime rates and police expenditures." American Journal of Sociology 82:565–604.

Letkemann, Peter
1973 Crime As Work. Englewood Cliffs: Prentice-Hall.

Lystad, Mary
1974 An Annotated Bibliography: Violence at Home. DHEW Publication No. (ADM 75–

136). Washington, D.C.: U.S. Government Printing Office.

Maddala, G. S., and A. S. Rao
1973   "Tests for serial correlation in regression models with lagged dependent variables and serially correlated errors." Econometrica 41:761–74.

Mansfield, Roger, Leroy Gould, and J. Zvi Namenwirth
1974   "A socioeconomic model for the prediction of societal rates of property theft." Social Forces 52:462–72.

Martin, John Bower
1952   My Life in Crime. New York: Harper.

Maurer, David W.
1964   Whiz Mob. New Haven: College and University Press.

Merchandising Week
1973   Statistical and Marketing Report (February). New York: Billboard Publications.
1976   Statistical and Marketing Report (March). New York: Billboard Publications.

National Commission on the Causes and Prevention of Violence
1969   Crimes of Violence. Vol. 13. Washington, D.C.: U.S. Government Printing Office.

Nettler, Gwynn
1974   Explaining Crime. New York: McGraw-Hill.

Newman, Oscar
1973   Defensible Space: Crime Prevention Through Urban Design. New York: Macmillan.

Office of Management and the Budget (OMB)
1973   Social Indicators 1973. Washington, D.C.: U.S. Government Printing Office.

Pope, Carl E.
1977a   Crime-Specific Analysis: The Characteristics of Burglary Incidents. U.S. Dept. of Justice, Law Enforcement Assistance Administration. Analytic Report 10. Washington, D.C.: U.S. Government Printing Office.
1977b   Crime-Specific Analysis: An Empirical Examination of Burglary Offense and Offender Characteristics. U.S. Dept. of Justice, Law Enforcement Assistance Administration. Analytical Report 12. Washington, D.C.: U.S. Government Printing Office.

Quètelet, Adolphe
1842   A Treatise on Man. Edinburgh: Chambers.

Reiss, Albert J.
1976   "Settling the frontiers of a pioneer in American criminology: Henry McKay." Pp. 64–88 in James F. Short, Jr. (ed.), Delinquency, Crime, and Society. Chicago: University of Chicago Press.

Reppetto, Thomas J.
1974   Residential Crime. Cambridge: Ballinger.

Roncek, Dennis
1975   Crime Rates and Residential Densities in Two Large Cities. Ph.D. dissertation, Department of Sociology, University of Illinois, Urbana.

Sagi, Phillip C. and Charles E. Wellford
1968   "Age composition and patterns of change in criminal statistics." Journal of Criminal Law, Criminology and Police Science 59:29–36.

Scarr, Harry A.
1972   Patterns of Burglary. U.S. Dept. of Justice, Law Enforcement Assistance Administration. Washington, D.C.: U.S. Government Printing Office.

Sears Catalogue
1960   Chicago: Sears.
1970   Chicago: Sears.

Shaw, Clifford R., Henry D. McKay, Frederick Zorbaugh and Leonard S. Cottrell
1929   Delinquency Areas. Chicago: University of Chicago Press.

Short, James F., and Fred Strodtbeck
1965   Group Process and Gang Delinquency. Chicago: University of Chicago Press.

Skogan, Wesley G.
1976   "The victims of crime: some material findings." Pp. 131–48 in Anthony L. Guenther (ed.), Criminal Behavior in Social Systems. Chicago: Rand McNally.

Sutherland, Edwin H.
1937   The Professional Thief. Chicago: University of Chicago Press.

Szalai, Alexander (ed.)
1972   The Use of Time: Daily Activities of Urban and Suburban Populations in Twelve Countries. The Hague: Mouton.

Theil, Henri
1971   Principles of Econometrics. New York: Wiley.

Tobias, J. J.
1967   Crime and Industrial Society in the Nineteenth Century. New York: Schocken Books.

U.S. Bureau of the Census (USBC)
1973a   Census of Transportation, 1972. U.S. Summary. Washington, D.C.: U.S. Government Printing Office.
1973b   Who's Home When. Working Paper 37. Washington, D.C.: U.S. Government Printing Office.
1975–   Statistical Abstract of the U.S. Washing-
1976   ton, D.C.: U.S. Government Printing Office.
1947–   Current Population Studies. P-25 Ser.
1976   Washington, D.C.: U.S. Government Printing Office.

U.S. Department of Justice (USDJ)
1974a   Preliminary Report of the Impact Cities, Crime Survey Results. Washington, D.C.: Law Enforcement Assistance Administration (NCJISS).
1974b   Crime in the Nation's Five Largest Cities: Advance Report. Washington, D.C.: Law Enforcement Assistance Administration (NCJISS).
1974c   Crimes and Victims: A Report on the Dayton-San Jose Pilot Survey of Victimization. Washington, D.C.: Law Enforcement Assistance Administration.
1976   Criminal Victimizations in the U.S., 1973. Washington, D.C.: Law Enforcement Assistance Administration (NCJISS).
1977   Criminal Victimizations in the U.S.: A

Comparison of 1974 and 1975 Findings. Washington, D.C.: Law Enforcement Assistance Administration (NCJISS).

Washnis, George J.
1976   Citizen Involvement in Crime Prevention. Lexington: Heath.

Wellford, Charles F.
1973   "Age composition and the increase in recorded crime." Criminology 11:61–70.

Wilks, Judith A.
1967   "Ecological correlates of crime and delinquency." Pp. 138–56 in President's Commission on Law Enforcement and the Administration of Justice Task Force Report: Crime and Its Impact—An Assessment. Appendix A. Washington, D.C.: U.S. Government Printing Office.

Williamson, Henry
1968   Hustler! New York: Doubleday.

Wolfgang, Marvin E.
1958   Patterns of Criminal Homicide. Philadelphia: University of Pennsylvania Press.

Lawrence E. Cohen is Associate Professor of Sociology at the University of Texas at Austin. His most recent articles have appeared in the American Sociological Review, American Journal of Sociology, Social Forces, *and the* Journal of Research in Crime and Delinquency.

26

THE EFFECT OF CRIME ON RESIDENTIAL RENTS AND PROPERTY VALUES

MARIO J. RIZZO

I. Introduction

The central purpose of this investigation is to remedy the defects of the direct estimate approach of the costs of crime to victims.[1] Traditionally, this method has included such costs as (a) the estimated market value of the goods and property stolen or destroyed, (b) the loss of earnings due to personal injury or death, and (c) crime prevention expenditures.[2] There are many inherent defects in these kinds of estimates, several of which are important to mention here. First, the *market* value of property or goods does not measure their *true* value to individuals when the consumer reservation demand price exceeds the market price. Second, the loss of earnings is neither the only nor, perhaps, the major cost involved in personal injury crimes. The price people would have to be paid to submit willingly to crimes against their person would no doubt exceed their lost pecuniary earnings. Third, the empirical identification of crime-avoidance expenditures is not always easy. When, for example, is a taxi ride home crime-related and when is it not? Finally, the fear of crime which usually does not manifest itself in ultimate actual victimization is a true cost. To the extent that people are risk-averse, the expected value of all losses will understate the cost of crime to the individual.

The examination of the impact of crime on rents and property values undertaken here can, in principle, capture all of these costs. The housing market is essentially an implicit market on which people reveal the costs of crime as they themselves perceive them. Consequently, it is thereby possible to obviate the problems inherent in an outside observer attempting to assign costs independently of the behavior of the individuals.

Improvement in the accuracy of crime-cost estimations can have at least two important consequences. We can begin to acquire the data necessary for first, the determination of optimal criminal penalties, as well as, second, the determination of optimal crime prevention expenditures by public agencies. This is, of course, only a beginning, for the issues involved are quite complex. Most importantly, they involve, in the second case, assigning an opportunity cost to the resources used in crime prevention. These resources may have their next best opportunity in the *public* sector and hence their market price will understate the true opportunity costs. Nevertheless, improved information as to the *value* of a given reduction in crime permits more intelligent decision-making in this regard.

II. Regression Analysis

1. The Data Base

The two basic sources of data for this study are the 1970 *Census of Housing* and the Chicago Police Department *Crime Summary Sheet*. The units of observation are the community areas into which Chicago has been divided by the Department of Development and Planning. Each of these communities is an aggregation of census tracts. Tracts, of course, are the largest intra-city unit for which the Census Bureau reports data. However, the Department of Development and Planning has summarized much of these data on a community basis (in the *Chicago Statistical Abstract*), and we have made use of it in the present study.

Unfortunately, crime data are generally not available on any official basis for the community area. The Police Department records reported crime data for 21 police districts in the city.[3] From this, crime rates were constructed by dividing the number of total index plus non-index crimes by the 1970 population in each of the 21 districts and, then, multiplying these ratios by 100,000 in order to yield the absolute number of crimes per 100,000 population. The number of crimes per 100,000 residents was estimated for each of the communities: 1) by assigning the police district value when more than 90 percent of the tracts in the community were in a single district; and 2) when less than 90 percent of its census tracts were in a given police district, the assigned crime figure was a weighted linear combination of those prevailing in the

From Mario J. Rizzo, "The Effect of Crime on Residential Rents and Property Values," 23(1) *The American Economist* 16-21 (Spring 1979). Copyright 1979 by Omicron Delta Epsilon. Reprinted with permission.

various crime districts (where the weights were determined by the proportion of census tracts in each district). The actual crime rate used in the regressions, however, was a three-year average (1969-71) of the rates so computed.[4]

2. *Ordinary Least Squares Results*

The empirical estimations consisted of an analysis of 71 communities in the city of Chicago. The rent or property value observations for these communities were regressed on measures of the characteristics of the housing as well as crime and non-crime environmental variables. The following non-crime variables were entered into the estimating equations:

LMNR   = log of median number of rooms
LNEW60 = log of proportion of housing built since 1960
WHPRO = proportion of whites in population
DISCBD = distance from central business district in miles
NSD   = North-South dummy: if community is north of Loop, assign 1
LD   = Lake dummy: if community borders Lake Michigan, assign 1
PUB   = proportion of total housing units which are public housing
LINC   = log of median family income for 1969

The median number of rooms (LMNR) and the proportion of housing constructed after 1960 (LNEW60) are both obviously characteristics which, *ceteris paribus*, will raise rents and property values. Income (LINC) is interpreted as a proxy for the quality elements which we have not captured in our other variables. It is especially important to take into account adequately the quality aspect because one might make a plausible case that high crime communities (also low-income areas) are low housing quality communities, and hence what *appears* to be the effect of crime on rents (and property values) is, in large part, the effect of low quality.

Distance from the central business district (DISCBD), the proportion of whites (WHPRO), the North-South dummy (NSD), the contiguity-to-Lake Michigan dummy (LD), and the proportion of public housing (PUB) can all be viewed as environmental factors which affect the quantity of housing services which can be produced with given land and capital. In other words, these variables affect the amount of housing services which are embodied in a certain *physically* specified quantity of housing. Hence, they will affect the price of an observed unit of housing. As a consequence, these factors must be held constant to isolate the effect of crime.

The natural log of rents or owner-estimated property values was regressed against the above quality characteristics of the housing, the non-crime environmental variables, and crime.[5] The crime variable was entered in logarithmic form. The log transformation of the crime variable is particularly important. On the assumption of equal percentage rates of underreporting in the crime statistics for the various communities (rather than equal *absolute* amounts of underreporting—a plausible a priori assumption), the log transformation was deemed beneficial.[6] This is because with equal percentage underreporting, the absolute differences among crime totals in the various communities are understated by the measured statistics as compared to the absolute differences among the *true* crime totals. By concerning ourselves only with percentage differences, we obviate this difficulty.

a) *Without Income*

1) *Rents.* Turning to equation (1) in Table 1, we ought first to pay some brief attention to the non-crime variables. Here there are a number of interesting results.

The public housing variable (PUB)—the proportion of public housing—has the expected impact in reducing rents both because of the subsidy effect on rents and the possible disamenity effect on the neighborhood.

The effect of an increase in the proportion of whites (WHPRO) is to *lower* rather than raise rents. The negative coefficient of WHPRO is consistent with the results found in many other studies.[7] This is normally interpreted as a discrimination effect: landlords will only rent to blacks at a premium.

The positive coefficient of the North-South dummy variable (NSD) indicates that we have still not captured all of the factors which make rents on the North Side of Chicago higher than on the South. Proximity to entertainment, shopping areas, etc., may play some role.

Two puzzling results are the relatively weak (low *t* values) coefficient for the proximity-to-the-lake dummy (LD) and the distance from State and Madison (DISCBD). Furthermore, the coefficient

TABLE 1: Chicago OLS Results

Independent Variables	Dependent Variables			
	LRENT (1)	LVAL (2)	LRENT (3)	LVAL (4)
C	6.51	11.06	1.02	1.31
LMNR	0.59 (2.34)	0.55 (2.45)	0.20 (0.78)	0.15 (0.66)*
LNEW60	0.12 (4.42)	0.11 (4.47)	0.09 (3.48)	0.08 (3.48)
WHPRO	−0.39 (5.36)	−0.13 (2.06)	−.051 (6.73)	−0.25 (3.91)
DISCBD	−0.008 (0.91)	0.007 (0.88)	−0.01 (1.26)	0.004 (0.66)
NSD	0.22 (5.21)	0.28 (7.31)	0.20 (4.86)	0.25 (7.24)
LD	0.08 (1.28)	0.07 (1.24)	0.04 (0.78)	0.03 (0.66)
PUB	−0.87 (4.82)	−0.22 (1.35)	−0.49 (2.44)	0.18 (1.03)
LINC			0.57 (3.42)	0.60 (4.14)
LTOT3	−0.24 (3.35)	−0.20 (3.20)	−0.15 (2.09)	−0.11 (1.70)
R^2	0.67	0.77	0.73	0.82
n	71	71	71	71

NOTE. The numbers in parentheses are the absolute values of the *t* statistics.

of the latter variable—even if statistically significant—is small. The low *t* values for LD and DISCBD in Table 1 is doubtless at least in part due to the 0.55 simple correlation coefficient which exists between LMNR and LD, as well as between LMNR and DISCBD.

LNEW60 is a quality proxy which behaves in the expected fashion: the greater the proportion of new structures in an area, the higher are rents (and property values). An additional aspect of this is that the existence of new structures may also raise the rents in old ones by conferring an external benefit.

Finally, examination of equation (1) reveals an elasticity of our overall crime measure (LTOT3) with respect to rents of −0.24. This is significant at the .01 level. It should be noted, before continuing, that LTOT3 is an unweighted measure which consists of the total of both non-index and index crimes.

2) *Property Values*. The property value data are for owner-occupied houses or buildings, the market value of which is estimated by the owner. Since only owner-occupied houses are covered, there is a much smaller degree of overlap with the units considered in the rent data than might otherwise be the case. Furthermore, it is important for any estimate of the dollar cost of crime based on our results to know to what extent owner-estimates deviate from true market values. The only study on this matter of which we are aware lends support to the belief that *averages* of owner-estimated values are not far off the mark. Kish and Lansing have found that for 568 homes the mean of the respondents' (home owners) estimates is only $350 higher than the mean of $9,200 for the professional appraisers' estimates.[8] An implication of this study is that since errors on an individual basis are frequently quite large, increasing the level of aggregation will decrease the divergence of the average owner-estimate from the professional appraisers' estimate (the market value proxy).

A comparison of columns (1) and (2) in Table 1 will show that the crime coefficients are whether property values or rents are the dependent variables case.

b. *With Income*

Regressions (1) and (2) in Table 1 were re-estimated with the natural log of median family income (LINC) included as an independent variable because the equation without income lacked any measure of the quality of the housing unit except LNEW60 and LMNR. Income, it was felt, would act as a proxy variable for the quality elements we have not captured. However, the introduction of LINC as a regressor creates serious multicollinearity problems; of special importance is the high negative (simple) correlation between our measures of crime and income (e.g., −0.80 between LTOT3 and LINC). The coefficients of the crime variables remain unbiased, of course, but their reliability decreases and it may become impossible to separate out the effect of crime from the effect of income.

Returning to Table 1, we find that the coefficients of the income variable are highly significant and of the expected positive sign. It is quite interesting to note that in equation (3) the coefficient of LTOT3 is (despite the collinearity problem) still significant at the .05 level with the usual negative sign. Expectedly, the coefficient has fallen in magnitude from −0.24 to −0.15. A plausible explanation of this fall is that it represents, at least in part, the degree to which low quality has been confounded with high crime in its effect on rents. A glance at Table 1 will show that the effect on the property value equations arising out of the introduction of LINC very closely parallels its effect on the rent equations.

3. Two-Stage Least Squares Results

The TSLS regression technique was employed because of considerations of a two-way "causal" relationship existing between crime and property values (and, of course, rents). There are several ways of generating this. First, high property values may attract crime because they serve as a proxy for the "take" available to, say, burglars. Second, it may be plausible to assume that high property values serve also as a proxy for high opportunity costs of crime (i.e., high-paying legitimate opportunities). This effect, on the other hand, would reduce the supply of offenses.

Finally, the greater the value of what is to be protected, the greater will be the quantity of self-protection employed. Property values can be viewed as a proxy for both the human and non-human capital placed at risk by the threat of crime. This also has a negative impact on the supply of offenses.

The procedure is to purge the crime variable of its dependence on property values (and rents) or, more exactly, of its correlation with the disturbance term in the equation. Specifically, we regressed the endogenous crime variable (LTOT3) on the predetermined variables in the system[9] in order to generate the purged variable LTOT3 with which we then re-estimated the original equation.

Turning our attention to the rent equations (without income) in Table 2, we see that the magnitude of the crime coefficient has changed considerably from the OLS results. This coefficient has nearly doubled in size, lending support to the position that the simultaneity problem was, indeed, significant. Furthermore, there was a substantial rise in the ratio of the estimated coefficient to the asymptotically unbiased (i.e., consistent) estimated standard error.

The effect described is even more pronounced in the property value (without income) equation. Here, the coefficient more than doubles and is significant at the .01 level.

Next, we estimated the second-stage rent regression equations with income (LINC) as an

TABLE 2: Chicago TSLS Results

Independent Variables	Dependent Variables			
	LRENT (1)	LVAL (2)	LRENT (3)	LVAL (4)
C	8.29	13.52	1.45	7.40
LMNR	0.48	0.41	0.20	0.16
	(1.80)	(1.60)	(0.78)	(0.68)
LNEW60	0.10	0.08	0.09	0.07
	(3.43)	(2.99)	(3.38)	(3.11)
WHPRO	−0.50	−0.29	−.052	−0.30
	(5.08)	(3.06)	(5.91)	(3.85)
DISCBD	−0.01	0.002	−0.01	0.003
	(1.20)	(0.27)	(1.27)	(0.42)
NSD	0.20	0.26	0.19	0.25
	(4.40)	(5.78)	(4.76)	(6.47)
LD	0.11	0.12	0.05	0.06
	(1.70)	(1.84)	(0.79)	(1.07)
PUB	−0.84	−0.18	−0.50	0.12
	(4.45)	(1.01)	(2.40)	(0.67)
LINC			0.55	0.49
			(2.78)	(2.79)
LTOT3	−0.41	−0.45	−0.17	−0.23
	(3.33)	(3.78)	(1.24)	(1.86)

NOTE: The numbers in parentheses are the absolute values of the ratio of the estimated coefficient to the asymptotic standard error.

independent variable. The reason for including income is the same as in the OLS case. However, the problem of collinearity is substantially worse. Here the simple correlation coefficient between LINC and LTOT3 (the fitted crime variable) is almost −0.90 as compared to −0.80 between LINC and LTOT3.

As is evident from a comparison of the rent equation, the introduction of income very substantially reduces the magnitude of the crime coefficient. More importantly, however, the level of significance falls considerably. Yet, the results are still very highly suggestive and in the expected direction.

The result of the property value equation is more "generous." Here again the coefficient drops substantially in magnitude but the significance level is higher.

III. The Cost of Crime to Victims

In the course of this section, we shall complete the analysis of the previous two by deriving from our regression coefficients some rough measures of the cost that crime imposes upon its victims and potential victims. This measure of cost will be an individualistic one, i.e., dependent upon the evaluations of individuals revealed through the housing market, rather than on "society's" evaluation of the harm done to particular people.

We have calculated crime costs by comparing the difference between the predicted value of property (or rents) at the mean crime rate and at a rate which is one-half of the mean.[10] The difference between the two property values answers the following question: If the crime rate in the city of Chicago were to fall from a level of 7,331 crimes per 100,000 to 3,604 per 100,000, what would be the savings in crime costs; or to put it in an equivalent way, what is the incremental cost of a rise in crime from one-half the (current) mean to the mean? This is the question we shall attempt to answer subject to the limitations of our methods of analysis. It is important to understand that we chose to ask this question rather than the more daring one: What is the cost of the total amount of existing crime? This is because of the large errors inherent in extrapolating a regression estimate beyond the range of any observations in the sample (3,604 crimes per 100,000 is the lowest crime level for any community in our sample).

In Table 3 we have presented four alternative measures of the partial cost of crime (index plus non-index) for Chicago — a different one for each method of estimation used. The TSLS results are perhaps the more reliable as they take account of the simultaneity issue discussed in the previous section. The range over the whole table is between $147 million and $509 million per year, with the more probable range being the narrower $211 million to $509 million.

In Table 4 these data are presented on five different bases including the per capita cost of crime and the average cost per crime. The former might reasonably be interpreted as the expected value of losses (directly or indirectly) through crime for the typical individual, and the latter as expected value of losses *given* victimization. Crime costs as a proportion of the rental or capital value of the unit (third and fourth categories) are also tabulated and represent some additional costs of

TABLE 3: Partial Yearly Cost of Crime in Chicago

Method	Rents (millions of dollars)	Property Values* (millions of dollars)	Total (millions of dollars)
OLS (without income)	174.67	77.97 (1,146.6)	252.64
OLS (with income)	105.61	41.45 (609.59)	147.06
TSLS (without income)	317.53	192.35 (2,828.79)	509.85
TSLS (with income)	120.63	90.65 (1,333.09)	211.28

* The first figures is a flow yearly estimate based on a conservative rate of interest: .068 — the rate prevailing on two- to seven-year government securities in 1969. The figures in parentheses are the total capital value impact. All of the entries are the per housing unit cost multiplied by the number of units.

TABLE 4: Chicago Crime Cost Summary Statistics

Basis	Method			
	OLS (without income)	OLS (with income)	TSLS (without income)	TSLS (with income)
Per Capita	$ 78	$ 46	$158	$ 66
Per Housing Unit	$238	$139	$480	$199
Cost per Renter Unit Mean Rent per Year	.198	.119	.360	.136
Cost per Owner Unit Mean Property Value*	.147	.078	.364	.171
Cost Crimes**	$1,755	$1,022	$3,542	$1,468

* Both the numerator and denominator are in capital value terms.
** The partial crime costs of Table 3 are divided by one-half the total number of crimes since it is the cost of the latter which is being measured.

living in a particular unit as a percentage of the direct outlays.

In conclusion, let us summarize briefly what has been shown by our estimates. We have measured the direct and indirect costs of crime as revealed by differential residential property values and rents. Since none of the observations in our samples has a zero crime rate, we have only extrapolated our results to crime rates within the range of the samples. Our results are therefore *partial* crime costs and not total crime costs.

Notes

1. A more complete version (both theoretically and empirically) of these results appears in *The Journal of Legal Studies*, January, 1979.
2. U.S. President's Commission on Law Enforcement and Administration of Justice, *Crime and Its Impact   An Assessment*, Task Force Reports (Washington D.C.: Government Printing Office, 1967), p. 44.
3. Crimes are also reported on a beat basis but the unit of observation is not geographically constant. A "beat" may change up to four times per year depending on the changes in police power deemed necessary in an area. A "beat" is actually a unit of police input, so if the crime rate rises in a given "beat" it may then become, say, two "beats." Hence the "beat" is generally an unreliable unit of observation for our purposes.
4. We have used three-year averages because we are interested in permanent, not transitory, crime rates. The Loop and the Near North Side were omitted from this study because of heavy daily transient populations. For the Near South Side (as well as the Loop) there were no available property value date from the *Census of Housing*, so it was omitted. Hyde Park and Kenwood were omitted because their

outlying position in a scatter of property values on crime indicated the presence of special factors. These communities were studied separately in Mario J. Rizzo, "The Cost of Crime to Victims: An Empirical Analysis," *Journal of Legal Studies*, January 1979.
5. It should be noted that lot size proxies were dropped from the property value equations in this chapter because their coefficients were insignificant and their impact on any of the other independent variables was virtually zero.
6. See I. Ehrlich, "Participation in Illegitimate Activities," *Journal of Political Economy*, 81 (May June 1973), p. 561.
7. See, for example, T. King and P. Mieszkowski, "Racial Discrimination, Segregation, and the Price of Housing," *Journal of Political Economy*, 81 (May June 1973), pp. 590 606, and J. Kain and J. Quigley, *Housing Markets and Racial Discrimination: A Microscopic Analysis* (New York: Columbia University Press for the National Bureau of Economic Research, 1975), Chapter 8.
8. L. Kish and J. Lansing, "Response Errors in Estimating the Value of Homes," *Journal of the American Statistical Association*, 49 (1954), pp. 520 32.
9. The predetermined variables are those included in this study LMNR, LNEW60, WHPRO, DISCBD, NSD, LD, PUB, LINC as well as those examined by Ehrlich the proportion of population between ages 15 and 24, median years of schooling, unemployment rate, population density, proportion of population receiving welfare, ratio of males to females, and the labor force participation rate. On exactly how the latter variables affect crime, see Ehrlich, "Participation in Illegitimate Activities."
10. Since we have estimated the equations in logarithmic form, the mean referred to here is the mean of the log of crime (not the log of the mean). This is simply the geometric mean of the crime rates in their natural form.

Mario J. Rizzo, Assistant Professor of Economics at New York University, received his Ph.D. from the University of Chicago and has been a postdoctoral fellow in law and economics, as well as in Austrian economics, at New York University. He has published articles in such journals as American Economist *and* Journal of Legal Studies *and has contributed to such volumes as* Assessing the Criminal: Restitutions, Retribution, and the Legal Process *and* New Directions in Austrian Economics. *Professor Rizzo's research interests are in the areas of economic theory, industrial organization, and the economic analysis of law.*

27

CRIME CONTROL AS ENERGY POLICY

STEVEN BALKIN

The effectiveness of energy conservation and the expansion of energy supplies depend on law enforcement. The author considers the energy problem in the United States from a crime-control perspective and suggests policies that would reduce energy demand and increase energy supply.

Through their effect on American lifestyles, crime and fear of crime have contributed to excess use of energy in the United States. In addition, energy conservation laws are often not as effective as they could be because of inadequate enforcement. Too strict regulation of energy supplies may, in some cases, constrain domestic energy supplies. I suggest here several approaches to crime control that could reduce the severity of the American energy problem.

REDUCING ENERGY CONSUMPTION
Transportation

Mass Transit—The lack of public confidence in the safety of mass transit encourages use of the private automobile. Crime and fear of crime associated with mass transit could, and to some extent have been, reduced by

- greater (and well-advertised) penalties for offenses committed on transit lines;
- more police patrol of transit stops and stations;
- large rewards for witnesses to offenses;
- prominent placement of television surveillance devices;
- readily accessible emergency phones;

From Steven Balkin, "Crime Control as Energy Policy." © 1978 by The Regents of the University of California. Reprinted from POLICY ANALYSIS, Vol. 5, No. 1, pp. 119-122, by permission of The Regents.

- clean, well-lit vehicles, stops, and stations;
- design of stops and stations so that stairways, corridors, platforms, and transit vehicles are more visible to the outside public;
- placement of stops only near centers of population activity;
- encouragement of considerate behavior on the part of passengers and transit personnel;
- prohibiting passengers from sitting in empty vehicles.

Underutilized mass transit lines and routes are energy inefficient and provoke high fear of crime. Since there is (perceived) safety in numbers, policies to increase the number of mass transit passengers, especially at off-peak hours, could themselves deter crime and reduce fear of crime. The staggering of work hours would distribute ridership more evenly across the day, creating a greater sense of safety, as well as making mass transit more energy-efficient. This policy may be hard to implement, however, since fear of crime at present off-peak hours is one reason why people are reluctant to switch from the usual day-shift. If workers, en masse, could be induced to stagger work shifts, the greater perceived safety resulting from more people using mass transit at off-peak hours would make the switch less undesirable. Underutilized mass transit service could be eliminated and/or partially served by rerouting. The greatest effort to reduce crime on mass transit should focus on those lines and routes with the highest degree of present use and the greatest likelihood of higher use in future.

Bicycles—Reducing the hazards involved in bicycle riding could make the bicycle a more attractive alternative transportation mode. Stronger enforcement of traffic laws affecting both automobiles and bicycles, inexpensive bicycle parking lots—patrolled to reduce theft —and increased emphasis on punishment for offenses committed against bicycle riders are policies relevant to this aim.

Hitchhiking—At present, as a crime prevention measure, many areas prohibit hitchhiking. If hitchhiking were well regulated, it could become an energy-saving alternative to other forms of transportation. Public, patrolled hitchhiking stops could be placed along major transportation routes. Every hitchhiker could have a hitchhiking identity card and number. Persons with criminal backgrounds could be denied such cards. At every hitchhiking stop the ride interaction could be noted by recording the license plate of the driver and the hitchhiker's number. If an offense occurred, the offender could be easily identified, which would increase the certainty of punishment for crimes associated with hitchhiking and thus significantly reduce the dangers of hitchhiking.

Compact Cars—Use of smaller, energy-efficient automobiles could be more easily encouraged if there were less likelihood of fatal impacts in collisions involving smaller automobiles. The frequency and seriousness of automobile accidents could be reduced by vigorous enforcement of traffic laws, especially against trucks and buses, and perhaps by restricting large-sized autos to certain streets, highways, or lanes. Increasing the safety of automobile use might also increase the use of automobiles, but if smaller cars were used this policy might not increase energy use even if people drove more.

Housing

Encouraging people to switch from single-family dwellings to energy-efficient high-rise apartment buildings could be accomplished by reducing the fear of crime associated with high-rise living. Crime-control measures could include twenty-four-hour doormen and elevator operators; use of transparent rather than opaque materials in lobbies, elevators, and stairwells; assigning individual tenants parcels of land adjacent to the building for gardening or other recreational purposes to encourage surveillance and protection of these outside areas; and establishing tenant associations to encourage acquaintanceship among neighbors so that strangers could be more easily distinguished and suspicious events reported.

Energy-Use Laws

Stricter enforcement of laws relating to energy use would further the cause of energy conservation. The 55 mile-per-hour speed limit is a notable example of an energy conservation law that tends not to be followed unless enforcement is emphasized. Higher fines for violation of the speed limit could be imposed that reflect the waste of energy caused by speeding. States could be denied revenue-sharing funds if enforcement of the 55 mile-per-hour limit were not above a certain level. Housing code violations, misreporting of tax deductions for energy conservation expenses, and meter tampering are other examples of crimes that waste energy and should be more strongly discouraged.

INCREASING ENERGY SUPPLY

Stricter enforcement of security and safety regulations at nuclear power plants would help reduce the threat of nuclear theft and nuclear accidents. If these threats were greatly diminished, there might be less resistance to the development of nuclear power sources. Stricter application of antitrust laws to the oil industry would reduce purposeful withholding of energy supplies and the manipulation of relative prices and quantities of different energy sources.

An argument can be made that in some instances weaker law enforcement would expand energy supplies. If government-regulated energy prices induce shortages by discouraging exploration, and if prohibitions on the use of high-sulfur fuel remove an abundant and inexpensive energy source, then allowing more "crime" in these areas would expand energy supplies. However, allowing more violations of these regulations might produce more income inequality, more white-collar criminals, and a dirtier environment.

CONCLUSION

There are many interconnections between crime-control policy and the energy "crisis" in the United States. Some of the policies suggested here might cause the retargeting of criminal activity— from transit stations to automobile parking lots, for instance. From a strict crime-reduction standpoint, the general incidence of criminal activity might not be diminished; from an energy conservation standpoint, however, certain types of displacement of criminal activity may be desirable. Crime control strategies should also consider the monetary, energy, and freedom costs of enforcement to ensure that they are not greater than the benefit of energy savings or supply expansion.

Steven Balkin is Assistant Professor of Criminal Justice at the University of Illinois at Chicago Circle. He has written a number of articles on victimization, deterrence, and crime control. His current research concerns alternative sentencing and environmental criminology.

Part V:

VICTIMS

Black's Law Dictionary contains no entry for "victims," and the term is not found frequently in the various indexes to the criminal law literature or jurisprudential writings generally. The omission may reflect a certain terminological conservatism quite common in law. In its original sense, "victims" were the persons or animals killed in religious sacrifices, and those using legal language may wish to avoid confusion. Beyond that, however, one must recognize that the law does not assign any starring parts to victims as such.

In civil procedure, plaintiffs get top billing, but it is a long way from being a crime victim to being a plaintiff. In the penal law, the victim does not even get a speaking part because "the legal order providing punishment as a sanction does not recognize as decisive the interest of the private individual directly violated by the delict."[1] The offended party is *The People*; and a person or persons who suffer some actual harm, loss, or injury are simply part of the *corpus delicti*—the "body"—of the crime. Historians of the role of the victim tread on uncertain ground when they suggest that archaic law was "the golden age of the victim."[2] There is little reason to suppose that *Wergeld* or its equivalents were intended, or functioned, as victim compensation as we might understand it. Instead, they were simply tokens of appeasement and they bought freedom from retribution. What seemed to matter most in the past, as it does today, was not that someone bled, hurt, or sustained a loss as the result of a transgression, but that an act took place that offended a legal norm. The king may have established his peace on the highways, but he never undertook to guarantee those who traveled on them their safety, even to the extent to which hosts and innkeepers were held accountable for the safety of their guests.

Victims have not fared much better in criminology than they have in criminal law. Serious efforts to study victims of crime began with the appearance of Hans von Hentig's *The Criminal and His Victim*[3] in 1948. These efforts have been increasing ever since. We think one can say that this new work is founded on two propositions that do not so much change the inherited meaning of crime as they bring into the open some vaguely appreciated implications that were always known, but neglected. The first is that crime is not merely an act but also an effect. As there is a person who does it, so there is a person who suffers it. Corresponding, for every assault there is an injury; and for every theft there is a loss. To be sure, not all the effects of criminal acts can be brought to account through studying the victim, but a great many can. Moreover, even with the flurry of recent studies, we still have only the most sketchy knowledge of the identities of the victims of criminal acts and the effects of crime upon them.

The second proposition upon which much current work on victims is based is that victims are not simply passive targets of criminal acts, but conscious, often actively participating, and sometimes contributing actors in highly complex events. Those events cannot be fully understood and explained without detailed knowledge of the characters and roles of victims. This matter obviously touches questions of legal responsibility. Theoretically, the criminal process knows only guilt or innocence and by implication, at least, a victim is an innocent victim. But we all know that in practice judges and juries are capable of perceiving flaws in victims and taking these into account in formulating verdicts.[4] Conversely, it is well known that some persons find it very difficult to establish themselves as *bona fide* victims in the eyes of the law.

For the most part, victims of crime suffer only neglect by legal functionaries. Sometimes, however, the state imposes certain expenses and indignities upon victims as it pursues, prosecutes, and punishes criminals. That society not only refuses to lend the strong arm of the law in aiding victims toward restitution but that it appears to act in ways that compound their losses and injuries is the main point of the angry and pessimistic review of the role of the crime victim in the United States by William McDonald. Though his view of the past is perhaps somewhat tinged by nostalgia, he is no doubt correct in emphasizing that the bureaucratized criminal process we known today often enough adds to the harms caused by the crime. One theme that is implicit throughout his article is that we have not yet worked out conceptions of rights of victims, and procedures to safeguard them, in a manner analogous to the way this has been accomplished on behalf of defendants. Obviously, the past will not be a lesson in this; it is not likely that predators will ever again be indentured to their victims to expiate their misdeeds.

The most actively pursued innovation points toward some manner of distributing losses resulting from crime. This takes the form of money indemnification paid to certain victims. In addition to the direct remedial effect these measures have, they are also expected to be of some help in increasing the effectiveness of the state's response to crime.[5] Victims who stand to gain from the successful prosecution of offenders will presumably be more likely to participate actively in the criminal process than they do now, thereby increasing the likelihood of convictions. Silverman and Doerner show, on the basis of Canadian data, that the intended effect is not in evidence, at least so far. It may well be, they say, that the small amounts of money involved and the cumbersome procedures instituted to release them discourage many victims. Moreover, it is likely, they add, that the availability of money compensation is not known to all the people who could be eligible for it.[6]

An altogether different victim right is identified by Ruben Castillo and his coworkers. They review a series of appellate court decisions which appear to have created a right not to be made a victim of a crime in certain settings, and a corresponding duty to afford protection and to pay damages when protection is inadequate. This appears to be the situation of common carriers now. It remains to be seen whether the determination resulting from the legal relationship between passenger and carrier can be generalized to other settings. Further, it remains to be seen whether the creation of an effective social responsibility toward victims might lead to the devising of new anticrime measures.

The problem of victims' rights is approached from yet another perspective by Nancy Wolfe. She reviews some factual materials bearing on the question of whether a defendant charged with homicide can advance having been a victim as a defense against the charge. The problems of self-defense of the particular victims of concern to Wolfe—battered wives—are distinguishable from the problems facing other persons accused of homicide in ways that the author makes clear. Wolfe does not present a legal analysis of these differences, but rather what might be called a factfinder's appreciation of them. And she identifies an effort on the part of some members of the bar to create law that would take account of the special characteristics of this class of victims. In trying to assess with what degree of malice, if any, a woman has slain the spouse who has tormented her, one must obviously take into account the special vulnerability of wives to being victimized by husbands within the modern household. It would take a quite extraordinary misogynist to settle the matter of guilt in these cases by holding that if women did not marry assaultive husbands, there would be no battered wives. Once one takes the step of trying to find even a part of the explanation for a crime in the victim, one is moved to a position from which it is difficult to hold the offender totally accountable. Further, outside the legal framework, if the nature of the prey explains some part of the act of the predator, then we ought to study it.

Hindelang, Gottfredson, and Garofalo are represented by a chapter from their major work on personal victimization. In that work, they present the results of massive studies of victims of certain crimes involving direct personal contact (e.g., robbery, assault, and rape); in the chapter included here, they outline a theory to account for personal victimization. The theory, emphasizing how "lifestyles" associated with different demographic characteristics expose persons differentially to criminal depredation, strikes us as both highly plausible and one that is likely to be fruitful in encouraging further thought and theorizing about the links between personal situations and public troubles. The final article in this section is based on the same data as the preceding one, and it extends the study of victims to one of the possible consequences of victimization, namely, increased fear of crime. Garofalo indicates that, although there does *not* appear to be a significant effect of the experience of victimization on the professed fear of crime, the data suggest that fear of crime may reduce exposure to victimization on the professed fear of crime, the data suggest that fear of crime may reduce exposure to victimization risk.[7]

The study of victims and the collection and analysis of materials drawn from surveys involving victims and potential victims is, perhaps, the most rapidly growing part of criminology. The publications we have collected deal, for the most part, with the victim's experiences, contributions to the criminal justice process, possibly developing rights, and vulnerability to crime. Little attention as yet (so far as we know) has been paid to the justifications for, or structural sources of, the legal situation of crime victims. These matters have mainly been treated in passing and deplored, as by McDonald, or an effort is made to document changes, as by Castillo and Wolfe. One part of the next stage of victimization studies hopefully will focus more directly on such questions, including clarifying victim's rights in the past and why they assumed the negligible role they apparently have.

Before closing these introductory remarks, we would like to mention one use to which data on victims is being put that is not represented among the articles we have collected, namely, its use in extending understanding of the incidence of crime and the characteristics of criminals. When data on victims were first collected, a major interest was to learn more about the incidence of crime. It was quickly and usefully learned that the "dark numbers" were high overall, different for different categories of crime, and that they bore no constant relation between jurisdictions to officially reported numbers. Criminologists seem to have quickly digested this information. Now, equally usefully, more detailed analyses are suggesting that even though all this is the case, the characteristics of offenders as seen through official numbers may not be strikingly different than the characteristics revealed by victimization data.[8] Of course, victims can only report on those who commit personal crime, and there is no reason to suppose that victims are totally unbiased sources of information. Still, the implications of these findings, if they withstand further scrutiny and interpretation, are potentially profound for what they tell us about both crime and criminal justice in the United States.

NOTES

1. Hans Kelsen, *General Theory of Law and State*. New York: Russell & Russell, 1961, p. 206.

2. Stephen Schafer, *The Victim and His Criminal*. New York: Random House, 1968, pp. 7ff.

3. Hans von Hentig, *The Criminal and His Victim*. Hew Haven, CT: Yale University Press, 1948.

4. What we all know is beginning to be documented systematically. For example, see Eugene Borgida and Phyllis White, "Social Perception of Rape Victims: The Impact of Legal Reform," 2(4) *Law and Human Behavior* 339-351 (1978). They found "jurors' close scrutiny of the victim's credibility and moral character was directly related to the conviction rate."

5. Victim assistance programs of all sorts should surely be studied to gauge the extent to which assistance to prosecutors comes to dominate assistance to victims.

6. One of the more enduring mysteries of many evaluations is whether the "experimental treatment" is ever or frequently delivered; this is one example of this problem. Another problem with the Silverman and Doerner data is that increases in the numbers of violent crimes may have

overwhelmed the short-run capacity of the justice system to deal with them. If this is so, then the programs they evaluated may be having the desired effect in some measure difficult to know with their dependent variable of conviction rates.

7. Garafalo speculates that victims may have lower rates because they adapt to fear of crime by reducing exposure. This is similar to Cook's idea, expressed in an article in the next section, that clearance rates may be lowered by criminals' shifts of crime styles in response to increases in criminal justice system effectiveness. Both ideas happily take the actors in criminal situations to be something other than passive pawns of forces totally beyond their control.

8. See, for example, Michael J. Hindelang, "Race and Involvement in Common Law Personal Crimes," 43(1) *American Sociological Review* 93-109 (1978).

28

THE ROLE OF THE VICTIM IN AMERICA
WILLIAM F. McDONALD

Before the American Revolution, criminals were required to pay back their victims. All defendants convicted of larceny, for example, were required to pay treble damages. If they could not pay, they were given to their victims in servitude for a length of time equal to the amount owed. If the victim preferred, he could sell the defendant. In 1769, a Massachusetts court sentenced defendant Powell to be sold for four years; in 1772, defendant Polydone to be sold for six months; and in 1773, defendant Smith to be sold for fourteen years. Victims who chose to sell their criminals rather than take them as servants were allowed one month in which to find a buyer. After that they had to pay for the criminal's maintenance in jail or the criminal would be released.[1]

The conception of crime in colonial America was very different than it is today. While criminal prosecutions were brought in the name of the state, they were in effect private prosecutions in which the state usually did not play an active role and did not have a vested interest. Crime was conceived of primarily as an injury to the individual victim, not an attack against society.[2] Today, the situation is reversed. Crime is regarded as an offense against the state. The damage to the individual victim is incidental and its redress is no longer regarded as a function of the criminal justice process. The victim is told that if he wants to recover his losses he should hire a lawyer and

1. William F. McDonald, "Towards a Bicentennial Revolution in Criminal Justice," *American Criminal Law Review* 13 (1976):649–73.

2. W. Nelson, "Emerging Notions of Modern Criminal Law in the Revolutionary Era: An Historical Perspective," in *Criminal Justice in America*, ed. Richard Quinney (Boston: Little, Brown and Co., 1974).

From William F. McDonald, "The Role of the Victim in America," pp. 295-307. Reprinted with permission from ASSESSING THE CRIMINAL: RESTITUTION, RETRIBUTION, AND THE LEGAL PROCESS, Copyright 1977, Ballinger Publishing Company.

sue in civil court. The criminal justice system is not for his benefit but for the community's. Its purposes are to deter crime, rehabilitate criminals, punish criminals, and do justice, but not to restore victims to their wholeness or to vindicate them.

One of the tremendous ironies in the development of the American criminal justice system lies in the changed status of the victim. He once was the central actor in the system and stood to benefit both financially and psychologically from it. Today, he is seen at best as the "forgotten man" of the system and at worst as being twice victimized, the second time by the system itself. The history of concern about criminal justice in this country has reversed. Enormous efforts are made on behalf of criminals. Vast sums have been spent in genuine efforts to humanize punishments, develop rehabilitative techniques, provide indigent persons with legal counsel, and to give all persons ample opportunity to challenge the state's case against them. However, in contrast, there has been little concern for the rights or treatment of victims or the proper role of victims in the administration of justice.

Unlike the criminal, the victim was better off before the Revolution than he is today. In colonial times, police departments and public prosecutors' offices did not exist as they are known today. The victim of crime was on his own. In the cities a victim could call for help from the nightwatchmen, but he was unlikely to do so. The nightwatch was only on duty during certain hours of the night and was composed of decrepid or dishonest old men. The watchmen might be persuaded to chase a fleeing criminal for a few blocks, but once he had gotten away the watchman's duty ended. The victim had to do his own detective work himself or hire someone to do it. If he sought the assistance of the sheriff, he was charged a fee. In Boston, one dollar bought twelve hours of "sheriff's aid in criminal cases." Once the criminal was located, there was an additional fee to the victim of thirty cents for service of criminal warrants.[3] It was not easy to get the sheriff interested in pursuing criminals—even if the victim were wealthy enough to afford these fees. The sheriff's fees for serving civil process were far more lucrative and less dangerous. Thus, the wealthier victims hired private detectives or posted rewards.

When the criminal was finally arrested, the victim's role was not over. He paid an attorney to draw up the indictment, and the victim either prosecuted the case himself or hired an attorney to prosecute it for him. For his efforts the victim reaped certain benefits. There

---

3. See, generally, Roger Lane, *Policing the City—Boston: 1822–1885* (Cambridge, Mass.: Harvard University Press, 1967).

was the satisfaction of seeing justice being done and tailoring it within the limits of the law to one's own needs. If property had been taken, it would unquestionably be ordered returned. In addition, there were the treble damages that had to be paid.[4]

THE DECLINE

The decline of the victim's importance in the criminal justice system occurred rapidly after the Revolution. The ideas of the Enlightenment, particularly those of the criminal law reformer Caesare Beccaria, were enthusiastically adopted by the young American nation.[5] The principles of his view were as follows: Crime is an offense against society. Punishment must be swift, certain, and equal to the harm done if it is to be effective. If used properly, the criminal justice system can deter crime and reclaim criminals from their fallen state. The Quakers in Pennsylvania had discovered a way to implement these idealistic goals. In contrast to the barbaric penological practices of the heartless British, the new republic would show the world that hardened criminals could be reclaimed by humane and natural methods.[6] Instead of whippings, forced servitude, or the hangman's noose, the Americans would place their criminals in prisons where they could read the Bible, meditate in silence, and come to see the error of their ways. The severity of the punishment could be easily proportioned to the harm done by varying the length of time in prison. The victim had no role to play under this new plan. In fact, his influence over the administration of justice had to be eliminated because it reduced the certainty of punishment. In 1778, the first prison opened in Philadelphia. Within thirty years, eleven states had prisons. In 1805, Massachusetts proudly opened its new prison.[7] Significantly, it was in that same year that a Massachusetts court imposed for the last time the sentence of paying treble damages to the victim of a crime.

During the next century, modern police departments were founded and grew into large bureaucracies; and the offices of public prosecutors assumed responsibility for prosecuting most crimes. The victim was displaced even further. Part of the rationale for the establishment of the police and the expansion of the responsibilities of the

4. Nelson, p. 108.

5. McDonald, pp. 654–56.

6. David J. Rothman, *The Discovery of the Asylum* (Boston: Little, Brown and Co., 1971), ch. 4.

7. Harry E. Allen and Clifford E. Simonsen, *Corrections in America: An Introduction* (Riverside, New Jersey: Glencoe Press, 1975), pp. 55–56.

public prosecutor is especially noteworthy. Reformers were concerned about the injustice of a system in which only wealthy victims could afford to buy law enforcement and justice. A publicly supported system would eliminate this inequity.[8]

THE VICTIM TODAY

In contemporary America, the victim's well-being and fair treatment are not the concern of the criminal justice system or any other institution. The victim has to fend for himself every step of the way. When there is a rash of burglaries in his neighborhood, for example, he will have to form a neighborhood vigilante system if he wants any real protection. The "increased police patrols" that the local police will provide amount to nothing more than a few extra passes of a squad car through the general vicinity. The victim might even try to concoct a trap in his house to catch an intruder. He may make a false arrest; or he may be charged with murder if a burglar breaks in and manages to get himself killed by the trap. But, in either case, he runs serious risks of violating the law himself.

When a victim's self-protective measures do lead him to violate the law, it is no defense to say that police protection was inadequate. In Washington, D.C., a retired old gentleman with a lifelong record of lawful behavior had been robbed each of the last two months after he had cashed his social security checks (his sole source of support). By now he was desperate for money. So, when he received his next check he took a pistol with him when he went to cash it. Incredibly, the pistol accidentally fell out of his pocket right in front of a policeman. He was convicted of carrying a dangerous weapon.

After a crime has occurred, the victim continues to be on his own. Some police departments will not even give him a free ride to the hospital.[9] Insurance restrictions permit the transportation of criminals but not of victims. If the victim goes to the hospital in an ambulance and happens to live in one of the few states that have victim compensation laws, the ambulance bill will be one of the items not covered by the law.[10] In cooperating with the prosecution of a criminal case, a victim incurs a variety of financial costs such as trans-

8. Christopher Hibbert, *The Roots of Evil* (Boston: Little, Brown, and Co., 1963).

9. M. Baluss, *Integrated Services for Victims of Crime: A County-Based Approach* (Monograph on file with the National Association of Counties, 1975).

10. G. Geis, "Crime Victims and Victim Compensation Programs," in *Criminal Justice and the Victim*, ed. W.F. McDonald (Beverly Hills, California: Sage Publications, 1976), pp. 237–59.

portation and parking, loss of wages, and babysitting expenses. Theoretically, the state helps victims defray the cost of assisting with the prosecution of the case. There are such things as witness fees, but not every jurisdiction has them; where they do exist they are grossly inadequate, mired down in red tape, and taxed, and most victims are not even told about them. Until recently in Philadelphia, Pennsylvania, a victim had to go to eleven different processing steps spread around the courthouse before he could claim his $20 a day witness fee, which was then subject to a city tax. Most victims did not know they were entitled to a fee, and those who had thrown their subpoena away were unable to establish their claim to the fee. In addition to losing a day's wages, the victim may even lose his job. Unlike the arrangement with jury duty, employers are not required to release their employees for witness duty or pay them their normal salaries.

There are also the endless delays and continuances. One trip to the courthouse is never enough. Even under ideal conditions it takes at least three or four trips: first for charging, then grand jury, then motions hearing, then trial, and finally, sentencing. Of course, the system never operates ideally. Thus, one regularly hears about victims who make fifteen or twenty trips to the courthouse. During his many trips the victim becomes very aware of his lowly status in the criminal justice system. The reserved parking is not for him but for the judges, prosecutors, police, clerks, and others. Sumptuous offices have been provided for the judges, but in many courthouses there is no room where the victim can wait comfortably until his case is called. He must either sit in a courtroom or pace the corridors and try to avoid being held in contempt of court for falling asleep in the courtroom or loitering in the hallways. In some jurisdictions he cannot even use the public restrooms. They are closed because of the crimes that have occurred in them.

The victim/witness "lounges" that have been provided in some jurisdictions are a stark contrast to the luxuriousness of the judicial chambers. The lounges are furnished in early American bus station, with rows of stiff plastic chairs lined up monotonously, facing nowhere. Defendants who are on pretrial release or their witnesses may be waiting in the same witness lounge as the victim. Open threats do not have to be made. A constant stare at the victim is adequate to intimidate. The victim arrives at 9:30 A.M. as ordered by the court and tries to keep from sliding out of his plastic seat until late in the afternoon when he is informed by the smiling young prosecutor that his case has been continued again.

The criminal justice system's interest in the victim is only as a means to an end not as an end in himself. The victim is a piece of evidence. The police want to know "just the facts," but the traumatized victim wants to tell the whole frightening story and more. Victims want to be reacted to as human beings and to be treated with care and solicitude. They resent the policeman's professional disinterest and detachment. But it is not just the police. No one in the criminal justice system gives the victim the sympathetic hearing, the opportunity for cathartic release, that victims feel they need. Prosecutors, like the police, only want to hear the relevant facts and to size the victim up regarding his or her articulateness, believability, and deservingness. How will he or she do on the witness stand? Will the typical local jury believe him? If so, will they sympathize with him? Victims who have done something stupid or who have prior criminal records, or who seem in some way to deserve the fate that has befallen them, cannot count on juries—or prosecutors—to vindicate them.

The modern public prosecutor conceives of his job as conservator of limited court resources. There are simply too many cases for the courts to handle. Thus, the prosecutor will keep cases involving unconvincing and unsympathetic victims from clogging the courts. Even if the case has merit, it will be marked for a giveaway type disposition. The prosecutor may refuse to charge the case; or may charge it and later drop it; or charge it and later plea bargain it on terms very favorable to the defendant. The implications here regarding class-biased justice for victims are substantial. Lower income groups are disproportionately represented among victims of crime. They are also more likely to have criminal records and to be less articulate witnesses. Thus, it is more likely that their cases are more frequently given away by the prosecutor than those of higher income victims. The irony of this is that historically the reason for establishing the office of public prosecutor was to ensure that poor victims could get the same kind of justice that the rich victims could afford.

Today's victim will not be told why his case was dropped or plea bargained; nor will he even be notified of the final disposition of the case.[11] For that he will have to call the courthouse and struggle through a labyrinth of referrals to other offices. In the end there is a good chance he will be unable to locate his case. The filing system of the courts and the prosecutors are not cross-referenced by the victim's name. Thus, unless the victim happened to catch the name of the stranger who attacked him, or the police officer who made the

11. R. Lynch, "Improving the Treatment of Victims: Some Guides for Action," in *Criminal Justice and the Victim*, pp. 172–74.

arrest, or the assistant prosecutor who handled the case, he may have to hire a lawyer to find out what happened to his case.

The modern public prosecutor does not have time to coddle victims, to listen to their emotional reactions, or to explain why he is going to take certain actions. Prosecutors claim they do not have the resources to notify victims of the final dispositions of their cases. Every prosecutorial dollar must count and must be used to suppress crime. But it must also be spent in a way that accommodates the realities of the prosecutor's office. Traditionally, that office has been used as a training ground for inexperienced young attorneys fresh out of law school and as launching platforms for careers in higher public offices (Chief Justice Earl Warren and United States Senator Thomas Eagleton are two examples). The high rate of staff turnover among prosecutors (usually two years) means that the prosecutors must use an assembly line organization for their work. Many of the assistant prosecutors will not have sufficient experience to see a case all the way through from beginning to end. For that and other reasons different prosecutors are stationed along the various stages of the process and handle all the cases that reach the processing plant. Typically, the least experienced prosecutors are stationed at the early screening stage end. The most experienced ones handle the trial stages of the most serious crimes. This means that the victim, who may have already explained his case to several different police officers, now has to retell it to each new prosecutor. It also means he experiences no sense of continuity.

When the case finally comes to sentencing, the victim in today's criminal justice system finds that he is not regarded as having a stake in the matter. In stark contrast to Colonial days, he cannot even expect to have restitution ordered, much less treble damages imposed. His views regarding what he believes would be an appropriate sentence are not represented to the judge. Defense counsel will be allowed to appeal to the judge, to beg for mercy, to try to sway the judge's emotions, and to recount in pathetic details his client's tragic childhood. If the defendant is indigent, this patent emotional appeal will be made by counsel paid for by the state. But the victim is not allowed to have his counsel make an appeal. The state does not supply indigent victims with attorneys at sentencing.

Some prosecutors will say that it is the function of the public prosecutor to represent the views of the victim, but this is not and cannot be so. There is a conflict of interests between representing the opinions and wishes of the victim and those of the state. The most frequent example of this is where the victim only wants to get his property back, while the state believes the defendant should be punished. To illustrate the "pro-defendant, anti-victim" mind set in contemporary criminal justice, it is worth mentioning an exquisite double standard. When reformers have urged recently that victims should have an attorney representing them at sentencing, the response has consistently been that that would be improper because the victim would play on the emotions of the judge!

While it is true that the victim's role in the criminal justice system has become less visible and less central since the Revolution, it has not been eliminated. Research in the last decade has shown that the victim's residual role is of critical importance. National surveys of victims have found that an extensive amount of crime is not even reported to the police. The President's Commission on Law Enforcement and Administration of Justice found that 35 percent of the robberies, 35 percent of the aggravated assaults, 40 percent of the larcenies over $50, 90 percent of the consumer fraud, and 74 percent of other frauds were not reported by victims.[12] It has also been found that the vast proportion of the more serious crime, i.e., excluding traffic offenses and disorderly conduct type offenses, that comes to the attention of the criminal justice system comes by way of complaints from victims and other citizens.[13] Very little is the result of on view arrests by police or other police-initiated actions. What is more, contrary to the television model, most detectives do not find new and ingenious sources of evidence. Solving crimes depends heavily upon the information supplied by the victim. It has also been discovered that of those victims who do report their victimizations to the police, many will subsequently refuse to cooperate with the prosecution. In Washington, D.C., the Institute for Law and Social Research found that of 5,042 cases of violent crimes referred for prosecution in the criminal courts in 1973, 52 percent were dropped at screening due to a problem related to the complaining witness.[14]

Once the victim is into the prosecution phase of the criminal justice process the role he plays is usually thought of entirely in terms of his function as a witness, but this is a superficial view that ignores the subrosa but vitally important role of the victim at this stage of the process. To understand this role one must first understand the criminal justice system as a human organization. When it is stripped

12. President's Commission on Law Enforcement and Administration of Justice, *The Challenge of Crime in a Free Society* 22 (New York: Arno Press, 1967).

13. Albert J. Reiss, *The Police and the Public* (New Haven, Connecticut: Yale University Press, 1971).

14. K. Williams, "The Effects of Victim Characteristics on the Disposition of Violent Crimes," in *Criminal Justice and the Victim*, p. 212, n. 15.

of all its mythology, ritual, and noble-sounding purposes, the criminal justice system is just like any other human organization that has been established to perform some function. As such it is subject to a phenomenon known to sociologists as "goal displacement," i.e., the tendency to substitute unofficial goals for the official goals of the organization.[15] One of the criminal justice system's unofficial goals is to minimize strain and maximize rewards for individuals within the organization as well as for the organization itself.[16] A constant potential source of strain is adverse criticism and publicity. Judges and prosecutors prefer to avoid such criticism and are always alert both to the possible sources of criticism and to the ways of deflecting it.

The victim's role can now be understood. He is a potential source of criticism who has to be neutralized. But, he also can be used as a convenient means of deflecting criticism. Prosecutors, judges, and defense counsel understand this and exploit, dupe, and use the unwitting victim accordingly. One widely used tactic for neutralizing the victim is known as "cooling the victim out." Victims are most vengeful, upset, and therefore, likely to be "a problem" immediately after the crime. Therefore, defense counsel will have the cases continued several months until the victim "cools off" and can be "reasonable."[17] Since defense counsel's obligation is to serve his client's interests, his use of this tactic is understandable. But prosecutors also use it. For them it is one of several methods of avoiding the victim's criticism.

If a prosecutor has a case that he believes does not merit prosecution, but he knows the victim will be upset (hence, potentially "a problem") if the case were dismissed or plea bargained, he may delay the case long enough so that either the victim cools down enough to be able to accept a dismissal or the evidence in the case will weaken— i.e., witnesses' memories fade—to the point where the victim can be easily persuaded that the prosecutor "had" to plea bargain the case to a lesser charge. Given the same case, an alternative to cooling the

15. See, generally, James D. Thompson, *Organizations in Action* (New York: McGraw-Hill Book Co., 1967), p. 79.

16. William Chambliss and Robert Seidman, *Law, Order and Power* (Reading, Massachusetts: Addison-Wesley Publishing Co., 1971), p. 266; see also, W.F. McDonald, "Plea Bargaining and the Criminal Justice Process: An Organizational Perspective" (Paper presented at the Annual Meeting of the American Political Science Association, Chicago, 1976, on file with author).

17. See, generally, William F. McDonald, "Notes on the Victim's Role in the American Criminal Justice Process" (Paper presented at the Second International Symposium on Victimology, Boston, 1976. Forthcoming in *Victimology: An International Journal.*)

victim out is to pin the blame for the unpopular decision elsewhere. There are several convenient scapegoats to choose from, including the victim himself.[18]

If the case is a really dangerous one, i.e., high adverse publicity potential, the prosecutor will not dismiss it himself but will take it to the grand jury and have that faceless body do the dirty work. Similarly, if he had a case that he believed was a second degree murder but he knows he would be criticized for being lenient if he did not charge it as first degree murder, he will charge the former and let the trial jury reduce it to the latter. The responsibility for some decisions is passed on to the judge. This is known among prosecutors as "putting the turd in the judge's pocket." It is yet another method of avoiding the appearance of leniency. Instead of recommending the sentence he believes is appropriate in a case, the prosecutor will either make no sentence recommendation or will recommend the maximum. The judge is then forced to go out on a limb and assume sole responsibility for setting the "realistic" sentence. If the case ever "backfires," i.e., the defendant recidivates, the judge will take the rap for having not imposed the maximum. Unfortunately for prosecutors, this ploy does not always work. Judges often recognize it for what it is and counter it by either insisting that the prosecutor commit himself to a realistic sentence recommendation or, if that fails, giving the prosecutor a hard time in other ways.

Sometimes the victim is the fall guy. Take for example the prosecutor who has a case that he would like to dismiss, but the victim is present in the courtroom and could be "a problem." The clever prosecutor waits for the victim to leave the courtroom for a few minutes' break and then quickly has the case called and dismisses it. When the victim returns, the prosecutor profusely apologizes to him, explaining that he should never have left the room. When he did, the case was called and had to be dismissed because he was not present. Sometimes it is the "system" in general that is to blame. For example, when the prosecutor has agreed to a plea bargain that specifies that the prosecutor will keep the victim away from the sentencing hearing, the resourceful prosecutor will notify the victim to come at 1:00 P.M. although the hearing is scheduled for 11:00 A.M. When the victim arrives he will be told that "the system" is to blame for "a last minute change in the schedule."[19]

Many case disposition decisions are contingent upon the assurance of a neutral victim. Defense counsel know that judges are more likely

18. Ibid.
19. Ibid.

to go along with motions to dismiss cases or proposals to reduce charges or impose light sentences if they can be assured that the victim won't complain. Thus, as part of their cooling out strategy, defense counsel will meet with victims, feel them out, see how mad they are and whether they could be satisfied with simple restitution in property offenses or a light sentence in other cases. The feeling out process is done casually and elliptically so as not to tip off the victim to the importance of these off the record remarks.

If it turns out that the victim would be satisfied with restitution or suggests a sentence that he naively believes is severe but in fact is lenient by current standards, counsel will argue to the judge that the victim's wishes should be honored. On the other hand, if the victim "wants blood," different tactics are used. Counsel may pull out his shopworn appeal for mercy and recount to the victim how sorry the defendant is, how he has a wife and kids, and how he grew up in a slum and was neglected by his parents. While this same appeal may get nowhere with judges who have heard it a million times before, its chances of success with victims is much greater.

A major alternative to suckering the victim is simply to keep him out of the matter altogether or at least as much as possible. By plea bargaining, a defendant avoids trial and thereby eliminates the emotional impact of the victim on the judge. In some places this is known as "sneaking the sun past the rooster." As long as the judge does not know and feel the full impact of the crime on the victim, he will be more amenable to a lighter sentence. Sometimes as an extra precaution, defense counsel will ask policemen or prosecutors to tone down their description to the judge of what was done to the victim. Instead of saying "the defendant slashed him with a switchblade big enough and sharp enough to carve up an elephant," say "the defendant inflicted some lacerations."

Victims can be used to help deflect criticism by being given a share in the responsibility for decisionmaking. If the victim agrees to a disposition—i.e., a case dismissal or a plea bargain or particular sentence—it gives prosecutors and judges something to fall back on if the case "backfires." They can always argue that the victim agreed to the disposition. This does not get them completely off the hook, but it helps blunt criticism. It also reduces the probability that the disposition will be criticized. Other than the press, the only likely source of criticism of any particular disposition is the victim. But if the victim has agreed to it, there is less to fear.

Prosecutors do seek the approval of victims for certain decisions. But this is done on a highly selective basis and is not to be regarded as evidence that contemporary prosecutors subscribe to the pre-revolutionary practice of allowing victims to control the prosecution of cases. On the contrary, modern prosecutors vehemently argue that prosecutorial decisions call for the exercise of professional judgment that only they with their learning and experience possess. It is on these grounds that they oppose the suggestion of reformers who lately have suggested that victims should be given more influence over disposition decisions. Yet the importance of professional judgment notwithstanding, prosecutors do seek out the victim's approval in two types of cases: (1) minor crimes that the prosecutor would like to get rid of to lower his caseload, and (2) very serious crimes with a high potential for adverse publicity that the prosecutor wants to or has to plea bargain to avoid losing the case altogether. To illustrate, in many jurisdictions today prosecutors are operating "early diversion" programs. Defendants charged with minor and not too minor crimes and who are first offenders are released pretrial for six months. If they do not recidivate, the charges are dropped. In effect, the prosecutor agrees not to prosecute these suspected criminals. In many of these programs, the prosecutor requires that the victim approve the decision to divert.

As for examples of the prosecutor turning to victims in cases involving serious crimes, there are many. Two will illustrate the point. When the Los Angeles District Attorney decided to plea bargain with Sirhan Sirhan for the assassination of Senator Robert F. Kennedy, he wrote to the Kennedy family to ask for their opinion of what a "suitable sentence" might be.[20] When the state's attorney in Chicago was faced with having to plea bargain in a "cop killer" case, he first held meetings with the relatives of the deceased officer, his fellow officers, and businessmen in the neighborhood where he grew up.[21] No doubt prosecutors can explain how the ends of justice are served by getting the victims' approval in these cases. A more detached observer will also see how the organizational and personal self-interest of the prosecutors also benefit from these practices.

SUMMARY

In the development of criminal justice in America, the victim has gone from central to peripheral actor in the system, from a prime beneficiary to an also-ran. In the name of equal justice for poor victims, bureaucracies were established to apprehend and prosecute

20. Robert G. Kaiser, *RFK Must Die* (New York: E.P. Dutton & Co., 1971), p. 519.

21. Albert Alschuler, "The Prosecutor's Role in Plea Bargaining," *University of Chicago Law Review* 36 (1968):50–112.

criminals. These organizations were supposed to serve the ends of justice better because they would be free of the elements of revenge and self-interest. But, they developed self-interests of their own. Today's victim has not been relieved of major costs in assisting with the prosecution of crimes. What is more, the criminal justice bureaucracies have denied him the satisfaction of participating in the justice process. If anything, the victim is exploited by criminal justice officials and defense attorneys to serve their personal and organizational self-interests.

A movement to improve the treatment of victims has begun in the last few years and has been supported by the Law Enforcement Assistance Administration. Victim-witness lounges are being built. Procedures for claiming witness fees are being streamlined. Special counselors contact victims; assess their social, medical, and financial needs; and refer them to community services. They also provide them with information about the disposition of their cases. Volunteers stay with frightened victims; home repair vans respond to burglarized victims and replace broken locks; and telephone alert systems allow witnesses to stay at home or at work if they can get to the courthouse on an hour's notice. In Sacramento, California, the police have had the courage to do what most bureaucracies would never do: they admit their failures. They write to victims after a period of time has passed and inform them if no arrest has been made in their cases.

The state of Minnesota has been successfully experimenting with a new restitution process. Felons convicted of selected property offenses are given early release from prison and are placed in a halfway house where they can work in the community and pay restitution to their victims on installment plans agreed to by the victims. As of January 1975, sixty-two offenders owed a total of $18,374, of which $5,627 had been paid; $3,505 would not be paid because the offenders had been returned to prison; and the remainder was expected to be paid on schedule. In Peoria, Illinois, an experimental effort is underway to bring the victim into the plea bargaining process. In Suffolk County, Massachusetts, the victim is being involved in shaping the sentencing recommendation to the judge.

These efforts are laudable. They may make the victim's visit to the courthouse more pleasant. But for the most part they are not directed at the fundamental reordering of priorities among criminal justice goals that is needed to achieve a true victim orientation in criminal justice. The interests of the state, the defendant, and the bureaucracy still dominate the criminal justice process in theory and in reality, and they are likely to do so for some time.

William F. McDonald is Research Director of the Institute of Criminal Law and Procedure and teaches in both the Sociology Department and the Law School of Georgetown University. In addition to having published numerous articles, Professor McDonald is also editor of Criminal Justice and the Victim, *and he is presently pursuing research on plea bargaining and other dimensions of the criminal justice system.*

29

THE EFFECT OF
VICTIM COMPENSATION PROGRAMS
UPON CONVICTION RATES

SUSAN STELZENMULLER SILVERMAN

WILLIAM G. DOERNER

After many years of neglect, the criminal justice
system is beginning to reintegrate the victim into the
resolution of criminal matters. Legislative interest in
victim compensation, for example, is mounting. New Zealand
enacted the first modern victim compensation program in 1963
and Great Britain followed suit the next year. Since then,
several countries and half the states of United States have
passed victim compensation legislation (Edelhertz and Geis,
1974; Meade, et al., 1976).

Victim compensation consists of reparation by the state
to defray the cost of violent crime victimization. However,
the victim must satisfy several conditions before compensation will be awarded. Most victim compensation laws
mandate that the crime be reported to the police and that
the victim cooperate fully with law enforcement agencies or
risk loss of compensation benefits. Thus, victim compensation contains an economic incentive to report the crime
and to participate in the prosecution of the criminal.

These properties of victim compensation have not gone
unnoticed. Some program officials speculate that victim
compensation transforms reticent victims into witnesses
willing to cooperate with the criminal justice system (State
of Maryland, 1977:6). The potential impact of victim compensation is tremendous. If compensation serves as an
incentive for the victim, then one would expect increased

From Susan Stelzenmuller Silverman and William G. Doerner, "The Effect of Victim Compensation
Programs upon Conviction Rates," *Sociological Symposium, No. 25* (Winter 1979) 40-60. Copyright
© 1979. Reprinted with permission.

crime reporting to the police. Furthermore, victim cooperation with law enforcement agencies should produce a higher
proportion of offenders apprehended, prosecuted, convicted
and punished. Thus, victim compensation has the capacity to
impact the entire criminal justice system.

Although victim compensation has the potential to
affect criminal justice operations at several junctures, a
distinct effect has yet to materialize. Earlier studies,
using both official and victimization survey data, show that
the introduction of victim compensation programs has not
stimulated increased crime reporting nor increased offender
apprehension rates (Doerner, et al., 1976; Doerner, 1978a;
Doerner, 1978b). However, it would be premature to assume,
especially in the absence of any empirical data, that other
segments of the criminal justice system remain unaffected by
victim compensation programs. Therefore, a logical research
step is to assess the impact of victim compensation upon
conviction rates.

The legislative provisions requiring crime reporting
and victim cooperation with law enforcement agencies justify
the expectation that conviction rates for violent crimes
will increase in response to program implementation. While
the linkage between greater victim cooperation with law
enforcement agencies and higher conviction rates extends
over several stages, victim compensation programs attempt to
promote this expected relationship. One condition of victim
compensation eligibility is proof that a crime occurred. A
routine investigation into a compensation application can
take months to complete. In view of this delay, most jurisdictions accept conviction in a criminal trial as sufficient
proof that a crime occurred. Therefore, the amount of time
required to process the claim is reduced and the victim
receives the compensation sooner. At the same time, conviction rates for property crimes should remain unchanged
because these crimes are not compensable acts under current
statutes. Therefore, property crime conviction rates will
be examined in order to guard against extraneous influences.

For purposes of analysis, the implementation of a
victim compensation program constitutes the experimental

legislative innovation. The period prior to program implementation represents the pretest period and the time subsequent to program implementation constitutes the posttest
period. Two research hypotheses follow:

1. Posttest conviction rates for violent crimes will
   be significantly higher than pretest conviction
   rates for violent crimes.

2. Posttest conviction rates for property crimes will
   not differ significantly from pretest conviction
   rates for property crimes.

THE STUDY GROUP

The selection of Canada as the research site for the
study described in this paper rests upon three factors.
First, there is a high degree of uniformity among the Canadian victim compensation statutes. The provinces which
compensate victims of violent crimes require both crime
reporting and victim cooperation with law enforcement agencies prior to an award. Second, Canada has operated a uniform crime reporting system since 1948, making report categories comparable from year to year and from province to
province. Third, examination of conviction rates is a
logical continuation of previous research studying the
impact of victim compensation upon crime rates in Canada
(Doerner, 1978a).

DATA AND DESIGN

This study employs a quasi-experimental "interrupted
time-series" design to determine the impact of victim compensation programs upon conviction rates. Unfortunately,
the annual Canadian Statistics of Criminal and Other Offenses, the data base for this study, are available only
through calendar year 1973. Thus, the universe for the
experimental group consists of those Canadian provinces
operating victim compensation programs prior to 1973.

The experimental group consists of Saskatchewan, which
implemented its victim compensation program in 1967, and
Ontario, which began its program in 1968.[1] The study period

for the experimental group ranges from 1962 to 1973. The pretest period for the experimental units extends from five to six years, while the posttest period ranges from four to five years. Although placement of units with differing implementation dates into the same research group runs the risk of contamination by the rival hypothesis history (Lempert, 1966:118), the present study minimizes this contingency by examining the provinces individually and not as an aggregate. The selection of Ontario and Saskatchewan as experimental units also insures a minimum of three posttest points. Such a strategy allows the researcher to distinguish true program impact from immediate short-term effects, a simple continuation of the pretest pattern or slope, and delayed effects.

The control group consists of Nova Scotia, Northwest Territories and the Yukon, Prince Edward Island, British Columbia and Newfoundland. Although all these provinces, except Nova Scotia, currently operate victim compensation programs, none of the provinces had implementation dates early enough to affect conviction rates during the study period. The chronology of implementation dates includes British Columbia and Newfoundland in 1972, Northwest Territories and Prince Edward Island in 1973, and the Yukon in 1975. Thus, the observation period for the control group extends from 1962 to 1972. Manitoba, New Brunswick and Quebec, the remaining Canadian provinces, are eliminated from the control group since they initiated programs in 1970, 1971 and early 1972, respectively. These implementation dates also do not leave a long enough posttest period for consideration in the experimental group.

As mentioned earlier, data for this study come from the annual Canadian Statistics of Criminal and Other Offenses. The violent crime conviction rate equals the total number of convictions for violent offenses (all degrees of murder, manslaughter, all degrees of assault, all degrees of rape and robbery) divided by the total number of charges for violent crimes, multiplied by one hundred. The property conviction rate (breaking and entering, plus all forms of theft and fraud) is computed in a similar fashion.

RESULTS

Hypothesis One

The first hypothesis predicts that violent crime conviction rates will increase in experimental units after
victim compensation program implementation. Figure 1 presents the relevant data. All three curves exhibit an overall downward trend in conviction rates, culminating in
pronounced drops for 1972 and 1973. Although several points
in the Saskatchewan posttest curve give the appearance of an
upward trend, examination of the control group curve for the
same period reveals a relatively similar pattern. The
Ontario plot takes a similar form. Thus, a visual inspection of Figure 1 suggests that both experimental units
mirror the control group.

A one-way analysis of variance was performed on the
posttest observations.[2] As Table 1 shows, the F-ratio for
violent crime conviction rates reaches significance at the
.05 level of analysis. Further investigation of the data
via the Newman-Keuls procedure shows that neither experimental unit differs significantly from the control group.
The disturbance occurs between the two experimental units.
A glance at Figure 1 confirms this finding. There is clearly a huge gap between the Ontario and Saskatchewan graphs.
The significant difference between the experimental units
stems, in part, from the small sample size underlying the
Saskatchewan conviction rates. In sum, the tentative conclusion is that posttest conviction rates do not differ
significantly from pretest observations.

Hypothesis Two

The second hypothesis anticipates no change in property
crime conviction rates throughout the study period. Figure
2 displays the graph for property conviction rates. All
three curves are relatively stable except for declines at
the end of the posttest period. Although Saskatchewan shows
an upward trend during the posttest period, the graph parallels the control group observations. Thus, a visual
inspection of Figure 2 confirms the second hypothesis.

A one-way analysis of variance, the results of which appear in Table 1, indicates there is a significant difference among the study groups. However, a Newman-Keuls analysis shows that the difference between Ontario and Saskatchewan account for the significant F-ratio. Therefore, the tentative conclusion is to accept the second hypothesis and to conclude that there is no difference between property crime conviction rates.

INTERNAL VALIDITY

A researcher is unable to exert much control over extraneous factors when utilizing a quasi-experimental design. Much of this difficulty stems from the absence of randomization procedures. Consequently, the researcher cannot attribute causality to the stimulus without ruling out other sources of bias. It should be pointed out that argumentation by elimination can be problematic, but that such a procedure is used to assure confidence in the results already obtained. Campbell and Stanley (1966:5) outline eight possible rival hypotheses which could constitute threats to internal validity and could lead to inappropriate conclusions.[3] These rival hypotheses include maturation, testing, instrumentation, statistical regression, selection, mortality, selection-maturation interaction and history. The purpose of this section is to consider the extent to which these factors could have confounded the results.

Maturation

Maturation constitutes one potential threat to the internal validity of this design and could occur if results attributed to the experimental stimulus are due to changes that accrue with the passage of time. In this case, the researcher could attribute increased conviction rates to improved investigative or prosecutorial skills, rather than to the availability of cooperative victims. Empirical evidence discounting this rival hypothesis is difficult to muster, but researchers view maturation as posing minimal threat to the internal validity of most legal impact studies (Lempert, 1966:117). Although the effect of maturation will not be examined empirically, its possible influence will be borne in mind.

Testing

This rival hypothesis commonly exists when sensitization or reactivity occurs in a test-retest situation. Since a retest procedure is not part of the study design, testing is not a crucial rival hypothesis.

Instrumentation

This rival hypothesis occurs when there are changes in the measuring instrument, scoring procedures or scorers that cause fluctuations during the observational period. Canada's adoption of a uniform reporting system in 1948 minimizes the variation assoicated with statistics reported over different jurisdictions. However, other objective conditions, such as an increased number of police, judges and prosecutors could affect how much crime the criminal justice system can process. Still other subjective factors, such as changes in the quality of investigation and prosecution could produce instrumentation biases. Unfortunately, the research undertaken was unable to obtain the appropriate data with which to assess this rival hypothesis. Consequently, the impact of instrumentation as a feasible alternative explanation cannot be discounted.

Statistical Regression

Regression may confound the results when a study unit falls within an extreme region of the pretest distribution and shows movement toward the mean during the posttest phase. One way to isolate regression effects is to examine the rank-order of provincial violent crime conviction rates during the pretest period. Conviction rates were arranged from highest to lowest and assigned ranks ranging from one to eleven. The information in Table 2 indicates that only Ontario falls into an extreme region. If Ontario had moved toward the mean, as evidenced by an increased posttest conviction rate, statistical regression could be a competing alternative explanation. Since Ontario's violent crime conviction rate declines, albeit very gradually, during the posttest period, regression effects are not a plausible alternative explanation for the observed results.

Selection

Experimental designs involve a random allocation of subjects to control and experimental groups, in the hope of rendering the groups equivalent before exposure to the stimulus. Quasi-experimental designs, however, lack random assignment. Therefore, one plausible explanation is that posttest changes reflect pretest nonequivalency. A one-way analysis of variance on pretest violent crime conviction rates shows a significant difference among the groups ($F=43.38$, $df_B=2$, $df_W=14$, $p > .05$). In this instance, a significant difference appears between the control group and both experimental provinces. These results suggest a lack of pretest equivalency and indicate that selection is a plausible rival hypothesis. However, the reader should be reminded that because of the implementation dates associated with the Canadian victim compensation programs and the limited availability of secondary data, Ontario and Saskatchewan were the only provinces available for membership in the experimental group.

Mortality

Mortality refers to incomplete observations or response decay. Only one province, Alberta, lacked complete judicial statistics; it was eliminated from the study. Complete data were available for all the remaining provinces. In addition, the standardized reporting categories insure comparability over time and space. Thus, mortality exercises minimal influence in this study.

Selection-Maturation Interaction

The interaction of selection and maturation occurs when nonrandom selection allows a misleadingly high maturation rate. Although the rival hypothesis selection poses some difficulty for the present study, the design controls for selection-maturation interaction in at least three ways. First, selection-maturation interaction is most problematic with live subjects. The use of secondary data avoids much of this difficulty. Second, multiple measures of the dependent variable allow longitudinal comparisons of experimental and control units. Third, the design facilitates comparison of posttest with pretest data. Campbell and Stanley (1966:55), therefore, regard this rival hypothesis as having minimal impact whenever a time-series design is used.

History

History consists of any event, other than the stimulus, that occurs during a study period and influences the observations. Quasi-experimental designs are particularly susceptible to the rival hypothesis history because these designs lack experimental isolation. Thus, any observed changes in the dependent variable may not be due to the stimulus alone. As the reader can imagine, history covers a myriad of influences which could impinge upon the data. For example, a police strike during the study period or a change in prosecutorial policy could affect the relative number of crimes reported and prosecuted. [4] In any event, the possibilities remain countless. Therefore, the rival hypothesis history cannot be disavowed.

DISCUSSION

The examination of internal validity suggests that some problems exist in the research design. Any increases in violent crime conviction rates could be due, in part or whole, to statistical regression, maturation, instrumentation, selection and history. However, violent crime conviction rates displayed a decrease during the posttest period. While the possibility exists that these problematic internal validity factors may have obscured the impact of victim compensation upon conviction rates and caused a decline in conviction rates, this explanation is unlikely for at least two reasons. First, the control group violent conviction rate displays a pattern that resembles the two experimental groups, suggesting similar forces were at work in all the provinces. Second, property crime conviction rates were relatively stable and comparable, although they did decline rapidly at the end of the posttest period. In any event, the conclusion is inescapable. The two jurisdictions operating a victim compensation program did not experience noticeable gains in their violent crime conviction rates.

As mentioned earlier, the present study is part of a series of investigations in which the effects of victim compensation upon other segments of the criminal justice system were examined. Earlier studies showed that the introduction of victim compensation programs in several jurisdictions does not stimulate increased crime reporting (Doerner, et al., 1976; Doerner, 1978b). Nor does victim compensation stimulate increased crime reporting and offender apprehension in Ontario and Saskatchewan (Doerner, 1978a), the two experimental units in the present study. Although all the studies in this vein suffer in varying degrees from problems associated with internal validity, one consistent result surfaces each and every time. That is, victim compensation programs have yet to demonstrate that they have any appreciable effects upon the remainder of the criminal justice system.

The finding that victim compensation programs fail to impact other segments of the criminal justice system should not be construed as meaning that these programs are wholly ineffective and should be abandoned. One explanation for these empirical results is that these programs are experiencing problems that block goal attainment. A processual analysis of Ontario's victim compensation program isolates at least three problematic areas: public awareness, a high rejection rate and the relative size of award.

The limited public awareness of victim compensation programs indicates that the target population, violent crime victims, is not being reached. Few people, including law enforcement personnel, understand or are even aware of victim compensation. A recent survey in Minnesota shows that while most police officers fail to inform victims of compensation benefits, those who do so averaged 2.2 victims per year (State of Minnesota, 1978). Ontario's program administrators were cognizant of informational difficulties and launched a massive public awareness campaign in 1976. Posters and brochures advertising compensation benefits were placed in hospitals, courthouses and shopping areas. However, the relative increase in applications for the next fiscal year was smaller than for the two previous years. Thus, one partial explanation for the finding of no systemic effect is that the program still does not reach the target population.

Problems with claim processing and service delivery is another factor that could obscure the impact of victim compensation upon conviction rates. To begin with, a substantial proportion of the applications for victim compensation never even reach the hearing stage. Further, during the first three years of operations, no more than half the Ontario victims who applied for compensation received an award. As the program grew, this figure increased so that about sixty percent of all applicants receive compensation today. Thus, the large proportion of disallowed claimants could spell victim disenchantment with compensation remedies and account for the lack of effect upon conviction rates.

The size of compensation is another point in question. At present, no information is available concerning victim satisfaction with compensation awarded. Feedback from compensated victims could be very helpful in isolating problem areas and improving administrative procedures. For example, victims may benefit more from small, but immediate, emergency awards than from larger awards that require months of processing. The possibility exists that a high rejection rate, coupled with slow turnaround, causes more victims to be disillusioned with the criminal justice system. Thus, if a victim feels inadequate compensation would be forthcoming, the award could lose its ability to act as an economic incentive for cooperating with the criminal justice system. Thus, the lack of change in violent crime conviction rates reflects the inability of victim compensation schemes to achieve their primary goal.

In conclusion, then, the unsatisfactory, inconsistent and arbitrary nature of current program procedures is likely to obscure any impact that victim compensation can expect to have upon the remainder of the criminal justice system.

SUMMARY

The explanations offered for the finding that victim compensation programs in Saskatchewan and Ontario do not influence violent crime conviction rates suggest that there is much room for improvement in program operations. The major flaw in current programs is that no one really knows what is being accomplished. Evaluation of program success depends upon the measurement criteria employed and this area of victim compensation research remains untouched. Until evaluative measures are studied and new policies implemented, the potential remedial power of victim compensation will remain underdeveloped.

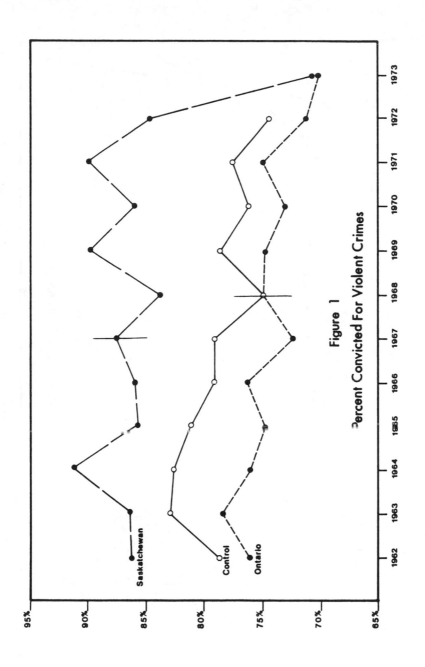

Figure 1

Percent Convicted For Violent Crimes

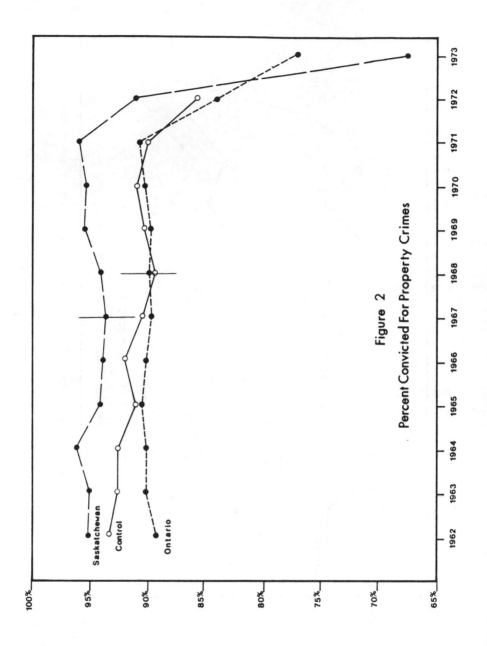

Figure 2

Percent Convicted For Property Crimes

TABLE 1

ONE-WAY ANOVA SUMMARY FOR POSTTEST OBSERVATIONS

Source of Variation	SS	df	MS	F-ratio
VIOLENT				
Between	323.72	2	161.86	6.44*
Within	276.70	11	25.15	
PROPERTY				
Between	26.72	2	13.36	5.91*
Within	24.82	11	2.26	

*Significant at the .05 level.

TABLE 2

RANK-ORDER OF VIOLENT CRIME CONVICTION
RATES DURING THE PRETEST PHASE*

Year	Ontario	Saskatchewan	Control
1962	10	6	6.0
1963	11	6	5.2
1964	11	5	5.6
1965	11	7	5.6
1966	11	4	7.4
1967	10	2	6.0
Mean	10.7	5.0	6.0

* A rank of eleven was assigned to the lowest violent crime conviction rate and a rank of one went to the highest violent crime conviction rate.

Footnotes

[1]Although Alberta implemented its victim compensation program in 1969, that province is excluded from the experimental group because it did not report full judicial statistics throughout the entire study period.

[2]The one-way analysis of variance is an interval-level statistic which, when used in conjunction with a technique like the Newman-Keuls procedure, mirrors the logic behind t-test comparisons. T-test requires independent observations, a condition not satisfied in the present study, and multiple t-test comparisons yield results that are prone to Type II errors (Newman, 1939; Winer, 1962). A superior strategy, then, is to apply a one-way analysis of variance. The one-way analysis of variance tests the null hypothesis that the smallest group mean is similar to the largest group mean. Whenever a significant difference exists between the two extremes, the question arises as to whether intermediate groups differ significantly. The Newman-Keuls technique is one statistic that can locate other disturbances in the data (Champion, 1970:124-127). Since the present study utilizes a control group, the focal point is any significant differences between the experimental and control groups. Differences between the two experimental units Ontario and Saskatchewan, are meaningless in the present study.

[3]An additional rival hypothesis, instability, surfaced in subsequent quasi-experimental work (Campbell and Ross, 1968:40; Campbell, 1969:410). However, a perusal of the graphs suggests that the observations are systematic and not influenced by this rival hypothesis.

[4]A spot-check of several Canadian legal journals failed to locate any legislative or prosecutorial changes which could influence conviction rates during the study period.

Acknowledgments

*The authors would like to thank Fred Faust, Richard Smith and the anonymous Sociological Symposium reviewers for their invaluable suggestions and comments during various phases of this study.

References

Brooks, James A.
    1975   "How Well Are Criminal Injury Compensation Boards Performing?" Crime and Delinquency 21:50-55.

Campbell, Donald T.
    1969   "Reforms as Experiments." American Psychologist 24:409-429.

Campbell, Donald T. and H. Laurence Ross
    1968   "The Connecticut Crackdown on Speeding: Time-Series Data in Quasi-Experimental Analysis." Law and Society Review 3:33-53.

Campbell, Donald T. and Julian C. Stanley
    1966   Experimental and Quasi-Experimental Designs for Research. Chicago: Rand McNally & Company.

Champion, Dean J.
    1970   Basic Statistics for Social Research. Scranton: Chandler Publishing Company.

Doerner, William G., Mary S. Knudten, Richard D. Knudten and Anthony C. Meade
    1976   "An Analysis of Victim Compensation Programs As a Time-Series Experiment." Victimology 1:295-313.

Doerner, William G.
    1977   "State Victim Compensation Programs in Action." Victimology 2:106-109.

    1978a   "A Quasi-Experimental Analysis of Selected Canadian Victim Compensation Programs." Canadian Journal of Criminology 20:239-251.

1978b   "An Examination of the Alleged Latent Effects of Victim Compensation Programs upon Crime Reporting." LAE Journal 41:71-76.

Edelhertz, Hubert and Gilbert Geis
    1974   Public Compensation to Victims of Crime. New York: Praeger.

Harris, Eugene C.
    1976   "Crime Victim Bill OK'd." The Milwaukee Journal March 21.

Lempert, Richard
    1966   "Strategies of Research Design in the Legal Impact Study: The Control of Plausible Rival Hypotheses." Law and Society Review 1:111-132.

Maryland, State of
    1977   Criminal Compensation Injuries Board Eighth Annual Report.

Matthews, Linda
    1972   "Few Taking Advantage of Law That Aids Victims of Crime." Los Angeles Times July 14.

Meade, Anthony C., Mary S. Knudten, William G. Doerner and Richard D. Knudten
    1976   "Discovery of a Forgotten Party: Trends in American Victim Compensation Legislation." Victimology 1:421-433.

Minnesota, State of
    1978   "An Analysis of the Public Information Effort of the Minnesota Crime Victims Reparations Board." St. Paul: Department of Administration.

Newman, D.
    1939   "The Distribution of Range in Samples from a Normal Population, Expressed in Terms of an Independent Estimate of Standard Deviation." Biometrika 31:20-30.

Winer, B.J.
   1962   Statistical   Principles   in   Experimental
           Design.   New York: McGraw-Hill Book Company.

Susan S. Silverman recently completed the master's program in the School of Criminology at Florida State University. She is currently a member of the research staff at the Florida Supreme Court. Her major areas of interest include victimology and court operations.

William G. Doerner is Assistant Professor in the School of Criminology at Florida State University. He has published several articles on victim compensation and also on southern homocide rates. He is President of the Florida Network of Victim/Witness Assistance. Currently he is conducting a study of victim compensation applicants and their attitudes toward the criminal justice system.

30

THE USE OF CIVIL LIABILITY TO AID CRIME VICTIMS

RUBEN CASTILLO   THOMAS W. DRESSLER

RICHARD FOGLIA   MICHAEL J. FABER

Our legal system is beginning to take note of the problems encountered by victims of crimes, whose rights until now have been largely overlooked.[1] The general focus of this concern has been the provision of adequate financial compensation for crime victims[2] through the use of insurance, restitution, state-funded compensation programs or civil actions.[3] Crime insurance and court-ordered restitution have been considered insubstantial in many cases, and also have been criticized because of the extent of their dependence on the individual discretion of insurance adjusters and judges.[4] Although nearly one-third of the states have enacted victim compensation programs,[5] such programs also have been criticized as ineffective because of their restrictions on recoveries for victims of violent crimes.[6] Civil actions to compensate crime victims

also have been generally ignored because of the difficulty of obtaining civil recovery from the perpetrator of the criminal act.[7]

However, several recent cases indicate that victims of crime have been successful in suits against common carriers for the criminal actions of third parties.[8] These suits have been aided by the increasing tendency of courts to find defendant carriers in violation of a duty to prevent crime against passengers and others. Similarly, victims also have found success in suits against other entities for the criminal acts of third parties, if a special legal relationship between the victim and the potential defendant is successfully pleaded. Such a special relationship giving rise to a duty to protect another from a criminal attack by a third person may exist, for example, in innkeeper-guest, landowner-invitee and custodian-ward situations.[9] Yet, the major source of litigation in the area of third person criminal attacks, and hence the prime focus of this article, still appears to arise from common carrier-passenger situations.

Recently, the Court of Appeals for the Third Circuit in *Kenny v. Southeastern Pennsylvania Transportation Authority,*[10] imposed civil liability on a common carrier for failing to protect adequately its passenger against criminal violence. In *Kenny,* a woman who was raped in a transit station sued the Southeastern Pennsylvania Transportation Au-

[1] *See* Denenberg, *Compensation for the Victims of Crime: Justice for the Victim as Well as the Criminal,* 1970 INS. L.J. 628; Comment, *Compensation For Victims Of Violent Crimes,* 26 KAN. L. REV. 227 (1978).

[2] *See* Inbau, *Forward* to Carrington, *Victim's Rights Litigation: a Wave of the Future?,* 11 U. RICH. L. REV. 447 (1977).

[3] *See* Lamborn, *Remedies for the Victims of Crime,* 43 S. CAL. L. REV. 22 (1970). In this work, the author reviews and evaluates the remedies currently available to those disabled by criminal conduct.

[4] *See* Harland, *Compensating the Victims of Crime,* 14 CRIM. L. BULL. 203 (1978). Professor Harland points out that there is a need for the imaginative use of restitution.

[5] *See* ALASKA STAT. §§ 18.67.010-18.67.180 (1974 & Supp. 1977); CAL. GOV'T CODE §§ 13959-74 (West Cum. Supp. 1977); DEL. CODE TIT. 11, §§ 9001-17 (Cum. Supp. 1976); HAW. REV. STAT. §§ 351-1 to 351-70 (1968 & Supp. 1975); ILL. ANN. STAT. ch. 70, §§ 71-84 (Smith-Hurd Cum. Supp. 1977); MD. ANN. CODE art. 26A, §§ 1-17 (1973 & Cum. Supp. 1977); MASS. GEN. LAWS ANN. ch. 258A, §§ 1-7 (West Cum. Supp. 1977-78); MINN. STAT. ANN. §§ 299B.01-299B.16 (West Cum. Supp. 1977); NEV. REV. STAT. §§ 217.010-217.350 (1977); N.J. STAT. ANN. §§ 52:4B-1 to 52:4B-21 (West Cum. Supp. 1977-78); N.Y. EXEC. LAW art. 22, §§ 620-35 (McKinney 1972 & Supp. 1972-77); N.D. CENT. CODE §§ 65-13-01 to 65-13-20 (Supp. 1977); OHIO REV. CODE ANN. §§ 2743.51-2743.72 (Page Supp. 1976); TENN. CODE ANN. §§ 23-3501 to 23-3517 (Cum. Supp. 1976); WASH. REV. CODE ANN. §§ 7.68.101-7.68.910 (Supp. 1977); WIS. STAT. ANN. §§ 949.01-949.18 (West Cum. Supp. 1977-78).

[6] Most of these programs fail to compensate the victim for pain and suffering and only provide relief for economic loss resulting from violence such as medical bills

and loss of wages. *See* Lamborn, note 3 *supra*; McAdam, *Emerging Issue: An Analysis Of Victim Compensation,* 8 URB. L. 346 (1976).

[7] "All victims of criminal violence have a remedy in tort, but the problems associated with civil recovery are legion. First, the suspect must be apprehended. If the suspect has no assets, the victim's civil recovery is completely frustrated," McAdam, *supra* note 6, at 347-48.

[8] *See* Kenny v. SEPTA, 581 F.2d 351 (3d Cir. 1978); McCoy v. CTA, 69 Ill. 2d 280, 371 N.E.2d 625 (1977).

[9] *See* Totten v. More Oakland Residential Housing, Inc., 63 Cal. App. 3d 538, 134 Cal. Rptr. 29 (1976). *See also* Carrington, *supra* note 2, at 459-67, for other potential applications of such civil liability. It should be noted that such civil suits allow a victim to seek damages for pain and suffering which are not generally available under the average state compensation program.

[10] 581 F.2d 351 (3d Cir. 1978).

From Ruben Castillo et al., "The Use of Civil Liability To Aid Crime Victims," 70(1) *Journal of Criminal Law & Criminology* pp. 57-62. Copyright © 1979 by Northwestern University School of Law.

thority[11] (hereinafter SEPTA) and the City of Philadelphia. The evidence showed that the plaintiff was attacked by another patron while awaiting the arrival of a train at an inadequately lighted station platform. The SEPTA employee on duty allegedly paid insufficient attention to platform conditions,[12] although SEPTA had previously acknowledged the existence of a crime problem on its transit system.

At trial, the jury concluded that the transit system had knowledge of the dangerous condition of the platform, and had negligently failed to provide adequate protection against such danger. This negligence was found to have been the proximate cause of the plaintiff's injuries. The jury also decided that the City of Philadelphia was not liable.[13] Nevertheless, the district court[14] entered judgment notwithstanding verdict in favor of SEPTA, finding that SEPTA had no reason to anticipate the criminal conduct of the assailant at the particular station involved.[15] The district court also rejected the plaintiff's alternative argument that the lack of adequate lighting and an adequate system of security devices, such as closed circuit TV coverage of the platform or telephone and warning devices, were the proximate cause of the assault.

On appeal, the Third Circuit reinstated the jury verdict in favor of the plaintiff. The court held that in view of SEPTA's knowledge that crime had been increasing on the transit system, the possibility of such an assault on the station platform should

have been foreseeable. The court then applied Section 344 of the Restatement (Second) of Torts[16] in finding that SEPTA had a duty to protect the plaintiff from foreseeable criminal acts. Under Section 344, a landholder is liable to its business invitees for physical harm caused by the intentional acts of third persons and the failure of the landholder reasonably to protect the invitee from foreseeable harm.[17] The court held that this duty was violated by SEPTA when it failed to provide adequate lighting at its transit station and when its employee failed to hear the plaintiff's screams and call the police.

Furthermore, the court claimed that the district court had erroneously narrowed the scope of SEPTA's potential liability by emphasizing the probability of the specific offense occurring at the particular location involved. The appellate court instead held that the duty to protect its patrons is to be determined, in such cases, by "whether the authority could have reasonably expected criminal activity from *anyone* at its station."[18] This statement of the scope of the carrier's duty may significantly increase the chances of proving that a carrier has been negligent in failing to provide adequate safe-

---

[11] SEPTA, Southeastern Pennsylvania Transit Authority, is an entity created by the Pennsylvania Legislature to provide mass transit in the greater Philadelphia area. *See* PA. STAT. ANN. tit. 66 §§ 2002-03 (Purdon Cum. Supp. 1978-79).

[12] The carrier's attendant who had been in the cashier's booth testified that he knew nothing of the attack and had not heard the plaintiff's screams. He admitted that he had a portable radio playing in the booth, but said that the radio was permitted by his employer. A telephone in the booth was connected with dispatches and security units but was not used that evening until after police had come to investigate the incident. 581 F.2d at 353.

[13] *Id.* at 354. Apparently, the jury did not agree with the plaintiff's argument that the Philadelphia Police Department, who were relied on by the transit system to provide protection for its patrons, were negligent in failing to protect the station platform or in responding to her cries for help. The jury awarded damages of $18,000 against SEPTA alone. *Id.* at 353.

[14] *Id.* Federal jurisdiction in this case was based upon diversity of citizenship. The federal court applied Pennsylvania law.

[15] *Id.* at 354.

[16] Section 344 of the RESTATEMENT (SECOND) OF TORTS (1965) states that:

A possessor of land who holds it open to the public for entry for his business purposes is subject to liability to members of the public while they are upon the land for such a purpose, for physical harm caused by the accidental, negligent, or intentionally harmful acts of third persons or animals, and by the failure of the possessor to exercise reasonable care to

(a) discover that such acts are being done or are likely to be done, or

(b) give a warning adequate to enable the visitors to avoid the harm, or otherwise to protect them against it.

See also Comment E to Section 344, which as pointed out by the *Kenney* Court, states that:

it may not be enough for the servants of [a] public utility to give a warning, which might be sufficient if it were merely a possessor holding its land open to the public for its private business purposes. The utility may then be required to take additional steps to control the conduct of the third person, or otherwise to protect the patron against it.

Section 344 of the RESTATEMENT SECOND OF TORTS (1965) had been cited with approval in Pennsylvania. *See* Moran v. Valley Forge Drive-In Theater, Inc., 431 Pa. 432, 246 A.2d 875 (1968) (a patron recovered from a theater for injuries received when rowdy teenagers exploded a firecracker near him).

[17] Section 344, RESTATEMENT (SECOND) OF TORTS (1965).

[18] 581 F.2d at 354 (emphasis added).

guards against criminal activities. The court's emphasis on the evidence which showed a high crime rate on Philadelphia's mass transit system also indicates that this standard may prove to be an effective tool for the plaintiff who is criminally assaulted in an area with a large volume of prior crime.[19]

The *Kenny* court has not been the only court to hold a carrier liable for the foreseeable criminal acts of non-related parties. Civil liability was also imposed on a common carrier for the criminal act of a third party by the Illinois Supreme Court in *McCoy v. Chicago Transit Authority*.[20] In that case, the plaintiff was injured when he was assaulted by a fellow passenger while riding a Chicago elevated train. Although the plaintiff obtained a jury verdict in his favor, the state appellate court held that verdict to be against the manifest weight of the evidence. On appeal, the Illinois Supreme Court reinstated the trial court's verdict holding the common carrier liable, under Illinois law, for a breach of its duty to prevent the commission of a foreseeable criminal act against a passenger.[21] The court looked to the case facts and noted that a Chicago Transit Authority (CTA) conductor had been aware of the presence of three loud and troublesome men on his train. The conductor had seen that these men were bothering the plaintiff but had failed to take any action. Later, it was these men who assaulted the plaintiff. Centering on the conductor's failure to take preventive action, as well as on the fact that this particular CTA transit line was in an area having a high incidence of on-board crime,[22] the court held that the verdict of liability must be sustained.

Prior Illinois cases[23] had indicated that two elements were necessary to support a finding of common carrier liability: (1) that the carrier knew or should have known that one of its passengers may be injured through the occurrence of a criminal act and (2) that the carrier had ample opportunity to take preventive measures to protect all passengers, but failed to do so. The court in *McCoy* found that these two elements were present in the plaintiff's evidence. The court reasoned that the CTA motorman should have been aware of the potential misconduct of the three boisterous passengers on the train.[24] The conduct of these passengers, who later assaulted the plaintiff, together with the existing high level of crime on the train's route, made the criminal injury of the plaintiff foreseeable. Furthermore, the court noted that the conductor could have prevented the assault through radio communication with the motorman, who in turn could have established radio contact with CTA headquarters to obtain help.[25]

Both *Kenny* and *McCoy* avoid the recurring tort law problem of determining foreseeability by focusing on the occurence of prior crimes on the respective transit lines. This is significant, especially in urban areas where transit crime is becoming commonplace. The use of evidence of prior assaults on persons using the defendant carrier's facilities is crucial in establishing the defendant's negligent breach of its duty to police its platform.[26]

---

[19] *See* Comment F to Section 344 of the RESTATEMENT (SECOND) OF TORTS (1965) which points out that a possessor of land may:

know or have reason to know, from past experience, that there is a likelihood of conduct on the part of third persons in general which is likely to endanger the safety of the visitor, even though he has no reason to expect it on the part of any particular individual. If the place or character of his business, or his past experience, is such that he should reasonably anticipate careless or criminal conduct on the part of third persons, either generally or at some particular time, he may be under a duty to take precautions against it, and to provide a reasonably sufficient number of servants to afford a reasonable protection.

See also 13 C.J.S. *Carriers* § 678 (1955) which notes that the duty to exercise care for a passenger's safety may vary according to time, place and circumstances.

[20] 69 Ill. 2d 280, 371 N.E.2d 625 (1977).

[21] *Id.* at 289, 371 N.E.2d at 629.

[22] *Id.* at 289, 371 N.E.2d at 627.

[23] The court reviewed three principal Illinois cases: Watson v. CTA, 52 Ill. 2d 503, 288 N.E.2d 476 (1972); Letsos v. Chicago Transit Authority, 47 Ill. 2d 437, 265 N.E.2d 650 (1970); Blackwell v. Fernandez, 324 Ill. App. 597, 59 N.E.2d 342 (1945).

In *Letsos*, the Illinois Supreme Court held that under the circumstances, the incident which caused the plaintiff's injury occurred so quickly and unexpectedly that the driver of the carrier, acting with the highest degree of care consistent with the safe operation of the bus, could not have averted it. In *Watson*, the transit authority was held liable upon a showing that the driver drove the bus for several blocks while the plaintiff was struggling with his assailant for a gun. The plaintiff in *Watson* was then subsequently shot when the driver purposefully opened the bus doors to throw out the struggling pair.

In *Blackwell*, an Illinois Appellate Court affirmed a jury verdict finding the carrier liable. The facts showed that the streetcar conducter allowed an intoxicated and quarrelsome passenger aboard who subsequently knifed the plaintiff in the case.

[24] The conductor had admitted in prior deposition testimony that he had thought that these passengers were "apparently . . . bent on mischief." 69 Ill. 2d at 284, 371 N.E.2d at 627.

[25] *Id.* at 282, 371 N.E.2d at 626.

[26] *See* Miller v. CTA, 78 Ill. App. 375, 223 N.E.2d 323 (1966). *But see* Sue v. CTA, 279 F.2d 416 (7th Cir.

This evidence may also lay the basis for the establishment of the carrier's willful or gross negligence in failing to fulfill its duty to provide safe passage for its passengers. Such negligence can result in the recovery of exemplary or punitive damages.[27]

It should also be noted that *Kenny* and *McCoy* both reinstated jury verdicts which had been overturned by trial court judges. This could indicate a trend toward greater jury discretion in determining the scope of a common carrier's liability. Thus liability may depend upon the jury's prediction of the likelihood of criminal injury to the plaintiff together with the potential of the defendant carrier to prevent the criminal conduct.

Other recent cases which have dealt with the imposition of civil liability on common carriers for the criminal acts of third parties have also emphasized the concept of foreseeability. The court, in one prominent case, *MacPherson v. Tamiami Trail Tours*,[28] held that a bus driver had not exercised a sufficient degree of care when he asked the plaintiff to move to the rear of the bus. The court stressed the fact that the bus driver knew that the plaintiff, who was black, had been threatened by some belligerent white passengers seated at the rear of the bus, so that the driver was sufficiently aware of the potential danger of a racially motivated attack on the plaintiff. Because of this knowledge, the court held the defendant carrier liable for the injuries which the plaintiff sustained during the ensuing criminal assault.[29]

In *Smith v. West Suburban Transit Lines*,[30] a bus passenger sued a bus company to recover damages for personal injuries sustained when he was assaulted by a motorist who had become angry at the bus's obstruction of traffic. The state appellate court reversed a directed verdict in favor of the bus company and ruled that the evidence permitted a conclusion that the motorist's attack upon the plaintiff could have been anticipated and prevented by the bus driver, since the motorist had threatened the bus driver and all of his passengers before the attack. As the court noted, "[t]he carrier must exercise the care required to protect the passenger from violence even by a stranger. . . . The

general rule is clear that, from whatever source the danger may arise, if it be known, care must be exercised to protect the passenger from that danger."[31]

The scope of a common carrier's duty to protect its passengers from the criminal acts of third parties may extend beyond the vehicle to the carrier's parking lot. In *Watson v. Adirondack Trailways*,[32] a New York appellate court affirmed a judgment against a common carrier, where the plaintiff was assaulted by an intoxicated passenger in the defendant's parking lot while walking to the bus terminal.[33]

Recent cases have also held that a common carrier has a duty to protect its passengers from the foreseeable criminal acts of a mob. In *Campo v. George*,[34] for instance, a Louisiana appellate court held that a bus driver must be aware of the possibility of gang violence when a group of rowdy people enter a bus. The court found that in such a situation a bus driver must "take such actions as may be practicable under the circumstances to prevent assault from being committed or to interfere with its execution."[35] Furthermore, the court seemed to ease the plaintiff's proof requirements by holding that "[t]he mere showing of injury to a fare-paying passenger, and [the passenger's] failure to reach his destination safely, establishes a *prima facie* case of negligence."[36]

A Pennsylvania appellate court, in addition, has

[31] *Id.* at 223, 326 N.E.2d at 451 (quoting Neering V. Illinois Central R.R., 383 Ill. 366, 378, 50 N.E.2d 497, 502 (1943)).

[32] 359 N.Y.S.2d 912, 45 A.2d 504 (1974)..

[33] It should be noted, however, that a person may lose passenger status if he leaves the premises of the carrier. *See* Ortiz v. Greyhound Corp., 275 F.2d 770 (4th Cir. 1960).

The determination of passenger status does not turn solely on the payment of a fare. *See* Suarez v. Trans-World Airlines, Inc., 498 F.2d 612 (7th Cir.1974).

The matters to be considered in determining the status of passenger are: (1) place (a place under the control of the carrier and provided for the use of persons who are about to enter carrier's conveyance); (2) time (a reasonable time before the time to enter the conveyance); (3) intention (a genuine intention to take passage upon carrier's conveyance); (4) control (a submission to the directions, express or implied, of the carrier); and (5) knowledge (a notice to the carrier either that the person is actually prepared to take passage or that persons awaiting passage may reasonably be expected at the time and place).

Katamay v. CTA, 53 Ill. 2d 27, 32, 289 N.E.2d 623, 626 (1972).

[34] 347 So. 2d 324 (La. App. 1977).

[35] *Id.* at 326.

[36] *Id.*

1960) "Prior occurrence evidence must be such as would establish that the carrier had notice of danger to its passengers at the *place* of the accident." *Id.* at 418 (emphasis added).

[27] 13 C.J.S. *Carriers* § 674 (1955).

[28] 383 F.2d 527 (5th Cir. 1967).

[29] The court also held that it was the duty of a bus company to acquaint a passenger with any threat of danger known to it.

[30] 27 Ill. App. 3d 220, 326 N.E.2d 449 (1975).

advanced what may be the broadest duty to protect passengers from criminal mob action. In *Mangini v. Southeastern Pennsylvania Transportation Authority,*[37] a bus driver opened a door of a trolley when a mob of boys were hurling objects against the trolley. The driver did not even attempt to get out of his seat to exert his influence when this mob boarded the trolley and attacked his passengers. In the resulting suit for damages, the court found that the driver had negligently failed to uphold his affirmative duty to protect, as best he could, his passengers from the criminal acts of third persons. The court maintained that a carrier must use every means at its command to protect its passengers and restrain, and if necessary remove, the disorderly parties. "If necessary, the employees of a carrier may enlist the assistance of willing passengers, police, or other authorities to quell a disturbance."[38] The court noted that a failure to use these measures may lead to the imposition of liability on the carrier if the carrier knew of violent human behavior which gave rise to a reasonable apprehension of injury, prior to the time a passenger is in fact injured.

Despite the recent trend in cases holding common carriers liable, the carriers have escaped liability in some instances. Those cases which have absolved a common carrier of any liability for the criminal acts of third persons against its passengers have focused on two factors: the non-foreseeability of the criminal act and the inability of the carrier to have prevented the crime through reasonable means. For example, in *Morris v. Chicago Transit Authority*[39] an Illinois appellate court relieved a carrier of liability because it was unable to reasonably foresee and avoid an injury to its passenger resulting from a brick being hurled into one of its buses. Similarly, in *Martin v. Erie-Lackawanna Railroad,*[40] a federal district court applying Ohio law, reversed a judgment for a victim-passenger because the evidence failed to show that the carrier should have known that the plaintiff would be a victim of an abortive purse-snatching attempt that would result in her sustaining bodily injuries.

Two recent cases in Louisiana, *Higgins v. New Orleans Public Service, Inc.*[41] and *Orr v. New Orleans Public Service, Inc.,*[42] also reflect the need to show

foreseeability before the court will impose liability on common carriers for the criminal acts of third parties. In *Higgins,* a 67-year-old bus passenger was assaulted by a group of boys. The court held that the bus driver could not have anticipated this assault and therefore was not negligent. Furthermore, the court narrowly defined the duty of a carrier by noting that the driver did not have any affirmative obligation to intervene in the assault and had fulfilled his duty by summoning the police.[43] In *Orr,* the court, as in *Higgins,* reversed a judgment for the plaintiff, holding that the evidence failed to show a reasonable foreseeability of the violence which was inflicted upon the plaintiff by a gang of youths. The court stated that the assault was so brief that the carrier could not have reasonably prevented it.

One recent case, *Hanback v. Seaboard Coastline Railroad,*[44] indicates that when a carrier's employee fails to respond adequately to a passenger's cries for help, the carrier may be held secondarily liable for the aggravation of injuries resulting from a criminal act even though the carrier was not primarily responsible for the occurrence of the act. In *Hanback,* the plaintiff was sexually assaulted on an Amtrak passenger train. The trial court found that the defendant carrier did not violate its duty to protect adequately the victim from the occurence of an unpredictable criminal act. However, the court held that the victim could recover for the injuries and damages suffered when an Amtrak employee failed to respond adequately to her screams.

In sum, the trend to allow passenger victims to recover from carriers for third party criminal acts represents a response to the need to provide adequate remedies for persons who have been victimized. However, the courts are reluctant to allow crime victims to use such civil liability in the absence of special legal relationships.[45] It should

---

[37] 344 A.2d 621 (Pa. Super ct. 1975).
[38] *Id.* at 623.
[39] 28 Ill. App. 3d 183, 328 N.E.2d 208 (1975).
[40] 388 F.2d 802 (6th Cir. 1968).
[41] 347 So. 2d 944 (La. App. 1977).
[42] 349 So. 2d 417 (La. App. 1977).
  The carrier is not obliged by its contract to provide armed guards, or even simply to hire only

burly wrestlers or boxers as drivers; otherwise it could not hire slightly built persons to drive its buses. Therefore the carrier cannot have the obligation to have its driver physically intervene in a beating. Thus even if a driver happens to be very strong, if he personally has some moral obligation arising out of his humanity to aid a weak person being beaten by a stronger one, the carrier does not have the obligation to intervene, but only to summon the police as speedily as possible.
347 So. 2d at 946.
[44] 396 F. Supp. 80 (D.S.C. 1975).
[45] *See* Totten v. More Oakland Residential Housing, Inc., 63 Cal. App. 3d 538, 134 Cal. Rptr. 29 (1977); Pippin v. CHA, 58 Ill. App. 3d 1029, 374 N.E.2d 1055 (1978).

nevertheless be emphasized that such legal relationships arise with great frequency in our social system. These relationships may effectively be used to provide a compensatory civil remedy for victims of criminal acts.[46] The rising rate of crime on premises which are open to the public for business purposes is a factor which may be used by a court to facilitate a finding that the occurrence of a criminal act on those premises was foreseeable.

[46] *See generally* Tarasoff v. Regents of the University of California, 17 Cal. 3d 425, 131 Cal. Rptr. 14, 551 P.2d 334 (1976); Carrington, *supra* note 2.

Such foreseeability can then in turn lead to the creation of a concurrent duty to protect one's business visitors from criminal actions.

If the plaintiff-victim can successfully allege the presence of a special legal relationship, as in the common carrier-passenger cases, he may be able to recover damages for his criminal injuries from a third party. The plaintiff need only show that the crime which resulted in his injury was foreseeable and could have been prevented by reasonable acts of the carrier.

31

VICTIM PROVOCATION
The Battered Wife and Legal Definition of Self Defense

NANCY WOLFE

It sometimes happens that an alteration in legal principle occurs that has not been prompted by changes in phenomena. Such a transition may be occurring in the doctrine of self-defense as it pertains to the trials of battered wives who kill their husbands.[1] Available statistics suggest that there has not been a significant increase in the number of women resorting to deadly force (Samuelson, 1978: 1562; Price, 1977: 103), but a body of law has been developing in cases in which wives claim that the homicide was justifiable because of prior abuse by husbands.

Judges, attorneys, and juries are clearly manifesting greater sympathy for self-defense arguments based on victim provocation—a shift of great potential impact (Macpherson, 1977: A 1). Although it is too soon for a definitive statement of a legal trend, a number of recent cases have demonstrated that the courts and the public are increasingly willing to endorse an expanded interpretation of a wife's right of self-protection, even to the extent of homicide. Very little has been written on this subject, particularly from the legal standpoint.

In theory, it is not the function of American courts to make law; rather, they are forums in which established legal doctrines are discerned and applied to particular cases. Under this principle, the law cannot be changed by judicial action; yet history has demonstrated that courts do respond to sociological and political changes and may, in fact, play an activist role in fostering change in both law and society. A perplexing legal dilemma arises from the concomitant effort to obliterate sex stereotypes and, at the same time, to protect a wife's rights *qua* woman. Attorneys who defend wives charged with committing homicide following abuse must address this problem squarely. Typical of the proponents of this defense tactic is Alan Eisenberg, an attorney who has successfully used the self-defense argument in this connection; he deems it hypocritical to punish a woman for obeying the natural urge of self-protection (Eisenberg and Seymour, 1978: 42). In the discussion which follows, defense arguments are reported as

From Nancy Wolfe, "Victim Provocation: The Battered Wife and Legal Definition of Self Defense," *Sociological Symposium*, No. 25 (Winter 1979) pp. 98-118. Copyright 1979 by the Sociological Symposium. Reprinted with permission.

given without consideration for the accuracy of the reports of abuse; the focus is on the nature of the defense rather than on reliability of testimony.

Battered wives face an unfavorable legal climate inasmuch as doctrines pertaining to the marriage relationship differ significantly from law covering the relationship of strangers. Under the feudal doctrine of coverture, when a woman married she lost her legal rights, and the husband and she as a wife then constituted a single legal entity (Kanowitz, 1977: 35). In the United States, despite modification of this harsh rule, there is, in the criminal law, still a definite distinction between married and single status. For example: until recently, some states prohibited a wife from bringing a charge of rape against her husband. And, until 1973 the laws of some states, such as Texas, New Mexico, and Utah, allowed a husband to kill a man he caught in the act of having intercourse with his wife (Inbau et al., 1974: 64-65); however, these laws did not accord the same right to the wife in a reverse situation. Other states had "unwritten" laws allowing such retaliation.

Six-linked legal tenets are crucial in instances where an abused wife kills her husband. Not only the statutes, but enforcement of laws differs in situations involving a man and wife. Traditional Anglo-American jurisprudence has held that a man's home is his castle, and governmental officials have hestitated to invade the sanctity of the marriage home.[2] A wife assaulted by her husband has found it difficult to gain effective protection from the criminal justice sytem; wife beating has been "all but condoned by our laws" (Goodman, 1977: 142-143; International Association of Chiefs of Police Training Key, 1977: 145; Steinmetz, 1977; Goode, 1969; U.S. News and World Report, 1978).

The extent of the phenomenon of homicide by battered wives is just beginning to be realized, according to Maria Roy of the New York Assistance Program, the Abused Women's Aid in Crisis. Women have lower rates of homicide than men, but when they kill, the victim is more likely to be their husbands than some other person (Goode, 1969: 954; Ward, 1968: 879; Hoffman-Bustamante, 1973: 121). Susan Steinmetz (1977), reporting on studies of interspousal violence, stated that the data suggest that the number of wives who killed their husbands was about equal to the number of husbands who have killed their wives (Gregory, 1976: 110-111).

The support for battered women now being provided by shelters has intensified research in interspousal homicide. A 1976 study of inmates of Cook County jail in Chicago indicated that as many as 40% of the women who killed their male partners reported having suffered physical abuse from the victim on several occasions. Claudia McCormick, the superintendent of the women's center, found that about 90% of such homicides by the women were not premeditated but were committed while under extreme emotional strain. A typical comment was that the woman had "picked up the first thing" to "get him off my back," ("Study of female killers finds 40% were abused," 1977: 20).

Several recent cases have given vivid life to abstract legal principles concerning victim-precipitated homicides. In December 1976, Roxanne Gay of

Clementon, New Jersey, knifed her husband Blenda after he allegedly had brutally beaten her repeatedly (Cook, 1978: B 3). The 25-year-old student nurse had sought police aid on prior occasions of the beatings but without success; the most the police did was to encourage the husband to take a walk to "cool off." In one instance, the police, whom she had called for protection, ended up discussing football with her husband, Blenda, who was a defensive lineman with the Philadelphia Eagles professional football team. Roxanne Gay was incarcerated for nearly a year awaiting trial ("Slaying suspect freed," 1977: 34). During her trial in the Camden County Superior court she was defended by Robert Ansell of Asbury park. Acquitted on grounds that she was insane when she killed her husband, she was ordered committed to a psychiatric hospital by Judge I. V. DiMartino (Janson, 1978: 27).

The following month, Marlene Roan Eagle, an American Indian in South Dakota, stabbed her husband through the heart, claiming that he threatened her with a broken broomstick (MacPherson, 1977: A 1). Again, there was a reported history of prior assaults, some occurring during the time that she was pregnant. The prosecution used the argument that the club with which she was being threatened "was not as big as some other clubs" (Eisenberg and Seymour, 1978: 34). Alan Eisenberg noted that this was a pathetic rationale, inasmuch as Mrs. Eagle's husband had successfully beaten her with his bare hands. Defended by Cleveland attorney Christopher Stanley, Marlene Roan Eagle won acquittal.

In March 1977, two dramatic homicides occurred. Jennifer Patri, a 32-year-old Waupaca, Wisconsin, farm wife, shot her husband Robert, buried the corpse in the smokehouse, then set fire to the smokehouse (Quindlen, 1977: B 4; "A killing excuse," 1977: 108). Made desperate by the husband's assaults, sexual abuse, and molestation of their 12-year-old daughter, Jennifer Patri bought a 12-gauge shotgun. Although she had felt dutybound to her marriage vows, she finally began divorce proceedings. The husband, who had gone to live with another woman, threatened to kidnap his daughters or to kill her. When he arrived to visit the children, his wife shot him in the back. Jennifer Patri's defense attorney, Alan Eisenberg, was unable to secure an aquittal and she was convicted of first degree murder and given a sentence of ten years.

In the same month, March 1977, Francine Hughes of Jackson, Michigan, poured gasoline around her sleeping husband James, then ignited it (Jacoby, 1977: C 2; Quindlen, 1977: B 4). The couple was divorced after seven years of marriage, but Francine returned to help nurse Hughes back to health after he suffered a near-fatal automobile crash. The assaultive behavior which had characterized their married relationship continued, and on the day of Hughes' homicide he had beaten Francine several times ("Killer of ex-husband acquitted," 1977: 928). Francine, 30 years old, was attending business school to be able to support herself rather than depend on welfare payments, and she was intensely distressed when her ex-husband forced her to burn her textbooks in the back yard. At the trial, in the Ingham County Circuit Court, she claimed that she was driven to the killing by years of physical abuse. Four policemen testified that

Francine was a troublemaker and had called them several times during the past few years. With a defense of insanity, her counsel, Aryon Greydanus, was able to plead convincingly to the jury of ten women and two men. They acquitted her after six and one-half hours of deliberation.

Criminal homicide, originally a single offense under the ancient common law of England (4 Bl. Comm. 177), has been divided into two categories under American jurisprudence: murder and manslaughter. Homicide is held to be murder if (1) committed with malice aforethought by (2) an individual in "an inexcusable, unjustified, and unmitigated person-endangering state of mind" (Wells and Weston, 1978: 179). State laws defining murder varies, but in most states, deliberate and premeditated homicide is designated first degree. Second-degree murder lacks the two elements cited above and is basically termed murder at common law. Manslaughter, under the law of most states is considered to be unlawful homicide committed without malice (Ferguson and Stokke, 1976: 201); it is "homicide mitigated out of tenderness to the frailty of human nature" (Commonwealth v. Webster, 59 Mass. 295. 1850).

In most early prosecutions of homicidal wives, the defense of insanity was used. Recently, however, there has been resistance on the part of defense lawyers to use the insanity defense plea as a routine tactic. Most of the tests for insanity (such as M'Naghten, Durham, Irresistible Impulse, or the Model Penal Code) require demonstration of irrationality, mental disease or defect on the part of the defendent, and it is possible that the woman acquitted by reason of insanity could be confined to an institution indefinitely. Although insanity might be an appropriate defense in some specific cases, issues raised in cases of homicide by abused wives can most appropriately be seen in the broad context of equal rights for men and women.

Voluminous literature spawned by the debates concerning the possible ratification of an equal rights amendment to the United States Constitution has heightened awareness of discriminatory attitudes toward the role of women and their legal position (Simon, 1976; Klein, 1973; Temin, 1973; Frankel, 1973; *inter alia*). Numerous organizations have investigated the plight of the battered wife and have made great strides in establishing means whereby such victims can seek both practical and legal aid.

Attorneys such as Elizabeth M. Schneider and Susan B. Jordan, who represent in the courts abused wives charged with homicide, stress the right of women to take the measures necessary to protect themselves against provocative or dangerous abuse. These attorneys use the argument of self-defense rather than insanity. Since free will's a presumption of the law, a woman who reacts with violence to spousal attack must either prove that the circumstances were such that she was justified in her homicidal action or that she was in some way deprived of her free will. Defense counsels for battered women charged with committing homicide increasingly are advising their clients to claim self-defense (MacPherson, 1977: 14). Thus, lawyers now argue that it is "reasonable" for a wife who cannot muster sufficient physical force to protect herself, or who cannot otherwise prevent abuse, to resort to violence.

A relatively new field—that of the study of victim precipitation—has already sparked numerous theories (Quinney, 1972; Silverman, 1974) and has affected homicide laws. Victim provocation, the legal counterpart of the behavioral concept of victim precipitation, has been invoked by many of the battered wives to justify their violent actions. When a victim creates in his assailant overwhelming emotions too difficult to control, such provocative conduct is often cited by the defendant as cause for violence (Bein, 1975: 55-56; Morris and Blom-Cooper, 1967: 70). A classic statement involving this principle was made by Hans von Hentig: "in a sense the victim shapes and moulds the criminal." (*The Criminal and His Victim*, 1967: 384). Although the law holds one responsible for the consequences of one's actions, it does take cognizance of victim provocation as a mitigating factor in cases of assault (Perkins, 1969: 53). As early as 1957, Marvin Wolfgang, in his study of victim-precipitated homicides in Philadelphia, found that "husbands more often than wives are major, precipitating factors in their own homicidal deaths."

An excellent example of manifest victim provocation is found in the 1975 charge of homicide brought against Eva Mae Heygood. She testified that her husband attempted to coerce her into having abnormal sexual relations, wielding a bed slat, he chased her around the bedroom, locked her in, and later returned with a gun. As she struggled with him, the gun was turned in his direction and discharged. The shot blew out his brains (MacPherson, 1977: A 14). Eva May then took her husband's body to the barn and hung it from the rafters.

A defense plea of victim provocation cannot be a sufficient legal basis for dismissal in cases of homicide, but it can result in reduction of the charge from murder to voluntary manslaughter (MacDonald, 1976: 186; Inbau et al., 1974: 261). Inevitably, the doctrine of victim precipitation entails the subjective element of mutual victimization; that is, if the wife perceives herself as being victimized, she could argue that her intent was to escape from the role of victim by killing the victimizer and could thus claim self-defense (Newman, 1975: 113).

Unlike a defense based on victim provocation, the claim of self-defense can lead to acquittal. In criminal cases the burden lies with the prosecutor to prove the charge true beyond a reasonable doubt. The affirmative nature of defense on the grounds of self-defense requires that the prosecutor disprove any contention that the defendent was in danger of great bodily harm or feared for his life. In many of the recent battered wife cases there was no evidence of impending harm to the defendant at the specific time of the killing, but the cumulative effect of prior assaults emerged as a pertinent circumstance (Schneider and Jordan, 1978: 156). Because Sharon McNearney of Marquette, Michigan, had reason to believe her husband intended to kill her, she fired a shotgun at him as he walked in the front door. Judge John E. McDonald of the Marquette County Circuit Court ruled that the prosecutor had failed to prove that Mrs. McNearney did not act in self-defense (MacPherson, 1977: A 1). In another case, in Orange County Superior

Court in California in 1977, the defendant Evelyn Ware used a defense of past beatings and won acquittal (MacPherson, 1977: A 1).

A critical legal issue in cases of battered wives accused of murder involves the admissibility of evidence concerning prior conduct of the deceased victim. Although courts have allowed introduction of evidence about reputation, they have been reluctant to admit evidence based on opinion and evidence concerning previous specific acts. In Michelson v. United States, 335 U.S. 469 (1945), the United States Supreme Court ruled that the defense could not introduce testimony of specific prior acts of the victim, but evidence concerning the victim's general character was allowable in order to establish the grounds for apprehension on the part of the defendant (1 A. L. R. 3d 574-575; 40 Am. Jr. 2d 568-577).

When the defense counsel does gain admission of evidence that the nature of the decedent was abusive, the tactic is often efficacious. David Landy describes a case in which Percy Foreman, the eminent criminal lawyer, was representing a woman who admitted having shot her husband. After Foreman had finished denigrating the deceased, "[t]he jury was ready to dig up" the husband and shoot him again (Landy and Aronson, 1969: 195).

A remarkable instance of this type of testimony was given in the trial of Sharon Brown of Fort Lauderdale, Florida, who emptied a gun into her husband on the front lawn of their home in March, 1978. Her husband had been married twice before and both former wives came to court to testify to his violent nature in behalf of the defendant (Quindlen, 1977: B 4).

Courts have broadened the rules of evidence. Wisconsin, since 1973, has held evidence of prior conduct admissible and does not confine the evidence on the entire pattern of conduct, including all prior violence (MacPherson, 1977: A 14). In September 1978, the Connecticut Supreme Court, in State v. Miranda, ruled that evidence of a homicide victim's violent character may be used to establish that the victim was aggressive thus buttressing a claim of self-defense by the defendant (24 Cr. L. 1001). The Court further stated that, although there is a difference of opinion among courts about admission of prior convictions, there was a growing number of jurisdictions allowing such admission ("Homicide victim's violent nature provable through his record," 1978: 1001-1002).

Prosecution of battered wives who kill their husbands raises the question of the amount of force which can be employed in self-defense. Although the right to use force to defend one's self is undisputed (Inbau et al., 1974: 264-265), the law is indecisive about the duty of the endangered person to retreat. The preponderant position in American jurisdictions is one recognizing the right to use deadly force for safety if it seems reasonably necessary; however, a substantial number (yet a minority) of jurisdictions along with the American Law Institute in its Model Penal Code have adopted a "retreat to the wall" doctrine whereby use of deadly force can be justifed only as a last resort (Perkins, 1969: 1005-1012). The retreat rule adopted in the Model Penal Code does not apply, however, within the home of the endangered person—an exception referred to as the 'castle doctrine." Therefore, a tactic of self-defense is available to the battered wife under the deadly force of retreat principles.

The critical legal issues are these: At what point does it become justifiable for a wife to react with violence? What amount of force is legitimate? In this regard sexual stereotypes are paramount. In confrontation situations, the law presumes equality, an interpretation which is virtually never accurate in male-female assaults. The law, in ascertaining "reasonableness" for the use of violence, seeks to determine the degree of apprehension of danger as well as imminence of danger on the part of the intended victim. This principle is well-stated in the oft-quoted dictum of Justice Oliver Wendell Holmes, Jr., that the "law does not require detached reflection in the presence of an upraised knife" (Brown v. United States, 156 U.S. 335, 1921: 343).

The general tenet is that like force may be employed against like force, but it is difficult to evaluate the amount of force in play when the involved antagonists are a male and female. Prevailing stereotypes of women imply that, aside from their inferiority in physical strength, women simply have not been socialized to react with force similar to that of men. Because of this difference, women are much more likely to try to equalize the force relationship through use of weapons. Defense counsel in battered wife cases have argued that a woman with a weapon may be considered evenly matched with an unarmed man. Roxanne Gay claimed that she seized a knife to defend herself when she was assaulted by her husband who was six and one-half feet tall and weighed two hundred and fifty-five pounds. Robert Ansell, representing Mrs. Gay, stressed the cumulative effect of beatings on a woman's consciousness and said that women should be allowed to quickly resort to use of a weapon ("A killing excuse," 1977: 108).

These crucial changes in legal theory and practice regarding the battered wife who commits homicides greater reliance on self-defense strategies, recognition of provocation as a mitigating factor, admission of evidence concerning specific acts of the decedent, and recognition of the greater need of women to resort to use of weapons—could not have been legally recognized without considerable public support. Courts, as Alexander Hamilton stated two hundred years ago, are the "least dangerous" branch of government; without enforcement power, they must take care to adhere to legal principles which the public will accept, and so they must, for the most part, function both as a reflection and as an indicator of societal values. Part of the significance of the legal trend in self-defense arguments lies in the modification of the stereotype of women which it entails.

For lawyers, judges, or juries to find validity in the self-defense argument based on a record of prior assaults, it is necessary to re-examine the principle of coverture. There is an inherent contradiction, however, in the arguments of attorneys such as Elizabeth M. Schneider and Susan B. Jordan (1978) who seek to obliterate the stereotypical approach of judges and counsel in cases involving homicide of husbands. On the one hand, they attempt to demonstrate the unreality of the image of the wifely role as one of submission, claiming that there is serious danger that the stereotype serves to control the kinds of information elicited. Yet at the same time, they make an effort to establish the special need for women to protect themselves in ways which transcend the traditional rules of self-defense. In other words, such defense counsel are urging that women as well as men be judged in homicide cases by the "reasonableness" rule, but they insist that the standard of "reasonableness" necessarily must be different for women. By emphasizing that role values internalized by women operate as a hindrance in self-defense situations, as well as do the physical characteristics of women, these lawyers are using a sex-oriented argument.

Even more difficult to measure precisely is the effect of these cases on the judicial system. The assistant prosecutor in the Sharon Brown case expressed his belief that previous cases had influenced the jurors. Apparently a similar attitudinal change is occurring in England; Michael Freeman wrote in 1977 that he suspected that judges and juries were more lenient in battered wife homicide cases than they would have been ten years ago (215). Alan Eisenberg sees the battered woman syndrome defense as a "wave of the future" (Quindlen, 1977: B 4). His reaction to the legal modification can be discerned in his statement that "[if] nothing else, the enlightened attitude on self-defense in these cases is a good inducement for every man to be a model husband" (MacPherson, 1977: A 14).

Excellent evidence of the national proportions of public concern about domestic abuse was demonstrated recently when the U.S. Senate passed a Domestic Violence Prevention Services Act (S 2759); the bill, sponsored by Representatives George Miller (Democrat-California), Barbara Mikulski (Democrat-Maryland), and Newton I. Steers, Jr. (Republican-Maryland), is still pending in the House (HR 1299). It would establish a new Center for Domestic Violence and Citizen Panels on Domestic Violence.

Women's rights organizations can rightfully claim much credit for augmenting public awareness of domestic violence. Their goals include elimination of differentiation in legal views of spouse abuse by either men or women; it is their hope to have more wife beating cases adjudicated in criminal rather than family courts (Cook, 1977: B 3). A frequent assertion of the feminists is that law enforcement officials fail to provide the early necessary aid when called in wife beating incidences and must therefore be held partly responsible for the eventual homicides. Feminists watched the Hughes trial closely, hoping it would prove to be a landmark case, but since Francine Hughes was acquitted on grounds of insanity, some feminists doubt that the case will set a useful precedent. Although her defense attorney believed that it would ("Michigan Woman," 1977: A 14), other proponents of women's rights were less sanguine about the trials implications. Susan Jacoby cautioned that the image of a woman driven by physical brutality and desperation into "such a state of psychic bondage that she could free herself. . . only by killing" violates the belief of feminists that women "can and should take control of their own lives" (New York Times, 1977: C 2).

In the homicide cases discussed above, feminist groups have provided support for the women on trial. For instance, the Women's Resource and Survival Center in Keyport, New Jersey, formed a defense committee for Roxanne Gay to raise money and hire a defense counsel; the North New Jersey Branch of the National

Organization for Women raised 10% of her bail ("Slaying suspect freed," 1977: 34). The legal liaison for the Women's Resource and Survival Center, Janice D. Miller, said that the Center viewed Roxanne Gay as a typical victim of wife abuse as well as an example of society's attitude toward the phenomenon (Cook, 1977: B 3). She added that the Center felt that the destiny of Mrs. Gay might have been her own violent death had she not taken protective action. Wisconsin feminists generated a defense fund for Jennifer Patri to publicize the right of wives to protect themselves against physical and emotional attack from their spouses ("A killing excuse," 1977: 108). Further indications of organized efforts are the studies of Claudia McCormick, superintendent of the women's center of Chicago's Cook County jail which were sparked by her anxiety about the bruised condition of incoming female inmates ("Study of female killers finds 40% were abused," 1977: 20) and the conference on the "Abused and Battered Women in Crisis," held in the Cardinal Spellman Head Start Center, New York City, January 23, 1975.[3]

Predictably, the acquittals on the basis of self-defense have prompted *ad horrendum* comments about possible increase in the use of violence by battered wives.[4] The brother of James Hughes, in a television interview, voiced concern that the exoneration of Francine would give women an "excuse" to take revenge (Jacoby, 1977: C 2). Before the Jennifer Patri trial, the Sheriff of Waupaca, Lawrence Schmies, said he expected there would be a lot more killings if she won her case ("A killing excuse," 1977: 108). Even the staunch campaigner for women's rights, Maria Roy, feared that an acquittal decision might encourage wives to solve their problems through violence. When contacted by the desperate women, Miss Roy cautions them against hope of acquittal on grounds of self-defense (Quindlen: 1977: B 4).

Homicide threatens the very essence of organized societies and virtually all legal systems have held it to be *malum in se,* an evil so fundamental that it is immoral as well as illegal. For the law to condone killing, there must be a proven need, either to the society (as in the case of war) or to the individual (as in self-defense). In particular instances, individual danger to wives had been sufficiently manifest to allow the law to exonerate some women who have resorted to homicide. Law evolves slowly, often by almost imperceptible degrees, and it cannot yet be determined whether the apparent willingness of courts to modify established legal doctrines of self-defense in cases of battered wives will constitute a continuing trend. It is evident, however, that there is legal recognition of the prevalence and severity of abusive marital relationships and thus a greater drive to ameliorate the distress.

NOTES

1. For recent analyses of domestic violence and possible legal remedies, see Flynn, 1978; Maidment, 1977; Freeman, 1977; Fromson, 1977; and Eisenberg and Seymour, 1978.

2. Perhaps it should be mentioned that married women who commit crimes do have a distinct advantage under the law; if the offense was committed in the presence of the husband, it is presumed that it was done through his coercion (Frankel, 1973: 489-490; Perkins, 1969: 909-911; Kanowitz, 1977: 88-99).

3. Among the spate of articles and books about battered women have been ones that scrutinize the reasons why women stay in such dangerous situations; e.g., Hanks and Rosenbaum, 1977; Gelles, 1976; U.S. News and World Report, 1978, "Battered wives: now they're fighting back"; Eisenberg and Micklow, 1977; Lystad, 1975; McCormick, 1977; Stark and McEvoy, 1970; and Tahourdin, 1976.

4. Rita Simon (a pre-eminent authority on female crime), to the contrary does not expect an increase in homicide and manslaughter by wives. She reasons that, as the position of women improves, their frustration level will be lowered and they will be less inclined to violence (Simon, 1975: 4).

REFERENCES

"Battered wives: now they're fighting back." (1978) U.S. News and World Report 82 (September 20): 47-48.

Bein, D. (1975) "The impact of the victim's behavior on the severity of the offender's sentence (with special reference to Israeli law). In Israel Drapkin and Emilio Viano. Victimology: A New Focus. Volume II. Lexingington, Mass.: Lexington Books; 49-65.

Cook, J. (1977) "Battered wife campaign focussing on woman charged with murder." New York Times (August 12): B 3.

Eisenberg, A.D., and E. J. Seymour (1978) "The self-defense plea and battered women." Trial 14 (July): 34-42, 68.

Eisenberg, S.E. and P. L. Micklow (1977) "The assaulted wife: 'catch 22' revisited." Women's Rights Law Reported 3 (Spring): 138-161.

Ferguson, R.W. and A.H. Stokke (1976) Concepts of Criminal Law. Boston: Holbrook Press.

Flynn, D. (1978) "Domestic relations—the Protection from Abuse Act—Pa. Stat. Ann. tit. 35 Sections 10181-10190 (Purden Supp. 1977). Temple Law Quarterly 51: 116-126.

Frankel, L. (1973) "Sex discrimination in the criminal law: the effect of the equal rights amendment." American Criminal Law Review 11 (Winter): 469-510.

Freeman, M.D.A. (1977) "Le Vice Anglais?—wife-battering in English and American law." Family Law Quarterly 11 (Fall): 199-251.

Gelles, R. J. (1976) "Abused wives: why do they stay." Journal of Marriage and Family 38 (November): 659-668.

Goode, W. (1969) "Violence among intimates." In Donald J. Mulvihill and Melvin M. Tumin, co-directors. Crimes of Violence. Washington: Government Printing Office. Appendix 19: 941-977.

Goodman, E.J. (1977) "Legal solutions: equal protection under the law." in Maria Roy, ed. Battered Women: a Psycho-sociological Study of Domestic Violence. New York: Van Nostrand Reinhold Company.

Gregory, M. (1976) "Battered wives." In Marie Borland, ed. Violence in the Family. Atlantic Highlands, New Jersey: Humanities Press; 107-128.

Hanks, S.E. and C.P. Rosenbaum (1977) "Battered women: a study of women who live with violent alcohol-abusing men." American Journal of Orthopsychiatry 47 (April): 291-306.

Hentig, Hans von. (1967) The Criminal and His Victim. [Hamden, Conn.] Archon Books.

Hoffman-Bustamante, D. (1973) "The nature of female criminality." Issues in Criminology 8 (Fall): 117-136.

"Homicide victim's violent nature provable through his record." (1978) Criminal Law Reporter 24 (October 4): 1001-1002.

Inbau, F.E., J.R. Thompson, and J.B. Zagel (1974) Criminal Law and Its Administration. Mineola, New York: Foundation Press, Inc.

"International Association of Chiefs of Police Training." (1977) "Key #245." In Maria Roy, ed. Battered Women: A Psycho-sociological Study of Domestic Violence. New York: Van Nostrand Reinhold Company.

Jacoby, S. (1977) "Hers." New York Times (December 1): C 2.

Janson, D. (1978) "Court rules woman was insane in killing." New York Times (March 11): 27.

Kanowitz, Leo (1977) Women and the Law: the Unfinished Revolution. Albuquerque: University of New Mexico Press.

"Killer of ex-husband acquitted." (1977) Facts on File 37 (December 3): 928.

"Killing excuse, A." (1977) Time 110 (November 28): 108.

Klein, D. (1973) "The etiology of female crime: A review of the literature." Issues in Criminology 8 (Fall, 1973): 3-30.

Landy, D. and E. Aronson (1969) "The influence of the character of the criminal and his victim on the decisions of simulated jurors." Journal of Experimental Social Psychology 5: 141-152.

Lystad, M.H. (1975) "Violence at home: a review of the literature." American Journal of Orthopsychiatry 45 (April): 328-345.

McCormick, C. (1977) Battered Women. Chicago, Illinois: Cook County Department of Corrections.

MacDonad, W.F. (1976) Criminal Justice and the Victim. Beverly Hills: Sage Publications.

MacPherson, M. (1977) "Battered wives and self-defense pleas." Washington Post (December 4): A 1, A 14.

Maidment, S. (1977) "The law's response to marital violence in England and the U.S.A." International and Comparative Law Quarterly 26 (April): 403-444.

"Michigan woman acquitted in ex-husband's slaying." (1977) New York Times (November 4): Λ 14.

Newman, J. (1975) "The offender as the victim." In Israel Drapkin and Emilio Viano. Victimology: A New Focus. Volume II. Lexington, Mass. Lexington Books: 113-120.

Perkins, R.M. (1969) Criminal Law. Mineola, New York: Foundation Press.

Price, R.R. (1977) "The forgotten female offender." Crime and Delinquency 23 (April): 101-108.

Quindlen, A. (1977) "Women who kill their spouses: the causes, the legal defense." New York Times (March 10): B 4.

Quinney, R. (1972) "Who is the victim?" Criminology 10: 314-323.

Samuelson, R.J. (1978) "When government steps in." National Journal (September 30): 1562.

Schneider, E.M. and S.B. Jordan. (1978) "Representation of women who defend themselves in response to physical or sexual assault." Women's Rights Reporter 4 (Spring): 149-163.

Silverman, R.A. (1974) "Victim precipitation: an examination of the concept." In Israel Drapkin and Emilio Viano. Victimology: A New Focus. Volume I. Lexington, Mass.: Lexington Books: 99-109.

"Slaying Suspect Freed." (1977) New York Times (November 12): 34.

Simon, R. (1975) The Contemporary Woman and Crime. Rockville, Maryland: Government Printing Office.

Stark, R. and J. McEvoy III. (1970) "Middle-class violence." Psychology Today 4 (November): 52-54, 110-112.

Steinmetz, S.K. (1977) "Wifebeating, husbandbeating—a comparison of the use of physical violence between spouses to resolve marital fights." In Maria Roy, ed. Battered Women: A Psycho-sociological Study of Domestic Violence. New York: Van Nostrand Reinhold Company.

"Study of female killers finds 40% were abused." (1977) New York Times (December 20): 20.

Tahourdin, B. (1976) "Battered wives: only a domestic affair." Comparative Criminology 20: 86-88.

Temin, C.E. (1973) "Discriminatory sentencing of women offenders: The argument for ERA in a nutshell." American Criminal Law Review 11 (Winter, 1973): 355-372.

, Ward, D.A., M. Jackson and R.E. Ward. (1968) "Crimes of violence by women." In D. J. Mulvihill and M.M. Tumin, eds. Crimes of Violence: a Staff Report Submitted to the National Commission on the Causes and Presentation of Violence. Volume 13, Appendix 13. Washington, D.C.: · Government Printing Office.

Wells, K.M. and P.B. Weston (1978) Criminal Law. Santa Monica, Calif.: Goodyear Publishing Company.

Wolfgang, M. (1957) "Victim-precipitated homicide." Journal of Criminal Law and Criminology and Police Science 48: 1-11.

Nancy Travis Wolfe is Assistant Professor in the Law Enforcement Administration Department at Western Illinois University. She is author of "Victim provocation: the battered wife and definition of self defense" in Sociological Symposium *and "Trends in extradition" accepted for publication in* Southern Journal of Criminal Justice.

32

TOWARD A THEORY OF
PERSONAL CRIMINAL VICTIMIZATION

MICHAEL J. HINDELANG
MICHAEL R. GOTTFREDSON
JAMES GAROFALO

INTRODUCTION

To this point, our work with the victimization survey data—and the work of most of those who have used the data—has been almost wholly empirical and methodological. On the basis of what is now known about victimization experiences, it is time to attempt to move beyond the data in order to postulate a theoretical model to help to account for these phenomena. Owing largely to the recency of victimization data and the complexity of victimization experiences, the theoretical model proposed in this chapter is a tentative, first step in constructing a theory of personal victimization. Although the theoretical model proposed here is, by and large, grounded in data about victims of crime, for many of the *explanatory mechanisms* that are postulated no data are currently available. Nonetheless, what is proposed in this model appears to be compatible with what is known about victims of personal crime from victimization surveys and other data.

Our theoretical model of the likelihood that an individual will suffer a personal victimization depends heavily on the concept of *lifestyle*. Briefly, lifestyle refers to routine daily activities, both vocational activities (work, school, keeping house, etc.) and leisure activities. What is offered is a theoretical model that postulates the antecedents of lifestyle and the mechanisms that link lifestyle with victimization. The findings that have been presented both in the earlier chapters and in other criminological research are then discussed within the context of the model.

From Michael J. Hindelang et al., "Toward a theory of personal criminal victimization," pp. 241-274. Reprinted with permission from VICTIMS OF PERSONAL CRIME: AN EMPIRICAL FOUNDATION FOR A THEORY OF PERSONAL VICTIMIZATION, Copyright 1978, Ballinger Publishing Company.

The basic model is shown in Figure 11-1. We postulate that role expectations and social structure impose constraints to which persons must adapt if they are to function smoothly in society.[2] Role expectations and structural constraints for any individual depend upon that individual's constellation of demographic characteristics. The use of dashed lines in connection with demographic characteristics in Figure 11-1 is meant to indicate that these characteristics do not cause role expectations and social structural constraints.

Role expectations as used here refers to cultural norms that are associated with achieved and ascribed statuses of individuals and that define preferred and anticipated behaviors. The role expectations with which we are concerned are those that pertain to central statuses of individuals—central in the sense of having a diffuse influence on the person occupying the status.[3] For example, role expectations vary dramatically with the age of the person; what is expected and/or deemed appropriate behavior for a child is generally not what is expected of an adult. Similarly, traditional American childrearing practices involve implicit and explicit definitions of role expectations—the differential propriety of dress, manner, expression of emotion, choice of play objects, etc.—depending on the sex of the child. Also, with respect to marital status, there are different role expectations for married versus unmarried persons; the former are generally expected to spend more time at home and in general to lead a more settled existence.

The other source of constraints identified in Figure 11-1 is the social structure. The *structural constraints* originating from this source can be defined as limitations on behavioral options that result from the particular arrangements existing within various institutional orders, such as the economic, familial, educational, and legal orders. For example, economic factors impose stringent limitations on the range of choices that individuals have with respect to such fundamentals as area of residence, nature of leisure activities, mode of transportation, and access to educational opportunities; to some extent racial barriers, particularly with regard to area of residence, are economically based. In addition, in the United States, the decline of the extended family structure has had an impact on the behavioral choices of family members. For example, parents must assume at-home responsibilities—including child supervision, cooking, and cleaning—that in former times were shared with grandparents and other relatives in the household.

No attempt is made to assign priorities to these institutional orders; they are certainly interdependent, and most people, at various times in their lives, are simultaneously constrained by several of them. By

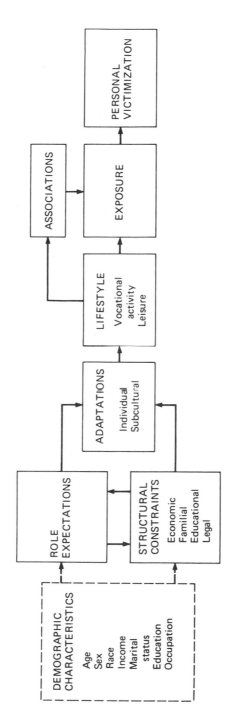

Figure 11-1. A Lifestyle/Exposure Model of Personal Victimization

way of illustration, adolescents under a certain age are constrained
by both legal and educational institutions. That is, the structure of
the educational system (e.g., school calendar and class times) as well
as legal requirements (e.g., compulsory attendance laws and child
labor laws) limit the behavioral options of adolescents.

Note that in Figure 11-1, role expectations and structural constraints are reciprocally related. In recent years, for example, sex role
expectations have been modified so that there has been some convergence in the role expectations for males and females. This change, in
turn, has been translated into structural changes, particularly in the
family and, to a lesser extent, in the economic realm. One might
argue that role expectations and structural constraints are indistin-
guishable, that social structure is simply a composite of social roles.
However, we believe the two are analytically distinct; for example,
the expectations associated with the role of parent may be quite
different in a social structure characterized by detached nuclear
families than in one characterized by an extended family structure
of communal childrearing.

As pointed out earlier and as illustrated in Figure 11-1, members
of society adapt to role expectations and structural constraints. Such
adaptations occur on both the individual and group levels. Each
person learns skills and attitudes that allow him or her to operate
with some individuality within the constraints imposed by role
expectations and social structure. Among the skills and attitudes that
an individual acquires in adapting to role expectations and structural
constraints, of particular interest in connection with personal victimization are attitudes and beliefs about crime, including fear of crime.
Once learned, these attitudes and beliefs are often incorporated into
the routine activities of the individual, frequently as limitations on
behavior.

Role expectations and structural constraints have similar effects
for people with the same demographic characteristics. Thus, *shared*
adaptations also emerge and can even be incorporated as norms
among subgroups of society. Such group adaptations are postulated
in Cohen's (1955) description of the "delinquent subculture" and
Wolfgang and Ferracuti's (1967) "subculture of violence" theory.

Individuals adapt to structural constraints and role expectations in
ways that result in regularities in behavioral patterns. What is important for our purposes is that these include such routine activities as
working outside of the home, going to school, or keeping house, as
well as typical leisure time pursuits. These daily routines constitute
lifestyle as we use the term here.

Our usage of lifestyle is similar to Havighurst's (1961:333): "a characteristic way of distributing one's time, one's interest, and one's talent among the common social roles of adult life—those of worker, parent, spouse, homemaker, citizen, friend, club or association member, and user of leisure time." Our definition differs from Havighurst's in that ours is not limited to adults; furthermore, our emphasis is heavily on *routine* activities.

In our model, lifestyle differences result from differences in role expectations, structural constraints, and individual and subcultural adaptations. Variations in lifestyles are related differentially to probabilities of being in particular places at particular times and coming into contact with persons who have particular characteristics; because criminal victimization is not randomly distributed across time and space and because offenders in personal crimes are not representative of the general population—but rather there are high-risk times, places, and people—this implies that lifestyle differences are associated with differences in *exposure* to situations that have a high victimization risk.

In the course of vocational and leisure pursuits, individuals spend a disproportionate amount of their time with others who have similar lifestyles. One reason why vocation—whether it be keeping house, going to school, or being employed—is so central to lifestyle is that it structures a large portion of daily activities. To the extent that these vocational activities are carried out as formal roles within institutional structures, the nature of an individual's interactions with others has a greater degree of predictability. That is, formal roles generally define socially acceptable daily routines that structure the lifestyles of those involved.

As shown in Figure 11-1, the major linkage between lifestyle and exposure to high victimization risk situations is direct. There is, however, another indirect link, which operates through associations. *Associations* refer to more or less sustained personal relationships among individuals that evolve as a result of similar lifestyles and hence similar interests shared by these individuals. Because offenders disproportionately have particular characteristics, association with people having these characteristics serves to increase exposure to personal victimization.

Personal victimization, the final element in the model, follows probabilistically from exposure to high victimization risk situations. Below, we will give additional attention, primarily in the form of a series of propositions, to the model and how it helps to explain variations in the likelihood of personal victimization. Before doing so, however, it is necessary to discuss more fully the key component in our model, lifestyle.

LIFESTYLE

Such diverse phenomena as life expectancy, morbidity, automobile accidents, suicide, and criminal victimization are all closely associated with demographic characteristics. For example, the life expectancy for women is about eight years longer than that for men and the life expectancy for whites is about seven years longer than for blacks (U.S. Bureau of the Census, 1974:58). Blacks have higher infant and maternal death rates than do whites (U.S. Bureau of the Census, 1974b:60). Younger drivers are more likely than middle-aged drivers to be involved in automobile accidents. Persons who have never married or who are separated, widowed, or divorced have suicide rates that are substantially higher than those for married persons (Gibbs, 1966). Males have higher suicide rates than females, particularly in older age groups (U.S. Bureau of the Census, 1974b:63). As we have shown throughout this book, demographic characteristics are also related to differential probabilities of personal victimization.

In terms of our model, these relationships between demographic variables and these diverse consequences, particularly personal victimization, can be attributed to differences in lifestyle. This is because various constellations of demographic characteristics are associated with role expectations and structural constraints that, mediated through individual and subcultural adaptations, channel lifestyles. For example, the lifestyles of young drivers can help account for their relatively high accident rates. They have less driving experience and relatively immature judgment; they are more likely to socialize in groups and to be influenced by group pressures to drive recklessly, drag race, and so on. Younger persons are typically more mobile and active than older persons and hence have a greater *exposure* to risks of automobile accidents. Similar inferences about differential lifestyles can be suggested to account for the relationship of demographic variables to the other consequences noted above: men are more likely than women to be exposed to the health hazards related to occupation; because of the relative economic constraints impinging on blacks and whites, blacks are more likely to live under conditions conducive to ill-health and are less able economically to take advantage of preventive medical care; unattached persons (single, divorced, widowed, or separated) may tend to spend more time alone and to have fewer dependents who rely upon them for nurturance and support.

It should not be surprising that lifestyle is closely tied to the most fundamental aspects of human existence: how long we live, how well we live, and how we die. The antecedents of lifestyle not only affect life chances in the long run, but also affect short-term life experiences. As conceptualized in our model, variations in lifestyles are attributable to the ways in which persons with various constellations of demographic characteristics adapt to role expectations and structural constraints. Our attention will now turn briefly to some examples of how lifestyle can be traced back to demographic characteristics in our model.

Age

Perhaps the clearest example of a demographic variable that dramatically affects lifestyle is age. Role expectations vary as a function of age. In addition, a variety of structural constraints—kinship, economic, educational, and legal—differentially impinge upon individuals according to age. In infancy and early childhood, the child's existence is highly structured according to parental expectations; that is, such things as when the child is fed, the stimuli within the child's environment, where the child is permitted to play, and with whom the child comes into contact are all largely under parental control. However, as the child approaches school age and begins to associate increasingly with others outside of the immediate family, parental control is less influential in restricting the extrafamilial exposure of the child—where the child is, with whom she or he comes into contact, and generally how the child's time is spent outside of the home.

During the years in which the child is completing her or his education, the child's lifestyle begins to shift dramatically. The waking hours spent outside of the home are largely structured by the activities involved in traveling to school, participating in curricular and extracurricular activities, and returning from school. As the child moves into adolescence, there is increasing autonomy; a greater proportion of time is spent in association with peers, and, by late adolescence, the activities of the child are by and large no longer within the institutional control of family or school. During early adulthood, lifestyles become increasingly determined by adaptations to the constraints of educational and occupational (economic) structures. For those pursuing neither occupational nor educational careers, there is considerably less institutional structure. The occupation of the person—that is, the role that the individual assumes within the economic structure—will have a substantial impact on that person's lifestyle throughout adulthood. This impact manifests itself with respect to where, when, and with whom time is spent. Of course, throughout the occupational career, age itself will also have an impact on lifestyle, especially in terms of time spent outside of the home, restrictions imposed by childrearing, and leisure time activities. As retirement years are reached, individuals begin to experience another dramatic shift in daily activities: mobility decreases, the number of interpersonal contacts decreases, and the experiential world of the individual becomes constricted generally. One of the important *adaptations* that occurs as age increases is a shift in attitudes, including an increased fear of crime. This increased fear contributes to limitations of activities, mobility, and contacts with strangers. By virtue of adaptations to role expectations and structural constraints that vary as a function of age, age itself an important indicator of lifestyle.

Parenthetically, it is important to note that throughout the life cycle, individuals are more likely to associate with and to come into contact with those occupying similar age-linked roles than with those occupying different roles: students with students, workers with workers, homemakers with homemakers, and retired persons with retired persons.

Sex

Despite the growing movement toward sexual equality in all institutional spheres and away from sex role differentiation, there remain structural constraints and differences in sex role expectations. Adaptations to these make sex an important indicator of lifestyle. Traditionally, the sex role socialization of females has been different from that of males. Because of sex role differentiation, sex is related to daily activities such as where time is spent, the number of interpersonal contacts, and the likelihood of encountering strangers. For example, females spend a greater proportion of their time inside the home because as adolescents they are more closely supervised than males, and as adults they are more likely than males to assume housekeeping responsibilities. Although sex is a major indicator of lifestyle, it is a weaker indicator for the youngest and oldest members of society. That is, in preadolescent and postretirement age groups, the lifestyles of males and females are less differentiated than in the intervening years, during which sex-linked differences in structural constraints and role expectations are more pronounced. For example, after retirement, both men and women are likely to be less mobile, to spend more time at home, and to have fewer contacts with persons outside of their primary groups; at this point in the life cycle (and in preadolescence as well), the role expectations and structural constraints associated with age tend to take precedence over those associated with sex.

Marital Status

Another variable that is closely tied to lifestyles through the processes shown in our model is marital status. Among adults, the lifestyles of those who are married can be expected to differ in several important respects from those who are not married. The common living arrangements associated with marriage (or cohabitation) introduce a form of structure that is less prominent in the lives of "unattached" persons. For example, married persons would be expected to spend proportionately more time within the home than would single persons; this is especially true of those who have children. Marital and familial ties result in an increased number of at-home responsibilities. In addition, leisure time spent out of the home is likely to be in the company of partners or with other persons of similar marital and familial statuses. Also, because the marital bond brings together two extended family networks, the likelihood of spending time with family members increases. On the other hand, single persons are likely to spend their time outside of the home more often unaccompanied or in the company of other single persons. The transition from an "unattached" to an "attached" status (e.g., single to married) generally implies a dramatic shift in lifestyle; this transition involves a shift in role expectations and structural constraints to which individuals must adapt. Thus, marital status is another indicator of where, when, and with whom individuals routinely spend their time.

Family Income and Race

Family income is closely· associated with life chances and life experiences because it is reflective of one's position in the economic structure, which is one of the most important constraints on behavioral options. As family income increases, so too does the flexibility to adjust one's lifestyle to one's wishes. This flexibility includes the ability to select the area in which to live, the mode of transportation that will be used in daily activities, the proportion of time spent in private surroundings versus public places, and the very nature of leisure time activities. It is important to note that the choices provided to those with sufficient family income often result in an income-linked segregation in housing, transportation, privacy, and many leisure time activities. Thus, patterns of *association* are also income-linked: those living in suburbs are likely to be of at least moderate income; those relying primarily on public modes of intracity transportation are likely to be less affluent; members of country clubs are likely to be relatively wealthy. Thus, those of similar family incomes tend to cluster in particular residential, recreational, and other social settings.

Like family income, race is closely tied with life chances and life experiences. Some of the importance of race as an indicator of life-style derives from its association with family income. However, whites and blacks of the same socioeconomic stratum live in quite different worlds. For example, noneconomic structural constraints associated with race result in segregated housing patterns, and thus blacks tend to live in more economically heterogeneous areas than do whites (Taeuber, 1968; Erbe, 1975). Such housing patterns have particularly strong implications for patterns of associations among blacks versus whites; among the latter, patterns of association will be more income-segregated than among the former. These differences are apparent throughout the life cycle, especially in the educational and recreational realms. For example, attending private schools and belonging to private clubs are much more common among whites than among blacks.

Our attention will now turn to an examination of some of the major victimization findings and to a discussion of ways in which patterns of victimization can be related to variations in lifestyles. Our discussion will draw on the analyses presented both in earlier chapters and in Hindelang (1976). In order to assist the reader, references to the tables in which particular findings are presented will be given as those findings are discussed. In addition, to the extent that the data are available, our discussion below will draw upon relevant findings of prior research.

VICTIMIZATION AND LIFESTYLE—A SET OF PROPOSITIONS

For a personal victimization to occur, several conditions must be met. First, the prime actors—the offender and the victim—must have occasion to intersect in time and space. Second, some source of dispute or claim must arise between the actors in which the victim is perceived by the offender as an appropriate object of the victimization. Third, the offender must be willing and able to threaten or use force (or stealth) in order to achieve the desired end. Fourth, the circumstances must be such that the offender views it as advantageous to use or threaten force (or stealth) to achieve the desired end. The probability of these conditions being met is related to the life circumstances of members of society.

Lifestyle is the central component in our theoretical model. In our view, the centrality of lifestyle derives primarily from its close association with *exposure* to victimization risk situations. Victimization is not a phenomenon that is uniformly distributed; it occurs disproportionately in particular times and places; it occurs disproportionately by offenders with particular demographic characteristics; it occurs disproportionately under certain circumstances (e.g., according to whether or not the person is alone); it occurs disproportionately according to the prior relationship between the potential victim and the potential offender; and so forth. Because different lifestyles imply different probabilities that individuals will be in particular places, at particular times, under particular circumstances, interacting with particular kinds of persons, lifestyle affects the probability of victimization. In the following discussion, we will suggest ways in which particular lifestyles have implications for exposure to personal victimization in light of the empirical properties of these victimizations. Although the format we will use involves the statement of a single proposition followed by a discussion of its theoretical and empirical tenability, it should be stressed at the outset that these propositions are interdependent. Therefore, for each proposition, the phrase "other things being equal" is implied.

Proposition 1: *The probability of suffering a personal victimization is directly related to the amount of time that a person spends in public places (e.g., on the street, in parks, etc.), and particularly in public places at night.*

Systematic analysis of the occurrence of criminal events has demonstrated repeatedly that the likelihood of a crime occurring is not uniformly distributed by time or place. In his study of robbery in Philadelphia, Normandeau (1968:221) found that 38 percent of the robberies studied occurred in the six-hour period from 8 P.M. to 2 A.M. Similarly, findings from both the President's Commission on Crime in the District of Columbia (1966:58) and McClintock and Gibson's (1961:131-2) London study are congruent with Normandeau's finding that robbery occurs disproportionately in the late evening and early morning hours.

In studies of police offense reports, rape has also been found to occur disproportionately in the late night and early morning hours. Chappell and Singer (1973:60) found that in New York City 37 percent of the rapes reported to the police occurred between the hours of 8 P.M. and 2 A.M.; Amir's (1971:84) study of Philadelphia rapes showed that nearly one-half of the rapes recorded in the police files occurred during the same time period. Likewise, the President's Commission on Crime in the District of Columbia (1966:48) found that nearly three-fifths of the rapes reported to the police in that city occurred between the hours of 6 P.M. and 3 A.M.—a finding congruent with MacDonald's (1971:30) study showing that 53 percent of the reported rapes in Denver occurred in the six-hour period between 10 P.M. and 4 A.M. The available studies using official data on assaults suggest that the majority of these crimes fall within the 6 P.M.–12 A.M. time period (President's Commission on Crime in the District of Columbia, 1966:70; Pokorny, 1965: Fig. 1; Pittman and Handy, 1964:45). Without exception, these studies of robbery, assault, and rape using police data demonstrate that late night and early morning carry the greatest risk of personal victimization. In the eight cities studied here, it was found that 40 percent of the total personal incidents occurred during the six-hour period from 6 P.M. to midnight (Hindelang, 1976:204).

What can the available data tell us about the places in which personal victimizations occur? Studies of robbery have uniformly shown that by far the greatest proportion of robbery incidents take place on the street. For example, Normandeau (1968:244), McClintock and Gibson (1961:130), Reiss (1967:22), Mulvihill, Tumin and Curtis (1969:221), and the President's Commission on Crime in the District of Columbia (1966:66) each found that about one-half of the robbery incidents recorded in police files took place on the street. For assault, similar findings have been reported (Pittman and Handy, 1964: Table 3.3; Reiss, 1967:34; Mulvihill et al., 1969:221), though the dominance of public places as the location of the crime is less than for robbery; in one study (President's Commission on Crime in the District of Columbia, 1966:79) assaults were found to have occurred more often in a residence than on the street (47 versus 37 percent). The results of studies of rapes known to the police indicate that this offense—unlike the crimes of robbery and aggravated assault—is most likely to occur within the residence of the victim or the offender (Amir, 1971:145; MacDonald, 1971:33; Reiss, 1967: 105; Mulvihill et al., 1969:221; Chappell and Singer, 1973:62). However, this finding is tempered by data that show that the most frequent place in which the victim and the offender came into initial contact is the street (Amir, 1971:139; MacDonald, 1971:32).[4]

Victimization survey results are consistent with studies of robbery and assault using official police data. About seven out of ten robberies and one out of two assaults occurred on the street and in other public places (Hindelang, 1976:206). In fact, victimization results indicate that this finding even holds for rape. In 1974, almost half of the rapes reported in the national sample were reported to have occurred on the street or in other open public places, compared to about one-third reported to have occurred inside of a home or other

(Table 1-1): those under twenty years of age had a rate of victimization that was three times the rate for those sixty-five years of age or older; to *sex* (Hindelang, 1976: Table 5-5): males had a rate that was 50 percent greater than the rate for females; to *marital status* (Hindelang, 1976: Table 5-7): those who were never married, divorced, or separated had total personal victimization rates that were more than twice as large as the rates for those who were married or widowed; to *vocation* (Figure 5-1): for example, young (sixteen to nineteen years old) males who were not in school had a risk of personal victimization that was 50 percent greater than the risk for young males who were in school, and young (sixteen to nineteen years old) females who were unemployed had a risk of personal victimization that was 50 percent greater than that of young females who were not unemployed; to *family income* (Hindelang, 1976: Table 5-7): there was a trend for rates of personal victimization to decrease as family income increased.

It should be pointed out here that although demographic indicators of lifestyle have been discussed as though they are independent of each other, clearly this is not the case. For example, in the earlier discussion of sex as predictive of lifestyle, it was suggested that sex would appear to be a poorer predictor of lifestyle for older persons than for young adults; that is, as dependent children leave the home and as retirement age approaches, the daily activities of males and females become more similar. The impact on personal victimization rates of this decreasing sex-based differentiation in lifestyles as a function of age was evident in the victimization survey results. In the youngest age groups surveyed (twelve to fifteen and sixteen to nineteen years old), males had a victimization rate that was nearly twice that of females; as age increased, the male-female rate differences decreased until in the sixty-five or older age category the rates of total personal victimization for males and females were virtually identical (Hindelang, 1976: Figure 5-2).[7]

Demands of lifestyle influence where an individual spends time. Those who work have a large portion of their daily activities structured in and around the workplace; those who raise children have a large portion of their time structured in and around the home; those in school have their time structured by school activities. Lifestyle includes not only these structured activities but also how leisure time is typically spent.

Both leisure time and work time activities are shaped by adaptations to structural constraints and role expectations. Earlier it was pointed out that attitudes are an important component of these adaptations. Of particular relevance to our present concern are atti-

building (Hindelang, Dunn, Sutton, and Aumick, 1976:356).[5] Overall, these data on personal victimizations suggest that the street and other public places are the places in which personal victimizations, especially robberies, are most likely to occur. There is evidence, then, to support the notion that personal victimizations occur disproportionately at night and in public places.

Proposition 2: *The probability of being in public places, particularly at night, varies as a function of lifestyle.*

In our earlier discussion of lifestyles, we suggested that, as a result of adaptations to role expectations and structural constraints, particular demographic characteristics are predictive of lifestyle differences. We suggested that younger persons (e.g., adolescents and young adults) are more likely than older persons to spend time outside of the home. Similarly, we posited that males and single persons are apt to spend a higher proportion of their time away from home than their similarly situated counterparts. Also, those whose daily routines are highly structured by involvement in conventional vocations (e.g., working or attending school)—although they spend a relatively high proportion of their time outside of the home—are more likely than those not involved in conventional vocations (e.g., unemployed or school dropout) to spend time in relatively structured, sheltered environments.[6] Finally, we argued that the higher one's family income, the greater the likelihood that time will be spent in semiprivate or private environs.

Some data supporting our contentions are available from studies of how people spend their time. DeGrazia (1961:121–124) found that away from home leisure activity tends to drop off sharply after the fifteen to nineteen year old group and then decline slowly, almost to zero among persons sixty or older; these age-specific differences were less pronounced for females than for males. Similarly, Chapin (1974:113) found that young persons and the elderly had more "free time" than persons in the middle age groups, but the elderly disproportionately spent their free time resting and watching television. Examining several variables simultaneously, Chapin (1974:144) discovered that "working full time, being a female, and having young children in the household each put constraints on the amount of discretionary time available".

How do these demographic characteristics, which we argue are predictive of lifestyle differences, relate to rates of personal victimization? As noted in Chapters 1 and 5, each of these lifestyle indicators is associated with rates of personal victimization. In the eight cities, rates of personal victimization are strongly related to *age*

tudes about crime. Chapter 8 as well as prior research (Hindelang, 1974b; Ennis, 1967) indicate that fear of crime and victimization are closely linked to respondent characteristics such as age and sex. For example, one of the most frequently asked "fear of crime" questions is: "Is there any area right around here—that is, within a mile—where you would be afraid to walk alone at night?"[8] Responses to this and similar questions consistently indicate that age and sex are both related to fear of crime. Older persons and females are more fearful than younger persons and males, respectively. These differences are especially pronounced when the referent is "on the streets."[9] Such fears would be expected to be translated by the respondent into avoidance of the feared situation whenever possible. The key words in the question quoted in the text above are "area" (i.e., public place), "alone," and "at night." Because these are the very conditions under which victimization is most probable, it follows that those who are fearful of these conditions and who therefore presumably try to avoid them will have a decreased *exposure* to personal victimizations.[10] Behavioral avoidance may be a powerful means of reducing one's likelihood of victimization. As pointed out in Chapter 9, however, such reductions may come about not by complete avoidance of exposure, but by subtle changes in such things as the times and the conditions (e.g., accompanied rather than alone) under which exposure occurs. As discussed in Chapter 8, in conjunction with age and sex, those with the highest levels of fear (older persons and females) have the lowest rates of personal victimization. These findings are quite consistent with the proposition that lifestyle (particularly leisure components), and hence, exposure to situations in which the risk of victimization is high, are shaped by personal attitudes and beliefs.

On the basis of a simultaneous consideration of Propositions 1 and 2, we are postulating that lifestyles are related to the probability of being in places (street, parks, and other public places) at times (especially nighttime) when victimizations are known to occur disproportionately. As will become clear below, lifestyle is related to victimization not only because it correlates with place-time exposure, but for other important reasons as well.

Proposition 3:   *Social contacts and interactions occur disproportionately among individuals who share similar lifestyles.*

Because they are predictive of lifestyle, demographic characteristics—such as family income, race, age, education, and marital status—are indicative of stratification processes that pattern social interactions. Not only are neighborhoods often segregated by race and income, but there are also housing developments and apartment complexes that are often segregated by age and marital status. Working, being in school, keeping house, as well as being unemployed and being a school dropout (routine activities that are a major component of lifestyle), all differ from each other along demographic dimensions.

People who are employed are different demographically from people who are unemployed. The latter are more likely to be younger, have less education, and be black (Executive Office of the President, 1973:113-14). Among the employed, people are more likely to interact with persons of similar socioeconomic statuses—blue collar workers with blue collar workers and white collar workers with white collar workers (Laumann, 1966). Within each of these groups (e.g., blue collar workers), patterns of interactions are likely to be further segregated by race, age, and sex. The interactions to which we refer here include both the formal structured aspects of the job as well as the informal unstructured aspects such as coffee breaks, lunch breaks, and relatively brief social interactions that occur in the process of going between work and home (e.g., stopping at a bar for a drink).

Just as those who are employed differ demographically from those who are not, so too do those in school differ from those of the same age who are not in school. Among those in school, segregation similar to that among workers is also evident. Those in school are obviously segregated by age. In addition, they tend to be segregated by income and race. Even within schools that are heterogeneous, the informal interactions are typically segregated by race, family income, sex, and age. Most of what we have said about those who are employed and those in school can be generalized to the other activities and statuses mentioned earlier.

The demographically segregated social interactions that occur within the structured school and work environs are also in evidence in the less structured social interactions that typically occur during leisure hours. As a result of role expectations and structural constraints, social interactions during leisure hours tend toward demographic homogeneity. Not only are the social interactions themselves segregated along demographic dimensions, but the places and situations in which these interactions occur are markedly different. For example, young single males and older married females might both go out of the home for entertainment during leisure hours, but the places they go are likely to be quite different from each other in the patrons they attract.

One of the consequences of the tendency toward demographically homogeneous social interactions is that criminal offenders have a greater probability of interacting with people who are demographically similar to themselves.

Proposition 4: *An individual's chances of personal victimization are dependent upon the extent to which the individual shares demographic characteristics with offenders.*

Data from the Federal Bureau of Investigation's *Uniform Crime Reports* show that individuals arrested for the personal crimes of interest here—rape, robbery, assault, and larceny—are much more likely (in relation to their representation in the general population) to be male, young, and black than female, old, and white. Data on arrests reported in the UCR for 1975 show that virtually all of those arrested for rape, about 90 percent of those arrested for robbery and aggravated assault, and nearly 70 percent of those arrested for larceny were males (Kelley, 1976:183).[11] About one-half of those arrested for index violent crimes and 60 percent of those arrested for larceny, were between the ages of fourteen and twenty-four (Kelley, 1976: 189), but only one-third of the general population fell into this age group (U.S. Bureau of the Census, 1974:31). The UCR data on race indicate that 31 percent of those arrested for larceny, 40 percent for aggravated assault, 45 percent for rape, and 59 percent for robbery were black (Kelley, 1976:192). For each of these crimes, the representation of blacks among arrestees is substantially above their 11 percent representation in the general population (U.S. Bureau of the Census, 1974b:33).

Data on the residence of the arrestee (e.g., urban versus rural) are not available from the UCR. However, arrest rates—the number of arrests divided by the general population—are available in the UCR for various city size groups. These data indicate that rates of arrest are related to extent of urbanization in much the same way as offense rates are related to extent of urbanization. In 1975, the arrest rate for rape in cities with populations of more than 250,000 was more than twice that in rural areas (21.2 per 100,000 versus 9.9 per 100,000). Similarly, for aggravated assault (163.0 versus 92.7), larceny (589.6 versus 204.6), and particularly robbery (163.1 versus 21.3), the rates of arrest per 100,000 persons in the general population were relatively high in large cities and tended to decrease as the extent of urbanization decreased. These data suggest that urban residence is also a characteristic of offenders, because offenders in personal crimes tend to commit crimes within a short distance of their residence (Turner, 1969; Hoover, 1966:23–27; Normandeau, 1968:249–77).

Although the findings reported above are generally accepted as demonstrating higher rates of offending by males, younger persons, and urban residents in the personal crimes of interest in this book, the findings on race are often questioned on the basis of alleged racial discrimination in the administration of justice (e.g., Quinney, 1970:129–30; Chambliss, 1969:856). In a recent paper (Hindelang, 1978), victimization survey data have been used as a source of information about the race of offenders as reported by victims. These data from the LEAA-Census 1974 national survey indicate that, according to victims' reports, seven out of ten of the offenders in personal larceny victimizations, six out of ten in robbery, four out of ten in rape, and three out of ten in assault are reported by victims to be black. The data, which are not subject to the criticism of reflecting biases in the administration of justice, are in close agreement with the UCR arrest data in showing that in the crimes of rape, robbery, assault, and personal larceny, blacks are substantially over-represented as offenders in relation to their representation in the general population.

Unfortunately, the UCR arrest data only provide information on the offender's age, race, and sex. Other offender characteristics, however, such as marital status, educational attainment, and income, are available from a variety of other sources. In the National Suvey of Jail Inmates conducted by the Bureau of the Census in 1972, it was found that fewer than one-quarter of those being held in jails, as compared to more than 60 percent of those in the general population of males fourteen years of age or older, were married (LEAA, 1977: Table C). This same survey indicated that the median number of years of education for the jail population was two years less than that of the general population of males fourteen years of age or older (ten versus twelve years; LEAA, 1977:Table 4). The income data available from this survey show that 44 percent of the jail inmates had annual incomes in the year prior to arrest and confinement of less than $2,000; this contrasts with 16 percent for males fourteen years of age or older in the general population. Further, only 6 percent of the inmates, but 35 percent of the general population of males fourteen years of age or older, had annual incomes of $10,000 or more (LEAA, 1977:20).[12]

Data available for specific offenses, such as robbery (Normandeau, 1968:ch. 6) and rape (Amir, 1971:ch. 5), are consistent with the profile of offenders conveyed by the jail survey data. In relation to the general population, offenders are less likely to be married and more likely to come from lower status occupations (and inferentially to have lower educational attainment), than the general population.

An earlier work (Hindelang, 1976) examined the joint distributions of victim and offender characteristics for race, sex, and age. These data for total personal incidents indicate that the vast majority of personal victimizations suffered by black/others were committed by black/others; similarly, victimizations suffered by males were committed by males, and those suffered by younger persons were committed by younger persons. Also, offenders with these characteristics were more likely to victimize those with the same characteristics than to victimize those with other characteristics.

To summarize, offenders involved in the types of crimes of interest here are disproportionately male, young, urban residents,[13] black, of lower socioeconomic status, unemployed (and not in school), and unmarried. In our brief review of victim characteristics above, and in earlier chapters, it was seen that victims disproportionately share these characteristics. It is of particular importance to note that when these characteristics are considered simultaneously, they are especially predictive of both rates of offending and rates of victimization. For example, from Figure 5-1 it can be seen that the likelihood of personal victimization for sixteen to nineteen year old males who are not in school was 143 per 1,000—nearly three times the overall likelihood of personal victimization in the eight cities. Data of this kind, which are standardized according to population characteristics, are not generally available in the literature for more than two *offender* characteristics at a time. Normandeau (1968:175) reports such data standardized by age and sex. The overall offending rate for robbery in Philadelphia was 17.7 per 10,000 general population; however, for fifteen to nineteen year olds the rates for males and females, respectively, were 55.6 and 3.1. Further, when race was taken into account, the rates ranged from 218.4 for fifteen to nineteen year old black males to zero for white females of the same age. Although there are some exceptions, the combinations of demographic characteristics that are predictive of offending for the personal crimes studied here are also predictive of victimization for these crimes.

Proposition 5: *The proportion of time that an individual spends among nonfamily members varies as a function of lifestyle.*[14]

Certain lifestyles insulate the individual from contacts with nonfamily members. For example, as children mature from infancy through adolescence, they spend a decreasing proportion of their time with family members. In early adulthood, individuals begin to marry and raise families and, consequently, spend an increasing proportion of time with their family of procreation. Because child-rearing responsibilities fall disproportionately on women, the result is that, among those who are married, females spend a greater proportion of their time with family members than do males. Also, as noted in our introductory discussion of lifestyle, as the retirement years approach, contacts outside of the home, and beyond a narrowing circle of close friends and family members, generally decrease. Thus, at the age extremes and among those who are married—particularly those with children—the proportion of time spent with nonfamily members is less than that for persons with other characteristics.

Proposition 6: *The probability of personal victimization, particularly personal theft, increases as a function of the proportion of time that an individual spends among nonfamily members.*

Our discussion regarding the general homogeneity of the victim-offender dyad does not necessarily imply, of course, that victims and offenders are likely to know each other. In fact, the victimization data from the eight cities indicate that four out of five personal victimizations reported to survey interviewers involved strangers as offenders (Hindelang, 1976:Table 7-1).[15] Offenders who were strangers predominated, particularly in theft-related offenses; in robberies, about 90 percent, and in personal larceny, about 95 percent of the victimizations reported to interviewers involved strangers. For assaultive victimizations not involving theft, the proportion of all offenders who were strangers was smaller; about seven out of ten of the rape and assault victimizations were by strangers (Hindelang, 1976:Table 7-1).

Studies using official statistics have repeatedly found that more than four out of five robbery victimizations involve strangers (Mulvihill et al., 1969; Normandeau, 1968; and McClintock and Gibson, 1961). Thus, for robbery, official statistics and victimization survey results are in agreement on this point. The official and victimization data on assault, and to a lesser extent rape, are not in as close agreement. For aggravated assault, Mulvihill et al. (1969) and the President's Commission on Crime in the District of Columbia (1966) report that only one out of five incidents involved offenders who were strangers to the victim. Thus, official data on aggravated assault show a percentage of stranger crimes that is less than one-third the percentage found in victimization survey data. The official data on rape are also at odds—but much less so than the assault data—with victimization survey results. Although the eight-city data show that about 70 percent of rape victimizations were committed by strangers, the percentages of strangers involved in rape victimizations as measured by official statistics reported in the literature range from 42 to 60 percent (Amir, 1971:42 percent; Mulvihill et al., 1969:53 percent; Chappell and Singer, 1973:58 percent; MacDonald, 1971:60 percent).

Reverse record checks can be used to estimate the extent to which differences between official and victimization data in the proportion of "stranger" offenders are method-linked. In such studies, victims are drawn from police files, and (ideally) interviewed in a double-blind design, about victimization during the reference period. These studies—which were limited to "known victims" (i.e., those selected from police files)—indicate that when the offender was a nonstranger, victims were slightly less likely to report aggravated assaults (50 percent versus 56 percent) to survey interviewers than when the offender was a stranger (LEAA, 1972: Appendix Table 5). According to reverse record checks, victimization surveys apparently undercount aggravated assault victimizations by nonstrangers only slightly (in comparison to official data). When an adjustment is made for this differential, victimization survey data still show that strangers predominate substantially as offenders in aggravated assault. Reverse record check results for rape indicate that when police files showed the offender as a stranger, 84 percent of the victimizations were reported to survey interviewers, compared to 54 percent of the nonstranger victimizations. If the victimization survey data are adjusted for this differential, the survey data for the eight cities would indicate that about 64 percent of the rapes were committed by strangers; this compares to an average of 53 percent for the four studies using official rape data cited above.

A point that is more critical to Proposition 6 is that our focus of interest is on nonfamily members rather than on strangers. We have reviewed the cited literature on *strangers* using official data because much of this literature does not report the results for *family members*. Those studies that do permit an examination of the proportion of offenders who are family members indicate that in rape the nonstranger offender is very rarely a family member. Amir (1971:234) reports for rape incidents that although 58 percent of all offenders were nonstrangers, only 2.5 percent of them were relatives of the victim. Similarly, Chappell and Singer (1973:64) found for rape incidents that 42 percent involved nonstrangers, but only 2.8 percent involved family members.[16] Mulvihill et al. (1969:217) found 47 percent nonstrangers and 6.9 percent family members in rape incidents.[17] For aggravated assault, the President's Commission on Crime in the District of Columbia (1966:78) reports that 60 percent of the victims and offenders were previously acquainted, but only 20 percent were relatives. These figures are similar to those for aggravated assault by Mulvihill et al. (1969:287); although only 21 percent of the aggravated assault victims were strangers, only 14 percent were relatives.

The victimization survey results are in close agreement with these official data in showing that a very small proportion of nonstranger offenders are members of the victim's family. In lone offender assaultive victimizations in the eight cities, only 7 percent were committed by family members (Hindelang, 1976: Table 7-2). Data from the national victimization survey indicate that in rape, 4 percent, and in assault, 7 percent of the victimizations involved offenders who were members of the victim's family. For robbery, victimization by family members accounted for fewer than 1 percent of the victimizations (Hindelang, Dunn, Sutton, and Aumick, 1976: Table 3-27).

Rates of personal victimization by age, race, and marital status are consistent with Propositions 5 and 6, jointly considered. In the eight cities, victimization rates increased through adolescence and decreased monotonically thereafter. Among the marital status categories, even when age was controlled, married persons consistently had rates of personal victimization that were about one-half of the rates for those who were not married. Also, regardless of employment status, available data indicate that females spend a larger portion of their time in "personal and family care" than do males (Executive Office of the President, 1973:214).

Proposition 7: *Variations in lifestyle are associated with variations in the ability of individuals to isolate themselves from persons with offender characteristics.*

In our introductory discussion of lifestyles, we indicated that family income, as it reflects economic structural constraints facing an individual, is an important determinant of lifestyle for a variety of reasons. Among the important consequences of family income are where one lives, how one lives, and with whom one comes into contact. Poor people have little choice about these matters; if the situation is undesirable in any respect, those in poverty have little choice but to cope. Greater family income provides flexibility to move one's place of residence from a less desirable to a more desirable location; to use private (e.g., personal automobiles) or more expensive (e.g., taxicabs, commuter trains, and airplanes) modes of transportation rather than inexpensive public modes of transportation; to change jobs; to have access to private environs for recreation; and to live in apartments and homes with elaborate security measures (e.g., security guards, video surveillance, and burglar alarms). Each of these concomitants of higher income has the effect of isolating the individual from exposure to persons with offender characteristics. Our review of offender characteristics under Proposition 4 indicates that the crimes of common theft and assault are simply much less often *com-*

mitted by those who can make these choices—that is, to live in exclusive suburbs, to ride commuter trains, and to go to the mountains for a weekend. Those with offender characteristics are much more likely to spend their time in core urban areas, to walk or to ride public transportation, and to be restricted to public places for recreation.

The flexibility that family income provides to make these choices in not independent of race. Because of de facto segregated housing patterns, higher income blacks do not have the same flexibility as higher income whites; that is, racial barriers are structural constraints that further limit the behavioral options of blacks. Sections of urban areas in which blacks are concentrated are more heterogeneous in family income than are areas in which whites are concentrated (Taeuber, 1968; Erbe, 1975). Further, the private clubs and environs that are open to higher income whites may be inhospitable or simply closed to blacks. As a result, blacks with incomes equal to those of whites are, in fact, less insulated from those with offender characteristics. All of this suggests that even when family income is controlled, blacks will have a higher rate of personal victimization than whites.

When rates of personal victimization in the eight cities are examined by race and family income, both racial groups showed generally decreasing rates as income increased. This pattern was slightly stronger for whites than for black/others (Hindelang, 1976; Table 5-6). When victimizations were weighted according to seriousness as measured by the Sellin-Wolfgang (1964) scale, the pattern was even more clear. The seriousness-weighted rate for whites in the less than $3,000 category was 70 percent greater than that for whites in the $15,000–24,999 category. For black/others, the rate for those in the lowest income category was 60 percent greater than that for black/others in the $15,000-24,999 category.[18] Furthermore, within each income category, the seriousness-weighted rate of personal victimization was greater, generally about 15 percent, for black/others than for whites (Hindelang, 1976: Table 6-5).

Variations in lifestyle are associated with variations in the ability to isolate oneself from persons with offender characteristics not only because family income affects lifestyle but also because the nature of the vocational activity in which an individual is involved—an important component of lifestyle—itself affects the freedom to isolate oneself from persons with offender characteristics. This vocationally linked potential for isolation is largely independent of income. Those who are students or employed outside of the home, although they are relatively insulated from personal victimization by the formal structure of their vocations once they are "on the job," nonetheless are exposed coming from, and going to, school or work. Those whose vocational activities do not demand that they be in particular places outside of the home at particular times have the ability to isolate themselves to a degree that those involved in vocations that have definite time and place demands do not. Those who are keeping house, retired, or unemployed can, within limits, control whether and when they will leave the relative security of their homes and expose themselves to those with offender characteristics. If she chooses, a housewife fearful of purse snatchers can shop during the day when many potential offenders are not on the streets. Similarly, retired couples need not go out after dark, because they are free to do what they wish to do or must do in public during safer daytime hours. Of course, the *freedom* to choose to isolate oneself from those with offender characteristics does not mean that that choice will be exercised; those who are unemployed have the same freedom to remain in the home and thus to isolate themselves from those with offender characteristics as do retired people and those keeping house. However, the unemployed are disproportionately young, male, poor, and urban, and ethnographic studies indicate that a great deal of their free time is spent on the street in interaction with others who have similar characteristics (Whyte, 1943; Liebow, 1967; Horton, 1972).

Proposition 8:   *Variations in lifestyle are associated with variations in the convenience, the desirability, and vincibility of the person as a target for personal victimizations.*

In the preceding seven propositions we have dealt with the implications of lifestyle for potential victims in terms of their exposure to high risk situations. Proposition 8 is concerned with the offender's perception of potential victims. Throughout our discussion of lifestyle, we have repeatedly emphasized the importance of *exposure* to persons with offender characteristics—particularly to persons who are nonfamily members—in public places during nighttime hours. One reason that this is important, we believe, is that the convenience of the victim as a target is a prime concern to the offender. From the offender's perspective, it is *convenient* to wait for a potential victim to come to a place (at a time) that is suitable to the offender for victimization. Public places, such as the streets and parks, offer the offender opportunities to victimize persons who have virtually no effective defensible space. Further, a patient offender can select from among potential victims a person who is most appropriate for the contemplated offense. Because these areas are public, if the victimization can be committed during times when these public places are less heavily traveled, the chances of observation or of intervention by another on the victim's behalf can be minimized. Although some robbery offenders engage, in effect, in door-to-door robberies (Reppetto, 1974), it is clear that from the offender's perspective, selection of targets in this way is extremely inconvenient. In such residential robberies, the offender approaches the victim within the victim's defensible space, in which the number of persons in the residence at the time of the robbery is unknown, in which the characteristics of the victim(s) (e.g., sex, age, and physical stature) may not be known, and in which the victim's access to weapons is increased.

The available literature suggests that offenders tend to commit their crimes within short distances of their residences (Hoover, 1966; Turner, 1969; Reiss, 1967; Normandeau, 1968; Amir, 1971). Amir (1971: Table 31) reports, for example, that seven out of ten of the rapes he studied for which the requisite location data were available were committed within the "vicinity" (five blocks) of the offender's residence. Normandeau (1968) reports that the median distance from the residence of Philadelphia robbers to the location of the robbery was 0.95 miles for juvenile offenders and 1.14 miles for adult offenders. From such data, it follows that those who live in or are frequent visitors to areas in which those with offender characteristics reside—that is, individuals who are convenient potential targets—have an increased risk of personal victimization. This helps to explain the finding that those who are among the least affluent (e.g., poor blacks) have the highest rate of personal theft victimization (Hindelang, 1976: Table 5-6).

The convenience of the target may also be a factor in assaults. Among those who are known to each other, the daily frustrations of living and the frictions that often arise among persons who are known to each other may combine with the result that a period of friction can trigger an aggressive outburst. The aggressor may have been "primed" for the outburst as frustration built up over time. A precipitating event—one that in the absence of the pent up frustration may have passed without incident—results in a convenient target (someone close to the aggressor) being the recipient of the aggression. In a similar way, a victim with no prior relationship with the offender can become a target of convenience in public places.

From the offender's perspective, not all individuals are equally *desirable* targets. In theft-motivated offenses, the apparent affluence of the potential victim may be an important consideration weighed by the offender. Another way that a potential victim's lifestyle influences the offender's perception of that person as a desirable target is whether the offender believes that the person is likely to report the crime to the police. For example, the lifestyles of some persons may occasionally place them in situations that involve violations of legal or other norms (e.g., visiting a prostitute, purchasing drugs, or seeking out a homosexual partner). In such situations, offenders may believe that the person would not report being robbed or assaulted out of fear of revealing the initial illegal involvement. Similarly, school-aged children may be desirable targets for assaults and thefts committed by other adolescents due to peer pressures not to inform the police.

The third component of Proposition 8 is *vincibility*. A person's vincibility to personal victimization increases to the extent that the potential victim is seen by the offender as less able to resist the offender successfully. Persons who are unaccompanied or under the influence of drugs or alcohol are relatively vincible to personal victimization. Although no "at risk" data are available regarding the probability of victimization for those who are alone versus those who are in the company of others when a potential offender is encountered, victimization survey results indicate that, in the eight cities, when personal incidents did occur, about nine out of ten victims were alone; only one out of fifty victims was accompanied by two or more persons (Hindelang, 1976:207). It seems reasonable to suppose that offenders will select lone victims in preference to accompanied victims because the former are liable to be less able and willing to resist; furthermore, the fewer the victims, the less likely it is that the offender will be subsequently identified. In our earlier discussion of lifestyles, we suggested that certain individuals—particularly young, single males—are more likely to be alone in public places. Also, the attitude data presented in Chapter 8 indicate that young males are nearly four times more likely than young females to say that they feel very safe about being out alone in their neighborhoods at night (Table 8-2). Of course, as the number of offenders increases, it becomes more feasible to confront multiple victims. It is interesting to note that although only one out of ten personal incidents in the eight cities involved multiple *victims*, nearly half of the personal incidents involved multiple *offenders*.

In addition to the vincibility indicator of number of victims, the sobriety of the potential victim is another indicator of vincibility. If a potential victim appears to be unable to resist and/or to provide the police with a description of the offender, then that person's apparent vincibility increases the likelihood of personal victimization. It is likely that variables predictive of lifestyle—particularly sex and socioeconomic status indicators—are related to the probability of being in a public place while intoxicated.

A NOTE ON VICTIM PRECIPITATION

One aspect of personal victimization that has had a prominent place in American criminological literature on aggressive crimes is that of victim precipitation. According to Wolfgang (1958:252):

> The term *victim-precipitated* is applied to those criminal homicides in which the victim is a direct, positive precipitator in the crime. The role of the victim is characterized by his having been the first in the homicide drama to use physical force directed against his subsequent slayer. The *victim-precipitated* cases are those in which the victim was the first to show and use a deadly weapon, to strike a blow in an altercation—in short, the first to commence the interplay or resort to physical violence.

A similar notion is embodied in Toch's typology of violent activity, which "is intended as a catalogue of ways of relating to people which carry a high probability of degenerating into contact of an aggressive nature" (Toch, 1969:135).

Compatible with these conceptions of victim precipitation is the notion that individuals and subcultural groups may subscribe to a set of values that result in an increased willingness to exhibit defiant or aggressive reactions to a wide range of stimuli. Wolfgang (1958:188) has pointed out that "the significance of a jostle, a slightly derogatory remark, or the appearance of a weapon in the hand of an adversary are stimuli differentially perceived and interpreted . . . ." These differential perceptions and interpretations can be expected to vary as a function of race, sex, age, and socioeconomic status. Wolfgang and Ferracuti's (1967) subculture of violence thesis postulates that such propensities are disproportionately found among young, black, lower-class males. In connection with assaultive crimes, such propensities on the part of the victim may serve to precipitate an event that might otherwise have not occurred or to escalate the level of violence in an event that otherwise would have been less violent.

Although the victimization survey results contain no information on victimizations that may have been victim-precipitated, the data presented in Chapter 3 do indicate that the rate of injury to victims is substantially greater for those victims who used a physical force self-protective measure than for those victims who did not (Figure 3-1). The victimization results in the eight cities show that males were more likely than females and younger persons more likely than older persons to use physical force self-protective measures; however, no race effects were found (Hindelang, 1976:260). Regardless of the tenability of the subculture of violence thesis, it seems reasonable to postulate that the propensity to precipitate or escalate violent victimization is not uniformly distributed among members of society.

Although a notion such as propensity to precipitate or escalate is implicitly subsumed in our model as a possible individual and/or subcultural adaptation to role expectation and structural constraints, we have not discussed this particular adaptation in our general presentation of the model. Because such a propensity is only one of a variety of possible specific adaptations, we believed that to have displayed it in the model in Figure 11.1 would have given to it undue prominence, perhaps to the exclusion of other important adaptations that are less widely discussed in the literature. In addition, propensity to precipitate or escalate—although it has been discussed and investigated by Normandeau (1968:286–92) in connection with robbery—does not, we believe, have applicability to the vast majority of theft-motivated offenses. It should be stressed that although some adaptations, such as propensity to precipitate, result in an increased likelihood of victimization, our model is equally concerned with common adaptations that decrease the likelihood of victimization. For example, adaptations to the role expectations of parenthood and the constraints of family structure lead to a lifestyle that involves spending more time with family members in the home and therefore decreases the exposure to high risk victimization situations.

INTERDEPENDENCE OF PROPOSITIONS

In this presentation of the lifestyle/exposure model of personal victimization, we have refrained from using the phrase "other things being equal." It should be clear, however, from the propositions themselves, that we have been generally discussing zero-order effects. This in no way implies, of course, that the propositions are independent in their effects on the likelihood of personal victimization. For example, the most desirable targets for theft-motivated crimes, as discussed in Proposition 8 (e.g., the affluent) may simultaneously be the individuals who are least likely to spend time in public places (Proposition 2). Predictions about victimization risks can be derived from a given proposition only when the other propositions are taken into account. Obviously, it would be easier to test this theoretical model if the propositions were independent of each other. This is especially true in light of the fact that many of the data required to operationalize the propositions adequately are not readily available. Unfortunately, the phenomenon of personal victimization, as is the case with most social phenomena, is sufficiently complex to preclude univariate explanations or multivariate explanations in which the critical dimensions are assumed to be orthogonal.

SOME EXPECTATIONS FROM
THE MODEL

In the course of discussing the individual propositions, we pointed to readily available research findings that are compatible with our lifestyle/exposure model. In addition, there are important expectations that can be derived from this model for which data are not as readily available. We believe that it would be helpful in explicating the model further to give brief attention to illustrations of some of these expectations.[19]

Our model suggests that as sex role expectations become increasingly less differentiated and sex-linked structural barriers become less rigid, with a corresponding convergence of the adaptations and lifestyles of males and females, rates of victimization for males and females will tend to converge. This is true primarily for two reasons. First, females generally will increase their exposure to nonfamily members, and hence their victimization rate should increase relative to the male rate. Second, if the *offending* rate among females increases, as some have suggested it will (Adler, 1975:251-52), then the lifestyle/exposure model predicts that females will have higher rates of victimization than would otherwise be expected. This is so because an offender characteristic (sex) would be shifting toward a characteristic of these individuals (female); according to Proposition 4, the more similar an individual's characteristics to those of offenders, the greater the chance of victimization.

To the extent that cohabitation outside of marriage continues to increase, we would expect that marital status will become less predictive of victimization. That is, persons who are not married (e.g., "single") but who are cohabiting will have adopted to some extent lifestyles that are normally associated with marriage. This would be especially true to the extent that cohabiting and married couples are equally likely to incur childrearing responsibilities.

The lifestyle/exposure model also suggests that to the extent that trends toward age segregation in housing patterns increase, rates of personal victimization among age groups will diverge; conversely, to the extent that housing arrangements become age-heterogeneous, rates of victimization among age groups will tend toward convergence. We are not suggesting, of course, that in an age-heterogeneous setting, variations in rates of personal victimization across age groups would not exist; there are too many other factors that affect differential likelihoods of victimization by age.

A society that is fully integrated—in terms of housing patterns, lifestyles, and patterns of personal interactions with regard to such dimensions as race, socioeconomic status, age, sex, etc.—would likely be relatively homogeneous with respect to many important social consequences, including criminal victimization. Conversely, to the extent that patterns of interaction occur more within race-age-sex clusters, rates of victimization for demographic subgroups can, on the basis of our model, be expected to diverge, provided that there are demographic correlates of offending behavior.

SUGGESTIONS FOR ADDITIONAL RESEARCH

There are a number of areas in which further research could have a bearing on our model in terms of refining, confirming, or falsifying portions of it. Some of these were mentioned in our discussion of the limitations of the NCS questionnaire in Chapter 10, but they will be repeated here in an attempt to draw together a group of suggestions for future research.

1. We defined lifestyle in terms of routine vocational and leisure activities. These activities are predictive of when, where, and with whom persons spend their time. Obviously, direct measures of these factors would be invaluable. There has already been a good deal of research in the realm of time budgeting that examines the spatial and temporal distribution of the subject's activities (cf. Chapin, 1974). The specific time, place, and activity categories used in prior time-budgeting research could be modified and used in a study that would yield information about lifestyle that is particularly relevant to the exposure to victimivation risk. If such direct measures of exposure were found to be unrelated to personal victimization, or if demographic characteristics were still found to be substantially related to personal victimization after such refined measures of exposure were controlled, then the model would be untenable as currently postulated.

2. In conjunction with the first suggestion, more information is needed about lifestyle variations within gross categories of major activity. For example, in this chapter we referred generally to persons employed outside the home, in contrast to homemakers, unemployed persons, retired persons, and so forth. But there are certainly variations within these categories—for example, related to *type* of occupation—that have major ramifications for lifestyle. For example, do those whose occupations involve work in public places have higher rates of personal victimization than those who work in private places?

3. To complement more specific information about the lifestyles of potential victims, more complete information about the locales of

victimizations are needed. In this work, we have been dealing with general locales such as "public places," but more specificity in our knowledge of high-risk locales would allow a more precise mapping of lifestyle variations to variations in exposure. If more detailed information about the locales of victimization were available, our model could be tested more precisely. It would have to be found that people with lifestyles that place them disproportionately in these specific types of public places where personal victimizations are likely to occur have higher victimization rates than do others.

4. In relation to victimization events, there is also a need for data about factors that immediately preceded the victimization (e.g., were the victim and offender drinking together in a bar?) and for more detailed information about the victim-offender relationship (e.g., was the offender a co-worker, a fellow student, a rival gang member?). Data of these sorts would be helpful for understanding the links between lifestyle and victimization, especially through the mechanism that was labeled "associations" in Figure 11–1.

5. Among the adaptations to role expectations and structural constraints that were identified were particular attitudes and response sets, such as the fear of crime and the propensity to precipitate or escalate violence. Further research is needed to determine how these adaptations are incorporated into individual lifestyles and how they, thereby, effect the likelihood and nature of personal victimization.

6. The theoretical model that has been postulated is grounded in cross-sectional research. Many of the important linkages in the model, however, can only be tested adequately with longitudinal data. As role expectations change according to the increasing age of the individual, do changing adaptations in fact result in lifestyle shifts that affect exposure and hence the probability of victimizations? Similar questions could be posed with respect to changes in marital status and income. As noted in Chapter 8, longitudinal data are also required to disentangle the time-dependent relationships among fear of crime, personal limiting of behaviors, and likelihood of victimization.

7. One test of our model would be in the realm of comparative research. That is, are the postulated mechanisms applicable under varying sets of role expectations and structural constraints that could be identified in cross-cultural research?

CONCLUDING REMARKS

The theoretical model that has been proposed grows primarily out of our research during the past four years on victimization survey results. Although the data and the theoretical model presented in this book deal with personal victimization, in prior research we have closely examined the correlates of household victimization—burglary, household larceny, and vehicle theft. We believe that with modifications the lifestyle/exposure model has some applicability to household victimization, primarily because lifestyles that disproportionately result in individuals being in public places also tend disproportionately to leave the households of those persons unoccupied and hence more vulnerable to household victimization. For example, age of head of household is inversely related to rates of household victimization; the lifestyles of younger persons which bring them into public places simultaneously tend disproportionately to expose their homes to household victimization. We are, however, pessimistic about the applicability of this model to victimization by corporate crime, white collar crime, and consumer fraud.

This lifestyle/exposure model of personal victimization has evolved as a result of a grounded theoretical approach. Although there are major advantages to a grounded approach to theory construction, there are some substantial shortcomings as well. Among the advantages are an intimate familiarity with the empirical patterns in the data, an empirical stance toward the concepts and indicators that are developed, and an appreciation for some of the measurement limitations inherent in the data. On the other hand, the greatest dangers are that grounded theory may be limited to ex post facto interpretation of the data and may not achieve a sufficiently high level of abstraction and generality. On balance, the advantages of a grounded theoretical approach seem to outweigh the disadvantages and such an approach has the greatest potential for advancing knowledge and explanations of social phenomena such as criminal victimization.

The lifestyle/exposure model is but a preliminary step toward an adequate explanation of personal victimization. Our own research will focus on testing, reformulating, and refining this theoretical model. To the extent that the model stimulates additional empirical and theoretical work on the part of others, it will have served an important function.

NOTES

1. Throughout this chapter, our intent is to construct a theoretical model of the personal victimizations discussed in this book—rape, assault, robbery, and personal larceny. Although the model has some implications for household, business, and other forms of victimization, our discussion is not specifically designed to address these types of victimizations.

2. We are not arguing that behavior is completely determined by role expec-

tations and social structure. The constraints imposed by these factors delimit a range of behaviors from which even conforming members of society can choose. In addition, the individual can, with varying degrees of risk and success, resist or rebel against the constraints. Our argument is that the constraints do act to produce typical ways of behaving.

3. This differentiation is similar to the one used by Becker (1963:31-35) in his designation of "master statuses."

4. MacDonald includes only stranger-to-stranger rapes in reporting this finding. Chappell and Singer (1973) found that in New York, the most frequent place of initial contact between the victim and the offender was a residence.

5. Part of the discrepancy between the official and victimization results is attributable to the greater proportion of rapes in police data committed by nonstrangers. When the victim and the offender are known to each other, victimization survey data show that the rape is most likely to occur inside of a home or other building (Hindelang, Dunn, Sutton, and Aumick, 1976:356).

6. There are, of course, some vocations—such as police officer and taxi driver—in which time on the job is not generally spent within a structured, sheltered setting.

7. We suggested earlier that for preadolescents, lifestyles would not be as differentiated by sex as among young and middle-aged adults. Although the victimization survey did not collect data for children under twelve years of age, our theory predicts that the male-female rates for these children would be more similar than those for young and middle-aged adults.

8. See generally, Chapter 2, Hindelang, Gottfredson, Dunn and Parisi (1977).

9. In addition to the question quoted in the text, the question, "Compared to a year ago, do you personally feel more afraid and uneasy on the streets today, less uneasy, or not much different than you felt a year ago?" has also been asked. For males 59 percent and for females 73 percent felt more uneasy. Within each sex group, the percentage tended to increase with age (Hindelang, Dunn, Aumick and Sutton, 1975:173).

10. We will discuss the victimizations of "lone" persons below.

11. The UCR larceny category includes larcenies from stores and homes, which are not counted as personal larcenies by the definition used in this book. Similarly, the UCR robbery category includes robberies of commercial establishments, which do not fall within the definition of personal robbery used herein.

12. Some of these data are also presented in Hindelang, Gottfredson, Dunn, and Parisi (1977: Tables 6-6, 6-9, 6-11).

13. In this book we have reported victimization data for urban areas only. Victimization results from the NCS national survey indicate that rates of personal victimization are positively associated with the extent of urbanization. See Hindelang, Gottfredson, Dunn, and Parisi (1977:368).

14. In our usage here, "family" refers to the extended family.

15. "Stranger" here includes persons whom the victim had never seen before, were known by sight only, or about whom the victim did not know whether or not they were strangers. When multiple offenders were involved in the victimization, if the victim did not know any of them, they were classified as strangers.

16. Chappell and Singer report that for 19 percent of their cases the victim-offender relationship was unknown.

17. It is possible that "rapes" by family members that come to the attention of the police are sometimes categorized as other crimes such as incest or child abuse. In addition, "rapes" by spouses probably do not generally appear in police files as rapes, because in most jurisdictions such events do not meet the legal criteria of rape.

18. In the $25,000 or more income category among black/others, the rate was higher than that for all other income categories except those under $7,500. However, fewer than 1 percent of the black/others in the eight cities had incomes of $25,000 or more; nearly three out of five black/others had incomes below $7,500.

19. Unless otherwise noted, in these illustrations we will be assuming that patterns of offender characteristics remain constant.

REFERENCES

Becker, H.S. (1963) *The Outsiders*. New York: Macmillan.

Chappel, D. and S. Singer. (1973) "Rape in New York City: A Study of Rape Materials in Police Files and Its Meaning." Albany: School of Criminal Justice, State University of New York at Albany. (mimeo)

Hindelang, M., C. Dunn, A. Aumick, and L. P. Sutton (1975) *Sourcebook of Criminal Justice Statistics: 1974*. Washington, DC: Government Printing Office.

Hindelang, M., C. Dunn, P. Sutton, and A. Aumick (1976) *Sourcebook of Criminal Justice Statistics: 1975*. Washington, DC: Government Printing Office.

Hindelang, M., M. Gottfredson, C. Dunn, and N. Parsi (1977) *Sourcebook of Criminal Justice Statistics: 1976*. Washington, DC: Government Printing Office,

Michael J. Hindelang is Professor of Criminal Justice at the Graduate School of Criminal Justice at the State University of New York at Albany. He has coauthored (with Michael R. Gottfredson and James Garofalo) Victims of Personal Crime *(Cambridge, MA: Ballinger, 1978), authored* Criminal Victimization in Eight American Cities *(Cambridge, MA: Ballinger, 1976), and coedits the annual* Sourcebook of Criminal Justice Statistics. *He directs research projects evaluating self-reported delinquency methods and victimization survey techniques.*

Michael R. Gottfredson is Assistant Professor of Criminal Justice at the Graduate School of Criminal Justice at the State University of New York at Albany. He has coauthored (with Michael J. Hindelange and James Garofalo) Victims of Personal Crime *(Cambridge, MA: Ballinger, 1978) and coedits the annual* Sourcebook of Criminal Justice Statistics. *He directs a research project aimed at understanding and structuring the discretion of bail decision makers.*

James Garofalo is Director of the Research Center East, National Council on Crime and Delinquency. His research interests are the fear of crime and victimization. He is the coauthor of Victims of Personal Crime: An Empirical Foundation for a Theory of Personal Victimization *(Cambridge, MA: Ballinger, 1978).*

33

VICTIMIZATION AND THE FEAR OF CRIME
JAMES GAROFALO

The determinants of the fear of crime are examined with special attention to how the risk and experience of criminal victimization affect that fear. Using data from victimization and attitude surveys in eight American cities, a model of the determinants of the fear of crime is developed and evaluated in a preliminary fashion. The major conclusion is that the fear of crime is not simply a function of the risk of and actual experiences with victimization.

The public's fear of crime has become the basis for a number of social-political decisions and programs in the United States. Unfortunately, while evidence of the fear of crime (e.g., from public opinion polls) is often cited as a justification for particular measures, assumptions about the sources of the fear are left unstated. Judging from the frequency with which fear of crime is cited as a justification for crime-reduction measures, a major assumption appears to be that the fear of crime is strongly and directly related to the risk or experiences of criminal victimization. Yet this assumption remains virtually untested; in fact, very little research has been devoted to examining any of the sources of the fear of crime.

In this paper a rough model of the determinants of the fear of crime will be presented and discussed. Then, using data from victimization and attitude surveys conducted in 1975, some indicators of the concepts in the model will be chosen, and the adequacy of the model will be evaluated. Finally, the shortcomings of the model will be discussed, with particular attention given to the areas in which our knowledge is still incomplete. Before addressing the substantive issues, however, a brief description of the data source for this paper is necessary.

JAMES GAROFALO: Director, Statistical Analysis Center, Division of Criminal Justice Services, State of New York, Albany, New York.

A slightly different version of this paper was presented at the annual conference of the American Association for Public Opinion Research, Buck Hill Falls, Pennsylvania, May 19–22, 1977. Parts of the research on which this paper is based were performed under federal grant #75-SS-99-6029, awarded to the Criminal Justice Research Center by the Statistics Division of the Law Enforcement Assistance Administration (LEAA). Points of view or opinions expressed in this paper are those of the author and do not necessarily represent the official position or policies of LEAA.

From James Garofalo, "Victimization and the Fear of Crime," *Journal of Research in Crime and Delinquency*, January 1979, pp. 80-97. Reprinted by permission.

THE NATIONAL CRIME SURVEY

In 1972, the Law Enforcement Assistance Administration (LEAA) of the U.S. Department of Justice began sponsoring a series of victimization surveys, known as the National Crime Survey (NCS). In each of the surveys, residents of a representative sample of households are interviewed concerning certain types of criminal victimizations that they may have suffered during some specified period preceding the interviews. Sampling, interviewing, coding, and data tabulations are performed for LEAA by the Bureau of the Census.

The NCS has had two major components: city surveys and national surveys. Because of methodological differences between the two components and because only the city surveys are used in this paper, the national surveys will not be discussed here.[1] In the city component of the NCS, interviews have been conducted in twenty-six major cities in the United States. Although data from all of the cities are used at one point in this paper, most of the information to be presented here is derived from interviews in eight cities—Atlanta, Baltimore, Cleveland, Dallas, Denver, Newark, Portland, and St. Louis—known collectively as the Impact Cities because of a particular federal program in which they participated.

Interviews were conducted in the eight Impact Cities during March, April, and May of 1975.[2] In each city, interviews were conducted in a representative sample of about 10,000 households. Within each household, members twelve years of age and older were eligible to be interviewed about certain criminal victimizations they might have suffered during the twelve months preceding the month of the interview. This resulted in interviews with about 21,000 persons in each city. The personal victimizations covered by the surveys were rape, robbery, assault, and larceny from the person (i.e., purse snatching and pocket picking without force or threat). Also covered were victimizations deemed to have been directed against the household as a unit (burglary, vehicle theft, and larcenies that involved no contact between the victim and the offender).

A supplemental "attitude questionnaire" was administered to a subsample of respondents in each city. A random half of the households selected for victimization interviewing were designated for administration of the supplemental questionnaire. In these households, every member age sixteen or older was interviewed with the supplemental questionnaire. Most of the analysis in this paper focuses on this subsample of about 70,000 respondents.

For each city a weighting scheme was designed to produce population esti-

---

1. Readers interested in a description of the national surveys should consult Garofalo and Hindelang, 1977.

2. The cities were also surveyed earlier, during July through November 1972. Five other cities in the NCS city component were also surveyed twice, so that data exist from thirty-nine surveys of the twenty-six cities.

mates from the sample data. The numbers reported in this paper are, therefore, estimates of population parameters based on the sample data. Furthermore, the results have been aggregated across the eight cities to take advantage of the large sample size. When the data are aggregated in this way, an average weighting factor of about 45 is applied to each interviewed individual in the attitude subsample.[3] The only point at which unweighted data are used in this paper is in the regression analysis presented in Figure 4.

A WORKING MODEL

As a first step in discussing the fear of crime, it should be noted that we will be working with a less-than-perfect indicator of the concept. Respondents in the NCS attitude subsample were asked: "How safe do you feel or would you feel being out alone in your neighborhood at night?" The four response categories were very safe, reasonably safe, somewhat unsafe, and very unsafe. Obviously, there are a number of problems in using this item as an indicator of the fear of crime. First, crime is not mentioned in the question. However, in the instrument the item was preceded by questions about crime trends, and the series of questions was introduced by the phrase, "Now I'd like to get your opinions about crime in general," so it is difficult to conceive of the respondent thinking about dangers other than crime. Second, the frame of reference for the question is the respondent's neighborhood, yet the meaning of the term *neighborhood* probably varies from respondent to respondent,[4] and some people may find it necessary to spend much of their time in areas that they perceive as more dangerous than their own. Third, the respondent is directed to think about being "alone," but there is probably great variability among people in the amount of time they spend outside unaccompanied.[5] Finally, the "do you feel or would you feel" portion of the question invites a mixing of actual feelings of fear with guesses about hypothetical situations. Despite these shortcomings, however, the item represents the best single indicator of the fear of crime available from the questionnaire.

In the introduction it was pointed out that studying the fear of crime is important because the proponents of many social programs invoke that fear as

3. For further details about sampling, interviewing, weighting, standard errors of the estimates, instruments, and so on, see Garofalo and Hindelang, 1977, and U.S. Bureau of the Census, 1976.

4. NCS interviewers are instructed that the term *neighborhood* "is defined, loosely, as the general area in which a person lives. The boundaries of this area would be whatever each individual feels is his 'neighborhood' " (U.S. Bureau of the Census, 1975:D5-2).

5. Even the term *alone* is ambiguous because some respondents may have interpreted it as meaning not being accompanied by another person or other persons, while other respondents may have assumed that it referred to situations in which there were no other people (even strangers) around.

Table 1.   Limiting of Behavior because of Crime
by Fear of Crime: Eight Impact Cities Aggregate, 1975

| | Limiting of Behavior | | |
Fear of Crime	No	Yes	Estimated Number*
Very safe	80%	20%	493,947
Reasonably safe	66%	34%	1,253,019
Somewhat unsafe	42%	58%	706,745
Very unsafe	27%	73%	727,441
Total	54%	46%	3,181,152

(Gamma = .56)
*Excludes persons who gave no response to either item.

a justification for their proposals. But the fear of crime is worthy of study in its own right. It is logical to assume that people who are very fearful of crime suffer psychological discomfort. There is also some indication that the fear of crime leads some people to restrict their behavior. For example, respondents in the NCS attitude subsample were asked: "In general, have you limited or changed your activities in the past few years because of crime?" Table 1 shows the relationship between responses to that question and the fear of crime indicator being used here. Overall, 46 percent of the eight-city residents said that they had limited their behavior. But the percentages vary greatly according to the level of fear expressed: from 20 percent for those who felt very safe to 73 percent for those who felt very unsafe.[6] Thus, a better understanding of the fear of crime could lead to action that will have the effect of improving the quality of life for many people.

A working model of the influences on the fear of crime is presented in Figure 1. Five general factors are seen as affecting fear: the actual risk of being victimized by a criminal act, past experiences of being victimized, the content of the socialization processes connected with particular social roles, the content of media presentations about crime and victimization, and the perceived effectiveness of official barriers that are placed between potential offenders and victims. Each of these factors will be discussed separately, and relevant data from the NCS Impact Cities surveys will be examined to determine the extent of empirical support for each factor. Then the model will be evaluated in a more systematic form using indicators that are available in the NCS.

6. Although the data are not presented here, the relationship maintains within age and sex groups, even though responses to both items vary with age and sex.

Figure 1.   Working Model of the Influences on the Fear of Crime

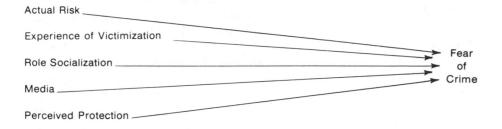

ACTUAL RISK OF VICTIMIZATION

Every person is unique, so it is theoretically possible to assign a unique risk factor (i.e., a probability of being victimized) to everyone in the sample. Our knowledge of the risk of victimization has not reached that stage, even though some work has been done on deriving a typology of persons based on the risk of victimization (Hindelang, Gottfredson, and Garofalo, 1978:ch. 5). Previous analyses of NCS victimization data have shown, however, that several personal characteristics are related more or less strongly to rates of victimization. Four of these characteristics—age, sex, race, and income—are also related to the fear of crime. It is possible, then, to examine how rates of victimization and the fear of crime co-vary among subgroups formed by age, sex, race, and income. The relevant data for the eight Impact Cities are presented in Table 2.

The rates of victimization in Table 2 refer to the personal victimizations of rape, robbery, assault, and larceny involving contact between the victim and offender; these crimes should be most relevant to the fear of crime. The rates are computed per 1,000 persons in the category. The numerator of each rate is the estimated count of the number of *victimizations* suffered by persons in the category, not the number of *persons* victimized. Thus, persons who suffered more than one victimization are counted more than once in the numerator. This provides a measure of risk for the category rather than for any individual within the category. The measure of fear in Table 2 is the summation of the percentages of persons in each category who answered "somewhat unsafe" or "very unsafe" to the question about feeling of safety at night that was described earlier.[7]

Table 2 shows that age has a negative relationship with victimization rates and a positive relationship with the fear of crime. That is, as age goes up, victimization rates decrease (from 125 per 1,000 to 34 per 1,000) and the fear of crime increases (from 37 percent to 63 percent). A similar reversal occurs for

7. The relationships do not change when the percentage who responded "very unsafe" is used as the measure of fear.

males and females: Males show a higher victimization rate (90 per 1,000 vs. 54 per 1,000) while females show a higher level of fear (60 percent vs. 26 percent). With race and income, however, the data are more in line with expectations. Whites have a slightly lower rate of victimization and fear-of-crime level than do blacks, and fear of crime and rates of victimization both decline as income goes up.

The correspondence between fear and risk of victimization among racial and income groups in Table 2 might be due to an areal effect. Because neighborhoods tend to be somewhat homogeneous with respect to race and income, and because areal crime rates also vary with race and income characteristics, the relationship between fear and risk of victimization for racial and income groups in Table 2 may be a reflection of the convergence of these factors in particular geographic locations. The same cannot be said of age and sex be-

**Table 2.   Estimated Rates of Victimization and Fear
of Crime among Age, Sex, Race, and Family Income Groups:
Eight Impact Cities Aggregate, 1975**

	Rates of Personal Victimization per 1,000 Persons*	Percent Responding Somewhat Unsafe or Very Unsafe
Age		
16–19	125	37
20–24	105	38
25–34	76	37
35–49	51	43
50–64	42	50
65 or older	34	63
Sex		
Male	90	26
Female	54	60
Race		
White	69	41
Black	72	54
Family income		
Less than $3,000	93	62
$3,000–$7,499	78	53
$7,500–$9,999	70	45
$10,000–$14,999	64	39
$15,000–$24,999	59	34
$25,000 or more	56	30

*Rape, robbery, assault, and larceny with victim/offender contact.

Table 3.   Fear of Crime by Dangerousness of Own Neighborhood Compared with Other Neighborhoods in the Metropolitan Area: Eight Impact Cities Aggregate, 1975

| Own Neighborhood | Fear of Crime | | | | Estimated Number* |
	Very Safe	Reasonably Safe	Somewhat Unsafe	Very Unsafe	
Much less dangerous	36%	39%	15%	10%	315,270
Less dangerous	19%	45%	20%	16%	1,182,990
About average	9%	37%	26%	28%	1,444,880
More dangerous	9%	26%	25%	40%	178,980
Much more dangerous	7%	17%	13%	63%	32,140

(Gamma = .36)
*Excludes persons who gave no response to either item.

cause, in general, neighborhoods are not strongly homogeneous on these factors. There appear to be differences among age and sex groups that override a possible conjunction between fear and risk of victimization; we will return to this issue later.

To specify the relationship between fear and risk for our model, we need some indicator that reflects geographic differences in risk. Unfortunately, the NCS data cannot be broken down by subareas of the cities, mainly because of rules of confidentiality maintained by the Census Bureau. As a proxy variable, we will use the supplemental questionnaire item: "How do you think your

Table 4.   Fear of Crime (Proportion Responding "Somewhat Unsafe" or "Very Unsafe") by Total Number of Personal Victimizations during the Twelve Months Preceding the Interview, by Sex and Age: Eight Impact Cities Aggregate, 1975

| Number of Personal Victimizations* | Males | | Females | |
	Less than 35	35 or Older	Less than 35	35 or Older
None	15% (551,974)**	32% (742,920)	54% (681,380)	64% (1,001,074)
One	22% (61,404)	54% (34,753)	63% (48,183)	77% (35,887)
Two or more	26% (15,930)	56% (6,181)	64% (8,196)	78% (3,021)

*Rape, robbery, assault, and larceny with contact between victim and offender.
**Estimated number of person in category; base on which percentage was computed.

neighborhood compares with others in this metropolitan area in terms of crime?" Responses to this item do vary with race and income, and, as shown in Table 3, the responses are also related to the fear of crime.

Use of the comparative neighborhood danger item as a measure of the actual risk of victimization requires the assumption that, in their replies, the respondents accurately reflect the objective risk of victimization in their neighborhoods. This assumption is probably not justified completely, but without information that is more geographic-specific, it will have to suffice for present purposes.

EXPERIENCE WITH VICTIMIZATION

For every individual interviewed in the NCS attitude subsample, information is available about certain victimizations suffered during the twelve months preceding the interview. Table 4 shows the relationship between the number of personal victimizations suffered during the reference period and the fear of crime expressed; age and sex have also been controlled here.

Table 4 indicates that being victimized is related to the fear of crime; within each age/sex group, nonvictims express less fear than do victims. However, the differences among the age and sex groups remain, regardless of experience with victimization. Furthermore, inspection of the numbers of persons on which the percentages in Table 4 were computed indicates that experience with victimization will not have a major effect in accounting for the total variability in the fear of crime because only a relatively small proportion of respondents were personally victimized during the survey reference period.[8]

Of course, the number of victimizations shown in Table 4 represents personal victimizations that occurred during the twelve months preceding the interview. It is possible that the results could change if information about victimizations were available over a longer period of time. However, it will be assumed here that victimizations that occurred more than twelve months before the interview—unless they were extremely serious—would have little effect on fear of crime at the time of the interview.

ROLE SOCIALIZATION

The findings that fear of crime and risk of victimization are inversely related across age and sex groups (Table 2) and that age and sex have much stronger effects on fear than does actual experience with personal victimization (Table 4) lead to a focus on differences in the life situations of people in the various age and sex groups. The hypothesis here is that sex- and age-specific socialization patterns are responsible for the disjunction between fear and risk.

8. In analysis not presented here, respondents were categorized more finely on victimization experiences: for example, from absolutely no contact with victimization to living in a household in which some *other* person was victimized to suffering a victimization that resulted in serious injury. The results of that analysis did not differ much from those shown in Table 4.

Regardless of the current push for greater equality for women, socialization into the female sex role has traditionally emphasized submissiveness; conversely, assertiveness has been stressed for males. According to some writers (Weis and Borges, 1973), one way submissiveness is achieved is by creating a fear of criminal attack—particularly a fear of rape—in females and thereby teaching them to feel dependent on males for protection. To the extent that these socialization goals are achieved, one would expect females to express more fear than males, regardless of the objective risks of victimization.

For older persons, a number of factors coalesce to produce dependency, isolation, and fear. The shift away from the extended family structure, public and private retirement policies, as well as purely physical changes such as declining health, all operate to place the elderly in positions that maximize feelings of vulnerability. Again, it is not surprising that older people express more fear than younger people, despite their lower risks of victimization.

It is possible that role socialization produces age and sex differences in expressed fear by a different mechanism. Younger people and males might be disinclined to *admit* fear to interviewers—whether or not they *feel* fear—because of the expectations associated with their roles. However, this possibility cannot be tested with the available NCS data, so we will take the fear of crime responses at their face value, as indicating the actual feelings of the respondents.

THE MEDIA

There have been a number of works dealing with the *content* of media treatment of crime and deviance (e.g., Cohen and Young, 1973). However, little has been done to determine the *effects* of the media presentations.[9] Although it would seem self-evident that the media have an influence on the public's fear of crime—if only by way of the pervasiveness of the media's messages—relevant data from the NCS are sparse.

Only one item in the NCS supplemental questionnaire deals directly with the media: "Crime is less (more, about as) serious than (as) the newspapers and TV say." In Table 5, responses to that item are cross-tabulated with the fear of crime. Looking at the row percentages in Table 5, the data show that respondents who thought that crime was actually less serious than portrayed in the media expressed somewhat less fear of crime than did other respondents. However, inspection of the column percentages reveals that, regardless of fear of crime, very few people thought that the media were underestimating the seriousness of crime. Even among those people who felt somewhat unsafe or very unsafe about being out alone in their neighborhoods at night, almost half

9. The exceptions are studies focusing on (a) the effects of violence in the media on attitudes toward violence and violent behavior and (b) the effects of pornography on sex crimes.

Table 5.   Fear of Crime by Perceived Seriousness of Crime Relative to What the Newspapers and Television Say: Eight Impact Cities Aggregate, 1975

Seriousness of Crime Relative to What Media Say	Fear of Crime				
	Very Safe	Reasonably Safe	Somewhat Unsafe	Very Unsafe	Estimated Number*
Less serious	28%**	42%	16%	13%	261,623
	15%***	9%	6%	5%	
About the same	15%	42%	23%	20%	1,514,438
	46%	51%	49%	42%	
More serious	13%	36%	23%	28%	1,292,171
	35%	37%	41%	50%	
Estimated number	474,850	1,208,236	683,365	701,781	3,068,232

(Gamma = .19)

*Excludes persons who gave no response to either item.

**Row percentages.

***Column percentages.

(49 percent and 42 percent) said that crime was about as serious as portrayed in the media. One can conclude from Table 5 that the media set "minimum standards" concerning perceptions of the seriousness of crime; other factors lead many people to perceive crime as being more serious than media portrayals, but few people believe that crime is actually less serious than depicted by the media.

The effects of the media can also be judged inferentially. The media provide both fictional and nonfictional accounts of crime. For the most part, the nonfictional accounts must be based on crimes that come to the attention of criminal justice officials. This means that media treatments of actual crimes are largely restricted to those crimes that are reported to the police, and the threat of crime communicated by the media will be shaped by those same crimes. Therefore, one would expect the fear of crime to be more strongly related to official measures of crime rates than to victimization survey rates which take into account crimes that are not reported to the police.

In order to test this notion indirectly, data from all the twenty-six cities surveyed in the NCS were used along with *Uniform Crime Reports* (UCR) data (Kelley, 1974 and 1975) from the same cities for the same time periods covered by the surveys. Fear of crime (the percentage of respondents in each city who replied somewhat or very unsafe to the fear of crime item) was regressed first on the personal victimization rate as found in the NCS and then on the UCR

Figure 2. Regression of Fear of Crime on NCS Personal Crime Rate: Twenty-six Cities, 1974–75

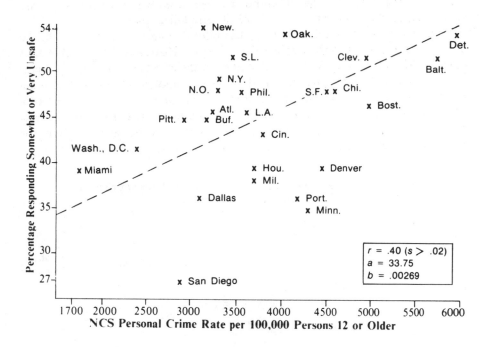

Cities: Atlanta, Baltimore, Boston, Buffalo, Chicago, Cincinnati, Cleveland, Dallas, Denver, Detroit, Houston, Los Angeles, Miami, Milwaukee, Minneapolis, Newark, New Orleans, New York, Oakland, Philadelphia, Pittsburgh, Portland, St. Louis, San Diego, San Francisco, Washington, D.C.

rate. For both crime measures, the crimes of rape, robbery, and aggravated assault were used. The UCR rates were expressed as the number of crimes per 100,000 total population in each city because that is the form in which those rates are communicated officially. The NCS rates were expressed as the number of victimizations per 100,000 persons age twelve years or older. The results are displayed in Figures 2 and 3.

The scattergrams show a much better grouping of the cities around the regression line when fear of crime is regressed on the UCR rate of crime (Figure 3) than on the NCS personal victimization rate (Figure 2). The summary statistics confirm the visual representation: The correlation between fear of crime and the NCS rates is .40, which is not significant at the .02 level, but the correlation is .66 between the UCR rates and fear of crime, a coefficient that is significant beyond the .01 level. However, using the procedure suggested by Blalock (1972:406–407), the difference between the two correlations is only significant at the .10 level (t = 1.41, 23 df, one-tailed test).

From the evidence in this section we can infer that media depictions of crime do have some effects on the public's fear of crime. However, the available data make it difficult to specify the exact nature of the effects or to quantify them. It should also be noted that the media factor cannot be considered as independent of the role socialization factor in the overall model because the media must be viewed as socialization agents. To the extent that the media depict females and the elderly as helpless and vulnerable in the face of crime, the processes noted in the discussion of role socialization will be reinforced.

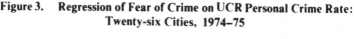

Figure 3.   Regression of Fear of Crime on UCR Personal Crime Rate: Twenty-six Cities, 1974–75

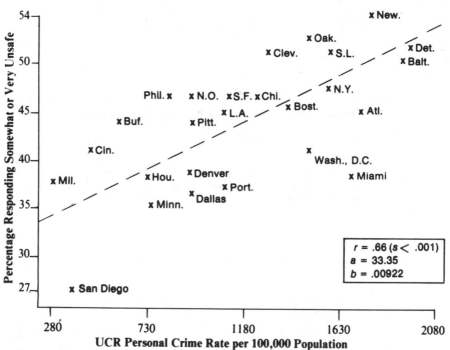

Cities: Atlanta, Baltimore, Boston, Buffalo, Chicago, Cincinnati, Cleveland, Dallas, Denver, Detroit, Houston, Los Angeles, Miami, Milwaukee, Minneapolis, Newark, New Orleans, New York, Oakland, Philadelphia, Pittsburgh, Portland, St. Louis, San Diego, San Francisco, Washington, D.C.

OFFICIAL BARRIERS AGAINST CRIME

If people feel adequately insulated from whatever crimes are occurring, it would seem reasonable to assume that they will not be very fearful of crime. To some extent a degree of insulation comes from knowing and trusting the people with whom one interacts. As a government commission pointed out, the fear of crime is basically a fear of strangers (President's Commission on Law Enforcement and Administration of Justice, 1967:165). In the modern, impersonal urban environment, however, the task of insulating people from crime tends to fall more and more on official government agencies, particularly the police. The confidence that people have in the police, then, should be related to their fear of crime.

Table 6. Fear of Crime by Evaluation of Police Performance: Eight Impact Cities Aggregate, 1975

Evaluation of Police Performance	Fear of Crime				
	Very Safe	Reasonably Safe	Somewhat Unsafe	Very Unsafe	Estimated Number*
Good	18%	39%	21%	22%	1,302,350
Average	14%	42%	24%	20%	1,345,100
Poor	14%	33%	21%	32%	394,640

(Gamma = .08)

*Excludes persons who gave no response to either item.

The supplemental NCS questionnaire contains the item: "Would you say, in general, that your local police are doing a good job, an average job, or a poor job?" In Table 6, responses to that item are cross-tabulated with the fear of crime responses. It is obvious from this table that, although the relatively small number of respondents who rated performance of their local police as poor were most likely to feel very unsafe, the relationship between evaluation of police performance and the fear of crime is not very strong (gamma = .08).

SPECIFYING THE MODEL

Each of the five factors in the working model (Figure 1) has been discussed at least briefly. The model can now be presented more systematically, using indicators that are available from the attitude subsample of the NCS Impact Cities surveys. The resulting model is shown in Figure 4.

Respondents' perceptions of the dangerousness of their own neighborhoods as compared with other neighborhoods in the same metropolitan area are used as a proxy measure of the actual risk of victimization. As mentioned earlier,

Figure 4.   Refinement of the Working Model of the Influences on the Fear of Crime

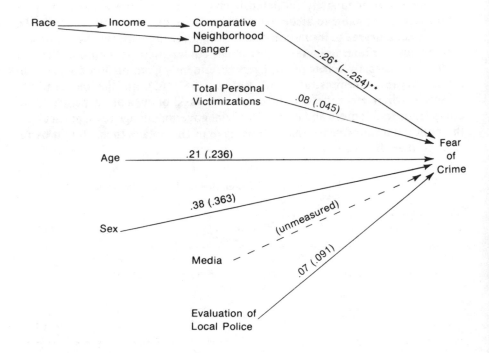

Note: All correlations were computed with unweighted sample cases; n = 65,579; cases with missing data on any of the variables were excluded.

*Simple r.

**Beta weight from multiple regression of fear of crime on comparative neighborhood danger, total personal victimizations, age, sex, and evaluation of local police. In the multiple regression, R = .51 and R^2 = .26.

use of this variable requires the assumption that respondents are relatively accurate in assessing the degree of threat present in their immediate environments. Because subcity geographic identifiers are not available in the data, subjective impressions about relative neighborhood dangerousness represent the best available indicator of local risk. Furthermore, it is probably true that respondents more accurately gauge the risk of victimization in their own neighborhoods than in more distant places.

The second component in the model—experience with victimization—is represented by the total number of personal victimizations reported to the interviewer as having occurred to the respondent during the twelve months pre-

earlier that the relationship of age and sex to fear cannot be accounted for by the risk of personal victimization, at least when risk is defined as the rates of personal victimization for sex and age subgroups in the sample. Actual experience with victimization cannot account for the relationships either, because females and older respondents, who express the highest levels of fear, have proportionately fewer encounters with victimization than do their male and younger counterparts. However, the possibility remains that females and older persons have low rates of victimization *because* of their fear of crime. That is, feelings of vulnerability lead them to stay indoors or to take other actions which insulate them from victimization. Role socialization can then be invoked as an explanation for the *initial* feelings of vulnerability and for the maintenance of those feelings in the face of risks of victimization that are lower than those faced by other segments of the population.

Figure 4 also shows that perceptions of the relative dangerousness of one's neighborhood also have a strong effect on the fear of crime. In the model, those perceptions are used as an indicator of actual risk, under the tenuous assumptions that respondents can make fairly accurate estimates about the dangerousness of their immediate surroundings and that those estimates are not influenced by the respondents' fear of crime. Geographic-specific data are needed for a more accurate measure of actual risk.

The effect of total personal victimizations suffered during the reference period is quite small in Figure 4. This is not surprising because of the relatively small numbers of persons who reported such victimizations during the interviews. Being victimized does appear to increase the fear of crime (see Table 4), but the number of victims in the population is so relatively small that their higher level of fear does not have a great effect on the overall level of fear in the population. Of course, a larger proportion of the population would be classified as having suffered victimizations if data were available for more than one year preceding the interviews. But even if such data were available, it is doubtful that victimizations suffered two, three, or more years before the interviews would have as much effect on the fear of crime as more recent victimizations.

A small effect is shown in Figure 4 for respondents' evaluations of their local police. There is a real measurement problem here. It is not unlikely that respondents have a low opinion of the criminal justice system's ability to protect them from crime yet believe that their local police are performing well; opinions about police officers already on the street do not have a necessary connection with opinions about overall criminal justice effectiveness. Further research is needed to determine the public's perception of how well the criminal justice system is protecting them from crime and whether variations in such perceptions are related to the fear of crime.

The effect of the fifth element of the model—the media—could not be estimated with any indicators available in the NCS, and it is left unmeasured in Figure 4.

Regression of fear of crime on the indicators that were available in the NCS

ceding the interview. This indicator, of course, is not sensitive to victimizations that might have occurred more than one year before the interview.[10] In addition, the variable covers a limited range of victimizations: rape, robbery, assault, and larceny involving contact between the victim and offender. As pointed out earlier, however, the most recent victimizations should have the greatest impact on the fear of crime, and the personal victimizations included in the variable would seem to be the ones most likely to create a fear of crime when they are experienced.

The indicators for role socialization were chosen on theoretical and empirical grounds. Both age and sex are master statuses, in the sense that they have a pervasive effect on all aspects of a person's life. Empirically, it was found that fear and risk were negatively associated across age and sex groups, so role socialization was invoked as a process which can override actual risk in determining the fear of crime in certain cases.

Figure 4 shows the influence of the media on the fear of crime as being unmeasured in this model. In the earlier discussion, some evidence was presented indicating that media presentations of crime do have some effect on the fear of crime. Unfortunately, no variable now exists in the NCS data set to measure the effect of the media adequately.

Finally, official barriers against crime are indicated by respondents' evaluations of how well their local police were performing. A focus on the police rather than on other parts of the criminal justice system in this context seems warranted because the police have more direct contact with the public than does any other criminal justice agency.

DISCUSSION OF THE MODEL

Figure 4 shows the zero-order correlation coefficients between the fear of crime and (1) the actual risk indicator, (2) the experience with victimization indicator, (3) age, (4) sex, and (5) the barrier against crime indicator. Also shown, in parentheses, are the standardized regression coefficients (beta weights) derived from a multiple-linear regression of fear of crime with those same five variables. No attempt has been made to present a complete path diagram of the relationships between all of the variables in this preliminary model.[11]

The beta weights in Figure 4 indicate that the effects of age and sex—the two role socialization variables—on the fear of crime are substantial. It was shown

10. Actually it is sensitive to earlier victimizations in the limited sense that once a person has been victimized, the probability of a subsequent victimization is higher than a simple multiplicative function of the probability of initial victimization; that is, some people are "victimization prone" (see Hindelang, Gottfredson, and Garofalo, 1978:ch. 6). We would expect, then, that people who had been victimized more than one year before the interview would be overrepresented among those who were victimized during the past year.

11. A correlation matrix of all of the variables is available in Garofalo, 1977:app. D.

produced an R^2 of .26, so there is a great deal of the variation in the fear of crime left unexplained. Some of the unexplained variation is probably due to measurement error: The variables used are imperfect indicators of the concepts in the model. In addition, one major factor—the effect of the media—remains unmeasured.

CONCLUSION

A model of the determinants of the fear of crime has been presented, discussed, and partially evaluated using data from victimization surveys conducted in eight American cities. Perhaps the major conclusion that can be drawn from this study is that the fear of crime is not a simple reflection of the risk or experience of being victimized. Social role expectations, in particular, are related to the fear of crime, regardless of—and even contrary to—the objective risk of and experience with personal victimization. Thus, policy makers should not necessarily expect a major decrease in the amount of fear if crime is successfully reduced.

On the other hand, the results do imply that the fear of crime can be reduced without waiting for progress on the difficult task of lowering the level of crime. As Skogan and Klecka (1977:43) note, however, few criminal justice policies "have been aimed specifically at reducing the fear of crime, although there is evidence that this fear is often independent of direct victimization and that it has its own consequences for city life." Programs which accomplish such things as increasing the visibility of the police to citizens, improving street lighting, or educating the public to the very mundane nature of most criminality (as opposed to the sensational portrayals elsewhere) could help to alleviate fear without having any impact on the actual amount of crime. Policies directed specifically at the fear of crime would seem to be justifiable simply in terms of improving the quality of life, especially for segments of the population such as the elderly.

REFERENCES

BLALOCK, H. M., JR.
   1972 *Social Statistics*, 2d ed. New York: McGraw-Hill.
COHEN, S., and J. YOUNG, eds.
   1973 *The Manufacture of News: Social Problems, Deviance and the Mass Media*. London, England: Constable.
GAROFALO, J.
   1977 *The Police and Public Opinion: An Analysis of Victimization and Attitude Data from 13 American Cities*. Analytic Report SD-VAD-3. Law Enforcement As-

sistance Administration, National Criminal Justice Information and Statistics Service. Washington, D.C.: Govt. Printing Office.

GAROFALO, J., and M. J. HINDELANG
   1977   *An Introduction to the National Crime Survey.* Analytic Report SD-VAD-4. Law Enforcement Assistance Administration, National Criminal Justice Information and Statistics Service. Washington, D.C.: Govt. Printing Office.

HINDELANG, M. J., M. R. GOTTFREDSON, and J. GAROFALO
   1978   *Victims of Personal Crime: An Empirical Foundation for a Theory of Personal Victimization.* Cambridge, Mass.: Ballinger.

KELLEY, C.
   1974   *Uniform Crime Reports—1973.* Federal Bureau of Investigation. Washington, D.C.: Govt. Printing Office.
   1975   *Uniform Crime Reports—1974.* Federal Bureau of Investigation. Washington, D.C.: Govt. Printing Office.

PRESIDENT'S COMMISSION ON LAW ENFORCEMENT AND ADMINISTRATION OF JUSTICE
   1967   *The Challenge of Crime in a Free Society.* Washington, D.C.: Govt. Printing Office.

SKOGAN, W. G., and W. R. KLECKA
   1977   *The Fear of Crime.* rev. ed. Supplementary Empirical Teaching Units in Political Science. Washington, D.C.: American Political Science Association.

U.S. BUREAU OF THE CENSUS
   1976   *Survey Documentation.* National Crime Survey, Central Cities Sample, 1975. Washington, D.C.: Govt. Printing Office.
   1975   *Interviewer's Manual.* National Crime Survey, Central Cities Sample. Washington, D.C.: Govt. Printing Office.

WEIS, K., and S. S. BORGES
   1973   "Victimology and Rape: The Case of the Legitimate Victim." *Issues in Criminology* 8 (Fall): 71–115.

James Garofalo is Director of the Research Center East, National Council on Crime and Delinquency. His research interests are the fear of crime and victimization. He is the coauthor of Victims of Personal Crime: An Empirical Foundation for a Theory of Personal Victimization *(Cambridge, MA: Ballinger, 1978).*

Part VI:

CONTINUITIES AND CONTROVERSIES

As noted in the first volume of this series, the *Yearbook* is "designed to assist students of crime and crime control in staying abreast of their rapidly growing and changing field." In adding a section entitled "Continuities and Controversies," we express our desire further to implement this design by establishing continuity among the *Yearbook* volumes. This editorial policy intends to drawn upon and add to debate in criminology. It is hardly necessary to argue the need for such debate to help counteract the tendency in the field—as in most of the disciplines contributing to it—toward unrelated or only terminologically linked projects and observations. Thus we extend an earnest and urgent invitation to readers to submit statements extending or taking issue with arguments or evidence presented in preceding volumes. We do not think that these pages would be put to best use if we publish contributions directed to specific technical points in particular articles of the sort one often finds in scholarly journals. Aside from this, however, we will welcome withering critiques, reminders of things forgotten but worth remembering, conceptual clarifications, observations that are relevant to some topic, and much else.

To get started, we are doing something we do not expect to repeat in the future —although we take no oath on the point. Namely, we are including three previously published articles in this section. Each related to a major section contained in the first volume of the *Yearbook*. But these selections are *not* intended to be a model for what we expect to publish in this section later.

Philip J. Cook's article probes the problematics connected with the economic approach to crime, the approach so ably outlined by Isaac Ehrlich in the first volume.[1] Cook raises a problem of quite extraordinary importance for those using, or hoping to benefit from, the economic approach to crime and crime control. Cook argues that it is not enough to attribute to potential offenders that quality and quantum of rationality required to be responsive to incentives; it is also necessary to assume that they will respond rationally to the range of incentives which reality presents to them. To be sure, he finally retreats from following the consequences of this assertion when he writes that measuring these effects "would entail the collection of highly detailed data on criminal opportunities . . . [and the] prospects for collecting such data appear slim indeed." One need not be insensitive to the technical difficulties behind Cook's pessimism to be disappointed by his ready surrender. To write of the "inevitable absence of data which is [sic] adequate to constructing an index of CJS effectiveness which is purified of the influence of criminal's adaptive behavior" represents a neglect of even the possibility of relating the economic approach with social psychological studies of criminal conduct. At the same time, of course, it identifies one locus of possible collaboration.

In the second article, Eric Monkkonen, a leading historian of criminal justice in the United States, introduces some of the difficulties and complexities of gaining access to, and evaluating, materials for the historical study of crime and its treatment. The article usefully extends related discussion by Michael S. Hindus in the first volume of the *Yearbook*. We are somewhat surprised that historians need such stern reminders of the problems resulting from the fact that inherited documentary evidence is a perspectively biased expression of studied institutions, rather than a neutral account of their workings. We had assumed that historians knew what to make of documents found in archives because they were cognizant of the ways the documents were produced, when they were produced; in fact, we assumed that this skill was the historian's stock in trade.[2] Be that as it may, we can only applaud historians' undertaking to combine the sociologists' skepticism about institutionally produced data with the economists' efforts to engage in formally rigorous, quantitative analysis of these materials. One hopes, however, that Monkkonen, even while he chastises historians such as Tobias, does not intend to deny narrative historiography its proper—we think high—value.

Judge David Bazelon's article enlarges considerably on the topic of discretion, treated by Arthur Rosett in the first volume. Though the article deals with decision making in areas of regulatory authority, in which the tension between technical findings and judical discretion is particularly prominent, the problem is present in other areas as well, including criminal justice. What is at issue here is not, of course, whether one ought to be guided by technical findings *or* value-infused judgments. Instead, the difficulty arises out of the fact that "the growing use of analytical tools such as cost-benefit analysis magnifies the chance that unrecognized value judgments will creep into apparently objective assessments." Judge Bazelon's views about the ways courts may assist in alleviating the mischief that arises from this fact may serve to suggest that, while our distrust of judges and other functionaries invested with the power of discretion may be well-warranted, the wisest choice may not be to keep untrustworthy judges and reduce their powers to cause harm. At least we ought not to rush into that solution without first assaying the possibilities of having more trustworthy judges. The latter recommends itself not only because in the recent past we have not been very successful in paring the powers of officials, whose apparent inventiveness in finding new means of having their way is truly awesome. Both Judge Bazelon and Arthur Rossett suggest another reason as well. To quote from Rossett's essay:

> When a system becomes preoccupied by its fear of fools and knaves it distrusts the discretion of all decision makers. In restricting all discretion to avoid the depredations of bad persons the system loses the capacity to fully realize the virtues

of good people in power. Harnessing talent, increasing responsiveness, improving the content of decisions are all aims that justify taking risks. To reconcile the prevalence of discretion in the criminal law, we must find ways to limit the risks of discretion to an acceptable level without eliminating the opportunity for wise decision.

NOTES

1. We should also like to recommend to readers Daniel Nagin's "Crime Rates, Sanction Levels, and Constraints on Prison Population," 12(3) *Law and Society Review* 341-366. In this article, Nagin argues that the negative association between crime rates and the sanction of imprisonment "is more readily interpreted as a negative effect of crime rates on sanction levels rather than its reverse—a deterrent effect."

2. We cannot resist calling to the attention of readers Josephine Tey's delightful detective novel, *Daughter of Time*. Berkeley, California: Berkeley Publishing Corporation, 1975. Tey's hero unravels the mystery of the murder of the Princes in the Tower by closely attending to the likely perspectives of those attesting to the guilt of Richard the Third. A more technical treatment may be found in Paul Murray Kendall, *Richard the Third*. Garden City, NY: Doubleday, (Anchor Books), 1965, Appendix I, "Who Murdered the Princes?" pp. 438-468; 554-558. It, too, is a fine read.

34

THE CLEARANCE RATE AS A MEASURE OF CRIMINAL JUSTICE SYSTEM EFFECTIVENESS

PHILIP J. COOK

The validity of the clearance rate as a measure of either criminal justice system (CJS) effectiveness or of the probability of punishment for crime can be questioned on the grounds that the relationship between CJS effectiveness and observed clearance rates is mediated by the choice behavior of criminals. If the clearance rate is endogenous in that sense, then recent econometric results concerning the deterrence effect of punishment are fundametally flawed. A model of criminal adaptation to changes in CJS effectiveness illustrates the basic problem.

1. Introduction

The fraction of crimes 'cleared' by arrest or conviction in a jurisdiction has long been used by police officials and others as an indicator of the effectiveness of that jurisdiction's criminal justice system (CJS). The various correlational studies of the criminal deterrence effect, published during the last decade, have adopted some variant of the clearance rate for a closely related use – measuring the jurisdiction-specific probability that a (potential) criminal will be punished if he chooses to commit a crime. A variety of such studies have reported negative relationships between crime rates and clearance rates across jurisdictions (precints, states, cities) and cited these results as evidence in favor of the hypothesis that increasing the certainty of punishment has a deterrent effect on potential criminals.[1]

The validity of clearance rates as a measure of either CJS effectiveness or the probability of punishment for crime has frequently been questioned on the basis of the inaccuracies in the data used to estimate these rates.[2] While this is indeed a serious problem in practice for most types of crime, there is at least a possibility that it can be overcome by the development of more accurate crime data. A more fundamental question concerning the validity of clearance rates in these uses is that the relationship between CJS effectiveness and observed clearance rates is mediated by the choice behavior of criminals.

*The author is Assistant Professor of Policy Sciences and Economics. Jan Chaiken, Franklin Fisher, and Charles Manski provided valuable comments on an earlier draft.

[1] These studies are reviewed and critiqued by Nagin (1978). The earliest published results appear in Gibbs (1968).

[2] See Cook (1977) for an illustration of how data inaccuracy can produce an artifactual negative correlation between crime rates and clearance rates.

From Philip J. Cook, "The Clearance Rate As A Measure of Criminal Justice System Effectiveness," 11(1) *Journal of Public Economics* 135-142 (February 1979). Copyright 1979 by North-Holland Publishing Company.

For example, robbers would be expected to adapt to an increase in the potential effectiveness of the system in solving robbery cases and gaining convictions for robbery defendants; if under the new more effective regime robbers tend to be more selective in choosing victims and more cautious in their modus operandi, the observed change in the clearance rate may be misleadingly small. In an extreme but not implausible case developed below, a change in the true effectiveness of the CJS will result in *no* change in the observed clearance rate.

The next section develops this argument and presents conclusions concerning the econometric methodology of deterrence research. The third section proposes a model to explain the incidence of violent crime and generates some intriguing results concerning the relationship between the clearance rate and criminal justice system effectiveness on the basis of this model. A final section presents my conclusions.

2. The measurement problem in the econometric study of deterrence

The current paradigm for the econometric study of deterrence was established by Ehrlich (1973), Carr-Hill and Stern (1973), and Sjoquist (1973). The focus of this literature is on measuring the responsiveness of crime rates to changes in the probability and severity of punishment by estimating the coefficients of an offense supply equation:

$$C = a_0 + a_1 \hat{p} + a'_2 X + \varepsilon_c \quad \text{(supply of offenses)}, \tag{1}$$

where:

C = the per capita rate of some category of offenses,

$\hat{p}$ = the number of people punished (arrested or incarcerated) for this offense category divided by the number of offenses committed,

X = a vector of other variables thought to influence the potential criminal's crime related decisions, usually including a measure of the average severity of punishment (e.g. median number of months served in prison for those convicts who are sentenced to prison for the offense in question),

ε_c = a random variable.

$\hat{p}$, which I will call the 'clearance rate', is included as a measure of the probability of punishment which is perceived by a potential criminal contemplating the commission of a criminal act. The consistent estimation of the 'deterrent effect',[3] a_1, was seen as requiring the simultaneous estimation of a CJS 'production function' to take account of the presumed effect of the

---

[3]This is more accurately labelled the 'preventive effect', since it may reflect incapacitation as well as deterrence effects [see Ehrlich (1973)].

crime rate on the clearance rate; an increase in the crime rate increases the workload on CJS resources, *ceteris paribus*, presumably resulting in a reduction in the clearance rate:

$$\hat{p} = b_0 + b_1 C + b'_2 Y + \varepsilon_p, \qquad \text{(CJS production function)}, \qquad (2)$$

where $Y=$ a vector of variables thought to influence the effectiveness of the CJS in clearing crimes.

More elaborate structures have been utilized in some studies,[4] but some form of equations (1) and (2) is included in virtually all recent econometric studies of deterrence.

While most authors report a significantly negative estimate for the 'deterrence effect', a_1, this result is not entirely robust with respect to the data set or the specification of the system.[5] A fundamental problem with this approach has for the most part been ignored by critics: If the estimate of a_1 is to be assigned its usual interpretation (deterrence effect), it is necessary that the clearance rate $\hat{p}$ be exogenous from the point of view· of the individual criminal. Yet it seems reasonable to suppose that the likelihood of a crime resulting in punishment is determined in part by choices made by the criminal; for a given environment of CJS threats, the likelihood that a particular crime will be cleared depends on the care exercised by the criminal in selecting his victim and in executing the crime (i.e. his *modus operandi*). Furthermore, one would expect that the criminal's choice of modus operandi is influenced by his perception of the effectiveness of the CJS, just as is his choice of crime commission frequency and crime type. Thus both the crime rate and the clearance rate reflect criminals' choices, which choices are influenced by the underlying (and unobserved) dimension, CJS effectiveness.[6]

The problem that the clearance rate reflects the choice behavior of criminals as well as the quality of criminal opportunities is analogous to problems which have been analyzed previously in the economics literature by Fisher (1964 and Pelzman (1976). In his discussion of the supply of wildcat drilling and of new discoveries of petroleum reserves, Fisher (1964, pp. 6–7)

[4]For example, a number of authors have added a third equation specifying the public's 'demand' for CJS inputs (CJS expenditures, number of police) as a function of the crime rate and other factors. See Carr-Hill and Stern (1973), Ehrlich (1973), and Avio and Clark (1974) among others.

[5]Forst finds little evidence of a deterrent effect in the 1970 cross section data on states. The identification problem for equations (1) and (2) is severe, and Nagin (1977) has made a strong empirical and theoretical case for the assertion that deterrence-like results generated by many authors from the 1960 state cross section are the result of unreasonable identification restrictions.

[6]Carr-Hill and Stern (1973) interpret their finding that the 'clear-up' rate is negatively related to the number of policemen per capita as the result of a 'weeding out' process; they assume 'that crimes deterred by the existence of more policemen are easier to solve than average i.e. with a given offense rate and extra police we expect the offense mix to be more 'professional' (p. 308).' While they are aware of this problem, they do not consider its implications for the specification and interpretation of their offense supply equation.

rejects the success ratio (the fraction of wildcat wells that are not dry holes) as a measure of 'natural conditions' confronting the individual operator:

> ...measures such as the success ratio and average size of average discoveries are not simply measures of properties of the distribution of opportunities presented to the industry in a given year; they are measures of the distribution of opportunities *accepted* by the industry and this is not at all the same thing. Such measures of industry performance depend both on the opportunities found in nature and presented for possible drilling, *and* on the drilling decisions made.

The analogy between this success ratio and the crime clearance rate should be clear.

Pelzman's analysis of the effect of auto safety regulations on the highway fatality rate gives both theoretical and empirical support to his claim that the regulation-induced increase in the protection which an automobile provides its passengers is not fully reflected in the resulting change in highway fatality rates – the increase in the intrinsic safety of an automobile simply shifts the schedule relating the probability of death to what Pelzman calls driving 'intensity', and drivers may choose to consume some part of this gain in the form of increased driving intensity. Thus, the change in the probability of death per passenger mile would be expected to provide an underestimate of the true effectiveness of the regulations.

The specific econometric problems posed by the use of the clearance rate as a measure of CJS effectiveness can be illustrated by displaying a new system of equations which incorporates an 'index of CJS effectiveness', I_E. This quantity index could be defined, for example, as the hypothetical clearance rate for a representative 'market basket' of criminal acts, where each act is described in detail as to circumstances and modus operandi.

As before, we have in the linear form:

$$C = \alpha_0 + \alpha_1 I_E + \alpha_2' X + \delta_c, \quad \text{(supply of offenses)}, \tag{3}$$

$$I_E = \beta_0 + \beta_1 C + \beta_2' Y + \delta_I, \quad \text{(CJS production function)}. \tag{4}$$

The discussion above suggests a third equation:

$$\hat{p} = \gamma_0 + \gamma_1 I_E + \gamma_2' X + \delta_p, \quad \text{(clearance rate)}. \tag{5}$$

Solving for I_E in equation (5) under the assumption that $\gamma_1 \neq 0$, and substituting in equation (3), yields

$$C = \left(\alpha_0 - \frac{\alpha_1}{\gamma_1}\gamma_0\right) + \frac{\alpha_1}{\gamma_1}\hat{p} + \left(\alpha_2 - \frac{\alpha_1}{\gamma_1}\gamma_2\right)X + \left(\delta_c - \frac{\alpha_1}{\gamma_1}\delta_p\right), \tag{6}$$

which suggests the interpretation of a_1 as the ratio of a true deterrence effect (α_1) and γ_1, a magnitude which measures the degree to which criminals adapt their modus operandi to changes in CJS effectiveness. This result makes the unwarranted assumption that the equation system is linear, and should be viewed as simply a concrete illustration of the problem at hand.

My basic criticism of the econometric estimation of the deterrence effect can now be summarized. Published studies have used the clearance rate $\hat{p}$ as a measure of the certainty of punishment, but this measure is unacceptable because it reflects the choice behavior of individual criminals as well as the threat level produced by the CJS. What is needed here is an index of CJS effectiveness, I_E, which is defined so as to be free of the influence of endogenous adjustments by criminals to the environment of CJS threats. The measurement of such an index would entail the collection of highly detailed data on criminal opportunities – both those opportunities which are actually accepted by criminals, and those which are not accepted (since an increase in CJS effectiveness may result in criminals becoming more selective about which opportunities they accept).[7] The prospects for collecting such data appear slim indeed, suggesting that the effort to estimate the supply of offenses function should be abandoned. However, the alternative of estimating the reduced form equation – the direct effect of CJS resources on the rate of crime commission – remains an attractive possibility with considerable relevance for CJS policy.

3. The relationship between the clearance rate and CJS effectiveness

Analysis of the relationship between the clearance rate and the effectiveness of the criminal justice system requires an explicit characterization of the criminal opportunities set. For some crimes of theft (e.g. shoplifting) it seems reasonable that a range of opportunities with known attributes are available at any point in time, with the locus of undominated opportunities being characterized by tradeoffs between hedonic attributes such as effort, the likelihood of punishment, and the expected 'take'. The thief then can be viewed as choosing a particular type of opportunity (*modus operandi*) from this set, and also choosing a crime commission rate. Such an approach might be developed as an extension of the model presented in Block and Heineke (1975).

A much different characterization of the opportunity set seems warranted in the case of many crimes of violence. An 'opportunity' to commit a violent crime can be defined as a circumstance in which the potential assailant would derive positive utility from a specified act of violence if the probability of punishment were zero. Such 'opportunities' are presumably rare for most

---

[7]The conceptually ideal approach is developed by Manski (1978), who presents the theoretical underpinnings for the estimation of individual criminal choice functions on the basis of detailed microdata on criminal opportunities.

people, and arise as an unintended byproduct of social intercourse. (A large fraction of murders and assaults, for example, occur in the immediate context of arguments between relatives and friends.) The decision of whether to accept a particular opportunity is presumably independent of both past opportunities and expected future opportunities.

Assume that each individual is confronted with a random sequence of opportunities to commit violent crimes, where each opportunity is identical in all respects except the (perceived) probability p that a decision to accept the opportunity will result in punishment. The individual accepts an opportunity if the expected utility of committing the crime exceeds the utility of remaining straight. Acceptance generates two possible states of the world: S_1 (crime results in apprehension and punishment), or S_2 (crime has no legal consequences.) He will accept the opportunity if the probability p of S_1 is less than p^*, where p^* is equal to the maximum value of p for which

$$p \, U(W, S_1) + (1-p) \, U(W, S_2) \geqq U(W, S_0). \tag{7}$$

In condition (7), W represents wealth and S_0 is the state of the world which results if he does not commit the crime.

Each period a maximum of one opportunity is produced by the individual's environment, drawn from a distribution represented by the density function $f(p, \alpha)$, where α is a parameter reflecting the effectiveness of the CJS. The probability of an opportunity arising during a period is equal to $\int_0^1 f(p, \alpha) \, dp \leqq 1$. Given the definition of 'opportunity', the value of this integral is independent of α.

The expected value of p for all opportunities which are *accepted* is

$$\hat{p} = \frac{\int_0^{p^*} pf(p, \alpha) \, dp}{\int_0^{p^*} f(p, \alpha) \, dp}. \tag{8}$$

$\hat{p}$ is the expected value of the clearance rate for any group of individuals who have identical opportunity density functions and 'cut points' p^*

Analysis of the effect of an increase in CJS effectiveness[8] requires assumptions about the opportunity density function $f(p, \alpha)$, and no general comparative statics results are available. It is even possible that $\hat{p}$ would fall in response to an increase in CJS effectiveness, if most of the change were concentrated on opportunities which had previously been barely acceptable to potential criminals.

In the context of this simple heterogeneous opportunities model, it is clear that any change in the criminal's environment which causes him to modify

[8] An unambiguous increase in CJS effectiveness ($\alpha_2 > \alpha_1$) requires that
$\int_0^x f(p, \alpha_2) dp \leqq \int_0^x f(p, \alpha_1) dp$ for $0 \leqq x \leqq 1$.

the 'cut point' p^* will result in a corresponding change in $\hat{p}$, assuming that the distribution of criminal opportunities is unchanged. For example, an increase in the average severity of punishment would result in a reduction in p^* and hence a reduction in $\hat{p}$. One implication of this result is that there should be a negative interjurisdiction relationship between the fraction of crimes which result in punishment and the average severity of punishment, *ceteris paribus*. In fact, the cross section correlations (for 1960 data on U.S. states) between median time served in prison and the fraction of crimes resulting in a prison sentence for each of the FBI's seven Index crimes are all negative, and significantly different from zero at the 5 percent level for assault, rape, robbery, and larceny.[9]

Several other variables should also influence p^* and hence $\hat{p}$; p^* would increase with increases in wealth, for example, if an increase in wealth increased the perceived opportunity cost of a prison term. Elaborations on the simple heterogeneous opportunities model should therefore be a source of testable hypotheses concerning the relationship between the distribution of criminal opportunities which are accepted by criminals and the various factors which influence this choice.

There is one circumstance in which an increase in CJS effectiveness is reliably signalled by a change in the clearance rate. In the short run it is likely that changes in the effectiveness of the system in producing threats will not be perceived by the relevant sector of the population. If so, the clearance rate will necessarily increase, since criminals will have made no adaptation to the new regime. Ironically, this short run instance is also characterized by a complete lack of any deterrence effect, precisely because the increase in effectiveness is not perceived.

4. Conclusions

From the time of Jeremy Bentham onward, it has been argued that the rational criminal will adjust his rate of crime commission to changes in the (perceived) effectiveness of the criminal justice system. I have argued that the criminal's crime decision is not limited to choosing a rate of crime commission, but also entails choosing the precise type of crime he will commit and the manner in which he will commit it. These latter choices influence the likelihood that he will be arrested and punished. The argument that these choices will be sensitive to changes in CJS effectiveness appears to be just as strong as the traditional argument that the rate of crime commission is sensitive to CJS effectiveness. The observed clearance rate is then the outcome of the interaction between the environment of threats generated by CJS and the adaptive choices of criminals, as illustrated by the model presented in section 3.

[9]Data are taken from Vandaele (1978, Appendix E).

In the inevitable absence of data which is adequate to constructing an index of CJS effectiveness which is purified of the influence of criminals' adaptive behavior, it would appear that the effort to estimate a 'supply of offenses' equation is doomed. The alternative is to estimate the reduced form equation relating CJS inputs to crime rates. The reduced form equation does not permit a distinction between the hypothesis that CJS effectiveness is not enhanced by marginal changes in CJS input mix or level, and the hypothesis that crime rates are insensitive to marginal changes in CJS effectiveness. However, the reduced form equation does not sacrifice anything in terms of policy relevance when compared with the structural equations.

References

Avio, Kenneth and Scott Clark, 1974, Property crime in Canada: An econometric study, prepared for the Ontario Economic Council.

Block, Michael and John Heineke, 1975, A labor theoretic analysis of the criminal choice, American Economic Review 65, no. 3, 314–325.

Carr-Hill, R.A. and N.H. Stern, 1973, An econometric model of the supply and control of offenses in England and Wales, Journal of Public Economics 2, November, 289–318.

Cook, Philip J., 1977, Punishment and crime: A critique of current findings concerning the preventive effects of punishment, Law and Contemporary Problems 41, no. 1.

Ehrlich, Isaac, 1973, Participation in illegitimate activities: A theoretical and empirical investigation, Journal of Political Economy 81, no. 3, 521–563.

Fisher, Franklin M., 1964, Supply and costs in the U.S. petroleum industry: Two econometric studies (Johns Hopkins Press, Baltimore).

Forst, Brian E., 1976, Participation in illegitimate activities: Further empirical findings, Policy Analysis 2, no. 3, 477–492.

Gibbs, Jack P., 1968, Crime, punishment, and deterrence, Southwestern Social Science Quarterly 48, 515–530.

Manski, Charles F., 1978, Prospects for inference on deterrence through empirical analysis of individual behavior, in: A. Blumstein, J. Cohen and D. Nagin, eds., Deterrence and incapacitation: Estimating the effects of criminal sanctions on crime rates (Washington, D.C.).

Nagin, Daniel, 1977, Crime rates and sanction levels in the context of an effective constraint on prison population, unpublished.

Nagin, Daniel, 1978, General deterrence: A review of the empirical evidence, Management Science, forthcoming.

Pelzman, Sam, 1975, The effects of automobile safety regulation, Journal of Political Economy 83, no. 4, 677–725.

Sjoquist, David L., 1973, Property crime and economic behavior: Some empirical results, American Economic Review 63, no. 3, 439–446.

Vandaele, Walter, 1978, Participation in illegal activities: Ehrlich revisited, in: A. Blumstein, J. Cohen and D. Nagin, eds., Deterrence and incapacitation: Estimating the effects of criminal sanctions on crime rates (Washington, D.C.).

Philip J. Cook is Associate Professor of Public Policy Studies and Economics at Duke University. His current research interests are gun control, preventive effects of punishment, and the public health effects of alcohol excise taxation. He is the author of the "The Effect of Gun Availability on Robbery and Robbery Murder: A Cross-Section Study of Fifty Cities" in Policy Studies Review Annual, *Vol. 3 (Beverly Hills, CA: Sage Publications, 1979).*

35

SYSTEMATIC CRIMINAL JUSTICE HISTORY
Some Suggestions

ERIC MONKKONEN

A recent article by Graff on the use of jail intake records for the study of criminal offenders in the past is misleadingly optimistic and underplays the critical role of theory and statistical methods. Jail records are indeed a rich source for social historical research. Yet one should not be as hopeful as Graff that these sources are abundant.[1]

Most historians who work with nineteenth-century criminal justice data are continually thwarted in their search for systematically preserved sources. Although court dockets, the most abstracted records, are most often preserved, my experience in searching for criminal court records indicates both a lack of availability and reasonable access. How many historians, for example, would be lucky enough to find the 1830s Oyer and Terminer dockets in a special closet at St. Francis College in Brooklyn? Further, for every court docket which has been preserved, few sets of papers have been saved, and to find primary jail records, police blotters, and other manuscript sources is a frustrating task.

The best place to begin for U.S. sources is the *Historical Records Survey* of the Work Progress Administration, but omission of desired papers from the *HRS* is not a sure sign of their nonexistence, just as the presence of a set of papers in a janitor's closet forty years ago when the surveys were made does not guarantee that these papers still exist. One can only hope that all researchers will find jail records as easily as Graff did. But even such good fortune should not suppress the importance of developing a careful theoretical and methodological perspective. Using this perspective, whatever specific ideological manifestation it takes, the historian must develop an awareness of the kinds of sources available: this note discusses sources accessible with enough regularity to constitute the basis for systematic social research.

1 Harvey J. Graff, "Crime and Punishment in the Nineteenth Century: A New Look at the Criminal," *Journal of Interdisciplinary History*, VII (1977), 477–491.

Reprinted from *The Journal of Interdisciplinary History*, IX (1979), 451–464, by permission of *The Journal of Interdisciplinary History* and The M.I.T. Press. Cambridge, Massachusetts. Copyright 1979 by the Massachusetts Institute of Technology and the editors of the *Journal of Interdisciplinary History*.

The greatest strength of the past two decades of social history has been its focus on individuals, on building up from the individual case level to make arguments and analyses which in many situations would have been impossible with pre-processed data. The list of innovative studies begins with Merle Curti, *The Making of an American Community* (Stanford, 1959), and continues through the Philadelphia Social History Project to the myriad of other projects underway around the world. Two of the main strengths of this new work have been its avoidance of the ecological fallacy and its ability, by using raw lists of names and attributes, to answer questions which the original compilers never had in mind.

But each of these strengths contains pitfalls. First, ecological problems can be confronted, if not abolished, without collecting individual level data, as the recent work of political historians has shown. Yet the work of these historians in using highly aggregated and pre-processed data—that is, data previously aggregated for specific needs—has not seemed to spur social historians to exploit the rich sources of pre-processed data compiled to record non-voting behavior. Only recently has there been a sign that researchers have begun to look at such data.[2] In a sense, the methodological focus on individuals, each of whom becomes a case in a data set specifically aggregated to answer the historian's questions, has encouraged social historians to forget about the potentials of pre-processed data. Part of the reason has been in the sheer fun of working with data on thousands of ordinary individuals, of saving from obscurity the obscure, and of answering questions which had never occurred to previous list compilers. But we have been too cautious, and in the push to compile data on an individual basis we have forgotten the need to establish larger parameters and to look at broad social trends. If social history is to build on its strengths and confront weaknesses, then social historians must do more work with aggregated pre-processed data, maintaining what has become a tradition of close

2   J. Morgan Kousser, "The 'New Political History': A Methodological Critique," *Reviews in American History,* IV (1976), 1–14; Samuel P. Hays, "The First Annual Meeting of the Social Science History Association," *Historical Methods Newsletter,* 10 (1976), 40; "News and Announcements" section in *ibid.,* 43; John Modell, "Changing Risks, Changing Adaptations: American Families in the 19th and 20th Centuries," Smithsonian Symposium on Kin and Community: The Peopling of America, 1977.

scrutiny of sources combined with careful theory and model building.[3]

The second problem relates to the first, for the wealth of data on individuals tempts any researcher to forget rigorous questions in favor of ad hoc generalizations. Often an endeavor which begins as a theory-directed search for sources and data with which to test specific hypotheses ends up as a search for theories to fit the data. One of the original strengths of building up data sets based on records compiled for other reasons then becomes subverted, and the social historian ends up recompiling and re-explaining the work of the original list makers: old wine in old bottles with new labels.

This problem is most seductive for those dealing with records generated by the criminal justice system. It is almost impossible to resist the "let the facts speak for themselves" temptations residing in a set of indictment rolls, court dockets, police blotters, or jail and prison records. And because of these temptations, the historian's approach to these records must be as calculated and careful as that exemplified in Hammarberg's research design for the Great Salt Basin Mormon Culture Area Project.[4]

Because most studies which exploit sources containing individual records will be case studies of some specific jurisdiction, several prior parameters must be established. First, what is the relative position of the unit being analyzed within the region or nation? A social scientific approach will select the unit for its relevant characteristics—size, rate of change or relative stability, position in an urban network, or developmental stage—and at this point the search for lists should begin. Unfortunately, there is no evidence that non-processed criminal justice record sources are abundant; critical lists are known to have been destroyed; and the researcher who finds complete manuscript sources usually

3 For an analysis of problems deriving from this means of creating data sets, see James Henretta, "The Study of Social Mobility: Ideological Assumptions and Conceptual Bias," *Labor History,* XVIII (1977), 165–178; also comments of Clyde Griffen, Michael Frisch, and Theodore Hershberg, "Social Mobility; New Directions," Social Science History Association Meeting, 1976; Hays, "The First Annual Meeting," 40–41.

4 For a use of civil court records which avoids the siren call of anecdotal history, see Lawrence M. Friedman and Robert V. Percival, "A Tale of Two Courts: Litigation in Alameda and San Benito Counties," *Law and Society Review,* X (1976), 267–302. Melvyn Hammarberg, "A Sampling Design for Mormon Utah," *Journal of Interdisciplinary History,* VII (1977), 453–476.

considers such a gold mine but often does not quite know why.[5] Until we know a good deal more about the creation and retention of manuscript sources generated by the criminal justice system in the nineteenth century, we might most wisely assume that complete files have been idiosyncratically preserved, and take this as a caution.

The researcher in criminal justice system sources must be aware of relevant parameters; when dealing with rates, whether arrest, jailing, conviction, or imprisonment, the behavior of comparable rates within the region or nation must be understood, or the researcher may well end up explaining national trends in terms of a model generated for purely local application. This *caveat* is difficult to attend to as the United States has no national statistics to compare to those used by Gatrell and Hadden for England.[6] My work in progress establishes urban arrest rates for 1860–1920 (for cities over 50,000), but this still leaves a blank for the pre-1860 period, for smaller cities and rural areas, and for rates other than arrests (jailings, trials, etc.). Over a dozen previous studies establish some sort of offense indicators, but the results tend to be contradictory and confusing. At this point, the researcher should examine these other studies in hopes of finding a comparable and useful set of data. If this does not work, the researcher must do two things: first, be alert to known "crime waves" such as that of 1855, and second, use pre-processed published data to establish comparable regional trends.[7]

5 See, for instance, the thorough source notes in Roger Lane, *Policing the City: Boston, 1822–1885* (Cambridge, 1967), 225–229, 239–248, where "it is clear no more primary sources remain to be exploited." The arrest blotters for nineteenth-century New York City have been destroyed, except for those of the draft riots of 1863, which have been preserved by Alfred J. Young, Curator, City of New York Police Academy Museum. Eugene Watts described some results of a systematic project based on complete manuscript sources at the Organization of American Historians meeting, 1976. This project began with careful prior questions and promises to show the potential of non-fragmentary records.

6 V. A. C. Gatrell and T. B. Hadden, "Criminal Statistics and Their Interpretation," in E. A. Wrigley (ed.), *Nineteenth-Century Society* (Cambridge, 1972), 336–396. Nevertheless, unpublished primary sources exist most systematically for felony level courts: see, for instance, Monkkonen, *The Dangerous Class: Crime and Poverty in Columbus, Ohio, 1860–1885* (Cambridge, 1975) for research utilizing such documents. For a recent state-wide survey see Michael S. Hindus, *The Records of the Massachusetts Superior Court and Its Predecessors; An Inventory and Guide* (Mass. Judicial Records Committee, n.d.).

7 See for example Charles N. Burrows, *Criminal Statistics in Iowa, University of Iowa Studies in the Social Sciences,* IX (1931); Waldo L. Cook, "Murders in Massachusetts,"

The researcher in criminal justice sources also must have some notion of the processes which generated these sources. Unfortunately, there is little literature on such processes in the nineteenth century, certainly nothing to compare to the study by Wright and Hunt and the whole critical literature on the census, recently well-summarized by Sharpless and Shortridge.[8] But the wealth of current literature should guide our thinking about the generation of official sources. For instance, a British study suggests both the dangers and possibilities in using reported suicides as any kind of consistent index; for the ultimate determination of whether or not most unnatural deaths are recorded as suicide depends upon whether the coroner thinks the deceased is the "kind of person" to have committed suicide. Thus the recording of the death as suicide serves as an indication of the coroner's perception of who commits suicide, as well as an indicator of who, in fact, commits suicide. This means that suicide rates can serve as a mixed indicator of perception and behavior, but may be questionable when used as an index to the actual incidence of suicide, or even more questionable when used as an index of a latent construct like "social tension."[9]

The complex bureaucratic processes involved in moving a person from freedom to prison are more visible than those pro-

---

American Statistical Association Journal, III (1893), 357–378; Theodore N. Ferdinand, "The Criminal Patterns of Boston since 1849," *American Journal of Sociology*, LXXIII (1967), 84–99; *idem*, "Politics, the Police and Arresting Policies in Salem, Massachusetts, since the Civil War," *Social Problems*, XIX (1972), 572–588; Arthur H. Hobbs, "Criminality in Philadelphia: 1810 Compared with 1937," *American Sociological Review*, VIII (1943), 198–202; Lane, "Urbanization and Criminal Violence in the 19th Century: Massachusetts as a Test Case," *Journal of Social History*, II (1968), 156–163; Monkkonen, "Toward a Dynamic Theory of Crime and the Police: A Criminal Justice Systems Perspective," *Historical Methods Newsletter*, 10 (1977), 157–165.

8   Carroll D. Wright and William C. Hunt, *History and Growth of the United States Census* (Washington, 1900); John B. Sharpless and Ray M. Shortridge, "Biased Underenumeration in Census Manuscripts: Methodological Implications," *Journal of Urban History*, I (1975), 409–439.

9   J. Maxwell Atkinson, "Societal Reactions to Suicide: The Role of Coroners' Definitions," in Stanley Cohen (ed.), *Images of Deviance* (Harmondsworth, 1971), 165–191. For two examples of the uncritical use of suicide rates see Sheldon Hackney, "Southern Violence," in Hugh D. Graham and Ted R. Gurr (eds.), *The History of Violence in America* (New York, 1969), 505–527; Vicent E. McHale and Eric A. Johnson, "Urbanization, Industrialization, and Crime in Nineteenth-Century Germany," *Social Science History*, I (1976), Pt. 1, 45–78; I, (1977), Pt. 2, 210–247. See also Albert Mandansky, "Latent Structure," *International Encyclopedia of the Social Sciences* (New York, 1958), IX, 33–38.

ducing arrests, but the measures generated provide less than clear indicators of official perceptions or the behavior of offenders. The best historical study of arrest practices in the nineteenth century is by Miller but, good as it is, his analysis does not show how we might treat records produced by the criminal justice system. Several studies of current arrest practices give more usable suggestions as to how we might understand the data. Although Skolnick's widely read *Justice without Trial* focuses mainly on felony level vice arrests, he makes clear the inherent ambiguities and negotiation processes of behavior which must be simplified in the source records. Likewise, Rubenstein's excellent description of the formal and informal constraints and incentives on police yields insight into the production of what becomes arrest records—of special interest is his analysis of the station house police culture and how this affects police officers as they work away from the station house. For the historian, the analyses of Skolnick and Rubenstein remind us to keep alert to the institutional dynamics of the source-producing agency; not only will the criminal justice system bureaucratize the predictable biases of the dominant society, but the system will have its own internal traditions. Its records, therefore, may not even be a clear indicator of social biases and expectations, for the institution mediates in some unknown way between the law makers and the law breakers.[10]

One useful way of dealing with this problem has been proposed by Kitsuse and Cicourel in an important research note which urged a sophisticated use of official data produced by various social systems processing persons with "deviant" behavior. Their main point, and one which few historians have heeded, was that the data must be interpreted as "indices of organizational processes rather than indices of the incidence of certain forms of behavior." In other words, criminal justice data measure system behavior, not necessarily individual offender behavior.[11]

10   Wilbur R. Miller, *Cops and Bobbies: Police Authority in New York and London, 1830–1870* (Chicago, 1977), 54–73; Perceval, "Municipal Justice in the Melting Pot: Arrest and Prosecution in Oakland, 1872–1910," unpub. ms. (Stanford Law School). See also Jerome Hall's classic article, "Legal and Social Aspects of Arrest Without A Warrant," *Harvard Law Review,* XLIX (1936), 566–592. Jerome H. Skolnick, *Justice Without Trial: Law Enforcement in Democratic Society* (New York, 1966); Jonathan Rubenstein, *City Police* (New York, 1973).
11   John I. Kitsuse and Aaron V. Cicourel, "A Note on the Uses of Official Statistics," *Social Problems,* II (1963), 137.

More recently Bottomley and Coleman carried the notion developed by Kitsuse and Cicourel one step further, examining "the relationship between central aspects of police work in discovering and detecting crime, and their subsequent influence upon the construction of official records of crime." Using some of the insights developed by the ethnomethodologist, Garfinkel, they examine the ways in which police construct their accounts: what their "'organizationally relevant purposes'" are and how these determine the form and content of the sources. They emphasize the important role that the public plays in reporting offenses with victims, not only in bringing the offense to the authority's attention, but also in defining the offense and determining the potential of its "clearance" by arrest. For anyone working with nineteenth-century crime data, these three critical variables—purpose of recording, role of the offense reporting, and the process of clearance by arrest—must be taken into account when analyzing the data.[12]

Stinchcombe adds yet another dimension to the problems posed by Kitsuse and Cicourel in his 1963 article which focuses on the notion of the population at risk for offenses where there is no complaining victim. Stinchcombe emphasizes that for various reasons some social groups, mainly the poor and young people, spend more time in public places than do other social groups, and thus are more often at risk for arrest than are other social groups. The importance of his insight is in its demonstration of systematic, built-in biases in criminal justice data which have nothing to do with other, more easily imputed biases, like racism or prejudice against age. For example, transient workers (tramps) may or may not have been drunk more often than white-collar clerks, and police may or may not have been biased against them as a social group, for there is a specific locational reason why they will have been arrested more than white-collar clerks.[13]

When dealing with the data produced by the nineteenth-century criminal justice system, the historian has two alternative modes of proceeding. The first is to conceive of the data as a

12 A. Keith Bottomley and Clive A. Coleman, "Criminal Statistics: The Police Role in the Discovery and Detection of Crime," *International Journal of Criminology and Penology*, IV (1976), 35; Harold Garfinkel, *Studies in Ethnomethodology* (Englewood Cliffs, 1967), 186–207, cited in *ibid.*, 37.
13 Arthur Stinchcombe, "Institutions of Privacy in the Determination of Police Administrative Practice," *American Journal of Sociology*, LXIX (1963), 150–158.

biased sample of all criminal behavior; although the biases cannot be precisely estimated, some logical aspects of their nature and direction can be determined. For instance, although local conditions probably have some role, we can say that the poor will have been more at risk for public drunkenness and related offenses. The discovery of the offender in crimes of stealth (e.g., burglary) will have depended, more than today, on police informants, meaning that offenders known in the community will have been more liable to arrest than strangers. Offenses where sophisticated technical proof was needed for arrest and conviction were likely to have been bungled, just as offenses requiring efficient information transfer to discover offenders and make arrests will also have met with inconsistent arrests. Perhaps in the latter two categories arrests will have been made, but the likelihood that the arrested person was also the offender was less in the pre-fingerprint, pre-telephone era. Only in the case of murder, where all suspicious deaths must be investigated, and where a high proportion of the offenders and victims know one another, is there a logically plausible isomorphic relationship between the criminal justice system records and actual offenses in society.[14]

The second way of dealing with data produced by the criminal justice system follows lines suggested by Kitsuse and Cicourel. The data must not be conceived as a sample but as a specific universe of formal interactions between the criminal justice system and the larger society; if it is a sample, it is a sample of all such interactions, not of all criminal behavior. Such an approach has both logical and methodological appeal—isomorphism is a given. Epistemological problems associated with the notion of "real" crime—the sum total of criminal behaviors occurring "out there"—are avoided. Consequently, the researcher's attention must remain focused on the interactional elements of the criminal justice system and society, keeping perilously vague notions and speculations about the "dark figure" of unreported

14   The famous investigation and trial of John Webster for the murder of George Parkman demonstrates most dramatically the erroneous and mistaken use of evidence in the mid-nineteenth century. See Robert Sullivan, *The Disappearance of Dr. Parkman* (Boston, 1971). The differential bias in arrests came partly from the non-linear relationship of police response time to the likelihood of arrest—today, if an arrest is not made within a half hour after the offense, there is little chance of any arrest. Current research by Lane on violent death in nineteenth-century Philadelphia has the promise of showing accurately the relationships between the various official records and actual violent deaths.

crime within bounds. And, as a sample or universe of all criminal justice system/offender interactions, the comparison should be to other cities, counties, states, or regions, rather than to unknown offenses.[15]

This approach raises the level of discourse about research from a groundless argument about the value of the indicators to a systematic and substantive discussion of differing criminal justice systems, and of differences between geo-political areas and social structures. And the latter is the most important aspect of the second way of conceiving the data, for it ultimately tells more about social structure, through the interaction of a bureaucracy and society, than does speculation about the actual number of burglaries and the nature of persons committing them.[16]

Although the original sources and records for criminal justice data from the nineteenth century often do not exist for the geographical area one wishes to analyze, pre-processed data abound. City police issued annual published reports to the mayor; although the content varied slightly, most reports usually included data ranging from an enumeration of specific offense arrest numbers, information on offenders (but not by offense), information on other business of the police (open sewers reported, mad dogs shot, lost children returned), and information on police personnel and expenses. County level information usually has been annually gathered and published by the state; included is information relating to the workings of county courts (usually felonious offenses) and jails. The states also annually published prison information—again, offenders, offenses, costs. And the U.S. Bureau of the Census made decadal surveys of local and state criminal justice institutions, culminating in the famous 1890 report by Wines.[17]

15   There are two recent comparative historical criminal justice studies: Gurr, et al., The Politics of Crime and Conflict: A Comparative History of Four Cities (Beverly Hills, 1977); Hindus, "Prison and Plantation: Criminal Justice in Nineteenth-Century Massachusetts and South Carolina," unpub. Ph.D. diss. (Univ. of California, Berkeley, 1975).

16   Despite a low and irregular current rate of clearance by arrest for burglary, for instance, historians persist in using various theft rates as indicators of the actual incidence of crimes against property. We are not alone in using this dubious measure, however: see Kenneth C. Land and Marcus Felson, "A General Framework for Building Macro Social Indicator Models: Including an Analysis of Changes in Crime Rates and Police Expenditures," American Journal of Sociology, LXXXII (1976), 586.

17   Frederick H. Wines, Report on Crime, Pauperism, and Benevolence in the United States at the Eleventh Census (Washington, 1895–1896), 2 v. See also his Report on the Defective, Dependent, and Delinquent Classes of the Population of the United States, as Returned at the

There is, clearly, a wealth of relatively accessible pre-processed data produced by the nineteenth-century criminal justice system.

The one thing these data cannot do, and the one area of research where original records must continue to be utilized, is to link individual information concerning the offender to the offense: here researchers must turn to original sources. But the work yet to be done with published, pre-processed data remains an exciting prospect for research in the nineteenth-century criminal justice system.

Each source has relative advantages and disadvantages: the annual city data have the greatest potential for suffering idiosyncratic errors which may escape the researcher's attention: Cleveland, for instance, showed a drop in total arrests per year from 30,418 to 6,018 between 1907 and 1909, a result of the application of the "Golden Rule" to drunks.[18] Such problems are hardly overwhelming and can be overcome, either by dropping the idiosyncratic years from the statistical analysis or by using high enough levels of aggregation to distribute such perturbances ran-

---

Tenth Census (Washington, 1888). Wright and Hunt's *History and Growth of the U.S. Census* has a description of the census questions related to crime and the criminal justice system, 212.

Perhaps my assertion that original records do not exist will be proven wrong. James Q. Graham has a project under way using the jail records of Toledo, Ohio. John C. Schneider's recent article, "Public Order and the Geography of the City: Crime, Violence, and the Police in Detroit, 1845–1875," *Journal of Urban History*, IV (1978), 183–208, utilizes jail records. Police reports usually are catalogued under the name of the individual city's department; often they were included in the complete bound volume of the annual mayor's report or report to the mayor. The Library of Congress has the most complete collection located in one place, but individual libraries sometimes have unexpected holdings. Occasionally police departments will have retained these records, but they should be the last rather than the first place to search. The reports for Washington, D.C., can be located by diligent search in the Congressional Serial Set. State level data can be found in the annual reports of the various Secretaries of State, and state departments of charities and welfare often published jail, prison, and other correctional data. The basic principle to remember (in searching for the records) is that all of these bureaucracies and institutions had public funding and had to show some form of accountability: they had to account for money spent and work done, the latter being the data of interest here.

18   These figures are from the *Annual Reports* of the police department. Mark H. Haller, "Historical Roots of Police Behavior: Chicago, 1890–1925," *Law and Society Review*, X (1976), 309, shows how the establishment of a Municipal Court system in Chicago caused arrests to decline by one-third between 1906 and 1907. Samuel Walker, *A Critical History of Police Reform: The Emergence of Professionalism* (Lexington, Mass., 1977), 94–98, has a discussion of the golden rule policy on drunks.

domly. The strengths of annual city data offset some of their weaknesses due to aggregation—great detail at the arrest level, information about the workings of the police, and the possibility of creating annual time series.

State collected and published county court and jail data suffer from the exclusion of misdemeanor offenses but compensate in thoroughness by including all counties on an annual basis. This means that annual series can be constructed, either on individual counties or on a typological basis (e.g., all urban counties, all rural counties). State collected data have the advantage of broadness and consistency in their sample of felony offenses. Like the published city data, this information may be unavailable for the earliest years of statehood, but with published data this kind of unavailability may well be a strength, forcing the researcher to exclude non-comparable kinds of criminal justice systems in the construction of a data base.

Information published in Federal Censuses has potential both as a primary source and for analysis to establish regional or national parameter estimates to compare with research focusing on smaller areas. Such national data can be used to make sure that the smaller area selected for analysis is not idiosyncratic; better, the national data can be used as a selection tool for a smaller area or areas destined for more intense analysis. And, the national data can be utilized in themselves for cross-sectional analysis.[19]

For example, I have drawn data from the 1880 and 1890 Federal Censuses to analyze a model which hypothesizes that average arrest rates from the decade of the 1880s depended on relative police strength, the amount of welfare assistance given by the police to homeless unemployed people—called "lodgers" by the police, "tramps" by the media—and the previous arrest rates of 1880 only, a variable which introduces a dynamic element in the analysis.[20] The results of a regression where all variables

19 Robert V. Perceval, "Municipal Justice," n. 23, thoughtfully uses national data from the 1907 census to show how Oakland police compared to other departments.
20 George E. Waring, *Report on the Social Statistics of Cities* (Washington, 1886–1887), 2 pts.; John S. Billings, *Report on the Social Statistics of Cities* (Washington, 1895). The research from which the two examples have been drawn is supported by a grant from the Academic Senate of the University of California, Los Angeles.

are in rates per 1,000 give the following parameters (with F ratios in parentheses and where Dw is a dummy for western cities and Dne is a dummy for northeastern cities; N = 129): Total Arrests = −50.5 + 0.32 Total Arrests$_{1880}$ + 73.9 Police Strength
$$(1.5) \qquad\qquad (61.1)$$
+ .39 Lodgers + 224.5 D$_w$ − 19.4 D$_{ne}$. Adjusted R^2 = .55 (Sig.
$$(23.2) \qquad (24.1) \qquad (1.2)$$
> .001). Although these results are not compatible with the time-series analysis which follows and will require more analysis, focusing on regional and city-specific differences, they do demonstrate the potential in pre-processed criminal justice data. At first glance, a startlingly high proportion of nineteenth-century arrests can be accounted for simply by the strength and welfare dispensation of police forces.

Time-series analysis is as promising as cross-sectional analysis of pre-processed criminal justice data, especially when it is utilized in conjunction with a more traditional narrative analysis of the subject. The precedents set by econometricians of crime such as Ehrlich may not be useful (or morally acceptable) to historians, but the recent work of Land and Felson provides an exciting research model. Land and Felson's evaluation of the utility of a careful theoretical and methodological approach to time-series analysis, which includes specifying and estimating dynamic equations—equations which account for change over time—consciously gears itself to researchers working with time-series criminal justice data. The model that they test has the singular strength of including both exogenous and endogenous variables, clearly reflecting their prior theoretical expectations concerning the internal dynamics of the criminal justice system and the relationship of external social conditions to the behavior of offenders. The major difference between their work and work which historians might wish to do comes from the kind of data available: they work with FBI processed data on crimes reported to the police while historians dealing with any pre-1930 era must create a data base from sources generated by the arrest rather than the reporting process. In some ways this gives historians an advantage, for FBI data represent highly selective processing by the FBI of data already processed by local police departments. In this sense, not only do the FBI data come from yet another level of derivation, but they are remarkably sketchy for the early years and bound to the FBI's scheme of categorization of offenses.[21]

The specific model developed and estimated by Land and Felson cannot work with historical data for which there is no way of creating a rate of crimes reported to the police; further, their model presumes isomorphism between the indicators of crime and the actual incidence of crime, an assumption which is risky, especially for the historian using arrest data. Thus an historical model must have both theoretical and data specific differences from the model of Land and Felson, but their general approach and the methodological techniques that they demonstrate do show potential for use with historical data.

For instance, preliminary results of an analysis based on arrest time-series created from annual police reports of the twenty-three largest U.S. cities, although not nearly as powerful as those obtained by Land and Felson, show an interesting parallel. In an equation covering the years 1860–1920, where all of the variables are per capita rates, the following equation has been estimated:

$$\text{Total Arrests} = 25.15 - \underset{(1.35)}{5.99} \text{ Police Strength} + \underset{(3.89)}{1.4} \text{ Homicide}$$
$$+ \underset{(4.21)}{.12} \text{ Lodgers} + \underset{(22.14)}{.53} \text{ Arrests}_{t-1}. \text{ Adjusted } R^2 = .66 \text{ (Sig.} > .001);$$

D-W $= 2.251$. Most notably, the police per capita measure, which can be interpreted as being roughly equivalent to Land and Felson's measure of police expenditures per capita, has a negative relationship to the arrest rate, as did their measure. The point here is not to belabor the as yet rather undeveloped substantive results of an analysis using time-series arrest data, but rather to make clear the research opportunities available with pre-processed data, opportunities which can take advantage of the theoretical and methodological advances in continuing non-historical work.

There certainly are measurement problems in criminal justice system produced data. But careful thinking about the nature and direction of the biases can make the data useful and powerful. To

---

21 Isaac Ehrlich, "The Deterrent Effect of Capital Punishment: A Question of Life and Death," *American Economic Review*, LXV (1975), 397–417; Brian E. Forst, "The Deterrent Effect of Capital Punishment: A Cross-State Analysis of the 1960's," *Minnesota Law Review*, LXI (1977), 743–767 for a critique of Ehrlich; Land and Felson, "Macro Social Indicator Models."

reject the use of recent theory, models, and statistical methods, as does Tobias, is both naive and irresponsible; nor should we be guilty of making the non-supportable assertion that certain kinds of arrest rates—theft, for instance—are isomorphic with the incidence of non-arrested theft offenses.[22] The use of individual level records to produce data has a rich potential, but the data must be used with sophistication, embedded in social theory, and be examined for its typicality by comparison with previous work and the available but under-utilized aggregate data. Until this happens, there can be no growth or dialogue in the social history of crime and criminal justice.

22 J. J. Tobias, *Urban Crime in Victorian England* (New York, 1972), rejects the use of statistics, 266.

36

RISK AND RESPONSIBILITY

DAVID L. BAZELON

Risk Regulation: A Problem for Democracy in the Technological Age

In 1906, Congress enacted the Pure Food and Drug Act, the first general food and drug safety law for the United States. Commenting on the provisions of the act, the House committee observed: "The question whether certain substances are poisonous or deleterious to health the bill does not undertake to determine, but leaves that to the determination of the Secretary . . . under the guidance of proper disinterested scientific authorities, after most careful study, examination, experiment and thorough research."

This statement reflected a deep faith in the ability of "disinterested" scientists to determine for society what substances posed an unacceptable risk. More than 70 years of regulation have called into question that naïve faith. We are no longer content to delegate the assessment of and response to risk to so-called disinterested scientists. Indeed, the very

The author is a Senior Circuit Judge, United States Court of Appeals for the District of Columbia Circuit, Washington, D.C. 20001. This article is based on a talk given at the American Bar Association National Institute on Law, Science, and Technology in Health Risk Regulations, Washington, D.C., 20 April 1979.

concept of objectivity embodied in the word disinterested is now discredited. The astounding explosion of scientific knowledge and the increasing sophistication of the public have radically transformed our attitude toward risk regulation. As governmental health and safety regulation has become pervasive, there is a pressing need to redefine the relation between science and law. This is one of the greatest challenges now facing government and, indeed, society as a whole.

Risk regulation poses a peculiar problem for government. Few favor risk for its own sake. But new risks are the inevitable price of the benefits of progress in an advanced industrial society. In order to have the energy necessary to run our homes and our factories, we incur risks of energy production, whether they be the risks of coal mining, nuclear reactor accidents, or the chance that a tree will fall on a man felling it to produce firewood. In order to have mobility, we risk auto accidents and illness from air pollution. In order to have variety and convenience in our food supply, we risk cancer or other toxic reactions to additives.

Ironically, scientific progress not only creates new risks but also uncovers previously unknown risks. As our understanding of the world grows ex-

ponentially, we are constantly learning that old activities, once thought safe, in fact pose substantial risks. The question then is not whether we will have risk at all, but how much risk, and from what source. Perhaps even more important, the question is who shall decide.

In our daily lives we do not confront the trade-off between dollars and lives very directly or self-consciously. But when we make societal policy decisions, such as how much to spend to eliminate disease-producing pollutants, we are painfully aware that we must make what Guido Calabresi has called "tragic choices."

In primitive societies these choices were often made by the tribal witch doctor. When the need to choose between cherished but conflicting values threatened to disrupt the society, the simplest path was decision by a shaman, or wizard, who claimed special and miraculous insight. In our time shamans carry the title doctor instead of wizard, and wear lab coats and black robes instead of religious garb.

But ours is an age of doubt and skepticism. The realist movement in law effectively stripped the judiciary of its Solomonic cloak. So, too, the public has come to realize the inherent limitations of scientific wisdom and knowledge. We have been cast from Eden, and must find ways to cope with our intellectual nakedness. To the basic question of how much risk is acceptable—a choice of values—we have learned that there is no one answer. To the problem of how much risk a given activity poses, we have learned that even our experts often lack the certain knowledge that would ease our decision-making tasks. Often the best we can say is that a product or an activity poses a "risk of risk."

From David L. Bazelon, "Risk and Responsibility," *Science* 277-280 (205, 4403) (July 20, 1979).

Who Decides? Scientists *v.* the Public

Under these circumstances, the questions of who decides and how that decision is made become all the more critical. Since we have no shaman we must have confidence in the decision-making process so that we may better tolerate the uncertainties of our decisions.

Courts are often thrust into the role of authoritative decision-makers. But in recent years there has been growing concern about the ability of the judiciary to cope with the complex scientific and technical issues that come before our courts. Critics note, quite correctly, that judges have little or no training to understand and resolve problems on the frontiers of nuclear physics, toxicology, hydrology, and a myriad of other specialties. And the problem is growing. Hardly a sitting in our court goes by without a case from the Environmental Protection Agency, the Food and Drug Administration, the Occupational Safety and Health Administration (OSHA), or the Nuclear Regulatory Commission (NRC). These cases often present questions that experts have grappled with for years, without coming to any consensus.

But the problem, of course, is not confined to the judicial branch. Legislators are daily faced with the same perplexing questions. They, too, lack the expertise to penetrate the deepest scientific mysteries at the core of important issues of public concern. This problem ultimately strikes at the very heart of democracy. The most important element of our government, the voter, simply cannot be expected to understand the scientific predicate of many issues he must face at the polls.

Some well-meaning scientists question the wisdom of leaving risk regulation to the scientifically untutored. They wonder, to themselves if not aloud, whether the public should be permitted to make decisions for society when it cannot understand the complex scientific questions that underlie the decisions. Some scientists point with relish to the contradictory and seemingly irrational response of the public to risk. They observe the public's alarm at the prospect of nuclear power and note that the same public tolerates 50,000 automobile deaths a year. They decry the Delaney clause, which singles out cancer among all serious risks and imposes a rigid ban, regardless of countervailing benefits.

Scientists are also concerned by the growing public involvement in decisions that, in the past, were left entirely to the scientific community. Many scientists believe that regulation has intruded too deeply into the sanctum sanctorum. The controversy ranges from the periphery of scientific pursuits, such as OSHA regulation of laboratory work conditions, to the heart of the scientific enterprise, such as the conflict over recombinant DNA research. Regulators are accused of stifling creativity and innovation in the name of the false god of safety. Science, once invoked as an ally to progressive government, more and more views the political process with hostility and disdain.

In reaction to the public's often emotional response to risk, scientists are tempted to disguise controversial value decisions in the cloak of scientific objectivity, obscuring those decisions from political accountability.

At its most extreme, I have heard scientists say that they would consider not disclosing risks which in their view are insignificant, but which might alarm the public if taken out of context. This problem is not mere speculation. Consider the recently released tapes of the NRC's deliberation over the accident at Three Mile Island. They illustrate dramatically how concern for minimizing public reaction can overwhelm scientific candor.

This attitude is doubly dangerous. First, it arrogates to the scientists the final say over which risks are important enough to merit public discussion. More important, it leads to the suppression of information that may be critical to developing new knowledge about risks or even to developing ways of avoiding those risks.

It is certainly true that the public's reaction to risk is not always in proportion to the seriousness of the threatened harm discounted by its probability. But the public's fears are real.

Scientists must resist the temptation to belittle these concerns, however irrational they may seem. The scientific community must not turn its back on the political processes to which we commit societal decisions. Scientists, like all citizens, must play an active role in the discussion of competing values. Their special expertise will inevitably and rightly give them a persuasive voice when issues are discussed in our assemblies and on our streets. But the choice must ultimately be made in a politically responsible fashion. To those who feel the public is incapable of comprehending the issues, and so unable to make informed value choices, I respond with the words of Thomas Jefferson:

I know no safe depository of the ultimate powers of the society but the people themselves; and if we think them not enlightened enough to exercise their control with a wholesome discretion, the remedy is not to take it from them, but to inform their discretion.

Scientist, regulator, lawyer, and layman must work together to reconcile the sometimes conflicting values that underlie their respective interest, perspectives, and goals. This cooperation can be achieved only through a greater understanding of the proper roles of the scientific, political, and legal communities in addressing the public regulation of risk. Only then can we achieve a program of risk regulation that accommodates the best of scientific learning with the demands of democracy.

Sorting Out Scientific Facts, Inferences, and Values in Risk Regulation

The starting point is to identify the fact and value questions involved in a risk regulation decision. In determining questions of fact, such as the magnitude of risk from an activity, we as a society must rely on those with the appropriate expertise. Judges and politicians have no special insights in this area. Where questions of risk regulation involve value choices such as how much risk is acceptable, we must turn to the political process.

But even this formulation leaves many problems unanswered. There is no bright line between questions of value and of fact. Even where a problem is appropriately characterized as one of scientific fact, consensus and certainty may very often be impossible even in the scientific community. Many problems of scientific inference lie in the realm of "trans-science" and cannot be resolved by scientific method and experimentation.

The recent National Academy of Sciences (NAS) report on saccharin vividly illustrates the problem of separating fact from value in risk regulation. Although there is a reasonable scientific consensus on the effects of saccharin in rats, the important question of human risks and the appropriate response to those risks remain controversial. On the basis of uncontroverted animal experimental data, the NAS panel could not conclude whether saccharin should be considered a substance posing a "high" risk of cancer, or only a "moderate" risk. Yet this lack of consensus should not surprise us. As Philip Handler, president of the NAS, observed in his preface to the report, "the difference of opinion which led to this ambivalent statement is not a differing interpretation of scientific fact or observation; it reflects, rather, seriously differing value systems."

Handler's statement reveals a critical issue in risk regulation. When the debate over saccharin is couched in terms of the degree of risk, it sounds as though there is a scientific issue, appropriate for resolution by trained scientists. In fact, however, the terms moderate and high do not conform to any differences in experimental data, but rather correspond to the scientists' view of the appropriate regulatory response.

The growing use of analytic tools such as cost-benefit analysis magnifies the chance that unrecognized value judgments will creep into apparently objective assessments. Even the most conscientious effort by experts not to exceed their sphere of competence may be inadequate to safeguard the validity of the decision-making process. Outside scrutiny may be imperative.

The Role of Courts

It is at this point that courts can make their contribution to sound decision-making. Courts cannot second-guess the decisions made by those who, by virtue of their expertise or their political accountability, have been entrusted with ultimate decisions. But courts can and have played a critical role in fostering the kind of dialogue and reflection that can improve the quality of those decisions.

Courts, standing outside both scientific and political debate, can help to make sure that decision-makers articulate the basis for their decisions. In the scientists' realm—the sphere of fact—courts can ask that the data be described, hypotheses articulated, and above all, in those areas where we lack knowledge, that ignorance be confessed. In the political realm—the sphere of values—courts can ask that decision-makers explain why they believe that a risk is too great to run, or why a particular trade-off is acceptable. Perhaps most important, at the interface of fact and value, courts can help ensure that the value component of decisions is explicitly acknowledged, not hidden in quasi-scientific jargon.

This role does not require, as some have suggested, that courts intrude excessively into an agency's processes. The demands of adequate process are not burdensome. Surely it is not unreasonable to suggest that agencies articulate the basis of their decisions or that they open their proceedings and deliberations to all interested participants and all relevant information.

These requirements are in everyone's best interest, including decision-makers

themselves. If the decision-making process is open and candid it will inspire more confidence in those who are affected. Futher, by opening the process to public scrutiny and criticism, we reduce the risk that important information will be overlooked or ignored. Finally, openness will promote peer review of both factual determinations and value judgments.

Coping with Uncertainty

Risk regulation in itself carries risks. No problem of any significance is so well understood that we can predict with confidence what the outcome of any decision will be. But there are two different kinds of uncertainty that plague risk regulation. Some uncertainty is inherent in regulating activities on the frontiers of scientific progress. For example, we simply do not know enough about the containment potential of salt domes to know with confidence whether they are adequate for storing nuclear wastes for thousands of years. In the face of such uncertainty society must decide whether or not to take a chance—to wait for more information before going ahead with nuclear production, or to go forward and gamble that solutions will be found in the future.

The other kind of uncertainty that infects risk regulation comes from a refusal to face the hard questions created by lack of knowledge. It is uncertainty produced by scientists and regulators who assure the public that there are no risks, but know that the answers are not at hand. Perhaps more important, it is a false sense of security because the hard questions have never been asked in the first place.

In the early days of nuclear plant licensing, for example, the problem of long-term waste disposal was never even an issue. Only after extensive prodding by environmental and citizens' groups did the industry and regulators show any awareness of waste disposal as a problem at all. Judges like myself became troubled when those charged with ensuring nuclear safety refused even to recognize the seriousness of the waste disposal issue, much less to propose a solution.

I expressed these concerns in *Natural Resources Defense Council v. Nuclear Regulatory Commission (1)*. In that case our court was asked to review the NRC's quantification of the environmental effects of the uranium fuel cycle, including the "back end" of the cycle, waste disposal and reprocessing.

The NRC concluded that those effects are "relatively insignificant." Yet the only evidence adduced in support of its assessment was the testimony of a single NRC expert. Most of the testimony was conclusory and the expert gave little or no explanation of the underlying basis for his optimism.

To my mind, that testimony, without more, provided an inadequate basis for making critical nuclear plant licensing decisions. My objection was not founded on any disagreement with the expert's conclusions. For all I knew then or know now, he may have been accurate in minimizing the risks from nuclear waste disposal. Nor do I criticize the NRC for failing to develop foolproof solutions to the problem of waste disposal. What I found unacceptable was the almost cavalier manner with which the NRC accepted the sanguine predictions and refused to come to grips with the limits of the agency's knowledge. I stated (2):

To the extent that uncertainties necessarily underlie predictions of this importance on the frontiers of science and technology, there is a concomitant necessity to confront and explore fully the depth and consequences of such uncertainties. Not only were the generalities relied on in this case not subject to rigorous probing—in any form—but when apparently substantial criticisms were brought to the Commission's attention, it simply ignored them, or brushed them aside. Without a thorough exploration of the problems involved in waste disposal, including past mistakes, and a forthright assessment of the uncertainties and differences in expert opinion, this type of agency action cannot pass muster as reasoned decisionmaking.

The "thorough exploration" that I found lacking is particularly important in technically complex matters such as nuclear waste disposal. Since courts lack the expertise to assess the merits of the scientific controversy, "society must depend largely on oversight by the technically trained members of the agency and the scientific community at large to monitor technical decisions." There were a number of avenues open to the NRC for the kind of exploration that permits meaningful oversight—but the agency adopted none of them.

The Supreme Court unanimously reversed our decision (3). They felt that we had imposed extra procedures on the NRC beyond those required by law for so-called informal rule-making under the 1946 Administrative Procedure Act. They returned the case to our court, however, to determine whether the record supported the substantive conclusions of the NRC.

Whether the Supreme Court's decision represents a fair reading of what our opinion in fact required the agency to do,

I leave to the legal scholars. My own view is that the Supreme Court's decision will have little impact because many of the new laws governing risk regulation explicitly direct agencies to use decision-making procedures that supplement the minimal requirements of informal rule-making under the Administrative Procedure Act. Statutes such as the Clean Air Act Amendments of 1977, the Clean Water Act of 1977, and the Toxic Substances Control Act of 1976 include procedural and record-enhancing features that will contribute substantially to the quality and accountability of agency decisions.

A Structured Approach to Decision-Making Under Uncertainty

I have never believed that procedures per se are a cure-all for solving regulatory problems. Rather, procedural safeguards serve an instrumental role, and it is the fullness of the inquiry that is paramount. If the inquiry is comprehensive and conscientious without additional procedural safeguards, it provides the best record we can hope for in making the difficult choices we now face. Conversely, even when all the procedural niceties are observed, if there is no commitment to a candid exploration of the issues, the predicate for good decision-making will be lacking.

Agencies are now revising their procedures to increase the availability of expert advice without abdicating agency responsibility for value decisions. Agencies have begun to encourage and fund public intervenors. These steps have increased the range of the administrative process, and have forced the

agencies to wrestle with the difficult questions which might otherwise escape public scrutiny. Restrictions on ex parte contacts have increased our confidence in agencies' impartiality and fairness. The visibility of decision-making processes and decisions themselves has been enhanced by Congress' and the courts' commitment to openness, through the Freedom of Information Act, the Advisory Committee Act, and the Sunshine Act. I am confident that the courts will continue vigorously to carry out Congress' mandate that decison-making be honest, open, thorough, rational, and fair.

The Problem of Delay

Considering all relevant data and viewpoints is essential to good decisions. This is why I am concerned by recent proposals to shorten the decision-making process for licensing nuclear reactors. I have no doubt that some of the current delay is unnecessary, and it may be that current proposals do not affect critical deliberative processes. I do not express any views on specific proposals. I only want to caution that in speeding up the process, we must take care not to sacrifice the valuable and productive safeguards that have come to be built into the decision-making process.

I do not favor delay caused by an unthinking rejection of progress. Delay from unjustified fear of the future can in the long run cause more harm than the risks it prevents. But delay that is necessary for calm reflection, full debate, and mature decision more than compensates for the additional costs it imposes. The Alaska Pipeline was embroiled in exten-

sive controversy in our courts, primarily by environmental groups who questioned whether sufficient attention was given to safety issues. The litigation imposed substantial costs, both the rising expenses for building the pipeline and the cost of postponing a major source of domestic energy. But in the subsequent attorneys' fees proceedings the companies themselves conceded that the litigation produced substantial safety improvements in the pipeline that Congress ultimately approved. Sometimes the benefits of delay can be dramatic. The American experience in avoiding the tragedy of thalidomide is a poignant but not unique example.

By strengthening the administrative process we provide a constructive and creative response to the inherent uncertainties of risk regulation. Approaching the decision to take or to step back from risks such as nuclear power is like coming to a busy intersection with our view partially obscured. Our instincts tell us to proceed with caution, because intersections are dangerous. Ultimately, the importance of our journey and the desirability of our goal may lead us to brave the traffic and pull out into the highway. But even when we decide to proceed, we should not omit the moment of reflection to observe the passing cars, and look both ways.

References and Notes

1. *Natural Resources Defense Council v. Nuclear Regulatory Commission.* Fed. Rep. 2nd Ser., vol. 547, p. 633 (D.C. Circuit 1976), reversed *sub nom. Vermont Yankee Nuclear Power Corp. v. Natural Resources Defense Council* (3). Nothing in these remarks should be taken to intimate any views of the merits of this case in its present posture, on remand from the Supreme Court.
2. *Ibid*., p. 653.
3. *Vermont Yankee Nuclear Power Corp. v. Natural Resources Defense Council,* U.S. Rep., vol. 435, p. 519 (1978).

David L. Bazelon is Lecturer in the Psychiatry Department, Johns Hopkins University School of Medicine. He sat on the U.S. Court of Appeals for the District of Columbia Circuit. He is the recipient of many lectureship and organization awards.

Part VII:

**CRIME AND CRIMINALS
IN THE UNITED STATES**

CRIME AND CRIMINALS IN THE UNITED STATES

JOSEPH G. WEIS
JAMES S. HENNEY

INTRODUCTION

This chapter, intended to serve as a reference resource, presents a brief and select review of data on contemporary crime and its control in the United States. Data have been included on: the public's attitudes toward crime; offenses known to the police and arrests; the ecological distribution of criminal activity; rates and characteristics of victimization by offense type; victims' perceptions of the characteristics of offenders; the extent to which victimizations are reported to the police; features of correctional supervision, including probation, admissions to institutions, parole, and other forms of release; and, finally, projections of arrest trends into the 1980s. The descriptions and discussions of these data will focus on those aspects which are among the topics of this volume—violent crime, demographic characteristics, ecological variations, and victimization.[1]

PUBLIC ATTITUDES TOWARD CRIME

Crime as a Social Problem

The overwhelming national concern with "law and order" in the 1960s seems to have been replaced in the 1970s by the pervasive feeling that economic problems are the most important confronting the United States. Annual Gallup Polls from 1970 to 1979 show that most Americans choose the high cost of living and inflation as the most important problem of the decade, followed by unemployment, international problems and foreign policy, and in the past few years by the energy situation. Crime and lawlessness is consistently perceived by a relatively small proportion of the population as the most important problem throughout the decade, but for most persons it seems to have become less important relative to other national problems over the past few years.[2] At the beginning of the decade, crime and lawlessness—and its close ally, drug abuse—taken together ranked second or third on the list of most important problems,

TABLE 1

Public Attitudes Toward the Most Important Problem Facing the Country, 1970-1979

QUESTION: "What do you think is the most important problem facing this country today?" (in percentages)[a]

Most Important Problem	1979	1978	1977	1976	1975	1974	1973	1972	1971	1970
High Cost of Living/Inflation	57	60	58	47	51	79	59	27	45	17
Unemployment	5	14	39	31	21	3	16	NA	NA	NA
International Problems/Foreign Policy	5	10	13	6	NA	NA	11	10	5	6
Energy Situation	33	4	23	NA	5	3	NA	NA	NA	NA
Crime and Lawlessness	2	3	15	6	5	3	17	8	12	7
Moral Decline/Lack of Religion	4	3	5	3	5	NA	5	2	2	4
Dissatisfaction with Government	3	3	4	6	9	7	NA	NA	NA	NA
Race Relations	NA	2	NA	NA	NA	NA	16	NA	NA	13
Drug Abuse	NA	1	NA	NA	NA	NA	20	9	2	NA
All Others	8	18	41	24	20	15	23	NA	NA	NA
Can't Say	2	3	2	4	2	2	11	NA	NA	NA

SOURCE: George H. Gallup, *The Gallup Poll*, 1970-1979 and SOURCEBOOK, 1979 and 1980.
a. Total does not add to 100 percent because of multiple responses and variation in response categories over the years.

but crime and lawlessness dropped to fifth in 1978 and slipped to seventh in 1979. Crime is still a major social concern, but compared to other national problems, the public's attitudes have changed—there is more concern for economic problems and less concern for crime problems.

The Fear of Crime

Paradoxically, although crime is perceived as less serious a national problem, a slightly higher proportion of the population was afraid of being victimized later in the decade, 1977 (45%), than earlier, 1973 (41%). The fear of becoming the victim of a crime is pervasive—almost one-half of the population is afraid of walking alone at night within a mile of their residence.

And, as one might expect, some citizens are more afraid than others. Women are about three times as likely as men to express fear of venturing out alone in the evening, while blacks are more likely to be afraid than whites. The less formally educated are more often apprehensive about their safety than the better educated; likewise the highest proportions of fearful persons are found among those in clerical and manual occupations and the lowest among professional occupations and farmers. The poor and the elderly are most likely to be afraid within income and age categories, respectively. Interestingly, the proportions of fearful young (18-20) and old ($\geqslant 50$) increased from 1973 to 1977, while the two intermediate age categories (21-29 and 30-49) remained virtually the same over these years. People in the urban population centers of the Northeast are somewhat more apprehensive than thier neighbors in the West and South and much more so than those in the Midwest. And, perhaps most interesting, those citizens with no declared religious belief and no traditional political party allegiance are less likely to be afraid of being victimized than those with more traditional religious and political affiliations.

CRIME IN THE 1970s—ITS NATURE AND ECOLOGY

Offenses Known and Arrests

Population estimates on the seven major "index" crimes—murder, rape, robbery, aggravated assault, burglary, larceny-theft, and motor vehicle theft— are derived each year by the Federal Bureau of Investigation from local law enforcement agencies' monthly reports of offenses known and arrests. A review of Table 3 demonstrates that both *violent* crime—murder, rape, robbery, and aggravated assault—and *property* crime—burglary, larceny, and motor vehicle theft—have steadily increased throughout the 1970s. The rate of known offenses increased by 34% for violent crime and 28% for property crime. Although violent offenses jumped higher than property offenses, the latter still far exceeded the former in frequency at the end of the decade. In 1970 the property-violent offense ratio was 10 to 1. By 1978 this ratio had only dropped to 9.5 to 1.

While the rates of the two major categories of known offenses exhibited growth in the 1970s, this growth was not at a constant rate. The violent crime rate rose by

TABLE 2

Fear of Walking Alone at Night by Demographic Characteristics
1973, 1974, 1976, and 1977

QUESTION: "Is there an area right around here—that is, within a mile—where you would be afraid to walk alone at night?" (in percentages)[a]

	1973		1974		1976		1977	
	Yes	No	Yes	No	Yes	No	Yes	No
National	41	59	45	55	44	56	45	54
Sex:								
Male	20	80	24	76	23	77	23	76
Female	59	40	63	36	61	39	63	37
Race:								
White	39	61	43	57	44	56	43	57
Black/other	54	45	60	40	48	51	59	40
Education:								
College	35	64	42	57	36	64	41	58
High school	44	55	44	55	47	52	46	53
Grade school	41	58	51	49	48	52	47	52
Occupation:								
Professional and business	38	62	39	60	40	60	40	60
Clerical	55	44	59	40	56	43	60	39
Manual	41	58	45	54	41	58	45	55
Farmer	26	72	18	82	27	72	22	78
Income:								
$15,000 and over	33	66	37	62	38	62	38	61
$10,000 to $14,999	44	55	41	58	40	60	38	61
$7,000 to $9,999	40	60	44	55	50	50	46	54
$5,000 to $6,999	40	59	44	55	51	49	53	46
$3,000 to $4,999	42	57	57	43	50	50	58	42
Under $3,000	46	53	58	42	50	50	52	46
Age:								
18 to 20 years	33	67	43	55	45	55	45	55
21 to 29 years	40	59	44	56	40	60	39	60
30 to 49 years	40	60	40	59	40	60	41	59
50 years and older	43	57	50	50	49	51	51	48
Region:								
Northeast	47	52	47	53	54	46	53	47
Midwest	40	60	39	60	34	66	36	63
South	39	61	47	53	42	58	47	52
West	38	61	48	51	50	50	46	54
Religion:								
Protestant	41	59	43	56	43	57	45	55
Catholic	43	56	50	48	46	54	45	54
Jewish	44	56	50	50	63	37	60	40
None	32	68	38	62	43	57	40	59

TABLE 2 (Continued)

	1973		1974		1976		1977	
	Yes	No	Yes	No	Yes	No	Yes	No
Politics:								
Republican	35	65	48	52	42	57	44	56
Democrat	46	53	45	54	49	50	48	52
Independent	39	61	42	58	39	61	41	58

SOURCE: Adapted from SOURCEBOOK, 1979, Table 2.9.
a. Percentages may not add to 100 because of small percentages of "Don't Know" responses excluded from the table.

over one-third from 1970 to 1978, but over 70% of this gain occurred during the first five years of the decade. Similarly, the property crime rate rose by 28% during 1970-1978, but three-quarters of that increase was completed by 1974. In short, although rates of criminal activity have increased throughout the decade, the past few years have seen somewhat of a leveling off.

Data on arrests and arrests rates show similar trends. Arrests for property crime far exceed those for crimes involving violence. In 1978 the ratio of property to violence arrests was 3.9 to 1. In addition, both types of arrest rates demonstrated decadelong increases. In 1970 the arrest rate for violent crime was 141.5 per 100,000 population. By 1978 it had risen to 217.6, a jump of 54%.

TABLE 3
Offenses Known and Arrests, Totals, and Rates, 1970-1978

	Offenses Known to the Police				Arrests			
	Violent Crime[a]		Property Crime[b]		Violent Crime		Property Crime	
	Total[c]	Rate[d]	Total	Rate	Total	Rate	Total	Rate
1970	738,820	363.5	7,359,200	3,621.0	287,550	141.5	1,259,600	619.9
1971	816,500	396.0	7,771,700	3,768.8	323,060	156.6	1,380,900	669.5
1972	834,900	401.0	7,413,900	3,560.4	350,410	168.3	1,370,000	657.9
1973	875,910	417.4	7,842,200	3,737,0	380,560	181.3	1,448,700	690.3
1974	974,720	461.1	9,278,700	4.389.3	429,350	203.1	1,731,000	818.9
1975	1,026,280	481.5	10,230,300	4,800.2	451,310	211.7	1,843,800	865.1
1976	986,580	459.8	10,318,200	4,806.8	411,630	191.7	1,746,900	813.8
1977	1,009,500	466.6	9,926,300	4,588.4	439,552	203.1	1,813,982	838.5
1978	1,061,830	486.9	10,079,500	4,622.4	474,598	217.6	1,833,128	840.6

SOURCE: Adapted from U.S. Department of Justice, Federal Bureau of Investigation, Uniform Crime Reports, 1970:119; 1971:115; 1972:119; 1973:121; 1974:179; 1975:49,181-187; 1976: 37,173; 1977:37,173-147; 1978:39,172-173; 1979:38,186-187.
a. Violent crimes include murder, rape, robbery, and aggravated assault.
b. Property crimes include burglary, larceny, theft, and motor vehicle theft.
c. Actual total for those agencies reporting plus an estimate for those not reporting.
d. Rate per 100,000 resident population. Population figures are U.S. Bureau of Census provisional estimates.

Meanwhile, arrests for property crime in 1970 were made at the rate of 619.9 per 100,000 population. In 1978 the same rate ws 840.6, a gain of 36%. Again, as was the case with know offense rates, the major portion of this increase in arrest rates had occurred by the end of 1974. From 1970 to 1974, the rate of arrest for violent crime jumped by 43% and for property crime by 32%.

In summary, the 1970s have seen substantial increases in both types of crime— property and violent offenses—and the rates of arrest for both. Violent crime seems to have jumped slightly more than property crime, and the same is true for the respective arrest rates. For both types of crime, the percentage gain in arrests outstrips that for number of offenses known.

Ecological Characteristics

Another important issue to be considered when discussing crime is its location. The data provided in Tables 4 and 5 show that crime tends to be more likely in certain parts of our society than others.

It is clear that crime is associated to a greater extent with certain geographical regions of the country than with others. With respect to both property and violent crime, offense rates for 1978 are at their highest in the western states and lowest in the middle regions of the country. The rate of property crime in the West is one and one-half times that recorded in the North Central region, 1.2 times the rate in the South, and 1.1 times that in the Northeast. With respect to violent crimes, the West has about 30% more crime than the other three regions. Interestingly, when rank ordering the regions according to level of known offenses, any two consecutive regions display substantial variation in rates of violent crime. However, property crime remains relatively constant across three of the four regions, with only the western states reporting a much higher level.

Looking at arrests, the patterns described above are repeated for the most part. One exception is that the Northeast, not the West, ranks first with respect to arrests for violent crimes. The rankings of the other two regions are concordant with their rankings on known offense rates. With respect to arrests for property crime, the rank order of the regions is the same as for offenses known.

If we are willing to assume that regions do not vary in the relative distributions of offense types—that is, that the number of offenders to number of offenses ratio is constant across regions—an assessment can also be made of how effective each region is in reacting to crime. Overall, the ratio of violent offenses to arrests is 2.23 to 1. Substantial variation does exist in this ratio across regions, however. It reaches its maximum value in the North Central states where there are slightly more than three offenses known for each arrest. In the West the ratio drops sharply to 2.3 to 1; in the South it is 2.1 to 1. In the Northeast it reaches its lowest level, with one arrest occurring for each 1.87 offenses known to police.

With respect to property crime, there are 5.59 crimes per arrest made. Looking at each region individually, both the southern (5.32) and northeastern (5.34) states fall below this standard. The West is near the mean at 5.66, with the North Central states again displaying the highest offense to arrest ratio at 5.99 to 1.

TABLE 4

Offenses Known and Arrest Rates for Violent and Property Crime
by Region of the Country, 1978

Region[a]	Population (100,000)	Offenses Known (Rate/100,000)		Arrests (Rate/100,000)	
		Violent	Property	Violent	Property
Northeast	49,082	528.6	4348.0	282.4	814.2
North Central	58,253	378.2	4244.7	122.8	708.0
South	69,962	469.1	4280.4	222.9	804.9
West	40,102	578.4	6079.0	251.4	1074.7
Total	217,399	478.3	4617.8	214.7	826.1

SOURCE: Adapted from U.S. Department of Justice, Federal Bureau of Investigation, *Uniform Crime Reports,* 1978:46-57,185.
a. The states included in each of the four regions are as follows: Northeast — Connecticut, Maine, Massachusetts, New Hampshire, New Jersey, New York, Pennsylvania, Rhode Island, Vermont; North Central — Illinois, Indiana, Iowa, Kansas, Michigan, Minnesota, Missouri, Nebraska, North Dakota, Ohio, South Dakota, Wisconsin; South — Alabama, Arkansas, Delaware, Florida, Georgia, Kentucky, Louisiana, Maryland, Mississippi, North Carolina, Oklahoma, South Carolina, Tennessee, Texas, Virginia, West Virginia; West — Alaska, Arizona, California, Colorado, Hawaii, Idaho, Montana, Nevada, New Mexico, Oregon, Utah, Washington, Wyoming.

Thus, holding constant the level of criminal activity, the Northeast and the South appear to be the most productive in arresting violent as well as property offenders. The West and North Central regions, on the other hand, seem to be the least successful.

One might argue that these results are misleading because of the failure to control for other types of ecological variables which may explain regional variations in crime. An example of such alternative variables is presented in Table 5. Here, offense patterns are examined according to varying levels of urbanization. Looking at the results displayed in the "Total" row, it is obvious that a positive correlation exists between extent of urbanization of a geographical unit and rates of both property and violent crime. Metropolitan areas have twice the rate of violent crime as other cities and more than three times the rate experienced in rural areas. Metropolitan areas also far exceed the other two types of areas in rates of property crime.

The critic may argue, then, that regions vary in the extent to which their populations are concentrated in Standard Metropolitan Statistical Areas (SMSAs), other cities, and rural areas, and that it is this phenomenon which creates the regional effect on crime rates. Several interesting findings emerge from an examination of Table 5. Of all SMSAs, those in the northeastern states possess the *lowest* levels of property crime, as do the other cities and rural areas in this region with respect to violent offenses. While holding constant the level of urbanization tends generally to lower the ranking of the Northeast with respect to criminal activity, the South emerges with a much higher ranking. The data

TABLE 5

Offense Rates by Extent of Urbanization and Region of the Country, 1978

Region[a]	Population (100,000)	Offenses Known (Rate/100,000)	
		Violence	Property
NORTHEAST			
Standard Metropolitan Statistical Area (SMSA)	41,718	591.7	4457.4
Other Cities	4,511	182.1	3898.5
Rural	2,852	137.8	2337.3
NORTH CENTRAL			
Standard Metropolitan Statistical Area	40,641	485.1	4930.9
Other Cities	7,440	186.1	4008.3
Rural	10,174	89.4	1624.4
SOUTH			
Standard Metropolitan Statistical Area	44,661	584.0	5424.6
Other Cities	9,830	360.9	3033.9
Rural	15,471	206.0	1498.9
WEST			
Standard Metropolitan Statistical Area	31,693	686.2	6510.4
Other Cities	4,119	397.3	5874.5
Rural	4,288	289.2	3120.5
TOTAL			
Standard Metropolitan Statistical Area	159,000	583.9	5286.3
Other Cities	26,000	285.4	4078.6
Rural	33,000	174.8	1823.1

SOURCE: Adapted from U.S. Department of Justice, Federal Bureau of Investigation, *Uniform Crime Reports*, 1978, pp. 46-57.
a. SMSA includes a core city with a population of 50,000 or more inhabitants and the surrounding county or counties. Other cities are urban places outside SMSAs. Rural areas are unincorporated portions of counties outside of urban places and SMSAs.

show that with respect to violent crime, the southern non-SMSA cities and rural areas exceed similar units in all other regions except the West. The rates of violence in Southern SMSAs approach those that exist in the large metropolitan areas of the Northeast, though cities in both regions trail the western cities by a substantial margin. Looking at the data on property crime, southern metropolitan areas exceed those in all other regions except the West in rates of known offenses.

These data, while not entirely consistent, tend to partially support the critic. The overwhelming edge in rates of violent and property crime that the western states maintain over other regions of the country is left unaffected by statistically controlling for urbanization levels. Meanwhile, it would appear that the rates of the Northeast are somewhat inflated by the fact that a disproportionate segment of its population (85%) lives in high-crime metropolitan areas. On the other hand, controlling for level of urbanization tends to point out that the South has a relatively greater crime problem than originally suspected. Ignoring for the moment the western states, the South reports the highest levels of crime in three of the six possible comparisons (extent of urbanization by type of offense) among the three remaining regions and ranks a very close second in a fourth.

In summary, the patterns of crime do tend to shift in accordance with macroscopic societal features. Geographical region and level of urbanization are two such features. An assessment of their individual and interactive effects provides somewhat confusing, yet interesting findings. The western region of the United States and large metropolitan areas appear to have the greatest susceptibility to crime. Furthermore, western states, along with North Central states, maintain the highest ratios of offenses known to arrests. The crime rankings of the South and the Northeast are particularly confounded by levels of urbanization. The analysis presented here suggests that when controlling the extent of urbanization, the states of the South fare just as poorly, if not worse, than those in the Northeast with respect to crime.

CRIME, CRIMINALS, AND THEIR VICTIMS

The statistical information which has been presented demonstrates the crime in an ever-increasing part of the contemporary American life. This section seeks to specify the phenomenon, focusing the discussion on some of the characteristics of the act, its perpetrator(s), and the individuals who are victimized by crime. The data presented are based, for the most part, on the responses of crime victims interviewed in the National Crime Survey (Law Enforcement Assistance Administration).

Characteristics of the Crime

Tables 6 and 7 examine three types of violent crime and the extent to which they vary with respect to a number of situational elements. It is obvious from the data that particular crimes have unique combinations of such factors.

TABLE 6
Violent Incidents by Number of Offenders Involved and Type of Offense, 1977

Characteristics of Incident	Rape and Attempted Rape			Robbery			Aggravated Assault		
	Total	(%)	% With Weapon	Total	(%)	% With Weapon	Total	(%)	% With Weapon
Total Number of Incidents	141,338	(100)	28	899,143	(100)	45	1,357,529	(100)	93
Number of Offenders									
Lone Offender	113,178	(80)	31	453,724	(50)	42	919,135	(68)	93
Multiple Offenders	27,037	(20)	19	423,232	(50)	49	378,499	(32)	95

SOURCE: Adapted from SOURCEBOOK, 1979, Tables 3.14, 3.16, 3.19, 3.20.
NOTE: Subcategories may not sum to total because of rounding.

The use of weapons. While rape, robbery, and aggravated assault are all classified as crimes of personal violence, the likelihood that a weapon is utilized by the offender varies greatly with the type of offense. Virtually all aggravated assaults (93%) involved the use of a gun, knife, or other weapon. Meanwhile, only about 3 of every 10 rapes included some sort of weapon. Thus, while rape is considered both legally and socially a more serious crime than assault, the risk of the appearance of some device of deadly force is greater in the latter than the former.

Number of offenders. While assault is most likely to involve weapons, robbery is the most likely of the three offenses to be perpetrated by more than one individual and rape is most likely to be a solitary offense.

Crime victims reported that in 80% of all rapes, a single offender was involved. Robbery was just as likely to involve a single offender as several offenders. Meanwhile, the majority of assaults (68%) were also single-offender crimes.

Cross-classifying the three violent offense types according to the two situational variables already discussed reveals other interesting findings. In the case of assault, the number of offenders tends to be unrelated to the presence of weapons. Regardless of the number of offenders involved, weapons are almost always a part of aggravated assaults. Rape, on the other hand, appears more likely to involve a weapon when only one offender engages in the act (31%) than when several individuals do (19%). Thus, while rapists rely to a greater extent on personal physical power than robbers or assaulters, this reliance is even greater when several actors are involved than when a lone offender commits the crime. Finally, robberies seem to show the reverse tendency—lone robbers are slightly less likely than robbers working in groups to carry weapons.

Relationship of offender to victim. Table 7 depicts the typical offender-victim interaction as involving people unknown to one another. However, the extent to which this statement is true depends upon the type of crime, as well as the sex and race of the victim. Of the three offenses, assault is most likely to involve people who are known to one another, while approximately three out of every four robberies bring together strangers. Blacks are much more likely than whites to be victimized by acquaintances, especially those black males who are assaulted. White males are more likely than white females to be victimized by strangers, regardless of offense. Among blacks, the data indicate a very slight tendency for females to be victimized to a greater extent by strangers.

Characteristics of the Offender

Table 8 provides some indications of the types of individuals who engage in criminal activity. The data are taken from National Opinion Research Center surveys of respondents who were asked if they had ever been arrested for a nontraffic offense.

The data clearly show males to be much more likely than females to report such an arrest. Furthermore, the data for the 1973-1977 period fail to support the notion that female crime is increasing at a faster rate than male crime. Over the

TABLE 7

Personal Victimization by Relationship of Offender to Victim,
Sex and Race of Victim and Type of Victimization, 1977

	Male		Female	
Type of Victimization	Black	White	Black	White
Rape/Attempted Rape				
Total	3,078	9,250	18,033	123,877
% Stranger	B	B	B	64
% Non-stranger	B	B	B	36
Robbery				
Total	178,225	546,864	82,838	275,010
% Stranger	77	82	76	72
% Non-stranger	23	18	24	28
Aggravated Assault				
Total	182,072	1,107,590	96,618	351,494
% Stranger	46	71	53	49
% Non-stranger	54	29	47	51

SOURCE: Adapted from SOURCEBOOK, 1979, Table 3.21.
B—denotes insufficient data to compute percentages.

same period, blacks were approximately twice as likely as whites to come into contact with law enforcement agencies.

Two of the traditional measures of socioeconomic status are also apparently related to the likelihood of one's experiencing an arrest. While college and high school graduates and those who completed only grade school do not seem to differ in self-reported arrest rates, occupation and income are negatively related to arrest. However, it should be noted that substantial differences exist only between the extremes of these two variables. Thus, professional, business, and clerical workers do not differ in the proportions of each type which have undergone arrest, but manual and rural laborers exhibited between two and three times the arrest rate of the first three groups. Similarly, people earning from $5,000 to over $15,000 do not vary substantially in arrest levels. The probability of arrest for those earning less than $5,000, however, approaches twice that of those earning over that amount.

A disproportionate fraction of criminal arrests are experienced by the youngest adults in society and by those who profess to have no ties to traditional religion. Finally, respondents in the western section of the the country report substantially higher arrest rates than respondents from any other region, a finding consistent with the earlier reported data on aggregate levels of known offenses and arrests.

Characteristics of the Victim

Males, the young, the economically disadvantaged, and blacks are responsible for a disproportionate share of criminal activity. Another important concern is

TABLE 8

Trends in Reporting a Nontraffic Arrest by Demographic Characteristics
(in percentages)

Characteristics	1973	1974	1976	1977
Sex:				
Male	19	18	16	20
Female	4	4	3	3
Race:				
White	10	9	8	9
Black	15	19	15	19
Education:				
College	11	10	9	10
High school	11	9	9	11
Grade school	10	13	8	9
Occupation:				
Professional and business	10	7	6	7
Clerical	4	6	4	4
Manual	14	13	13	14
Farmer	18	20	13	21
Income:				
$15,000 and over	11	7	7	8
$10,000 to $14,999	8	12	7	10
$ 7,000 to $ 9,999	8	10	10	12
$ 5,000 to $ 6,999	14	12	8	10
$ 3,000 to $ 4,999	13	13	13	17
Under $3,000	15	15	11	15
Age:				
18 to 20 years	25	18	22	20
21 to 29 years	15	17	13	19
30 to 49 years	12	10	8	10
50 years or older	6	6	5	6
Region:				
Northeast	9	10	7	10
Midwest	8	10	8	10
South	9	8	8	11
West	20	15	13	11
Religion:				
Protestant	9	9	7	10
Catholic	12	8	8	10
Jewish	0	5	8	9
None	29	25	23	17

SOURCE: Adapted from SOURCEBOOK, 1979, Table 4.19.

the identity of the victim against whom such activity is carried out, as well as the discretion as practiced by the victim. Contemporary criminology has explored in great detail the discretionary practices of police, prosecutors, judges and juries, and parole and probation officers in dealing with criminal offenders. The focus here is on the initial discretionary step—that of the victim in deciding whether to bring a crime to the attention of the formal criminal justice machinery.

Personal victimization. According to the data presented in Table 9, males and the young tend to make up a disproportionate share of the victim population. For all offenses except rape and personal larceny with contact, and in all age categories, the rate of victimization for males exceeds that for females. This tendency toward a preponderance of male victimization reaches its maximum among 12-19 and 20-34 age groups with respect to robbery and among 35- to 49-year-olds with respect to assault. In these groups the male/female victimization ratio generally exceeds 2:1 and in one instance (assault among 35- to 49-year-olds) it is greater than 6:1. In terms of the age criterion, among males the two youngest age groups report higher rates of victimization than the other three on all five offenses sampled. Among females the same generalization holds true except in the case of personal larceny with contact (purse snatching, pickpocketing, and so on), for which 50- to 64-year-old females are most likely to be victimized.

The data displayed in Table 10 show that regardless of age, nonwhites are more likely than whites to be robbery victims and to experience a personal larceny with contact. Whites, on the other hand, are more likely to experience a personal larceny without contact at all age levels. In the cases of the other two types of victimization, an Age x Race interaction is evident. At earlier ages, whites tend to have higher levels of assault victimization than nonwhites, while the reverse is true for persons over 50. With respect to rape, young nonwhites (ages 12-19) and whites are victimized at very similar rates, while at older ages whites appear to stand a greater risk of being victims.

Those who are more likely to become the criminals' victims are also the most likely *not* to report an incident. In each crime examined (except rape), individuals between the ages of 12 and 19 years had the highest rates of nonreporting. This age differential in reporting tends to hold true across sex and race categories. The trends in nonreporting attributable to sex and race are not nearly as simple. In 19 comparisons of male and female nonreporting rates, males had higher levels in 11 instances, females in 8. In the majority of age categories, males tended to be less likely than females to report robberies, assaults, and larceny with contact.

Turning to the white-nonwhite distinction, one finds that among 15 comparisons, 8 showed whites to exhibit greater reluctance to report the incident to police, while the other 7 showed lower rates of reporting by nonwhites. In all age groups, whites were less likely to report an assault than nonwhites, which may reflect a greater likelihood that the nonwhite victim knows his or her assailant (see Table 7). Nonwhites, in general, exhibited a slightly greater reluctance to

TABLE 9

Total Personal Victimizations, Estimated Rate of Victimization, and Percentage not Reported by Sex and Age of Victim and Type of Victimization, 1977

| | Age of Victim | | | | | | | | | |
| | 12–19 | | 20–34 | | 35–49 | | 50–64 | | 65 & Older | |
Type of Victimization	Male	Female	Male	Female	Male	Female	Male	Female	Male	Female
Rape										
Total	5,493	64,573	5,632	58,703	0	13,394	1,202	2,311	0	2,748
Rate (per 100,000)	25.3	402.1	15.3	226.8	0.0	74.8	8.1	13.5	0.0	20.9
% not Reported	B	29	B	51	0	B	B	B	0	B
Robbery										
Total	248,860	81,989	258,869	123,763	99,599	57,811	79,313	56,911	38,448	37,373
Rate (per 100,000)	1524.8	510.1	1006.3	465.0	585.4	320.8	528.8	335.7	414.1	283.2
% not Reported	5	64	45	27	40	22	43.1	37.1	20.1	26.1
Assault										
Total	1,120,460	497,983	1,450,286	710,681	322,966	202,468	174,279	94,941	59,338	30,423
Rate (per 100,000)	6722.0	3089.2	5657.5	2680.0	1905.8	257.4	1147.1	564.0	639.6	230.4
% not Reported	66	59	54	51	46	38	47	48	53	60
Personal Larceny with Contact										
Total	56,332	25,968	63,647	93,434	39,412	47,250	27,250	53,167	16,264	38,290
Rate (per 100,000)	345.5	161.3	246.5	266.8	230.0	262.6	178.9	315.0	175.4	288.4
% not Reported	78	61	70	61	77	57	49	60	B	41
Personal Larceny w/o Contact										
Total	2,607,924	2,083,004	3,510,490	083,359	1,459,534	1,490,381	954,529	804,135	263,679	212,120
Rate (per 100,000)	15967.2	12914.4	13691.8	11578.2	8613.3	8300.8	6279.3	4787.3	2843.0	1612.7
% not Reported	85	89	71	72	70	64	68	63	67	72

SOURCE: Adapted from SOURCEBOOK, 1979, Tables 3.3, 3.11.

TABLE 10

Total Personal Victimizations, Estimated Rate of Victimization, and Percentage not Reported by Sex and Race of Victim and Type of Victimization, 1977

	Age of Victim									
	12–19		20–34		35–49		50–64		65 & Older	
Type of Victimization	White	Nonwhite	White	Nonwhite	White	Nonwhite	White	Nonwhite	White	Nonwhite
Rape										
Total	63,604	6,642	51,609	12,727	11,652	1,742	3,512	0	2,748	0
Rate (per 100,000)	232.3	132.1	113.9	183.7	38.2	40.4	12.2	0.0	13.5	0.0
% not Reported	34	B	52	B	B	B	B	0	B	0
Robbery										
Total	249,824	81,025	311,407	71,225	118,008	39,323	82,540	53,684	60,015	15,805
Rate (per 100,000)	912.4	1611.2	687.3	1027.9	385.6	912.9	286.6	1669.5	295.7	737.2
% not Reported	61	54	40	34	32	37	37	45	21	B
Assault										
Total	1,416,097	202,347	1,887,189	273,779	463,560	61,875	233,948	35,272	78,655	11,106
Rate (per 100,000)	5171.7	4023.7	4165.4	3951.0	1514.9	1436.5	812.2	1046.9	387.5	518.0
% not Reported	65	56	54	48	44	37	49	37	58	B
Personal Larceny with Contact										
Total	62,282	20,018	110,375	46,706	63,036	23,626	68,047	12,370	33,490	21,064
Rate (per 100,000)	223.9	398.1	243.6	674.0	206.0	548.5	236.2	384.7	165.0	103.8
% not Reported	67	B	62	70	62	79	59	B	38	B
Personal Larceny w/o Contact										
Total	4,202,052	488,876	5,787,982	805,867	2,618,800	331,114	1,581,629	177,035	435,487	40,311
Rate (per 100,000)	15346.2	9721.3	12775.1	11629.7	8558.3	7687.5	5491.1	5505.6	2145.7	1986.2
% not Reported	87	88	71	75	68	63	65	67	70	66

SOURCE: Adapted from SOURCEBOOK, 1979, Tables 3.4, 3.11.

report larceny than whites. Finally, among younger victims, more whites failed to contact the police about a robbery than nonwhites, while the reverse situation appears among victims over 35 years old.

It would appear, then, that from the point of view of having his/her criminal act come to the attention of law enforcement officials, the violent offender is selecting victims—the young and male—among whom the unreported victimization levels are the highest.

Household victimization. While the economically deprived are overrepresented in the official criminal population, the data in Table 11 indicate that a postive relationship exists between family income and probability of household victimization. The only exception occurs with respect to burglary, for which the relationship is generally negative. In the case of larceny, families making over $7,500 but less than $10,000 possess the highest rates of victimization, with families whose incomes exceed $25,000 following closely. For motor vehicle theft, the highest risk is borne by the wealthiest families.

Like personal victimization, household victimization is a mixed bag when it comes to racial characterization. At all income levels, nonwhites are subject to a greater likelihood of burglary than whites. This is generally true also when considering household larceny. However, whites are more likely than nonwhites to suffer motor vehicle theft, except in higher income settings (above $10,000) for which the victimization rate for nonwhites is twice that for whites.

Socioeconomic status of the victim appears to be moderately associated with the probability of reporting a crime. The nonreporting percentages for burglary, larceny, and motor vehicle theft among whites with incomes less than $3,000 are 61%, 78%, and 41%, respectively. Comparable percentages for whites whose incomes exceed $25,000 are 45%, 69%, and 29%. Of the three property crimes examined, burglary shows the clearest income-based differential in probability of reporting. For larceny, the income differences are virtually nonexistent.

Earlier, in regard to personal victimization, it was reported that the relationship between race and reporting of victimization was quite ambiguous. When one examines the same topic within the context of household victimizations, a similar conclusion is reached. In four of six income categories, white families are less likely to report a burglary than are nonwhites. However, in the case of larceny, in all but the lowest income groups, nonwhites show greater reluctance to contact the police. Finally, when white-nonwhite comparisons on reporting of theft are possible, whites consistently fail to report victimizations in greater proportions than do nonwhites.

In summary, types of crime examined here typically involve a lone offender acting against an unknown victim and these events, except in the case of aggravated assault, take place without the presence of any sort of weapon. The typical offender is male, black, economically disadvantaged, and below the age of 30. The victim, on the other hand, also tends to be a young male and nonwhite; and, similarly, reporting the episode tends to be least likely if the victim is a male, is relatively young, or is from a low-income background.

TABLE 11

Total Household Victimizations, Estimated Rate of Victimization and Percentage not Reported to Police by Race of Head of Household, Family Income and Type of Victimization

	Family Income											
	Under $3,000		$3,000 to $7,499		$7,500 to $9,999		$10,000 to $14,999		$15,000 to $24,999		$25,000+	
Type of Victimization	White	Nonwhite	White	Nonwhite	White	Nonwhite	White	Nonwhite	White	Nonwhite	White	Nonwhite
BURGLARY												
Total	561,318	207,680	1,205,711	381,250	547,215	129,941	1,095,220	172,999	1,143,928	112,175	604,544	33,422
Rate (per 100,000)	11033.7	12749.7	8825.3	13569.8	8746.8	14497.3	7837.2	12276.7	7699.0	10379.8	9623.0	9734.2
% not Reported	61	63	53	51	58	55	46	42	47	51	45	36
LARCENY												
Total	525,013	138,631	1,530,615	331,482	883,193	138,652	1,825,364	190,385	1,986,438	133,008	876,617	52,215
Rate (per 100,000)	10320.1	8510.6	11203.4	11798.4	14117.1	15469.1	13062.0	13510.5	13369.3	12307.6	13953.6	15207.7
% not Reported	78	76	75	81	76	84	75	79	72	72	69	75
VEHICLE THEFT												
Total	44,803	5,466	195,762	36,425	88,435	11,978	243,513	47,653	273,031	56,221	144,611	16,556
Rate (per 100,000)	880.7	335.6	1432.9	1296.5	1413.6	1336.4	1742.5	3381.7	1837.6	5202.3	2301.9	4822.0
% not Reported	41	B	33	29	28	B	32	25	30	26	29	B

SOURCE: Adapted from SOURCEBOOK, 1979, Tables 3.5, 3.31.

CORRECTIONAL SUPERVISION

There are a number of types of correctional supervision, ranging from jail to probation, institutionalization, and parole. Each deals with different types of offenders at different points in the criminal justice process. At any point in time, there may be approximately two million citizens under correctional supervision in jails, on probation, institutionalized, or on parole, and this is a conservative estimate which does not include, for example, all of those supervised in community treatment contexts. If one controls for age, say 12 years or older, perhaps 5% of the age-eligible population of the country could be under some kind of correctional supervision on any given day. Even more startling, it seems possible that 20% to 25% of all juveniles will have been under some form of correctional supervision by age 18. Of course, these are gross estimates which depend not only on the reliability of the various data sources but also on how one counts or measures the different aspects of correctional supervision. And it is also clear that there are interesting variations within types of correctional supervision by region, jurisdiction, sex, age, race, admission and release characteristics, and so on.

Jail as Dentention and Confinement

Between the 1972 and 1978 National Jail Censuses and Surveys of Inmates of Local Jails, there has been an increase of 12% in the number of persons detained or confined in jail. Approximately 60% are confined for misdemeanor convictions, and 40% are detained for a variety of reasons, usually awaiting action on a charge. The largest proportion of those who do time in jail are young, underemployed, urban males. Although the trend, for legal and humanitarian reasons, has been to separate juveniles and adults throughout the criminal justice process, there were still many juveniles in jails in 1978: 1% of the jail population in 1978 consisted of juveniles, and the sex ratio is smaller (5:1) among juveniles than adults (16:1) in jail. This means that among those who spend time in jail, there is a higher proportion of juvenile than adult females who are detained or confined. (See Table 12.)

Regional differences in the sex and age composition of those jailed and in the incarceration rate are illuminating. The Northeast has the best record regarding juveniles in jail with less than 100 incarcerated, while approximately 2% of the jail population in the North Central states consists of juveniles. The Northeast also jails the smallest proportion of females (5%), followed very closely by states in the South (5%), then North Central (7%), and the West (9%). And two of the regions have rates of detention and confinement higher than the national average of 76/100,000 population. States in the West jail the highest proportion of the population (100) followed closely by the South (98). The Northeast is substantially lower (54) than the national rate, and the lowest rate is to be found in the North Central states (49).

TABLE 12

Jail Inmates by Region, Sex, and Age and Rate of Detention by Region, 1978

Region	All Inmates			Adults			Juveniles			Rate Per 100,000 Population
	Total	Male	Female	Total	Male	Female	Total	Male	Female	
United States	158,394	148,839	9,555	156,783	147,506	9,277	1,611	1,333	278	76
Northeast	24,228	23,039	1,189	24,129	22,984	1,145	99	55	44	54
North Central	28,452	26,687	1,765	27,937	26,256	1,681	515	431	84	49
South	67,444	63,992	3,452	66,775	63,420	3,355	669	572	97	98
West	38,270	35,121	3,149	37,942	34,846	3,096	328	275	53	100

SOURCE: Adapted from U.S. Department of Justice, Census of Jails and Survey of Jail Inmates, 1978, National Prisoner Statistics Bulletin, No. SD-NPS-J-6P, February 1979, Table 3.

Probation and Parole Supervision

Probation and parole are the most frequent forms of correctional supervision in the community. The former is typically carried out as a dispositional alternative to incarceration, while the latter is usually a postincarceration supervised transition to discharge and complete freedom. Perhaps three-fourths of the total under correctional supervision are in the community as probationers or parolees, with 83% of these on probation and 17% on parole. Probation by itself could account for almost two-thirds of the correctionally supervised.

Among both the probationers and parolees, approximately 75% are adults and 25% are juveniles. However, the sex ratio among juvenile probationers is one-half that among adult probationers, and among juvenile parolees it is one-third that among adult parolees. There is a higher proportion of female juvenile (23%) than adult (14%) probationers, and an even greater discrepancy between female juvenile (20%) and adult (7%) parolees. Apparently, probation is twice as likely as parole for adult females, while approximately the same proportion of juvenile probationers and parolees are female (see Table 13).

Adults in Prison

Perhaps 15% of the total under correctional supervision are adults incarcerated in state and federal institutions. Over the past decade, there has been approximately a 40% increase in the number of felons in state and federal institutions; the incarceration rate has increased from 90 to 129; the percentage increase has been larger among women (76%) than men (40%), meaning that more women are now being incarcerated and a higher proportion of prisoners are women; the number released to parole also increased, although as a proportion of the number imprisoned has remained at around 30% over the years; and parole remains the favored type of release, with approximately 85% of those imprisoned being released to parole.

The latest data on the movement of sentenced prisoners in state and federal institutions show a 6% increase in the number of prisoners institutionalized on the last day of 1976 and 1977, respectively. This increase may also be seen as the difference between the number of admissions and releases, which are measures of the number of prisoners who are admitted to or released from institutions during the course of the year. However, these two general categories and the movements within them may also represent transactions rather than discrete prisoners, because some prisoners may be involved in more than one movement during the year. For example, an individual prisoner might be counted as a release for an escape, but within the same year also be counted as an admission if caught and returned to an institution and, though unlikely, perhaps released from the institution before the last day of the same year. Therefore, this individual prisoner would be involved in and counted as three transactions (or movements) for the year but not be included in the end of the year count of the total number of prisoners in state and federal institutions (see Table 14).

TABLE 13

Adults and Juveniles under Probation and Parole Supervision by Sex, 1976

Type of Supervision	Total Population	Adults			Juveniles		
		Total	Male	Female	Total	Male	Female
Total	1,461,459	1,079,258	939,845	139,413	382,201	294,484	87,717
Probation	1,251,918	923,064	795,231	127,833	328,854	251,781	77,073
Parole	209,541	156,194	144,614	11,580	53,347	42,703	10,644

SOURCE: Adapted from SOURCEBOOK, 1979, Table 6.1.

TABLE 14

Movement of Sentenced Prisoners in State and Federal Institutions by Region and Jurisdiction, 1977

Region and Jurisdiction	Number of Prisoners on 12/31/76	Admissions				Releases				Number of Prisoners on 12/31/77			Incarceration Rate (per 100,000)
		Total	New Commitments from Courts	Parole or Conditional Release Violators Returned	Other[a]	Total	Conditional Releases[b]	Unconditional Releases[c]	Other[d]	Total	Male	Female	
United States, Total	262,833	163,203	128,050	21,746	13,407	147,895	100,230	24,052	23,613	278,141	267,097	11,044	129
Federal Institutions, Total	26,980	17,685	13,820	2,129	1,736	16,015	5,248	3,021	6,946	28,650	26,956	1,694	13
State Institutions, Total	235,853	145,518	114,230	19,617	11,671	131,880	94,982	20,231	16,667	249,491	240,141	9,350	116
Northeast	36,180	22,135	16,233	3,867	2,035	20,474	16,154	1,779	2,541	37,841	36,766	1,075	77
North Central	54,765	33,795	26,726	5,074	1,995	30,295	25,216	2,463	2,616	58,265	56,119	2,146	108
South	110,030	67,832	54,870	6,830	6,132	60,237	36,196	14,598	9,443	117,625	112,956	4,669	169
West	34,878	21,756	16,401	3,846	1,509	20,874	17,416	1,391	2,067	35,760	34,300	1,460	92

SOURCE: Adapted from SOURCEBOOK, 1979, Tables 6.28 and 6.24.
a. Escapes returned, transfers from other jurisdictions, and other admissions.
b. Parole, probation, supervised mandatory release, other.
c. Expiration of sentence, commutation of sentence, other.
d. Deaths, escapes, transfers to other jurisdictions, other.

As with jailing, there are interesting regional differences in the rate of increase in the number of offenders incarcerated, incarceration rates, sex composition of prisoners, and the use of different types of admissions and releases. The North Central region had a percentage increase in the number of prisoners identical to the national average of 6% while the Northeast (5%) and West (3%) had smaller percentage increases and the South (7%) was the only region higher than the national average. And almost as many people in the South are imprisoned as the other three regions combined. This is reflected in the extremely high incarceration rate in the South (169), which is followed at a distant second by the North Central states (108), then the West (92), and lastly the Northeast region (77).

Examining the sex composition of the imprisoned population, one finds a higher proportion of women in federal than state institutions, and one noteworthy regional deviation from the national prisoner sex ratio. The Northeast has a larger sex ratio (34:1) than the other three regions, which are very similar to the national average of 24:1.

There is also an interesting regional anomaly in release patterns. Across the types of admission to prison, the regions are relatively similar to the national averages for new commitments (78%), parole or conditional release violators returned (13%), and other admissions (9%). However, the South differs substantially from the other three regions in the use of different types of release from an institution. Approximately 80% of the releases in the Northeast, North Central, and Western regions are conditional releases, while the comparable figure in the South is only 60%. Since almost 90% of conditional releases are to parole, this suggests that parole is not as favored a form of correctional supervision in the South as elsewhere, while unconditional releases—for example, expiration of sentence—account for a concomitantly higher proportion of releases than in the other three areas of the country. Overall, the data seem to support the belief that correctional policy in the South is much more traditional and conservative than in other parts of the country.

Juveniles in Custody

As the incarceration rate for adults continues to increase, institutionalization becomes a less popular form of correctional supervision for juveniles. In fact, there is a trend toward decarceration of juveniles, with a corresponding increase in the utilization of community alternatives to institutionalization. Between the 1975 and 1977 Law Enforcement Assistance Administration censuses of juvenile facilities, there was a 2% decrease in the population of juveniles in custody, continuing the trend started at the beginning of the decade. However, the balance between "public" and "private" supervision is shifting—there has been a 7% increase in residents of private juvenile custody facilities but a 7% decrease in residents of public juvenile custody facilities. This growth in the private sector reflects compliance with provisions of the Juvenile Justice and Delinquency Prevention Act of 1974, especially those regarding the deinstitutionalization and return to the community of status offenders. The "open" residential facility had become more typical in the private sector, while "institutional" facilities are the domain of the public sector. Approximately one-third of the juveniles in private facilities are delinquents—most are status offenders and nonoffenders, including the neglected, mentally retarded, and disturbed. On the other hand, in long-term public facilities, almost 90% are juvenile criminals. It is apparent that the juvenile justice system will have even more responsibility for the correctional supervision of juvenile delinquents, and that other kinds of juvenile offenders and nonoffenders who have special needs will be supervised and helped in the community in private facilities.

About 60% of juveniles in custody in 1977 were confined or detained in public facilities. Reflecting a historical sex difference in the illegal behavior and custody of juveniles, a higher proportion of the boys are in public than in private facilities, while a higher proportion of the girls are in private than in public facilities, and within the private facilities the sex ratio (5:1) is much larger than in the public facilities (2:1). The boys are more likely delinquents and, therefore, more likely residents of long-term public facilities. This is also likely for adults—interestingly, approximately 3% of the population in juvenile facilities are adults, the overwhelming majority (86%) of whom are confined in public facilities (see Table 15).

There are equally interesting race differences. Among whites and other nonwhites, about equal proportions are in custody in private and public facilities, but a substantially larger percentage of black juveniles (71%) are in public facilities. And within public facilities, approximately two-thirds of the population is white, one-third is black, and a tiny fraction is other nonwhites. The population white within private facilities is even larger (75%) and the proportion black even smaller (21%). Clearly, blacks are overrepresented in public facilities, which are more typically institutions for juvenile delinquents, as well as in the overall population of children in custody where their representation is twice that of black juveniles in the general population.

These data on juveniles in custody show even more clearly the variety of ways of counting or measuring correctional supervision. The number of admissions and departures, as one would expect, is very similar for the year, and the ratio of both public to private admissions and departures is about 9:1. The larger ratio of admissions (or departures) to number of residents at year end (about 7:1) suggests substantial movement and turnover in the population of juveniles in custody, most attributable perhaps to the short terms served. After all, the average daily number of residents—the mean of the daily counts, including the end of year count—is not only close to the end of year count but may also be a better measure of the number of juveniles in custody and of the capacity of the system over a year.

Curiously, the average length of stay in private custodial facilities (9 months) is two and one-half times as long as in public facilities. The discrepancy seems to be a consequence of the characteristics of the two types of facilities and the juveniles they serve. Almost two-thirds of the total number of juvenile custodial facilities are private, and a very high proportion (73%) of the long-term facilities

TABLE 15

Selected Characteristics of Public and Private Juvenile Custody
Residents and Facilities, 1977

Characteristic	Public	Private	Total
Number of residents	45,920	29,377	75,297
Juvenile	44,096	29,070	73,166
Male	36,921	20,387	57,308
Female	7,175	8,683	15,858
Adult	1,824	307	2,131
Race	44,096	29,070	73,166
White	27,963	21,917	49,880
Black	14,865	6,005	20,870
Other	1,045	1,148	2,193
Number of admissions[1]	614,385	67,045	681,430
Number of departures[1]	622,151	61,571	683,722
Average daily number of residents[1]	48,032	29,611	77,643
Average length of stay (days)	107	270	189($\overline{X}$)
Number of facilities	992	1,600	2,592
Short term	448	126	574
Long term	544	1,474	2,018
Per capita operating cost (dollars)[2]	14,123	12,269	13,196($\overline{X}$)

SOURCE: Adapted from "Children in Custody: Advance Report on the 1977 Census of Public Juvenile Facilities" and "Children in Custody: Advance Report on the 1977 Census of Private Juvenile Facilities," both Law Enforcement Assistance Administration.
NOTE: Data for 1977 are as of December 31, except for figures on admissions and departures, average daily number of residents, and operating costs, which are for an annual period, either calendar or fiscal year.
1. Based on all residents (juvenile and adult).
2. Based on average daily number of residents.

(e.g., training schools) are private, while a smaller proportion (22%) of the short-term facilities (e.g., detention centers) are private. And among the public facilities, almost half are short term and half are long term, while among the private facilities only 8% are short term and the remainder are long term. Clearly, the private custodial facilities (e.g., group homes) are not detention facilities but rather places to which juveniles are sent for rehabilitation and care. In the public facilities, the average length of stay in a short-term facility is 14 days, while in a long-term facility it is 184 days. In the private facilities, the comparable figures are 20 days and 291 days. So, not only are there more private long-term facilities but also those youngsters who are in these facilities are averaging about three months more time under supervision than those in public long-term facilities. Finally, although both public and private juvenile custody costs are high, the private facilities are approximately $2000 less expensive per capita.

CRIME IN THE 1980s

With the decade of the 1970s behind us, it is tempting to consider what the new decade may hold in the area of crime and its control. Of course, it is impossible to predict the future, but based on experience one can make informal guesses—projections or forecasts—about likely trends. Projection techniques have become relatively sophisticated in the past few years, but here only simple linear projections of arrest rate trends for the UCR Total, Property, and Violence indexes are presented.

For each index the actual arrest rate for each year from 1964 to 1977 is plotted (solid line), as well as the linear projection of arrest rates from 1964 to 1990 (dotted line). The projected yearly average rate of increase is derived from the average increase per year in the actual rates from 1964 to 1977. For example, the projected increment for the total index arrest rate is 796 per year. The straight trend line is based on this projected yearly average rate of increase, while the changes in the actual rates fluctuate and constitute the more jagged line. The R^2 for each of the three index rates indicates the "fit" of the projection line on the actual rates line. Otherwise put, it is an estimate of the amount of variance in the actual rates accounted for by the projected rates. The latter is the best-fit line, the one that maximizes explained variance. A perfect fit between the actual and projected rates lines would account for all of the variance and allow perfect prediction.

Examining the total index arrest rates first, it is clear that the trend has been and seems likely to be ever-increasing rates through the 1980s. Of course, the linear projection is based on an all-other-things-remaining-equal assumption. It does not take into account the possible changes in other variables which may affect the arrest rates—for example, the age structure, unemployment rates, criminal justice resources, sex differences in crime, or differential fertility rates by ethnicity. However, if the amount of variance explained (.863) can be used as a measure of the probability that the total index arrest rate will increase as projected, then one can "predict" with some confidence that by 1990 the arrest rate could be approximately one-fourth higher than in 1977 (see Table 16).

The property index arrest rates show similar prospects. If anything, the rate of increase may be higher for property than total crimes, as well as the probability that the projection will be correct. The R^2 (.900) is higher than for the total index, and it is conceivable that by 1990 the property index arrest rate could increase by more than one-half over 1977 (see Table 17).

Finally, the violence index arrest rates mirror the patterns for the other two indexes. The rate of increase may be even higher than for the property index, with a virtually identical (.898) amount of the variance in the actual rates explained by the linear projection. And perhaps some cause for alarm, it is possible that by 1990 the arrest rate for violent crimes could increase by two-thirds over the rate in 1977[3] (see Table 18).

(text continued on page 727)

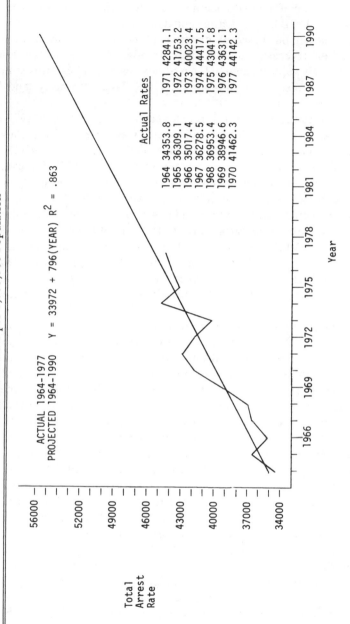

TABLE 16

Total Arrest Rate per 1,000,000 Population

ACTUAL 1964-1977
PROJECTED 1964-1990   Y = 33972 + 796(YEAR) R^2 = .863

Actual Rates

1964 34353.8   1971 42841.1
1965 36309.1   1972 41753.2
1966 35017.4   1973 40023.4
1967 36278.5   1974 44417.5
1968 36953.4   1975 43041.8
1969 38946.6   1976 43631.1
1970 41462.3   1977 44142.3

Total
Arrest
Rate

56000
52000
49000
46000
43000
40000
37000
34000

1966 1969 1972 1975 1978 1981 1984 1987 1990

Year

TABLE 17

Property Arrest Rate per 1,000,000 Population

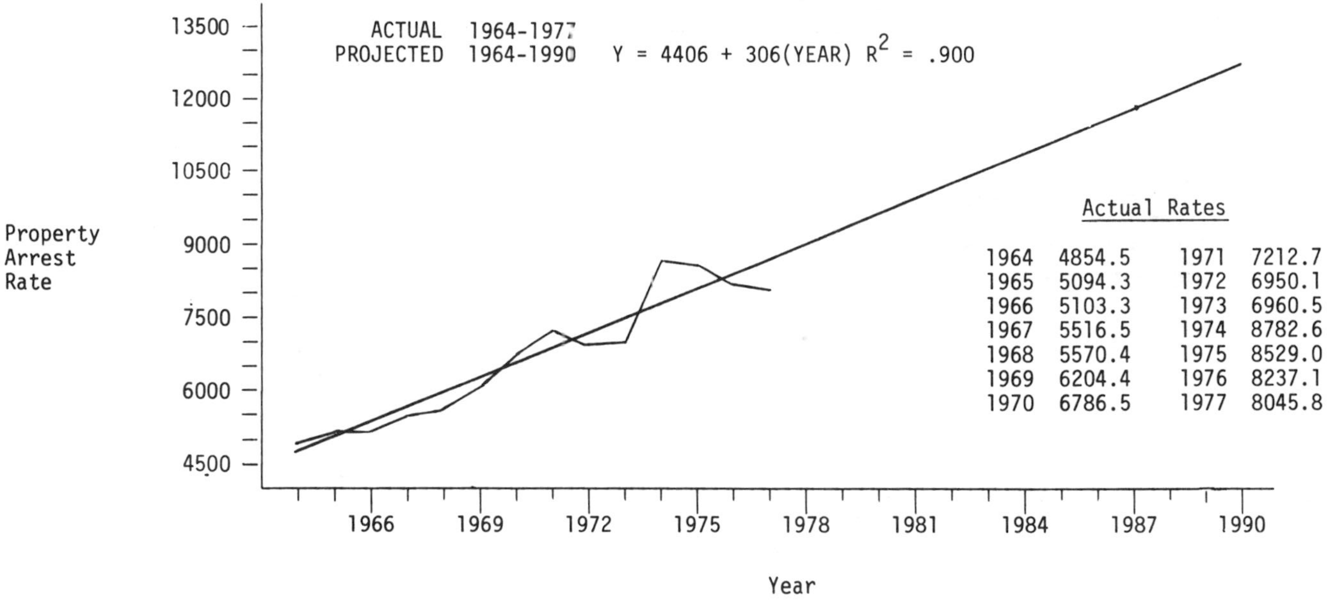

ACTUAL 1964-1977 $Y = 4406 + 306(YEAR)$ $R^2 = .900$
PROJECTED 1964-1990

Property Arrest Rate

Year

Actual Rates

1964	4854.5	1971	7212.7
1965	5094.3	1972	6950.1
1966	5103.3	1973	6960.5
1967	5516.5	1974	8782.6
1968	5570.4	1975	8529.0
1969	6204.4	1976	8237.1
1970	6786.5	1977	8045.8

13500 12000 10500 9000 7500 6000 4500

1966 1969 1972 1975 1978 1981 1984 1987 1990

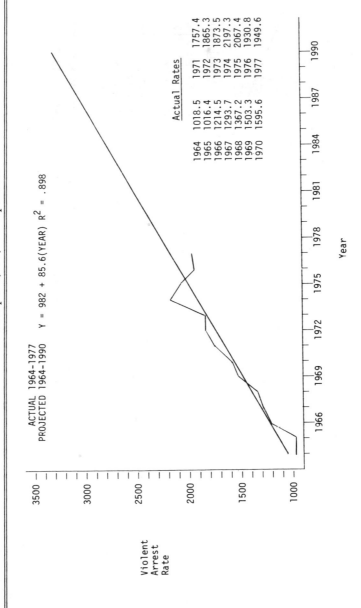

TABLE 18

Violent Arrest Rate per 1,000,000 Population

ACTUAL 1964-1977   Y = 982 + 85.6(YEAR) R² = .898
PROJECTED 1964-1990

Actual Rates

1964	1018.5	1971	1757.4
1965	1016.4	1972	1865.3
1966	1214.5	1973	1873.5
1967	1293.7	1974	2197.3
1968	1367.2	1975	2067.4
1969	1503.3	1976	1930.8
1970	1595.6	1977	1949.6

In general, these data suggest that there may be continuing increases in arrest rates over the next decade, with perhaps the greatest relative increases for violent crimes. But, again, for these observations to become true, one must assume that the next decade will unfold in the same way as the past. Who knows?

NOTES

1. We would like to acknowledge the assistance of Ann L. Pastore, Editorial Specialist of the *Sourcebook of Criminal Justice Statistics,* for providing data which will appear in the 1979 and 1980 editions of the *Sourcebook.*

2. These data must be interpreted somewhat cautiously, particularly the 1973 and 1977 data, which are based on the respondents' perceptions of the first and second most important problems.

3. It should be noted that projections using more sophisticated analytic techniques which take into account changes in variables which may affect arrest rates suggest similar trends, particularly for violent crime arrest rates.

CRIMINOLOGY REVIEW YEARBOOK

CONTENTS FROM VOLUME 1

ABOUT THE EDITORS

EGON BITTNER received his Ph.D. from the University of California, Los Angeles in 1961. He taught at the University of California, Riverside, and was a Research Social Scientist at the Langley Porter Neuropsychiatric Institute, University of California Medical School, San Francisco. He is presently Harry Coplan Professor in the Social Sciences and Chairman of the Sociology Department at Brandeis University.

SHELDON L. MESSINGER is Professor of Law at the University of California, Berkeley and continues to be associated with the Center for the Study of Law and Society there. Formerly, he was Professor and Dean of the School of Criminology at the University of California, Berkeley.